Composing Electronic Music

Composing Electronic Music

A NEW AESTHETIC

Curtis Roads

OXFORD
UNIVERSITY PRESS

OXFORD
UNIVERSITY PRESS

Oxford University Press is a department of the University of Oxford. It furthers the University's objective of excellence in research, scholarship, and education by publishing worldwide.

Oxford New York
Auckland Cape Town Dar es Salaam Hong Kong Karachi
Kuala Lumpur Madrid Melbourne Mexico City Nairobi
New Delhi Shanghai Taipei Toronto

With offices in
Argentina Austria Brazil Chile Czech Republic France Greece
Guatemala Hungary Italy Japan Poland Portugal Singapore
South Korea Switzerland Thailand Turkey Ukraine Vietnam

Published in the United States of America by
Oxford University Press
198 Madison Avenue, New York, NY 10016

Library of Congress Cataloging-in-Publication Data
Roads, Curtis.
Composing electronic music : a new aesthetic / Curtis Roads.
pages cm
Includes bibliographical references and index.
ISBN 978-0-19-537323-3 (cloth: alk. paper) — ISBN 978-0-19-537324-0 (pbk.: alk. paper)
1. Electronic music—Instruction and study. I. Title.
MT724.R73 2015
786.7'13—dc23
2014027116

CONTENTS

ABOUT THE COMPANION WEBSITE

www.oup.com/us/composingelectronicmusic

Oxford has created a website to accompany *Composing Electronic Music*, and the reader is encouraged to take advantage of it. Over 150 sound examples illustrate the concepts and techniques described in the book and are essential for understanding the ideas discussed in the book, which are ultimately grounded in the medium of sound. Recorded examples available online are found throughout the text and are indicated by the Oxford University Press symbol

PREFACE

Composition is evolving. The practice of electronic music continues to generate a flow of new materials, tools, and novel methods of organization. The music produced by these means evokes new sensations, feelings, and thoughts in both composers and listeners.

Every path to composition engages tools, be it a pencil, a drum, a piano, an oscillator, a pair of dice, a computer program, or a phone application. Each tool opens up aesthetic possibilities but also imposes aesthetic constraints. This book sketches a new theory of composition based on the toolkit of electronic music. The theory consists of a framework of concepts and a vocabulary of terms describing musical materials, their transformation, and their organization.

Back in 1954, Werner Meyer-Eppler, the visionary of the Cologne electronic music studio, wrote:

> The music composition that can be produced with electric tone sources differs so much from the conventional that only in exceptional cases will it be possible to extrapolate some of the "assets" of traditional orchestration methods into the new regions of sound. Anyone entering the new field of electronic music will be confronted with entirely different conditions and unexpected as well as unfamiliar phenomena.

Today, after decades of experimentation, electronic music is not entirely new. Many texts describe its technology, yet the compositional implications of these tools have rarely been analyzed in detail. Now is an appropriate moment to step back and reevaluate all that has changed under the ground of compositional practice. One of my goals is to update the conceptual framework and vocabulary in order to be able to speak precisely about the task at hand.

This book is not a how-to manual. It offers little in the way of recipes and recommended practices. (The exception is chapter 12 on mixing and mastering.) Chapter 9, on multiscale organization, comes closest to describing a methodology, which in any case is specific to my practice. If anything, *Composing Electronic Music* is more of a guidebook: a tour of facts, history, commentary, opinions, and pointers to interesting ideas to consider and explore.

Here at the beginning, allow me to state an important point. My intention is not to argue the case for pure electronic music in opposition to other means of musical expression. Exceptional music continues to be written for traditional acoustic instruments and voice; some of it incorporates electronic elements. The teaching of traditional composition and electronic music composition are not diametrically opposed; they should be complementary. However, the target of this book is specifically electronic music, and thus I focus on its intrinsic characteristics. Certain compositional strategies can only be freely and fully exploited using electronic technology; exploring and mapping these aesthetic implications are primary goals of this text.

What is electronic music?

Myriad labels have been applied to this medium. It has been called electric music, elektronische Musik, musique concrète, electroacoustic music, sonic art, and tape music, for example (Landy 2007). Groups of artists cluster under umbrellas such as acousmatic, electronica, intelligent dance music, electroacoustic, feminist, interactive, algorithmic, soundscape, laptop, microsound, noise, glitch, live coding, and so on.[i] Many more labels will inevitably emerge in order to differentiate social networks and aesthetic schools (Rodgers 2010). While aesthetic, cultural, and philosophical differences separate composers, the common tool of the computer has unified the technical means. To the public, however, the term "computer music" is often linked with the notion of algorithmic composition. At the same time, we see a resurgent trend toward modular synthesizers, a hybrid of analog and digital modules under the regime of voltage control. For this book, I needed one term, and I chose electronic music to refer to the general category of analog and digital technologies, concrète and synthetic sound sources, and systematic and intuitive composition strategies.

Origins of this book

The practice of electronic music has grown out of long-established music traditions based on acoustic instruments. However, the traditional canon of Western music theory, with its emphasis on 12-note equal-tempered pitch relations, offers limited help in understanding the materials and organization of the electronic medium. Traditional music theory is note-oriented and score-bound. Few theorists study music as a sonic, spatial, or psychoacoustic phenomenon.

The notes of traditional music represent a closed, homogeneous set. In contrast, the sound objects of electronic music are extremely heterogeneous, and sonic transformation is ubiquitous. The symbolic world of paper notations, textual abstractions, and mathematical algorithms can only take us so far in describing this perceptually complex world: Electronic music must be directly heard in order to be understood.

Twentieth-century manuals of traditional composition such as those by Hindemith (1941) and Schoenberg (1967) remain rooted in 19th-century practice, not even touching on dodecaphony. Books released since the 1960s updated the discourse by introducing serial and other strategies (e.g., Cope 1977, 1997; Morris 1987). However, they were never intended to cover the full range of possibilities offered by the electronic medium.

A wave of books on electronic music composition appeared in the 1970s, prompted by the initial surge of popularity of analog instruments such as the Moog, Arp, EMS, and Buchla synthesizers. These texts tended to explain the craft in terms of technical skills like tape splicing or operating a synthesizer. Other books, such as those by Kaegi (1967) and Strange (1983) interspersed technical explanations with descriptions of specific pieces. Since that era, incessant advances in technology have altered the terrain of possibilities.

In parallel with technological developments, focused artistic practice has fostered a profound evolution in musical aesthetics and style. This convergence of technical and aesthetic trends prompts the need for a new text focused on a *sound-oriented, multiscale approach* to composition of electronic music. By sound-oriented, I mean a practice that takes place in the presence of sound. Here formal schemes can serve as guides, but the sonic result is the ultimate reference point. This is perceptual—not conceptual—art. As Igor Stravinsky (1936) wrote in his *Autobiography*:

> It is a thousand times better to compose in direct contact with the physical medium of sound than to work in the abstract medium produced by one's own imagination.

By multiscale, I mean an approach to composition that takes into account the perceptual and physical reality of multiple, interacting timescales—each of which can be composed.

I had many motivations for writing this book. Foremost was a desire to reflect on my composition praxis, to assess what I had already done as a foundation for determining what to do next.

I did not begin with a preconceived theory. Through analysis, I examined what had been a mostly intuitive process of working with the tools of electronic music. I scrutinized both the interaction and the tools in order to better understand their ramifications. This reflection was a way of trying to understand the past in order to see how it could be transformed and projected in new directions in the future. As Luc Ferrari (quoted in Caux 2002) observed:

> Creation places us in front of a fantastic abyss. This has always interested me: to recognize that in this abyss there is something to do, that there are elements whose capacity one does not yet know, but which one is going to use.

Another motivation came about through teaching. The teaching of composition, particularly in lecture and classroom settings, forces one to think through the implications of technical and aesthetic trends. Rendering these thoughts to text took much time; I started several chapters as early as 1990, when I was teaching at the Oberlin Conservatory. At the end of the day, it made sense to gather my lectures into an integrated document that could serve as the basis for future courses. I sketched an outline for the book in Santa Barbara in 1998. After *Microsound* was completed in 2000, I began in earnest. By the summer of 2011, I began to see light at the end of the tunnel, but progress was slowed by my duties as chair of Media Arts and Technology at the University of California, Santa Barbara (UCSB). It was not until my sabbatical in spring 2014 that I was able to devote all my creative time to completing the manuscript.

Disclaimer

> It was my teacher, Lisette Model, who finally made it clear to me
> that the more specific you are, the more general it will be.
>
> —DIANE ARBUS (2007)

Musical meaning finds expression in diverse idioms. It is as likely to appear in indigenous cultures as it is in the most calculated cosmopolitan conception. It can emerge from careful logical planning or erupt spontaneously by emotional force. Thus the process of composition follows myriad paths.

Reflecting this situation, I originally conceived this text as an encyclopedic survey of compositional methodologies covering a wide range of styles and approaches, like *The Computer Music Tutorial* of composition. As I began writing, however, it became clear that the original plan was not viable. I realized that it would be impossible for me to do justice to topics that are not central to my practice. As the musicologist Demers (2010) observed:

> Electronic music is not one single genre but rather a nexus of numerous genres, styles, and subgenres, divided not only geographically but also institutionally, culturally, technologically, and economically. Because of this breadth of activity, no one single participant or informant can speak about all of electronic music with equal facility.

Rather than trying to survey every possible approach to composition, I decided to focus on ideas that guide my work. Thus this text is stamped by my own aesthetic philosophy, a working hypothesis starting from a set of assumptions formed by intuition and experience. For this reason, certain opinions might seem pointed.[ii] This book, however, is not intended as a prescription for anyone else's practice; its ideas represent nothing more than my current point of view on what I do. Here is my disclaimer: What the text loses in generality and objectivity, it gains in authenticity. I have attempted to present my views without polemic or hyperbole.

While this text reflects my biases, I believe it will interest others. Several readers of the draft manuscript commented that the more engaging parts were those in which I recounted personal experiences, observations, and opinions. It is not a question of identifying or agreeing with everything I said. No two composers have identical aesthetics. I vividly recall reading *Stockhausen on Music* (Maconie 1989) at Oberlin soon after it was published. Stockhausen expressed numerous opinions, many of which concerned things I had never before considered. Ultimately, I did not agree with him on many points, but only because I was stimulated by his opinions to formulate my own.

Even a single artist's aesthetics are not fixed in stone. We hope that the creative artist evolves and is sensitive to the opportunities of the day, while at the same time not being distracted by ephemeral fads that time-stamp and stereotype the results.

In any case, many ideas developed here transcend my practice. For example, I already wrote the chapter on multiscale organization when I came across a similar description of heterarchical graph structures in Morris's (1987) book, which represents a different aesthetic. His description apparently derived from Hofstadter (1979). Later, the same notion turned up in Polansky (1996). The fact that we found a common paradigm points to the generality of the concept. Many of the aesthetic and philosophical issues addressed by this book, particularly in the chapters on organization, generative strategies, and aesthetics, are shared by other arts. Indeed, I took cues from visual arts texts such as Klee's *Pedagogical Sketchbook* (1925) and Kandinsky's *Point et ligne sur plan* (1926). These books convey specific theories and techniques gathered through artistic practice, while also articulating personal aesthetic visions. Certain books on electronic music, such as Trevor Wishart's *Audible Design* (1994), François Bayle's *Musique acousmatique* (1993), Stockhausen's *Texte* (1963, 1964, 1971, 1978), and, of course, Xenakis's *Formalized Music* (1971, 1992) take a similar approach.

Researching this book afforded me the great pleasure of reading inspiring texts by and about composers such as Barlow, Barrett, Berio, Brün, Ferrari, Harvey, Ligeti, Messiaen, Morris, Stravinsky, and Vaggione, among others. I enjoyed rereading Kostelanetz's (1988) compilation of interviews with John Cage and was struck again by Cage's original synthesis of ideas, even though his positions are foreign to me.

Varèse is my guiding light. It was a special treat to read his complete *Écrits* (Hirbour 1983) kindly conveyed to me by my colleague at the Université de

Paris 8, Anne Sedes. For most of his life, Varèse engaged in a fierce struggle with critics, the musical establishment, and corporate management (Varèse 1957; Trieb 1996). This sharpened his opinions. I found many spicy quotations to season my dull prose.[iii]

It is important to speak as precisely about sonic phenomena and their perception. Thus, for the chapters on the nature of sound, pitch, and rhythm, I consulted many texts on acoustics, psychoacoustics, and music psychology. Relevant texts in music theory are also cited.

As I listen and compose, I inevitably formulate new techniques and aesthetic concepts. This text is a continuation of a sustained effort to articulate these ideas. My book *Composers and the Computer* (1985) gathered the voices of nine practitioners into a single volume. That anthology was an attempt to advance the aesthetic discourse in the nascent field of computer music composition. Much later, *Microsound* (2001b) presented a chapter of aesthetic reflections and offered sound examples and excerpts of compositions on an attached disc. *Composing Electronic Music* is my latest attempt to foster aesthetic discourse. I have tried to spell out ideas as clearly as I can, to map the terrain of electronic music and point out many largely unexplored paths.

A new aesthetic?

Composing Electronic Music: A New Aesthetic: What's new about it? First, it is not the newest aesthetic. The newest aesthetic tends to engage the latest gadgets and social fads. In contrast, the core aesthetic tenets in this book derive from the 20th century, beginning with Varèse's *Liberation of sound*, which was published after his death but conceived decades earlier (Varèse 1966). Due to the state of technology, however, some of these ideas remained more like dreams than reality. The technical conditions for Varèse's aesthetic to fully bloom only became widespread in the 1990s, with the availability of personal computers, quality audio interfaces, graphical sound editors and mixers, real-time synthesis, and interactive tools for sound granulation and sound transformation in general. Inextricably bound with these technical changes came a change in musical culture that was more accepting of the new sound world.

What are some of the tenets of the aesthetic traced in this book? It

- opens the door to any sound possible in composition, an unlimited universe of heterogeneous sound objects;
- exploits the specific capabilities of electronic music technology (see chapter 1);
- composes all timescales down to the micro and even the sample level;
- accepts spatialization as an integral aspect of composition;
- focuses on sound transformation as a core structural strategy;

- organizes flowing mesostructures (sound masses, clouds, streams) that emerge as consequences of new materials and tools;
- integrates the possibility of sounds that can coalesce, evaporate, and mutate in identity on multiple timescales;
- plays with *zones of morphosis*—thresholds where quantitative changes in sound parameters result in qualitative changes to the listener (see chapter 5);
- treats pitch as a flowing and ephemeral substance that can be bent, modulated, or dissolved into noise;
- encourages microtonality but also free intonation;
- treats time as a plastic medium that can be generated, modulated, reversed, bent, granulated, and scrambled—not merely as a fixed duration subdivided by ratios;
- weaves the undulation of envelopes and modulations into the fiber of musical structure;
- applies the power tools of algorithmic methods, but allows the freedom to edit and rearrange their results;
- addresses the issue of narrative in composition; and
- considers human perception/cognition as a baseline for theory and practice.

Taken together, these tenets constitute game-changing possibilities.

Topics not covered

Following the disclaimer, I would like to address the omission of three topics: live performance and improvisation, graphical representations, and timbre.

LIVE PERFORMANCE AND IMPROVISATION

Live performance has a long tradition and is an important domain of electronic music.[iv] Recent texts by Borgo (2005), Barbosa (2008), Jordà (2007), Collins (2007), Dean (2009a), Perkis (2009), Tanaka (2009), Lewis (2009), Oliveros (2009), and Pellegrino (2010), among many others, explore the issues that surround live performance, including extensions into network-based interaction.

In the bad old days of computer music, there was no live performance. Algorithmic composition, sound synthesis, and sound processing could not be realized in real time. Today real-time interactive performance is common. I frequently perform with synthesizers and sound transformation tools, even if it is in the studio and not live onstage. Continued technical research in support of live performance is essential. This involves the design of new electronic instruments and modalities of performance interaction.

The risks associated with improvisation onstage can instill a live performance with dramatic and emotional impact. A key to success in such performances is virtuosity, a combination of talent plus rigorous practice. We hear this in Earl Howard's *Strasser 60* (2009), a tour de force of sonic textures played live on a sampling synthesizer. Behind such a piece are months of sound design and rehearsal to prepare the 20-minute performance.

Sound example 0.1. *Strasser 60* by Earl Howard. Performed live at Roulette, New York City, Nov. 12, 2009.

Richard Devine's *Disturbances* (2013), which he performed live on a modular synthesizer at UCSB, is another impressive demonstration of virtuosic control.

When I project my music in a hall, another kind of live performance takes place: sound projection or diffusion. This consists of varying the dynamics, equalization, and spatialization of music that is already composed in order to take advantage of a particular space and its sound system. Virtuosity drives such performances, but this is based as much on intimate knowledge of the music being projected as it is on physical dexterity. The key is knowing precisely when and how to change the projection, keeping in mind the resources of a given hall and its sound system. (For a discussion of the aesthetic significance of sound projection as a performance interpretation, see Hoffman 2013.)

The idea of combining acoustic instruments and electronic tape has a venerable tradition, dating back to the early concerts of the Groupe de Recherche de Musique Concrète, in which Pierre Schaeffer and Pierre Henry collaborated to make *Orphée 51* for soprano and tape (Chion 1982). Extending this line, many composers, such as my colleague JoAnn Kuchera-Morin, write mixed pieces that combine a virtuoso instrumental score with electronic sound and interactive processing. Mixed pieces pose many aesthetic challenges, and I admire those who master that difficult medium. For more on live interactive electronic music with instruments, see, for example, Rowe (1993, 2001).

In contrast, my compositional practice is studio based. Playing an instrument in real time is central to my studio work, keeping in mind that "playing" and "instrument" go beyond traditional modalities to encompass interaction with software. I record these (sometimes improvised, sometimes planned) performances, and this is often how I generate the raw material for a composition. Due to the nature of my music, however, which is organized in detail on multiple timescales down to the microscale, it is impossible for me to generate it in real time onstage.

Studio practice affords the ultimate in flexibility and access to the entire field of time on multiple scales. The ability to zoom in and out from the micro to the macro and back, as well as move forward and backward in time (e.g., compose the end before the beginning, change the beginning without modifying the rest of the piece), are hallmarks of studio practice. Sounds can be reversed and their time support can be freely modified with varispeed and pitch-time changing or utterly scrambled by granulation. Once the macroform of a composition has been designed, I sometimes finish it by sprinkling it with a filigree of transients—like a dash of salt and pepper here and there in time.

These kinds of detailed studio practices take time. Indeed, a journalist emphasized the glacial timescale of my composition process, which to me is merely the natural pace of the work (Davis 2008). In order to construct an intricate sequence of sound events, I often listen at half speed or even slower. A passage of a few seconds may take a week to design. The process often begins as an improvisation. I try an experiment, listen to it, revise it, then perhaps backtrack and throw it away (deleting the past). I write notes and make a plan for the next improvisation. I reach a dead end and leave a piece for weeks in order to come back with a fresh perspective. My composition process takes place over months or years. *Epicurus* was composed over the period of 2000–2010. The original sound material in *Always* (2013) dates to 1999, and the piece was assembled over a period of three years.

Sound example 0.2. Excerpt of *Always* (2013) by Curtis Roads. 

Thus it makes no sense for me to pretend to have anything particularly interesting to say about onstage live performance of electronic music. I leave this for others.

GRAPHICAL REPRESENTATIONS OF ELECTRONIC MUSIC

Another topic not covered in this book is graphical representations of electronic music. This stands at the nexus of several intersecting research areas in between sound, image, and music notation:

- Study scores for electronic music, comprising still images that intermingle traditional notation with sonographic, iconic, and symbolic representations
- Interactive composing environments based on drawing and manipulation of images of waveforms, envelopes, and sonographic spectra (e.g., Xenakis's UPIC system)
- Scientific visualizations of sonic data based on analysis (e.g., sonograms, wivigrams, etc.)
- Scientific sonification of image (or other data) to sound (also known as *auditory display*)
- Artistic visualizations of music, either abstract or representational music animations or *visual music* (von Amelunxen et al. 2009; Brougher et al. 2005; Evans 2005; Woolman 2000) (an example would be the brilliant visualizations designed by Brian O'Reilly to accompany our DVD of *POINT LINE CLOUD* [figure 0.1])

Sound example 0.3. Excerpt of *Fluxon* (2003) by Curtis Roads. 

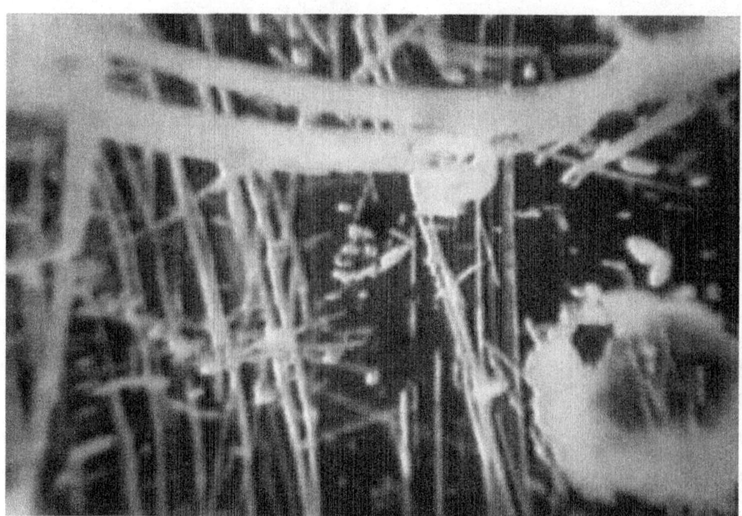

FIGURE 0.1 Still image by Brian O'Reilly from the DVD of *Fluxon* (2003) by Curtis Roads on *POINT LINE CLOUD* (2004).

Technological advances have accelerated efforts to both visualize and sonify. Software translations between sound and image that were once the province of laboratory specialists are now accessible to anyone with a computer and video jockey (VJ) software. As a result, activity in all these intertwined areas is rapidly evolving.

This general area remains a research interest of mine. I have worked with a number of collaborators—both artists and engineers—to realize visualizations of my music. I have also managed the development of new tools for scientific visualization.[v] I supervise graduate students who develop generative algorithms for both sound and image. Thus I am confident that one of my younger colleagues will eventually tackle this book-length topic.

TIMBRE

The synthesis and transformation of timbre is central to the practice of electronic music, yet no chapter in this book is devoted exclusively to it. Why is this? Timbre is a problematic topic. According to definition, timbre is "an attribute of auditory sensation" that enables a listener to distinguish two sounds having the same loudness and pitch (American National Standards Institute 1999). This definition is obviously lacking. (See Smalley 1994 and Houtsma 1997 for critiques.) To begin with, it describes timbre as a perceptual phenomenon, and not an attribute of a physical sound. Despite this, everyone has an intuitive sense of timbre as an attribute of a sound like pitch or loudness (e.g., "the bassoon timbre" or "Coltrane's saxophone sound"). From a compositional point of view, we are interested in the physical nature of timbre. We want to know how timbre can be made operational, in order to manipulate it for aesthetic purposes.

Everyone agrees that timbre is a "multidimensional property," but there is no general scientific agreement about what these dimensions are or how to measure them. Spectrum and amplitude envelope are clearly parts of the story, but so are many other factors. Thus, timbre has been called "the psychoacoustician's multidimensional wastebasket" (McAdams and Bregman 1979) as it serves as a catchall for sundry phenomena (Plomp 1970). As Houtsma (1997) asked:

> One can match the loudnesses of two sounds that differ in frequency or spectral content and one can match the pitches of two sounds that differ in intensity or spectral content. Would it be possible to match the timbres of two sounds across differences in intensity (loudness) and fundamental frequency (pitch)? The author is not aware of any such experiment reported in the psychoacoustical literature.

In musical practice, what we call timbre is an undeniably powerful force and has always been used creatively by composers under the rubric of orchestration. Generalized to include the entire range of sonic phenomena, it appears as a vast *n*-dimensional space. Ever since the early days of computer music, musicians have dreamed of taming the domain of timbre by means of a psychophysical timbre space (Wessel 1979; Lerdahl 1987). However, the fruits of such research are not yet ripe. Nonetheless, our student Daniel Mintz (2007) demonstrated a proof of concept of how this agenda could be furthered. (See the description in chapter 3.)

How does timbre convey musical structure? At a minimum, for an element of timbre to be morphophoric, it must be perceivable as differentiable. That is, we need to perceive a continuum between two contrasting poles along some dimension, or a set of distinct ordered classes along this same dimension. Functional relations between timbral elements must allow for the accumulation and release of tension or perceived intensity. Moreover, the patterns designed out of timbre must permit some form of invariance under transformation, like a melody that remains identifiable when it is transposed. Despite the absence of a formal or standardized theory, composers of electronic music have always exploited these properties. Examples include manipulations of the following timbral elements, among many others:

- Contrasting sharp versus smooth attack shapes
- Contrasting harmonic versus inharmonic spectra
- Modulating, including changes in modulation frequency, waveform, and depth
- Filtering, including filter sweeps, and changes in resonance
- Sliding along the continuum from pitch to colored noise to white noise
- Changing bandwidth in both tone clusters and noise
- Contrasting registers in both tone clusters and noise (e.g., gongs and cymbals of different sizes, other unpitched percussion)
- Manipulating grain density, duration, and envelope in granular clouds

Recent progress in formulating precise mathematical descriptors of timbral attributes is encouraging, specifically the MPEG-7 multimedia standard (International Standards Organization 2002; Martinez 2004; Casey 2010). However, MPEG-7 is only a beginning and by no means a complete scientific account of timbre. (See the discussion in chapter 3 for more on the MPEG-7 timbral descriptors.)

The anachronistic term "timbre" will likely be superseded by a more precise taxonomy of sound qualities, at least in scientific discourse. In any case, timbral issues are unavoidable in electronic music. Thus the reader will find focused discussions of specific aspects of timbre synthesis, transformation, and organization interwoven throughout the book.

Intended audience

The intended audience for this book is practicing composers, sound artists, theorists, and aestheticians of music and media arts, including students in these disciplines. This text is less technical than my previous books, but it still assumes a basic familiarity with electronic music techniques and a willingness to discuss sound phenomena in terms of the scientific theory of acoustics and signal processing. Technical terms inevitably pop into the discussion. Rather than loading down every term with cumbersome explanatory notes, I have tried to cite references to the literature so that curious readers can follow up as they see fit. In general, my book *The Computer Music Tutorial* (Roads 1996) could serve as a technical companion to this text. (A revised edition of *The Computer Music Tutorial* is forthcoming.)

Please note that chapters 3 (The nature of sound) and 4 (Creating sound materials) are more introductory than the other chapters. Even so, I have cast these topics within an aesthetic frame that could be of interest even to advanced readers.

Pedagogy in music composition

Pedagogy in music composition is still bound by tradition, yet continues to evolve. Given the diversity of paths and inherently interdisciplinary nature of electronic music composition, it is difficult to prescribe a single curriculum that would be ideal for all students. It is clear, however, that students with scientific training in areas like audio engineering, software programming, and digital signal processing are better able to work independently, design their own tools, and follow the research literature. In this way, they can grow as the field evolves and tools and technical concepts change. To cite one example, 20 years ago, time-frequency analysis/transformation and convolution-based effects were rare laboratory tools. Today, such tools are built into common software applications for sound editing and transformation. Yet in order to use these tools effectively, scientific knowledge is essential.

TRAINING AND TALENT

Pedagogy in composition faces a well-known paradox. No amount of training makes a difference if the student is devoid of artistic vision, acute listening, and that combination of attributes we call talent:

> Obviously, the aptitudes on which ultimate quality depends—imagination, invention, vitality, daring, temperament—cannot be taught; and while a teacher can and should communicate attitudes [and enthusiasms] toward music, his primary function is not that of teaching his pupil to write "great" or even "good" or "interesting" music. This of course cannot be taught.
>
> —ROGER SESSIONS (1971)

Thus one must be clear about the boundaries of teaching composition. A standard approach, which I use in my classroom teaching, is to assign a series of graduated exercises, going from simple to more advanced constructions, while learning a set of tools and also benefiting from critical feedback from peers, as well as the instructor. At the same time, we listen to notable works in class, and I present technical analyses or ask the students to offer their own.

Just as any intelligent person can learn to write grammatically correct sentences or computer programs, certain skills can be taught to any musician, regardless of talent. No one pretends that rote mastery can imbue the student with talent as defined above; this can only emerge from within.

The conservatory model of composition involves a period of apprenticeship with a senior composer. The student receives feedback and learns of the teacher's techniques and aesthetic philosophy. The teacher may direct students to important scores and recordings and provide clues about their organization. When the teaching is done in a group setting, the students have the opportunity to share ideas with fellow students. This informal sharing among students working at similar levels is often as valuable as anything the teacher says.

COMPOSITION STRATEGY VERSUS MUSIC ANALYSIS

In my teaching, I occasionally present analyses of works of my own and others. One reviewer of a draft of this book opined that the main focus of a text on composition should be analytical examples. However, analysis is not a goal of this book. I draw a distinction between music analysis and composition strategy.

Music analysis is a problematic endeavor. The task of analysis based on a printed score is fairly straightforward, though it is hardly a science. The starting point—a score—is already a simplified high-level symbolic representation of a more complex phenomenon: a pattern of air vibrations. In contrast, when analyzing electronic music, a main goal is precisely to try to find a score (a repertoire of symbols) in the waveforms. In practice, this is difficult, as there are often no standardized, homogeneous units like notes in electronic music (Bossis 2006). Many analytical accounts of electronic music tend toward the anecdotal or philosophical

(Griffiths 1979; Smalley 1993; Lyon and Teruggi 2002; Heikinheimo 1972; Roads 2005; Roy 2003; Hinkle-Turner 2006; Vande Gorne 2011; Young 2004).[vi]

The central narrative in electronic music often revolves around timbral elements projected in virtual spaces. Thus the development of a proto-science of electronic music analysis depends on the ability to describe both timbres and spaces, their combinations, and their time-varying mutations. Yet the development of a vocabulary of descriptors for timbre is in its infancy, and the practice of virtual spatialization is far ahead of any descriptive aesthetic theory.

As already stated, timbre is an ill-defined multidimensional attribute. In order to describe timbral phenomena, studies of electronic music frequently turn to time-frequency visualizations such as sonograms (Cogan 1984; Simoni 2006; Licata 2002). While helpful, sonograms require interpretation; they display the result of a mathematical transformation that does not correspond directly to what we hear (Smalley 1997). Even a simple chord progression, which is easily readable in common music notation, appears as a dense pattern of stratified bands with fuzzy edges (figure 0.2). More complex sounds (noises that are easy to recognize audibly) are projected by sonograms as amorphous clouds.[vii]

Beyond current technical limitations on musical sound analysis, epistemological conundrums inherent in analysis are well known. Music analysis is often driven by a traditional philosophy of *organicism*—a tendency to search for unity, even at the cost of gross simplifications. As the musicologist Joseph Kerman (1981) pointed out:

> [New] music may not be "organic" in any useful sense of the word, or its organicism may be a more or less automatic and trivial characteristic.

A more basic problem is that no general or universal method of analysis exists; anything can be analyzed in innumerable ways. Moreover, there is no limit to the number of goals one could have for analyzing: Seek and ye shall find. As G. M. Koenig (1971) observed:

> Musical analysis presents great difficulties, as the problems involved are still a matter of debate; once the musicologist knows what aspect he wishes to investigate, the main problem is already solved.

The point of a music analysis could be to "explain what we hear," "to uncover hidden structures," "to find semiotic oppositions," "to find pitch rows," "to find the most compact representation," "to find the grammatical structure," "to determine the statistical structure," "to recreate the generative algorithm," "to trace its implications and realizations," "to find borrowings from previous works," "to situate a work within a cultural context," "to correlate the music with the composer's psychology," and so on. The meaning of an analysis is intimately tied to its goals, which are defined by the chosen analysis model. Yet for an analysis to be of use to a creator, it needs to teach the techniques used by the composer, rather than the analyst.

Finally, we must recognize the limits of analysis. As Varèse (1923) bluntly observed:

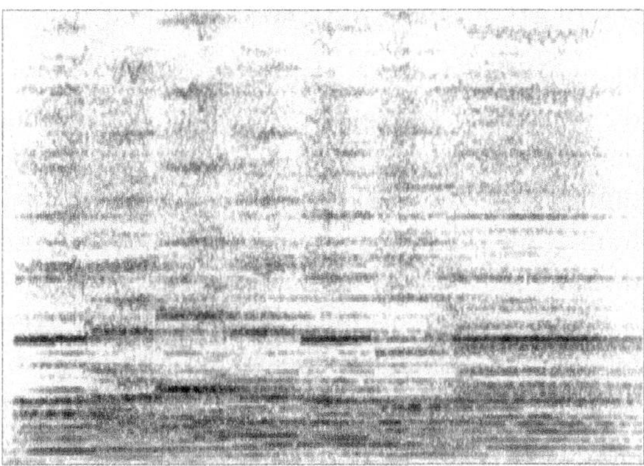

FIGURE 0.2 Score of a stanza sung by a chorus (SATB + continuo) from J. S. Bach's cantata *Brich dem Hungrigen dein Brot*, BWV 39 (left) and its sonogram (right). The duration of the sonogram (horizontal scale) is 7.21 seconds. The vertical frequency scale extends to 3000 Hz.

> Analysis is sterile by definition.

One analyst spent his life trying to give a "reason" for every note in a Beethoven sonata. What could be the significance of such elaborate rationalizations? Any composition is merely an instance of a deeper compositional vision. Many surface details are arbitrarily chosen; they could have been composed this way or that. In the course of composition, I often compose alternative versions of phrases that would be as equally "valid" as the one that is actually used.[viii]

Ultimately, what is missing from current discourse on composition is not necessarily analysis of individual works, but a deeper analysis of the opportunities of the medium of electronic music itself. This is a question of aesthetic philosophy, and it is the subject of this book.

In contrast to music analysis, a composition strategy is a collection of ideas that a composer uses to organize his or her thoughts, to conceptualize and realize a piece. In extreme cases, a composition strategy may be only indirectly related to the perceived sonic result. Consider the piece *Kontakte* (1960) by Stockhausen. This work is organized according to serial principles, but does anyone pretend to hear the serial organization behind this work? As James Dashow (1985) wisely observed:

> [Labels] do not really tell us what we are hearing. As a result, just like many other techniques that have been developed in this century, it is merely something for the composer to hang his hat on, something to get him going, something equivalent to his cup of coffee in the morning and his glass of wine at night or whatever he needs to keep going.

The point is that a composition strategy is by its nature subjective and arbitrary. Moreover, it is almost always incomplete; it does not account for every aspect of a finished work.

CONCEPTS AND VOCABULARY

Electronic music composition is the product of many intellectual streams, among them aesthetic philosophy, acoustics and psychoacoustics, music theory, composition strategy, and technical knowledge. Every composer can benefit from thinking as clearly as possible about the métier. Students can benefit from a framework of concepts and a vocabulary of terms about musical materials and their organization. This book attempts to address these two points.

Part of compositional training involves the study of instrumental techniques. Many composers learn to write for each instrument by working with virtuosos on solo works. Here they learn to appreciate the "best" notes, the "sweetest" combinations, performance tricks known to instrumentalists, and the secrets of notating unusual sonorities. A similar kind of learning takes place in the electronic music studio. Each device and program has particular strengths and limitations. One must beware of falling into the trap of complacency with respect to one's tools. Even general-purpose toolkits impose aesthetic, technical, and sonic biases. Anything may be possible in theory, but is it easy to design and interact with, and is the sonic result worth the development effort?

Composition and research

To me, composition has always been a domain of research, as well as a métier of practice. As Varèse (1930) observed:

> For all new conceptions there must be new means. I do not believe in a return to the past.

Creativity, by its nature, involves experiments. Based on a given hypothesis, experiments succeed, prove inconclusive, or fail. Risk is inherent. Backtracking (discarding a failed experiment and returning to a previous point) is a necessary strategy. Often one has to try something in order to arrive at the conclusion that it will not work. Strategic retreat is not a waste of time; indeed it is an essential phase of the composition process!

Since our experiments involve acoustical phenomena, one can never learn enough about the physics and psychophysics of sound. New methods of synthesis, analysis, and transformation are always pertinent. At the same time, it is obvious that technical methods cannot, in themselves, resolve all problems of musical expression or organization.

Another form of research is scholarly inquiry. It was gratifying to study the ideas and impressions of the many composers and scholars that appear in the references. Days spent reading analyses of works while listening to the music and studying scores were rewarding, even if they resulted in nothing more than a single sentence in the final book.

Overview of the book

The first chapter of *Composing Electronic Music* begins by examining the specificity of the electronic medium. It points out the unique possibilities offered by this medium. At the same time, it also describes what electronic music shares with traditional composition.

Chapter 2 discusses fundamental aesthetic issues raised by the practice of electronic music.

As mentioned previously, chapters 3 and 4 are introductory and can be skipped by advanced readers. Chapter 3 describes the nature of sound from a scientific perspective, while chapter 4 surveys the range of sound materials available to the composer and discusses how sounds are gathered, organized, and performed.

Chapter 5 presents a theory of sound transformation that analyzes the aesthetic ramifications of transformation.

In much Western music, metered rhythms and equal-tempered pitches are primary compositional ingredients. Chapters 6 and 7 reexamine the dominance of these two elements from a wider perspective.

Chapter 8 discusses sound in virtual and physical space, an especially important dimension of electronic music.

Chapters 9 and 10 are effectively the core chapters of this book, as they focus on the new possibilities of musical organization and sonic narrative.

Chapter 11 discusses the complex aesthetic issues surrounding generative strategies.

Chapter 12 is devoted to the art of sound mixing and mastering. It is perhaps the most practical chapter with its list of "magic frequencies" and specific tactics.

For the reader's convenience, I have invested a major effort in the name and subject indices of this book.

Sound examples and compositions cited

In 1980, I had a meeting with the director of the MIT Press at the time, Frank Urbanowski. He suggested that I write a listener's guide to electronic music. Although this was not one of the original goals of this book, as the text evolved, I realized that I was citing more and more pieces. Thus one of the threads of this book evolved into an informal and personal listener's guide, citing dozens of compositions, listed in the index. This subproject consumed many hours. For various reasons, it was not possible to include sound examples for every piece cited in the text. However, I am pleased to include a subset of 155 sound examples cited throughout the text and listed in appendix A. These mostly excerpted sounds are available online at Oxford University Press and on my website (www.mat.ucsb.edu/~clang). I encourage readers to seek out these works in their entirety from the copyright holders.[ix]

Just as this book does not pretend to be an all-inclusive historical examination of the field, neither the list of cited works nor the set of sound examples are meant to be in any sense comprehensive. Most of the musical works I cite in this book focus on the mid-century modern classics that inspired me.[x] Today's musical harvest is the product of this experimental and revolutionary period. I trust that young readers who take the time to become familiar with some of the best works of the past will make the connection to trends in today's constantly changing scene.[xi]

Acknowledgments

I thank many people for their comments on the lectures that formed the basis of this text. Chapter 1 derives from a lecture first given at UCSB in 1997 and presented at Dartmouth and Bennington colleges later that year. I tested other chapters in short courses and lectures at Centre de Création Iannis Xenakis (CCMIX, Paris), Prometeo Studio (Parma), the Université Paris 8, the Maison des Sciences de l'Homme (Paris), the Centro di Ricerca Musicale/Goethe Institute (Rome), the Ionian University (Corfu), the Royal Music Academy of Aarhus, the Catholic University of Porto, the Zürcher Hochschule der Künste, LaSalle College of the Arts (Singapore), the Beijing Central Conservatory, and the Center for New Music and Audio Technologies, University of California, Berkeley, between 1998 and 2013.

Reviewers of chapter drafts included Ori Barel, Clarence Barlow, Natasha Barrett, Nicola Bernardini, Thom Blum, Andres Cabrera, Anil Camçi, Alberto de Campo, Pablo Colapinto, Nick Collins, James Dashow, Brian Hansen, James Harley, Lawrence Harvey, Florian Hecker, Michael Hetrick, Henkjan Honing, Christopher Jette, Zbigniew Karkowski, Douglas Keislar, Garry Kling, Stefanie Ku, Jennifer Logan, Paulo Lopes-Ferreira, Aaron McLeran, Dennis Miller, Gerard Pape, Stephen Pope, Jean de Reydellet, Muhammad Hafiz Wan Rosli, Chad Skopp, Marcus Schmickler, Bob Sturm, Martino Traversa, Horacio Vaggione, Matthew Wright, and Michael Winter. I am most grateful for their critical feedback. Others who supplied information included Alessandro Cipriani.

I should mention my special debt to Horacio Vaggione, who contributed valuable insights to this text through his music and writings and also via numerous discussions in Paris. I would also like to thank my colleague JoAnn Kuchera-Morin at UCSB. Since my arrival in Santa Barbara in 1996, I have been inspired by her vision of a transdisciplinary research community. With her and several other colleagues, we created the Media Arts and Technology (MAT) graduate program at UCSB, an extraordinary group of colleagues and students. I thank my mother, Marjorie Roads, for a lifetime of love and understanding.

The writing of this book was aided by travel breaks, which provided an opportunity to escape mundane obligations and dream on a higher plane (literally). How wonderful to put to good use the hours spent in airplanes, airports, and hotel rooms! I offer my deep thanks to those who made these lecture and concert trips possible.

This book is dedicated to the memory of several departed souls I was fortunate to know: Luc Ferrari, Bebe Barron, and Iannis Xenakis. I would also like to mention the memory of a student who briefly studied with me in Santa Barbara, Agostino Peliti. Electronic music was his refuge, as it is mine. I salute his father, Professor Luca Peliti of the Department of Physics at the University of Naples (where I was once a visiting faculty member), who contributed significantly to our AlloSphere research in Santa Barbara as a visiting professor of physics at UCSB.

Please note that we have taken all reasonable measures to identify and duly credit the owners of derivative rights. In the event you believe you have not received due credit for your work, please notify the publisher.

1

The electronic medium

To be a composer means that one enjoys solving puzzles of pitch, rhythm, sound color, phrase structure, and process, but also questions of taste and feeling. To be an electronic music composer, however, requires a particular disposition because of the unique predicament of this medium.

This chapter compares traditional instrumental and vocal composition with that of electronic music, pointing out their similarities and differences. We examine the specificities of the electronic medium and, in particular, the unique challenges and opportunities it presents to composers.

Acoustic versus electronic?

One of the most important trends in the present compositional situation is a tendency away from an exclusive focus on pitch-centric note patterns and toward a timbral and textural approach. This is true in the domain of electronic music, as well as in certain genres of acoustic instrumental music.[1]

This being said, a note-by-note approach is in no danger of extinction. Indeed, such an approach is fully compatible with electronic music technology.

Wendy Carlos's *Switched-on Bach* (1968), realized on a Moog synthesizer recorded to an Ampex 8-track tape recorder, brought electronic music technology to the forefront of popular awareness through the language of traditional harmony and counterpoint.

Sound example 1.1. Excerpt of *Brandenburg Concerto No. 3, Allegro movement* (1721) by J. S. Bach, from *Switched-On Bach* (1968) by Wendy Carlos.

Sound example 1.2. Excerpt of *Sheep may safely graze, from Cantata 208* (1713) by J. S. Bach, from *Switched-On Bach II* (1973) by Wendy Carlos.

Early experiments in tape music composition featured the sounds of traditional instruments modified by simple processes such as tape echo.

Sound example 1.3. Excerpt of *Underwater Waltz* (1952) by Vladimir Ussachevsky. Transcribed from a long-play vinyl record.

Electronic synthesis was a natural extension of the academic serial style of the 1960s. Pioneering electronic works such as *Composition for Synthesizer* (1961) by Milton Babbitt highlighted atonal counterpoint in precise rhythmic patterns.

Sound example 1.4. Excerpt of *Composition for Synthesizer* (1961) by Milton Babbitt.

Today, tools such as common music notation software, MIDI sequencers, and keyboard controllers lend themselves to note-based styles. Consider *Wall Me Do* (1987) by Carl Stone, an example of electronic music in a tonal context.

Sound example 1.5. Excerpt of *Wall Me Do* (1987) by Carl Stone.

Moreover, increasingly realistic simulations of traditional instruments make it easier than ever to compose in a conventional manner.

Sound example 1.6. Additive synthesis simulation of a string quartet playing Beethoven's *Opus 132* using the application Synful Orchestra sequenced by Eric Lindemann.

At the same time, timbral/textural composition has been explored in the domain of acoustic instrumental music by Gyorgy Ligeti, Helmut Lachenmann, Giacinto Scelsi, Gérard Grisey, Natasha Barrett, Iannis Xenakis, and others. These works play with the continuum between pitch and noise and are not necessarily aligned to a regular metric grid. In these pieces, variations in timbre and voice density play a structural role. As Ligeti (undated) said of certain works in his texture period (1958–1970):

> My personal development began with serial music, but today I have passed beyond serialism. . . . I have attempted to supercede the structural approach to music which once in turn superceded the motivic-thematic approach, and to establish a new textural concept of music.

Consider the use of pitch as pure register in Ligeti's magnificent *Volumina* (1962) for pipe organ. This work functions by means of changes in density and register, articulated by additive and subtractive processes on pitch clusters and sound masses that express no harmonic or intervallic function.

Sound example 1.7. Excerpt of *Volumina* (1962) by Gyorgy Ligeti. 

In a different genre altogether, a cadre of musicians following the example of the "free music" school launched in the 1950s and the tradition of live electronic music continue to explore territories of timbre/texture from the standpoint of improvisation. (The New York-based musician Earl Howard comes to mind.)

Here we confront a question that inevitably emerges out of this discourse: Rather than focusing on electronic means, isn't the contrast between note-based versus timbral/textural composition more pertinent? Both acoustic and electronic media support either approach.

As pointed out in the preface, the focus of this book centers on my aesthetic practice: studio composition in the electronic medium. I must in all humility leave the task of analyzing instrumental and improvisatory practices to experts in those domains. Moreover, I see no contradiction between note-based and timbral/textural organization; indeed they can operate simultaneously within a piece. In works such as my *Purity* (1994), I explore a combination of microtonal (note-based) harmony, nonfunctional pitch clusters, and freely gliding glissandi.

Sound example 1.8. Excerpt of *Purity* (1994) by Curtis Roads. 

My composition *Pictor alpha* (2003) features repeating pitch loops. In works such as *Epicurus* (2010), I intersperse noisy granular textures with pitched impulse trains.

Sound example 1.9. Excerpt of *Epicurus* (2010) by Curtis Roads. 

The situation of electronic music

This section examines the situation of electronic music within the broader musical world of critics, media coverage, and audiences. Such an examination could easily be turned into a book-length sociocultural analysis. I am neither sociologist nor musicologist, however, so my treatment is intentionally brief. (For more on this topic, see, for example, Landy 2007.)

In instrumental composition, the basic materials—the notes—evolved out of a long tradition. Their properties are well known. It takes only a second to inscribe a note on staff paper. This situation stands in stark contrast to that of electronic music, where the first stage of composition is the potentially time-consuming construction of the sound materials to be deployed in the piece. Therefore, the composer in this medium must love working directly and intimately with sound material. One spends a great deal of time exploring the gamut of sounds, and the creation of a single sound object may take a long time. One must be patient.

The legacy of electronic instruments dates back more than a full century (Roads 1996b). However, the impact of the electronic medium was slow in coming. The visionary composer Edgard Varèse (1936a) predicted the "liberation of sound":

> When the new instruments will allow me to write music as I conceive it, taking the place of linear counterpoint, the movement of sound masses, of shifting planes will be clearly perceived. When these sound masses collide, the phenomena of penetration or repulsion will seem to occur. Certain transmutations taking place on certain planes will seem to be projected onto other planes, moving at different speeds and at different angles. There will no longer be the old conception of melody or interplay of melodies. The entire work will be a melodic totality. The entire work will flow as a river flows.

It took many decades for this aesthetic—which seemed radical at the time it was proposed—to be accepted.[2] Varèse first gained access to an electronic music facility only in 1954, at Pierre Schaeffer's Studio d'Essai. He was 71 years old and was able to complete only two electronic pieces before his death.[3]

The electronic music instruments of the pre-World War II period tended to mimic traditional instruments. They were played, for the most part, within the context of established genres.[4] In the 1930s, Paul Hindemith, for example, wrote works for electronic Trautonium instrument—for example, *Langsames Stück und Rondo für Trautonium* (1935)—in which the instrument is treated as a melodic voice, essentially like a clarinet, but with a wider tessitura.

Sound example 1.10. Excerpt of *Langsames Stück und Rondo für Trautonium* (1935) by Paul Hindemith.

As another example, Joanna M. Beyer's *Music of the Spheres* (1938) could be performed either by "electrical instruments" or strings (Kennedy and Polansky 1996).

In general, it was only after 1945 that the aesthetic implications of electronic music composition per se (as advocated by Varèse) began to be understood. As Herbert Eimert, who founded the Cologne electronic music studio observed (1954):

> [Electronic music] is not a cautious departure from certain traditional paths, but rather, in the radical character of its techniques, gives access to sound phenomena hitherto unknown in the field of music. This bursting open of our familiar world of sound by electronic means leads to new musical possibilities of a wholly unpredictable nature.

In contrast to Eimert, whose conception of electronic music was narrowly defined both in terms of its materials and methods of organization (Chadabe 1997), the cornerstone of Varèse's electronic music aesthetic is an open approach to sound. This means that any sound, from any source, can serve a function in an appropriate musical context. This fundamental premise already projects us far beyond the limits of traditional instruments and voice. An open approach to sound poses many challenges, however.

In traditional music, the repertoire of instruments is generally limited to a fixed set. In certain pieces, a rare and exotic instrument may augment this set, but the usual set of instruments is well known. Moreover, the instruments are visible onstage, and we witness the correlation between the performer's gestures and the sounds they produce. Thus the identity of the sound sources is unambiguous. In contrast, in music played back from a tablet computer, for example, the source of a given sound and its identity are often ambiguous. The unlimited variety of sampled sounds means that the space of possible sources is much larger. Moreover, many transformations obscure the identity of the original source, making source identification difficult.

This expansion of available sound led to an issue identified early on by Pierre Schaeffer (1966; Chion 2009), the situation of *acousmatic listening*. As an adjective, acousmatic refers to a sound that one hears without seeing the source that caused it. Phonograph records and radio imported the acousmatic listening experience into the home. Consciously acousmatic works play with issues of reference, source identity, and sound causation (Barrett 2007). They often feature recognizable concrète sounds or soundscapes, quotations, and other highly referential material. A classic example is Luc Ferrari's groundbreaking *Presque rien no. 1* (1967–1970), the first composition to expand the timescale of musique concrète from short sound objects to long environmental soundscapes in shifting background and foreground relationships.

Sound example 1.11. Excerpt of *Presque rien no. 1* (1970) by Luc Ferrari. 

Natasha Barrett's *Industrial Revelations* (2001) plays with the ambiguity between the recognizable and the non-recognizable, which provokes an emotional reaction by means of the immersive physicality of the acousmatic gesture.

Sound example 1.12. Excerpt of *Industrial Revelations* (2001) by Natasha Barrett. 

On the other hand, electronic music can also explore—just as effectively—the cosmos of abstract synthetic sound. In works such as Stockhausen's *Kontakte* (1960) or my own *Now* (2003), the sounds are generated purely electronically. Like objects in an abstract painting, the sounds are not necessarily recognizable in terms of a familiar reference; any resemblance to the external world is purely coincidental.

Sound example 1.13. Excerpt of *Now* (2003) by Curtis Roads.

The open approach to sound and the myriad possibilities for transforming it pose another major challenge: the need for new paradigms for the organization of musical structure. Opening a Pandora's box of sound had the inevitable side-effect of expanding possibilities of musical form. Material and formal structure are interdependent; an architect creating structures with sprayed fiberglass foam will not create the same types of structures as an architect working with bricks or steel. Thus new forms have emerged, some successful, some not. The point is that heterogeneity in sound material led to heterogeneity in musical structure. These innovations show no sign of slowing down.

Pitch relations in traditional occidental music have been formalized (albeit incompletely) by means of a symbolic algebra of notes, scales, harmonic relations, and counterpoint. In contrast, Western rhythmic theory is less developed. It varies according to style, but often without much aesthetic or philosophical justification.

A comprehensive formal theory of electronic music seems far away. The vague term "timbre" is ill defined; one hopes that it will be superceded in the future by a more precise scientific terminology.[5] Thus composers must have a personality that can cope with the fresh and informal liberty offered by the electronic medium. They must not be overwhelmed with or too mystified by the possibilities, in order to choose realistic goals. Fortunately, a number of exemplary masterworks have been composed, and an increasing corpus of clichés or known gestures are accumulating. These serve as signposts in the vast, mostly uncharted territories of the electronic medium.

Today, electronic music exists as a subculture of the musical world. It does not, in general, enjoy the high-culture prestige associated with the dominion of symphonies, operas, major commissions, and prizes. It is rare to see any kind of electronics in, for example, a symphony concert.

Non-pop electronic music does not have the mass audience appeal of a Metropolitan Opera broadcast or a spectacle that fills a casino showroom. This predicament, however, is not new. As Varèse (1965a) observed in regard to audiences:

> There is no such thing as an avant-garde artist. This is an idea fabricated by a lazy public and by the critics that hold them on a leash. The artist is always part of his epoch, because his mission is to create this epoch. It is the public that trails behind, forming an *arrière-garde.*

Indeed, electronic music is ignored by mainstream music critics, even as the star of mainstream journalism fades.[6]

Composers are sometimes asked, who is your ideal listener? As Gérard Grisey (1987) wrote:

> The ideal listener only exists like a utopia that allows us to create in the face of and in spite of everything.

Perhaps the wisest assessment of the audience is this remark attributed to Mario Davidovsky:

> The audience is an abstraction.

Indeed, the audience is not a monolith, and in any case, it is something over which a composer has little control.

Confounding the impression is a curious tendency for composers to dabble in electronic music—for whatever reason—and then afterward "see the light" and reject the electronic medium in a public confession to a major news outlet.[7]

Despite these factors, electronic music is more widespread now than it has ever been. Untold millions of people have used the tools of electronic music in popular applications with built-in virtual synthesizers. Electronic music has a major presence on the Internet. The impact of electronic music on pop music genres is indisputable. The culture of electronic music production is now supported by a diverse industrial base devoted to the development, marketing, and sales of music technology. The commercial mentality is counterbalanced by a lively alternative market of exotic instruments and freeware.

Pedagogy in electronic music has been in place in academia since the 1970s. Research centers around the world generate scientific papers that are read in a variety of international conferences. Electronic music rides advances in science and technology, which positions it favorably for future development. As Jean-Claude Risset (2007) observed, we are still in the infancy of computing, and this bodes well for this medium.[8] After decades of research and development—both artistic and technical—Varèse's vision for the liberation of sound is our reality. For this reason, I call this a "golden age of electronic music" because the conditions for composing in this medium have never been better.[9]

Commonalities between electronic music and traditional music

Electronic music is both a continuation of and a break with traditional music practice. This section discusses the properties it shares with established musical theory and practice. The next section describes the unique potential of the electronic medium.

1. Electronic music inherits centuries of musical thinking. There is no aspect of traditional music theory (scales, melodies, harmonies, rhythms) that electronic music cannot exploit, if a composer so chooses.
2. Electronic music is not a musical genre per se. The toolkit of electronic music is flexible and does not impose a particular style. The medium serves as a vehicle for different genres and styles.
3. The sound palette of electronic music can, if desired, closely approximate that of traditional instruments through techniques such as sampling, additive synthesis, and synthesis by physical models (Roads 1996; Lindemann 2001; Cook 2007; Smith 2010).

4. In addition to the toolkit of the studio, electronic music is also a virtuoso performance medium. Many types of instrumental controllers have been developed, making possible both solo and ensemble performance. A legacy of electronic music performance exists, including traditional instruments modified with electronic pickups or processed through live electronics.
5. The tools and practices of electronic music can be combined with traditional musical tools and practices, leading to "mixed" pieces in traditional styles or in stylistic hybrids that combine known elements with the new possibilities introduced by the electronic medium.
6. Problems of musical organization remain universal, regardless of the medium. Design of melody, harmonic texture, dynamic profile, rhythm, phrase, timbre flow, form, and meaning are essential in any music. Issues like symmetry versus asymmetry, linear versus nonlinear narrative, repetition versus non-repetition, density of voicing, and orchestration come up in any case.
7. Any musical medium, including electronic music, may be a platform for the expression of "extramusical" ideas, which inform the work of many composers. These may include dramatical/theatrical, cultural/political, formal/algorithmical, conceptual/philosophical, and psychological/spiritual issues.
8. Both traditional and electronic music require study and practice in order to achieve significant results. Talent is real and applies in both domains.
9. As in traditional music, electronic music benefits from visual representations. The composer's interface to an electronic music system may be a traditional score or its equivalent in alphanumeric text (a list of notes). Creative graphic representations may be used, as they have been in instrumental music. These scores may serve as a guide for an instrumental performer, as a document of the piece's construction, or as an illustration of an analysis by a music scholar.

Thus electronic music shares many things with acoustic music. Indeed, as we have already pointed out, it is possible to compose electronic music in a conventionally notated way in traditional styles with a result that sounds almost indistinguishable from acoustic performance.[10] Nor is it a matter of one medium being "easier" then the other. As Varèse observed:

> The principles are the same, whether a musician writes for the orchestra or for magnetic tape. The most difficult problems remain rhythm and form. These are also the two elements in music that, in general, are the most poorly understood.

A similar sentiment was expressed by George Crumb (2011):

> It is obvious that the electronic medium in itself solves none of the composer's major problems, which have to do with creating a viable style, inventing distinguished thematic material, and articulating form.

The specificity of electronic music

> Stimulated by science, the music of today is trying to liberate itself from the conventions of East and West—thus penetrating deeper into the world of pure sound, becoming nearer to nature, richer in means of expression, freer from the limitations of musical conventions. . . . The appearance of electronic devices of sound production and the introduction of scientifically conceived new musical instruments are of primary importance and opens an entirely new way for the composer of today.
>
> —ALEXANDER TCHEREPNIN (1971)

We have surveyed what electronic music shares with acoustical instruments. Now what is the specificity of the electronic medium? Nine characteristics that we can briefly summarize set electronic music apart, Each could be elaborated upon at much greater length. In some cases, the specificity is a matter of degree, but this makes a qualitative difference.

1. Electronic music opens the domain of composition from a closed, homogeneous set of notes to an unlimited universe of heterogeneous sound objects. Varèse called this opening the "liberation of sound." The notes of traditional music are a homogeneous system. Each note can be described by the same four properties: pitch, dynamic marking, duration, and instrument timbre. A note at a certain pitch, duration, dynamic, and instrument timbre is functionally equivalent to another note with the same properties. The properties of a pair of notes can be compared and a distance or interval can be measured. The notions of equivalence and distance lead to the concept of *invariants*, or intervallic distances that are preserved across transformations.[11] In contrast, heterogeneity implies that diverse musical materials may not share common properties. Moreover, in these objects, we allow the possibility of time-varying morphologies and even mutations of identity. We can extend heterogeneity even further, down to the level of microsound, where each constituent grain of sound can be unique. However, the diversity of sound made available by electronic music comes at a price: the loss of note homogeneity and, with it, the foundation of a standardized symbolic language (common music notation). To enter the realm of heterogeneous sound objects is to be cast into a strange new acousmatic land without conventional language.
2. It extends the temporal domain of composition to a *multiscale* conception, where we can manipulate an entire composition, or its sections, phrases, and individual sounds with equal ease. A single operation can affect any level. This control extends to the previously invisible realm of microsound: the grains, pulsars, etc., even down to the individual sample. Using detailed knowledge about sound, we can edit

a microsound until it has just the right timbre, weight, proportion, and shape within a phrase. As Stockhausen showed in the 1950s, electronic instruments unify the time field between the audio or intoned frequencies above about 20 Hz and the infrasonic or rhythmic frequencies below this threshold. This means that we can compose throughout this zone, where rhythms morph into tones and vice versa.

3. Sound spatialization has evolved into an integral component of composition. It presents two facets: the virtual and the physical. In the virtual reality of the studio, composers spatialize sounds by means of techniques that lend the illusion of sounds emerging from imaginary environments. Each sound can even articulate a unique virtual space, if desired. As a complement to this virtual approach, in the physical concert hall, we see a strong trend toward the use of pluriphonic or multi-loudspeaker sound projection systems involving dozens or hundreds of loudspeakers around the audience, occupying the entire front stage, positioned vertically, and even within the audience. The convergence of the virtual and the physical makes it possible to paint rich sonic soundscapes. Here there is an interplay between foreground and background elements in three dimensions, with sounds tracing arbitrary trajectories in space. In the concert hall, the composer is often called upon to perform the spatial projection of the work.
4. New materials and tools mean new organizational strategies. Not only pitch and time, but also timbre and space are *morphophoric* (capable of conveying structure). Thus compositional processes can be based on timbral mutations, timbral and spatial counterpoint, detailed control of complex sound masses, juxtapositions of virtual and real soundscapes, sound coalescence and disintegration, and the multiscale interplay between the micro timescale and the other timescales that cannot be realized to the same degree by acoustic instruments.
5. The composer is the performer in the electronic music studio. (There is a subset of composers of instrumental music who are also performers, so this distinction does not apply to them.) As Varèse observed:

> On an instrument played by a human being you have to impose a musical thought through notation, then much later the player has to prepare himself in various ways to produce what will—one hopes—emerge as that sound. This is all so indirect compared to electronics, where you generate something "live" that can appear and disappear instantly and unpredictably.
>
> —QUOTED IN SCHULLER 1971

In the studio, the composer often performs the sound materials using keyboards and other gestural controllers.[12] The electronic medium is demanding. Many composers hire assistants or quit electronic music when they realize that they must become virtuosi of technical studio technique in order to achieve a significant work. This is a formidable medium to master.

6. The notation of electronic music is often graphical rather than symbolic. Figure 1.1 is an excerpt of Edgard Varèse's sketch of the *Poème électronique* (1958). We see an increasing tendency in music software to portray sound structure graphically, for example, in the *sonographic* or frequency-versus-time plane. In some cases, the interface resembles a painting or drawing program for sound. The representation of sound spectra is increasingly explicit, rather than hidden by the note symbol.
7. The frequency precision of the medium opens up new possibilities for pitch organization, such as an unlimited array of microtonal scales, the combination of scales in polytonal constructions, and the exploitation of the continuum between pitch and noise. At the same time, dependence on pitch as an organizing principle is reduced due to expanded control over other dimensions.
8. The temporal precision of the medium makes it possible to realize mathematically exact rhythmic structures and polyrhythms. At the same time, dependence on the grid of meter, which is necessary in order

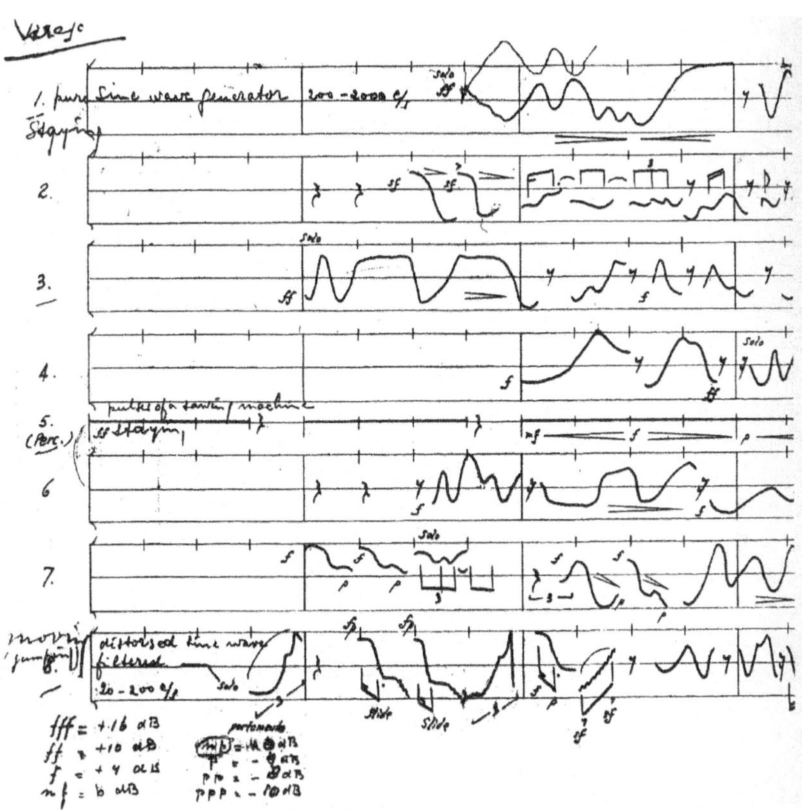

FIGURE 1.1 Excerpt of Varèse's graphic score for the *Poème électronique* (Philips).

to synchronize players in instrumental music, is reduced to an optional structuring principle in electronic music.

9. Memorized control (i.e., playback from a stored function or sequence) and algorithmic control (i.e., playback according to a set of logical rules) let a composer organize more layers and dimensions of music than can be handled manually and greatly expand the capabilities of interactive performance.

These possibilities change the rules of the game of composition. Any one of these nine possibilities may be enough to draw a composer to the medium, even if the composer rejects all the other possibilities.

Conclusion

The impact of electronic technology on music can be seen as an opening. Varèse called for the "liberation of sound," and we see this manifest in the acceptance of any sound possible as a musical resource.

Of course, "liberation" is a charged word. Earle Brown (1967) put it in context:

> Where there is so much talk of "liberation" there are sure to be very disturbing reverberations within the world of established, acceptable criteria. The "liberation" of words, objects, sounds, etc., should be seen as different from the confusions surrounding the idea of making them "free." They are already free, before anyone thinks of using them. The idea of them being "liberated" is relative to the use that they have been put to (and enslaved by) in the past.[13]

The point is that electronic technology is an opening to new musical possibilities. Thus technology has effectively liberated time, since any sound can be sped up, slowed down, played backward, or cut into tiny pieces to be stretched, shrunk, or scrambled. Pitch is liberated from 12-note equal temperament to any scale or no scale at all. It can flow into noise, slow into pulsation, or evaporate and coalesce. Timbre is liberated by the availability of dozens of synthesis toolkits, hundreds of sample libraries, and thousands of new software and hardware instruments. Space is liberated by a panoply of tools for choreographing sounds and the deployment of immersive multi-loudspeaker playback systems.

It has been said that in the hands of a virtuoso, a single instrument becomes an infinite resource of possibilities. This may be true, but some infinities are bigger than others. Cantor's theory of the transfinite numbers showed that the infinite set of real numbers is greater than the infinite set of integers. Thus the infinite set of possibilities of a full orchestra is greater than the infinite set of possibilities of a cello, because an orchestra already contains all the possibilities of the cello as a subset. With electronic music, we extend the possibilities to the infinite set of all possible sounds.

Some would argue that electronic music presents too many possibilities, and blame this for a flood of bad electronic pieces. Yet the world is full of mediocre paintings; we cannot blame the availability of brushes and paint. The ability to select the right problems to solve, regardless of the means, is one of the hallmarks of talent. As Varèse (1966) observed:

> Good music and bad music will be composed by electronic means, just as good and bad music have been composed for instruments. The computing machine is a marvelous invention and seems almost superhuman. But, in reality, it is as limited as the mind of the individual who feeds it material. Like the computer, the machines we use for making music can only give back what we put into them.

To summarize, the electronic medium is an art of unusual independence. But this does not come free of charge. One pays a price, both in terms of the extra work it takes to accomplish something significant in the electronic medium, and also in terms of its mixed and contradictory social acceptance.

2

Aesthetic foundations

This chapter presents a number of fundamental aesthetic issues confronting the field of electronic music. My goal is to foreshadow a range of topics that we encounter in subsequent chapters. Some of the ideas presented here derive from chapter 8 of my book *Microsound* (2001); however, this presentation contains many additions and refinements.

The principle of economy of selection

> To Generalize is to be an Idiot; To Particularize is the Alone Distinction of Merit.
>
> —WILLIAM BLAKE (c. 1798)

A central theme of this book is the principle of *economy of selection*, which means choosing one or a few aesthetically optimal or salient choices from a vast desert of unremarkable possibilities.

Making the inspired, intuitive choice from myriad possibilities remains the exclusive domain of human talent. As Stuckenschmidt (1970) observed:

> Bach was as well versed in the possible uses of the three mirror forms of a melody as any Netherlands polyphonist of the fifteenth or sixteenth century. He did not omit to use one or another of them out of forgetfulness or a defective grasp of the full range of possibilities. He knew that a two-part invention can occupy only a limited amount of space. The ability to make the right choice from the million or more possible forms is a creative secret that cannot be uncovered by science or technology. Here, too, is where the astonishing capabilities of computers prove to have limitations.

Long seen as a gift from the gods, inspiration seems difficult to teach to human beings, and even more so to computers. Indeed, what makes a choice inspired is hard to define, as it is particular to its context. Sometimes it is the surprising or atypical choice, but other times it is simply emotionally satisfying, optimal, or salient in a way that is not easy to formalize.

In discussing inspired choice, it is not a question of idealizing either the composer or the selection. Here "optimal" does not imply perfection; it is simply a particularly satisfactory choice given the context. Indeed, it would be hard to prove by scientific argument that a specific solution to a musical problem is inspired, satisfying, or optimal. It may simply "satisfice," to use Herbert Simon's (1969) term for "sufficiently satisfactory." Indeed, in many compositional decisions, more than one choice would be equally effective, but the composer simply had to pick one. Caprice is integral to the composition process.

Economy of selection is an important concept because it emphasizes the role of subjective intuitive choice in all compositional strategies. Even in formalized generative composition, the algorithms are chosen according to subjective preferences. The rules are inevitably loosely constrained or incorporate randomness in order to allow many possible "correct" solutions. Computer programs can solve for and enumerate many of these correct solutions, but carefully picking the "best" or "optimal" solution is a human talent.

Choices in the moment create our lives. I would go so far as to say that the talent of a composer lies primarily in his or her ability to listen and understand deeply enough to make optimal choices. This begins with choosing the right compositional problems to solve—a question of strategy, tactics, tools, and materials.

The philosophy of organized sound

Composition today has been profoundly altered by the philosophy of *organized sound*. First proposed by Varèse, this philosophy extended the boundaries of accepted musical material—and hence the scope of composition—from a tiny set of instrumental and vocal sounds to a vast range of acoustic phenomena. Unlike the Italian Futurists, who wanted to imitate the sounds of the external world,

Varèse's vision, expressed as early as 1916 (quoted in Hirbour 1983), extended to the entire range of sonic phenomena, both real and imaginary:

> I have always sensed in my work the need for new means of expression. I refuse to submit to sounds that have already been heard. What I seek are new technical means that are able to convey any expression of thought.

In their own ways, musicians such as Henry Cowell (1930) and John Cage (1937) echoed these views. Creative musicians sought beauty not only in the traditional, but also in the strange. Broad acceptance of this philosophy was slow in coming, and Varèse encountered much rejection (Chou Wen-Chung 1966; Stuckenschmidt 1969). What critics initially dismissed as "unmusical noise," however, is now accepted as a potent resource in the palette of the composer.

The idea finally took hold in the 1950s. At the same time, experiments with aleatoric and serial organization contributed to a feeling that the traditional materials and methods of harmonic and rhythmic organization were nearly exhausted. As Herbert Brün (1970) observed:

> The history of music and of musical thought is the story of artificial systems, their inception, bloom, and decline, their absorption or replacement by other artificial systems. . . . Recent developments in the field of musical composition have shown that the limited and conditioned system of musical elements, considered musical material for several hundred years, has now entered the administrative stage, where all possible permutations will no longer possess any new meaning.

Simultaneous with this sense of historical crisis, new forms of music were inexorably emerging from fresh musical materials introduced by electronics technology. These included Pierre Schaeffer's musique concrète, which brought familiar recorded sounds into the mix, and electronic generators, which ushered in a new era of synthetic sound.

Sound example 2.1. Excerpt of *Crystal Skull of Lubaantum* (1999) by Jeremy Haladyna. The sounds are produced entirely by sampled glass crystal, including a glass rod striking glass.

Sound example 2.2. Excerpt of *Aquaforms* (1985) by JoAnn Kuchera-Morin. The sound palette is entirely computer-generated.

Fresh materials forced composers to think in new ways about compositional organization. The new world of sounds is immeasurably more heterogeneous than the previous note-based model. Electronic sounds have unique morphologies that tend to make the abstract notions of symbolic equivalence and structural invariance less germane as an organizing principle. For this reason, elaborate combinatorial strategies make little sense when applied to more diverse sonic materials. We see this weakness in the early musique concrète etudes of Boulez and Stockhausen. These works attempted to tame raw sounds by imposing an ineffective rationalistic order on them, rather than designing new forms and strategies to fit the material. (See further discussion of these pieces in chapter 4.)

Ultimately, material determines form just as form determines material. Thus composers had to wend a path away from abstract symbol manipulation to new methods of organization based on the specific nature of the sound material and the emerging technologies of sound transformation. For example, we can see how an openness to sound leads to a more fluid approach to organization in Natasha Barrett's *The utility of space* (2000).

Sound example 2.3. Excerpt of *The utility of space* (2000) by Natasha Barrett. 

The philosophy of organized sound places great emphasis on the initial stage of composition—the construction and selection of the sound materials. Just as the molecular properties of mud, thatch, wood, stone, steel, glass, and concrete determine the architectural structures that one can construct with them, sonic morphology inevitably shapes the higher layers of musical structure. These interrelationships confirm what musicians have known all along: Material, transformation, and organization work together to construct a musical code. It is through this context that a given sound accrues meaning.

Expansion of the temporal field

Along with the philosophy of organized sound, technology changed the nature of temporal organization in music. Specifically, the emergence of film sound recording prompted a call for an expanded temporal field by composers such as Henry Cowell (1930) and John Cage (1937), who predicted micro control of musical time:

> In the future . . . the composer (or organizer of sound) will be faced not only with the entire field of sound but also with the entire field of time. The "frame" or fraction of a second, following established film technique, will probably be the basic unit in the measurement of time. No rhythm will be beyond the composer's reach.

It was impractical to manipulate film sound on a micro timescale, but the medium of magnetic tape, which became available in the 1950s, made detailed splicing manageable. Tape splicing opened paths to the formerly inaccessible territories of microsound. Composers such as Stockhausen, Koenig, Xenakis, Davidovsky, and Parmegiani began to explore the microtemporal limits of organization. At a typical tape speed of 38 cm/sec, a 1-cm fragment represented a microtemporal interval of about 26 ms. With digital audio technology, we are now blessed with sample-accurate editing on a timescale of millionths of a second.

Not only could sound on tape be edited on a microscale, its time support could be varied; the duration of a sound was no longer fixed, and sounds could be played in reverse. Varispeed tape loops permitted indefinitely long time extension with pitch shifting (figure 2.1). Pioneering electromechanical devices such as Gabor's Kinematical Frequency Converter demonstrated that one could also stretch or shrink the duration of a sound without changing its pitch (Gabor 1946). Today, the digital domain provides a sophisticated array of tools for pitch-time changing. These range from simple granulation techniques that "freeze" a sound to experimental techniques such as *dictionary-based pursuit* in which the time base of time-frequency grains within a sound can be altered on a grain-by-grain basis (Sturm, Daudet, and Roads 2006; Sturm et al. 2008). The aesthetic implication of these technical advances is that the temporal support of a given sound is more-or-less freely composable. It also means that we can realize arbitrarily complicated rhythmic structures with ultra-fine precision, as we discuss further in chapter 6.

The possibility of manipulating sound on any timescale has opened up a wide range of transformations. Manipulations on the micro timescale, in particular, enable new compositional processes (see Roads 2001b for details):

- Coalescence and disintegration of sounds through manipulations of particle density
- Time stretching and shrinking of sound patterns with or without pitch change
- Lamination of multiple sound layers with microtemporal delays

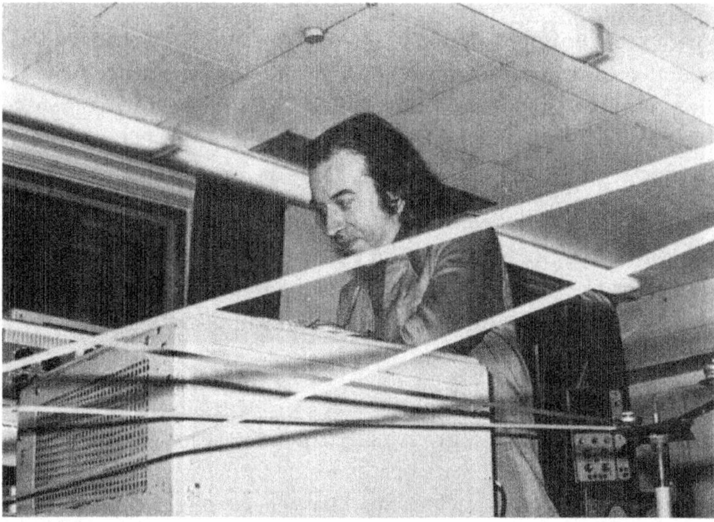

FIGURE 2.1 Jean-Claude Eloy working with multiple tape loops in composing his work *Shanti* (1974) in the WDR Cologne Electronic Music Studio. (Volker Müller, Cologne; from Marietta Moraska-Büngeler, 1988.)

- Spatialization on a micro timescale (see chapter 8)
- Precise polymetric rhythms, created by superimposing multiple particle streams
- Pulses and tones with multiple formant streams, each with their own time-varying frequency and spatial trajectory (Roads 2001a)
- Microsurgery to extract the chaotic, harmonic, loudest, softest, or other selected components within a sound and reassemble it with alterations (Sturm et al. 2008)

Such operations expand the practice of composition and mandate a rethinking of compositional strategy and architecture. To cite one example, as Horacio Vaggione's *Harrison Variations* (2004) demonstrated, it is possible to grow an entire composition—full of heterogeneity—from a single "cell" sound.[14]

Sound example 2.4. *Harrison Variations* (2004) by Horacio Vaggione. 

Multiscale planning and intervention

Another theme of this book is the concept of multiscale planning and intervention. This section briefly introduces the idea and its aesthetic ramifications. Later we devote much of chapter 9 to explaining this perspective in detail.

The basic idea of multiscale composition is that all levels of temporal organization are freely composable at all steps in the compositional process. At any step, for example, we can vary the scope of a synthesis, editing, or transformation operation by applying it to the appropriate timescale, from the macroform, to sections, phrases, individual sound objects, grains, even individual samples.

This contrasts with compositional strategies that preplan a high-level structure or low-level process and then, for the sake of consistency, restrict the composer's freedom thereafter. These plans usually start with either a preconceived macroform (top-down organization) or a formalized generative process (bottom-up organization).

In contrast, a multiscale approach to composition recognizes the reality that a composition comes together in multiple stages and on multiple levels. To work in the widest possible zone of creativity, the composer wants to navigate freely across timescale boundaries, to reevaluate and modify strategy at any stage. This means not only making corrections but also opportunistically taking advantage of insights gained in the reevaluation, perhaps elaborating on an idea that appeared in the initial process. All timescales can be planned and organized, but these plans need not be rigid; we can adapt as the terrain of composition shifts, as it inevitably does during the course of any realization. To generate, delete, rearrange, and transform sounds on any timescale at any step, this is the multiscale approach to composition.

Aesthetic oppositions in composing electronic music

It seems inevitable that we seek to define and understand phenomena through positing their opposites. High cannot be understood outside the context of low, and likewise with near and far, big and small, and so on. Similarly, a given aesthetic tendency can be seen as confronting its opposite, and examining this tension can sometimes lead to insight. This section explores certain aesthetic oppositions raised in composing electronic music, including the following:

- Formalism versus intuitionism
- Coherence/unity versus invention/diversity
- Spontaneity versus reflection
- Intervals versus morphologies
- Smoothness versus roughness
- Attraction versus repulsion in time
- Parameter variation versus strategy variation
- Simplicity versus complexity in synthesis
- Sensation versus communication

Many of these themes echo throughout the rest of the book.

FORMALISM VERSUS INTUITIONISM

Composition embodies an ancient dualism: formalism/intuitionism. Formal models of process are natural to musical thinking. As we listen, part of us drinks in the sensual experience of sound, while another part is setting up cognitive expectations—hypotheses of musical process.

Since the dawn of music notation, composers have been able to manipulate musical materials as symbols on paper, separated from the act of producing sound in time. Therein lies a fundamental schism. Because formal symbols can be organized abstractly, such manipulations have been closely identified with the organization of musical structure. As Schillinger (1946) demonstrated, one can make a music generator out of any found mathematical formula or dataset. Lejaren Hiller's pioneering experiments with automated composition in the 1950s proved that the computer could model arbitrary formal procedures (Hiller and Isaacson 1959; Hiller 1970). Music, however, is more than an abstract formal discipline; it is eventually rendered into perceived sound. Thus it remains rooted in acoustics, auditory perception, and psychology.

A computer translates every human gesture into a formal operation. This system is encoded in the logic of a programming language and executed according to the algebra of the machine hardware. A crucial question is this: At what level of musical structure do such formalisms operate? Consider a pianist practicing on a digital piano, which is one type of computer music system. She is not concerned that her performance is triggering a flurry of memory accesses and data transfers. The familiarity of the clavier and the sampled piano sounds makes the interaction seem direct and natural. This is a great illusion, however. With a change of formal logic, the same equipment that produces piano tones could just as well synthesize granular clouds, as we showed in the Creatovox instrument (Roads 2001b; De Campo and Roads 2003).

Applied at different strata of compositional organization, formal algorithms can be powerful means of invention. An algorithm for spawning sound grains can organize millions of microsonic details. Other algorithms can rapidly iterate through myriad variations, offering the composer a wide range of selections from which to choose. Interactive performance systems try to balance programmed automation with spontaneous decisions and expressive gestures. Many composers mix algorithmic and intuitive strategies.

While formal algorithms enable interaction with a machine, strict formalism in composition means imposing constraints on one's self. The formalist composer follows a systematic plan from beginning to end. The plan must ultimately be translated into the real world of acoustics, psychoacoustics, music cognition, and emotional response. It is in this translation that the game is often lost.

COHERENCE/UNITY VERSUS INVENTION/DIVERSITY

> Coherence must bear some relation to the listener's subconscious perspective. But is this its only function? Has it not another of bringing outer or new things into wider coherence?
>
> —CHARLES IVES (1962)

In academic theory, formal coherence is one of the most vaunted characteristics of musical composition. In general, coherence signifies "logical integration and consistency." This quality is not always easy to measure in practice. In its most obvious form, coherence manifests itself as a limitation in the choice of compositional materials and a consistency in the operations applied to those materials.

One way to ensure formal consistency is to place a composition under the regime of an algorithm. In this case, the operations ensure that the piece always remains within the boundaries of the formal rules. Such an approach makes for a tidy package, free from anomalies and logical inconsistencies. The compositions it produces can be proven to be formally consistent, even if they are dull or incomprehensible.

The problem is, as Vaggione (1996c) observed:

> The rigor of the generative process does not guarantee the musical coherence of the work.

To reiterate, music is not a purely formal system; rather, it is grounded in acoustics, auditory perception, and psychology. Musical coherence seems to be a poorly understood psychological category. It is one of those ubiquitous terms in aesthetic discourse that everyone uses subjectively and no one has ever studied from a scientific viewpoint.

Thus we might focus our attention on other criteria in the way that we compose. I would suggest that inventiveness is at least as important as coherence. The legal profession's definition of a novel invention as a "non-obvious extrapolation of prior art" is a reasonable starting point. Novelty depends on historical and cultural context. What was not obvious to composers in 1913 was demonstrated by the Paris premiere of Stravinsky's brilliant invention *The Rite of Spring*.[15]

Like coherence, the related notion of unity is often emphasized as an aesthetic ideal, and "the unity of all things" is a common theme in spiritual teachings. What strikes me as equally profound is the endless differentiation in nature. Every snowflake, every blade of grass, every living thing is unique! We speak of a human body as one thing as if it were not a fantastically diverse and ever-changing community of trillions of different cells with their own lives hosting an even greater number of microbes. Such diversity is the product of the fantastic inventiveness of nature.

Besides embracing diversity as a goal in itself, we need to accept the notion that unity can emerge from diversity. The most obvious example in the musical domain is the well-established notion of variations on a theme, where diverse variations echo a common theme, but this principal can be extended to all timescales and dimensions of musical organization.

SPONTANEITY VERSUS REFLECTION

We find in electronic music new examples of a venerable opposition in music-making, pitting the immediate spontaneity of improvised performance onstage against the careful, reflective process of studio-based composition. It is not a matter of which is better than the other; they are different worlds—like the distinction between acting and playwriting.

Intuitive decision-making occurs in both domains, as does planning. The main difference is the immediate timescale associated with live performance. Onstage, there is no backtracking; the deed is done. In the studio, deeds can be undone and revised. Another important difference is the greater scope of operation allowed by the studio environment:

- Studio decision-making can take into account the entire range of timescales, from macro to micro. For example, one can adjust a single grain until it has precisely the right morphology, or filter the entire composition in one operation.
- The time support of any sound can be modified arbitrarily: stretched or shrunk with or without pitch correction, varispeed playback, reverse playback, or scrambled in time by granulation processes.
- Due to the possibility of revision, the composition does not have to be through-composed. For example, the ending can be composed before the middle; or, based on how the ending turns out, the beginning can be modified.
- An arbitrary number of independent musical threads can be superimposed precisely via mixing.

Once a piece of studio-realized music is finished, it exists in a fixed medium as a file. This contrasts with the situation in traditional instrumental music, where countless interpreters take on the classics. In some circles, there is a tendency to criticize electronic music in fixed media. In answer to this, the composer Conlon Nancarrow (1987) observed:

> They never say that they would like to have *War and Peace* different each time or Rembrandt's this or van Gogh's that or the Shakespeare sonnets different each time. . . . But they insist that each time a piece of music is played, it should be different. I do not understand why.

Nancarrow, of course, did not compose electronic music. He is mainly known for his mechanical music, sequenced on player piano rolls. His *Study #41* (undated) was called "One of the most astonishing pieces in the entire literature of 20th century music" by James Tenney (1991).

Onstage virtuosity can be dazzling, eliciting a rousing reaction from an audience in spite of the ordinariness of the composition being performed. However, the studio environment is the ultimate choice for the composer who seeks the greatest possible space of creative control.

This is not to say that studio-based reflection is without downside risk. Indeed, an ever-present hazard in studio work is overproduction, resulting in a contrived result. We hear this in pieces that have been overdesigned to impress in a showy way with superficial technical virtuosity or overuse of effects for their own sake, lacking any deeper statement. (A similar tension exists between the dramatic and the melodramatic.)

INTERVALS VERSUS MORPHOLOGIES

> Atomism compels us to give up the idea of sharply and statically defining bounding surfaces of solid bodies.
>
> —EINSTEIN (1952)

A classical aesthetic—dating back to the Greeks—assigned great value to works of art that conformed to certain simply defined numerical proportions, ratios, and intervals. This aesthetic imprints itself throughout the history of music, particularly in the domain of pitch relations. It is also implicit in the treatment of metrical rhythms, with its scale of durational values based on duple and triple divisions of the beat.

Intertwined with intervallic thought is the notion of scales. As Karlheinz Stockhausen observed (1957, 1962), any continuous musical parameter (spatial position, filter setting, etc.) can be subdivided into an arbitrary scale and then manipulated in terms of intervallic relations. The 20th century saw the introduction of serial, spectral, and minimalist aesthetic theories, which were all intervallic. The main difference among them was in regard to which intervals and scales were the most important.

Yet perceptual reality is more complicated than the simplifications of intervallic thought. The momentary frequency of most acoustic instruments is constantly changing. Noise is ubiquitous. Difference thresholds limit all aspects of perception. Masking and other nonlinear effects complicate perception. Training and mood strongly influence musical hearing.

To think in terms of the full range of sound materials and procedures is to shift the aesthetic focus away from sharply defined intervals toward continuously varying and fuzzy boundaries. Just as it has become possible to sculpt habitats from fiberglass foam, or construct any shape by means of a three-dimensional printer, the flowing structures that we can now design and generate do not necessarily resemble the usual angular forms of musical architecture. To the contrary, they often tend toward streamlike or cloudlike morphologies in continuous evolution.

Sound example 2.5. Excerpt of *Altars of Science* (2007) by Markus Schmickler.

It is not a matter of avoiding or excluding intervallic structures, but rather of accepting plasticity: allowing rigid structures to metamorphose into fluid structures and back again.

Through the use of microsonic processing, we can dissolve solid notes into more supple materials that cannot always be measured in terms of definite intervals (Roads 2001b). As a result, sound objects can exhibit "fuzzy edges," that is, ambiguous pitch and indefinite starting and ending times (due to evaporation, coalescence, and mutation). Variations on a micro timescale melt the frozen abstractions of traditional music theory such as "continuous tone," "pitch," "instrumental timbre," and "dynamic marking," reducing them to a constantly evolving stream of micro-morphologies. Intervals may emerge, but they are not the indispensable grid. Rather, there is interplay between intervallic and non-intervallic material. An example is found in the final minute of my composition *Tenth vortex* (2000), when pitched tones emerge out of a noisy granular stream.

Sound example 2.6. *Tenth vortex* (2000) by Curtis Roads.

Within these flowing structures, the quality of grain density—which determines the transparency of the material—takes on prime importance. Increasing grain density induces tone fusion, lifting a cloud into the foreground. Decreasing density induces evaporation, dissolving a continuous sound band into a pointillist rhythm or a vaporous background texture. Keeping density constant, a change in the characteristics of the grains themselves induces mutation—an open-ended transformation.

SMOOTHNESS VERSUS ROUGHNESS

> The shapes of classical geometry are lines and planes, circles and spheres, triangles and cones. They inspired a powerful philosophy of Platonic harmony. . . . [But] clouds are not spheres. . . . Mountains are not cones. Lightning does not travel in a straight line. The new geometry models a universe that is rough, not rounded, scabrous, not smooth. It is the geometry of the pitted, pocked, and broken up, the twisted, tangled, and intertwined. . . . The pits and tangles are more than blemishes distorting the classical shapes of Euclidean geometry. They are often the keys to the essence of the thing.
>
> —JAMES GLEICK (1988)

Intervallic organization depends on stable materials; the pitches in a chord should not suddenly destabilize and disintegrate in the middle. Electronic sound synthesis techniques can generate ultra-smooth and stable continua; the ultimate example is the pure sine tone. However, these same techniques can also be programmed to generate intermittent and nonstationary textures, which in the extreme tend toward chaotic noise bands. The determinants of pitched continua are stable waveforms, rounded envelopes, and long grain or note durations. In contrast, the determinants of noisy signals are irregular waveforms, jagged envelopes, and brief grain durations.

This contrast between smooth and rough timbres can serve as an element of tension in composition, akin to the tension between tonic and dominant or consonance and dissonance. As in these classical musical oppositions, transitions between the two extremes act as a bridges.

ATTRACTION VERSUS REPULSION IN THE TIME DOMAIN

The universal principle of attraction and repulsion governed the emergence of the universe, as well as the inner structure of the atomic particles. It manifests itself in physical biology in terms of the experiences of pleasure and pain, and in the psychological experiences of love and hate, lust and disgust. It rules over individual human relationships, as well as relations between tribes and cultures.

We can apply the principle of attraction and repulsion in music by means of processes that converge or diverge to specific points on the timeline. For example, Igor Stravinsky (1947) used attraction as a means of organizing the time structure of a composition:

> Composing leads to a search for the . . . center upon which the series of sounds . . . should converge. Thus if a center is given, I shall have to find a combination that converges on it. If, on the other hand, an as yet unoriented combination has been found, I shall have to find a center towards which it will lead.

Varèse (1966) thought that it might be possible to adapt the principle of repulsion as an organizing principle:

> When new instruments will allow me to write music as I conceive it, taking the place of the linear counterpoint, the movement of sound-masses, or shifting planes, will be clearly perceived. When these sound-masses collide, the phenomena of penetration or repulsion will seem to occur.

Temporal attraction takes three forms:

- Attraction to a point (see the description of gravitational fields in chapter 6)
- Attraction to a pattern
- Attraction to a meter

When numerous grains or impulses gravitate toward a specific time point, the clustering results in a swarm or explosion. The opposite of attracting sounds to a point is sound repulsion or silence. I have applied these concepts in my pieces *Clang-tint* (1994) and *Half-life* (1999), where points of attraction shape the density of sonic events.

Sound example 2.7. Point of attraction in *Organic*, part 2 of *Clang-tint* (1994) by Curtis Roads.

Attraction to a pattern refers to a strong tendency toward reoccurrence of a given rhythmic motive. The isorhythms of ancient music exemplify this phenomenon. Repulsion from a pattern refers to the absence or avoidance of regularity in motivic figuration.

Metric attraction is a tendency to align to a regular pulsation. A strong metric beat attracts a metric response. It is easy to synchronize multiple layers on top of a regular pulse. The opposite of metric attraction is metric repulsion, found in the rich realm of ametric (or aleatoric) rhythms. (An ametric rhythm is not the same as syncopation; syncopation reinforces meter by emphasizing subdivisions of it.) It is difficult to synchronize or overdub on top of an ametric rhythm. (For more on the topic of temporal attraction and repulsion, see chapter 6.)

PARAMETER VARIATION VERSUS STRATEGY VARIATION

Every technique of sound synthesis is controlled by a limited number of parameters. Consider the technique of frequency modulation (FM) as pioneered by John Chowning (1973). The timbre of many computer music pieces of the 1970s and '80s relied on variations of a handful of FM parameters. We have witnessed a similar phenomenon with respect to granular synthesis since the late 1990s.

As a strategy, parameter variation maintains consistency within a predefined space of possible variations, potentially leading to a monochromatic palette of timbres. As an alternative to this somewhat restricted situation, the synthesis method can itself be the subject of variations. A switch to a different synthesis technique (or source sound) alters the set of parameters that can be varied, which can be a refreshing contrast.

A parallel situation appears in performances using algorithmic composition programs or patches controlled by a few variables. This is a common strategy in live performance. Here the composition process is based on parameter variation of a single algorithm or patch. This tends toward a restricted range of gestures, since no developments can occur that cannot be derived from the predefined parameter set. A switch to a different algorithm, with different parameters to control, is an escape from this finite cage. Another strategic change is to step up or down to control a different level of structure. Such juxtapositions revitalize the senses by breaking the closed cycle of permutations and combinations on a single timescale.

SIMPLICITY VERSUS COMPLEXITY IN SOUND SYNTHESIS

Certain basic sounds, like the pure and magical sine waves, can be made expressive with only a touch of vibrato and tremolo, and perhaps a dash of reverberation. Most other interesting sounds, however, are somewhat complicated in their time-varying behavior. In creating such sounds, one question is whether to embed complexity within an elaborate synthesis instrument, or whether to use a simple instrument in a complex way. My preference is toward the latter. Rather than designing the equivalent of a grand Wurlitzer organ controlled by dozens of parameters (figure 2.2), I prefer an ensemble of small, distinct instruments, each with its own articulators and modes of performance.

In this approach, the score serves as the source of synthesis complexity, as it does in traditional orchestration. In electronic music, of course, the "score" does not necessarily take the form of a traditional staff. It can be a collection of sound events and envelopes, as in the note lists of the Music-N languages, or the graphical regions of a sound mixing program. It can also be generated by an algorithmic composition program or produced in real time by means of gestural interaction.

Consider granular synthesis. An individual grain is an elementary signal created by a simple instrument. Yet by combining hundreds or thousands of elementary grains per second, we generate rich and complex textures. As the traditional practice of orchestration teaches us, by selecting and combining different instruments, each of which is limited in its sonic range, we can manipulate a broad palette of timbral colors. The score interweaves these colors in detail.

As an example of algorithmic control, my 1975 granular synthesis program PLFKLANG written in the ALGOL language spawned thousands of individual grain specifications. We see a similar approach today in the form of high-level generators of microsonic behavior. For example, James McCartney's SuperCollider language provides a set of high-level event generators, called Spawn, Tspawn, OverlapTexture, and XFadeTexture. These emit a variety of sonic behaviors that can be edited and adjusted by users. For example, OverlapTexture generates a

FIGURE 2.2 Wurlitzer theater organ, 1929. (Berlin Musical Instrument Museum)

series of overlapped sounds, where the sounds are produced by a user-supplied synthesis instrument. By adjusting the parameters of the OverlapTexture, and randomizing some of them within specific limits, one can create a wide variety of ambient textures. Many commercial synthesizers also offer ambient textures in which several interacting layers form a complex sonic behavior.

Ultimately, a synthesis technique is a means to an end. In my work, synthesis is the starting point for sound design, which is itself only the beginning of composition. I inevitably edit and alter raw sound material with a myriad of transformations. This editing involves trial-and-error testing and refinement. Because of this, my strategy would be impossible to bundle into a real-time synthesis algorithm.

SENSATION VERSUS COMMUNICATION

Sound waves speak directly to perception. They can be likened to the immediate sensation of touch, if touch could penetrate to the inner ear. As the biologist Walter Freeman (1991) observed:

> Within a fraction of a second after the eyes, nose, ears, tongue or skin is stimulated, one knows the object is familiar and whether it is desirable or dangerous. How does such recognition, which psychologists call preattentive

> perception, happen so accurately and quickly, even when the stimuli are complex and the context in which they arise varies?

The experience of music is a cognitive response to a perceptual reaction. Music directly touches emotions and associations; intellectualization is a side-effect.

Traditional musical languages adhere to familiar grammars. This familiarity acts as a framework for setting up small surprises. We see this in the scores of Mozart where, despite a great deal of apparent repetition in the structure, nearly every measure of the score contains a grain of novelty. In creative electronic music, where the grammar is not familiar, the surprise often consists in finding familiarity.

In this music, the role of the composer is to create a pattern of acoustic sensations in the form of a code. The code organizes the sensations into a meaningful structure. (I do not attempt to define "meaningful" here.) The intellectual challenges and emotions experienced by the composer in creating this structure may be profound and intense (or not). In any case, they are independent of those experienced by the listener. The composer cannot hope to account for the mindset carried into the concert hall by the listener. Acoustic sensations are inevitably filtered by the listener through the narrow sieve of subjective mood and personality. These interpretations trigger a halo of emotions and reflections that are unique to each person.

Music can be seen as a form of communication in the sense that it can serve as a medium for sharing emotions and meaningful gestures. "Ideal" musical communication would imply a direct transmission from composer to listener. Yet music perception is not a point-to-point transmission. The listener modulates the signal, just as the signal modulates the listener, as Daphne Oram (1972) observed:

> The signal reaching your consciousness is as much about you as it is the music. It is the sum and difference of you and the music.

Music stimulates listeners with organized sensations. As Xenakis (1978) observed:

> Any musical piece is akin to a boulder with complex forms, with striations and engraved designs atop and within, which men can decipher in a thousand different ways without ever finding the right answer or the best one.

We could say that the composer is at the helm of a ship that sails the listener on a fantastic voyage. Each listener experiences their own story within this voyage.

Intuition, subliminal perception, and magic

> Art may tell us more about the direction of our journey and the adventures that await us than we can learn from other facts of so-called real life.
>
> —ERNST KRENEK (1939)

> Our whole inner world is a reality; it is perhaps more real than the visible world.
>
> —MARC CHAGALL (1963)

Subliminal perception is perception without conscious awareness. It occurs when stimuli that are below the threshold or *limen* for awareness are found to influence thoughts, feelings, or actions. The term is also applied generally to describe situations in which stimuli are perceived but not actively noticed. Scientific experiments confirm the effects of unnoticed stimuli (Carey 2007). A related phenomenon is *tacit knowledge* based on ingrained experience of music (Rosner and Meyer 1982). We anticipate, recall, and understand music without being able to articulate why or how.

The domain of subliminal perception is much broader than it is often assumed to be. For example, how many listeners in a concert hall are aware of the unfolding technical mechanisms at work in Beethoven's late string quartets, much less those of Bartok? They may hear the notes, but they are only half aware of the structural connections that the notes form; only detailed technical analysis reveals these structures. Yet if they focus their attention and concentrate, they find that they are able to follow an intricate ebb and flow; in essence, they "read" the musical narrative. Understanding a specific musical idiom well enough to be able to parse and label its component parts and/or processes requires academic training, but the underlying capability is innate. As Lerdahl and Jackendoff (1983) observed:

> Much of the complexity of musical intuition is not learned, but is given by the inherent organization of the mind, itself determined by human genetic inheritance.

The composer Paul Lansky (Clark 1997) was direct about the role of the unconscious in understanding music:

> Q: Have you ever included any kind of subliminal messaging in any of your works?
>
> A: I think subliminal messaging is really what music is all about.

In this sense then, the effect of music is largely magical—beyond explanation. Indeed, many scholars today would deny that music theory is a science. Some composers believe that using magic squares, the Golden Section, Fibonacci series, and ratio numerology imbues their music with mysterious powers. In her fascinating book *Music, Science, and Natural Magic in Seventeenth Century England*, Penelope Gouk (1999) quotes the English philosopher Francis Bacon (1561–1626), who defined magic as follows:

> The science which applies the knowledge of hidden forms to the production of wonderful operations.

Gouk notes how consonance ("musical sympathy") and dissonance were considered magical (i.e., inexplicable) phenomena in 17th-century England. Moreover, combinatorial mathematics and mechanical devices (the software and hardware of traditional music) were seen as central to the proper practice of "natural magic" or "experimental philosophy." Prayer, alchemy, and music were seen together as means of reaching higher truths.

Creating music can itself be a magical process when it is informed by deep inspiration and guided at key moments by intuition.

Conclusion: music, body, brain

> Our brain is computing value at every fraction of a second. Everything that we look at, we form an implicit preference. Some of those make it into our awareness; some of them remain at the level of our unconscious, but . . . what our brain is for, what our brain has evolved for, is to find what is of value in our environment.
>
> —STEVEN QUARTZ (2009)

Over a million years ago, the human ancestor *Homo ergaster* walked upright on two legs. According to archaeologist Steven Mithen (2006), this capability, called bipedalism, had significant implications for the evolution of human linguistic and musical abilities. He speculates that the increased demands on sensorimotor control fostered changes in brain structure and the position of the larynx. Increased sensorimotor control meant more rhythmic sensitivity—the ability to move hands expressively and to dance. The lowering of the position of the larynx lengthened the vocal tract and enabled singing.

The universal appeal of music is proof that *Homo sapiens* are designed to appreciate it. Our auditory systems and brains work in symphony to extract aesthetic content from organized sound. As neuroscientists have observed:

> Emotional appreciation of music requires . . . the use of sophisticated knowledge of musical structure. Nevertheless, recourse to this knowledge appears to be immediate, and available to the layman without conscious reflection and with little effort.
>
> —PERETZ ET AL. (1998)

Other scientists observed:

> Just as a bat's ability to use echolocation is related to the unique organization of its auditory system, so the human nervous system may be considered as being organized such that it enables people to readily understand speech and music.
>
> —ZATORRE ET AL. (2002)

From a neuroscience perspective, music can be viewed as a kind of dance around the auditory cortex—tightly interconnected with the rest of the brain, intellectually and emotionally.

Music inevitably invokes psychological states that are bound up with emotional responses. Even "technical" music like the Bach *Two and Three-part Inventions* (BWV 772–801) evokes affective reactions. This tightly constrained and orderly music is at turns comforting, exhilarating, wistful, dazzling, contemplative, and delightfully inventive.

Aesthetic understanding engages mental agents that seek to differentiate between good and bad: beautiful versus ugly, original versus ordinary, engaging versus boring, etc. These are not rational judgments. It is obvious that aesthetic meaning is as much about feelings as it is about logical rationalizations. As Varèse (1937) observed:

> Art is not born by reason. It is the buried treasure of the unconscious—an unconscious that has more comprehension than our lucid mind.

One can be deeply touched without understanding why or how:

> I think it was Sartre who said: music is meaningful, but it doesn't mean anything. It doesn't designate anything. It's like a dream. You wake up in the morning. You really knew what the dream was about. Most of the time you can't explain it—and yet there seems to be an intuition that you really do know.
>
> —MORTON SUBOTNICK (1992)

A fundamental example of aesthetic meaning is the mysterious process of human attraction. The aesthetic reactions of lust and disgust, love and hate, are basic to the human spirit and are clearly a survival mechanism. We seek desirable partners, delicious food and drink, beautiful surroundings, and sensory delight. The alternatives are depressing and debilitating, counter to survival.

Yet why is something desirable, delicious, or beautiful? Why are we attracted to one thing and not another? It is not something that we can always articulate; we just know. Aesthetic perception is dominated by subliminal and unconscious forces.

3

The nature of sound

The material of music is sound—a physical phenomenon. As Varèse (1939) observed:

> When you listen to music do you ever stop to realize that you are being subjected to a physical phenomenon? . . . In order to anticipate the result, a composer must understand the mechanics of the instruments and must know just as much as possible about acoustics.

The phenomenon of sound requires the dimensions of time and space, but also a vibrating medium. Unlike light, which penetrates a vacuum, sound is mechanical energy. That is, it needs a medium that can be vibrated—typically air in the Earth's troposphere.

Understanding the nature of sound, its properties and physics, is of prime importance for composers today. The terrain of music is sound, and the more one knows the terrain, the better one can navigate within it.

The science of acoustics deals with the physical properties of sound. Acoustics has theoretical, experimental, and practical sides. Acoustical theory describes the physics of wave mechanics by means of mathematical models (Morse 1981). Experimental acoustics is concerned with the development of new acoustic devices—microphones and loudspeakers, for example—and overlaps with electrical engineering. Architectural acousticians design auditoria, concert halls, and recording studios. A branch of practical acoustics focuses on the pernicious problem of noise pollution.

Sound touches the body and penetrates rapidly to the brain in the form of electrochemical signals. Once it reaches our awareness, we inevitably dissect it to decode its messages. Thus, in contrast to acoustics, psychoacoustics explores the impact of sound on human beings—our bodily and psychological responses to it. It overlaps with the science of hearing, which is tied to anatomy and the neuroscience of the auditory system (Avanzini et al. 2003). In the rest of this chapter, we examine both acoustic and psychoacoustic phenomena.

While some of the material in this chapter is basic, other parts disclose new facts or perspectives. Advanced readers might quickly scan both this chapter and chapter 4 on sound materials.

What is sound?

> Sound is an alternation in pressure, particle displacement, or particle velocity propagated in an elastic material.
>
> —HARRY F. OLSON (1957)

Sound results from vibration in a material medium. Vibration occurs when mechanical energy interacts with the medium. In acoustical terminology, the energy is referred to as the *excitation,* and the vibration that it induces is the *response* or *resonance.* For example, a cellist vibrates a taut string by drawing a bow across it. This grating sound is amplified and filtered by the resonances of the cello body.

We hear sound because we live on the bottom of a vast ocean of air,[16] a vibrational medium. In scientific parlance, the word "sound" refers not only to phenomena in air responsible for the sensation of hearing but also "whatever else is governed by analogous physical principles" (Pierce 1994). Sound can be defined in a general sense as mechanical radiant energy that is transmitted by pressure waves in a material medium. Thus, besides the airborne frequencies that our ears perceive, one can speak of underwater sound, sound in solids, or structure-borne sound. Mechanical vibrations even take place on the inaudible atomic level, resulting in quantum units of sound energy called phonons. The term "acoustics" is likewise independent of air and human perception, and is distinguished from optics in that it involves mechanical—rather than electromagnetic—wave motion.

How does sound affect human beings?

Sound is heard by the ear but also felt by the body. As Stockhausen (1972) observed:

> Sound waves penetrate very deep into the molecular and atomic layers of our selves. Whenever we hear sounds, we are changed. We are no longer the same. . . . This is more the case when we hear organized sounds, sounds organized by a human being: music.

Airborne sounds enter the body via the ear. The ear is a miraculously sensitive organ connected to a complicated neural structure known as the *central auditory system*, extending deep into the brain. The outer ear takes in sound pressure waves and transduces them into mechanical vibrations in the middle ear. From this point, mechanical vibrations are transduced into liquid vibrations in the inner ear, and then into electrical impulses transmitted via nerves leading to the brain.

At dangerous intensities, sound affects the entire body (Miller 1978a, 1978b, 1978c). At the same time, experiments show that when sound waves are projected on a naked human body, it is almost entirely reflected; little energy penetrates the skin (Conti et al. 2003, 2004). This is because the unadorned human body is acoustically similar to a bag of water, which tends to reflect sound. When human beings don several layers of clothing, they become sound absorbers. Thus a thousand people dressed in several layers of clothing in a concert hall have a damping effect on the acoustics of the hall.

We do not need ears to sense sound vibrations. Mobile phones and other vibrating devices transmit sound energy directly to the body by the sense of touch, bypassing the auditory system.

At a basic level, the human body is an electrochemical system; chemical changes trigger electrical signals (Galambos 1962). For example, muscles are batteries, and muscle fatigue is literally a drop in electrical charge. The sensation of sound provokes immediate and major electrochemical changes in the paralimbic system, which includes the amygdala, hippocampus, and other brain structures associated with emotional responses (Brown et al. 2004; Molavi 2005). These in turn affect the hypothalamus and the pituitary gland—the brain's regulators, which emit hormonal secretions that affect the rest of the nervous system.

Hormones affect muscle tone, breathing rate and depth, blood pressure, and heart pulse, among other involuntary bodily functions. Meanwhile, the mind takes in conscious and unconscious sensations; it remembers what has happened and anticipates what is to come, that is, it constructs a narrative. Depending on the path of this narrative, intense emotional reactions can occur, covering the gamut from tears of joy to insufferable boredom and abject torment. Here is a universal principle: Every music, even the most coldly conceptual and unromantic in inspiration, triggers emotional reactions. The aesthetic implications of this principle are profound: All music is perceived emotionally and romantically. This should not be a surprise, as Meyer (1956) observed:

> Thinking and feeling need not be viewed as polar opposites but as different manifestations of a single psychological process.

Or as Marvin Minsky (2006) observed, human beings never think purely rationally because our minds are always affected by assumptions and preferences (values and beliefs) and driven by goals (desires).

Sound waveforms

Let us now look at visualizations of sound from a scientific perspective. A direct method of visualizing sound waveforms is to draw them in the form of a graph of air pressure versus time (figure 3.1).

This is called a *time-domain* representation or *pressure graph*. When the curved line is descending, the air pressure is decreasing. When the curve is rising, the air pressure is increasing. The *amplitude* of the waveform is the amount

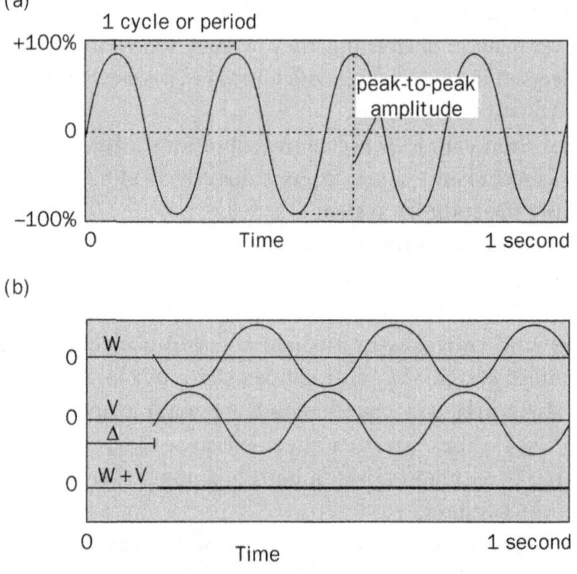

FIGURE 3.1 Time-domain representation of waveforms. (a) The distance between repetitions of a waveform is a cycle or a period. The peak-to-peak amplitude is the distance between the highest peak and the lowest trough. In this diagram, the amplitude scale is measured in percentage, but other scales, such as decibels, can be used. (b) This diagram shows two waveforms *W* and *V*, one of which is phase-shifted with respect to the other by the delay time Δ. The two waveforms are out of phase (i.e., not phase-aligned). Indeed, waveform *V* is phase-inverted with respect to *W*. If we were to add *W* and *V*, the result would be zero amplitude, shown in the third example. This is called *destructive interference*.

of air pressure change; we can measure amplitude as the vertical distance from the zero pressure point (in the middle) to the highest (or lowest) points of a given waveform segment.

Digital audio editing programs usually display pressure graphs, which plot the amplitude profile on a linear scale, that is, from 0% (silence) to ±100% (positive maximum and negative maximum). Some editors let users see the amplitude in terms of the numerical sample values. For example, for a 16-bit sound, the samples range from a high of +32767 to a low of −32768 (corresponding to 2^{16} different values), where one bit is reserved for indicating the positive or negative sign.

The positive and negative excursions of the waveform correspond to compression and rarefaction of air molecules when sound energy passes through air. Any vibrating source causes such effects. For example, a loudspeaker creates sound by moving a membrane back and forth according to changes in an electronic signal. As the loudspeaker pushes outward, the air pressure near the loudspeaker is raised (compression). When the loudspeaker pulls inward from its position at rest, the air pressure decreases (rarefaction).

PERIODICITY AND FREQUENCY

Figure 3.1a portrays a simple sinusoidal wave. A sine repeats at exactly constant intervals of time. Repeating waveforms are called *periodic*. If there is no discernible repetition pattern, it is called *aperiodic* or *noise*. In between the extremes of periodic and aperiodic is a vast domain of quasi-periodic tones.

The rate of repetition of a periodic sound is called its *fundamental frequency*, measured in cycles per second. The scientific term for cycles per second is *hertz* (abbreviated Hz) after the acoustician Heinrich Hertz. Logically, as the interval of the period increases, the frequency decreases, and vice versa. Specifically, the period is 1/frequency. Thus the period of a waveform at 100 Hz is 1/100th of a second.

PHASE

The starting point of a periodic waveform on the *y* or amplitude axis is its *initial phase*. The cycle of periodic waveform repetition can be mapped to rotation around a circle, where one complete cycle is 360 degrees. For example, a sine wave starts at the amplitude point 0 and completes its cycle at 0. If we displace the starting point by 90 degrees (a quarter of a 360-degree cycle) then the sinusoidal wave starts at 1 on the amplitude axis. By convention, this is called a cosine wave. In effect, a cosine is equivalent to a sine wave that is *phase-shifted* by −90 degrees.

When identical waveforms start at the same initial phase, they are said to be *in phase* or *phase-aligned*. (It makes little sense to compare the phases of non-identical waveforms.) Conversely, when two waveforms start at different initial phases, they are said to be *out of phase*. In figure 3.1b, sine wave *W* starts at 0 on the amplitude axis. Notice that sine wave *V* starts after a half-cycle delay. Thus *V* is 180 degrees out of phase with respect to *W*. When two identical signals are

180 degrees out of phase, we say that they are *phase-inverted* with respect to one another. One could also say that *V* has *reversed polarity* with respect to *W*.

Notice the zero-valued waveform ($W + V$) in figure 3.1b. When summing two signals that are exactly out of phase, they cancel out each other.

Phase manipulations are behind a variety of audio transformations, including filtering and spatialization among others (Roads 1996). See Laitinen et al. (2013) for more on phase perception.

Spectra: the frequency domain

Many frequencies can superimpose in a waveform. A *frequency-domain* or *spectrum* representation shows the distribution of frequency energy in a sound. We can view a sound in the frequency domain after transforming it from the time domain to the frequency domain via *spectrum analysis* or *estimation*.

A working definition of spectrum is: a measure of the distribution of signal energy as a function of frequency. Such a definition may seem straightforward, but in practice, different analysis techniques measure properties that they each call "spectrum" with diverging results. Except for isolated test cases, the practice of spectrum analysis is not an exact science (see Marple 1987 for a thorough discussion). The results are typically an approximation of the actual energy. (Roads 1996 presents a variety of different methods of spectrum estimation.)

Individual frequency components of the spectrum are referred to as *partials*. *Harmonic partials* (or simply *harmonics*) are a special case. Harmonics are simple integer multiples of the fundamental frequency (2:1, 3:1, 4:1, etc.). Thus, assuming a fundamental or first harmonic of 440 Hz, its second harmonic is 880 Hz (2 × 440), its third harmonic is 1320 Hz (3 × 440), and so on. More generally, any frequency component can be called a partial, whether or not it is an integer multiple of a fundamental. Indeed, many complex sounds have many partials but no particular fundamental frequency.

The frequency content of a waveform can be displayed in myriad ways. A standard method is to plot each partial as a vertical line along an *x*-axis. This is called a *line spectrum*. The height of each line indicates the amplitude of each frequency component. The purest signal is a sine, which represents just one frequency component. If the segment being analyzed is exactly one period of the sine, then the spectrum shows a single line at the frequency corresponding to that period. Figure 3.2 depicts the time-domain and frequency-domain representations of several waveforms.

Another type of static plot is a *continuous spectrum*, which plots both inharmonic and harmonic energy. Figure 3.3 shows a typical continuous spectrum plot. The line and continuous spectral plots are static, timeless descriptions. They plot all the energy that occurs over a snapshot of time, but they do not indicate when this energy occurred within the snapshot. Since musical signals are non-stationary (i.e., constantly changing), these static views only describe a

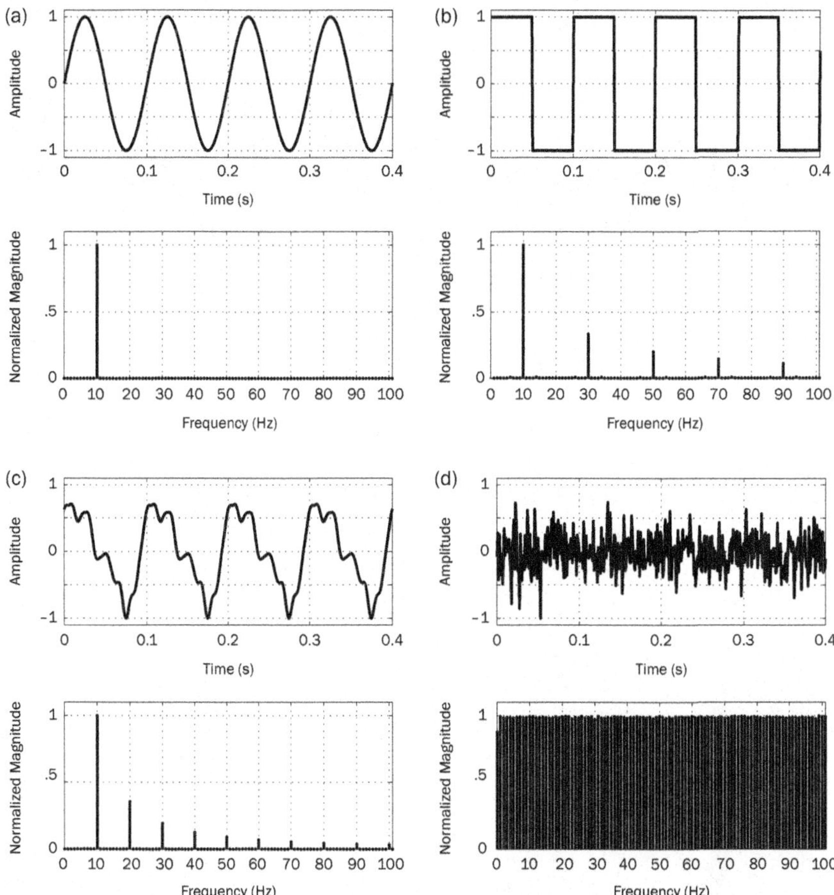

FIGURE 3.2 Time and frequency-domain representations of four audio signals. At the top is the waveform and underneath is its corresponding line spectrum. (a) 10 Hz sine, (b) 10 Hz square, (c) 10 Hz harmonic signal, (d) pink noise (notice the broad spectrum).

narrow window of time—usually less than a tenth of a second. Thus another type of plot is needed to capture variations of energy over time. One can design a time-varying visualization by analyzing sequential pieces of the signal, in the same way that a movie is nothing more than a series of snapshots.

A common time-varying plot is a *sonogram* (also called a *spectrogram*). Figure 3.4 shows a sonogram of speech, which plots frequency versus time. The darkness of the traces indicates the energy at a given frequency. The advantage of this display is that it provides a time-varying record of the sound—akin to a score—that can be studied in detail.

The sonogram is a venerable technique, with roots dating back to the "visible speech" of the 1930s (Dudley 1939). In digital form, it is implemented using the *Fast Fourier Transform* or FFT (Rabiner and Gold 1975; Allen and Rabiner 1977; Roads 1996).

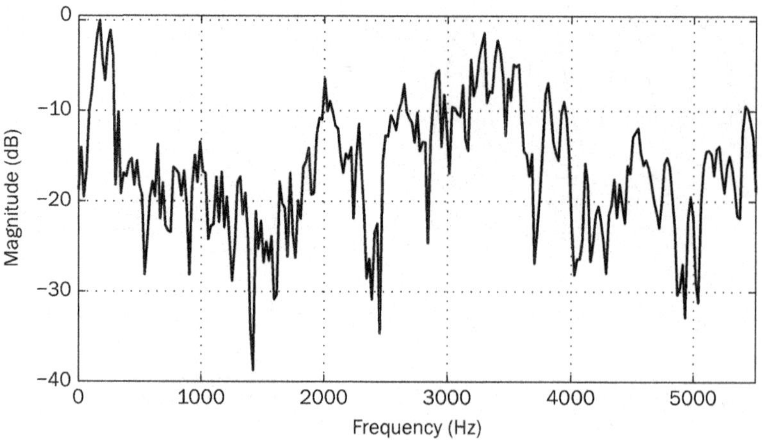

FIGURE 3.3 Continuous spectrum from 0 to 5.5 kHz of a speech sibilant noise, "shhh." The *x*-axis is frequency and the *y*-axis is magnitude. Notice the peak of energy between 3 and 4 kHz.

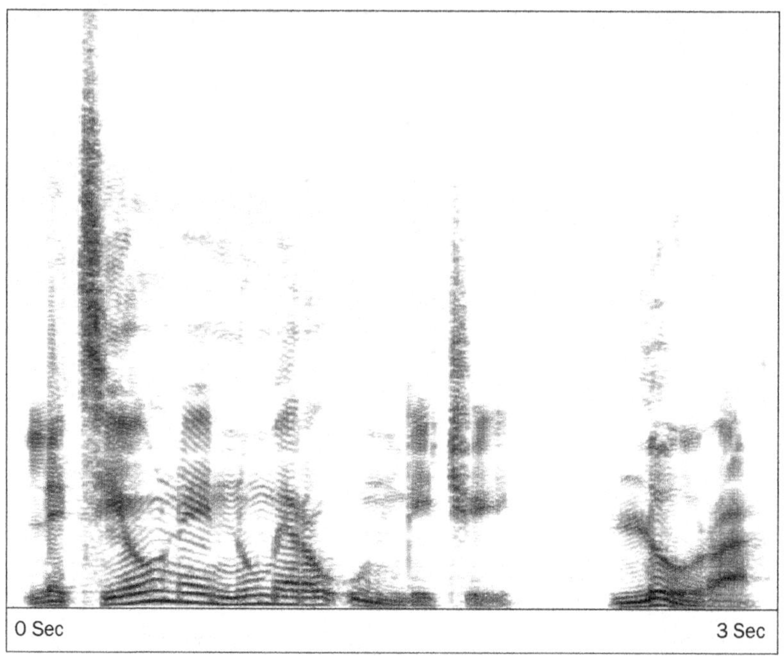

FIGURE 3.4 Sonogram projection of time-frequency energy of the Italian phrase "Lezione numero undice, l'ora" spoken by a male voice. The horizontal scale is time. The vertical scale represents frequency from 0 Hz to 12 kHz. Notice the wideband noise of the hard "z" in "Lezione" near the beginning.

Myriad alternatives to Fourier-based spectrum estimation exist (Roads 1996). Among them, one family is of particular interest, as they decompose a sound into a collection of *sound atoms* (analogous to grains). The resulting decomposition is called an *atomic time-frequency representation* of a sound. The first step in this method is to define a dictionary of all different types of atoms—long, short, high-frequency, low-frequency, etc. The next step is to analyze the sound by seeing if there is a match between the time-frequency energy in the sound and a given atom. The analysis looks at the sound and then searches through the dictionary, looking for an ideal match. If it finds one, it adds an atom to the atomic representation and subtracts that energy from the original signal. The process proceeds iteratively until all the important energy in the original is matched.

These techniques are called by various names, including *sparse approximations* and *dictionary-based pursuit* (Mallat and Zhang 1993; Mallat 1998; Sturm et al. 2009). They are called "sparse" because the atomic representation can closely approximate the original signal with a small number of atoms.

Dictionary-based pursuit is an analytical counterpart to granular synthesis (Roads 2001b). *Matching pursuit* (MP) decomposition is one sparse approximation technique. It offers a number of attractive properties, including excellent localization of time/frequency energy, customizable feature extraction, and malleability. This latter property means that the analysis data are robust under a variety of transformations. These transformations can easily be carried out in real time (Kling and Roads 2004; Sturm et al. 2008, 2009). Figure 3.5 is an analysis plot generated by the MP technique.

Sound magnitude

We all have an intuitive notion of sound level or magnitude. Even a small child understands the function of a volume knob. Dozens of terms have been devised by scientists and engineers to describe the magnitude of a sound. The following are among many:

- Peak-to-peak amplitude
- RMS amplitude
- Gain
- Sound energy
- Sound power
- Sound intensity
- Sound pressure level
- Loudness

From a scientific point of view, these are all different. In a scientific paper on acoustical measurements, a physicist should use precise and appropriate definitions. In discussing compositional issues, however, the extreme precision required by physicists is not always necessary. From a commonsense point of view, the terms listed above are all correlated and proportional to one another: A significant

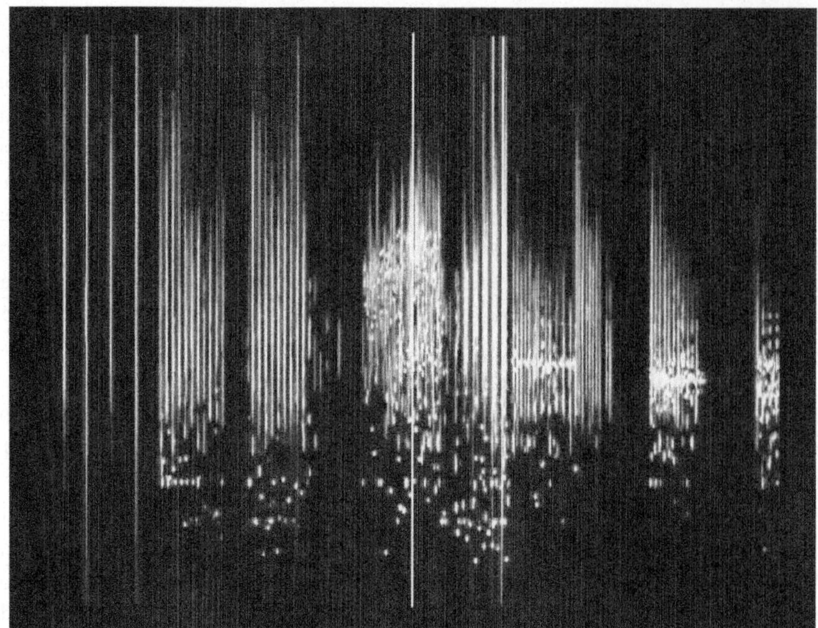

FIGURE 3.5 Frame of animation of *Pictor Alpha* (2003) by Curtis Roads. The display shows a white line in the center that signifies the now. To the left of center is the past and to the right is the future. Notice how noise around the "now" line takes the form of a cluster of atoms or grains. Animation by Garry Kling. From the DVD *POINT LINE CLOUD* (Asphodel 2004).

boost in one corresponds to a boost in all. Our ears are sharply attuned to sound level, so the concept of magnitude is physical and directly perceivable.

From a compositional point of view, the most useful terms are peak-to-peak and RMS amplitude (as seen in a sound editor), gain (a standard term for boosting or attenuating a sound), sound pressure level (what a sound level meter measures in the air), and loudness (perceived magnitude). Sound energy, power, and intensity are technical terms used by physicists to describe measures of sound magnitude in terms of the amount of work done (i.e., how much energy it takes to vibrate a medium).

Table 3.1 summarizes the formal definitions of these terms. The rest of this section explains the useful concept of *decibels* (dB).

DECIBELS

The ear is an extremely sensitive organ. Suppose that we are sitting three meters in front of a loudspeaker that is generating a sine tone at 1000 Hz, which we perceive as being very loud. Amazingly, one can reduce the power by a factor of one million and the tone is still audible. In a laboratory where all external sounds are eliminated, the reduction extends to a factor of more than one billion (Rossing 1990; Backus 1969).

TABLE 3.1

Units for measuring sound magnitude

Peak-to-peak amplitude	A measure of the peak-to-peak difference in waveform values expressed in percentage or dB (see figure 3.6). Useful for describing the magnitude of periodic waveforms in particular.
RMS amplitude	For complex signals such as noise, root mean squared (RMS) amplitude describes the average power of the waveform. RMS amplitude is the square root of the mean over time of the square of the vertical distance of the waveform from the rest position. (see figure 3.6).
Gain	Gain is a measure of the ratio of the input and the output amplitude (or power) of a process, usually measured in dB. A gain of greater than one is a boost, and a gain of less than one corresponds to attenuation.
Sound energy	A measure of work, sound energy is the ability to vibrate a medium, expressed in joules. A joule is a unit of energy corresponding to the work done by a force of one newton traveling through a distance of one meter. A newton is equal to the amount of force required to give a mass of one kilogram an acceleration of one meter per second squared.
Sound power	The rate at which work is done or energy is used. The standard unit of power is the watt, corresponding to one joule per second. One watt is the rate at which work is done when an object is moving at one meter per second against a force of one newton.
Sound intensity	Sound power per unit area, measured in watts per square meter.
Sound pressure level	Air pressure at a particular point, given in dB as a ratio of sound pressure to a reference sound pressure of 20 micropascals. A pascal is a unit of pressure equivalent to the force of one newton per square meter.
Loudness	A psychoacoustic measure based on queries of human subjects, measured in phons. One phon equals one dB SPL at one kHz.

Sound transports energy generated by the vibration of a source. The range of sound energy encompasses everything from the subsonic flutterings of a butterfly to massive explosions. A whisper produces only a few billionths of a watt. In contrast, a large rocket launch generates about 10 million watts of power.

The dB unit compresses these exponential variations into a smaller range by means of logarithms. It can be applied to myriad physical phenomena; however, the definition changes according to the phenomenon being measured. A standard unit in audio is dB SPL (*sound pressure level*). This compares a given SPL with a standard reference level. The logarithm (base 10) of this ratio is the level in decibels, hence:

$$\text{SPL in decibels} = 20 \log_{10} (W/W_0),$$

where W is the actual SPL of the signal being measured and W_0 is a standard reference level of 20 micropascals of pressure. This corresponds to the quietest sound that a human being can hear.

To calculate the dB value of a digital audio waveform, we compare a sample value to a reference level. For a 16-bit audio file, the sample values vary from −32768 to +32767, a range of 65536. Thus, for such a digital audio file, the dynamic range is

$$20 \log_{10} (65536/1) = 96.32 \text{ dB}.$$

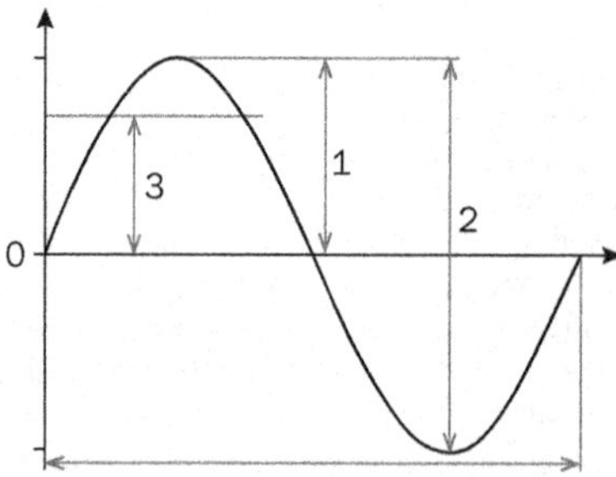

FIGURE 3.6 Measures of amplitude. (1) Peak amplitude. (2) Peak-to-peak amplitude. (3) RMS amplitude.

TABLE 3.2
Amplitude in percent versus decibels

100%	0 dB
70%	–3 dB
50%	–6 dB
25%	–12 dB
12.5%	–18 dB
6.25%	–24 dB
3.125%	–30 dB
1.562%	–36 dB
0.781%	–42 dB
0.39%	–48 dB
0.195%	–54 dB
0.097%	–60 dB
0.048%	–66 dB
0.024%	–72 dB
0.012%	–78 dB
0.006%	–84 dB
0.003%	–90 dB

Describing sound levels in terms of dB enables a wide range of amplitudes Table 3.2 shows how the decibel unit compresses large changes in percentage amplitude into relatively small changes in dB.[17]

As we move away from a sound source, its SPL diminishes according to the distance. Specifically, each doubling of distance decreases SPL by about 6 dB, which represents a 50% decrease in its amplitude. This is the famous *inverse square law*: Intensity diminishes as the square of the distance.

So far we have been talking in terms of amplitude and SPL. Another two concepts—*volume* or *loudness*—are intuitive. Technically, loudness refers to perceived or subjective intensity measured through psychoacoustic tests on human beings, not to sound pressure level measured by laboratory instruments. For example,

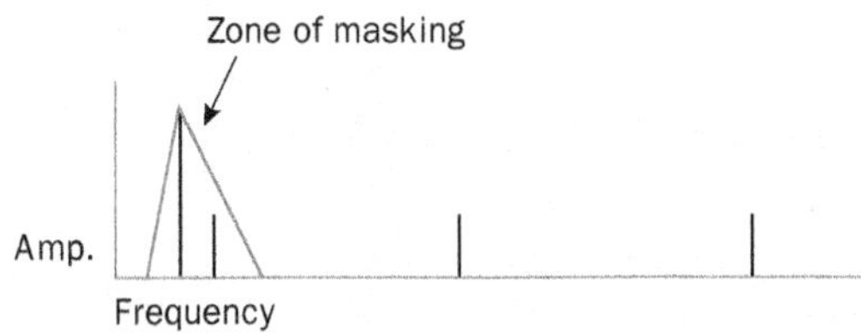

FIGURE 3.7 A loud low-frequency tone masks soft tones nearby. It does not mask tones outside the zone of masking.

the ear is especially sensitive to frequencies between 1000 Hz and 4000 Hz. Tones in this region sound louder than tones of equal intensity in other frequencies. Thus the measurement of loudness falls under the realm of psychoacoustics. In order to differentiate loudness level (a perceptual characteristic) from sound pressure level (a physical characteristic), a unit *phon* (rhymes with John) is used. For example, to sound equally loud (60 phons), a tone at about 30 Hz needs to be boosted 40 dB more than a 1000 Hz tone.

The ear is quite sensitive to sound intensity. A classical question of psychoacoustics is: What is the minimal intensity difference between two sounds, otherwise identical, that allows a listener to reliably report that one sound is louder than another? This is the *just noticeable difference* (JND). Interestingly, this is not a constant, but varies according to the frequency and intensity of the signal, and also from person to person. For example, in the ear's most sensitive range, at 70 dB between 1000 and 4000 Hz, the JND is less than 0.5 dB (Scharf 1978). However, the JND expands to 10 dB for low-frequency (35 Hz), low-intensity (30 dB) tones.

MASKING AND CRITICAL BANDS

The subject of *masking* inevitably arises in discussions of loudness perception. In its most basic form, masking describes a phenomenon wherein a low-level sound is obscured by a higher-level sound (figure 3.7).

For example, standing in a shower masks many sounds, such as someone speaking nearby. Masking is the process by which the threshold of inaudibility of one sound is raised by the presence of another sound. In this case, the voice, which would normally be perceived clearly, is reduced in apparent loudness. This effect is called *partial masking* because the masking signal does not completely eliminate the masked signal. Partial masking depends not only on the intensity of the masker, but also on the frequency of the masking signal relative to the frequency of the masked signal.

Human hearing can be considered as divided into a number of overlapping frequency bands. The interactions between sounds within adjacent bands can lead to a variety of frequency- and bandwidth-dependent loudness phenomena. For example, if we play two sine waves that are very close in frequency, the total loudness we perceive is less than the sum of the two loudnesses we would hear from the tones played separately. As we separate the tones in frequency, this loudness remains constant up to a point, but then a certain frequency difference is reached where the loudness increases. This frequency difference corresponds to the *critical band*. Similarly, the loudness of a band of noise does not increase as the bandwidth increases, but only up to a certain critical bandwidth. Beyond this bandwidth, the loudness increases (Whitfield 1978). (As we see in chapter 7, the critical band plays a role in the perceived "roughness" or *sensory dissonance* of a pitch combination.)

PERCEPTUAL CODING AND DATA COMPRESSION

Taking advantage of the fact that the presence of one sound can partially or completely mask a second sound, *perceptual coding* techniques are designed for *data compression*—a large reduction in the amount of data needed to transmit an audio signal. These techniques estimate which frequency bands are being masked so that they can throw them away before transmission. Common data reduction schemes like MPEG-1 Audio Layer 3 (or MP3) and Advanced Audio Coding (AAC) are based on such methods, which are also called *lossy compression* schemes. A large research literature surrounds this topic.

So far we have discussed *simultaneous masking* effects. Two other types of masking effects are time-based: *forward* and *backward masking*. Consider a short sound that ends abruptly. The human auditory system continues to react for a short time (about a half second) after the sound ends (Zwislocki 1978). This "resonance" can blur our perception of the onset of a second sound. Indeed, when the time interval between impulses is less than about 50 ms, the ear no longer perceives them as separate impulses but collectively as continuous tones. Thus forward masking is strongly related to our perception of pitch.

Backward masking is a curious phenomenon. Basically, a loud click or noise coming less than 100 ms after another sound can obscure our perception of the earlier sound (Zwislocki 1978). The masking sound can disrupt the brain's ability to hear a preceding sound, hence the term backward).

It is interesting that both forward masking and backward masking occur in the visual domain as well. This would suggest that they are indicators of the limitations of the brain in handling events that are too closely spaced in time. We continue this discussion in the next section.

Zones of frequency and intensity

Some sounds we can hear; other sounds we cannot. The *audio* frequencies are perceptible to the ear. They span the range of about 20 Hz to 20 kHz, where the specific boundaries vary depending on age and the individual.

Low-frequency impulsive events are perceived as rhythms. These are the *infrasonic frequencies* in the range below about 20 Hz. The infectious beating rhythms of percussion instruments fall within this range. (Note that sine waves in this same frequency range are, in general, imperceptible, because they have little bandwidth.) Structure-borne sound is vibration that one can feel, like the vibration caused by a train rumbling down nearby tracks. These are typically low-frequency vibrations that one's ear may be able to hear, but they are also felt through the body. Of course, we can also feel high frequencies, such as the buzzing of an electric razor, which is felt by the hand, as well as heard by the ear.

Ultrasound comprises the domain of high frequencies beyond the range of human audibility. The threshold of ultrasound varies according to the individual, their age, and the test conditions.

Some sounds are too soft to be perceived by the human ear, such as a caterpillar's delicate march across a leaf. The softest sounds we can hear stand at the *absolute threshold of hearing* (Zwikcker and Feldtkeller 1999). Below this is the zone of the *subabsolute* intensities, sounds too feeble to be perceived by the ear. This zone of faint sounds can sometimes be captured by a microphone and amplified into the realm of the audible to spectacular effect—a classic technique of musique concrète.

Other sounds are so loud that to perceive them directly is dangerous, since they are destructive to the human body. Very loud impulses can permanently damage the inner ear. Sustained exposure (typically in a noisy work environment) to sound levels above 85 dB induces permanent hearing loss. As the intensity increases, it takes less and less time to induce permanent loss. Around 130 dB, sound is not only heard but also felt as a painful pressure wave by the exposed tissues of the body (Pierce 1983). The loudest possible sound in air is about 194 dB, the point at which the nominal air pressure is reduced to from an average of 100,000 pascals to 0 pascals, creating a vacuum.

The dangerous zone of intensities extends into a range of highly destructive acoustic phenomena. The detonation of a high explosive device, for example, results in an intense acoustic shock wave. For lack of a better term, I call these the *perisonic* intensities (from the Latin "periculos" meaning dangerous). The *audible* intensities fall between these two ranges. Figure 3.8 depicts the zones of sound intensity and frequency. What I call the *alphazone* in the center is where the audio frequencies intersect with the audible intensities, enabling hearing. Notice that the α-zone is only a fraction of a larger range of sonic phenomena.

Timescales of sound and music

Music theory has long recognized a temporal hierarchy of structure in music compositions. Adopting the terminology of mathematical graph theory (Bobrow and Arfib 1974; Aldous and Wilson 2000), this hierarchy can be plotted as an inverted tree structure (figure 3.9). The topmost vertex or *root* represents the entire piece (the *global* level). The root splits into multiple arcs, which connect to vertices that represent substructures of the piece. These in turn split into further

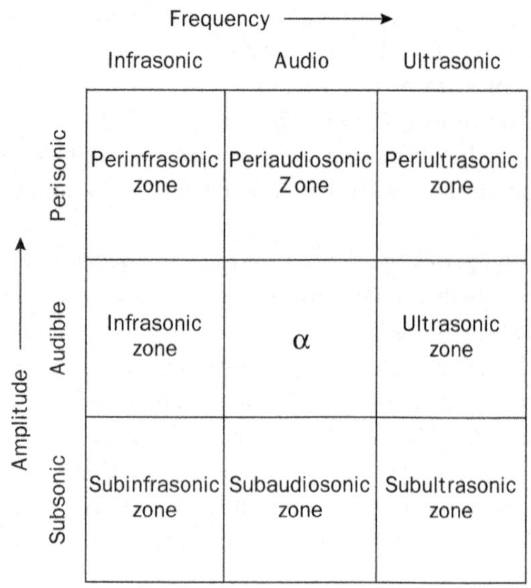

Frequency →

Amplitude ↑	Infrasonic	Audio	Ultrasonic
Perisonic	Perinfrasonic zone	Periaudiosonic Zone	Periultrasonic zone
Audible	Infrasonic zone	α	Ultrasonic zone
Subsonic	Subinfrasonic zone	Subaudiosonic zone	Subultrasonic zone

FIGURE 3.8 Zones of intensities and frequencies.

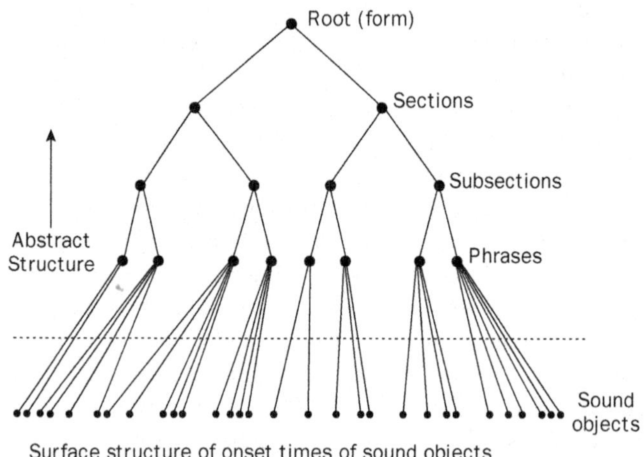

FIGURE 3.9 Idealized graph of hierarchical musical structure. This is a simple musical structure, typical of nursery rhymes.

substructures, ultimately arriving at the bottom or *terminal* layer of individual notes or sound objects (the *local* level).

This hierarchy, however, is incomplete. Above the level of an individual piece are the cultural time spans defining the oeuvre of a composer or a stylistic period. Beneath the level of the note lies another multilayered stratum, the microsonic hierarchy. Modern tools let us view and manipulate the microsonic layers, from which all acoustic phenomena emerge. Beyond these physical timescales,

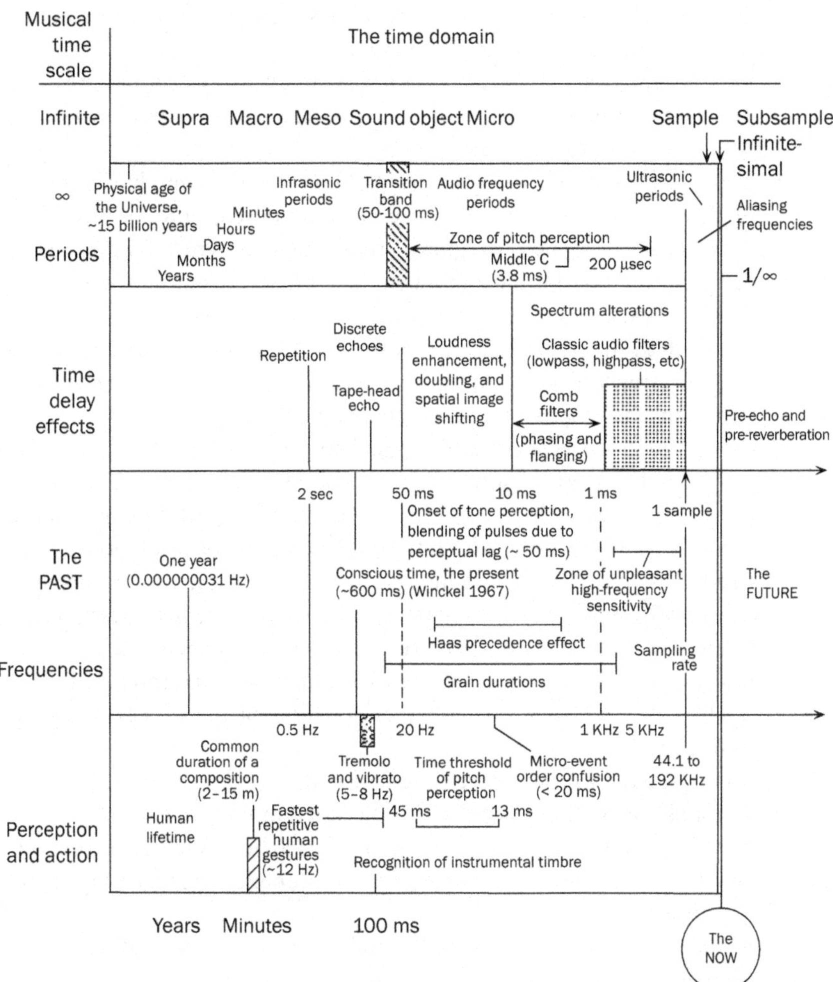

FIGURE 3.10 The time domain. Ranges are not drawn to scale.

mathematics defines two ideal temporal boundaries—the infinite and the infinitesimal, which appear in the theory of Fourier analysis.

Understanding the multiscale nature of sound is essential to the practice of composition today. Taking a comprehensive view, we distinguish nine timescales of music, as shown in figure 3.10.

The nine timescales are as follows:

1. *Infinite*—The ideal time span of mathematical durations such as the infinite sine waves of classical Fourier analysis. Harking back to a theological perspective, Messiaen (1994) called this *eternity.*
2. *Supra*—A timescale beyond that of an individual composition and extending into months, years, decades, and centuries. Musical cultures

are constructed out of supratemporal bricks: the eras of instruments, of styles, of musicians, and of composers.

3. *Macro*—The timescale of overall musical architecture or form, measured in minutes or hours, or in extreme cases, days (as in Wagner's *Ring* cycle, Japanese Kabuki rituals, etc.).
4. *Meso*—Divisions of form, groupings of sound objects into hierarchies of phrase structures of various sizes, measured in minutes or seconds. This "local" as opposed to "global" timescale is extremely important in composition. For it is most often on the meso level that the sequences, combinations, and transmutations that constitute musical ideas unfold. Local rhythmic patterns, as well as melodic, harmonic, and contrapuntal relations transpire at the meso layer, as do processes such as theme and variations, development, progression, and juxtaposition.
5. *Sound object*—A basic unit of musical structure, generalizing the traditional concept of note to include complex and mutating sound events on a timescale ranging from a fraction of a second to several seconds. Whereas notes are static and homogeneous (each note has a fixed pitch, duration, dynamic, and instrument name), sound objects can vary in time (they can mutate) and they are very heterogeneous. In electronic music, any sound from any source may serve a musical function. Thus the influence of the traditional intervallic pitch-duration grid (which assumes note homogeneity) is greatly diminished.
6. *Micro*—Sound particles on a timescale that extends down to the thresholds of auditory perception (measured in thousandths of a second or milliseconds). Thousands of microsonic particles such as grains and wavelets can serve as building blocks for a complex time-varying sound (Roads 2002).
7. *Sample*—The lowest level of digital audio systems: individual binary samples or numerical amplitude values, one following another at a fixed time interval. The period between samples is measured in millionths of a second (microseconds).
8. *Subsample*—Fluctuations on a timescale that are too brief to be properly recorded or perceived, measured in nano-, pico-, fempto-, atto-, zepto-, and yoctoseconds (1×10^{-24} seconds). The subsample timescale encompasses an enormous range of phenomena, from the perceptible to the imperceptible: aliased artifacts, ultrasounds, and the Planck interval (see Roads 2001b).
9. *Infinitesimal*—The ideal time span of mathematical durations such as the infinitely brief delta functions. One application of the delta function in signal processing is to tether the mathematical explanation of sampling (see Roads 2001b).

Notice in the middle of figure 3.8, in the frequency column, a line indicating "Conscious time, the present (~600 ms)." This line marks off Winckel's (1967) estimate of the "thickness of the present." The thickness extends to the line at the right indicating the physical NOW. This temporal interval constitutes an estimate of the accumulated lag time of the perceptual and cognitive mechanisms associated with hearing. Here is but one example of a disparity between *chronos* (physical time) and *tempus* (perceived time).

As a sound's duration passes from one timescale to another, it crosses perceptual boundaries. It seems to change quality. This is because human perception processes each timescale differently. Consider one period of a simple sinusoid wave transposed to several timescales (1 μsec, 1 ms, 1 sec, 1 minute, 1 hour). The waveform shape is identical, but one would have difficulty classifying auditory experiences of these waveforms in the same qualitative family.

In some cases, the borders between timescales are demarcated clearly, but ambiguous zones surround other boundaries. The ultrasonic threshold, for example, could be said to be different for each person, changing with age. Moreover, training and culture condition the perception of certain temporal phenomena. To notice a flat pitch or a dragging beat, for example, is to detect a temporal anomaly on a microscale that might not be noticed by everyone.

It is easy to distinguish the boundary separating the sample timescale from the subsample timescale. This boundary is the Nyquist frequency, or half the sampling frequency. However, the perceived effect of crossing this boundary is not always evident. Low-level aliased frequencies from the subsample time domain may mix unobtrusively with high frequencies in the sample time domain.

The border between other timescales is context-dependent. Between the sample and micro timescales, for example, is a region of transient events—too brief to evoke a sense of pitch but rich in timbral content. Between the micro and the object timescales is a stratum of brief events like short staccato notes. Another zone of ambiguity is the border between the sound object and meso levels, exemplified by an evolving texture. Consider a granular cloud lasting a minute or more; it is perceived as a unified entity but it may be constantly mutating. Sound art installations that are set up for weeks at a time blur the boundary between the macro and the supratemporal timescales. Indeed, an algorithmic composition system can spawn non-repeating musical patterns indefinitely, given a sufficiently large parameter space to explore (Collins 2002).

Timescales are interlinked, since the musical structure at each level comprises events on lower levels and is simultaneously subsumed by higher timescales. Hence, to operate on one level is to affect other levels. The nonlinear nature of musical structure means, however, that linear incremental changes in the parameters on one timescale cannot guarantee a linear perceptible effect on adjacent timescales. The most common example is a beating pulse at 1 Hz, which when sped up linearly, passes through several zones of perception (figure 3.8). At 20 Hz, it forms a continuous tone without identifiable pitch. Increasing the frequency of this tone, it turns into a pitched tone at about 40 Hz. However, the perception of pitch evaporates again at about 5 kHz. Increasing the frequency still further to 9 kHz, the tone becomes piercing to the ear, while at 12.5 kHz, it gives a sense of transparency and air. The tone disappears from awareness altogether somewhere about 20 kHz, yet it is still registered by the brain considerably beyond this frequency threshold (Oohashi et al. 1991, 1993).

Sound phenomena on one timescale may travel by transposition to another timescale, but the voyage is not linear. Pertinent characteristics may not be maintained. In other words, the perceptual properties of a given timescale are not necessarily invariant across dilations and contractions. To cite an example, a melody loses all sense of pitch when transposed very high or very low. This inconsistency, of course, does not prevent us from applying such transpositions. It merely means that we must recognize that each timescale abides by its own rules.

The speed of sound

Sound propagates at different rates, depending on the medium of propagation. As the mathematician and physicist Leonard Euler wrote in his 1726 doctoral dissertation "De Sono":

> [As] both the density or weight and pressure of the air surrounding the earth are subject to various changes, the speed of sound is constantly changing also. Hence the maximum speed of sound will be [found] on the hottest days with a clear sky. . . . With the harshest cold and the fiercest storm, the speed of sound should be a minimum.

Sound traveling in a sparse medium of dry air propagates at about 331 meters (1100 feet) per second at 0 degrees centrigrade. In contrast, sound waves travel slowly in rubber—an absorbent medium—at speeds as low as 40 meters per second (Eargle 1995).

Sound travels much faster in water (1429 meters per second). The speed of sound in a bubbly medium is slowed, however, due to interference by the bubbles. Bubbles transport their own sounds. A gurgling brook releases bubbles of air, and as these air pockets contact the surface, they pop with a resonance according to the size of the bubble. Large bubbles make low-frequency sounds while the tiny bubbles in a glass of fine champagne emit a high fizzing sound.

Finally, sound travels fastest in solid metal media, such as a bar of steel, in which longitudinal sound waves travel over 5000 meters per second (Rossing 1990; Eargle 1995).

If the source producing the sound is moving toward or away from a listener, this affects what they hear. The *Doppler shift* effect is a continuous pitch bending that occurs when a moving sound source passes a stationary listener. If we are standing by the railroad tracks and a train approaches at high speed, we hear the pitch shift upward as it approaches and shift downward as it passes by. The pitch shift upward is attributable to the shortening of the wavefronts as the sound

FIGURE 3.11 Boeing F-18 jet at Mach 1. A condensation cloud can appear around aircraft traveling at transonic velocities. (Photo: John Gay, www.navy.mil/navydata/images/hornetsb.jpg)

approaches, and the pitch shift downward is attributable to the corresponding lengthening of the wavefronts as it recedes into the distance.

MACH 1 AND BEYOND

The speed of sound, referred to as Mach 1, is approximately 1224 km/hour (761 mph) in air at sea level. When a sound-emitting source moves at *transonic* velocity (Mach 1), it is effectively aligned with its own sonic shock wave (figure 3.11). When it passes overhead, one hears a very loud impulse that represents its sonic history (Dowling and Williams 1983).

A curious effect occurs at exactly twice the speed of sound: Mach 2. The sound plays in reverse! As the source is ahead of its sound wave, the most recent sounds are heard first, and the earlier sounds arrive later. To the people in the airplane, the noise is heard normally.[18]

Sounds at extreme sonic velocities are destructive. Explosives can generate powerful transonic shock wave air currents traveling at up to 8000 meters per second, corresponding to Mach 24. These destroy everything in their path.

Shape, direction, and size of sounds

Sounds sculpt space. They form individual shapes of different sizes radiating in specific directions. This section examines these spatial attributes.

SOUND SHAPE

Sound waves in air tend to radiate spherically in three dimensions from a source. The direction and shape of the sound waves are variously called the *dispersion pattern, direction pattern,* or *radiation pattern,* and they can vary depending on the frequency band and the source. The dispersion pattern of a loudspeaker is usually fixed, whereas the dispersion pattern of an acoustic instrument varies as a function of frequency (figure 3.12).

A special-purpose *superdirectional* loudspeaker projects a narrowly focused sound beam—less than 50 cm in diameter at a distance of 2 meters (Holosonics 2010). A typical application is a museum installation, where listeners standing under a sound beam can hear a narrative description of a work of art, while others standing nearby cannot. (For more on superdirectional sound beams, see chapter 10.)

THE SIZE OF SOUNDS

Sounds have a specific physical size as well as shape. A quiet sound is physically petite. One has to put one's ear close to it because the body of air it perturbs is tiny. Other sound waves are gigantic, such as the Krakatoa explosion of August 1883. It was heard 4800 kilometers away, and the pressure wave traveled around the earth for 127 hours (Miller 1935). The shape of the sound is partly determined by the dispersion pattern of its source and also by the architecture of the space in

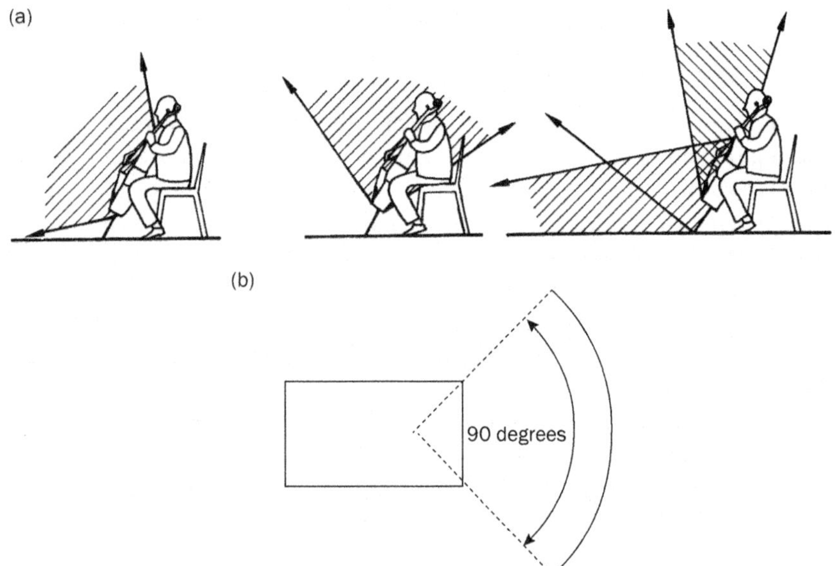

FIGURE 3.12 Comparison of dispersion pattern of a cello and a loudspeaker. (a) The dispersion pattern of a cello varies according to frequency (after Dickreiter 1989). (b) View of a loudspeaker from above. A typical loudspeaker dispersion pattern is relatively consistent for all frequencies.

which it is projected. For example, striking a triangle produces a spherical shape wave, while a sound beam emitted by a superdirectional loudspeaker is narrow. The reflections from a spherical sound wave tend to produce generalized reverberation, while a narrow sound beam will reflect like a beam of light, with echoes heard only in certain locations.

We can think of a sound wave as "unfolding" longitudinally from its source. Since sound takes time to travel in the air, we can measure the physical distance it takes for one period at a given frequency to unfold. This distance is called the *wavelength.* Since sound travels at 331 meters/second in air, the wavelength of a 331 Hz sine tone is one meter.

For loudspeaker listening, a room that is long (i.e., the distance between the loudspeakers and the rear wall is large) is preferable to a short room, since bass frequencies need space to unfold without distortion. For example, a deep bass tone at 68 Hz needs four meters to take form. In small rooms, parts of bass waveforms are reflecting back and colliding with other bass waveforms. There may be deep bass, but room-induced resonances (standing waves) can distort the tones produced by the loudspeakers.

PERCEPTION OF THE RATE OF SOUND EVENTS

In the world of acoustic music, the rate of successive sound events is limited by human performance. A virtuoso pianist can only play at maximum about 12 events per second. A skilled drummer can multiply this rate through the technique of the double-stroke or triple-stroke roll, in which every stroke produces two or three bounces, resulting in rolls that sound almost continuous due to the forward masking effect discussed in a previous section.

Not only is our muscular performance constrained, so is our perception. When events fly by too quickly, they "blur" in our brain. As Milton Babbitt (1964) observed:

> The constant self-question of the composer of the past, "Does what I have written exceed the capacities of the performer?" is now replaced by "Does what I have produced exceed the perceptual capacities of the trained listener?

Consider the effect of tempo on perception. I conducted an experiment with a MIDI score file of Mozart's familiar K .331 *Sonata for Piano Number 11*, the *Rondo Alla Turca: Allegretto* movement (ca. 1783). In a sequencer, one can change the playback tempo without altering the pitches. Here is what I observed when I steadily increased the playback tempo:

1 × tempo (the movement has a duration of 3 min, 45 sec): normal performance
2 × tempo: It is no longer playable by a human musician, but the ear follows it readily as an uptempo version of K .331.
3 × tempo: Certain melodic details are lost, but the identity of the piece is still unmistakable.

4 × tempo: Some melodic passages morph into glissandi, as if the pianist is skimming a finger up and down the keyboard.
6 × tempo (37 seconds duration): The piece loses structural coherence; certain parts sound like arbitrary glissandi.
12 × tempo (18 seconds duration): The sound degenerates into an unrecognizable swirl of grains.

The potential for uptempo performance was recognized in the early days of computer music. It led to a new genre of *machine music* characterized by superhuman speed and rhythmic precision. *Sonatina for CDC 3600* (1966) by Arthur Roberts is a classic example (on a recording accompanying Von Foerster and Beauchamp 1969).

Sound example 3.1. Excerpt of *Sonatina for CDC 3600* (1966) by Arthur Roberts.

Machine music found an echo in the manic sequenced electronica of the early 2000s, for example, *District Line II* (2003) by Squarepusher (Jenkinson 2003).

Sound example 3.2. Excerpt of *District Line II* (2003) by Squarepusher.

Psychoacousticians have studied a variety of perceptual effects that occur in the region between individuated event streams and continuous flows. These are mainly focused on processes of *fission* where alternating tones appear to be part of separate lines or streams, versus *fusion* in which they appear to be part of the same line or stream (Bregman 1978; Deutsch 1982). As in other aspects of perception, the laws of Gestalt psychology strongly influence how we segregate or group phenomena together. For example, the rule of "common fate" says that we tend to group together phenomena that change at the same time in the same way. (See chapter 6 for more on Gestalt grouping mechanisms.)

The perceptual threshold between individual events and a continuous flow is of great interest from an aesthetic point of view. For example, when discrete melodies are sped up, they lose their melodic quality and morph into continuous timbres. When rhythms are sped up, they morph into tones. When modulations like tremolo and vibrato are sped up, they morph into complex spectra. Streaming around the thresholds of this zone of morphosis—where discrete events turn into continuous tones—is intrinsically fascinating. It challenges our ability to keep pace with the flow. An example is Mario Davidovsky's *Synchronisms Number 6 for Piano and Electronic Sounds* (1970), which features glittering melodic strands; at one point, 14 tones flash by in just 1.14 seconds, each tone lasting 70 to 80 ms.

Sound example 3.3. Excerpt of *Synchronisms Number 6 for Piano and Electronic Sounds* by Mario Davidovsky.

A similar event rate appears at the end of my *Eleventh vortex* (2001), in which a burst of 40 sounds occurs in less than four seconds.

Sound example 3.4. Excerpt of *Eleventh vortex* by Curtis Roads. 

Timbre

> A compound color is produced by the admixture of two or more simple ones, and an assemblage of tones, such as we obtain when the fundamental tone and the harmonics of a string sound together, is called by the Germans *Klang*. May we not employ the English word clang to denote the same thing, and thus give the term a precise scientific meaning akin to its popular one? And may we not, like Helmholtz, add the word color or tint, to denote the character of the clang, using the term clang-tint as the equivalent of *Klangfarbe*?
>
> —JOHN TYNDALL (1875)

> Music theorists have directed little attention towards the compositional control of timbre. The primary emphasis has been on harmony and counterpoint. The reason for this probably lies in the fact that most acoustical instruments provide for very accurate control over pitch but provide little in the way of compositionally specifiable manipulation of timbre. With the potential of electroacoustic instruments the situation is quite different. Indeed one can now think in terms of providing accurate specifications for, by way of example, sequences of notes that change timbre one after another.
>
> —DAVID WESSEL (1979)

> In this day and age, the timbre of electroacoustic music could be expected to be the result of the compositional process as a whole, be it algorithmic or not.
>
> —CLARENCE BARLOW (2006)

As discussed in the preface, the standard definition of the term "timbre" is inadequate. The American National Standards Institute (1999) defines it as "an attribute of auditory sensation" that enables a listener to distinguish two sounds having the same loudness and pitch. This definition describes timbre as a perceptual phenomenon, and not an attribute of a physical sound. Despite this, everyone has an intuitive sense of timbre as a descriptive attribute of a sound (e.g., a gong sound, muted trumpet, voice-like sound, toy piano, etc.). Moreover, the spectrum of most instrumental sounds changes when they are played at different pitches, loudnesses, and durations, so even one instrument has many timbres.

Everyone agrees that timbre is a "multidimensional property," but there is no general scientific agreement about what these properties are or how to measure them.

Recognizing that the vast range of sound material opened up by musique concrète was largely undefined and unclassified, Pierre Schaeffer made a pioneering attempt to describe the correlates of timbre in his *Traité* (1966, 1976, 1977; Chion 2009) and the disc plus booklet *Solfège de l'object sonore* (Schaeffer, Reibel, and Ferreyra 1967). Although the vocabulary he developed is idiosyncratic, there is no question that Schaeffer made many discoveries on the nature of sound color.

Most scientific research on timbre has focused on traditional instrument and vocal tones. A classic example is the research of John Grey, who made a three-dimensional map of the perceived timbre space for different instrumental tones (Grey 1975, 1978). Tones that sound similar were close together in this space, while dissimilar tones were far apart. Wessel (1979) devised a scheme for navigating timbre space by means of additive synthesis. Only a few heroic attempts have been made to classify the vast universe of sound outside the territory of pitched acoustic instruments (Schaeffer 1977; Schaeffer, Reibel, and Ferreyra 1967).[19]

Numerous attributes of sounds inform timbre perception. These include the amplitude envelope of a sound (especially the attack shape), undulations due to vibrato and tremolo, perceived loudness, duration, and the time-varying spectrum envelope (the distribution of frequency energy over time) (Schaeffer 1966, 1976, 1977; Risset 1991; McAdams and Bregman 1979; McAdams 1987; Gordon and Grey 1977).

Certain tones, such as simple sawtooth waveforms, have a spectrum envelope that is *monotonic* (i.e., attenuating or rolling off linearly with increasing frequency; Mathews 1999). Other tones, such as spoken vowels, exhibit several sharp peaks called *formants* in their spectrum envelopes (figure 3.13). The formants move around as we speak to create the various phonemes of speech. For synthetic tones, we can choose to make the formant frequencies either independent of or dependent on pitch. In the latter case, the waveshape tends to be constant, and only the pitch period changes. For speech-like tones, the formants are in the range of 250 Hz to 4 kHz (Cook 1999).

MPEG-7 TIMBRAL DESCRIPTORS

Until the development of the MPEG-7 timbral descriptors in 2001, timbre was a vaguely defined territory described by numerous and incompatible maps. The MPEG-7 multimedia content description standard changed this situation. It provided a standard set of mathematically defined terms to describe a number of important aspects of timbre. Thus it represents a significant advance in timbral description.

A media file that conforms to the MPEG-7 format contains *metadata* (i.e., descriptors of the contents of the file). One category of descriptors built into this

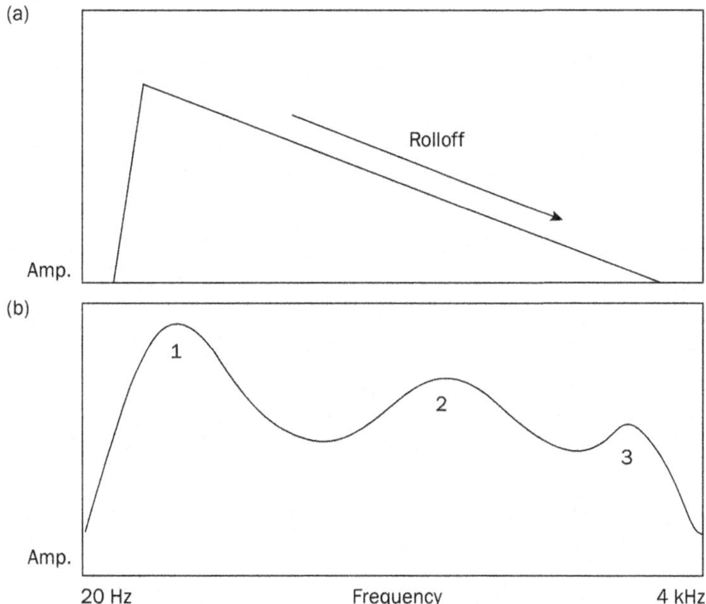

FIGURE 3.13 Spectrum envelopes. (a) Spectrum envelope with monotonic high-frequency rolloff. (b) Spectrum envelope with three labeled formants.

standard concerns timbre. Table 3.3 is a list of these descriptors, with capsule definitions adapted from Martinez (2004).

Although the definitions are described in capsule form here, in the standard, they are precisely defined mathematically. Indeed, my student Daniel Mintz (2007) developed a software synthesizer that could analyze a sound and synthesize similar sounds based on its MPEG-7 descriptors. For software resources in support of MPEG-7, see Casey (2010).

The descriptors form a solid scientific beginning for a taxonomy of timbre. It is only a beginning, however, because MPEG-7 is not a complete account of timbre. Its focus is specifically on harmonic, coherent, sustained sounds, and non-sustained percussive sounds.

Descriptors for the vast world of noises remain to be developed. Here the granular paradigm should prove useful, particularly since variations in granular density are characteristic of many noises.

FEATURE VECTORS

In parallel with the MPEG-7 standard, both academic and industrial researchers have developed schemes to analyze music (including its timbral aspects) for applications like *music information retrieval* (MIR) for categorization, recognition, retrieval, and recommendation of music (Wold et al. 1996). A typical MIR system takes a popular song and analyzes it according to dozens or even hundreds of quantified *feature vectors* (some similar to the MPEG-7 timbre

TABLE 3.3
MPEG-7 timbral descriptors

Audio waveform	The audio waveform envelope (minimum and maximum), typically for display purposes.
Audio power	Describes the temporally smoothed instantaneous power, which is useful as a quick summary of a signal, and in conjunction with the power spectrum.
Log-frequency power spectrum	Logarithmic-frequency spectrum, spaced by a power-of-two divisor or multiple of an octave.
Audio spectral envelope	A vector that describes the short-term power spectrum of an audio signal. It may be used to display a spectrogram, to synthesize a crude "auralization" of the data, or as a general-purpose descriptor for search and comparison.
Audio spectral centroid	Describes the center of gravity of the log-frequency power spectrum. A general indicator of "brightness," this is a concise description of the shape of the power spectrum, indicating whether the spectral content of a signal is dominated by high or low frequencies.
Audio spectral spread	Describes the second moment of the log-frequency power spectrum, indicating whether the power spectrum is centered near the spectral centroid, or spread out over the spectrum. This can help distinguish between pure-tone and noise-like sounds.
Audio spectral flatness	Describes the flatness properties of the spectrum of an audio signal for each of a number of frequency bands. When this vector indicates a high deviation from a flat spectral shape for a given band, it may signal the presence of tonal components.
Fundamental frequency	Describes the fundamental frequency of an audio signal. The representation of this descriptor allows for a confidence measure in recognition of the fact that the various extraction methods, commonly called "pitch-tracking," are not perfectly accurate, and in recognition of the fact that there may be sections of a signal (e.g., noise) for which no fundamental frequency may be extracted. Applies chiefly to periodic or quasi-periodic signals.
Harmonicity	Represents the distinction between sounds with a harmonic spectrum (e.g., musical tones or voiced speech [e.g., vowels]), sounds with an inharmonic spectrum (e.g., metallic or bell-like sounds), and sounds with a non-harmonic spectrum (e.g., noise, unvoiced speech [e.g., fricatives like "f"], or dense mixtures of instruments).
Log attack time	Characterizes the attack of a sound, the time it takes for the signal to rise from silence to the maximum amplitude. This feature signifies the difference between a sudden and a smooth sound.
Temporal centroid	Characterizes the signal envelope, representing where in time the energy of a signal is focused. This descriptor may, for example, distinguish between a decaying piano note and a sustained organ note when the lengths and the attacks of the two notes are identical.
Harmonic spectral centroid	The amplitude-weighted mean of the harmonic peaks of the spectrum. As such, it is very similar to the audio spectral centroid, but specialized for use in distinguishing musical instrument timbres. It is has a high correlation with the perceptual feature of the "sharpness" of a sound.
Harmonic spectral deviation	Indicates the spectral deviation of log-amplitude components from a global spectral envelope.

(continued)

TABLE 3.3 Continued

Harmonic spectral spread	Describes the amplitude-weighted standard deviation of the harmonic peaks of the spectrum, normalized by the instantaneous harmonic spectral centroid.
Harmonic spectral variation	The normalized correlation between the amplitude of the harmonic peaks between two subsequent time slices of the signal.
Audio spectrum basis (ASB)	A tool for indexing audio media using statistical methods. The ASB is a low-dimensional (data-reduced) projection of a high-dimensional spectral space consisting of a series of potentially time-varying and/or statistically independent basis functions derived from a normalized power spectrum. See Casey (2001), Casey et al. (2001), and Casey (2010) for details.
Audio spectrum projection (ASP)	A tool for indexing audio media using statistical methods. Used together with the ASB descriptor, the ASP represents low-dimensional features of a spectrum and is used to segregate different sources (e.g., instruments) in an audio document. See Casey (2001), Casey et al. (2001), and Casey (2010) for details.
Silent segment	Indicates a silent segment; can aid further segmentation of the audio stream or hint not to process a segment.

descriptors) that characterize many attributes of the sound. These can include low-level signal properties (e.g., zero-crossing rate, bandwidth, spectral centroid, signal energy), mel-frequency cepstral coefficients (often used in speech recognition), psychoacoustic features (e.g., roughness, loudness, sharpness), and auditory models. Layered on top of these can be myriad analyzers of pitch, event onset, instrumentation, melody, harmony, rhythmic organization, formal musical structure, genre, mood, artist, and so on (Tzanetakis and Cook 2002).

Conclusion

This chapter examined both the physical and psychoacoustical properties of sound materials: time domain waveforms, the time-frequency domain, sound magnitude, zones of frequency and intensity, timescales of sound, the speed of sound, the size and shape of sounds, the perception of the rate of sound events, and timbre. Understanding the physical nature of sound and its psychophysical impact is central to the practice of electronic music. Acquiring this knowledge is a gradual process, requiring book study (concepts, terminology, physical laws), as well as much listening.

Advances in technology have fostered enormous progress in tools for sound analysis, synthesis, and transformation. As composers become more knowledgeable, their use of these tools should become more sophisticated. Yet with each new tool, layers of psychoacoustic phenomena remain inexplicable. As one researcher observed:

> It is the immense difference between the physical acoustic signal on the one hand and the perceptual-cognitive world on the other hand that has

> frustrated theorists and researchers. The acoustical signal and the perceptual world seem to bear no simple one-to-one resemblance to each other.
>
> —STEPHEN HANDEL (1989)

By necessity, psychoacousticians tend to work with the simplest of audio stimuli; complicated sounds introduce too many variables into experiments. Notwithstanding monumental efforts by scientists like Helmholtz and his current counterparts (see Brunson and Sundberg 2006), the science of music cognition remains on a rudimentary plane. Yet in order to be able to understand the effects of sound and speak precisely about them, musicians will continue to need detailed scientific knowledge about sound and its impact on the hearts and minds of living creatures.

4

Creating sound materials

Beginning with a look at the physicality of sound, this chapter points out the interdependencies among sound material, its transformation, the tools used to generate and transform it, and musical organization. Following this discussion, we survey the various sources of sound, including concrète samples, and analog and digital synthesis.

The physicality of music

Music is more than a conceptual strategy or game of abstract logic. It takes material form in a medium. As Varèse (1955) pointed out:

> In speaking of music, what one must never forget is that in order to hear music, the listener must be subjected to a physical phenomenon; if an atmospheric disturbance between the source and the listener does not take place, there is no music.

The physical power of vibrating air can be easily felt in the hand four centimeters away from a loudspeaker radiating at 90 dB SPL. Even a score, which by itself makes no sound, exists in a material medium like paper or digital memory.

We have all known people who supposedly had great ideas, but were never able to realize them in the physical world; that is not our concern here. As Xenakis (1955) asserted:

> The hypothesis of non-materialized art is a piece of absurd sophistry.

Sound is mechanical vibration. We can hear it with our ears and also feel it with our bodies. Using special techniques, it is possible to see and photograph sound waves (figure 4.1).

FIGURE 4.1 Photograph of the pattern of sound intensity caused by a pyramidal horn loudspeaker. The aperture of the horn is 38 square centimeters. The radiated sound waves represent a pure sinusoid with a frequency of 9000 Hz. (Photo: F. K. Harvey, Bell Telephone Laboratories, in Kock 1971.)

By means of an elaborate process of audition, listeners turn physical vibrations into thoughts and feelings, which have a material basis in electrochemical changes in neurotransmitters that radiate from the brain and circulate throughout the body.

Organized sound

The 20th century brought many changes to compositional practice. None was more important than the expansion of the sound material made available to composers. The sound palette expanded from a fixed set of orchestral instruments to take in any sound from any source. Through this expansion, music evolved into what Varèse (figure 4.2) called *organized sound*—a rethinking of the process of composition to take into account the totality of sound material (Vivier 1973). As Varèse (1966) said:

> We are now in possession of scientific means not merely of realistic reproduction of sounds but production of entirely new combinations of sound, with the possibility of creating new emotions, awakening dulled sensibilities.

FIGURE 4.2 Varèse with Ampex magnetic tape recorder in his studio, New York, 1959. Photograph by Roy Hyrkin.

Varèse was encouraged by early advances in music technology, embodied in new instruments such as the Telharmonium, Thereminovox, and the Ondes Martenot (Cahill 1897; Rhea 1972, 1984; Chadabe 1997; Weidenaar 1989, 1995). In the 1920s, he briefly championed the experimental performances of the Futurist musicians, builders of "noise instruments." The Futurist composer Luigi Russolo (1916) wrote:

> I insist upon the charm of combinations of noise instruments. But to appreciate this quality, the most absolute silence is necessary in the concert hall. No one can imagine what charm is attained with harmonic modulations and held chords produced, for example, by the blend of low and medium howlers, low whistler, and hummer. What a marvelous contrast results if a high crackler suddenly enters above this group to inflect a theme, or a gurgler to hold some notes or point up the rhythm! It is an effect that is completely unknown in orchestras, since no orchestra but that of the noise instruments can produce this sensation of excited and pulsing life, exalted through the intensity and rhythmic variety found in the combination of [the noise instruments].

Throughout the 20th century, creative musicians sought beauty not only in the traditional, but also in the realm of strange and exotic sounds. Unusual juxtapositions of timbre and texture found favor (Cowell 1930; Cage 1937). For example, Luigi Nono's *Omaggio a Emilio Vedova* (1960) featured a sound palette of metallic noises.

Sound example 4.1. Excerpt of *Omaggio a Emilio Vedova* (1960) by Luigi Nono.

John Cage's theatrical *Water Walk* (1959) used a water pitcher, an iron pipe, a goose call, a bottle of wine, an electric mixer, a whistle, a sprinkling can, ice cubes, two cymbals, a mechanical fish, a quail call, a rubber duck, a tape recorder, a vase of roses, a seltzer siphon, five radios, a bathtub, and a grand piano (figure 4.3).

Sound example 4.2. Excerpt of *Water Walk* (1959) by John Cage.

What reactionary critics dismissed as "unmusical noise" is increasingly accepted today as a potent resource for composition. The philosophy of organized sound extended the boundaries of accepted musical material, and hence the scope of composition itself.

THE OPEN UNIVERSE OF SOUND

Photography is limitless, because a new visual world is being born at each instant, and so it is with audio recording. With even a single microphone, the number of original sounds one can discover is endless. Vast territories of sound remain undiscovered, uncharted, and unnamed.

FIGURE 4.3 John Cage performing *Water walk* in a 1959 broadcast of the show *I've Got a Secret* on American television.

A digital recording can be viewed as a kind of synthesis from millions of individual impulses, where each impulse is a sample of a waveform. Many digital synthesis techniques can generate realistic emulations of known sounds. For example, physical modeling synthesis emulates the mechanical and analog processes that produce instrumental sounds (Roads 1996; Cook 2007; Smith 2010).

Beyond recording and emulation lies the immense territory of artificial waveforms. How large is this space? A simple way to quantify it is to analyze how many different waveforms could exist within a limited duration (e.g., 10 seconds). Assuming a stereo sound at a sampling rate of 96 kHz, a 24-bit sample length yields over 32 trillion possible waveforms. A more complex way to measure it would be to ask how many different 10-second sounds can be distinguished by a human being? This would mean quantifying this space using perceptual constraints such as just noticeable difference thresholds and masking effects. The space is still huge. Consider, for example, the sound of all possible 10-second utterances in every language recorded by each person in the world in different sound environments. This enormous set is merely a tiny subset of all possible sounds.

Meanwhile, the field of digital sound synthesis is open-ended; new methods continue to be invented, as do refinements of existing techniques. Some of these techniques make little attempt to emulate the world of natural acoustics; rather, they harness the limitless power of algorithms to explore the open universe of abstract sound.

Yet new sound worlds pose compositional challenges. How to compose with strange new sounds? This question remains at the forefront of aesthetic pertinence.

From homogeneous notes to heterogeneous sound objects

> The former common paradigm of instrumental music . . . required a kind of "neutrality of the material" . . . an imperative for a compositional practice that was based on the autonomy of symbolic manipulations. To realize a pure permutational combinatoric, it was necessary to play with notes as "atoms" or primitive building blocks. Here, electroacoustic music has caused a real paradigm shift, introducing the sound object and the idea of morphological multiplicity.
>
> —HORACIO VAGGIONE (BUDÓN 2000)

As chapter 1 explained, electronic music extended the domain of composition from a closed, homogeneous set of notes to an open universe of heterogeneous sound objects (Roads 1985a). In the world of traditional music, limiting musical material to a homogeneous set of stable notes fosters abstraction in musical language. It serves as the basis for operations such as transposition, orchestration and reduction, the algebras of tonal harmony and counterpoint, and atonal and serial manipulations. The MIDI protocol extended this homogeneity into the domain of electronic music with its standardized note sequences that play on any synthesizer. The merits of the homogeneous note system are secure. Using common music notation, elegant structures have been designed with instruments inherited from past centuries. Since the dawn of the 20th century, however, a recurring aesthetic dream has been an expansion from a fixed, homogeneous set of notes to a much larger superset of heterogeneous sound objects. In these sound objects, we allow the possibility of instability (i.e., of time-varying morphologies and transmutations of identity). Thus, the notion of sound object generalizes the note concept in two ways:

- It replaces the restriction of a common set of properties in favor of a heterogeneous collection of properties, where certain objects do not share common properties with certain other objects. Sound objects can function as unique singularities; entire pieces can be constructed from nothing but singularities.
- It discards the notion of static, time-invariant properties in favor of time-varying *mutations and transmutations*. (See chapter 5 for an explanation of the distinction between these two terms.)

Sound objects fall into diverse classes. This has two important compositional implications:

- Each class of sound objects accommodates specific types of transformations; thus materials and their transformations are intertwined. Transformations applied to one class may not be appropriate when applied to another class. For example, a band-pass filter effectively sculpts a broadband noise texture, but is wasted on a single sine wave. Chapter 5 explores these implications more extensively.
- Each class lends itself to specific organizations; thus material and organization are intertwined. (See the next section.)

MATERIAL AND ORGANIZATION ARE INTERTWINED

As Pierre Schaeffer (1976) observed:

> In music, as elsewhere, organization is conditioned by material.

This is a fundamental point. In architecture, the choice of material—whether mud, thatch, bricks, concrete, wood, glass, steel, or fiberglass—shapes the architectural design forms. So too, in music, the choice of sound materials shapes the musical architecture. Just as traditional notes suggest structures full of melody, harmony, and counterpoint, granular materials suggest liquid-like streaming and cloud formations. For example, listen to Hugh LeCaine's pioneering *Dripsody* (1955), an etude for variable-speed tape recorder made out of copies and transpositions of a single drop of water, which predates Xenakis's first experiments in analog granular synthesis.

Sound example 4.3. Excerpt of *Dripsody* (1955) by Hugh LeCaine. 

The birth of frequency modulation (FM) synthesis prompted a multitude of works in which waves of inharmonic clusters and variations in the modulation index served as the primary musical narrative. Analog materials are often shaped by manual gestures, low-frequency oscillators (LFOs), and unstable circuits, which in turn become molders of phrase structure. Digital synthesis can be programmed in detail, enabling works of superhuman speed and precision. Concrète material inevitably plays the acousmatic card—a game of source recognition or hidden identity. (See the section on the acousmatic school later.)

Even simple materials can be highly expressive in the right hands. For Tod Dockstadter's *Quatermass* (1964), the basic sound source is a balloon that is processed by tape techniques into an expressive tour de force.

Sound example 4.4. Excerpt of *Quatermass* (1964) by Tod Dockstadter.

Consider the fascinating *Preludes for Magnetic Tape* (1967) by Ilhan Mimaroglu (featured in Federico Fellini's film *Satyricon*), a 15-minute suite in which the sound sources are nothing more than a piano, an electronic organ, a rubber band, a clarinet, the open strings of an acoustic guitar, and spoken voice. *Prelude II* features a Thomas electronic organ with an analog percussion unit.

Sound example 4.5. Excerpt of *Prelude II* (1967) by Ilhan Mimaroglu.

In *Prelude XI*, the sound source is a rubber band "whose rich timbres cannot be fully perceptible to the unaided ear, but can be beautifully captured by sensitive microphones" (Mimaroglu 1967).

Sound example 4.6. Excerpt of *Prelude XI* (1967) by Ilhan Mimaroglu.

In these works, Mimaroglu makes extensive use of simple but always effective transformations such as tape speed change, backward play, reverberation, and ring modulation to create a personal garden of sound, often organized sparsely such that each sound counts.

A more recent example is *eb + flo* (2003) by the British artist Kaffe Matthews. The staple material consists of sinusoids and other simple electronic tones, often shimmering with modulation. The sound material is artfully arranged in hypnotic looping patterns subject to sudden interruption or interplay with jagged electronic noise elements. In this case, the stripped-down material and the minimalist methods of organization complement each other, framing a convincing compositional statement.

Sound example 4.7. *Corner* (2003) by Kaffe Matthews from *eb + flo* (Annette Works AWCD0005-6).

In contrast, when the method of organization and the sound materials are mismatched, the results can be disastrous. Take, for example, the *Études I* and *II* composed in the primordial period of 1951 by Pierre Boulez. As François Bayle (2006) observed:

> The very first composers [of musique concrète] placed their faith in the absolute preciseness they thought could be achieved by combinations between machine and tape editing. One particular idea . . . appeared captivating: to take just a single sound as the initial material, then slowing, accelerating, and filtering it to extract one or a series of modes, coherence being maintained by a single root [sound].

The *Études* were designed according to a systematic procedure ill-suited to the chosen sound material, a "clicking" sound. The results are, as Bayle notes euphemistically: "stern in tone." Rather than confess to a personal artistic failure, Boulez (1958) heaped blame on the medium of musique concrète itself:

> Our "concrète musicians" are condemned to nonexistence. Let us add here the grief of producing sounds which, technically speaking, from the point of view of quality, are execrable. . . . As for the "works," which have nothing but these quotation marks to pretend to posterity, stripped of all bones of compositional intention, they are limited to montages of little ingenuity or variation, counting always on the same effects, nothing pointing to a coherent method.

Issued two years after Stockhausen's masterwork of musique concrète and electronic sounds, *Gesang der Jünglinge* (1956), this statement is patently unfair. The problems in Boulez's *Études* were not the fault of the medium (the entire gamut of recorded sound) or the operations that can be applied to them (the entire gamut of audio signal processing transformations) but rather of the mismatch between the sound material chosen by Boulez and the methods of organization that he chose to apply to them.

TOOLS, MATERIALS, AND ORGANIZATION INTERTWINE

We organize materials through actions mediated by specific tools. The critical influence of tools on the compositional process is a fundamental principle recognized early on by Pierre Schaeffer in his conception of musique concrète (Schaeffer 1966, 1977). By cutting into the grooves of a vinyl disc with a knife, Schaeffer created repeating loops. The tape recorder enabled razor-based splicing and rearrangement of arbitrary segments of time, as well as varispeed and backward playback. Following the example of Gabor's kinematical frequency converter (1946), which could stretch or shrink the duration of a sound without changing its pitch, Schaeffer's engineer Jacques Poullin developed the Phonogène pitch-time changer and the Morphophone echo machine (Manning 2004). The aesthetic implication of these technical advances is that the time support of a given sound is more-or-less freely composable. In effect, these tools enabled "the liberation of time."

More generally, all aspects of music are both enabled and limited by available tools (instruments, composing strategies, etc.). Technical advances often open up new aesthetic possibilities, as Stockhausen (2007) observed:

> Music is now very closely related to the equipment on which it is made.

In addition to the pure tones emitted by audio generators, the technology of recording let composers integrate rich and multicolored concrète textures into the musical fabric. Beginning in the 1950s, the computer introduced a new set of possibilities. These expanded the toolkit of available brushes and other implements with which to apply and manipulate sound color. This toolkit derives from the automation and flexibility of software. Today's sound tools allow precise control over all ranges of audio phenomena, from the level of elementary sound grains to massive sound clouds (Roads 1991).

To cite only a few examples of the impact of software tools, what is enabled by having not 4, 8, 16, or 24 tracks but instead hundreds of tracks? Not only can we create dense multilayered textures, but also elaborate filigrees of interconnected microsounds like intricate lacework. Digital multitrack recording and playback with automation enabled not only intricate control of mixing, but also highly sophisticated techniques of pluriphonic spatialization and time-varying effects. The simple ability to zoom in and out of a waveform, spectrum, or multitrack timeline display is taken for granted today. Yet this innovation, dating from the late 1980s, changed both the theory and practice of electronic music by enabling operations on multiple timescales, from the micro to the macro. Another advance is a granular spray jet, a new type of musical instrument that lets us paint novel morphologies and macroforms. Most importantly, the composer who is also a programmer has the ability to create his or her own tools designed for highly specific musical tasks.

To summarize, many aspects of music have seen an opening as a result of technology. As mentioned in chapter 1, electronic synthesis means that pitch can flow into noise, slow into pulsation, evaporate and coalesce, and align to a scale or not. Timbre has been liberated by the availability of thousands of new software instruments (Csound, Max/MSP, PureData, SuperCollider, Chuck, Nyquist, Reaktor, and many more). Space has been liberated by tools for choreographing sounds and the deployment of immersive multi-loudspeaker playback systems.

Inside a sound object: the domain of microsound

In traditional Western music, the note is like a brick—a basic building block of musical structure. With the exception of expressive effects like tremolo and vibrato, the possibilities for transition within a note are limited by theory, style, and the physical limitations of the acoustic instruments.

In order to liberate the note from its solid state, we must analyze its constituent components. Through this process, we can view its internal morphology.
In the 1960s, Jean-Claude Risset pioneered a technique for inspecting the internal morphology of a note on a microsonic timescale. His spectrum analyses portrayed a note as a combination of individual harmonic frequencies, each with its own time-varying envelope (figure 4.4):

> I recorded trumpet samples, analyzed them with the sound spectrograph and with the computer, displaying the evolution in time of the individual harmonic's amplitudes. From this analysis, it was possible to imitate isolated tones. . . . I used a different envelope function for each harmonic, approximating the curves yielded by the analysis in terms of piecewise linear functions.
>
> —RISSET (1985)

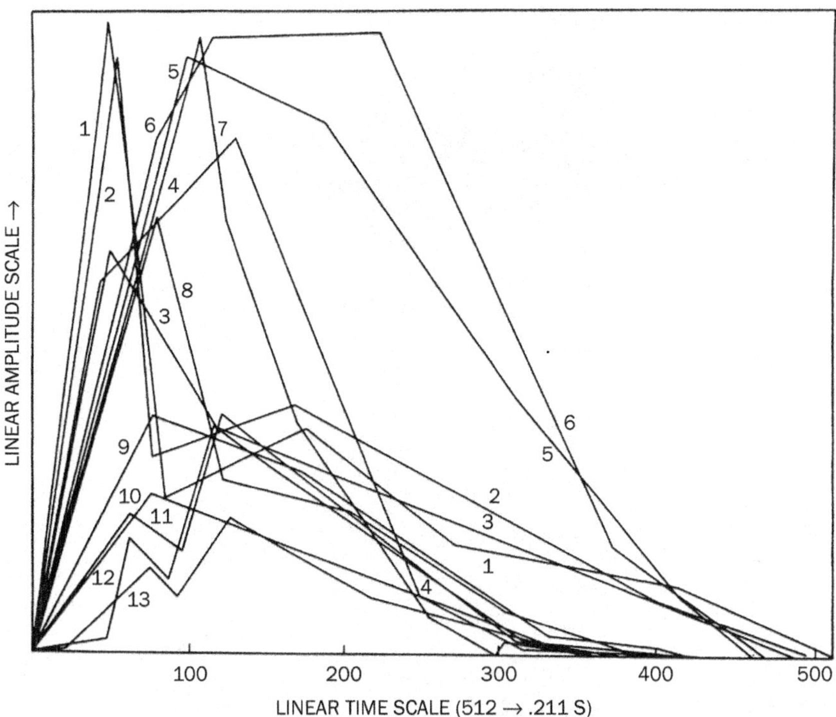

FIGURE 4.4 Line segment functions that approximate the evolution in time of 13 harmonics of a D4 trumpet tone (Risset 1965). Linear amplitude is the vertical scale and time is the horizonal scale.

Risset could then edit the analyzed envelopes and resynthesize the tones to realize variations on the original sounds. Of course, the idea that instrumental tones are purely harmonic is idealized, as many instruments generate inharmonic partials and noise, as well as harmonics. However, the point of this research was to prove how the timbre of complex sounds is the result of evolutions from one spectral state to others on a micro timescale. Risset later explored inharmonic and noisy sounds in his landmark compositions *Mutations* (1969) and *Inharmonique* (1977).)

In synthetic sounds, we can generalize the notion of time-varying envelopes and apply them not only to the frequency partials of a sound, but also to the pitch, amplitude, spatial position, and multiple determinants of timbre. Moreover, these variations may take place over timescales much longer than those associated with conventional notes, as we are not limited to physical limitations like breathing and muscular gestures.

As early as the 1940s, the physicist Dennis Gabor (1946, 1947) observed that it is possible to subdivide a sound object not only by its frequency spectrum but also by its temporal states (figure 4.5).[20] These granular or microtemporal states of a sound can be composed directly or decomposed from an existing sound and rearranged with tools such as granulators, time-frequency analyzers, and other software. By means of granular-scale operations, the

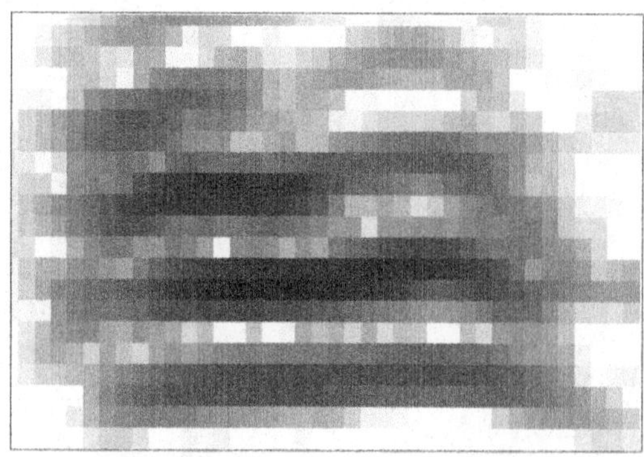

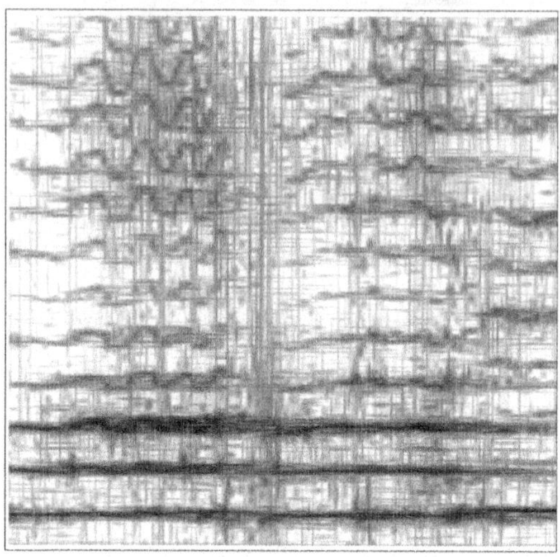

FIGURE 4.5 Sound as a sequence of microtemporal states. In both images, time is the horizontal dimension while frequency is the vertical dimension. (Top) Phase vocoder representation of sound as a matrix of time-frequency energy cells. This image depicts a zoomed-in 22 ms fragment of a vocal tone; the frequency range is 20-470 Hz. (Bottom) Time-frequency representation of a 1-second fragment of a soprano singing. Dictionary- based pursuit methods decompose a sound into a collection of time-frequency atoms. Individual atoms are clearly visible. The frequency range is from 20-4000 Hz. (Image courtesy of Bob L. Sturm.)

solid bricks of musical architecture—the notes—can be replaced by a more fluid concept of sound objects whose morphology mutates from one state to another over time.

Sonic density, opacity, and transparency

Not only can we visualize the scattered particulate nature of sound energy, we can also shape sonic matter in terms of its particle density and opacity. Particle density (expressed in terms of number of particles per second) has become a

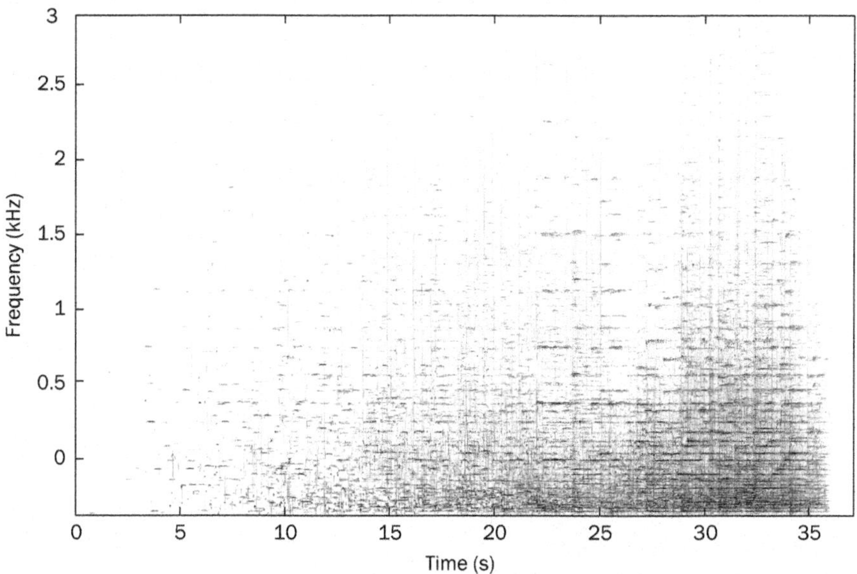

FIGURE 4.6 Wivigram of 200,000 grains coalescing from low density to high density. Image courtesy of Bob L. Sturm.

prime compositional parameter. Through manipulations of density, processes such as coalescence (formation) and disintegration (evaporation) can occur in sonic form. Figure 4.6 shows an image of a sound coalescing by means of a dictionary-based method (*matching pursuit*) both the time and frequency domains (Sturm et al. 2009).

Sound examples 4.8a and 4.8b. Granular coalescence of a sound by means of time-domain granulation. 

Opacity correlates to density. If the density of microsonic events is sufficient, the temporal dimension appears to cohere, and one perceives a continuous texture on the sound object level. Thus by controlling the density and size of sound particles, we have a handle on the quality of sonic opacity. Coalescence takes place when particle density increases to the point that tone continuity takes hold. An opaque sound tends to block out other sounds that cross into its time-frequency zone.

Going in the opposite direction, we can cause a sound to evaporate by reducing its particle density. A sparse sound cloud is transparent, since we can easily hear other sounds through it. A diaphanous cloud only partially obscures other sounds, perhaps only in certain spectral regions.

Sound example 4.9. The effects of cavitation on a sound. 

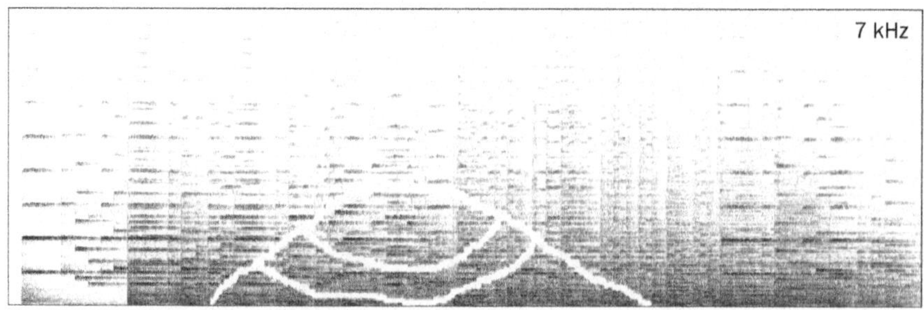

FIGURE 4.7 Sonogram of carving holes in the time-frequency spectrum of a sound by sonogram filtering. The duration is 30 seconds.

For example, by means of sonogram filtering, we can create cavities—holes in the spectrum of a sound (figure 4.7). These could also provide a window onto another layer of sound beneath.

The practice of electronic music

Creation of sound material is one step in the practice of electronic music composition—a multi-staged process (figure 4.8).

Viewed from a high level, this practice can be seen as three stages:

1. Gathering material
   For synthetic sources: programming and testing, rehearsal and performance
   For acoustic sources: writing, rehearsal, microphone selection and setup, selecting preamplifiers and analog-to-digital converters, performance
2. Organizing the material
   - Cataloging—listening, annotating, sorting, selecting
   - Editing—pruning, splicing, fading
   - Transformation—filtering, panning, reverberating, granulating, etc.
   - Multichannel montage—assembly of materials in time and space onto a medium
3. Performing the material
   - Playback—in the studio or concert hall
   - Mastering—preparing final versions for specific media
   - Sound projection—spatializing the sound to multiple loudspeakers in a concert hall
   - Interaction—in pieces that provide for real-time interaction, using gestural controllers to shape the sound or affect a musical process

Sound materials generally come from one of two sources: *concrète* and *synthetic:*

Concrète or sampled sounds recorded by one or more microphones:

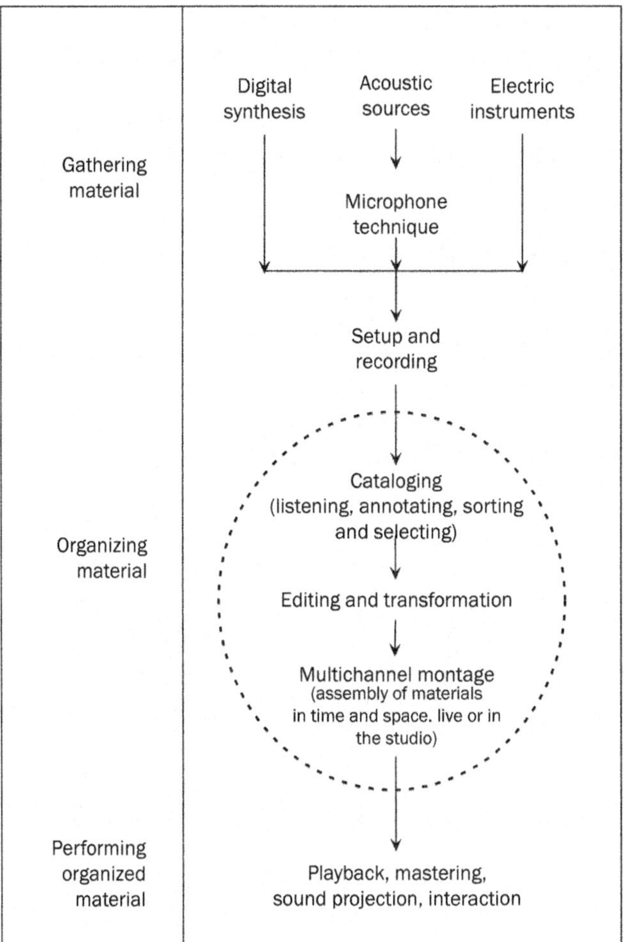

FIGURE 4.8 The multistaged process of electronic music composition.

- Environmental sounds induced by natural forces (wind, waves, thunder, volcanoes, etc.)
- Cries of animals (including human beings), birds, reptiles, insects, and fish
- Sounds excited by human actions (e.g., the voice and acoustic music instruments)
- Mechanically produced sounds (spring-driven mechanisms, gear-and-pulley devices, pump-driven mechanical organs, etc.)
- Amplified electrical, electromechanical, and electro-optical instruments (electric piano, organ, guitar, etc.)

Synthetic tones:

- Analog signal generation (including oscillators, analog synthesizers, radiosonic modulations, etc.)

- Digital sound synthesis (including techniques based on microsounds, which were difficult or impossible with analog techniques)

In either case (concrète or synthetic), generative algorithms can be deployed in the creation and/or selection and rearrangement of the material.

Sound material and musical structure

The *morphology* of a sound describes its shape (i.e., the inner evolution of its properties in time; Schaeffer 1966; Bayle 1993). The morphologies of electronic sound are extremely heterogeneous. This heterogeneity derives partly from the diversity of possible sources, and partly from the diversity of morphologies that can be generated by transforming even a single source. Sound properties can be static (constant) or time-varying. As Varèse (1954a) observed:

> Music can be considered as evolving in opposing planes and volumes, producing the impression of movement in space. But although the intervals between the notes determine these always changing volumes and contrasting planes, they are not founded on a preset assemblage of intervals such as a scale, series, or whatever principle existing in musical mensuration. They are determined by the exigencies of a particular work.

We can think of the temporal morphology of a sound as an *n*-dimensional space of envelopes and constants, such as the amplitude envelope, the pitch envelope, the spectral envelope, the spatial envelope, and envelopes on any number of effects (figure 4.9).

Each sound's morphology is unique and the number of dimensions it occupies is arbitrary. Thus analyzing the difference between two sounds is not a simple matter of comparing intervals between pitches. We must compare correlations or distance functions between fluid morphologies in multiple dimensions. This is a complicated business, however, and there is no standard method of comparing two sounds in this way. Alternatively, a technique like *multidimensional scaling* can be used to collapse many dimensions into a much smaller set (Wessel 1979).

One of the most important properties of a sound is its duration. Certain sonic processes require a sufficient duration to unfold. For example, the sweep of the cutoff frequency of a filter is most effective on a timescale greater than 100 ms. When the duration of any sound is very short (e.g., less than 20 ms), it is perceived as a transient event, regardless of its inner structure. As the duration of an event shrinks toward 1 ms, its amplitude envelope affects its spectrum more than its waveform, due to the effects of convolution.

As already stressed, the molecular properties of building materials determine the possible architectural structures that can be built with them. Thus the properties of sound materials inevitably shape the higher timescales of musical structure. Sound material and musical structure are interrelated. As Schaeffer (1966) pointed out, it makes little sense to talk of the meaning or function of an

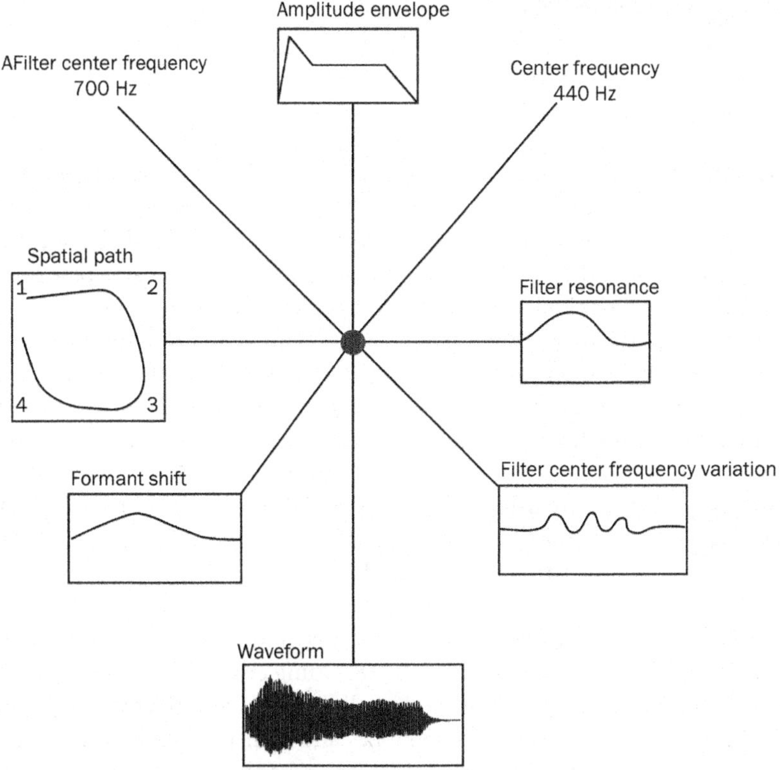

FIGURE 4.9 A single sound's morphology can be viewed as an *n*-dimensional space of envelopes and constants.

isolated sound. Depending on its structural context, it could serve any number of functions: background, foreground, transition, continuation, contrast, consonance, dissonance, passing tone, climax, etc.

The middle layers of musical structure (gestures and phrases) arise as the composer interacts with sonic material. To sculpt sonic material into gestures or phrases involves mediation between raw waveforms and the will of the composer. This mediation is not always immediately successful, which is part of the struggle of composition. If the initial result is unsatisfactory, the composer has two choices. The first is to develop new materials that will more easily fit a preconceived phrase mold. The second choice is to abandon the mold, which means following the "inner tensions"—to use Kandinsky's phrase—of the sonic material (Kandinsky 1926). In this case, the material "suggests" its own mesostructures. Later, the composer can intervene to reshape these structures from the vantage point of other timescales. These interrelationships between sound and structure confirm what the best composers have known all along: material, organization, and transformation must work together to construct a coherent musical code—a context. Sound accrues meaning through the structure in which it is heard, and structure accrues meaning through the sounds that articulate it.

Concrète sound material

> I find first. I search later.
>
> —PABLO PICASSO (CITED IN MIMAROGLU CA. 1968)

Concrète sound material refers to recorded or sampled sounds, as opposed to sounds synthesized by circuits or algorithms (Schaeffer 1966, 1976, 1977; Chion 2009). Schaeffer experimented extensively with recorded sounds beginning in the late 1940s. He and Pierre Henry used vinyl discs and later analog tape recorders to record and manipulate concrète sounds (Schaeffer 1966).

Schaeffer also meant the term "concrète" to refer to a studio-oriented manner of composition based on interaction with specific tools. In this sense, the concrète approach to composition stands squarely in opposition to abstract formal methods. The concrète method is empirical; it starts from a harvest of *found sounds* (i.e., recorded sound portraits) and moves toward a musical macrostructure using available tools. In contrast, traditional classical music tends to start from a musical schema that is notated on paper in terms of abstract notes that are only expressed in sound as a final phase, when the score is performed.

Since concrète sound depends on recording, it follows that the audio quality depends greatly on the resolution of the recording chain (microphones, preamplifiers, and the recording medium). Equally important is the technique of the sound engineer. The choice of microphones and their positioning are especially critical to this technique (Dickreiter 1989; Streicher and Everest 1998). Even for a single source, differences in microphones and positions can yield a multiplicity of different audio images. Like different lenses and camera angles, these variables can be played with creatively.

VOCAL SOUNDS

Vocal sounds (both spoken and sung) are privileged by the human brain:

> Acoustically produced speech is a very special sound to our ears and brain. Humans are able to extract the information in a spoken message extremely efficiently, even if the speech energy is lower than any competing background sound.
>
> —KOLLMEIER ET AL. (2008)

Vocal material attracts instinctive human interest. It immediately injects all of the referential baggage of language (narrative, literal meaning, etc.) and has inspired a large body of text-sound compositions (Bodin 2004). As Denis Smalley (1993) observed:

> It is no wonder that the human voice, both real and simulated, is prevalent in electroacoustic works. We can quickly distinguish between the real and the unreal, between reality and fantasy, and appreciate the passage between

> them. The voice's humanity, directness, universality, expressiveness, and wide and subtle sonic repertory offer a scope that no other source-cause can rival.

In other words, as Luciano Berio (2006) observed:

> The voice, whatever it does, even the simplest noise, is inescapably meaningful: it always triggers associations.

When text is involved, musical structure can serve a supporting role. Consider *Gesang der Jünglinge* (1956) by Stockhausen with its biblical texts repeating "Preiset den Herrn" (Praise the Lord), but also isolated words and phonemes. In the same studio, Ernst Krenek composed his eerie *Spiritus Intelligentiae Sanctus* (1956), which combined spoken voice with electronically manipulated voices on tape and a microtonal electronic part. The text stands out in Luigi Nono's evocative *La fabricca illuminata* (1964) featuring the sounds of a factory overlaid with a soprano singing a protest against industrial labor.

At the same time, as Griffiths (1979) observed, electronic music can resolve an antagonism between music and text since words themselves can be transformed. Extreme distortions obscure the meanings of the words, so that the sonic contours of the vocalisms are more important than their literal sense. Moreover, the freedom of the electronic medium encourages composers to make smooth connections between vocal and non-vocal material.

Certain pieces deconstruct an existing narrative into a jumble of words and phrases. Mel Powell's *Events* (1963) creates a scrambled collage out of three actors reading Hart Crane's poem *Legend* (1924). In Berio's *Thema (Omaggio a Joyce)* (1958), the text consists of utterances quoted from *Ulysses* by James Joyce. Here, with its nonsensical onomatopoetic wordplay, the voice serves as a vehicle of pure sonic expression. As Berio (1958) described it:

> By selecting and reorganizing the phonetic and semantic elements of Joyce's text, Mister Bloom's day in Dublin . . . follows an unexpected direction in which it is no longer possible to make distinctions between word and sound, sound and noise, poetry or prose, or poetry and music.

Sound example 4.10. Excerpt of *Thema (Omaggio a Joyce)* by Luciano Berio (1958). 

ORCHESTRAL INSTRUMENT SOUNDS

The familiar sounds of orchestral instruments: strings, brass, woodwinds, and percussion are heavily laden with historical context. Yet when acoustic instruments are played or combined in unconventional ways, the result can sometimes sound like electronic music. Ligeti's *Volumina* (1962) for pipe organ (cited in chapter 1) is an outstanding example of pure sound composition, as is Xenakis's remarkable *Tetras* (1983) for string quartet.

The mixture of instrumental sounds with other sounds can be highly effective and is featured in countless electronic pieces, dating back to the earliest experiments in musique concrète and tape music. Classic works such as François Bayle's *L'oiseau chanteur* (1963) seamlessly splice electronic tones and vocalisms with sounds from a French horn, oboe, and harpsichord.

Sound example 4.11. Excerpt of *L'oiseau chanteur* (1964) by François Bayle.

Percussion instruments (i.e., anything that can be struck) are especially interesting. It is easy to create dozens of variations on a drum sample, for example, through effects such as pitch-shifting, frequency-shifting (single sideband modulation), ring modulation, and filtering. As John Cage (1937) wrote:

> Percussion music is the contemporary transition from keyboard-influenced music to the all-sound music of the future. Any sound is acceptable to the composer of percussion music: he explores the academically forbidden "non-musical" field of sound insofar as is manually possible.

The twelve *Synchronisms* (1962–2006) of Mario Davidovsky contrast instruments (including percussion) with electronically generated tones.

Sound example 4.12. Excerpt of Synchronisms Number 5 for percussion ensemble and electronic sounds (1969) by Mario Davidovsky.

A more recent example of a seamless blend is the *Quartetto per viola solo* (2006) by Martino Traversa, featuring the violist Garth Knox multiplied into an ensemble by means of multitrack recording and editing techniques.

Sound example 4.13. Excerpt of *Quartetto per viola solo* (2006) by Martino Traversa.

The combination of sampled piano tones and percussion features in a series of effective works by Horacio Vaggione, beginning with *Schall* (1994), *Nodal* (1997), and *Agon* (1998). His later works expand the palette of sampled sounds to a variety of orchestral instruments—for example, *Préludes Suspendus* (2000), *Taleas* (2002), *Arenas* (2007), *Préludes suspendues III* and *IV* (2009), and *Points critiques* (2011).

ENVIRONMENTAL SOUNDSCAPES

An increasingly relevant resource of concrète material is the environment, including natural and urban *soundscapes*. This has led to a genre of sound design based on field recordings. These include sound portraits of natural environments, cities, people talking, etc., that serve as a kind of sonic documentation. Walter Ruttman's 1930 composition *Weekend* (recorded on optical film) was an extraordinary foreshadowing of musique concrète and soundscape design. A sound portrait of Berlin meant for radio broadcast, the piece consists of a montage of speech, street noises, and industrial sounds—spliced rapidly in an unpredictable sequence.[21]

Sound example 4.14. Excerpt of *Weekend* (1930) by Walter Ruttmann. 

Another example, Makoto Shinohara's *City Visit* (1979) is a 40-minute collage of New York City soundscape recordings without additional processing. Coming out of similar documentary experiments by R. Murray Schafer and others, the field of *acoustic ecology* has emerged as a hybrid of soundscape art, ecology, and environmental studies (Truax 1999a; Norman 2004; Westercamp 2006). Along these lines, the British sound recordist Chris Watson has carved a career out of "putting a microphone where you can't put your ears," such as an Icelandic glacier, capturing the groaning of melting ice (Watson 2009). Scientists have gone even further, simulating the acoustic effects of events in different planetary atmospheres (Leighton and Petculescu 2009a, 2009b). A more down-to-earth example of soundscape art is Hildegard Westercamp's *Cricket Voice* (1987), which processes sound materials found in the desert to evoke an impression of an arid terrain.

VIRTUAL SOUNDSCAPES

Virtual soundscapes are interesting from an aesthetic viewpoint. A virtual soundscape is composed by mixing field recordings made in different locations together with other sounds (instruments, electronic sounds, voice, etc.) to create a phantasmagorical composite.

The French composer Luc Ferrari (figure 4.10) was a master of this genre. Seizing on the introduction of the first portable tape recorders in 1962, Ferrari became an inveterate field recordist, amassing a large archive of recorded sound. He was intrigued by the element of chance in soundscape recording and the concept of the *objet trouvé* or found [sound] object (Ferrari 2002). Based on field recordings, Ferrari pioneered the use of what he called *anecdotal* sound in composition, first in his composition *Hétérozygote* (1964). As he observed (Caux 2002):

> When I made Hétérozygote in 1963–4, I used sounds that were no longer in the world of music, which were not the concrète noises. I left the dogma [of musique concrète] just as I had left the serial [dogma]. . . . I reasoned that the microphone is made for registering noises and recording them on a medium. Whether it was in the studio, in society, on the street, or in intimate situations, it recorded just the same. It was thus consistent for me to introduce anecdotal noises into musical discourse. . . . I found it so beautiful to juxtapose abstract sounds and recognizable sounds, anecdotes; one could visualize them. I did it by intuition and sensuality. Later I was more conceptual, for example in *Music promenade* (1969) and in *Presque rien no. 1* (1968)

FIGURE 4.10 Luc Ferrari recording at the Grand Canyon, 1998. Photograph courtesy of Brunhild Ferrari.

Sound example 4.15. Excerpt of *Hétérozygote* (1964) by Luc Ferrari.

Presque rien no. 1 (1967–1970), *Presque rien no. 2* (1977), *Presque rien avec filles* (1989), and *Cycle des souvenirs* (2001) exemplify his original and inimitable art. In all these works, we experience an improbable but fascinating mix of soundscapes, voices, and looping elements—turning an ordinary documentary recording into a kind of artificial augmented reality.

Sound example 4.16. Excerpt of *Presque rien, numéro 1, le lever du jour au bord de la mer* (1970) by Luc Ferrari.

THE ACOUSMATIC SCHOOL

One school of composers, originally associated with the Groupe de Recherches Musicales (GRM) in Paris, but now worldwide, refers to their music as *acousmatic* (Schaeffer 1966). The term derives from the Greek philosopher-scientist Pythagoras, who gave lectures from behind a curtain so that his students would pay attention to the sound of his words. Today, the term "acousmatic" refers to compositions in which external reference—or the hiding of it—is central to the meaning of the work. A sound emanating from a loudspeaker emerges from behind a curtain, as it were, so we do not see the original source.

Acousmatic works tell stories. The sound of a door opening or closing, for example, might signal a new musical scene about to unfold. People whisper, storms gather, a train passes by. The meaning is sometimes veiled by various strategies, such as familiar sounds placed in unusual contexts (Bayle 1997). Acousmatic works play with recognizability, mimesis, reference, meaning, and semantic allusion (Barrett 1997; Bodin 2004). For example, in works like *Viva La Selva* (1999), Natasha Barrett explores *surrogacy* as a compositional strategy, wherein a sound recorded in nature (e.g., monkeys) is mimicked temporally and spatially by a surrogate sound (the human voice).

Of course, the manipulation of familiar material has the potential to enable deep emotional expression. Natasha Barrett (2002) went so far as to state:

> Electroacoustic and computer music can be more closely connected with emotion, to a larger degree use material from nature and human relationships, and appeal more directly to our perception and memories than does performed instrumental music.

Whether or not this is the case, the use of concrète sound material certainly opens a door to a wide range of expression.

An acousmatic agenda is explicit in many works by the iconic GRM composer François Bayle. In his *Tremblement de terre très doux* (1978), we hear a succession of auditory scenes, which the composer describes in the program notes (Bayle 1980) as follows:

Chronometer	Character	Instrument	Familiar sounds	Hidden sounds
0:00–1:37	climate I mobility (. . . like the awakening of birds at dawn . . .)	electronic flux	wind	deaf blows
1:37–3:18	transit	images/mirages impacts	trap door female voice	vertical transfer balls
3:19–6:40	landscape	rolled, shocked pulsed, inverted	rolling, sizzling light wind	slight shifts

The ambiguity of these descriptions—metaphorical rather than literal—is characteristic of the acousmatic sensibility, which often incorporates poetry or other spoken allusions.

In contrast, in certain acousmatic works, there is no attempt to disguise the sources, but the game of identification and reference is secondary to appreciation of the work. As the critic Paul Griffiths (1979) wrote:

> Xenakis's works [such as *Concret PH*, *Bohor*, and *Orient-Occident*] . . . exemplify the use of musique concrète to abstract ends; the origins of the sounds

are not that important, and the composer does not attempt to invest them with metaphysical significance.

In other works, sources are transformed beyond recognition. In these compositions, we encounter a distinction defined by Schaeffer as *écoute réduite* or *reduced listening* (Schaeffer 1966). Reduced listening means focusing on an event as a pure sound object, that is, in terms of its acoustic qualities, separate from its source and the meaning this may convey. Many acousmatic works obscure the source and so encourage reduced listening. Consider the abstract transformations of instrumental sounds in *Pentes* (realized at the GRM studios in 1974) by Denis Smalley. The sole recognizable source sound (a Northumbrian pipe instrument) emerges from the mix only after nine minutes of this 12-minute composition.

HYPERREALISM AND MAGNIFICATION OF SUBSONIC SOUNDS

A unique and interesting possibility offered by concrète techniques is *hyperreal magnification*—the exaggeration of feeble sounds for expressive effect. This is analogous to the blowup technique in photography, which greatly magnifies a detail of an image. Consider the intimate, gentle quality of an acoustic guitar recorded in stereo with high-quality microphones in close proximity to the instrument. This intimate acoustic image can be magnified with a dash of reverberation and amplification in a concert hall with widely spaced loudspeakers; suddenly, the guitar takes on huge proportions.

A variation on this is a method used by many composers of musique concrète: magnifying nearly subsonic sounds into massive sonic events. Recall that a subsonic sound is one that is too faint to be heard by the human ear. In this method, the sound engineer positions a microphone or a pair of microphones in close proximity to a quiet sound source, such as raw rice being poured into a bowl. This quiet sound can be greatly amplified, pitch-shifted downward, or time-stretched. When this amplified, pitch-shifted, and time-stretched sound is projected in a large concert hall, tiny events are magnified into massive dramatic gestures, like an avalanche of boulders. In Maggi Payne's *FIZZ* (2004), a quiet water fizzing sound is magnified by means of granular time expansion into a massive crescendo.

 **Sound example 4.17.** Excerpt of *FIZZ* (2004) by Maggi Payne.

SAMPLE LIBRARIES

> Sampling makes a system of recording into a creative instrument and turns sound production into sound consumption (making choices from existing materials).
>
> —CHRIS CUTLER (2007)

Catalogs of prerecorded samples are available on digital media and the Internet. These should not be ignored, as they contain many sounds that would be difficult to prepare on one's own. For example, in my collection, I have many commercial recordings of natural environments and machines. One of these captures the sounds of Niagara Falls from different perspectives, and this complex sound is one of my preferred sources of broadband noise.

The use of commercial samples opens up a debate. Apart from questions of authorship and rights, which we will not enter into here, the issue of originality stands out. Certain musicians depend almost completely on commercial samples; as a result, their music has a "canned" sound palette, deriving from the generic quality of these samples. A saxophone sample purchased from a commercial sound library captures a generic saxophone played by a generic saxophonist. This generic quality stamps all music that uses such a sample, creating an aesthetic problem that must be overcome somehow; thus one needs to be judicious in their use.[22]

Analog synthesis

One of the most important resources in electronic music is the sound of analog synthesis (figure 4.11).

FIGURE 4.11 Analog tape recorders (foreground), tone generators, mixers, and patch bay in the Cologne Electronic Music Studio, designed in the 1950s. (Photo from *Der WDR als Kulturakteur. Anspruch-Erwartung-Wirklichkeit.* G. Schulz, S. Ernst, O. Zimmermann. German Cultural Council. Berlin, 2009.)

Over a century of invention has gone into the design of analog instruments (Roads 1996b). In contrast to digital circuits, which generate audio samples at a fixed sampling rate, analog circuits generate continuous signals that vary freely within a specified voltage range. The behavior of analog circuits can be predicted according to the flow of voltage and current in interaction with circuit properties such as resistance, capacitance, and inductance (Chirlian 1971; Benedict 1976; Black 1953).[23] Differences between analog instruments can be traced to variations in circuit topologies, but also the individual components or parts within a circuit. For example, a vacuum tube circuit will behave differently than a transistor circuit. Every component contributes to the overall sound.

Equally important is the design of the physical control panel (i.e., the layout of faders, knobs, buttons, sliders, and indicators [lights, numerical displays, etc.]). The design of this control interface has a strong influence on the types of sounds and gestures that can be obtained from a synthesizer.

Milton Babbitt (2000) described the process of working in the 1960s with the RCA Electronic Music Synthesizer, Mark II:

> When you're walking into the studio up at 125th Street (Columbia) with a piece in your head and eventually, you're able to walk out with a finished piece and a tape under your arm, it's an unparalleled experience. You're not dependent on anyone but yourself. . . . Remember, all of this is analog. We were not working digitally, for which I am most grateful. In the most serious sense, it's a matter of just being the master of everything. Your decisions are your decisions. You convey them to a machine of course. Learning how to convey them to a machine was a big problem at the time. . . . There were no set-ups or samplers. We had to start from scratch and do everything from the beginning. Remember, I started working with the machine in 1957 and I didn't produce a piece with it until 1961.

Modular synthesizers have seen a tremendous resurgence in the 21st century, with dozens of companies producing hundreds of modules. Modular analog synthesizers sport dozens of knobs that allow immediate access to synthesis controls. This stands in contradistinction to some poorly designed digital devices that present a series of nested menus with a single multifunction control knob, permitting manipulation of only one parameter at a time out of dozens of parameters that can only be accessed on other submenus.

ANALOG WAVEFORMS

An analog waveform generator or oscillator is restricted by its circuit topology to a limited range of waveshapes. Many texts have been devoted to the art of analog waveform synthesis (e.g., Strauss 1960; Douglas 1968, 1973; Hutchins 2012), but the reality is that waveform flexibility is not the strong suit of analog devices.[24]

Figure 4.12 depicts the basic palette of electronic waveforms (Olson 1952). (In the most recent Eurorack analog synthesizers, one can find additional variations

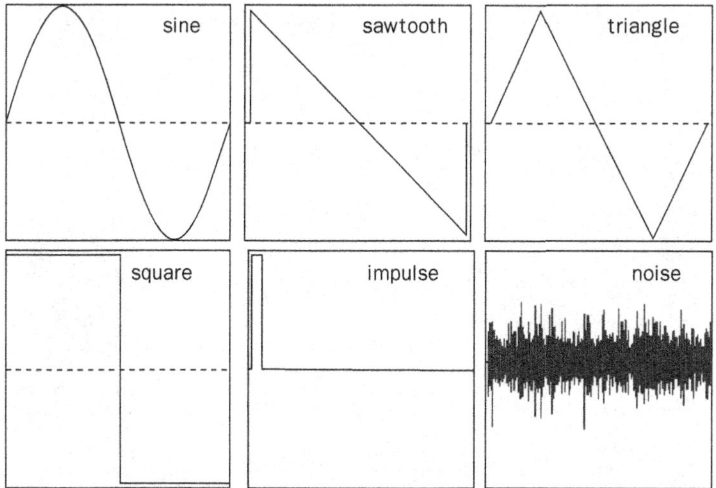

FIGURE 4.12 The six basic analog waveforms: sine, sawtooth, triangle, square, impulse, and noise.

of these.) Analog oscillators often allow continuous transitions between these waveforms; such transitions are characteristic of analog synthesis.

The sine wave is special. Pure sine waves are rare in nature; thus they have an ideal quality. As Varèse (1926) observed on the combination of sine tones with traditional instrument tones:

> It is surprising how pure sound, without overtones, lends another dimension to the quality of musical notes that surround it. The use of pure sounds does to harmonics what a crystal prism does to pure light. It scatters it into a thousand varied and unexpected vibrations.

Prior to the 1960s, the majority of electronic music instruments were fixed by the manufacturer to produce a certain class of sounds. Classic vacuum-tube oscillator instruments such as the Theremin (1920) and the Ondes Martenot (1928), for example, did not provide a wide range of timbral variation. Musicians achieved expressivity with these instruments primarily through sensitive variations in pitch and loudness. The classic electronic music studios built in the 1950s were equipped with laboratory test equipment, which had to be adapted for musical use.

In contrast, Georges Jenny's Ondioline (Fourier 1994) was designed as a virtuoso instrument (figure 4.13). This brilliantly designed monophonic keyboard instrument was based on the principle of filtered pulse trains controlled by a clever combination of input devices. These included a spring-mounted keyboard (for vibrato), an octave button (allowing an instantaneous switch to any of eight octaves), a knee pedal (for volume), and 27 multi-way switches and knobs for waveform and filter control.

FIGURE 4.13 Jean-Jacques Perrey's Ondioline. Photograph by the author.

Electronic sound production in the 1970s was typified by grand-scale modular voltage-controlled synthesizers (figure 4.14), such as the one used by Wendy Carlos to make the top-selling *Switched-On Bach* (1968). These systems allowed musicians to interconnect different synthesis and processing modules by means of patch cords. By the principle of voltage control, one module could control the behavior of another. Some modules in a synthesizer generate or process control signals in the manner of an analog computer (Ulmann 2013). Such modules include logic gates (AND, OR, XOR, etc.), envelope followers, lag processors/slew limiters, sample-and-hold units, comparators, switches, gates, triggers, timers/clocks, rectifiers, slope generators, etc. They also incorporated the first analog sequencers, allowing composers to program a sequential series of events, typically from eight to 48 steps.

UNIQUENESS OF ANALOG SYNTHESIS

One of the most recognizable sonic characteristics of analog synthesis is the effect of time-varying filters. Analog filters are not limited by the frequency ceiling imposed by a digital sampling rate. While digital filters are limited to a few basic circuit types, analog filters allow for a wide variety of circuit topologies. Moreover, the individual circuit components in an analog filter have a strong influence on the sound quality. For these reasons, there is greater heterogeneity in analog filters than in the digital domain. Certain analog filters impose a sound

FIGURE 4.14 Moog IIIp synthesizer, 1971.

FIGURE 4.15 Krohn-Hite 3550 analog filter.

that would be impossible to find in a digital system. For this reason, analog filters remain irreplaceable instruments for shaping sound.

An example is the classic Krohn-Hite 3550 filter (figure 4.15), which can be applied over a range of 2 Hz to 200 kHz (Krohn-Hite 1978). This filter has a unique sound quality, especially in the high audio frequencies between 10 kHz and 20kHz. There are other interesting filters; the point is that certain analog filters have distinct personalities.

ANALOG MODULATION

Central to analog synthesis is the use of modulations: ring, amplitude, frequency, and so on (Roads 1996a). The spectra generated by a modulation are constrained to fixed kinds of behavior. In practice, this means that each type of modulation has a characteristic signature that can be discerned after some exposure to the technique. However, not all analog modulators are the same. For example, the sound of analog ring modulation depends on the circuit design, the individual component parts in the circuit, and even the temperature of the circuit (Roads 1996a; Hoffmann-Burchardi 2008, 2009). This is in stark contrast to digital ring modulation, which simply multiplies two signals.

Modulation is a signature sound, and this signature can either be an annoying cliché or an attractive musical force. In the latter category, Louis and Bebe Barron's electronic music soundtrack to the science-fiction film *Forbidden Planet* (1956) stands out as an outstanding example of musical use of analog modulation (figure 4.16). Listen to works like Morton Subotnick's *Silver Apples of the Moon* (1967) or Christian Clozier's *Quasars* (1980) that were realized in the fantastic analog studio Charybde in Bourges, France. Even as more elaborate synthesis techniques are developed, there will remain something deeply evocative about artfully deployed analog modulation.

ANALOG EMULATION

In recent years, many musicians have rediscovered the power of analog synthesis and voltage control, and the value of vintage analog instruments has

FIGURE 4.16 Louis and Bebe Barron in their New York studio in the 1950s. Photograph by Walter Daran.

increased. Recognizing the trend, manufacturers have introduced a wave of new analog synthesizers and modules into the marketplace, including some that are similar to the older instruments. In addition, a new breed of *analog modeling* or *analog emulating* instruments has appeared. These use digital technology to simulate the expressive characteristics of analog synthesis. We see a corresponding trend in the world of audio products, where software products attempt to mimic the compression characteristics of vacuum tubes, the noise and distortion of analog tape, and even the crackling of scratched vinyl records. Evidently, the classic sound of analog circuits is still appreciated by many musicians.

VOLTAGE-CONTROLLED DIGITAL MODULES

Another important new phenomenon is the development of digital hardware modules that can be voltage-controlled with patch cords, like any other analog module. This opens the door to universal waveform synthesis and sampling, liberating the modular world from the inherent limitations of analog oscillators. It also integrates digital processes like granulation and other *digital signal processing* (DSP) operations within the modular framework. The modular framework changes the DSP game by putting it under the regime of voltage control and the type of real-time knob-and-button fiddling that is central to the modular paradigm.

Digital synthesis

Edgard Varèse opened the Pandora's box of sound in 1916:

> I refuse to submit to only those sounds that have already been heard.

The capability of synthesizing any possible waveform has opened up the entire universe of sound to digital synthesis. Digital waveform synthesis began in the early years of computing following WWII. The earliest efforts at sound production by computer produced primitive beeping sounds, melodies with no control over the waveform (Doornbusch 2005).

Beginning in 1957, however, an acoustical research group at Bell Telephone Laboratories in New Jersey began a series of experiments with waveform synthesis using an IBM 704 computer (figure 4.17) interfaced with the world's only digital-to-analog converter (DAC) (Roads 1996a). By means of the DAC, any possible waveform could be produced, limited only by the resolution of the converter.

After years of experiments, the secrets of digital waveform synthesis were revealed to the general public in the program notes to a phonograph record, *Music from Mathematics* (Strasser and Mathews 1961), and an article in the *Journal of Music Theory* (Tenney 1963). James Tenney's 46-page article reads like a user's manual to the Music III language (invented by Max V. Mathews in collaboration

FIGURE 4.17 Operating console of the room-sized IBM Electronic Data Processing Machine, type 704, ca. 1957. This computer was used in the first experiments of digital waveform synthesis by Max Mathews and his colleagues at Bell Telephone Laboratories.

with Joan E. Miller). Music III was the first modular synthesis language, in which a user could design a synthesis instrument as a collection of interconnected modules or *unit generators* (Mathews 1969). The output of a noise generator module, for example, could be connected via software to the input of a filter module to produce filtered noise. In this same period, Jean-Claude Risset wrote the first "cookbook" for digital sound synthesis (Risset 1969), which gave precise descriptions of how to produce sounds similar to flutes, brass, reeds, plucked strings, pianos, drums, and gongs, as well as synthetic sounds like glissandi and ring modulation.

Digital synthesis can employ any computable function. Thus it is theoretically unlimited in its scope and potential for sound generation. Current practice encompasses a broad range of techniques, from simple wavetable lookup to arbitrarily complicated methods. Digital techniques can realize methods that would be difficult or impossible to synthesize by other means. Examples include the following:

- Granular synthesis
- Physical modeling, including speech synthesis and analog emulation
- Sampling synthesis
- Graphical synthesis
- Stochastic and chaotic synthesis
- Analysis-based additive synthesis

Some of these methods have been attempted with analog techniques, but the precision and programmability of the digital medium takes these methods to another realm. (See Roads 1996a for a review of the full range of digital synthesis techniques.)

SYNTHESIS OF COMPOUND SOUNDS

Certain musicians rely on generic sounds created by preset patches that are bundled with synthesizers or loaded from a library.[25] They may transform such sounds in an attempt to make them more interesting, but they rarely think of combining them with other sounds in order to construct a *compound sound*. The notion of compound sounds can be traced to Pierre Schaeffer (1966). He observed that the components of a complex sound can be perceived as part of a single entity (i.e., a compound sound) or remain separate to form what he called a sound mixture. (In chapter 12 on mixing, we refer to these processes as *fusion* versus *fission*, respectively.) In the digital domain, the synthesis of compound sounds is a wide-open territory. By mixing sound B at 20 dB below sound A, one alters A in a subtle way without changing its perceived identity. Especially interesting are those fusions that add harmonic or inharmonic color and are thus heard as timbral variations. Many samplers facilitate the design of sound compounds through their *wavestacking* capabilities (Roads 1996a, forthcoming). Wavestacking adds together several waveforms (typically four to eight on commercial synthesizers), where each waveform can be a complicated signal, such as a sampled sound. By layering several sampled sounds, one can create hybrid timbres like saxophone/flutes or violin/clarinets. Each waveform in the stack has its own amplitude envelope, so sounds fade in and out of the stack in the course of a sound event. When four to eight complex waveforms are stacked, deep and rich hybrid textures can be created for each sound event.

Sound example 4.18. A long compound sound fusing a time-varying harmonic component, a broadband noise component, and an undulating bass component. 

ADVANTAGES AND DISADVANTAGES OF DIGITAL SYNTHESIS

Digital synthesizers can be embodied in software or hardware. Software synthesizers fall into two main categories: fixed plugins/applications versus configurable languages/toolkits. There is much to be said for a fixed application that is designed to do one thing and do it well. On the other hand, languages and toolkits let one design one's own circuit or *instrument patch* that is tailored with a specific compositional goal in mind. For example, *In Winter Shine* (1983) by James Dashow used custom instruments designed by the composer in the Music-11 language, the precursor to Csound.

Sound example 4.19. Excerpt of *In Winter Shine* (1983) by James Dashow.

The main advantages of digital software synthesis are as follows:

- Programmable control—a digital synthesizer can be programmed to precisely and automatically perform control operations that would be too complicated for human beings.
- Rich graphical user interfaces—interfaces can be designed to support multiple levels of operation and complexity (i.e., expert mode, novice mode); graphical synthesis techniques let users control synthesis by drawing and other graphical operations.
- Memorization—settings can be saved and recalled at the touch of a button.
- Scalable with increasing computer power—as computers become more powerful, the range of synthesis techniques will continue to grow as developers take advantage of increasing speed and larger memories.

The downside of software synthesis is the rapid obsolescence of software—computers and operating systems become obsolete, along with the software that ran on them. Music software companies come and go. Some of the most interesting software is shareware or freeware developed by an individual; however, few such programs are maintained over long periods of time.

This disadvantage is not as applicable to digital synthesizers embodied in hardware. Hardware synthesizers are generally not dependent on a host computer, so they work for decades.[26] Hardware synthesizers have several advantages, including physical controllers (knobs, buttons, sliders, keys) and immunity from the rapid pace of software obsolescence.

The universe of noises

Noise is a large and heterogeneous category of sound. Although noise sounds have long been part of the musical tradition, they were sometimes given little regard. As Rimsky-Korsakov (1891) observed:

> Instruments in this group, such as triangle, castanets, little bells, tambourine, side or military drum, cymbals, bass drum, and Chinese gong do not take any harmonic or melodic part in the orchestra, and can only be considered as ornamental instruments pure and simple. They have no intrinsic musical meaning.

It suffices to say that in the intervening period, the percussion and noise components of musical sound have emerged as a central resource. Indeed, they form one of the most vital elements of the compositional palette. As Cage (1937) said:

> I believe that the use of noise to make music will continue and increase until we reach a music produced through electrical instruments. . . . Whereas in the past, the point of disagreement has been between dissonance and consonance, it will be, in the immediate future, between noise and so-called musical sounds.

In 1980, Cage wrote:

> One difference between Harry Partch and myself—also a difference between me and Lou Harrison—is that they became interested in intonation and the control of microtones, whereas I went from the twelve tones into the whole territory of sound. I took noise as the basis.

Given its importance, I dedicate a major section of this chapter to noise. We first examine the problem of the definition of noise. We then point out the continuum between pitch and noise and its potential role in composition. Next, we survey the use of noise in composition, beginning with the Futurists and leading into the digital age. We list some mathematically defined colored noises and describe other sources of noise.

DEFINING NOISE

The dictionary definition of noise describes it subjectively as an unwanted disturbance. In engineering, noise is usually presented as a contamination in a signal channel, like buzz, hum, or hiss, that interferes with a meaningful message.

> Noise limits our ability to communicate. If there were no noise, we could communicate messages electronically to the end of the universe using an infinitely small amount of power.
>
> —L. COUCH II (2005)

These definitions carry negative connotations, with noise portrayed as an obstruction or intruder. Moreover, they say nothing about the objective nature of the signal.

The 19th-century acoustical pioneer Hermann Helmholtz (1885) defined the sensation of noise succinctly:

> The sensation of noise is due to non-periodic motions.

This allusion to aperiodicity captures the essence of the thing. In the acoustic world, there is a continuum of sound between periodic and aperiodic waveforms. Pitched noises, for example, stand somewhere between unpitched white noise and a pure sine wave.

In the time domain, noise can be defined as sound in which the amplitude over time changes with a degree of randomness. The amplitude is maximally random in *white noise*. In the spectral or frequency domain, noise can be defined as sound that has a continuous power spectral density (measured in watts per hertz) over a certain frequency bandwidth. The power spectral density of all frequencies is equal in white noise. Indeed, as we will see, certain ideal noises can be described precisely according to their statistical properties.

However, many noises in the real world are mixtures of periodic and aperiodic waveforms (the sounds of cars, refrigerators, etc.). They are driven by processes that are complicated and turbulent, with embedded periodicities, not necessarily "random" in nature. Thus, like the fuzzy term "timbre," "noise" serves as a kind of linguistic placeholder for a large class of complex, not always understood, signals. For example, certain static tone clusters are broadband and inharmonic, but they do not exhibit the asynchronous jitter (constant fluctuation) we associate with the statistical noises. In any case, let us not forget the rich domain of transient and intermittent noises. Thus any musical definition of noise must allow for flexible boundaries.

THE PITCH-NOISE CONTINUUM

Pitched tones and noise tones stand at opposite ends of a sonic continuum. Starting with a pitched tone, we can modulate it by a random function. If the noise is low in frequency, the result is a random tremolo (in the case of amplitude modulation) or vibrato around a central pitch (in the case of frequency modulation). As the frequency and intensity of the noise modulation increase, the sense of pitch becomes ambiguous. In the extreme, the modulation obliterates the sense of pitch altogether and we hear only a broadband noise.

Proceeding in the opposite direction, we can start with a broadband noise and apply a band-pass filter to it to obtain a narrowband noise. As the filter bandwidth is narrowed, we approach a single resonating pitch carved out of the noise. In the limit, this becomes a pure sine wave.

The continuum between pitch and noise can be exploited as a compositional opposition, with pitch functioning, for example, as the more relaxed stable pole, and noise as the tenser unstable pole. The intermediate pitched and colored noises provide for stepwise motion between the two.

It would be too simple, however, to portray pitch and noise as entirely segregated phenomena. Sounds in the real world often combine pitch and noise. Bending pitches and tone clusters are often embedded in complex noises. In natural and industrial sounds, we hear noisy crackling, crunching, creaking, and buzzing, but also pitched squealing, groaning, and humming. The same could be said for many animal sounds combining pitch and noise, like the purring of a cat.

THE ROLE OF NOISE IN MUSIC

Noisy sounds have always played a role in music, particularly in the unpitched percussion (snare drum, tom-tom, cymbals, woodblock, etc.). However, noise is also present in other instrumental sounds, such as the scraping of a cello bow on a string or in breathy or raucous wind tones. Only in the 20th century, however, was noise material gradually accepted into the family of "musical sounds."

FIGURE 4.18 Futurist composer Luigi Russolo in 1930 with his Russolophone noise instrument.

In the early 1900s, the Italian Futurist composers proposed an "art of noises" (Russolo 1916; Hultberg 2001):

> Musical sound is too limited in its variety of timbres. The most complicated orchestras can be reduced to four or five classes of instruments in different timbres of sound: bowed instruments, brass, woodwinds, and percussion. Modern music flounders within this tiny circle, vainly striving to create new varieties of timbre. We must break out of this limited circle of sounds and conquer the infinite variety of noise-sounds!
>
> —LUIGI RUSSOLO (1916)

The Futurists designed *intonarumori* ("noise-tone") instruments for performance (figure 4.18). Twenty-seven varieties of intonarumori were made, with different names according to the sound produced: howler, scraper, thunderer, crackler, crumpler, exploder, gurgler, buzzer, hisser, and so on. Compositions such as Russolo's *Risveglio di una Citta* (*Awakening of a City*) (1913) attempted to mimic the soundscape of an industrial morning. Their early performances were marked by riotous reactions, leading one Futurist, Marinetti, to observe derisively:

> It was like showing a steam engine to a herd of cows.
>
> —QUOTED IN HAYWARD (2004)

Russolo identified six categories of noise (I to VI) (Hayward 2004) summarized in table 4.1.

TABLE 4.1

The six categories of noise, according to Russolo

I	II	III	IV	V Beating on	VI Voices of humans and animals
thunder	whistling	whispering	screeching	metal	shouts
roars	hissing	murmuring	creaking	wood	screams
explosions	puffing	mumbling	rustling	skin	shrieks
hissing roars		muttering	humming	stone	wails
bangs		gurgling	crackling	pottery	hoots
booms			scraping		howls
			wheezing		
			sobbing		

Their work extended to radio broadcasts. For example, Marinetti's *Five Radio Syntheses* (1933) is a precisely scored script featuring the sounds of water, metal, short samples of recorded music, crowd noises, motors, and individual tones, interspersed with pregnant silences (Lombardi 1978).

Varèse's *Ionisation* (1931) for 13 percussionists was a historical breakthrough. In this original work, musical structure is articulated by changes in rhythm and timbre rather than melody and harmony. Note also John Cage's works for percussion, such as *First Construction in Metal* (1939), and his many pieces for prepared piano (1940–1954) as precursors of noise music in the realm of acoustic instruments.

The surge in electronic music after WWII led to a wave of experiments with noise materials. One of the first studies was carried out by the pioneer of musique concrète, Pierre Schaeffer. His *Cinq études de bruit (Five Noise Studies)* (1948) featured the sounds of trains, an orchestra tuning up, pots and pans, and the inside of a piano struck by mallets, among other sources.

Other composers filtered the sound produced by analog noise generators (figure 4.19) to experiment with bands of filtered noise. Karlheinz Stockhausen's *Studie II* (1954), for example, is a pioneering but otherwise unremarkable etude based on noise bands. More interesting is his *Gesang der Jünglinge* (1956), which features filtered noises mixed with sine waves and human voices. Stockhausen's colleague Gottfried Michael Koenig realized a series of noisy works using analog generators, including *Klangfiguren* (1956), *Essay* (1958), and *Terminus I* and *II* (1962 and 1967, respectively).

Xenakis's composition *Bohor* (1962) deploys the sounds of a Laotian mouth organ (slowed down greatly), small crotale bells, and hammerings on the inside of a piano to create a hypnotic and monumental sound mass. The last two minutes consist of sheets of broadband noise, which provoked a reaction at a Paris concert:

> By the end of the piece, some were affected by the high sound level to the point of screaming; others were standing and cheering. "Seventy-five percent

FIGURE 4.19 General Radio analog noise generator.

> of the people loved it and twenty-five percent hated it," estimated the composer from his own private survey following the performance.
>
> —BRODY (1971)

Bernard Parmegiani's *Capture éphémère* (1967), an analog tape composition, brilliantly anticipated the sound world of digital granular synthesis. His *Géologie sonore* from the masterpiece *De natura sonorum* (1976) explores noise textures as a sequence of sound masses move in and out of view.

In the earliest days of computer music, Max Mathews and James Tenney created pioneering studies in digital noise synthesis using Mathews's programming language Music III, which featured the first noise generator defined in software (Mathews and Pierce 1962). Considering the primitive technical conditions, both were notable achievements. Mathews's study *The Second Law* (1961), a reference to the law of entropy, contrasts all manner of pitched and unpitched noises. James Tenney's *Analog #1: Noise Study* (1961), despite its title, was synthesized by an IBM 7090 computer (Polansky 1983).

Sound example 4.20. Excerpt of *Analog #1: Noise Study* (1961) by James Tenney. 

Ushering in the age of digital sampling, *Sud* (1985) by J.-C. Risset deftly contrasted pure sine wave clusters and the broadband noise of ocean waves. Using a bank of highly resonant filters, he explored the continuum between periodic (resonating) and aperiodic (nonresonating) textures (Teruggi 2008).

Although Milton Babbitt routinely disdained the search for new sounds and never spoke of noise in his theoretical writings or interviews, his early electronic compositions feature hard-edged noise sequences.

Sound example 4.21. Excerpt of *Composition for Synthesizer* (1961) by Milton Babbitt.

These precursors of noise composition set the stage for many to follow. Indeed, an entire genre devoted to noise is by now firmly established; artists such as Zbigniew Karkowski (who died December 13, 2013), Russell Haswell (*Live Salvage* 1997–2000), and Florian Hecker (*Blackest Ever Black* 2007), among many others, till these fields. Laptop musicians from many countries have embraced the noise genre, with extreme volume levels that emphasize the physicality of sonic phenomena.

Sound example 4.22. Excerpt of *Live at Queen Elizabeth Hall* (1998) by Russell Haswell.

Long before the laptop, however, composers like Henri Pousseur and Toshi Ichiyanagi were exploring the extreme sound world of particulated and sustained noises.

Sound example 4.23. Excerpt of *Scambi* (1957) by Henri Pousseur.

Sound example 4.24. Excerpt of *Appearance* (1967) for three instruments, two oscillators, and two ring modulators by Toshi Ichiyanagi.

COLORED NOISES

Any noise with a limited bandwidth can be considered a *colored noise.* A common way to obtain a colored noise is to start from a broadband noise and pass it through a band-pass filter. The filter limits the frequency range of the noise. Colored noises have been a staple of the electronic medium since the 1950s.

The color analogy derives, of course, from light, where each color represents a certain frequency range in the electromagnetic spectrum. This analogy can be applied to the sound spectrum. Thus scientists have defined certain types of noises according to their spectra analyzed statistically over time.

Table 4.2 is a list of noises labeled by a color name. While most have a mathematical description, in two cases, the color names are simply those of the scientists Elisha Gray and Robert Brown. It is not claimed that this list of noises is comprehensive or complete; every field has its own catalog of noises.

Sound example 4.25. White, pink, and brown noise.

TABLE 4.2

Colored noises

White noise: If the frequency spectrum is flat (equal energy at all frequencies), then the noise is called white, by analogy to the spectrum of white light, in which all colors (frequencies) are present with approximately the same intensity.

Pink noise (1/f noise or flicker noise): Pink noise also contains energy at all frequencies, but its energy distribution or amplitude curve varies for different frequencies. Pink noise contains equal energy per octave and is often represented as $1/f$ or *fractal noise.* In terms of perception, pink noise has more bass rumble than white noise, as it falls off in amplitude at a rate of 3 dB per octave with increasing frequency. A 3 dB change is equivalent to a halving of power, thus doubling the frequency halves the power, which is equivalent to saying that power is proportional to 1/frequency.

Blue noise (azure noise): According to Federal Standard 1037C, in blue noise, the spectral density or power per hertz is proportional to the frequency. Blue noise power density increases 3 dB per octave with increasing frequency over a finite frequency range. In effect, blue noise is high-pass filtered white noise.

Purple noise (violet noise): Purple noise's power density increases 6 dB per octave with increasing frequency over a finite frequency range.

Green noise: Strange (1983) extended the color analogy to describe *green noise* as a white noise with boosted mid frequencies. There is no mathematical definition, however.

Red noise (brown noise): Continuing with the color analogy, *red noise* means a boost in low frequencies, more extreme than pink noise. It falls off in the high frequencies by a factor of 6 dB per octave. Some definitions construe it to be the same as *brown noise* ($1/f^2$ noise), named after botanist Robert Brown (1773–1858).

Gray noise: Gray noise results from flipping random bits in an integer representation of a sample stream. The spectrum is stronger in the lower frequencies (Castine 2002). Like brown noise, it is named not for its relationship to light but due to its relation to the code developed by Elisha Gray.

Grey noise: Random noise subjected to a psychoacoustic equal loudness curve (such as an inverted C-weighting curve) over a given range of frequencies, giving the listener the perception that it is equally loud at all frequencies.

Black noise: Black noise has several different definitions. According to one definition, it is "darker" than red or brown noise, characterized by a falloff of about 18 dB per octave (Castine 2002). Federal Standard 1037C states that black noise "has a frequency spectrum of predominately zero power level over all frequencies except for a few narrow bands or spikes. An example of black noise in a facsimile transmission system is the spectrum that might be obtained when scanning a black area in which there are a few random white spots. Thus, in the time domain, a few random pulses occur while scanning." Another, contrasting definition of black noise is that it is inverted white noise. This is the noise that cancels out white noise, an "anti-noise." Informally, the definition of black noise has been broadened to cover the inverse of any noise, for example, in reducing the roar in the passenger cabins of airplanes on noise-reducing headphones.

Infrared noise: A random fluctuation or rhythm in the infrasonic frequencies.

Beyond the colored noises is an open-ended space of algorithmically defined pseudorandom noises. For musical purposes, Peter Castine (2002) created a library of some 50 different stochastic noise generators. These include well-known distributions such as binomial, linear, exponential, Poisson, and Gaussian, as well as fractal noise generators and many of the colored noises listed in table 4.1.

PSEUDORANDOM NOISE

In the ideal, a source of noise should generate random values. To define an algorithm for generating truly random numbers is, however, impossible mathematically (Chaitin 1975, 1998). Any software method for random number generation ultimately rests on a finite, deterministic procedure. Hence, an algorithm for generating "random" numbers is actually a *pseudorandom number generator*, since the sequence generated by a finite algorithm ultimately repeats after a finite number of iterations. Programming language environments provide pseudorandom number generators with different characteristics, such as the frequency range and the length of the sequence before it repeats. Stephen Wolfram (2002) famously developed a new type of pseudorandom number generator that he called rule 30 based on a cellular automata algorithm that is much more random than previous algorithms.

A main challenge for digital synthesis is creating more sophisticated algorithmic models for noise. The global statistical criteria that define a pseudorandom numerical sequence, for example, are not optimum for describing many interesting noisy sounds.

SOURCES OF NOISE

Natural wind, sea spray, waterfalls, and thunder are excellent sources of wideband noise. Speech and animal sounds contain many evocative noises, especially the fricatives and plosives of speech [s], [z], [sh], [f], [k], [t], [p], [g], and so on. I have already mentioned the rich noises of the unpitched percussion instruments. Collections of samples recorded at industrial sites are available. These feature the sounds of crushing, creaking, scraping, squealing, squeaking, and grinding. A metal scrapyard is a particularly noise-intensive environment. I used the evocative sound of a burst of steam in *Half-life* (1998).

Analog devices produce some of the most complex and unstable noises. For example, the noise from a diode section of a transistor is widely considered to be one of the most random phenomena in nature; it can be amplified to make an analog noise generator or a cryptographic-quality random noise source (Comscire 2011).

Analog FM radios emit rich noises in the high region around 108 MHz where few stations broadcast.

Certain digital distortions such as aliasing and overload sound chaotic but are highly correlated with the input signal. That is, given the same input, they produce the same output, so they are deterministic rather than random.

In general, the colored noises of table 4.2 are too consistent to be sonically interesting for more than a few seconds. The ear is attracted to changes in noise, to trends. Thus the static global statistical criteria that define a pseudorandom numerical sequence are not optimum for describing the evolution of interesting acoustical noises. As early drum machines taught us, white noise is a poor substitute for a cymbal crash. The paradigm of *nonlinear chaos*—deterministic algorithms that generate complex behavior—has replaced stochastic models of certain phenomena observed by scientists (Gleick 1988).

NOISE AND DIGITAL SYNTHESIS

Many digital synthesis techniques can generate interesting chaotic noises. Long ago at the University of California, San Diego, I heard the results of an experiment to produce white noise by sine wave additive synthesis. It took about 90 sine waves to create a convincing noise band that was one-third of an octave in width, or about 270 sine waves per octave of noise. (This works out to be about 22 divisions per semitone.) Clearly, synthesizing noise by adding sine waves together is not efficient from a computational standpoint.

A basic law of signal processing states that the shorter a sound, the broader its spectrum. The briefest possible noise in a digital audio system is a single impulse. Thus we see its bandwidth extends to the Nyquist frequency (figure 4.20a). In figure 4.20(b), we see that a series of impulses in the time domain results in a series of impulses in the spectrum. Broadband noises can be synthesized from pure impulses. One method of noise generation creates a series of impulses regularly spaced in time but of irregular amplitude (figure 4.20c). Another method generates a series of impulses irregularly spaced in time, where each impulse has the same amplitude (figure 4.20d). These can be thought of as amplitude modulation (AM) and frequency modulation (FM), respectively.

Beginning with just two sine waves, FM using a high modulation index can produce dense unstable noises. Other techniques, such as nonlinear waveshaping, physical models, granular synthesis, and stochastic synthesis, can also create broadband noises. An example of the latter is Xenakis's GENDYN program (Xenakis 1992; Hoffmann 2000), which was used to realize *GENDY3* (1991) and *S.709* (1992), for example.

The sound of silence

The most expressive sound is silence. This is well known from speech. When a speaker injects pregnant pauses into his or her speech, the words seem to accrue great significance, and listeners pay attention. The famous Hollywood actor Alan Ladd (1953) once said:

> I may not be the greatest actor in the world, but I'm great on my pauses.

The pianist Artur Schnabel (cited in Margulis 2007) expressed a similar sentiment:

> The notes I handle no better than many pianists. But the pauses between the notes—Ah, that is where the art resides.

One style of 20th-century music took the insertion of pauses to an extreme. The music of Morton Feldman interposed sparse events framed by weighty silences

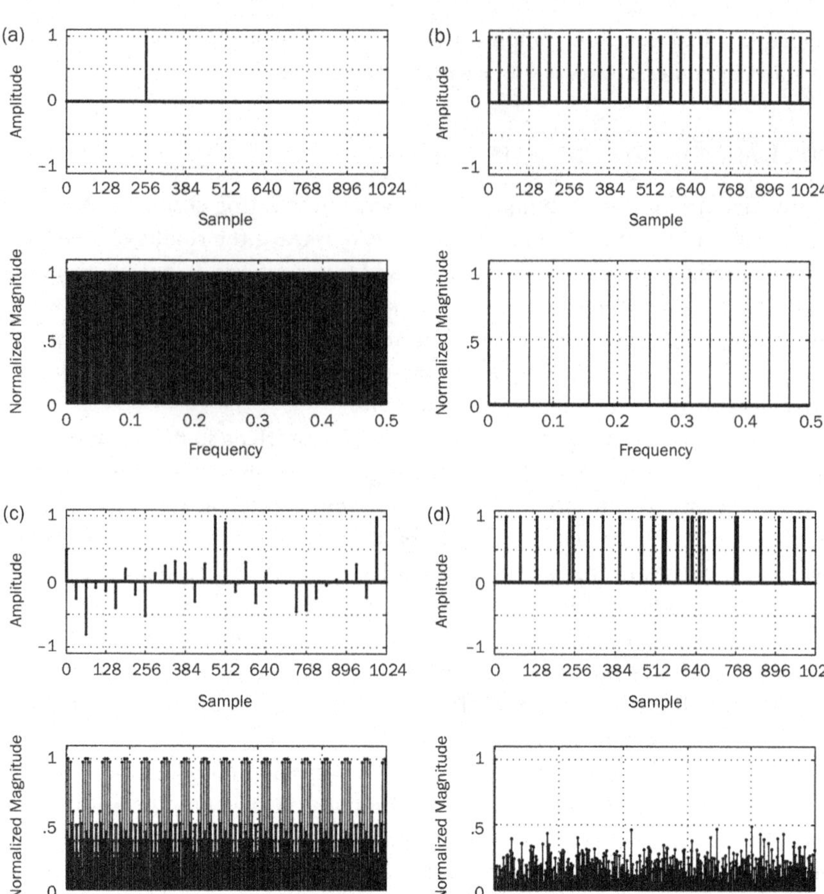

FIGURE 4.20 Four example signals and their normalized magnitude spectra extending to the Nyquist frequency (labeled 0.5 meaning "half the sampling rate"). The time domain signals are on top and the spectrum plots are below. (a) Single impulse. (b) Impulse train with period of 32 samples. (c) Series of impulses at random amplitudes. (d) 25 impulses at random times, generated by a uniform probability distribution.

in long compositions. Such a tactic places a high burden of expectation on the coming events. Of course, the iconic composition *4'33"* (1952) by John Cage presented the musical equivalent of the blank canvas: Listeners hear only the relentless chatter of their minds, as well as any incidental noises of the space in which we experience it.

Absolute physical silence is difficult to find. Most anechoic chambers still have a residual noise level of 10 to 20 dB. Of course, musical silence need not be physically silent; a drop in amplitude by 20 to 30 dB can be as dramatic as a complete pause. This sudden shift of attention can reveal a soft background texture that was masked by the foreground action, what Stockhausen called *colored pauses* (Coenen 1994).

Of course, to subtract sound (i.e., cut sound material) is as old as the practice of composition. We must distinguish between simply deleting a sound (thereby shortening the passage) and pruning, which makes a passage sparser without affecting its total duration. One of the great benefits of working in a studio is that a composer can prune on any timescale, backtracking from a nonproductive cul de sac. A performing artist cannot—whatever was expressed onstage is now part of collective history.

Software techniques provide a number of new ways of composing directly with silence by means of subtractive processes. A number of such techniques exist, including spectral filters, tracking phase vocoders, graphical synthesis interfaces, and matching pursuit decomposition. The important property of all of these methods is that they operate selectively in both time and frequency. Thus composing subtractively is not a question of zeroing the amplitude of a time-domain waveform, but of a systematic process of poking holes in both frequency and time. See chapter 5 on sound transformation for an explication of these cavitation processes.

Conclusion: material and organization

> I was not influenced by composers as much as by natural objects and physical phenomena. As a child, I was tremendously impressed by the qualities and character of the granite I found in Burgundy, where I often visited my grandfather. . . . So I was always in touch with things of stone and with this kind of pure structural architecture—without frills or unnecessary decoration. All of this became an integral part of my thinking at a very early stage.
>
> —EDGARD VARÈSE (1965B)

In the first half of the 20th century, Varèse (1939) dreamed of opening the compositional palette to any sound from any source:

> The raw material of music is sound. . . . Today when science is equipped to help the composer realize what was never before possible—all of what Beethoven dreamed, all that Berlioz imagined possible—the composer continues to be obsessed by traditions which are nothing but the limitations of his predecessors. Composers like anyone else today are delighted to use the many gadgets continually put on the market for our daily comfort. But when they hear sounds that no violins, wind instruments, or percussion of the orchestra can produce, it does not occur to them to demand those sounds. . . . Yet science is even now equipped to give them everything they can require.

Not all practitioners of electronic music agreed with the philosophy behind the "liberation of sound." To Milton Babbitt (1967), the main attraction of the electronic medium was its rhythmic precision, not new sounds:

> It is rather depressing to realize that people still talk about the new sounds that composers are trying to find. . . . This reflects a very deep misunderstanding. Composers did not turn to these [electronic] media for a new sound, for ephemeral titillation of the sonic surface.

Directly opposed to this point of view stood Pierre Schaeffer (1976). He saw technology as opening a door to an entirely new sound-oriented approach to composition:

> The *Traité* [*des objets musicaux*] argues against a conception of musical "progress" that expects from modern technology a simple improvement in performances (with serial music one expected electronic music to provide a more precise division of values, of duration and pitch). The emergence in the musical domain of "concrete" and "electronic" sounds does not constitute a perfecting of but rather a break with the previous [musical] system.

While Schaeffer championed concrète sources, the early Cologne school tried to ban them; they were thought to be too loaded with acousmatic associations. As Stockhausen (1989) observed:

> All recognizable sounds were avoided in [1950s Cologne aesthetic] electronic music. I used to say, don't imitate a car sound or a bird, because then people start thinking of the bird and of the car rather than listening to the music.

However, the purist view with respect to sound material faded away, as Stockhausen (1989) admitted:

> It was basically a weakness to have to demand a kind of exclusivity for each aspect of music, always to define music in terms of taboos.

Today we see a wide gamut of approaches to sound material. Consider the computer music pioneer Hubert S. Howe Jr., whose work *19-tone Clusters* (2010) is a systematically organized construction based on sine wave additive synthesis. Yet the composer has also realized a version of the same piece where, instead of sine tones, the piece is played with instrumental samples. The reorchestration makes it a different piece altogether.

Sound example 4.26. *19-tone Clusters* (2010) with sine waves by Hubert Howe.

Sound example 4.27. *19-tone Clusters* (2010) with instrumental samples by Hubert Howe.

New sounds are always possible, if only from the infinite possibilities of mixing sounds into compounds. Of course, a search for new sounds is meaningless as an end unto itself. As Luciano Berio (1958) stated:

> For me, the significance of electronic music lies not so much in the discovery of "new sounds" but more in the unique opportunity to enlarge the domain of sound phenomena and to integrate them into a musical thought that justifies and provokes further extensions.

In other words, the challenge posed by new sounds is always how to organize them compositionally.

In linguistic discourse, the sign (written or acoustic) is relatively neutral or arbitrary (i.e., the same concept can be expressed in many different languages with completely different sounds). This is somewhat true of traditional notated music. In some cases, it is possible to substitute a piano, for example, in place of a harpsichord, without radically affecting the composer's message. In other cases of reorchestration, such as substituting tubas for double basses in a Mozart symphony, this would constitute musical heresy. If musical meaning includes the interpretation and/or the orchestration, then they are not the same, even if listeners recognize the piece in both forms.

To a much greater degree, in electronic music, the specific nature of each sound informs its function within the flow of organized sounds. The substitution of new sounds tends to deeply alter the impression of a given piece. Material and organization are deeply intertwined, as Stockhausen (1989) observed:

> There is a very subtle relationship today between form and material. I would even go so far as to say that form and material have to be considered as one and the same. A given material determines its own form out of its inner nature.

Along the same lines, consider this remark by Horacio Vaggione (2000):

> I assume there is no difference of nature between structure and sound materials; we are just confronting different operating levels, corresponding to different timescales to compose.

Indeed, today we can extend the interplay of material and form to all levels of musical structure.

5

Sound transformation

Sound material is malleable and mutable. The plasticity inherent in the electronic medium was recognized early in the history of electronic music by pioneers like Werner Meyer-Eppler (1960). It has profound implications for composition. As Trevor Wishart (1993) observed:

> The signal processing power of the computer means that sound itself can now be manipulated. Like the chemist, we can take apart what were once the raw materials of music, reconstitute them, or transform them into new and undreamt of musical materials. . . . The shift in emphasis is as radical as possible—from a finite set of carefully chosen archetypal properties governed by traditional "architectural" principles—to a continuum of unique sound events and the possibility to stretch, mould, and transform this continuum in any way we choose, to build new worlds of musical connectedness.

Digital recording and synthesis make it possible to generate and store enormous sound libraries, which can be accessed and auditioned instantaneously (Harvey 2010). This furnishes a virtually endless supply of material for sound transformation techniques.

The transformation of sound is central to the methodology of electronic music composition. The choices of what sound to transform, which transformation to apply, when to apply it, and with what parameter settings are crucial compositional decisions. They depend entirely on the plans, goals, expertise, and sensitivity of the composer. As Wishart (1994) observed:

> One cannot simply apply a process, "turn the handle," and expect to get a perceptually similar transformation with whatever sound source one puts into the process.

The meaning or function of a sound transformation depends on the musical context in which it appears. Certain sound transformations seem to be *ornamental* (i.e., they alter a sound in a way that does not have major structural implications). Other transformations seem to be more *structural* (i.e., they alter the organization of the composition). However, the nature of music is such that it is difficult to draw a neat line between the ornamental and the structural. Indeed, this ambiguity is part of the charm and interest of music. Consider sound example 5.1, a transformation of a santur by Ivan Tcherepnin from his *Santur Opera* (1977). The melody and harmony are preserved but the processing stamps this as an electronic idiom.

Sound example 5.1. Excerpt of *Santur Opera* (1977) for santur and electronics by Ivan Tcherepnin.

Let us assume, however, that use of a mute on a trumpet in the context of a jazz ballad can be seen as an ornamental timbre transformation in the sense that the notes remain the same. We see the same essentially nonstructural transformation in compositions that have been adapted for different instruments, such as keyboard reductions of ensemble works. On the other hand, it is clear that skillful orchestrations of keyboard works (which go from monotimbral to polytimbral) articulate structural functions by highlighting particular voices at crucial moments. Moreover, a device such as a mute on a trumpet helps to inform a genre. Similarly, an adaptation from piano to distorted electric guitar is not a neutral change. Just as a performer can render a novel performance of a piece without deviating from the notated score, certain electronic transformations inject nuances that make a piece more expressive or evocative.

At the opposite end of the spectrum, some transformations are so extreme as to make the input sound unrecognizable.

Sound example 5.2. Excerpt of *E Cosi Via* (*And so on*) (1985) for piano and tape by Daniel Teruggi. The piano sound is heavily modified. Signal processing techniques include harmonizing, delays, feedback loops, controlled distortion, resonant filters, and reverberation.

Sound transformation can serve as a means of spawning musical material to be organized in a separate phase of composition. Going further, transformation can also serve as a compositional methodology—a means of progression—by deriving new material from old. In this case, the transformations serve the structural function of *variation.*[27] Derived variations can be generalized to multiple timescales: from transformations on individual samples, grains, a part of a sound (i.e., its attack), an entire sound object, a phrase of several sounds, a section, to a complete piece. This multiplicity of scope creates a large space of possible variants, even for a basic operation such as re-enveloping (changing the amplitude profile of a signal).

The goal of the rest of this chapter is to analyze the central role played by sound transformation in the composition of electronic music. We first look at sound transformation in vocal and instrumental music. Then we clarify the notion of sound signal transformation and explain how it has taken on structural functions in electronic music compositions. The final section presents a survey of categories of sound transformation, including their different control regimes and a basic taxonomy of effects.

Sound transformation in vocal and instrumental music

The last half of the 20th century saw extensive experimentation in new performance methods. *Extended techniques*, as they were called, aimed at transforming the sound of the voice and traditional instruments. A famous example is John Cage's invention of the prepared piano, created by inserting objects on and in between the strings of a conventional piano. In the same vein, vocalists experimented with Sprechstimme and other unconventional vocalisms. String performers practiced unusual bowing techniques (such as sul ponticello) and tapping on the body of the instrument. Woodwind and brass performers used overblowing and multiphonics, among other means (Erickson 1975). The domain of percussion instruments expanded from a limited set to include almost any object that produced sound when hit.

After several decades and hundreds of pieces incorporating extended techniques, these once novel effects are now more familiar. Familiarity, or a "decay of information," as Herbert Brün referred to it is not necessarily negative (Hamlin and Roads 1985); there is nothing wrong with familiar sounds in music. Indeed, electronic music has many familiar elements that once were exotic.

Yet there is something to be celebrated about novelty in any dimension of artistic creativity. In the instrumental and vocal domain, sonic novelty is increasingly rare. It is fair to say that the mine of new orchestral instrument sounds to be found is nearly exhausted. This is meant as an observation, not a polemical statement.[28]

The situation is objectively different in the electronic medium, not the least because it incorporates the domain of all recordable sounds, of which the instrumental sounds are a tiny subset. Even this enormous resource can be considered merely a base set, however, since any sound can then be electronically transformed in limitless ways. Consider, for example, Milton Babbitt's *Philomel* (1964) for voice and tape, in which the composer electronically processed vocal sounds on tape through the RCA Mark II synthesizer (Babbitt 1997, 2000).

> We got the first 4-track Ampex tape [recorder] that was ever made. . . . We could go from machine [RCA synthesizer] to tape and from tape back to machine. You could play through this machine too. You could use it entirely as a processor. There was a way of entering a signal and processing it internally within the machine, which I did in *Philomel.*

Sound example 5.3. Excerpt of *Philomel* (1964) for soprano, recorded soprano, and synthesized tape by Milton Babbitt. 

Sound signal transformation

Music information can be represented in myriad ways (Roads 1984; DePoli et al. 1991). For each representation, a class of meaningful transformations exists. This is reflected in the notion of *data type* in computer science, in which the set of admissible operations on a given datum depends on its type. For example, the integer type admits operations such as add, subtract, multiply, and divide, while the string type admits operations such as copy, append, compare, insert, etc. Music data encompasses myriad types such as waveforms, spectra, time-frequency representations, MIDI and OSC data, fonts and notation data, graphical scores, etc. Although basic operations such as copy and delete might apply to all types, certain operations, such as a fadeout, are only meaningful when applied to a specific type (waveform). Thus materials and admissible transformations are interlinked.

Moreover, a transformation has different effects depending on the nature of the data to which it applies. For example, if the music data consists of pitch-class sets represented by integers, then even simple transformations—when translated into sound—change the musical material in perceptually salient ways. Consider a simple transformation on a set of MIDI notes that randomly adds or subtracts 1 to each note's pitch class value—this has a major effect on the melody and harmony. Yet the same plus-or-minus 1 operation applied to sample values in a sound file will produce thousands of variations that are perceptually indistinguishable from one another.

Transformation has always been a means of development in music. Traditional methods of development include dividing base material into smaller figures, regrouping motifs or figures into new phrases, altering the contour of the motifs, and exploring harmonic variations and digressions (Apel 1972). Similar transformations on MIDI pitch-time data have been developed over the past two decades, many built into music programming languages. Some sequencers feature such transformations in their menus.

In this chapter, however, we are concerned specifically with *sound signal transformation*, where the sound to be transformed exists as an analog or digital signal. (In the rest of this chapter, the word transformation refers to sound signal transformation.) The range of transformative operations is open-ended; new methods are continually being invented. Meanwhile, creative musicians combine classic techniques in fresh and idiosyncratic ways.

TRANSFORMATION AS VARIATION AND DEVELOPMENT

Transformation serves two main functions in electronic music. First, starting from a base set of sounds, transformations generate families of derived sounds, multiplying the diversity of the sound palette. Even a small set of operations (e.g., granulation + ring modulation + pitch shifting) can generate a vast space of possible morphological variations on a given sound. A given set of transformations forms a composable network of permutations and combinations. To chart and organize this outside-time space of possibilities can be part of the initial phase of composition in electronic music (Vaggione 2006). Consider a simple snare drum hit processed through a frequency shifter. Each frequency that it is modulated with produces a different spectrum. So from one sound, we can easily create a hundred mutations. These possibilities were recognized early in the development of electronic music (Ussachevsky 1958); see figure 5.1.

In recent years, the technics of manipulating sounds on magnetic tape by mechanical and electro-acoustical means have brought the possibilities of timbre control into a new dimension, in some respects greatly exceeding the possible variations obtained on conventional musical instruments. To the timbre

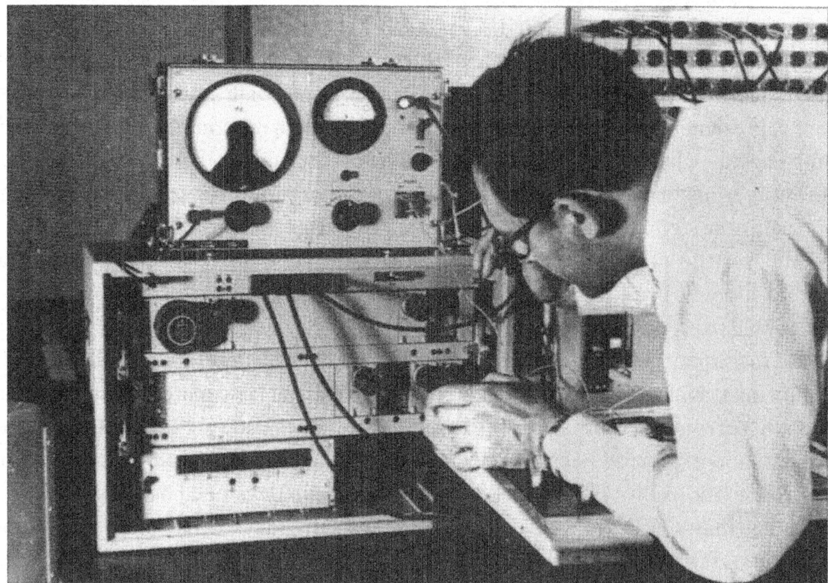

FIGURE 5.1 Vladimir Ussachevsky operating the Klangumwandler (frequency shifter) at the studios of the Southwest German Radio in 1958.

mutations of recorded sounds by tape-speed variation, band-pass filters, and resonators, etc., can now be added a radical alteration of the ratios among the harmonics within any sound.

Going further, modern techniques of audio transformation create new means of continuous musical development or progression, including variations of amplitude, pitch, spectrum, spatial position, and granular texture. Operations such as pitch-time changing, convolution, frequency shifting, adaptive concatenation, and granulation can impose radical changes, extending the time base of the material, density, and basic texture. Such alterations affect the very fiber or internal structure of a sound, potentially changing its structural role.

In many works by Trevor Wishart, including *Red Bird* (1977), sound transformation plays a role analogous to variation in traditional music (Wishart 2000). All sounds in his 25-minute *Imago* (2002) derive from transformations of a one-second clip of two wine glasses clinking. As cited in chapter 2, Horacio Vaggione's *Harrison Variations* (2002) is a 10-minute composition derived from the same clip. Despite reliance on a single sound as the germ of the entire work, both compositions exhibit remarkable acoustic heterogeneity. The lesson is that it is possible to start with any sound and derive a cornucopia of diverse sounds from it through transformation.

Going in the opposite direction, certain transformations sequenced in reverse can function as revelations. They begin with an obscure sound (derived by means of a series of previous transformations) whose identity is gradually revealed by means of clarifying transformations that effectively "undo" the derived sequence (Smalley 1993).

SOURCE-CAUSE VERSUS SPECTROMORPHOLOGICAL TRANSFORMATION

Smalley (1993) made an important distinction between two types of transformations according to the perceptual effect they create:

- *Source-cause* transformations affect our perception of the provenance of the sound.
- *Spectromorphological* transformations change the spectral and morphological properties of a sound.

The first category of transformations is of particular interest to the acousmatic school of composition (see chapter 4), where the musical narrative is concerned with identifying and tracking a sound's *source* (a named vibratory system) and *cause* (an activity or gesture that excited the vibration). Together, these constitute what Smalley calls a sound's *base identity*. For certain types of sounds, such as the voice, recognition of the base identity is undoubtedly innate to the human auditory system. We instantly recognize a voice like that of Billie Holiday, and we continue to recognize it in recordings made in different times and places. Any transformation that affects the base identity to the extent that we no longer recognize it will be meaningful, as in "That's not Billie Holiday." Hiding the origin of the sound is a source-cause transformation.

The second category of transformations is more general because it affects all sounds, whether or not we recognize their base identity. Concerning John Chowning's *Turenas* (1972), Smalley (1993) wrote:

> There is nothing "realistic" about the timbres; there is no viable real cause, and any extrinsic link will relate to the velocity and spatial articulation of imagined sound sources.

Spectromorphological transformations involve an alteration of a sound's perceived acoustic properties, such as pitch, duration, loudness, spectrum, spatial position, etc. These transformations apply to abstract electronic tones, as well as concrete sources. *Wind Chimes* (1987) by Denis Smalley is a case in point, wherein the sound palette is derived primarily from the transformation of strikes on ceramic wind chimes (Gayou 2011):

> It was not so much the ringing pitches which were attractive but rather the bright, gritty, rich, almost metallic qualities of a single struck pipe or a pair of scraped pipes. These qualities proved a very fruitful basis for many transformations. . . . Not that the listener is supposed to or can always recognize the source, but in this case it is audible in its natural state near the beginning of the piece, and the ceramic quality is never far away throughout.

Sound example 5.4. Excerpt of *Wind Chimes* (1987) by Denis Smalley.

Elena Ungeheuer (1994) referred to the span of transformations as a *Klangfarbenkontinuum (sound-color or timbre continuum)*:

> Attempts to achieve a continuous change of timbre can be found all over the landscape of electronic composing. Inasmuch as timbre is a complex parameter that fuses together all the different properties of sound into its "character," the Klangfarbenkontinuum figures not only as an exotic effect in the universe of electronic sounds but links a musical utopia with an acoustic premise and electrotechnical reality. . . . Electrotechnical transformations articulate the continuum of musical derivation.

The next section explores this continuum of effects and perceptions.

THE IDENTITY CONTINUUM: MUTATION AND TRANSMUTATION

Certain transformations have a stronger effect than others from a perceptual point of view. A *unit* or *identity* transformation, such as a 180-degree phase inversion of a monaural sound, has no perceived effect. We call a mild transformation, in which the sound is altered but the perceived source identity or signature of the sound is retained, a *mutation*. In a mutation, we can tell by listening that a second sound is derived from an initial sound. An important class of mutations is composed of the *automorphisms* that map an object onto itself while preserving the structural connections among elements. The structural connections inform the identity of the element being transformed. For example, if you rotate an apple, it is still an apple. The transposition of a chord or melody can be seen as an automorphism in the sense that it preserves intervallic relations.

In contrast, radical transformations obliterate the source identity of the sound being transformed. We call such radical transformations *transmutations*. This range of effects is the *identity continuum*:

identity—mutation—transmutation

An example of a transmutation would be the sound produced by a convolution of a voice with a cloud of grains. This produces a radical temporal scrambling of the voice (figure 5.2).[29]

Many other transformations are less radical. Indeed, we can establish a perceptual continuum of effects, from subtle mutations to unrecognizable transmutations.

Here we enter into issues central to the acousmatic discourse: recognizability, reference, meaning, and allusion (see chapter 4, "Creating sound materials"). The

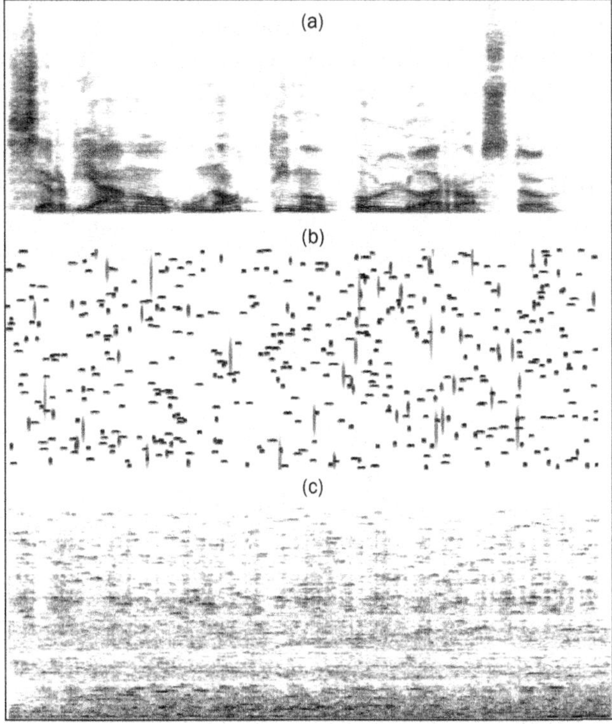

FIGURE 5.2 Time-frequency sonogram: (a) a six-second vocal utterance; (b) a cloud of grains; (c) their convolution product. It is not clear from either visual inspection or listening that (c) was derived from (a).

choice of whether to alter a sound beyond recognition depends on its function in a compositional context. Certain transformations color the result with noise and artifacts. This is neither good nor bad, since the goal of a given compositional decision could be precisely to color the original to the point of causing a mutation. For this reason, there are no universally "good" filters or "bad" reverberators in the absolute sense, just as there are no inherently "good" or "bad" sounds. Everything depends on the context in which the transformation is applied.

DERIVING SOUND FAMILIES THROUGH TRANSFORMATION AND INTERPOLATION

Transformation lets one generate families of related sounds from a single parent sound. In figure 5.3, the parent sound is a snare drum hit. We derive children from it by ring modulation (RM) at various modulation frequencies. The event time structure is preserved by RM. Grandchildren and great-grandchildren sounds are produced by subsequent operations. These sound families can be used to produce either equivalence classes (functional substitutions) of the parent sound or, in contrast, a series of differentiated sounds that can be used to construct progressions on higher timescales.

Sound example 5.5. Deriving a family of sounds through a single transformation. We hear a vocal sample followed by eight variations, all produced with a multiband frequency-shifting effect (Virsyn PRISM).

A classic example of a composition based on a system of sound transformations is Gottfried Michael Koenig's *Terminus I* (1962), the last piece he realized at the Cologne Electronic Music Studio (Ungeheuer 1994). In this work, five electronic glissandi were manipulated by transposition, amplitude modulation,

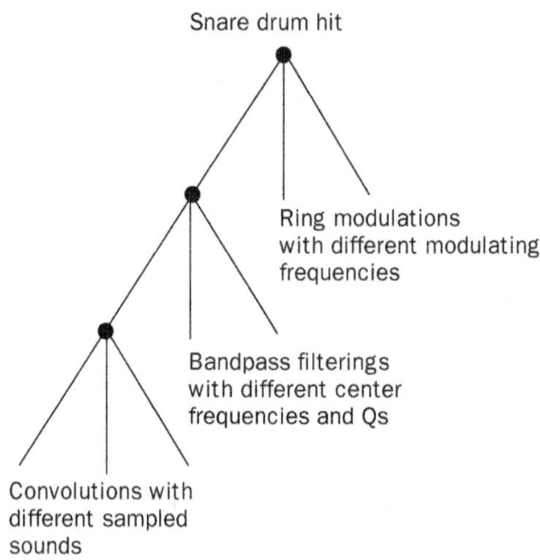

FIGURE 5.3 Deriving families of sounds through transformations.

reverberation, and RM. Koenig's formal plan of the work shows a tree structure of derivations (figure 5.4).

Sound example 5.6. Excerpt of *Terminus I* (1962) by Gottfried Michael Koenig. 

Techniques like granulation can radically transform the time structure of an original sound (Thall 2004a, 2004b; Roads and Thall 2008). In combination with other operations at the granular level (pitch shifting, filtering, amplitude variation, grain size variation, spatial variations, etc.), a given sound can be exploded into a wide variety of cloud forms. These can range from dense continua to sparsely scattered grains, as in Stéphane Roy's *Mimetismo* (1992) for guitar and tape, which deftly blends a strummed, plucked, and tapped acoustic guitar with rapid-fire splicing and processing of these materials.

Sound example 5.7. Excerpt of *Mimetismo* (1992) for guitar and tape by Stéphane Roy. 

Another class of derived sounds is obtainable by *morphing* or *interpolation* processes between two sounds, prepared by an analysis phase (Fitz and Fulop 2009). Morphing is not the same as crossfading. If the two sounds being morphed have different pitches, for example, we should hear the sound glissando from the first pitch to the second pitch. A general theory of sound interpolation was proposed by Trevor Wishart (1993, 1994). He cites an example where the source sound is the sea and the target sound is a voice. The recognition of a change from one to the other may be sudden or gradual ("the talking sea"). Interpolation effects can be achieved by a variety of technical means: analysis-based spectral interpolation, vocoding, or granulation with interpolation, for example.

THE ROLE OF SOUND ANALYSIS IN TRANSFORMATION

Certain transformations start from an analysis of an existing sound. An example would be a time-stretching transformation based on a phase vocoder spectrum analysis (Roads 1996a). The power of analysis-based sound transformation was recognized by Luciano Berio (2006):

> Analysis is not just a form of speculative pleasure or a theoretical instrument for the conceptualization of music; when it contributes to . . . the transformation of sound forms . . . it can make a profound and concrete contribution to the creative process.

In simple forms of analysis, one can perform the analysis and transformation in real time. In other cases, the analysis and transformation are performed as two separate steps.

Every method of analysis should be viewed as fitting the input signal to an assumed model. For example, spectrum estimation methods based on Fourier

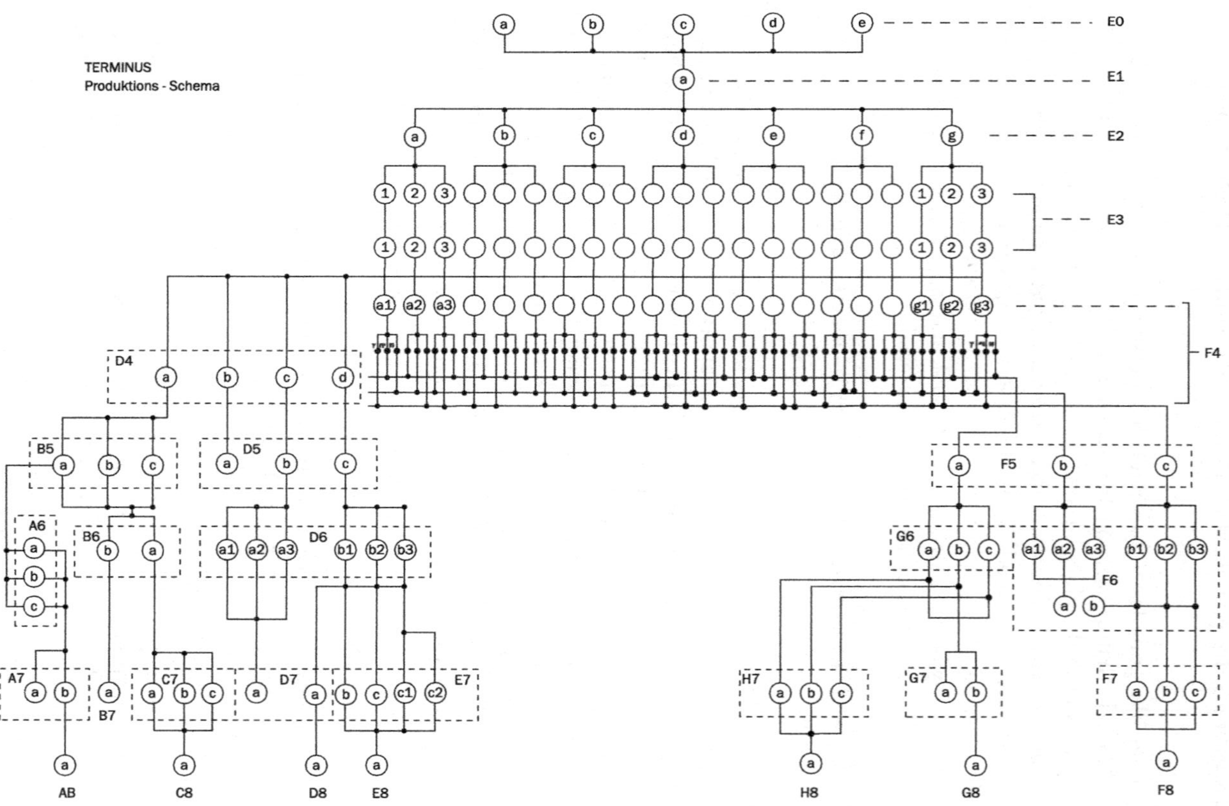

FIGURE 5.4 Production scheme of transformations of five glissandi (at top) *a, b, c, d, e* in Koenig's *Terminus I* (1962). After Ungeheuer (1994).

analysis model an input sound as a sum of harmonically related sinusoids—which it may or may not be. Other techniques model an input signal as a collection of atoms in a dictionary, a sum of square waves, a combination of inharmonically related sinusoids, a set of formant peaks with added noise, or a set of equations that represent the mechanical vibration of a traditional instrument. Innumerable other models are conceivable. Variations in performance among the different methods can often be attributed to how well the assumed model matches the signal being analyzed. No method of sound analysis is ideal for all applications. Hence it is important to choose the appropriate analysis method for a given sound transformation.

One of the ways to test an analysis method is to resynthesize the sound based on the analyzed data. Some analysis methods, such as the tracking phase vocoder (Roads 1996a), must be carefully tuned to the characteristics of the analyzed sound (harmonic, percussive, noisy, etc.) in order to produce a convincing resynthesis. Other methods, such as the non-tracking phase vocoder and dictionary-based pursuit, require less tuning.

The result of any analysis method is a representation of a sound based on the analysis model. Certain representations are more malleable than others with respect to transformation. Some representations are brittle (i.e., they cannot be easily transformed without producing audible artifacts). Wavelet-based transformations come to mind (Ramakrishnan 2003). Other methods, such as the tracking phase vocoder and dictionary-based pursuit, produce a more malleable representation (Sturm et al. 2009).

TRANSFORMATION AND ZONES OF MORPHOSIS

Transformation of sound is fundamental to composition in the electronic medium. It is common to design a gesture in which the musical process consists of X turning into X' (a mutation) or even Y (a transmutation) over time. Such transformations can become the theme or subject of the composition (Stockhausen 1989). In effect, the transformations become the process that produces the musical structure.

Just as states of matter undergo critical phase transitions from solid to liquid to gas to plasma, sound phenomena can pass from one state to another as they dance on the edges of perceptual thresholds. These *zones of morphosis* are of extreme interest from an aesthetic point of view, as they are intrinsically exciting and fascinating. Zones of morphosis can be seen as the places where a continuous change in a plastic medium confronts context-dependent thresholds of human perception. They occur when a change in quantity in some parameter appears as a qualitative change to the listener.

One of the most ubiquitous zones of morphosis is the simple crossfade. Depending on the source and destination materials, we gradually change the ratio of the amplitudes of two or more signals to effect a sonic mutation. Similarly, an analysis-based morphing algorithm creates a zone of morphosis.

Other zones of morphosis appear when sounds are transposed. By means of tape-speed change, pioneers like Stockhausen could speed up discrete melodies to the point where they lost their melodic quality and morphed into continuous timbres. In a similar manner, rhythms, when sped up, change state and morph into tones. Modulations like tremolo and vibrato, when sped up, morph into complex spectra.

Another zone of morphosis is a change in a *just noticeable difference* (JND) where a barely perceptible alteration is occurring. Bernard Parmegiani was a master of this game. His *de natura sonorum* (1975) is full of subtle details in which slight clicks, detunings, filter changes, modulations, panning motions, or beating phenomena become the focus of the composition—as if he applied a JND of change (sound example 5.8).

Sound example 5.8. Excerpt of *de natura sonorum* (1975) by Bernard Parmegiani.

Another zone of morphosis is a point of emergence or disappearance, as something comes into being and goes out of being through a critical phase transition. This approach is fostered by treating musical material as a continuous and fluid energy, rather than as a pattern of discrete notes. By means of synthesis and processing, pitch, for example, can be manipulated as a flowing and ephemeral substance to be bent, modulated, or dissolved into noise. Similarly, by means of technology, time becomes a plastic medium that can be generated, modulated, reversed, bent, granulated, and scrambled. The undulations of envelopes and modulations weave into the fiber of musical structure on multiple timescales.

Categories of sound transformations

> There does not seem to be any general or optimal paradigm to either analyze or synthesize any type of sound.
>
> —JEAN-CLAUDE RISSET (1991)

A detailed technical study of sound signal transformations would constitute a book unto itself. Here we distinguish several basic categories of sound transformation and their control regimes. Later we present a taxonomy of effects as a guide to the possibilities.

UNIVALENT VERSUS MULTIVALENT TRANSFORMATIONS

Univalent transformations alter a single property of a sound without significantly affecting our perception of its other properties. An example would be a low-pass filter effect. Univalent transformations are, however, usually an exceptional case.

Typically, when we alter one property of a sound, it has a side-effect on other properties. As a simple example of a *multivalent* effect, by varying the playback rate of a sound file, we shift its pitch and spectrum but also modify its duration. (This is called a *multidimensional effect* in Zölzer 2011, which includes a table of effects and the perceptual attributes they modify.) A classic multivalent transformation is convolution, which can alter both the spectrum and the time structure of a sound.

Another multivalent example is *sonographical transformation* based on manipulations of an image of sound on a frequency-versus-time plane (Roads 2001b). The UPIC system, operational in 1977, was an early example (Xenakis 1992). Today many software systems let one inscribe graphical traces on a frequency-time grid, where the traces can be converted directly into sound. In effect, one can paint the sound, erase it, or touch it up with all the flexibility of a software painting program. For example, a sound can be transformed using image processing techniques such as blurring or rotation (figure 5.5). The MetaSynth application is a prime example of a sonographic synthesizer (Wenger and Spiegel 2009).

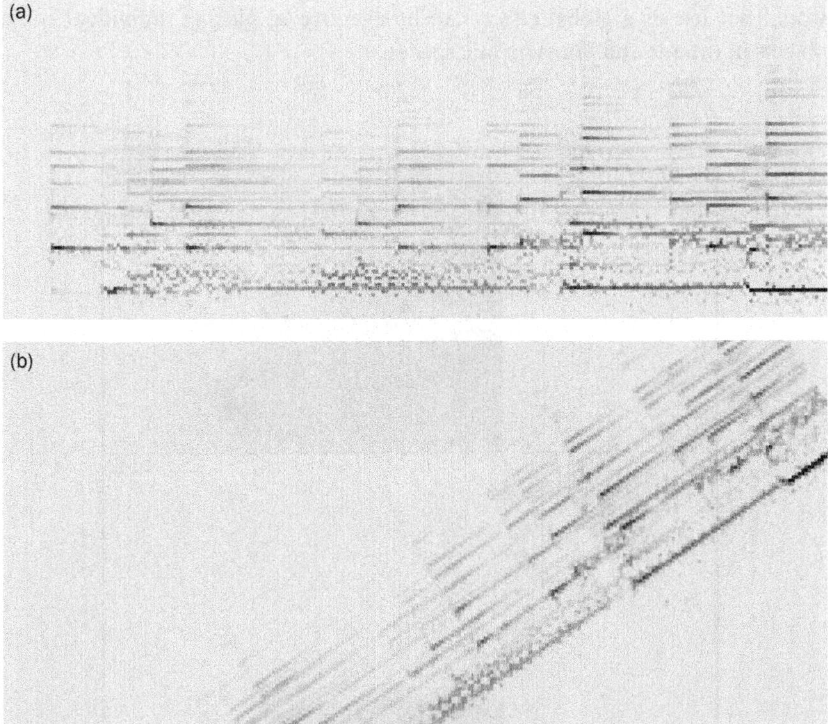

FIGURE 5.5 The top image (a) is the spectrum of a classical guitar passage. The bottom image (b) is the same spectrum rotated in a graphical synthesis program. When resynthesized, the original identity of the sound is not perceptible. However, using small angles of rotation, one can establish a continuum from subtle mutations to unrecognizable transmutations.

Another multivalent operation is to alter the amplitude envelope of a sound; this also changes its spectrum due to a fundamental law of convolution: Multiplication in the time domain is equivalent to convolution in the frequency domain. Since a change in envelope is essentially a multiplication by a new envelope function, it follows that the spectrum changes. This is easily demonstrated (figure 5.6).

In certain cases, perceived changes derive from nonlinearities of the human auditory system. For example, attenuating the amplitude of a sound may make it seem simultaneously duller and less bassy, since hearing is acute in the midband of the spectrum at low levels. (Indeed, buttons for "loudness" on audio receivers boost the bass and the highs so one can listen at low level without missing parts of the spectrum.) In contrast, at higher amplitudes, the ear hears spectrum more linearly.

Finally, other side-effects can occur due to imperfections in the transformation algorithm itself; many effects processors introduce artifacts at certain settings. These artifacts take many forms: noise, distortion, DC offset, resonances, time aliasing (echoes), phase anomalies, clicks, etc. In some cases, the coloration induced by an effect is part of its charm. For example, when used creatively on individual sounds, highly colored (i.e., band-limited) reverberators, which one would not use as a global effect, can be effective in placing individual sound objects in unique and idiosyncratic spaces.

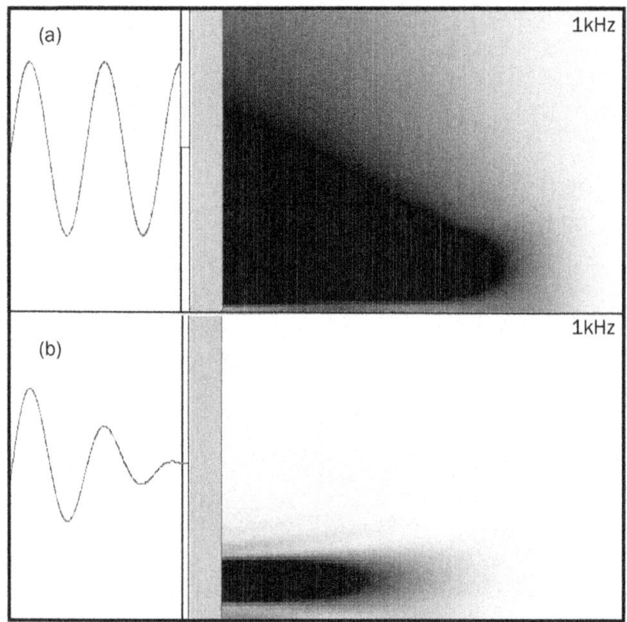

FIGURE 5.6 Effect of envelope change on spectrum. (a) A sound consisting of a 120 Hz sine wave lasting 39 ms and its spectrum plotted up to 1 kHz. (b) The same sound as (a) with a fadeout. Notice how radically its spectrum is narrowed.

CONTROL REGIMES FOR TRANSFORMATION

This section looks at how transformation operations are controlled: static versus time-varying, real time versus non-real time, manual versus automatic, as well as content-based transformations.

Static versus time-varying control

Sound transformations can be *static* or *time-varying*. Static transformations apply to the entirety of a sound (on whatever timescale) and do not change over time. Examples of static transformations include a fixed boost in gain or a global reverberation applied to an entire track. Devices with switched controls (rather than continuously variable controls) are designed for static transformations and are often imposed on an entire track. A typical example would be a classic Neve 1073 or API 550B hardware equalizer; these have detented knobs set to discrete frequency settings. Because effects in pop music are usually applied to an entire track, devices with static settings are staples of the trade. In more general applications, however, we want to be able to vary transformation parameters in either discrete or continuous modes.

Manual versus automatic control

Certain transformations can be controlled by a musician in real time as a sound is being played. This lets them stamp the transformation with a human gesture. In other cases, it is desirable to automate the control of a parameter.

An early form of automation was *voltage control*, introduced in the analog synthesizers of the late 1960s. In an analog synthesizer, one module (such as a low-frequency oscillator or LFO) can control another module (such as the center frequency of a filter). Voltage control allowed musicians to control a dozen or more parameters in real time. Built into a number of modular analog synthesizers were modules for the processing of control signals. These allowed composers to perform analog computations: adding, subtracting, scaling, inverting, integrating, interpolating, smoothing, and sampling, for example.

The most advanced synthesizers, then and now, incorporate the generality of *matrix modulation* into their design (figure 5.7). Matrix modulation means that any control source can control any parameter. Moreover, the degree of control—the index of modulation—is also a control parameter.

Modern sound editing and mixing programs let users control synthesizers and effects by drawing envelope curves that automatically modify multiple parameters in time (figure 5.8).

Control by oracle

Gareth Loy (2006) observed that artists sometimes delegate control to an external process or oracle:

> The characteristic feature of art of all kinds is that it combines *objective criteria and methods with choice making*. The difference between art and

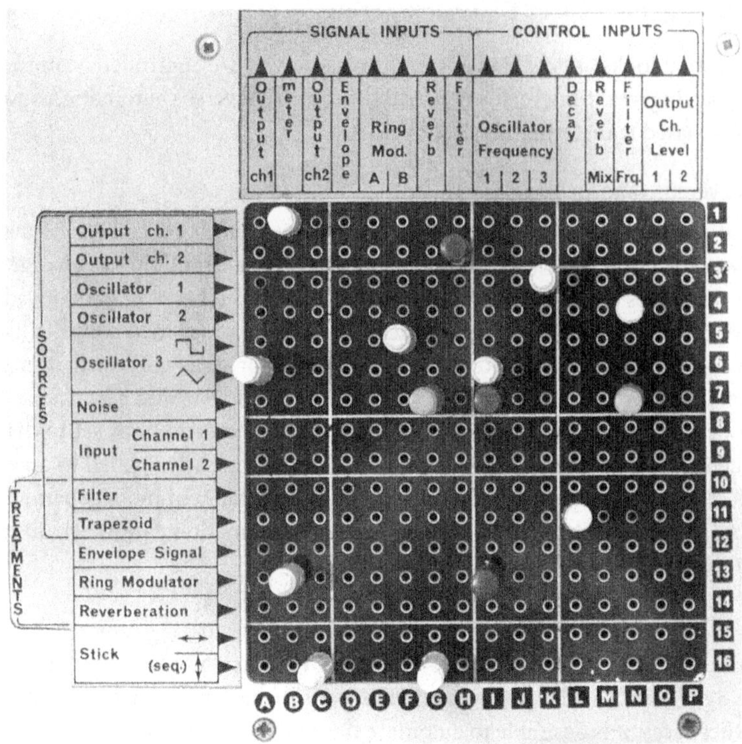

FIGURE 5.7 Routing matrix of an EMS VCS3 synthesizer, taken at the Musikinstrumentenmuseum in Berlin. Users inserted pins into the panel to connect the output of a control source (rows on the left) to the control input of another module (columns left to right). (Photograph by FallingOutside, Creative Commons license.)

> algorithm is that deterministic methodology (algorithm) always produces the same result with the same inputs. . . . So-called objective choice, such as tossing a six-sided die, is actually just the delegation of subjective choice to an external process. . . . A delegated external choice-making entity is an *oracle*.

Facilities for random or aleatoric control of sound processing go back to the earliest modular analog synthesizers in the 1960s. The output of noise generators could be low pass filtered and converted into low-frequency random voltages in order to control other sound modules.

Such processes echo the compositional methodologies of John Cage. Cage designed compositional decision processes in which sonic details were determined by aleatoric means, what he called "chance operations." These could be activities in his studio like throwing dice, splattering ink, or drawing from a deck of cards, or produced from indeterminant computer algorithms, as in his collaboration with Lejaren Hiller on *HPSCHD* (1969). They could also be delegated to a performer to choose from a set of options or to improvise on the spot. Finally,

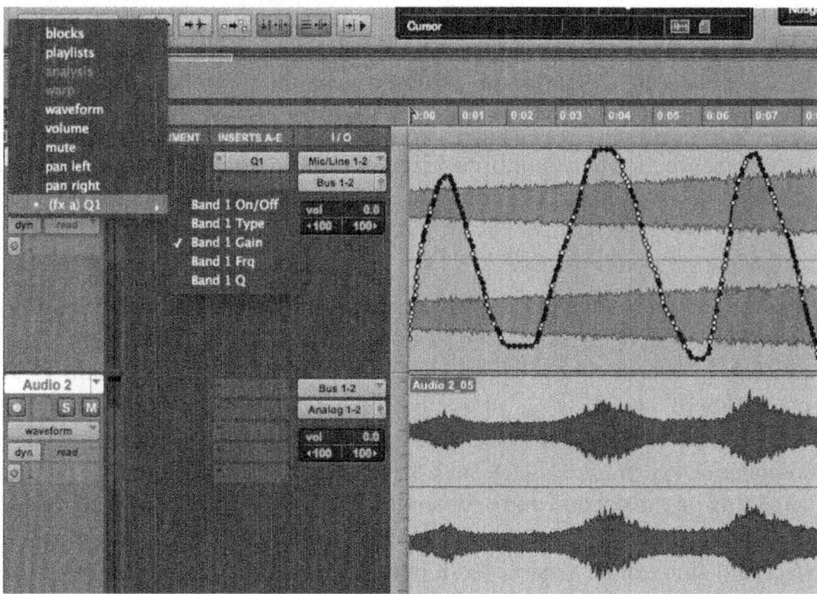

FIGURE 5.8 Automation control of a plug-in effect in a sound editor. The menu at upper left selects what effect parameter is displayed. In this case, it is the gain of a band-pass filter. The control envelope is shown overlaying the top stereo track. The bottom stereo track shows the result of the effect on a band of white noise.

a number of his compositions depend on external conditions: for example, radio broadcasts whose content is not known in advance. One could say that Cage delegated compositional decisions to oracles.

A modern-day electronic oracle is the Model 266e Source of Uncertainty in the Buchla 200e Electric Music Box:

> The Model 266e Source of Uncertainty is a general source of musical unpredictability. Divided into 4 sections, each section serves a unique function.
>
> Noise comes in three flavors. White noise is electrically flat, but acoustically balanced toward the high end of the spectrum (+3 db/octave). Integrated white noise has a low spectral bias (−3 db/octave). Musically flat noise has a flat spectrum (constant energy per octave) and is a particularly useful source for subsequent processing.
>
> Fluctuating Random Voltages are continuously variable, with voltage control of bandwidth over the range of .05 to 50 Hz, making possible changes that vary from barely perceptible movement to rapid fluctuation.
>
> Quantized Random Voltages change on receipt of pulses. Their number of states is voltage controllable from two to twenty-four, and their distribution can be varied both spatially and temporally.

Stored Random Voltages have three parameters under voltage control. Degree varies the amount of randomness; chaos alters the distribution from just a little uncertain to total chaos; while skew biases the randomness toward one extreme or the other.

Control by oracle is built into many electronic transformation processes, including all my granulation engines (Roads 2001b; Roads and Thall 2008).

Content-based transformations

An interesting new class of transformations has emerged in recent years called *content-based transformations* or *adaptive effects*. This borrows from signal processing, information retrieval, and machine learning (Amatriain et al. 2003; Dubnov and Assayag 2012; Eigenfeldt and Pasquier 2012). The most basic example of a content-based transformation is an automatic gain control (compressor/expander/limiter). Such a system can reduce or increase its gain depending on the relationship between the level of the input signal and a given amplitude threshold. This scheme uses the input signal's level to control the effect, but this can be generalized to any feature of the input signal that can be extracted by analysis. Researchers have developed effects that react according to the fundamental frequency, the spectral centroid, and other features extracted from an analyzed sound. An example would be a time-stretching algorithm that applies only to the (voiced) vowels of speech and not the (unvoiced) consonants.

Sometimes an analysis stage can be skipped because the input signal already contains metadata that can be used in the transformation process. An example of such a transformation would be an equalization setting that applies to a genre of music, where the metadata describes the genre. (The MPEG-7 standard described in chapter 3 supports embedded metadata in sound files.)

Higher-level musical transformations can even be developed to manipulate structural features of music such as tempo and instrumental articulation. This, of course, implies that an analysis or feature extraction phase is able to derive these features from the input signal.

A BASIC TAXONOMY OF EFFECTS

This section presents a list of common effects, broken down according to categories in the manner of a taxonomy. I present this here mainly for the benefit of those who are new to the field. It is by no means a complete list; new methods are constantly being invented. Moreover, some of the techniques listed here could be classified under more than one category. (For example, reverberation is listed as a convolution effect while convolution is listed under reverberation techniques.) Hence this is really more of a quick overview of possibilities than it is a scientifically inclusive taxonomy. Further information on transformation techniques can be found in Roads

(1996, 2002); Roads et al. (1997); Dodge and Jerse (1997); Moore (1990); Steiglitz (1996); and Zölzer (2002, 2011); as well as many conference proceedings (International Computer Music Conference, Digital Audio Effects, Audio Engineering Society, etc.).

Conclusion

The transformation of sound plays a central role in the practice of electronic music composition. Mutation (modification of identity) and transmutation (switch of identity) are omnipresent possibilities. By means of transformation, we can—if desired—start from a tiny corpus of source sound and derive from it most or all the material needed for an entire composition. For example, my composition *Always* (2013) is the product of a fourth-order granulation process that produced three other compositions: *Volt air III, Now,* and *Never.* The primary source material for all these pieces was a single click (sound example 5.9) granulated into an 800 ms sound object (sound example 5.10).

Sound example 5.9. An impulse generated by the author in 1999.

Sound example 5.10. An 800 ms sound object created by granulating the impulse of example 5.9.

Sound example 5.11. Excerpt of *Volt air III* (2003) by Curtis Roads, much of which was derived from granulating the sound in example 5.10.

Sound example 5.12. Excerpt of *Now* (2003) by Curtis Roads, much of which was derived by granulating *Volt air III* in sound example 5.11.

Sound example 5.13. Excerpt of *Never* (2010) by Curtis Roads, much of which was derived by granulating *Now* in sound example 5.12.

Sound example 5.14. Excerpt of *Always* (2013) by Curtis Roads, much of which was derived by granulating *Never* in sound example 5.13.

As Trevor Wishart (1994) observed:

> The precision of computer signal processing means that previously evanescent . . . features of sounds may be analyzed, understood, transferred, and transformed in rigorously definable ways. A minute audible feature of a sound can be magnified by time-stretching or brought into focus by cyclic repetition. . . . The evolving spectrum of a complex sonic event can be pared

TABLE 5.1

A basic taxonomy of effects

Signal mixing	
Balance mixing	Combine tracks while retaining the identity and individuality of each one.
Fusion mixing	Blend a low-level sound in order to fuse it with another sound.
Re-recording	
Acoustic re-recording	Play a sound through an amplifier and loudspeaker within a specific room and record with a particular microphone in order to impose the characteristics of the recording chain on the sound.
Electronic re-recording	Play a sound through a device such as a (real or emulated) vacuum-tube preamplifier or analog tape recorder and record it in order to impose the characteristics of the recording chain on the sound.
Reverse and inverse	
Time reversal	Flip the time axis, play the sound backward.
Phase inversion	Flip the amplitude axis, positive becomes negative.
Amplitude (dynamic range) processing	
Gain adjustments	Boost or attenuate by a fixed factor in dB.
Normalization	Scale a sound so that its peak amplitude matches a given target value.
Envelope reshaping	Scale a sound according to a drawn envelope function.
Tremolo	Slow amplitude modulation.
Compression	Compresses variations in dynamic range. When the input signal rises above a specified threshold, the compressor attenuates it. The overall level of the input signal can be raised by means of a makeup gain parameter.
Limiting	Strong compression with a hard threshold that cannot be exceeded.
Expansion	Expands small variations in dynamic range into large variations.
Multiband dynamics processing	Performs compression or expansion on multiple frequency bands simultaneously. The amount of compression or expansion can be adjusted for each band.
Pitch processing	
Vibrato	Slow frequency modulation (6-9 Hz).
Pitch shifting	Transposition.
Pitch bending	Continuous pitch alteration in time by a variable factor.
Pitch-time changing	Changing pitch while keeping the duration of a sound constant, or changing the duration while keeping the pitch constant.
Harmonization	Automatic accompaniment at one or more arbitrary musical intervals.
Time-domain spectrum filters	
Low-pass	Attenuates high frequencies above a designated cutoff frequency.
High-pass	Attenuates low frequencies below a designated cutoff frequency.

(continued)

TABLE 5.1 Continued

Band-pass	Boosts all frequencies between high and low cutoff frequencies.
Band reject	Attenuates all frequencies between high and low cutoff frequencies.
Shelving filters	Shelving filters boost or cut all frequencies above or below a given threshold. Their names can be confusing, because a high shelving filter acts like a low-pass filter when it is adjusted to cut high frequencies, and a low shelving filter acts like a high-pass filter when it is adjusted to cut low frequencies.
Linear-phase filter	A filter in which all frequencies have equal delay times, resulting in no phase distortion.
Graphic equalization	A graphic equalizer has a control panel that mirrors the shape of the filter's frequency response curve. Each filter has a fixed center frequency and a fixed bandwidth (typically one-third of an octave).
Comb filters	A comb filter has several regular sharp curves in its frequency response. When viewed as a plot of frequency (*x*) versus amplitude (*y*), they resemble the teeth of a comb. One type of comb filter has deep notches in its response, while the other has steep peaks.
All-pass filters	For a steady-state (unchanging) sound fed into it, an all-pass filter passes all frequencies equally well with unity gain—hence its name. The purpose of an all-pass filter is to introduce a frequency-dependent phase shift. All filters introduce some phase shift while attenuating or boosting certain frequencies, but the main effect of an all-pass filter is to shift phase. If the input signal is not steady-state, the all-pass filter colors the signal, due to the frequency-dependent phase-shifting effects. This coloration is particularly evident on transient sounds where phase relations are so important to sound quality.
Spectrum processing in the frequency domain	
Transient extraction	Extracts only the transient energy (attacks); usually implemented with wavelet analysis or matching pursuit decomposition.
Spectrum blurring	Applies a low-pass filter to the spectral changes from one window to the next, progressively "smearing" the sound (Norris 2007).
Spectrum freezing	Each frequency bin is watched until its amplitude reaches a peak. It is then held at that peak until it is exceeded by another peak in that bin (Norris 2007).
Spectrum tracing	Spectral tracing analyzes a sound and retains only the loudest or softest *N*% of the partials in the spectrum. To extract the transient part of a spoken voice, one retains only the softest 1 percent of the analyzed spectra. The sound quality of this 1 percent is like noisy whispering, after the result is high-pass filtered.
Spectrum harmonizer	The spectrum is transposed up or down by a set series of intervals.
Spectrum pitch shift	Spectral peaks (presumed to be fundamental pitches) are tracked and shifted.
Spectrum shift	Shifts the entire spectrum up or down by a stipulated number of frequency bins.
Spectrum stretching	Spectral peaks are tracked and shifted by an amount that varies according to frequency.

(*continued*)

TABLE 5.1 Continued

Spectrum filter bank	A bank of narrow band-pass filters.
Spectrum randomizer	Applies a random variation in amplitude to a stipulated percentage of frequency bins.
Sonographical transformations (not based on linear system theory)	
Rotation	Graphical rotation of the spectrum image.
Sonogram filters	Select a frequency region graphically, then boost or cut.
Graphical translation	Cut/copy/paste a part of the spectrum image to a different time-frequency region.
Displacement map	Distort a sonographical representation according to a graphic image.
Change contrast and brightness	Changes the amplitude of sounds.
Blur	Smears the image and smooths the attack and decay of sounds.
Trace edges	Highlights the amplitude profile of a sound.
Emboss left and right	Emphasizes the attack and decay, respectively.
Expand/contract	Expands/contracts the pixel spacing, changing the spectrum of the sounds.
Invert pitch	Flip the canvas vertically to shift the pitch.
Graphical echo and pre-echo	Repeat pixels to the right (echo) or to the left (pre-echo) of a graphical image, creating echo and pre-echo effects when the image is synthesized. The echoed pixels are not as bright as the original.
Graphical reverberation	Extend and fade the durations of all pixels.
Graphical repeat	Repeat pixels across a picture at a distance stipulated by the user.
Pulse	Carves graphical vertical cuts (removing pixels) at a distance stipulated by the user to create a pulsating effect.
Dictionary-based atomic transformations (Sturm et al. 2009)	
Transient extraction	Deleting all atoms longer than a given duration.
Deleting short atoms	Deleting all atoms shorter than a given duration.
Changing playback speed	Scale the duration of the atoms.
Changing playback pitch	Scale the pitch of the atoms.
Deleting loud atoms	Delete all atoms above a given amplitude threshold.
Deleting atoms by time	Delete all atoms below a given amplitude threshold.
Deleting short atoms	Delete all atoms within a given span of time.
Atomic filtration	Cut or boost all atoms within a given frequency band.
Time-frequency filtering	Cut or boost all atoms within a given span of time and frequency band.
Transposition	Changing pitch while keep harmonic ratios between atoms constant.
Atom translation	Moving a group of atoms to a different time-frequency region.
Atomic scrubbing	Moving the playback cursor back and forth for forward and backward playback at variable speed.
Time delay processing	
Echo	Time-delayed repeat of a sound. With feedback, the echo itself repeats several times.
Reverse echo	An effect made by reversing a sound, applying echo to it, and reversing it again. The echo precedes the sound.

(continued)

TABLE 5.1 Continued

Chorus	Any effect in which a single "voice" is transformed into a set of slightly pitch-shifted and delayed voices.
Flanging	Mixing a variable-time-delayed signal with itself, producing a set of equally-spaced peaks or nulls in the spectrum that sweep up or down.
Phasing	Phasing is similar in effect to flanging, but the "churning" sound produced by the sweeping comb filter is usually not as pronounced. In phasing, a spectrally rich signal is typically sent through a series of all-pass filters.
Tape echo feedback	A wide range of effects, from echoes to self-sustaining feedback with continuous pitch shifting and narrow filtered resonances.
Granulation	
Pitch-time changing	Stretch or shrink the timescale of a sound without affecting its pitch.
Freezing	Stopping the grain read pointer. A single grain is read repeatedly, effectively "freezing" the sound.
Deterministic selection	The read pointer moves from left to right (in time order).
Random selection (scattering)	The read pointer selects from random points in the sound file.
Pitch-time changing	Stretch or shrink the timescale of a sound without affecting its pitch.
Grain size variation	Short grains induce noise into the signal.
Granulation with pitch-shifting	Each grain is pitch-shifted by a random amount within a range set by the user.
Granulation with filtering	Applying a band-pass filter to each grain, where the filter center frequency is random within a range set by the user.
Formant shifting	Granulation with a variable formant shift that is independent of pitch.
Convolution	
Spatial mapping	Mapping an arbitrary sound to a spatial pattern captured by an impulse response.
Reverberation with real and synthetic IRs	Applying reverberation to an arbitrary sound, where the reverberation is the impulse response of either a real or synthetic space.
Rhythm mapping	Mapping an arbitrary sound to a rhythmic pattern captured by an impulse response.
Cross-synthesis	Crossing the spectrum of one sound with the spectrum of another.
Spatialization	
Panning	Moves the sound from one channel to another.
Panning with Doppler shift	Models a change in pitch that results when a sound source and the listener are moving relative to each other. Specifically, Doppler shift is a perceptual cue to the radial velocity of a source relative to a listener.
Image widening and narrowing	Modifies the spatial image of a sound.
Image shifting	Inverting the phase of one channel of a stereo pair to cause a shift in the stereo image in the uninverted channel; most interesting when applied to individual sound objects.
Channel swapping	The sound in channel A trades places with the sound in channel B and vice-versa. Most effective when applied intermittently to relatively short sound segments.

(*continued*)

TABLE 5.1 Continued

Filtering to induce vertical illusions	Certain filters can induce vertical illusions, particularly on sounds heard on headphones.
Reverberation	
Schroeder reverberation	Classical digital reverberation with comb and all-pass filters.
Convolution reverberation	Imposes the impulse response of a real space on a signal.
Geometric, waveguide, and feedback delay network (FDN) reverberators	Reverberation based on physical models of simulated spaces.
Reverse or pre-reverberation	Playing a sound in reverse while reverberating it, then reversing it so that the reverberation is heard before the sound.
Modulations and distortions	
Waveshaping and wavefolding	Nonlinear waveform distortion, where the shaping function can be designed to emphasize specific harmonics or simply distort in idiosyncratic ways.
Rectifying	Makes a bipolar waveform unipolar.
Amplitude modulation (AM) (audio rate)	Varies the amplitude of the carrier wave according to the modulator; generates spectral components that are the sums and differences of the carrier and modulator waves; in AM the modulator is unipolar (the entire waveform is above zero).
Ring modulation (RM) (audio rate)	Generates spectral components that are the sums and differences of the carrier and modulator waves.
Frequency shifting or single-sideband modulation (SSBM)	Adds a constant amount to all frequencies.
Frequency modulation (FM) (audio rate)	Varies the frequency of the carrier according to the frequency of the modulator, producing rich spectra.
Waveset operations (units of three zero-crossings)	
Waveset and wavecycle operations	See table 5.1 in *Microsound* (Roads 2001b) for a list of over 30 transformations. See also Wishart (1994).
Concatenations	
Granular remapping	Substituting grains from an arbitrary database of sound A in another sound B according to similarities between the features of the grains in A and B; enables radical transmutations (Sturm 2006).

away until only a few of the remaining partials remain, transforming something that was perhaps coarse and jagged into something aetherial.

In another approach, families of related sounds can be derived from a source sound to form functional progressions. Indeed, a single sound object can serve as the core of an entire macrostructure full of variation. (See Table 5.1) In this case, compositional organization and sound transformation are one and the same.

6

Processes of rhythm

All is inscribed in the scroll of time. Pulses mark points; tones trace lines. Envelopes shape undulations. Swells and swarms of grains form bubbling streams and clouds in time. Accents top off peaks; echoes prolong them; fadeouts and rests discharge musical energy.

Rhythm is the most fundamental element in all forms of musical expression. This chapter examines the gamut of possibilities for organizing the rhythmic structure of electronic music. We show that the full range of rhythmic expression is much larger than has been taught in traditional music curricula. Specifically, electronic means deliver new rhythmic options, from mathematically precise polyrhythms to the time warping of any rhythmic pattern.

However marvelous technology is, it requires a conceptual framework in order to be exploited effectively. Thus we need a theory of rhythm, even if it is only a partial one, that takes the new technical potential into account. Here is the primary goal of this chapter: to think through the gamut of possibilities for rhythmic organization and lay them out as an interconnected system of patterns on multiple timescales.

Agenda

We begin by examining the concept of rhythm. As we will see, rhythm is inseparably bound up with other elements of music on multiple timescales. For example, we could speak of the rhythm of harmonic changes (meso timescale) or the rhythm of vibrato (micro timescale). Next we look at the scope of rhythm: how time, amplitude, pitch, space, and timbre all function as articulators of rhythm. Then we examine the perception of rhythm and how human beings tend to anticipate and group events into specific rhythmic patterns. Next we briefly trace the history of rhythmic thinking from ancient times through Varèse up to today, leading to the notion of a rhythmic continuum. We discuss how the paradigm-shifting technologies of recording, editing, granulation, and programming fundamentally altered the rhythmic playing field. We then dissect that most ubiquitous rhythmic pattern: pulsation and meter. The controversial subject of algorithmically generated rhythm is the next topic, including stochastic rhythms and rhythmic sieves. Then we examine rhythmic organization in the electronic medium, including timescales of rhythm, polyrhythmic grids and fields, new possibilities for sequenced rhythm, and the role of undulation, modulation, and envelopes in rhythmic organization. The penultimate section presents a table of rhythmic oppositions—ways of pitting one rhythmic behavior against another, either in succession or in parallel. The final section presents a capsule overview of rhythmic processes in my music.

The concept of rhythm

The concept of rhythm continues to evolve. On the most general plane, rhythm is any temporal structure or pattern. In simple cases and within specific perceptual limits, rhythm is a quantifiable pattern; we can perceive basic rhythms clearly and immediately notate them. However, the scope of rhythm goes beyond simple onset time and duration. As Varèse (1959) observed:

> Rhythm is too often confused with metrics. Cadence or the regular succession of beats has little to do with the rhythm of a composition. Rhythm is the element in music that gives life to a work and holds it together. It is the element of stability, the generator of form.

Not only does rhythm articulate form on multiple timescales, it also subsumes the undulations internal to a sound, such as accents, swells, vibrato, and tremolo, which can be generalized to fluctuations in any parameter.[30]

Unlike the simple rhythm of a drumbeat, the rhythmic pattern of certain sounds is far from clear because of fundamental ontological issues. The onset time, duration, and even the existence of a sound is not always sharply defined. Consider these factors:

- The attack of a sound can slowly fade in, obscuring its *perceptual attack time* (Wright 2008, 2011). Moreover, its release can slowly fade out, obscuring its perceptual end.
- One sound can mask or unmask the presence of another sound.
- Undulations and modulations can obscure the duration of events.
- In the middle of a transmutating sound, when does one sound end and another begin?
- Sounds can split apart into separate components, or converge from several sounds into one composite.
- Sounds can coalesce and disintegrate by gradual changes in grain density (adding and removing grains) or spectral components (adding and removing sinusoids or other basis functions)

Thus we should view rhythm not as a series of points and intervals on a timeline grid, but rather as a continuously flowing temporal substrate.[31] We will return to this important point later.

RHYTHM IS THE SUM PRODUCT OF ALL PARAMETERS

Part of the difficulty in studying rhythm is that it is inseparably bound up with other elements of music. As Berry (1987) stated:

> The most complex [musical] element of all, that of rhythm, is in a sense the product of the actions of the other elements.

As Narmour (1984) observed with respect to meter:

> Meter is a summarizing result of all parameter interactions . . . rather than the cause of them.

Studies have shown, for example, that listeners infer rhythmic organization from melodic structure (Ahlbäck 2004).

Rhythm rarely appears in a pure form. In order to create a pure rhythm, isolated from all other musical elements, one would need to vary the onset times and durations of a sound while keeping all other sonic dimensions (i.e., loudness, pitch, timbre, and spatial position) constant. Of course, in real music, all these dimensions are changing simultaneously. Thus rhythm simultaneously organizes and is itself organized by these elements.

Consider a series of eighth notes, where every other note is accented, every third note is repositioned in space, every fourth note has vibrato, every fifth note is ring-modulated, and every sixth note changes pitch. Here the onset times are regular and the durations are all the same. The perceived rhythm is a function of patterns in dynamics, space, ornamentation, timbre, and pitch. Thus we can speak of the rhythm of a given dynamic, space, ornamentation, timbre, or pitch change, which can be a sudden discrete transition or a continuous variation over time.

Rhythm unfolds on multiple timescales simultaneously, from the microrhythms of the waveform, to the undulations within a note, to the higher layers of phrases and macroform. As Cooper and Meyer (1960) observed:

> As a piece of music unfolds, its rhythmic structure is perceived not as a series of discrete independent units strung together . . . but as an organic process in which smaller rhythmic motives, while possessing a shape and structure all their own, also function as integral parts of a larger rhythmic organization.

To summarize, music expresses rhythm on multiple timescales through patterns of pitch, amplitude, timbre, and space, in undulations, modulations, and changes of density, as well as by onsets and durations.

The scope of rhythm

Music students learn to associate their body gestures with music notation: the onset times and durations of notes with respect to a beat. The virtuoso musician knows how to alter the ideal values notated in the score in order to render an evocative interpretation. Musical rhythm also includes the time pattern of continuous variations (crescendi, diminuendi, undulations, and modulations) in all musical parameters. In electronic music, we call these undulating morphologies *envelopes*, and we speak of amplitude envelopes, spatial envelopes, vibrato envelopes, filter envelopes, and so on.

Table 6.1 charts musical elements that articulate rhythm. Taking advantage of the full range of possibilities, one can not only organize the rhythm of a melody, but also the rhythm of spatial, dynamic, and timbral patterns.

TABLE 6.1
Articulators of rhythm

Parameter	Articulator of rhythm
Time	onset
	duration
	silence
	patterns of onset, duration, silence
Pitch	specific isolated pitches
	glissandi (pitch trajectories)
	melodic patterns (sequential pitches)
	contrapuntal patterns
	harmonic patterns
Space	specific spatial positions (lateral, vertical, proximital, i.e., how near or far)
	panning (spatial trajectories)
	spatial chords (emanates from several locations at once)
	sequential spatial patterns
Amplitude	specific intensities
	accent patterns (groupings of strong-week attack patterns)
	envelope morphologies
Timbre	specific timbres
	continuous timbre mutation (timbral trajectories)
	timbre melodies (sequential timbres)
	timbral chords (combinations of simultaneous timbres)

Perception of rhythm: physical and psychological time

> [Perceptual] laws do not explain music any more than gravity explains the art of architecture. But there is not an architect who ignores gravity any more than there is a musical rhythm that does not respect perceptual laws.
>
> —FRAISSE (1982)

> We do not have a rhythmic center in the brain, nor do we have specialized time receptors. There is no component of the acoustic signal that can uniquely specify the rhythm.
>
> —HANDEL (1989)

Rhythm is the skeleton of musical structure, from the microtime of waveforms to the macrotime of musical form. One element of rhythm can be a periodic beat. If the fluctuations are periodic between about 10 beats per minute (BPM) and about 360 BPM, we feel a regular pulse.[32]

In most music, the dominant rhythmic expression is closely aligned to the pace of human muscle movement: breathing, talking, singing, dancing, tapping, rocking, and other bodily gestures. As is evident from pop music, the most easily perceived patterns are tightly aligned to a metric grid between 80 and 120 beats per minute (Fraisse 1982). The correspondence between rhythm and muscular gestures goes only so far, because rhythmic perception far exceeds human muscular performance. That is, one can easily hear rhythms on a timescale that one could not possibly perform with the body. Green (1971) observed that *temporal auditory acuity* (the ability of the ear to detect discrete events and discern their order) extends down to durations as short as 1 ms. Our sensitivity to shifts in periodicity and phase extends down to the microseconds.

This timing sensitivity, however, is at odds with another fact. Although absolute pitch is well known, the phenomenon of "absolute duration" in the absence of a metric grid does not exist (Fraisse 1982). That is, listeners can neither name nor play accurately specific durations. Our ability to estimate a duration without counting becomes poor when a sound is longer than several seconds. Moreover, it is difficult to align a human performance to a rhythm that is not synchronized to an underlying pulse.

London (2002, 2006) identified a number of perceptual/cognitive constraints on the perception of metric rhythms. These are akin to some of the perceptual/cognitive constraints on pitch perception cited in chapter 7. London's constraints included, among others:

- Upper and lower bounds for perception of musical meter (6 seconds to 100 ms, respectively)
- Longest and shortest periods for stimuli that subjects tend to group into twos or threes (2 seconds and 100 ms, respectively)
- Preferred tempo: the rate at which subjects are most comfortable at producing a steady beat (around 600 ms)
- Range in which subjects are most likely to hear a pulse (around 600 ms)
- Duration of the psychological present (5–6 seconds), a temporal envelope for patterns of musical rhythm and meter

Note that most of these constraints fall into the category of preferences and norms (sweet spots) rather than absolute limits per se.

Cognition itself is a play of rhythms, repetitions, and variations. Anyone who has meditated (or tried to fall asleep) has noticed that the mind generates new thoughts every second. A single thought immediately mutates. We can also think in parallel. For example, I am typing this sentence while also listening to music. Innate mental rhythms (rapid shifts of attention and perception) impose themselves upon music cognition. Musical problem-solving (including analytical listening, pattern recognition, and many other compositional tasks) takes time, and psychologists have devised a variety of tests to measure these mental processing delays (Posner 2005).

CHRONOS VERSUS TEMPUS

A disparity between measurable or objective time (*chronos*) and perceived or subjective time (*tempus*) has long been observed. Olivier Messiaen's monumental *Traité* (1994) places great emphasis on the distinction between "chronometric" or measured time and "duration" or perceived time. He devised several heuristics on how duration is experienced in musical rhythms. For example, his *law of attack-duration* can be stated as follows: A brief sound followed by silence appears longer than a sustained sound of the same duration. As a consequence, a melody played staccato appears longer than one played legato, even if the total duration is the same. Moreover, he asserts that factors such as attack shape, intensity, register, and timbre also influence the perceived duration. These issues were taken up by Stockhausen (1955) in his essay on what he called *experiential time.*

Music scientists study the perception of rhythm (tempus) in carefully contrived experiments (Honing and Ladinig 2008). Many rhythms are easy to learn; thus psychological factors such as remembrance and expectation have a profound effect on temporal perception.

> Even in improvised music, with the notion of learned riffs, Indian paltas and other improvisation training methods, each beat is performed within the context of intended future beats as well as those beats already performed. . . . Listeners use their corpus of learned rhythms as a reference point to subsume the new performance. A purely causal model will be limited in its success because it is not taking into account the prediction and retrospection possible of the performance as it proceeds.
>
> —SMITH AND HONING (2008)

Anticipation affects the listener's attention and informs their reaction as to whether their expectation is met or not (Huron 2006).

> Expectation and memory are intimately related. I wait for the return of a theme to the degree that I remember it. . . . In musical duration . . . there is a prevalence to wait for the past to occur again.
>
> —GISÈLE BRELET (QUOTED IN MESSIAEN 1994)

Thus anticipation informs the process of perceptual grouping, as discussed next.

GROUPING AND GESTALT PERCEPTION

When we listen to music, we tend to parse or group sonic events into a smaller number of higher-level rhythmic units. In this way, objective rhythm becomes subjective rhythm. According to scientific studies, listeners spontaneously group patterns of unaccented taps into units of two, three, or four. For example, a pattern of nine unaccented events such as - - - - - - - - - tends to be heard as (+ - -) (+ - -) (+ - -) (i.e., as a repetition of a small group of three events; Handel 1989).

Accents and other articulations trigger perceptual grouping mechanisms. Meyer (1956) and later Tenney (1961) and Deutsch (1982, 1999) isolated five mechanisms of Gestalt perception behind grouping:

- *Proximity*—closely spaced events form a group, especially if the time interval between any two events is less than 1.5 seconds.
- *Similarity*—perceptually similar events form a group.
- *Good continuation*—an arpeggio or glissando is perceived as a unified entity because it continues or unfolds in one direction.
- *Common fate*—events that change in the same way at the same time form a group.
- *Familiarity*—a known pattern forms a perceptual group (we all know dozens of dance rhythms, for example, and we can be taught a new rhythm in a composition).

Another Gestalt principle is *closure*, whereby we "fill in the blank" to complete a known but incomplete pattern.

All of these Gestalt mechanisms can be used as compositional tactics, either to unify or differentiate a sequence of sounds.

PERCEPTUAL ADAPTATION

Listeners adapt to expressive timing deviations. They tend to simplify rhythms, rounding them off to fit an inferred rhythm (Handel 1989). Within certain ranges, tempo variation or rubato does not detract from hearing the simpler abstract rhythmic structure that is being slowed down or sped up. Studies indicate that diverse performers exhibit similarity in the way they deviate from the notated score, which suggests the existence of implicit rhythmic preference rules (Bengtsson and Gabrielson 1983; Clarke 1999).

LIMITS OF SCIENTIFIC UNDERSTANDING OF RHYTHM PERCEPTION

As it is currently practiced, the scientific study of rhythm perception can only go so far, because scientific method is generally reductionist. Scientists take a complicated phenomenon and break it into small pieces that can be studied in isolation. In this way, knowledge accumulates from details. Rigorous experiments demand controlled laboratory conditions in which extraneous influences are systematically eliminated. Thus studies of rhythm often focus on short patterns of isolated taps. For example, London's (2002) report on cognitive constraints on metric systems, cited above, was qualified by the author as follows:

> The values reported are largely from experiments that used nonmusical (or perhaps "quasi-musical") stimuli and contexts; for the most part, this research lacks ecological validity relative to real-life listening situations. Moreover, this research has shown that various thresholds, acuities, and so on are heavily dependent upon task, stimulus, context, and so forth.

Attempts to model aspects of human music perception have been limited to elementary tasks like tracking the beat of a musical performance (Sethares 2007) or following a score as played by a performer. I do not diminish the challenge of teaching machines how to mimic basic aspects of human music cognition. However, we need to acknowledge the true complexity of music. Electronic music, in particular, is not merely a beat machine. It *undulates* (under envelope control), *modulates* (under low-frequency oscillator or LFO control), and *triggers*, as well as beats. These phenomena are the result of many simultaneous clocks and functions of time applied to pitch, timbre, space, etc., all of which express their own rhythms. Moreover, broken and jagged beats, loops and diced loops are common currency of electronic music discourse. Electronic music can deploy overlapping polyrhythms generated by algorithms and advanced clocking schemes that ambulate around zones of rhythmic morphosis. Moreover, the local temporal context is always functioning within a hierarchy of larger timescales. In all these ways, the art of rhythm is far ahead of science's ability to track it, much less explain it.

The evolution of rhythmic theory

This section briefly traces the evolution of rhythmic music theory from antiquity to the present era. The design of instruments and the abstractions of music theory and notation enable the organization of music *outside time*, as Xenakis (1971) called it. Outside-time organization means that a composer can design or select instruments, scales, abstract rhythmic patterns, and other formal schemes prior to mapping them to a specific piece and point in a timeline. The outside-time domain is sometimes also referred to as the "precomposition" stage of composition, although in our conception, it is an integral part of the compositional process.

Perhaps the earliest systematic organization of rhythm emerged from the Indian tradition. From about 2000 BC, Indian music established the *tala* or *tal* (a pattern of hand claps) as a rhythmical structure of a composition. Each composition aligns to a tala, and as a piece is performed by a melodic artist, a percussionist plays the pattern repeatedly. This is not to say that the pattern is perceived as simply repetitive. Indeed, the cycle of repetition can be as long as 108 beats (Clayton 2000). Much of the perceived complexity of Indian rhythm comes from structures that play against the tal pattern such as syncopations, phrases that go against the tal but then resolve to the downbeat, and polymetric subdivisions (Wright 2009). The tala and the associated pitch pattern or *raga* are monophonic. Classical Indian rhythmic structure is subtle and sophisticated on its own terms, but remains deeply rooted in traditional practices and rituals. Unlike Western music, with its experimental tradition, we do not hear much about theoretical extrapolation or advances.

The development of European music notation took hundreds of years. In the 13th century, rhythmic notation distinguished only two duration types: *longa* versus *brevis*. In the late 14th century, musicians gradually adopted more note duration values, reflecting a desire for increased temporal precision. Notation also codified the ordering and duration of silent rests, as well as sounding events. The symbolic language of common music notation (CMN) evolved around the 15th century. CMN prompted musicians to stipulate their intentions more precisely than before.

The epoch of the 14th-century Ars Nova in music, which saw the introduction of notated tempi (Yeston 1976), was also the age of the earliest mechanical clocks, which divided time into minutes (Klemm 1964). Prior to this, the smallest durational unit in common use was the hour, viewed in daylight by means of a sundial. At the end of the 16th century, scientists like Galileo and Huygens constructed accurate pendulum clocks that established time as a fundamental measurable quantity. This ushered in the classical era of clockwork time, idealized by Isaac Newton, who posited the existence of an "absolute, true, and mathematical time" that "flows equably without relation to anything external" (Newton 1687). The promulgation of Newtonian clockwork time coincided with the birth of the classical masters J. S. Bach, G. F. Handel, and D. Scarlatti, around 1685. In their lifetimes, new musical rules for structuring time came into common practice, including time signatures, bar lines, and tempo indications, which divided time according to a uniform grid. These devices allowed composers to express rhythmic intentions with ever more precision.

RHYTHM AND NOTATION

Textbooks on CMN such as Read (1978, 1979) offer tutorials on the symbolic representation of complex rhythms. Notation of rhythm can be arbitrarily complicated, to the point of being unreadable and/or unplayable with any degree of accuracy.[33] CMN was designed to enable human performance, but when CMN is pushed beyond the limits of human legibility or playability, it no longer serves this function. Yet while myriad rhythms are beyond the scope of readable or playable CMN, our ability to hear and distinguish temporal structures far exceeds our ability to read or perform them.

Electronic music, with its sequencers, clock generators (see below), generative processes, and detailed micro-organization, is full of such complex rhythms. Since the sound is produced directly by a synthesizer or computer, without the intermediary of a human performer, the issues of readability and playability are moot.

Notation can, however, serve other purposes besides that of a performance script. For example, it can be instructive to study a score and follow along with a recording. In doing so, we see how a piece is put together. Composers have lamented the absence of reading scores for electronic music, an issue that we pointed out in the notes to the preface. As part of a research project in music notation, in 2002, I commissioned James Ingram, who was Stockhausen's assistant for years, to create a reading score for my composition *Sonal atoms* (1998). Ingram's meticulous work showed that it is possible to extend CMN-like rhythmic notation down to the threshold of microsound in a largely timbral/textural composition (figure 6.1).

Sound example 6.1. Excerpt of "Sonal atoms," Part 1 of *Half-life* (1999) by Curtis Roads.

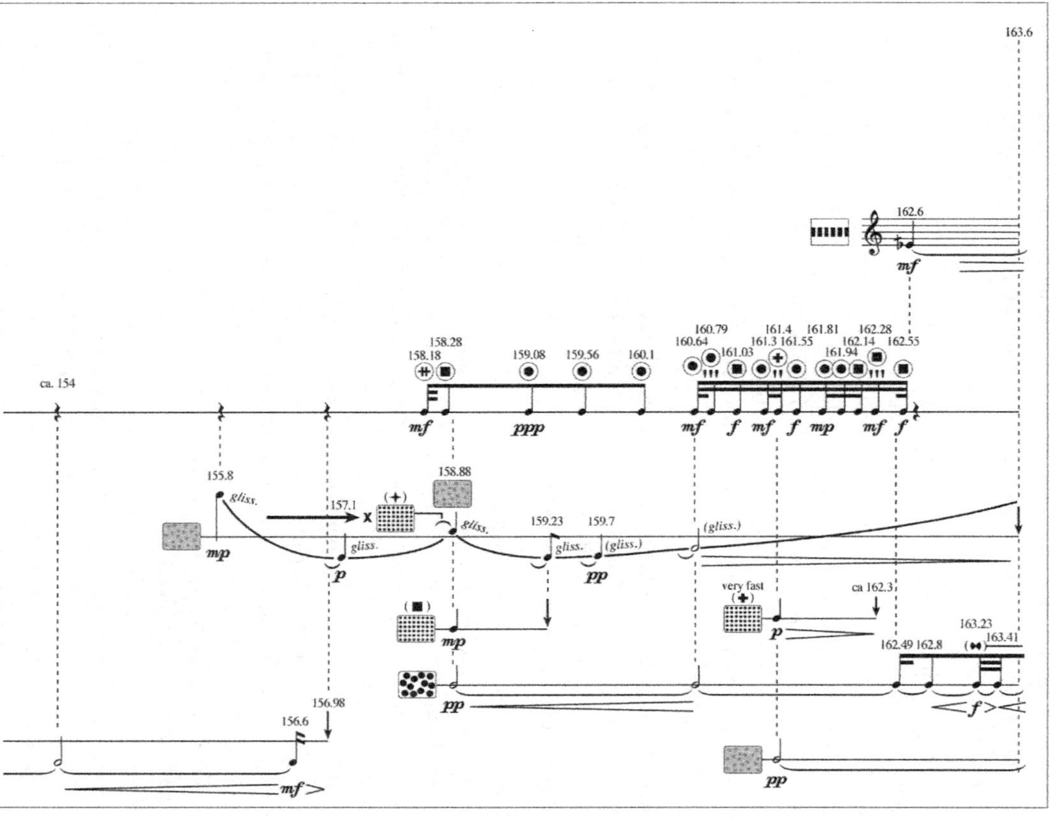

FIGURE 6.1 Excerpt of page 14 (154 to 163.6 seconds) of the score to "Sonal atoms," Part 1 of *Half-life* (1999) by Curtis Roads, notated by James Ingram. The rectangular icons to the left of each line represent timbre classes. To view the entire score, see Roads (2004b).

EMERGENCE OF A NEW CONCEPT OF MUSICAL TIME

In the classical era, rhythmic structure was subordinate to harmonic and melodic organization (Yeston 1976). This tended to limit the rhythmic possibilities, as Handel (1989) observed:

> Fraisse studied rhythms in music from Beethoven to Bartok and found that composers tend to use only two durations extensively. The ratio of the two durations is 2:1. In one composition, 85% of the notes were of these two durations.

Twentieth-century music inherited the master grid of classical time: synchronous beats and measures bent by occasional rubato (local temporal deformations) with accelerando and rallentando gestures. In the first decade of the 20th century, however, the master grid began to loosen. The seeds of a new concept of musical time were planted by the so-called Impressionist composers. Debussy blurred not only tonal harmony, but also rhythmic organization. In his piece *Jeux* (1913), for example, the ebb and flow of rhythm is part of a "fleeting and ever-changing sonic landscape" (Cox 1974). As Grout (1973) observed:

> Rhythm, in the kind of music one often thinks of as "impressionistic," is nonpulsatile, vague, concealed by syncopations and irregular subdivisions of the beat. Outlines of phrases and the formal structure as a whole may be deliberately blurred and indistinct.

The Impressionist composers deformed the grid of meter by means of overlapping textures, ambiguous beginnings and endings, and a wavelike swelling of tempo that often dissipates into chaos. This was intertwined with colorful orchestration and rapidly shifting harmonic passages that played with the tonal expectations of listeners.

Igor Stravinsky took further liberties. His early compositions freed rhythm from the "tyranny of the barline" (Grout 1973) by injecting irregular rhythmic patterns after regular ones, and positioning a repeating rhythmic motive at different points in the bar. The most famous example is, of course, *Le sacre du printemps* (*The Rite of Spring*, 1913) with its juxtaposed sequences of time signatures (e.g., 2/16, 3/16, 2/8, 5/16, etc).

Henry Cowell's book *New Musical Resources* (1930) introduced fresh ideas concerning the composition of rhythm, the most important of which was the notion of the *rhythmic continuum*, about which I will elaborate further. John Cage began composing for percussion ensemble in the late 1930s and introduced many unconventional rhythmic sources such as prepared piano, tin cans, conch shells, anvils, water gongs, wastebaskets, and brake drums. By the 1950s, certain of his scores did away with common music notation in favor of a scripted timeline. For example, the score of his *Water Walk* (1959) consists of a list of objects, a floor plan showing the placement of the objects, and a timeline with descriptions and pictographic notations of events and these instructions: "Start watch and then time actions as closely as possible to their appearance in the score."

THE PROCESS OF RHYTHM IN VARÈSE'S MUSIC

> Three principles are the basis for every composition: inertia, force, and rhythm, with all the contradictions that these contain.
>
> —EDGARD VARÈSE (1936B)

One of the most original figures in 20th-century music is Varèse, not the least because of his novel and sophisticated rhythmic processes, which are central to his musical language (Carter 1979). Varèse's rhythmic model remains compelling, both perceptually and conceptually, and could serve as a basis for further extensions.[34] In Varèse's music, rhythm is propelled by a constant tension: either in a sustained note or cluster that crosses between two phrases or in "the clicking and rattling of complex machinery that seems to produce broken out-of-phase cycles of sound" (Carter 1979). The root of Varèse's rhythm is the rhythmic cell. A typical gesture is the obsessive repetition (with variations) of rhythmic cells, either pitched or unpitched. Linked with this is a strong emphasis on percussion instruments, explained early on by Henry Cowell (1928):

> It is perhaps his desire to focus the interest on the . . . sound qualities alone—without the distraction of harmonies of pitch—or on chords of rhythms, that has led Varèse to develop his interest in percussion instruments. He probably uses more such instruments, proportionally, than any other composer. For example in *Hyperprism* there are seventeen percussion against nine melodic instruments.

Notice the phrase "chords of rhythms" to denote the presence of simultaneous but independent rhythms in Varèse's music. Even pitched instruments are sometimes deployed as a kind of percussion effect, repeating short patterns of one or two pitches.

In Varèse's orchestral works such as *Amériques*, unpitched percussion does not merely ornament or punctuate the pitched instruments, as it often did in traditional scores. Instead, the percussion hews a separate path in parallel to the pitched instruments, so that both elements contribute independently to the overall texture.

Sound example 6.2. Excerpt of *Amériques* by Edgard Varèse. 

As Morgan (1979b) observed about Varèse's use of percussion:

> A sense of constant variation and renewal . . . stems from the continuous metamorphosis of the highly colorful surface of the percussion, providing an essential foil for the relatively fixed timbral and registral quality of the pitch component.

Sound example 6.3. Excerpt of *Ionisation* (1931) by Edgard Varèse.

Varèse's pioneering *Ionisation* (1931) was created for percussion, with 13 musicians playing 37 instruments.[35] Although some instruments are associated with jazz and Latin music, *Ionisation* went beyond these connotations. Unpitched percussion dominates the piece, which was a radical idea at the time (figure 6.2). Indeed, *Ionisation* shifts the musical focus from specific pitches to register (Solomos 1995). A striking characteristic of *Ionisation* and other works of Varèse are passages consisting of multiple overlapping asynchronous rhythmic patterns interrupted by the sudden vertical alignment of all rhythmic elements in a synchronous pattern. As Varèse (1959) described it:

FIGURE 6.2 Score page from *Ionisation* (1931) by Edgard Varèse. Reprinted with permission of G. Ricordi & Co., Milan.

> In my own works, rhythm derives from the simultaneous interplay of elements that convene at calculated, but not regular time periods.

An analogy to the behavior of self-organizing systems is unavoidable. In a self-organizing system, a feedback process leads to phase transitions, as in physical processes such as spontaneous crystallization or biological processes such as morphogenesis, in which specific genes or viruses emerge out of materials devoid of specificity (Wiener 1961).

THE RHYTHMIC CONTINUUM

Fundamental to the modern concept of rhythm is the recognition of the continuum between rhythm and tone (i.e., between the infrasonic frequencies—periodic and aperiodic rhythms—and the audible frequencies—pitched and unpitched tones). As mentioned previously, Cowell described this relationship in 1930:

> Rhythm and tone, which have been thought to be entirely separate musical fundamentals . . . are definitely related through overtone ratios. . . . Assume that we have two melodies in parallel to each other, the first written in whole notes and the second in half-notes. If the time for each note were to be indicated by the tapping of a stick, the taps for the second melody would recur with double the rapidity of those of the first. If now the taps were to be increased greatly in rapidity without changing the relative speed, it will be seen that when the taps for the first melody reach sixteen to the second, those for the second melody will be thirty-two to the second. In other words, the vibrations from the taps of one melody will give the musical tone C, while those of the other will give the tone C one octave higher. Time has been translated, as it were, into musical tone.

Thus Cowell explained how sped-up rhythms become tones. He also introduced the concept of *undertones* at fractional intervals beneath a fundamental—a sub-pulse. In order to represent divisions of time that are not handled easily by common music notation, Cowell proposed a *shape note* scheme, where the note heads are squares or diamonds, for example. He observed how a series of partial frequencies, as seen in spectra, could also be used to build a scale of meters or a scale of tempi, with different tempi running simultaneously and various rates of accelerando and ritardando notated graphically.

Sound example 6.4. (a) Speedup from pure pulsation to pitched tone and back. (b) Speedup of burst pattern (3-on, 3-off) to pitched tone and back. Notice the subharmonic pitch.

More than two decades later, Karlheinz Stockhausen (1955) formulated another theory of the continuum between rhythm and pitch in the context of serial music:

> If the rate of beat is gradually increased beyond the time constant of the filter and the limits beyond which the ear can no longer differentiate, what started

> as a rhythmically repeated note becomes continuous. . . . We see a continuous transition between what might be called durational intervals which are characterized as rhythmic intervals and durational intervals characterized as pitch levels.

In his piece *Kontakte* (1960), the composer used an impulse generator to create pulse trains. To the output signal of this generator, he applied a narrow band-pass filter, which gave each pulsation a variable resonance. If the band was narrow enough, the impulse resonated at a specific pitch. If the pulse train was irregular, the infrasonic impulses generated ametrical rhythms. By transposing these rhythms (via changes in tape speed—see the next section) up into the audible frequency range, he could build noises from aperiodic impulse trains.

Stockhausen's text "The unity of musical time" proposed an integrated approach to temporal composition. As he points out, the acoustical frequency continuum is broken into a number of different phenomena by human perception:

> [In working with an impulse generator], one must proceed from a basic concept of a single unified musical time; and the different perceptual categories such as color, harmony and melody, meter and rhythm, dynamics, and form must be regarded as corresponding to the different components of this unified time.
>
> —STOCKHAUSEN (1962)

Of course, Cowell's ideas on the continuum precede those of Stockhausen by almost 30 years and demonstrate that a comprehensive multiscale view of time can be separated completely from serial theory.

The continuum was also central to the foundations of the spectral school of composition, which emerged in the 1980s (Murail 1991). A founding member of this school, Gérard Grisey, explicated a theory of temporal organization (Grisey 1987). Grisey sketched a rhythmic continuum similar to figure 6.3.

Let us briefly examine each category in turn. The most orderly morphology is the smooth category, corresponding to unchanging seamless tones like drones. Pure silence also falls into the smooth category; without audible change, any perceived rhythm is imaginary.

Periodic rhythms encompass all patterns based on a fundamental pulse, including syncopated patterns. The effect of predictable events is to heighten perception of deviations from periodicity.

Continuous dynamic rhythms (acceleration and deceleration) can be either linear or curved in profile. By controlling the steepness of the curve, one controls the degree of tension in the unfolding process. For example, a rapidly accelerating pattern tends to generate more tension than one with no acceleration. Speeding up and slowing down are basic musical motors. They inject directionality, but as Grisey points out, a repetitious alternation between acceleration and deceleration is tiresome.

Discontinuous dynamic curves make sudden jumps in speed as they accelerate or decelerate, and so break up the predictability of common logarithmic

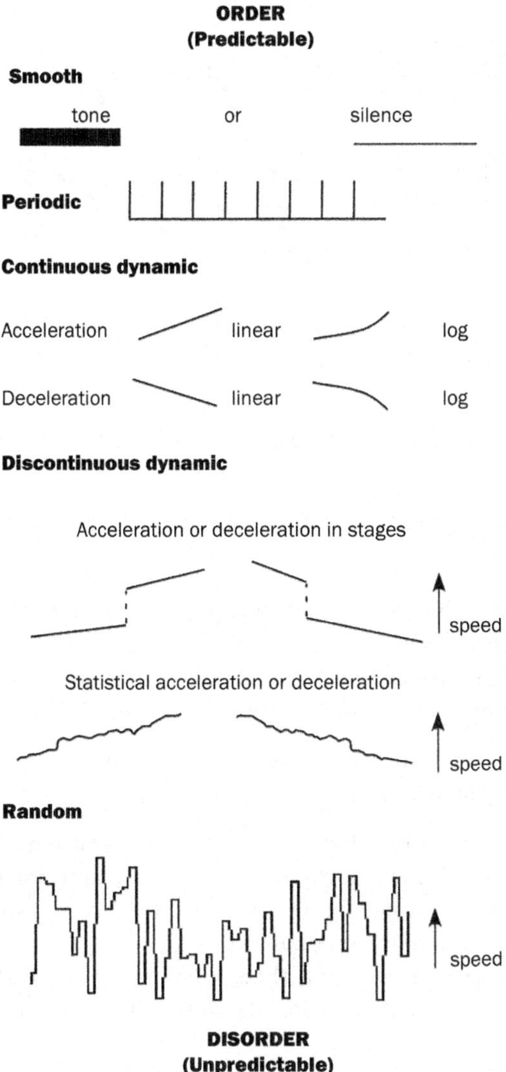

FIGURE 6.3 Grisey's continuum of rhythm, from order (top) to disorder.

curves. "Statistical" acceleration/deceleration meanders in speed while maintaining a global upward or downward direction.

GRISEY'S CRITIQUE OF ABSTRACT RHYTHMS

Grisey based his rhythmic theory on perception, rejecting approaches based purely on simple mathematical abstractions such as prime numbers, Fibonacci series, and so on. He did not reject mathematics, but he felt that algorithms needed to take perception into account. As he pointed out, in Stockhausen's

FIGURE 6.4 A palindromic or non-retrogradable rhythm in the lower staff, from Messiaen's *Prélude, Instants défunts* (1929), Éditions Durand.

Gruppen (1957) for three orchestras, the work's rhythmic structure is highly organized in terms of tempi but unfathomable to the listener:

> The tempi have great structural importance. Who perceives them?
>
> —GRISEY (1987)

Grisey took issue with rhythmic abstractions promoted by the integral serialists, who were strongly influenced by Messiaen's book *Technique de mon langage musicale* (1944). One of the techniques described by Messiaen was *non-retrogradable rhythm*, or rhythmic palindrome (figure 6.4). He defined these as follows:

> Whether one reads them from right to left or from left to right, the order of their values remains the same.

Messiaen's student Pierre Boulez experimented with related methods of generating symmetric and asymmetric rhythmic figures by transformation of rhythmic cells. For example, he created figures that were the rhythmic inverse of another figure (i.e., notes replaced by rests and vice-versa).

As Grisey (1987) pointed out, these kinds of rhythmic abstractions (i.e., permutational and symmetrical note relations) make absurd assumptions about perception:

> Such a distinction, whatever its operational value, has no perceptible value. . . . What a utopia this spatial and static [notion] of time was, a veritable straight line at the center of which the listener sits implicitly, possessing not only a memory but also a prescience that allows him to apprehend the symmetrical moment at the time it occurs! Unless, of course, our superman were gifted with a memory that enabled him to reconstruct the entirety of the durations so that he could, a posteriori, classify them as symmetrical or not!

LIBERATION OF TIME FROM METER

The mechanical metronome was a product of the classical period in Western music, which peaked around 1820. This period, which included Mozart, Haydn, and the early works of Beethoven, was based on regular and orderly structures. Meter was synonymous with steady metronomic tempi. In contrast, rubato (speeding up or slowing down the tempo) is more characteristic of the music of the romantic period. It involves the performer stretching or hurrying the tempo to lend elasticity and expression to the performance. Rubato gives flexibility to meter, but does not negate it. In classical music, perhaps the freest rhythmic passages appear in recitatives, in which a continuo adopts the rhythm of human speech, and in the often-improvised cadenza sections of concertos.

After a century of rhythmic experimentation, by the 1950s, serial procedures fragmented meter such that it was no longer felt by the audience and served only as the conductor's clock for timing events with no obvious pulse. Into this disjointed scene came one of the most important technologies in the organization of musical time: the audio tape recorder. As Milton Babbitt (1988) observed:

> If there is one dimension of the music totality, one component which originally led composers to the electronic medium, it was and is the temporal domain.... Those who originally turned to electronic tape were obviously attracted to the element of control. After all, the tape was not a source of sound. Tape is for storage. You can, however, control time as a measurable distance of tape. Here we are talking about rhythm in every sense of the word. Not only durational rhythm, but also the time rate of changes of register, of timbre, of volume, and of those many musical dimensions that were unforeseen until we tried to find out how we heard and how we could structure the temporal.

As a tool of composition, the tape recorder liberated the dimension of musical time from dependence on any kind of meter, whether regular or fragmented. Reliance on a conductor's beat, which is necessary in order to synchronize players in instrumental music, was reduced to an optional structuring principle in electronic music. By using a tape recorder with a varispeed control, musical time could be continuously sped up, slowed down, played backward, or freely modulated.

Cutting and splicing of tape made it possible to segment time into arbitrary fragments, which could be rearranged in order at a micro timescale (figure 6.5). The practice of precisely juxtaposing sounds or weaving filigrees by splicing tiny fragments was taken up by many composers. As John Cage (in Kostelanetz 1988) said of his *Williams Mix* (1953), which was realized in the studios of Louis and Bebe Barron:

> What was so fascinating about the tape possibility was that a second, which we had always thought was a relatively short space of time, became fifteen inches. It became something quite long that could be cut up.

Sound example 6.5 Excerpt of *Electronic Study Number 3* (1965) by Mario Davidovsky. 

Sound example 6.6. Excerpt of *Laborintus 2* (1965) by Luciano Berio. 

Early examples of extraordinary splicing technique include Xenakis's *Concret PH* (1958) and *Analogique B* (1959), both assembled from hundreds of tiny splices, Parmegiani's masterful montage *De natura sonorum* (1976), Davidovsky's detailed *Electronic Study Number 3* (1965), and Berio's expressive *Laborintus 2*, Part II (1965). The editing in these works crossed into the threshold of detailed microsonic rhythmic organization.

The gradual introduction of multitrack tape recorders, beginning in the 1960s with four-track machines, made it possible to overdub new tracks while listening to previously recorded tracks, enabling the construction of polyrhythmic textures and free counterpoint.

Another tape technique, the loop (a segment of tape of arbitrary length, with the end spliced to the beginning so that it recycles endlessly), articulated either an indefinitely sustained tone or a repeating pattern. For example, in *Kontakte* (1960), Stockhausen designed rhythms by splicing together pieces of tape with various pulse patterns and making tape loops of the rhythms. Long loops were wrapped around stands to keep them taut, a typical practice in that day (figure 6.6).[36] Several loops running simultaneously ran for long periods, and the mixed result was recorded. As Stockhausen noted (quoted in Kurtz 1992):

FIGURE 6.5 Bruno Maderna and Luciano Berio at the Studio di Fonologia, Milan, in the 1950s, with fragments of magnetic tape used in composing. (Photo: RAI.)

> So there were loops running everywhere and you could see it between the glass windows of the studios. Finally I used fast-forward on the tape recorder to accelerate the tapes so they were already four or five octaves up, then the result went up four octaves—so then I was up eight octaves—until I finally got into an area where the rhythms are heard as pitches and timbres.

One composer who made extensive use of loops was Luc Ferrari. Indeed, loops are a signature of his tape music, appearing and disappearing as background ostinati underneath a foreground texture. Classic examples include *Presque rien avec filles* (1989) and his hypnotically repetitious *Cycle des souvenirs* (2000). In contrast, loops take the foreground in minimalist electronic music (e.g., Steve Reich's *It's Gonna Rain* [1965]), where small shifts in the phases of several loops create dramatic cascades of sound.

Sound example 6.7. Opening of *Cycle des souvenirs* (2000) by Luc Ferrari. 

FIGURE 6.6 Karlheinz Stockhausen with tape loops in the Cologne studio (1964). Photograph by Arnold Newman; used with permission of Getty Images.

Beginning with Gabor's (1946) Kinematic Frequency Converter experiments, it became possible to stretch or shrink the duration of a sound without changing its pitch, thereby expanding the gamut of rhythmic possibilities. Since that time, we have witnessed increasingly sophisticated tools for flexible pitch-time changing. These range from digital granulation techniques that slow or "freeze" a sound, even allowing granulation in reverse, to specialized pitch editors that separate out the different notes in a chord, letting users adjust the pitch and timing of each note independently (Hoenig et al. 2010). For even greater pitch-time precision, dictionary-based pursuit lets one alter the time base of each of the time-frequency grains within a sound on a grain-by-grain basis (Sturm, Daudet, and Roads 2006; Sturm et al. 2008).

As we will see, studio-based practice affords the ultimate in flexibility and access to the entire field of rhythm on multiple scales. We can zoom in and out from the micro to the macro and back, as well as move forward and backward in time (e.g., compose the end before the beginning or change the beginning without modifying the rest of the piece). Rhythms can be reversed and their time support can be freely modified with varispeed and pitch-time changing, or scrambled by granulation.

RHYTHM ON THE MICRO TIMESCALE

The ability to generate discrete events lasting fewer than 100 ms is not new; as we have already pointed out, the drum roll is the original granular cloud. However, the capability of easily editing any sound directly on a variety of timescales is recent from a historical perspective. As Stockhausen, Parmegiani, Babbitt, and others showed in the 1960s, it could be accomplished with analog sequencing and tape techniques and a great deal of painstaking labor. As Babbitt (2000) observed about his electronic music:

> I could produce things faster than any pianist could play or any listener could hear. We were able to work with greater speeds. That was one of the things that interested me the most: the timbre, the rhythmic aspect. And we learned a great deal. [The RCA Synthesizer] was an analog device and it was given digital information and switching instructions (for envelope, spectrum, and other aspects of tone) passing over very expensive gold wires that scanned the information and then recorded it on tape. I could change certain qualities of a tone while keeping other qualities, like the pitch, consistent. I could hear what I was playing as I was playing it, using trial and error. We had no precedent and we were extrapolating from no known theory. Theories about what could be heard and what couldn't be heard were essentially wrong because they had never been tested in those conditions.

By the 1990s, digital recording and sound editing technology became widespread. Part of the reason that we are now fascinated with microsonic musical materials is precisely because they became accessible recently. It would not have made much sense for a musician to be concerned with the microstructure of sound a century ago.

Digital technology provided four important new capabilities: high temporal accuracy, intuitive and editable waveform displays, pitch-time changing, and programmability. These capabilities have deeply altered the playing field of rhythm, which affects all of composition in its wake.

- Accuracy means that events can be edited and arranged on a timescale of microseconds, corresponding to the sampling rate of the audio system. (One microsecond is one millionth of a second.)
- The simple ability to view sound waveforms and zoom in and out while editing them—taken for granted today—has since 1988 had a tremendous impact on the craft of electronic music composition. It took us from splicing tape or typing codes to intuitive graphical editing, with a picture window on the formerly invisible realm of microsound (figure 6.7).
- A sound's duration is no longer fixed; it can be varied independently of its pitch, and vice-versa using sophisticated tools like the phase vocoder and dictionary-based pursuit. Any sound can be elongated or shrunk by granulation, and the order of the grains in time can be scrambled at will.
- Algorithms can spawn rhythmic processes, generating patterns of arbitrary complexity.

The ramifications of these changes are profound. In traditional music, the dimension of pitch was the object of obsessive compositional concern. When I was a student in the 1970s, I heard many lectures by composers in which their approach was defined primarily by the pitches and pitch organization methods they chose

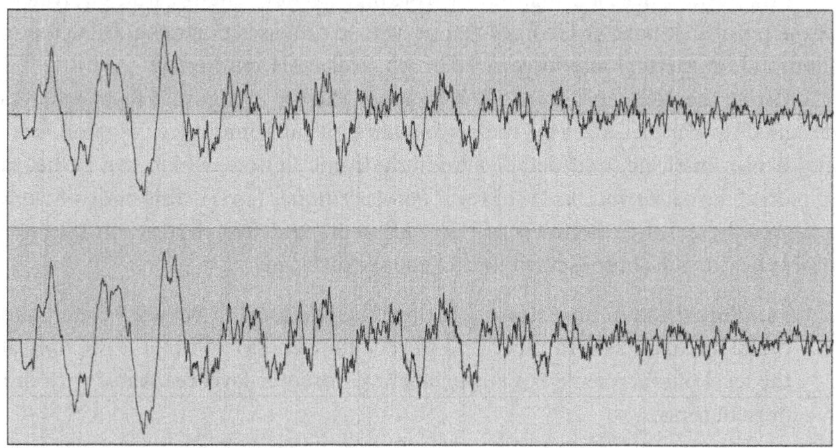

FIGURE 6.7 A sound editor's display zoomed in to the first 75 ms of a snare drum hit recorded by the author. Notice the subtle differences between the two channels. Such an image can be projected on an arbitrarily large display to enable precise visual editing.

to use. Today the facile manipulation of the time domain, as well as corresponding advances in the control of other musical parameters, means that the dimension of pitch need no longer always be the dominant compositional parameter. Rhythm, timbre, dynamics, space, and pitch now stand on more-or-less-equal ground.

The notion of "musical parameter" has itself also changed. In the world of homogeneous musical notes, one can enumerate the parameters of a musical event in terms of a short list: pitch, duration, dynamic marking, and instrumental timbre. In contrast, the heterogeneous world of electronic sounds is controlled by myriad synthesis and processing parameters, such as index of modulation, carrier-to-modulator ratio, echo density, center frequency, grain density, delay time, and so on, all of which can vary in time according to individual envelopes.

DESIGNING MICRORHYTHM

Two quite different composers have done extensive work in the domain of microrhythm. Paul Lansky composed a series of works realized using an automatic mixing program he developed. In *Idle Chatter* (1985), the raw material consists of vocal phoneme fragments of about 80 ms in duration scattered metrically with a constantly shifting accent pattern. His subsequent pieces *just more idle chatter* (1987), *Notjustmoreidlechatter* (1988), and *Idle Chatter Junior* (1999) continue along the same line, with strong emphases on articulation of meter and tonal harmonic progressions.

In contrast, the composer Horacio Vaggione deploys microsounds in a non-metrical manner. Micromontage is an essential component of the Vaggione style. In micromontage, the composer extracts short grains from sound files and rearranges them in time. The term "montage" derives from the world of cinema where it refers to cutting, splicing, dissolving, and other film editing operations. The term "micro" refers to the timescale of these operations (usually less than 100 ms). In this detailed manner of working, we have the musical equivalent of the pointillist painter Georges Seurat, whose canvases portray a dense sea of thousands of meticulously organized brush strokes (Homer 1964).

Using the IRIN program (Caires 2005) shown in figure 6.8, which was designed by Carlos Caires for the organization of micromontage, Vaggione creates dense, intricate, and detailed microrhythmic figures, which can be heard in pieces like *24 Variations* (2002) and *Points critiques* (2011). This body of work explores the contrast between metrical elements and free rhythm on multiple timescales, as the composer (in Budón 2000) explained:

> I am interested in investigating further the relationship between meter (as a cyclic force) and rhythm (as a non-cyclic movement) and this is not only at the level of macrotime but at the most microscopic level reachable with our present tools.

Careful listening reveals the organization of the microrhythmic figures as they repeat, play forward and backward, and combine with other figures. The composer sustains these low-level scintillating textures for up to 20 seconds or

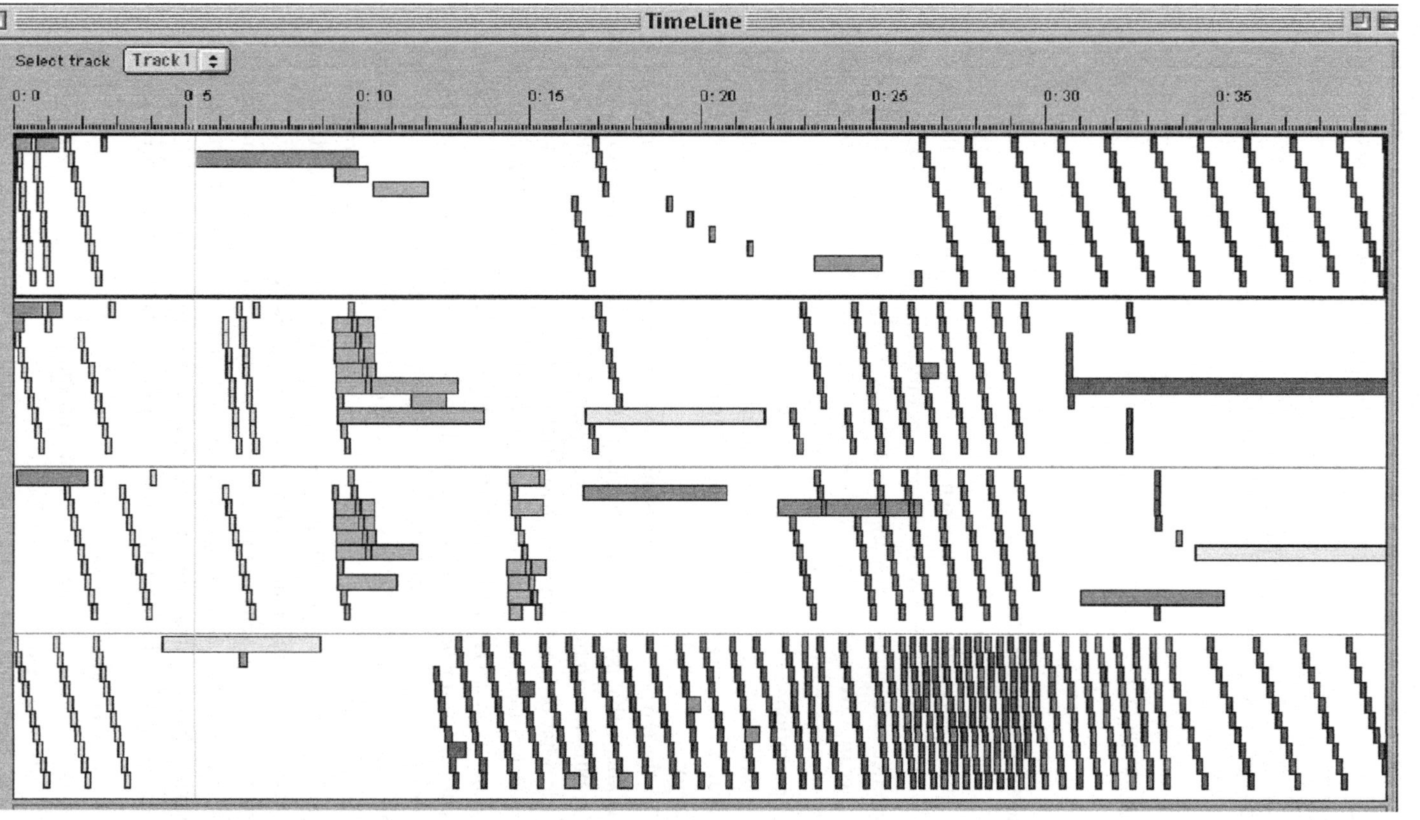

FIGURE 6.8 A 40-second excerpt of the score of Vaggione's *24 variations* (version 2), showing the four-track timeline designed with the IRIN program. Each rectangle represents a sound clip or sample. The vertical position of a sample within a track is not significant (i.e., it does not correspond to pitch). IRIN lets one encapsulate figures within a track and represents them as a single fragment, permitting one to build up mesostructure hierarchically.

more at a time, keeping the listener engaged while he prepares the next explosive release. Like any highly detailed background pattern, their intricate design emerges into the foreground only when nothing else is superimposed upon them for several seconds.

Sound example 6.8. Excerpt of *24 Variations* (2002) by Horacio Vaggione.

Sound example 6.9. Excerpt of *Points critiques* (2011) by Horacio Vaggione.

Anatomy of beat pulsation

Human perception is exquisitely sensitive to pulsation. Thus beat pulsation is a ubiquitous element of rhythmic expression. Pulsation marks a recurring period. Recurrence and periodicity play out in the natural cycles of breathing, heartbeats, ocean waves, geysers, sunrises, planetary orbits, and countless other natural phenomena extending down to the subatomic realm.

A pulsation can be generalized from a single event to a recurring pattern of events, what Xenakis referred to as a "self-reproduction" or "reincarnation" of a temporal pattern (Xenakis 1971, 1992). This is pulsation as sequential rhythmic regularity.

For the purpose of this discussion, I constrain the term "pulsation" to a rate of periodicity that is perceived by humans as a beat. The typical way to measure a regular pulsation in music is in terms of tempo in beats per minute (BPM), which in music notation is associated with Maelzel's metronome (MM) (e.g., ♩ = 60 MM). By this definition, beat pulsation concerns repetitions on a timescale of about 50 ms (MM = 1200, 20 Hz) to about 8 seconds (MM= 7.5, 0.125 Hz), where our ability to accurately estimate periodicity begins to break down. Of course, although we can perceive a pulsation within these ranges, what we perceive as "the beat" may be some subdivision of this rate, depending on the context. The practical limits of ensemble performance with traditional instruments are much narrower, in the range of about 60 to 120 MM (Apel 1972). (A 32nd note at 120 MM lasts only 63 ms.) Some electronic dance music unfolds as fast as MM = 190.

In contrast, the general notion of frequency is essentially unlimited in its range, encapsulating a vast domain of periodic phenomena that are above (ultrasound) and below (infrasound) the range of human perception.

A pulsation can be dissected into four components, as shown in figure 6.9:

- Instant of attack (onset or time point)
- Duration of pulsating event (note duration)
- Interval between attack instants
- Interval between the end of one pulsating event and the beginning of the next attack (the *entry delay*)

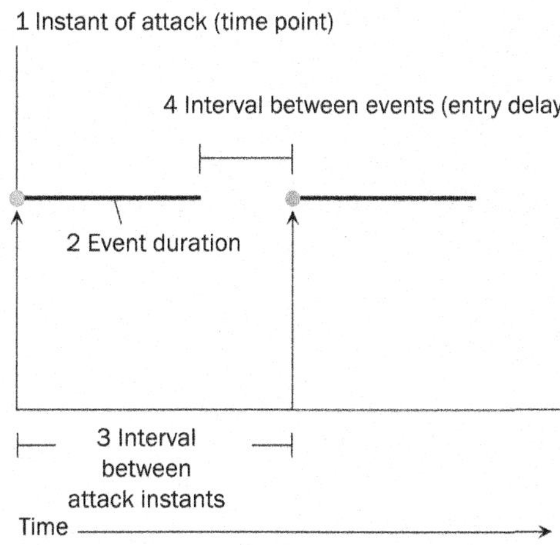

FIGURE 6.9 Anatomy of pulsation.

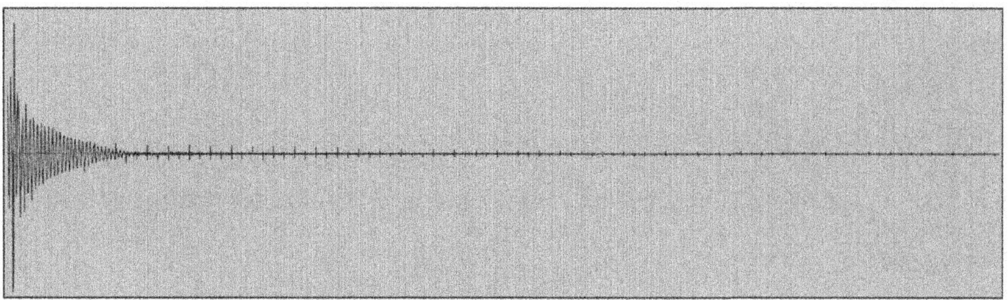

FIGURE 6.10 Pulsating grain echo in *Half-life* at 1:09 to 1:16.

Any of these components can be varied to construct a rhythmic process. Pulsation can also be a regular silence, not just a regular sound. In this case, the interpretations of the components in figure 6.8 invert (sound becomes silence, and silence becomes sound).

Pulsation can appear on multiple timescales in various configurations. In popular music, it is typical that the beat never changes on a macroscale throughout an entire piece. Even in this case, one can set up a situation where the musical voices play a subdivided pulsation that is initiated by, but not necessarily aligned with, the main beat (Howard 2011).

Pulsation can also function as an emergent force that surfaces from the flux and flow of sonic energy. For example, in certain pieces, such as *Half-life* (1999), I used pulsation to create fading echoes resulting from grain singularities (figure 6.10). Here the fading pulsation acted as a transition, continuing the past. Nor is such a pulsation limited to the regular or periodic case. A slowing-down or speeding-up pulsation is a common gesture in electronic music.

Sound example 6.10. Pulsating grain echo in "Sonal atoms," Part 1 of *Half-life* (1999) by Curtis Roads. 

BROKEN BEATS

In other interesting cases, pulsation is "broken" into a combination of regular and irregular beats. An early example is *Touch* (1969) by Morton Subotnick. In this work, the composer recorded onto tape the tones to the clockwork output of a Buchla sequencer. To break up the regular beat, he then spliced in brief interruptions to create an irregular pulsation.

Sound example 6.11. Excerpt of *Touch* (1969) by Morton Subotnick.

A broken beat style is characteristic of pieces by, among others, Autechre (e.g., the *Confield* [2001] album). Pulsation can also be interspersed with non-pulsating phrases on a meso timescale.

Sound example 6.12. Transition from tracks 8 to 9 on the album *Confield* (2001) by Autechre.

METRIC FIELD STRENGTH

Related to pulsation is the sense of regular meter. A simple repeating rhythm like

♩♩♩♩. . .

provides strong cues as to the underlying beat, whereas a more complicated figure over the same time period may not convey beat cues so clearly. Stockhausen's jagged *Klavierstücke 8* (1965) (see an excerpt in chapter 11) is an extreme example; it has no measure lines and unfolds as an arbitrary sequence of durations and rests in 64th note resolution.

Could there be a way to measure the metric strength and then vary this measure in an algorithmic composition system? This is the goal that Clarence Barlow set out to achieve in his composing programs (Barlow 1980, 1985, 2001). Specifically, he developed an algorithm for determining the degree to which a particular point in a measure contributes to a sense of regular meter, since a given time signature can be divided according to note values into a hierarchy of strata or divisions. For example, 4/4 can be subdivided as follows:

𝅝, 𝅗𝅥𝅗𝅥, ♩♩♩♩, ♪♪♪♪♪♪♪♪, etc.

Each of these attack pulses on every stratum can be measured for its importance in contributing to a sense of meter. Notes that strongly reinforce a sense of beat or meter have a higher *indispensability* value, according to his algorithm. As the algorithm was built into a generative composition system, this gave him control over what he calls the *metric field strength* at a given point in a composition:

> The metric field strength can thereby be increased or decreased, with the rhythm varying from metric (with a clearly recognizable basic pulse) to

> ametric (without a recognizable basic pulse). This can happen by defining and employing pulse-strength in such a way, that in order to support the meter the stronger pulses appear more frequently than the weaker; in an ametric rhythm, pulses of all strengths would be equally frequent.
>
> —BARLOW (2012)

For example, here are the indispensabilities of the twelve 16th notes of the third hierarchical level (quarter, eighth, sixteenth) of the meters 3/4, 6/8, and 12/16:

Pulse-point position	1	2	3	4	5	6	7	8	9	10	11	12
3/4	11	0	6	3	9	1	7	4	10	2	8	5
6/8	11	0	6	2	8	4	10	1	7	3	9	5
12/16	11	0	4	8	2	6	10	1	5	9	2	7

These integers indicate the relative importance (indispensability) of each pulse point in the measure in establishing a meter on a scale of 0 to *N*-1, where *N* is the last pulse point. Notice that at all levels, the indispensability of the first pulse is always highest, and that of the second pulse is always zero. That the first downbeat reinforces meter is not surprising, nor is it surprising that a displacement by a 16th note (the second pulse-point position) would tend to subvert a sense of meter. In the 3/4 measure, every fourth note (1, 5, 9) is indispensable as it is on the beat. Since in 12/16, the 16th notes are grouped in threes, every third note (1, 4, 7, 10) is indispensable.

Extending this reasoning to polymetric design, Barlow then calculated the coherence or affinity of two different superimposed meters by multiplying the indispensability values of each meter. Finally, extending the same idea to the audio frequencies, Barlow wonders:

> If one were to consider an audible pitch as an extremely rapid series of pulses, of which the tempo is the pitch's frequency (I call this the frhyquency, the "rhythm-frequency"), the harmonicity would be have to be a kind of "micro-metric coherence"!
>
> —BARLOW (2012)

In this extrapolation to the continuum between rhythm and tone, he revisits the territory of his former teacher Stockhausen (1957).

Automatic rhythm generation

Automatic drum machines date at least as far back as Jacques de Vaucanson's flute-and- drum-playing mechanical robot or android of 1738 (Ord-Hume 1973). Many 19th-century orchestrions incorporated percussion. These automatic instruments were driven by preprogrammed sequences encoded on punched rolls or pinned cylinders.

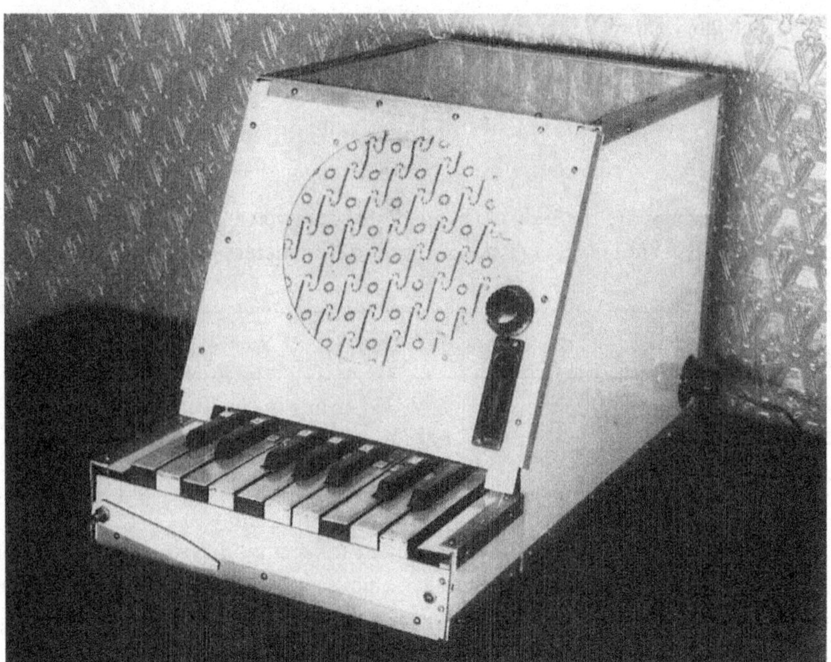

FIGURE 6.11 Theremin Rhythmicon. Photograph from the Theremin Center, Moscow, by Andrej Smirnov.

The 20th century saw the development of electronic rhythm generators. The 1931 Rhythmicon developed by Leon Theremin and Henry Cowell was a keyboard-controlled optoelectronic tone generator. Each key controls a lamp whose light triggers a repeated tone by means of mirrors, two rotating wheels (one for pitch and one for rhythm), plus a photocell. Pitches and rhythms follow the same harmonic progression as the harmonic series (Rhea 1972). That is, for every one beat of the fundamental, the second harmonic beat twice, the third three times, the fourth four times, and so on, through the 16th harmonic. The performer could sound any combination of the harmonics by means of a keyboard. The speed of repetition could be controlled independently of the rhythm.

In the same time period, William Miessner patented another automatic rhythm generator, which he coincidentally also called the Rhythmicon (Mooney 2003; Miessner 1931).

Figure 6.12 shows the flexible rhythmic encoding scheme of Miessner's invention, where users could insert different celluloid patterns into a circular "record" of a rhythm that was scanned by an electromechanical device.

Beginning in the 1950s, many electronic organs for the home featured "rhythm machines" that produced simple repeating patterns for dance styles like tango, waltz, samba, and so on (figure 6.13). These devices used analog circuits to generate their percussion patterns (Douglas 1968).

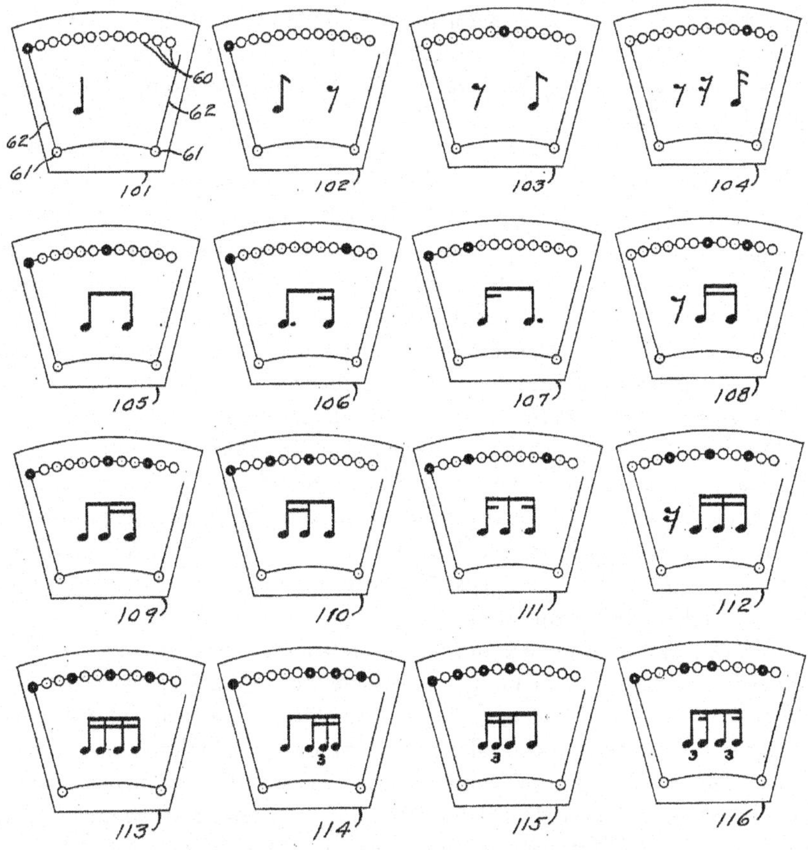

FIGURE 6.12 Miessner's Rhythmicon patterns, from the 1931 U.S. Patent 1,887,857. Each pattern represents a different division of a quarter note.

FIGURE 6.13 Detail of an analog Hammond Rhythm II unit, a part of a Hammond T-422 organ manufactured in 1969. This unit allows two dance rhythms to be superimposed on top of each other with a variable tempo control.

Sound example 6.13 Pattern generated by Hammond Rhythm II percussion unit on a 1969 Hammond T422 organ by pressing pattern selection buttons and turning a tempo knob. The reverberation effect is provided by the built-in spring reverberator.

Today's drum machines, groove boxes, and loop-oriented sequencer software play sampled drum patterns (including samples of the older analog drum machines) in popular dance styles. In typical uses of these devices, dependence on the grid of meter is virtually absolute. In many cases, the sounds and rhythmic patterns are so formulaic that sometimes the only thing distinguishing one artist from another is the choice of tempo. However, as we will see, aesthetic trends and technology push and pull each other, so that a new generation of devices and software is liberating rhythm from the tyranny of the lockstep beat.

Technology does not in itself solve problems of musical innovation, creativity, or expression. Thus there will always be a privileged place for a talented human percussionist. By means of expressive microvariations in timing, amplitude, and timbre, a virtuosic performer can breathe life into an otherwise mechanical meter. The "life" in this case consists of selective temporal asymmetries, timbral nuances, and amplitude variations.

The grid of meter is a necessary foundation in certain musics, such as works in which multiple instrumentalists must synchronize, or when the goal is to induce dance or trance. When music is liberated from the constraint of an unrelenting beat, however, we can take a freer approach to rhythmic organization. Such an approach to rhythm is embodied in our PulsarGenerator program (De Campo and Roads 2001a; Roads 2001b). Figure 6.14 shows a screen image of one panel of the control interface of PulsarGenerator. The fundamental frequency parameter, for example, is controlled by a continuous envelope and can sweep across and between infrasonic pulsations and audio frequencies.

Sound example 6.14. Sound created by the author using PulsarGenerator to crisscross between rhythm and tone, corresponding to figure 6.14.

Using similar tools, temporal formulas that are impossible to perform precisely by human musicians can be realized automatically, including sudden and extreme shifts in speed. Of special importance is the ability to cross effortlessly between the previously segregated infrasonic and audio timescales: from rhythm to tone and back.

ALGORITHMIC RHYTHM GENERATION

Compositional algorithms spawn material according to a systematic procedure. Exploration of algorithmic rhythm continues to drive generative composition. Harnessing the power of software toolkits, composers have developed elaborate schemes for rhythm production. The complexity of these schemes far exceeds

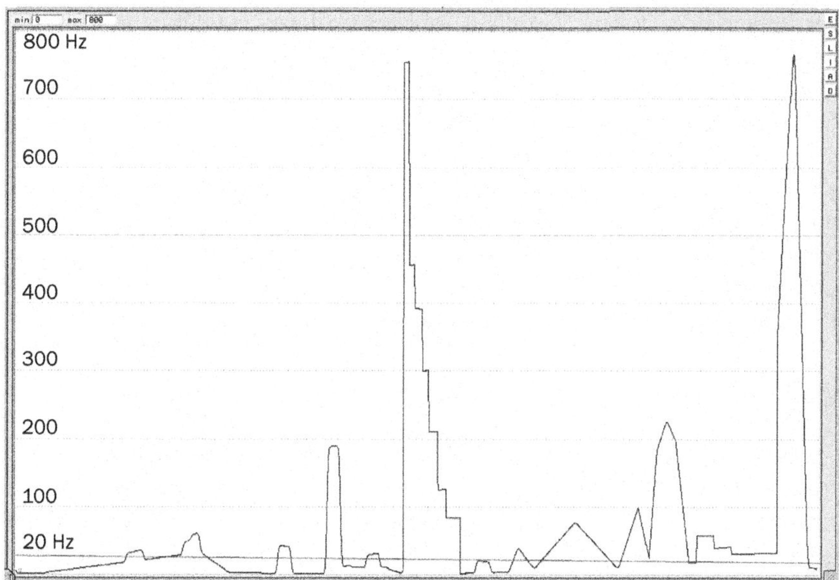

FIGURE 6.14 PulsarGenerator graphical interface for fundamental frequency with envelope control. This is one of a panel of malleable envelope controls built into the interface. In this example, the melody interpolates between rhythm and tone. A horizontal line is overlaid near the bottom to show the 20 Hz boundary. The duration is 29 seconds.

what a composer could assemble without a computer. These can include elaborate nested, rhythmic canons, canonic modulations, fractal rhythms, multiple tempi in fixed or variable ratios, polyrhythmic canons featuring common subdivisions between canons of different periods, etc. Rhythmic structures can be encoded as lists of numbers representing either onset time or duration. These lists can be subjected to arbitrary symbolic manipulations (rotation, permutation and combination, cell insertion/substitution, modulo divisions, interpolations, etc.). The rhythms generated by such operations are anything but perceptually simple. When they are transcribed into common music notation, which was never optimized for complex time patterns, they tend toward patterns that are not readable by human performers. A typical example would be a sequence of irregular tuplet patterns such as 6:4, followed by 7:8, followed by 3:2, in 64th-note resolution with interspersed rests (Agon et al. 2006). Unplayable as such rhythms are for a human performer, machines have no problem realizing them.

We return to a common theme of aesthetic philosophy (i.e., what does it mean to compose a structure that no one can perceive as such?). Of course, this issue is not specific to the computer age and is pervasive in all approaches to compositional organization.

The deployment of algorithms varies widely among composers. At one extreme, generative algorithms represent the holy grail of formal purity. Purist composers like Pierre Barbaud regarded deviations from the algorithm as a corruption that "invalidated" the compositional process. To others, notably Iannis Xenakis, an algorithm is merely one means of generating raw material. The material may be taken in whole, in part, or not at all. Furthermore, Xenakis felt free to rearrange and modify the generated material to suit an overriding compositional intention (Roads 1973).

Chapter 11 investigates generative strategies and dissects some of the complicated aesthetic issues they raise. Generative rhythm in itself could be the subject of a major treatise. In the rest of this section, we focus narrowly on three aspects of generative rhythm: the recent history of formalized rhythm, stochastic rhythmic processes, and rhythmic scales and sieves.

RECENT HISTORY OF FORMALIZED RHYTHM

Systematic or formalized procedures to spawn rhythmic patterns are ancient (e.g., isorhythmic techniques in the 14th century), but they emerged into the forefront in the mid-20th century. For example, the composer Alban Berg used a repeating durational series in parts of his operas *Wozzeck* (1922) and *Lulu* (1935) (Stuckenschmidt 1970). In the 1940s, Olivier Messiaen (1994, Tome I) described several new rhythmic innovations, including rhythmic modes (arbitrary patterns that are subject to variations analogous to serial pitch operations), non-retrogradable rhythms (palindromes), and rhythmic series:

> What is there to prevent our rhythmic thinker to choose . . . a short fragment, to superpose this short fragment on itself in diverse permutations, and to then cut within the superposition and to superimpose this cut to another cut of the same fragment, to realize a third cut on this last superposition, and so on? This process of choosing and repeated mixing is one of the natural tendencies of our thought.

Messiaen used rhythmic series techniques as early as 1940 in his *Quartet for the End of Time.* For example, in his *Ile de Feu* 2, part of *Four Etudes of Rhythm* (1950), he created a rotational permutation algorithm for sets of attack qualities, intensities, pitch classes, and a set of 12 durations based on a multiple of a single note duration. For example, one could build a set of duration classes on multiples of a sixteenth note:

{1 × 𝅘𝅥𝅯, 2 × 𝅘𝅥𝅯, . . ., 12 × 𝅘𝅥𝅯}

In another part, *Modes de valeurs et d'intensités*, he used a rhythmic series of 24 durations cycling over a series of 12 pitches (Stuckenschmidt 1970). Messiaen's rhythmic techniques were appropriated by a number of European composers, including Luigi Nono (Dodge and Jerse 1997). An analogy can be made between a rhythmic series and the chromatic scale: both are formed by iterating an interval 12 times. This analogy led to the famous discourse by Stockhausen on " . . . how time passes . . . " (Stockhausen 1957; see an analysis of this text in Roads 2001b).

Later, Milton Babbitt (1962) proposed an alternative rhythmic scheme for serial music called *time point sets* that used the measure as a kind of octave equivalent, so that two attacks that started exactly in the beginning of successive measures could be seen as forming an "octave-like" time interval. Unfortunately, the time point set pertained only to intervals between durationless instants of attack, and not the actual duration of sounding notes, making it perceptually opaque.

Serial techniques tend to be deterministic. In contrast, stochastic methods incorporate random variables. Stochastic rhythm generation can be as simple as throwing dice (à la Mozart) or coins (à la Cage) in order to select a rhythmic pattern. All that is needed is an arbitrary mapping between possible outcomes and corresponding rhythmic patterns. Lejaren Hiller and Leonard Isaacson (1959) conducted pioneering experiments in algorithmic rhythm generation. After two experiments in counterpoint where the notes all had the same duration, their third experiment concentrated on generating stochastic rhythm patterns. They first generated a random seed rhythm—a combination of eighth, quarter, half, and whole notes constrained to a single bar in 4/8 meter. They calculated how long this rhythm would repeat in one voice of a four-part composition. They then introduced another constraint that imposed vertical as well as horizontal redundancy by dynamically assigning certain voices as "masters" whose rhythm had to be followed by "slave" voices. The vertical rule took precedence over the horizontal rule. Their *Illiac Suite for String Quartet* (1956) showcased these experiments.

A handful of brave algorithmic composers followed in the immediate wake of Hiller. These include Herbert Brün and John Myhill (Urbana-Champaign), James Tenney (Murray Hill), Pierre Barbaud, Michel Phillipot, Iannis Xenakis (Paris), and G. M. Koenig (Utrecht). It has now been many years since the first generation of algorithmic composition. Today we are fortunate to see a variety of sophisticated environments and languages, some of which are specifically designed to support algorithmic composition.[37] These and programming languages like LISP provide a wide range of functions that can be applied to the generation of rhythm (see, e.g., Lorrain 2009). Hence, at this time, the possibilities for algorithmic rhythm generation are practically without limit.

STOCHASTIC RHYTHMIC PROCESSES

Stochastic rhythm generators scatter events irregularly in time. Xenakis (1960, 1971, 1992) used the metaphor of clouds to describe the sound masses heard in his pioneering orchestral works *Metastasis* (1954) and *Pithoprakta* (1956). We encounter similarly dense and irregular sound masses in his electronic constructions, including *Concret PH* (1958), *Bohor* (1962), *Persepolis* (1971), *Polytope de Cluny* (1972), and *La legende d'Eer* (1978). In these pieces, sounds crackle irregularly (*Concret PH* captured the sound of burning embers) or appear and disappear like bubbles in boiling liquid—hardly traditional models for rhythmic structure.

We distinguish two types of stochastic rhythmic processes: *stationary* versus *weighted* (or *biased*). A stationary rhythmic process exhibits random behavior without a trend or long-term movement as measured by a moving average, for example (Kendall 1973). It fluctuates around a constant mean with a constant deviation. We can hear it varying, but we can also perceive it as a predictable Gestalt. We see these characteristics in certain sound-mass textures created with granular synthesis. Consider a dense cloud of grains scattered over a wide bandwidth; it meanders irregularly but never evolves, and is therefore a stationary texture. Stationary rhythmic textures are fertile material for composition. One can place them at low amplitude in the background layer, where they lend depth to the musical landscape. Positioned in the foreground, their constant presence introduces dramatic tension and sets up an expectation of change. The ear notices any change, whether slow or sudden, as a deviation from the stationary texture.

To impose a trend is to bias the texture, sending it in a direction. Such a transformation can take place instantaneously or slowly on a meso timescale (i.e., many seconds). The presence of a trend transforms a stationary texture into a weighted stochastic texture. One can introduce a trend by changing the density of events, changing the amplitude, widening or narrowing the bandwidth, altering the spectral centroid, or by any other perceptible time-varying operation.

Sudden changes in event density create intermittent textures. Intermittencies are irregular rhythmic patterns that break up the stationary texture by injecting loud particles or silent micro-intervals. This latter technique—composing with silence—is largely unexplored, but it can be effective. The basic idea is to begin with a stationary texture and introduce silent intervals within it. Here one works like a sculptor, carving rhythmic patterns by subtraction.

OUTSIDE-TIME STRUCTURES: RHYTHMIC SCALES AND SIEVES

So far we have been discussing methods of algorithmically generating events in time. This section explores the synthesis of what Xenakis called outside-time structures (mentioned earlier in this chapter). A pitch scale is an outside-time structure. It enumerates a set of pitches and the intervals between them, but it does not indicate when any given pitch should be played; thus it is independent (outside) of time.

By analogy, a rhythmic scale provides a set of durations or time intervals, but it does not stipulate the order in which the elements of this set will be used. Intrinsic in the notion of a grid of time are subdivisions of the grid by multiples of simple ratios like 1/2, 1/3, 1/5, etc. One can also construct a rhythmic scale consisting of not just a simple ratio, but of multiple subdivisions of a given grid. Xenakis (1971, 1990, 1992) called these *sieves*[38]:

> In music, the question of symmetries . . . or of periodicities . . . plays a fundamental role at all levels: from a sample in sound synthesis by computer to the architecture of a piece. It is thus necessary to formulate a theory permitting the construction of symmetries which are as complex as one might want, and inversely, to retrieve from a given series of events or objects in space

or time the symmetries that constitute the series. We shall call these series "sieves."

—XENAKIS (1992)

Sieve-theory methods can be applied to pitch, rhythm, or any kind of parameter that is divided by intervals. For example, Xenakis suggested that sieves could be used to control sound synthesis, constraining the waveform to certain amplitude and time values. However, here we are mainly concerned with rhythmic scales produced by sieves.

The term "sieve" is a metaphor for a process that selects certain sets by filtering specific intervals, particularly by means of the modulo operation. Two integers are said to be *congruent modulo n* if their difference $(a-b)$ is a multiple of n. Thus 39 and 15 are congruent modulo 12, because $39 - 15 = 24$, which is a multiple of 12. Congruence of a and b is another way of stating that these two numbers have the same remainder after dividing by the modulus n ($39 \bmod 12 = 3$, and $15 \bmod 12 = 3$). Congruence modulo n is an equivalence relation, so 39 and 15 are equivalent with respect to mod 12, and the class of integers that are equivalent in this way is called the *congruence class* or *residue class* of a modulo n. In mathematics, sieves are called *residue class sets.* An exegesis of the theory of residue class sets is outside the scope of this text, so I limit my remarks to a few observations. For more on the theory of sieves, see Gibson (2001), Jones (2001), and Ariza (2005).

Xenakis's use of sieves involved the generation of multiple subdivisions of a given span using different moduli. He then applied logical operations such as intersections and unions to construct scales that pick different elements from the various subdivisions. Intersections find points of common periodicity (the smallest common multiple), since only those elements that are in common intersect. Unions merge sieves, taking into account the periodicities of all the moduli. By simultaneous combination of these two logical operators, intricate sieves can be designed; their internal symmetries are not obvious. Using more logical operators (such as exclusive-OR and complementation) enables the design of even more complicated sieves (Ariza 2005).

Sieve constructors allow one to design ordered patterns of any degree of regularity (symmetry) or irregularity (asymmetry). Xenakis and Marino's sieves program is a specific implementation of applied sieve theory, with limited options, rather than a generalized sieve toolkit. Based on my experiments with the published sieves application that I corrected and compiled, I was impressed with the variety and complexity of the numerical results it produced. Unless one constrains the sieve to the simplest of integer relationships, the series it generates quickly becomes unpredictable. In certain cases, the resulting patterns are so complex that they resemble stochastic processes.

Sieve theory is a means of designing grids of diverse kinds, whether in pitch, time, or another parameter. These grids can be simple or arbitrarily complex and abstract. The beauty of Xenakis's conception is that he reserved them for the design of outside- time structures. Rhythmic scales designed by sieves say nothing about what will be done with them in time. That is, sieves lay out the game board, but do not define the rules of the game or mention how the game plays out in time. (Of course, the design of the game board shapes the design of the rules and how the game is played.) The design of effective sieves and of compositional algorithms that will unveil their properties remains a research opportunity.[39]

Rhythm and the electronic medium

The precision and programmability of electronic music let us effectively organize and control more layers and dimensions of musical structure than were previously possible. This section presents some new possibilities opened up by these enhancements, specifically, extension of the timescales of rhythm, polyrhythmic grids, "machine music" or extreme uptempo performance, new approaches to sequential rhythm programming, and the rarely discussed domain of rhythmic undulations and envelopes in relation to spectromorphology.

EXTENDING THE TIMESCALES OF RHYTHM

In traditional Western music, the longest musical notes are measured in seconds. Although a pipe organ can hold a note indefinitely, very long note durations (> 8 seconds) are untypical. In contrast, classical Indian music plays out over a timeless drone that spans an entire work from an instrument such as the tamboura or harmonium.

The shortest musical notes are measured in fractions of a second. For example, at a tempo of 120 BPM for a quarter note, a 32nd note lasts 62.5 ms (1/16th of a second). Events as short as this occur primarily in ornaments such as mordents and fast keyboard runs, as in J. S. Bach's *Concerti* for harpsichord. I analyzed one recorded passage lasting merely 1.035 seconds, yet containing 18 notes. The average note duration was 57.5 ms.

Conlon Nancarrow (1912–1997) made amazingly precise music using mechanically driven instruments. Operating a custom-built hole-punching machine, he produced piano rolls that drove two synchronized player pianos. Nancarrow was obsessed with the simultaneous layering of multiple tempo strands, where the tempi were related by a mathematical ratio. For example, in his *Study for Player Piano 41a* (1965), the tempi are related by an irrational factor, and cascades of notes sweep up and down the keyboard at superhuman speed (Tenney 1991).

The technology of the magnetic tape recorder effectively liberated time. By simply varying the recording or playback controls, one could slow down, speed up, or reverse the flow of audio time. Tape cutting and splicing enable time segmentation and the free arrangement of tape segments on the timeline. Combining the idea of tempo change and time segmentation, Gabor constructed a sound granulator based on an optical film sound recording system (Gabor 1946). He used this device to make pioneering pitch-time changing experiments—changing the pitch of a sound without changing its duration, and vice-versa.

The synthesis of sound by digital computer opened the doors to dramatically expanded control over the time domain. The most obvious extrapolation was the pursuit of superhuman precision and speed. Uptempo beats were among the earliest rhythmic effects to be exploited in the primeval days of computer music (e.g., in Arthur Roberts's 1961 landmark *Sonatina for CDC 3600*; see sound example 3.1).

Since that time, one thread of computer music research has involved the design and exploration of microsonic materials. Granular processes are a widely available rhythmic resource. This can take two forms of organization: manual and automatic. In micromontage, a composer carefully sequences a pattern of tiny grains to make microfigures on the smallest perceptible timescale (Roads 2001b). In contrast, automatic granulation processes tend to shift the aesthetic focus from sharply defined intervals of time toward continuously variable and fuzzy boundaries. Just as it has become possible to generate new freeform 3D sculptures with rapid prototyping machines, the flowing morphologies that we can create with microsonic materials do not resemble the usual angular forms of musical architecture. On the contrary, they tend toward stream or cloudlike structures of variable density. Starting and stopping times of perceived events may be ambiguous due to processes of coalescence, evaporation, or mutation. Here we experience rhythms of undulating texture, rather than metered syncopation. Time intervals may emerge, but they are not an indispensable grid. There is instead an interplay between intervallic and non-intervallic material.

Manual and automatic methods of micro-organization can be interspersed. For example, the organization of my composition *Touche pas* (2009) combined an initial phase of granulation followed by a long period of detailed micromontage with a goal of constructing intricate rhythmic patterns on multiple timescales.

POLYRHYTHMIC GRIDS AND GRAVITATIONAL FIELDS

In his monumental study of polyrhythm in the music of sub-Saharan Africa, Simha Arom (1991) defines polyrhythm as a set of superimposed rhythmic patterns that share "a common temporal reference unit." This implies simple integer ratios such as 1/2, 1/3, 2/3, 3/4, and so on, but can also be extended to more complicated patterns such as found in the Carnatic music tradition, where complicated cycles can be constructed. Here a polyrhythm can be expressed by superimposing different accent patterns on top of onset figures to create patterns like 7/3 against 7/4 (Adler 2011).

Arom's definition, however, is too restrictive for our purposes, given the essentially unlimited flexibility and precision of the electronic medium. In particular, there is no technical or musical reason why multiple rhythms must share a common reference unit or complete a cycle.

As Messaien (1994, Tome I) observed, all music is polyrhythmic when it is viewed on multiple timescales.

> The universe and man make superimposed rhythms. . . . The substance of the world is thus polyrhythmic. What a lesson for the musician! All musicians should be rhythmicians and polyrhythmicians!

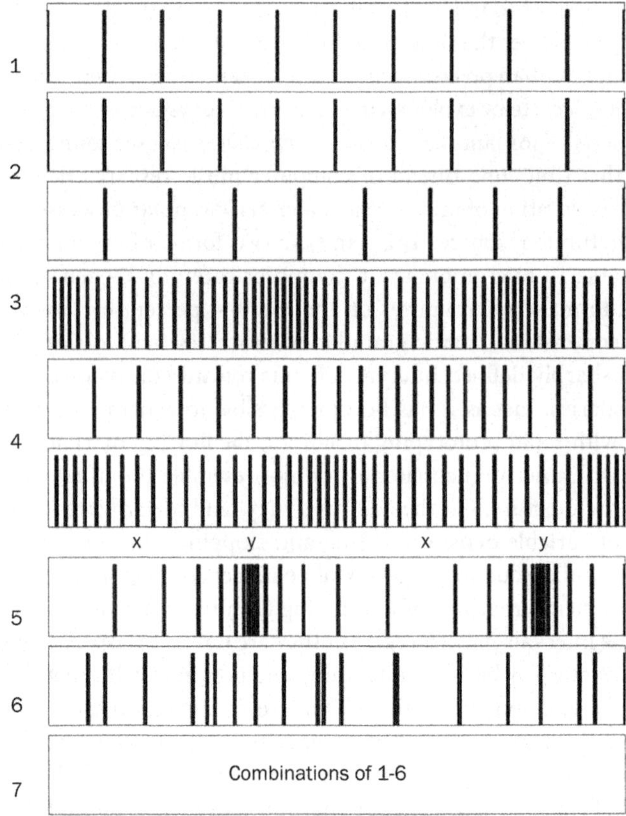

FIGURE 6.15 Rhythmic grids and fields. See text for explanation.

What we hear is always an intersection of patterns unfolding on several levels, each with their own rhythm. Below the level of macroform, for example, mesostructures divide time into sections, which transpire over minutes. Each mesostructure encapsulates smaller phrases and individual sound objects that articulate the surface structure of musical time. Within a single sound object, we experience the morphological rhythm of tremolo, vibrato, spectral variations, and spatial modulations. Subdividing time still further, we enter into the rhythm of microsounds: grains and microrhythmic figures that can morph into pitched tones and timbral variations.

Earlier in this chapter, we described Clarence Barlow's measure of metric field strength as a way of determining the attractive force of a rhythmic grid. We can also define non-grid-based *points of attraction/repulsion* or *gravitational fields*. These fields attract events in clusters around specific centroids.

Put in a more general framework, we can view all rhythmic spaces as falling into one of seven categories with respect to rhythmic grids and gravitational fields (figure 6.15):

1. Aligned to a constant metrical grid
2. Aligned to more than one simultaneous metric grid

3. Aligned to a variable metrical grid
4. Aligned to more than one variable metrical grid
5. Gravitating around points of attraction (y) and away from points of repulsion (x)
6. Unaligned to a metrical grid or gravitational points
7. Combinations of (1) to (6)

Thus at any given time, there is not necessarily a single temporal grid, but possibly many grids and gravitational fields operating on different timescales.

In case (2), pulsations at different fixed rates can overlap. Let us call this *contrapulsation* and classify the ratios between the pulsation rates according to three types:

- *Multiples* (e.g., 4/2) where pulses are subdivided equally
- *Small integer ratios* (e.g., 4/3) where pulses come in and out of phase with noticeable regularity
- *Complex ratios* (e.g., 43/11) where periodicity occurs on such a large timescale that it is not noticeable, as well as irrational ratios (e.g., 4:π) where there is no true periodicity

Complex contrapulsations can lead to chaotic cloud textures whose internal rhythm can only be perceived statistically. A classic example is Ligeti's *Poème Symphonique* (1962) for 100 metronomes, where each metronome is set to a different tempo (Toop 1999). In my own work, contrapulsations are often realized with synchronous streams of grains and pulsars.

Some digital audio mixing applications let the user set the grid or time signature on a per-track or even per-clip basis. These temporal grids need not be rigid. Rather, their tempi can be elastic, deforming in the presence of pivotal sound events, analogous to the way that spacetime is warped by the presence of matter (Einstein 1916). In the extreme, the grids may evaporate, leading to free and open temporal spaces (case 5).

As Messiaen (1994) observed, when combining multiple simultaneous rhythms, one confronts "neutralizing forces" that prevent clear perception of their superimposition. In general, these forces pertain to any kind of similarity between the various rhythmic voices, be it timbral, registral, harmonic, durational, or similarity of intensity and attack time. Messiaen was especially insistent on how isochronous pulsations destroy the polyrhythmic "scaffolding" (*échafaudage*). Messiaen (1994, Tome I) suggested that polyrhythms be articulated by polytonality and polymodality:

> Rigorous serial music is poorly adapted to polyrhythm. The cohesive force of the series engulfs everything as a banal tonal chromatic succession distributed in all voices.

Finally, we should mention the well-known strategy of crossing from one grid of pulsation to another, known as *beat modulation* or *metric modulation* (Duckworth and Brown 1978). In this technique pioneered by Elliot Carter (e.g.,

First String Quartet, 1951), a pulsation common to two beat speeds serves as a bridge from one to the other. That is, one sets a beat and then subdivides it by some factor, where the subdivision becomes the new beat (Tingley 1981).

ELECTRONIC RHYTHM SEQUENCING

An electronic sequencer is a recording and playback system with a programmable memory. It can be packaged as either a dedicated hardware box (analog or digital) with buttons and knobs or a software application. Traditionally, a sequencer recorded only the *control* or *performance data* needed to regenerate a series of musical events. For analog sequencers, this meant control voltages, while digital sequencers communicated MIDI messages (IMA 1983).

Early sequencers were analog and were programmed by adjusting knobs for each of the discrete steps of the sequence. Later, the advent of digital sequencers made it possible to record performances in real time. For example, when a musician performed on a keyboard, key presses were recorded by the sequencer as MIDI messages. At a later time, the sequencer could play this sequence back and send the MIDI messages to a synthesizer to recreate the musician's performance.

A new generation of sequencing technology has pushed exploration of rhythmic structure into new territories. The latest analog sequencers encourage elaborate clocking and control circuits. Advanced digital sequencers incorporate multiple clocks and multiple independent sequences of varying lengths. Moreover, they integrate sampling and signal processing (i.e., they sample and process audio in real time, as well as trigger existing sounds). They can send and receive Open Sound Control (OSC), as well as MIDI (Wright and Freed 1997; Wright 2002; Wright 2005). Moreover, in keeping with general aesthetic trends in electronic music, they extend the range of rhythmic organization by operating in the realm of microsound (Roads 2001b).

Many types of sequencers are available. Each type is a specialized instrument that provides an interface and workflow optimized for a specific task. For example, the interface of an analog sequencer tends toward flashing lights, physical knobs and buttons, input/output jacks, and patch cables. In contrast, sequencers built into digital audio workstation (DAW) software, like Avid Pro Tools, tend toward graphical drawing interfaces driven by a single clock tempo that can also be drawn.

Sequencing of electronic music has a long history (see Roads 1996a). Two important landmarks were the sequence-controlled RCA Mark I (1955) and II (1964) synthesizers at the Columbia/Princeton Electronic Music Center. Only a handful of composers ever mastered the operation of these room-sized vacuum tube machines (Olson and Belar 1955; Olson 1952). Notably, Milton Babbitt used them in iconic compositions such as *Vision and Prayer* (1961), *Ensembles* (1964), and *Philomel* (1964), in which precise rhythmic performance was paramount.

The commercial introduction of *modular voltage-controlled synthesizers* by companies such as Moog, Arp, Buchla, and EMS in the 1960s and 1970s brought new possibilities for musical expression to several thousand musicians worldwide. These transistorized systems contained a dozen or more modules that could be interconnected via patch cords. Voltage control meant that sound parameters could be controlled either by input devices such as keyboards or automatically by signals from other modules—opening up a new field of sonic possibilities.

The analog sequencer module was central to large synthesizers. The musician tuned a series of knobs, each corresponding to a voltage that controlled a sonic parameter (such as the pitch of an oscillator). At the push of a button, the sequencer then stepped through these voltages sequentially, sending each voltage in turn to the module connected to it by a patch cord (e.g., an oscillator). If desired, the sequence could be set up to loop, thus realizing, for example, a repeating melody. More generally, the voltage sequence could control any module, such as filter center frequency, the gain of an amplifier, etc.

The rate at which the sequencer stepped was set by a knob for an internal clock or controlled from another clocking source. When the sequencer stepped according to the internal clock, the result was a lockstep metric sequence, usually set to loop indefinitely. However, the sequencer could also be stepped by other triggers to create complicated rhythmic patterns.

A major technical limitation in analog sequencers was the number of different steps that they could store. The Moog 960 sequencer module offered 24 steps, while the Arp 1027 module provided 30 (figure 6.16), and the Buchla 246 sequencer had 48 steps. In these sequencers, when more than one parameter was controlled at each step, the number of steps was reduced by that factor. For example, a 24-step Moog sequencer could control the pitch, duration, and amplitude of just eight notes (24 divided by three parameters). To add more notes, one needed another sequencer module. Moreover, each parameter at every step had to be tuned by hand with a control knob; it was not possible to program the sequencer by playing. For this, digital memory technology was needed.

Peter Zinovieff and his associates at Electronic Music Studio (EMS), London, developed the first commercial digital sequencer in 1971. Unlike knob-oriented analog sequencers, the EMS AKS sequencer could record and play up to 256 events played on a keyboard, with each event having six parameters, for a total of 1536 stored values. This control information was stored in digital form. As soon as the MIDI protocol was introduced in 1983, digital sequencing became widespread.

NEW GENERATION ANALOG SEQUENCERS

During the 1980s, most developers of analog synthesizers were swept out of the marketplace by the spread of the new digital technology. Since that time, a new appreciation of analog technology has emerged. This, in turn, has inspired an explosion of new sequencer designs. These can be roughly separated into two

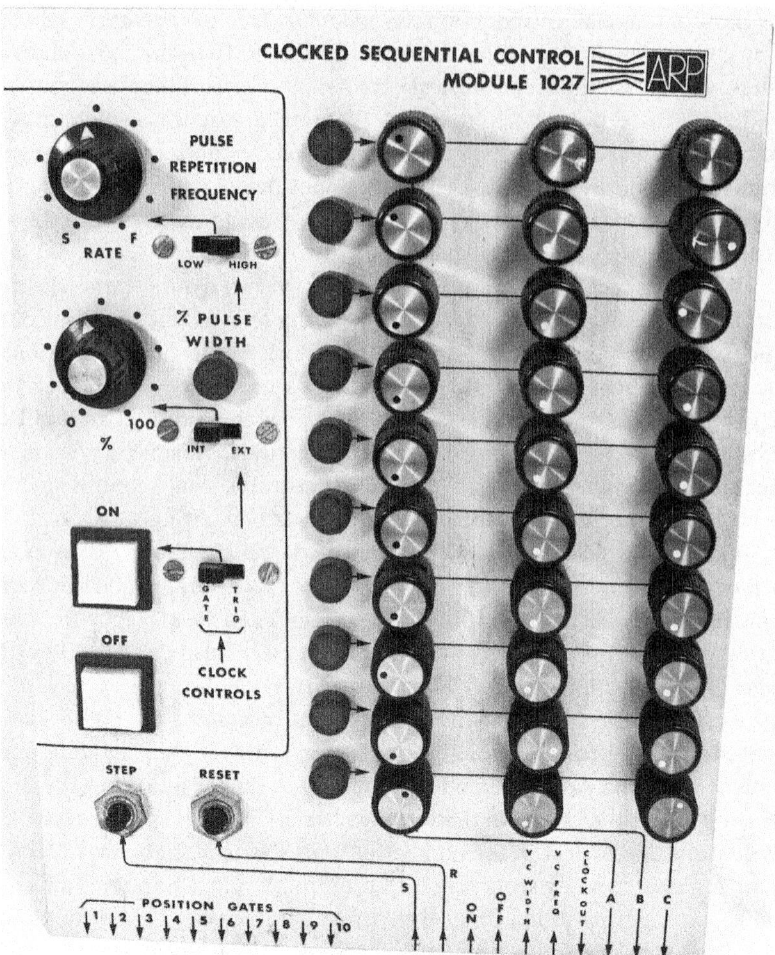

FIGURE 6.16 The Arp 1027 sequencer module of the Arp 2500 analog synthesizer. The internal clock is on the left. (Photograph from www.flickr.com/photos/switchedonaustin.)

categories: analog hardware sequencers with elaborate clocking schemes versus digital sequencers with sophisticated sampling, signal processing, and logic capabilities. New analog hardware sequencers accent the following features:

- Input from multiple clock sources, including some with exotic series patterns (e.g., burst, sweep, prime, Fibonacci, etc.)
- Generation of clocks from audio signals using comparators and threshold gates
- Clock processing modules (dividers, ping-pong switches, logic gates, delays)
- Flexible output routing permitting multichannel spatialization
- Interactive or multiple clock control of sequence direction (left-right, up-down)

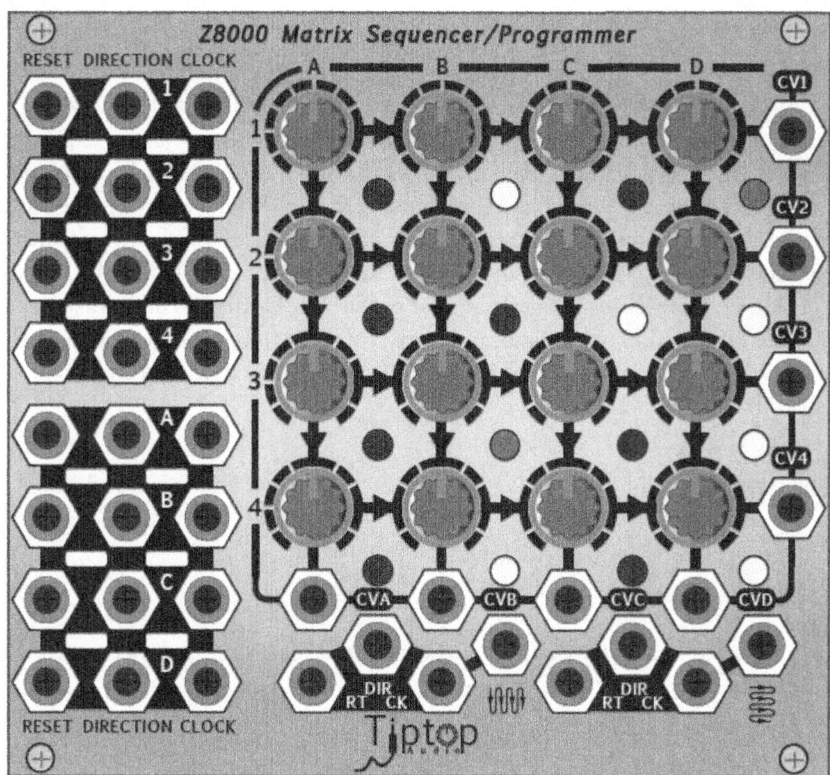

FIGURE 6.17 Tiptop Z8000 Matrix Sequencer/Programmer.

- Multiple steps playing simultaneously
- Real-time manipulation of sequence length

The current state of analog hardware sequencers is a hotbed of innovation, with a number of small companies making sequencers with distinct personalities. A characteristic example is the Tiptop Audio Z8000 sequencer (figure 6.17), which can operate in several different modes:

- Four 4-step sequencers on the horizontal (1/2/3/4)
- Four 4-step sequencers on the vertical (A/B/C/D)
  - One 16-step sequencer aggregating all four horizontal 4-step sequencers in order from top to bottom, left to right (A1, B1, C1, D1, A2, B2, etc.)
  - One 16-step sequencer aggregating all four vertical 4-step sequencers in order from left to right, top to bottom (A1, A2, A3, A4, B1, B2, etc.)

Sound example 6.15. *Tiptop Z8000 Acid jam and experiments*, Part 1 (2010) by Richard Devine and Josh Kay. The patch uses two Z3000 voltage-controlled oscillators, Doepfer A-145, and the Tiptop Z-DSP with Bat Filter card for processing.

NEW GENERATION CLOCKS

Some sequencers, including the Z8000 above, can process multiple clock inputs. Indeed, another area where novel features are emerging is in the design of the clocks that can either drive sequencers or act as timed event triggers without a sequencer. These feature *clock manipulation operations* include dividing, variable resolution (number of ticks per quarter note), fractional and step shifting (delay), pulse width modulation, and stochastic functions. In certain cases, these functions can be voltage-controlled, which adds an additional layer of complexity to their behavior.

An example of a new generation clock is the Eardrill Pendulum/Ratchet module (figure 6.18), with its stochastic density function, arithmetic series generators, and multiple clock division possibilities. Such modules can trigger themselves in complex ways.

Sound example 6.16. Eardrill Pendulum/Ratchet clock module demonstration.

NEW GENERATION DIGITAL SOFTWARE SEQUENCERS

In contrast to analog hardware sequencers, digital software sequencers focus on different capabilities:

- Integration of sampled sounds (not just MIDI control data) including well-stocked sample libraries with thousands of samples
- Compatibility with Open Sound Control (OSC) and all the flexibility and networking that this enables (Wright 2005)
- Sequenced control of signal processing with live interaction
- Sequencing of envelope curves
- Generation of DC voltages to control analog synthesizer modules
- Subsequences can be assigned to keys of a keyboard or any triggering scheme. For example, by pressing various keys, the musician can start multiple subsequences running concurrently to generate polyrhythmic sequences.
- Conditional sequencing (if-then rules). For example, the start of sequence B may depend on the start of an event in sequence A. Using toolkits like Max/MSP or SuperCollider, arbitrarily complicated schemes can be designed.
- Continuous tempo control from infrasonic to audio frequencies. The tempo of 60 BPM corresponds to a clock frequency of 1 Hz. An audio rate clock running at, say 100 Hz, would correspond to a tempo of 6000 BPM.
- Flexible real-time loop manipulation

Rhythmic composition with sequencers

Many people associate sequencers with ostinato backdrops for pop music. Even this simple functionality can be effective when it is overlaid creatively. An

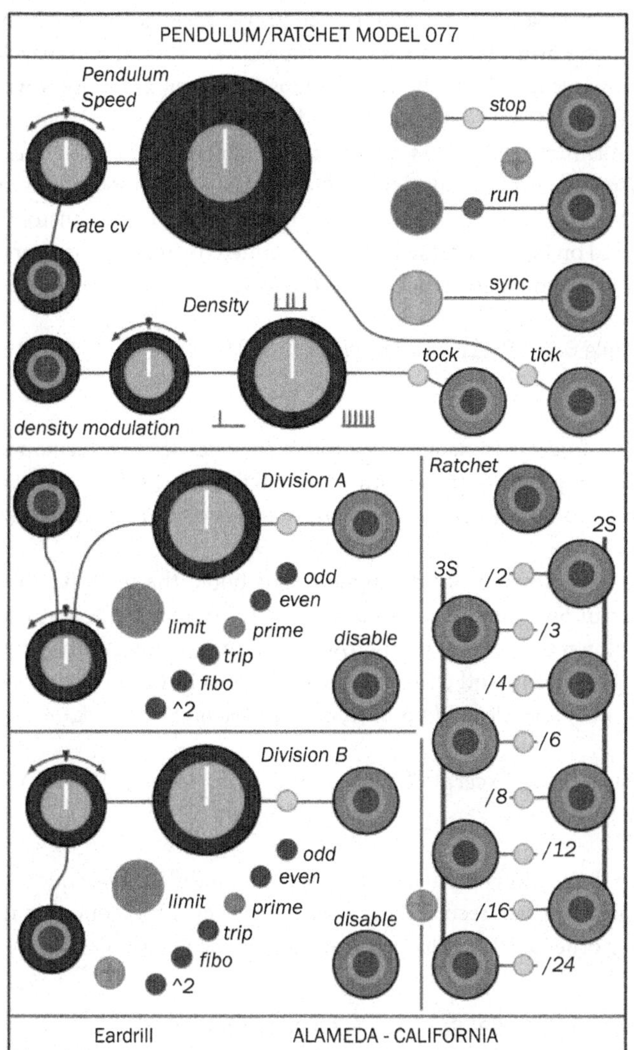

FIGURE 6.18 Eardrill Pendulum/Ratchet clock module. Pendulum section: The main clock varies from 8.5 sec to 10 ms (100 Hz). With the density control all the way up, the "tock" output is the same as the "tick" output. Turning density down creates a pulse train that randomly picks pulses from the clock to send out the tock output. Division A and B are variable ratchet divisors that can be freely positioned from a divisor of one to over 100. The divisor values can be limited to some interesting number sets, including primes and the Fibonacci series. The transport controls: stop, run are obvious. Sync resets all clocks and divisors. The ratchet section can be clocked from an external source. Fixed divisors include duplets and triplets.

example is *Ten-Day Interval* (1998) by the group Tortoise, in which the ostinato eventually fades away, leaving the layering tracks, which themselves fade into a concrète soundscape. As early as the 1960s, however, composers were designing synthesizer patches that implemented an elaborate control logic incorporating random timings, as well as interactively triggered sequences of complicated rhythmic/spatial events. Consider the *Funktionen* (1968–1969) series of works by Gottfried Michael Koenig, in which the control signals from a custom sequencer were recorded on tape, processed, and then routed to analog generators to control both the micro and macrostructures of the works.

Sound example 6.17. Excerpt of *Funktion Grau* (1969) by Gottfried Michael Koenig.

Much of the interest in sequencing today involves live performance, where a musician can reprogram the circuit with patch cords (in the case of analog) or continuously fiddle with the timings and settings of a sampled loop (in the case of digital).

As we have pointed out throughout this book, the most flexible approach to rhythm can only be realized in a studio environment, where it is possible to freely edit down to the level of microsonic rhythm. Consider the jittering lines, sudden interruptions, and chirping sound gardens in works like *Silver Apples of the Moon* (1967) and *The Wild Bull* (1968) by Morton Subotnick.

Sound example 6.18. Excerpt of *Silver Apples of the Moon* (1967) by Morton Subotnick.

As noted in the section on pulsation, Subotnick modified raw sequencer rhythms by manipulating their recordings in the studio, cutting sequences into pieces, and splicing other sounds into and around sequenced passages.

UNDULATION, ENVELOPES, AND SPECTROMORPHOLOGY

Pulsation articulates a periodic pattern with a sharp onset, in contrast to undulations, smooth waves of energy unfolding in time. An undulation is the result of the slow fluctuation or modulation of a sonic parameter. The source of fluctuation does not have to be periodic; it can be a random function. Even Messiaen (1976), an ardent proponent of divide-down fractional durations, observed:

> Most people believe that rhythm means the regular values of a military march. Whereas, in fact, rhythm is an unequal element, following fluctuations, like the waves of the sea, like the noise of the wind, like the shape of tree branches.

Undulations are usually discussed in the realm of their expressive and emotional impact, but they are also important conveyers of musical structure. For example, a typical undulation is a crescendo that unfolds over many seconds as several successive waves of increasing intensity. On a smaller timescale, undulations take the form of accents and modulations within a single sound object. Thus the scope of undulation includes the expressive morphologies of envelopes, first studied in detail by Pierre Schaeffer (1966, 1976, 1977; Chion 2009) and documented in the *Solfège des objets musicaux* (Schaeffer, Reibel, and Ferreyra 1967). On a larger timescale, sound shapes contribute to the perception of meso and macrostructure.

Spectromorphology and undulations

Denis Smalley's (1986, 1997) theory of *spectromorphology* deserves mention in this context. Spectromorphology is a collection of descriptors for sound shapes and their structural functions. It was designed for analyzing the experience of listening to electronic music. It consists of a taxonomy of terms aimed at describing the following features:

- *Structural function*—departure, transition, closure, etc.
- *Motion and growth processes*—ascent, oscillation, contraction, etc.
- *Texture motion*—streaming, flocking, twisting, turbulence.
- *Behavior*—dominance/subordination, conflict/coexistence, etc.

Finally, to account for spatial behavior, Smalley outlined a theory of *spatial morphology*, which resembles, at least in part, the spatial oppositions that I present in table 8.1.

In general, these descriptors apply to the sound object and meso levels of organization, where gestures play out individually and in larger phrases. The motion and growth descriptors are of special interest here, as they describe undulations like crescendi. Smalley isolated four basic types of motion and growth processes:

- *Unidirectional*—ascent, plane, descent
- *Reciprocal*—oscillation, etc.
- *Cyclic/centric*—rotation, spiral, vortex, etc.
- *Multidirectional*—coalescence and disintegration, dilation/contraction, divergence/convergence, exogeny and endogeny, etc.

To walk through every aspect of spectromorphological theory is beyond the scope of this chapter. It suffices to say that undulation processes on the meso timescale impose their own rhythms and thereby articulate musical structure.

Rhythmic oppositions

All music is a play of forces, attracting and repulsing, uniting and opposing. Attracting and unifying forces play with similarities, while repulsing and opposing forces play with dissimilarities and contrasts. The playing field of rhythm can be laid out as a set of oppositions, pitting one tendency against another as depicted in table 6.2.

TABLE 6.2
Rhythmic oppositions

Slow	Fast
Constant slowing down (rallentando)	Constant speeding up (accelerando)
Constant rate	Variable rate (rubato)
Constant measure (loop) length	Variable measure (loop) length
Synchronous (metric)	Asynchronous (ametric)
Simple symmetry (aligned to meter)	Complex symmetry (syncopation)
Sparse	Dense
Regular (no intermittencies)	Regular intermittencies stipulated as a burst ratio
Regular intermittencies	Stochastically timed intermittencies
Simple unitary pulse (a single beat)	Complicated repeating pattern (clustered events or repeating phrase)
Synchronous polyrhythm (aligned to one grid)	Asynchronous polyrhythm (aligned to a multiple grids)
Fixed polyrhythm	Drifting, fractional polyrhythm ("phasing")
Pulse emerging out of chaos	Pulse fading into chaos
Pulse sound as independent element	Pulse as metrical alignment for other sounds

Rhythmic processes in my music

This section synopsizes my approach to rhythmic process, as played out through a number of aesthetic themes.

PHRASES AND FIGURES

Rhythmic organization in my music often begins with a performance in the studio using synthesis (e.g., pulsar synthesis, frequency modulation, etc.) or processing (e.g., granulation, tape echo feedback, pitch-shifted sample playback, etc.) controlled by gestural interaction (using a musical keyboard, mouse, sliders, knobs, etc.). Rhythmic behavior is already specific in this initial stage, as it is part of the conception. The result is a set of sound files of varying lengths. Subsequent to this stage, I take a multiscale approach to organization. This involves detailed editing at the lowest levels of sound structure, but at any time, I can intervene on higher levels of structure, rearranging mesostructures or generating new sound material.

The goal at the initial stage is the design of phrases. Many phrases are structured around *figures*—rhythmic patterns consisting of discrete events. The figures often have a distinct morphology of beginning, middle, and end lasting several seconds.

However, and this is important, I also sculpt meaningful phrases even in a continuous cloud, where there are no discrete events per se, before I begin editing. (See the discussion of streams and clouds below.)

Phrase design in *Clang-tint*

For me, *Clang-tint* (1994) was a breakthrough in terms of phrase design. A commission from the Japanese Ministry of Culture and the Kunitachi College of Music, *Clang-tint* exists in three parts.

The first part, "Purity," opens with a slow and deliberate keyboard performance using the Bohlen-Pierce scale. This performance, which is not aligned to a regular pulse, was prepared by months of experimentation with the melodic and harmonic possibilities of this scale. After this performance, at 2:49, sustained undulating sine waves enter the scene. Certain sounds tremolo, fluttering at 7 Hz. At 4:47, echoing rhythms begin with repetitions at 400 ms. The finale features a long sustained tone with pitch bend, arching over 50 seconds.

The second part of *Clang-tint*, called "Organic," opens with a pulsar cloud, leading to an explosive crescendo with many different percussion timbres. Subsequent phrases feature sustained tones that build to a rapid-fire release followed by another sustained texture. Pulsations weave in and out. The pulsation slows at 1:28–1:41, breaking open a sustained ocean sound. Several pulsations begin again at different tempi. This is followed by a slow phrase with pulses every four seconds. Another sustained tone builds to the final explosive crescendo.

The third part, *Filth*, opens with a high-impact percussive tone. The rhythmic organization is again based on phrases, with long "straining" tones (like stretching a rubber band before it breaks) leading to crescendi with many clicking and snapping impulses that move into a continuous noise texture punctuated by percussive hits. The textures fade to a low-intensity noise cloud lasting 20 seconds. A tone appears, punctuated by burning ember-like sounds. The finale consists of three widely spaced percussive hits in reverberation, one 7.8 seconds after the first and the final hit 10.1 seconds after the second.

Mesostructure in *Volt air*

Mesostructure is the focus in *Volt air* (2003), a four-part exploration of a granular synthesis texture. Part 1, with its electronic woodblock-like sound palette, explores short-term pulsation as a means of forward motion. A rhythmic signature of the piece is the frequent double articulation of a single impulse. Another characteristic is the use of short flutters like 8 impulses in 300 ms, but also dozens of short pulse bursts (less than 10 pulses) in the 6–10 Hz range. Accelerations and decelerations of pulse trains are common. Silent intervals sometimes punctuate the phrases.

Sound example 6.19. Excerpt of *Volt air*, Part 1 (2003) by Curtis Roads. 

Part 2 uses the same sound palette. This rhythmically complicated piece involves both pulsation and continuous transformations, such as in the middle section (1:10–1:48), which is based on continuous tape echo feedback.

Sound example 6.20. Excerpt of *Volt air*, Part 2 (2003) by Curtis Roads.

Part 3 opens with a long (55 seconds) sustained crescendo that builds toward an anticlimax. Following this, the form is designed as a set of six climaxes over the subsequent 1 minute and 20 seconds. I am most pleased with the irregular phrase between 1:57 and 2:03, which intermingles several pulsation frequencies.

Part 4 features pulsations at different frequencies, interspersed with continuous tones. The climax of a phrase is often a breakup of a continuous texture into a sparse sprinkling of percussive impulses. Between 1:06 and 1:14, I invoke a beloved cliché of electronic rhythm: the exponentially decelerating pulsation.

PARTICLE-BASED RHYTHMIC DISCOURSE

Most of my works, with the exception of *Clang-tint* (1994), explore a particle-based rhythmic discourse. Microsonic processes can unfold as a more-or-less continuous granulation, a sparse pulsation, or by means of a manual practice of detailed assembly of microrhythmic figures or *micromontage*. One characteristic figure is a high-density spray or "avalanche" of particles, which creates a rattling or hissing sound, depending on the spectrum of the particles. As a cadential gesture at the end of a phrase, such an avalanche has the function of releasing accumulated energy, like letting off steam. (See the description of "Sonal atoms" below.)

POLYRHYTHMIC PROCESSES AND PAUSES

I am interested in Varèse-inspired rhythmic processes in which independent strands align at critical mesostructural boundaries. An example is *Always* (2013), which features polyrhythmic processes on multiple timescales. Due to this work's initial construction, as a real-time combination of six stereo sound files played simultaneously from a sampler on 10 keys (with pitch shifting according to each key, totaling 120 tracks), *Always* is especially complicated from the standpoint of rhythm. The work is divided in two sections. The first section is dissipative. The second section is fast-paced and scintillating, characterized by thousands of clicks and hissing grains underpinned by a lively melodic/bass line.

Pacing is critical. Much of my music consists of rapid-fire rhythmic processes on multiple timescales—a high rate of information density. This is also why my works tend to be short and concentrated. This rate of information density becomes tiresome if it is extended for too long without a break. Thus in high-velocity works like *Touche pas* (2009), the second half of the composition process consisted of slowing down an initial granulation. This meant selecting phrases and transposing them down in pitch (by an octave, for example) and rhythmic speed, then inserting reverberation cadences and pauses to make the work breathe in between the fireworks.

Sound example 6.21. Excerpt of *Touche pas*, Part 1 (2009) by Curtis Roads. 

SHAPING STREAMS AND CLOUDS

Exploring the new musical resource of streams and clouds of grains is central to my practice. At the core of these processes is an engine for grain emission. The valves that regulate the rate of granular flow are central. These control the number of streams and their granular density. In effect, they control the microrhythm of the granular emission as it is being generated in real time.

Once these textures have been recorded as sound files, as a rhythmic tactic, I seek to articulate mesostructural highlights within the granular flow (figure 6.19). Through micro-editing, I create internal fluctuations and accents of individual grains that sometimes sound like the crackling of a wood fire, except that the crackles are composed precisely to articulate the unfolding of

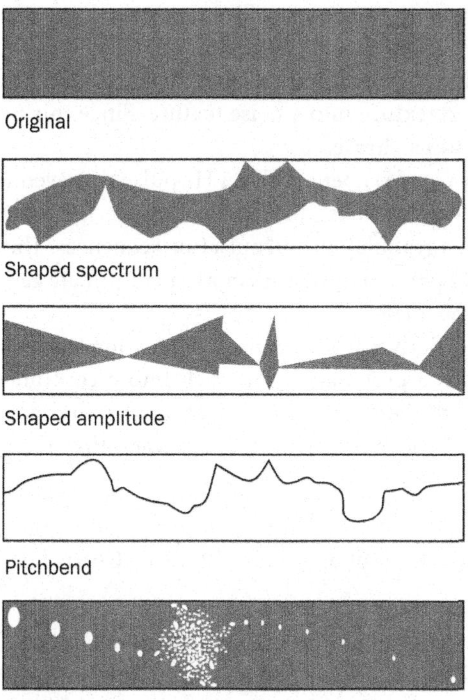

FIGURE 6.19 A texture cloud, represented by the grey rectangle at the top, can be shaped by transformations of spectrum, amplitude, pitch bending, and cavitation to create intermittencies.

mesostructural processes. I shape the continuous clouds with pitch-bending curves to obtain an effect of speeding up or slowing down. I also vary the grain durations over time, which has the effect of moving back and forth between pitch and noise. I often apply envelopes that lead to forceful accents. Indeed, I seek clear articulation of accents. However, accents are not always important structural boundaries; there can be a strong accent within a phrase merely as a point of articulation, not just at the beginning and end of a mesostructural boundary.

In terms of finally understanding how to organize granular materials, *Half-life* (1999) was a breakthrough composition (Roads 2004a). I began to compose with stream and cloud morphologies in *Half-life*. For example, the second part of *Half-life*, called "Granules" was spawned by a single real-time granulation of a file created by pulsar synthesis. I extensively edited and rearranged this texture with a goal of maintaining the illusion that the end result could have somehow been generated in real time, with no pauses. The macrostructure of "Granules" is a slow dissipation of energy, bubbling down to the depths, proceeding inexorably to a sputtering end.

Like *Half-life*, *Tenth vortex* (2001) was originally a real-time granulation of a pulsar synthesis file. It unfolds as a continuous cloud texture characterized rhythmically by expressive undulations, spectral fluctuations, and accents rather than a series of discrete events. Mesostructure is often articulated by spectral processes that unfold over several seconds, such as a bandwidth widening induced by shrinking the grain durations (Roads 2001b). This has the effect of dissolving a pitched texture into a noise texture. Since this unfolds over several seconds, it articulates a phrase.

Eleventh vortex (2001) opens with a 4 Hz pulse that eventually dissolves into an irregular granulation. Rhythmically, *Eleventh vortex* is a play of oppositions between continuous granulation and pulsating sequences. These pulsations often appear at the end of phrase boundaries or as a penultimate gesture before an ending fadeout as in the finale.

Sculptor (2001) derives from a driving percussion track sent to me by drummer John McEntire. I granulated this track into a continuous cloud, turning it into a flow of undulations, spectral fluctuations, and accents. The individual grains reveal themselves only in the end when they form a rapid rhythmic pattern.

Sound example 6.22. Excerpt of *Sculptor* (2001) by Curtis Roads.

Fluxon (2002) is a continuous granulation of a sampled sound marked by undulations, spectral fluctuations, and accents, combined with fluttering amplitude modulations in the 14–18 Hz range. The jittering cloud form articulates the central theme of pitch bending toward local climaxes.

The three movements of *Never* (2010) are similarly outcomes of continuous granulation marked by undulations, spectral fluctuations, and accents. The granulation is regularly broken up into high-velocity particle figures. A bass line serves as a rhythmic counterpoint to the granular figures.

FIELDS OF ATTRACTION AND REPULSION

In several works, including *Half-life*, Part 1 (1998) and Part 2 of *Clang-tint* (1994), I set up gravitational fields of attraction and repulsion. An attractive field serves as a magnet for a dense avalanche (i.e., a micromontage of dozens of discrete events). A repulsive field disperses events to create a rhythmically sparse texture.

CREATING PULSATION AND PITCHED TONES BY PARTICLE REPLICATION

In this music, both pulsation (at infrasonic frequencies) and tone formation (at audio frequencies) are emergent qualities of particle repetition. Thus, although the compositions as a whole are rarely aligned to a meter, within each piece, I create metric figures on multiple timescales including the audio timescale. For example, in the first part of *Half-life* (1999) called "Sonal atoms," the pitched phrase at 2:18 was created by replicating grains at audio rates to form tones. Most of this piece contrasts long clouds of more-or-less-continuous granular noise, punctuated by discrete rhythmic figures (using individual grains), such as bursts of grain repetitions in the 7–14 Hz range. The work makes explicit use of individual pinpoint grains as accents. Silent gaps of up to 1.65 seconds appear in the middle, gradually increasing granular density beginning at 1:45. A first avalanche of short grains is centered at 2:02, followed by low-level pulsation interrupted by sharp isolated impulses and a return to noisy granulation. The pitched phrase at 2:18 was created by replicating grains at audio rates to form tones. In the final minute of the piece, phrases often conclude with grain avalanches that fade away with pulsation. The finale consists of an accelerando with a speeding-up phrase repeated five times that ends in an explosive granular avalanche. The finishing gesture is a decaying pulse train at 10 Hz.

REVERBERANT SPACE AS A CADENCE

A phrase that ends with a long reverberation pause is typical in several recent works, including *Epicurus* (2010). The tripartite form of *Epicurus* determined its rhythmic structure. The opening section unfolds at high velocity. This is followed by a slow section and succeeded by a grand finale. All three sections transpire in the space of just 3 minutes and 6 seconds. The 18-second opening introduces all the elements of the piece: sharp impulses, low-amplitude granulation, replicated particle patterns, and long (10-second) reverberation cadences. The next 20 seconds form a continuous granulation that is finally broken up at a pattern of particle replications (37.5 to 40 seconds). The second, slow section starts at 1:22.5. The finale, starting at 2:03, deals with long reverberated decays ranging from 5.7 seconds to a long 16.8 seconds.

The reverberations are compound sounds or *reverberation chords* consisting of several pitch-shifted copies of the same reverberation cloud. (See chapter 7.)

OSTINATO AND INTERMITTENCY

I am interested in the tension between repetition and interruption, between ostinato and intermittency. For example, *Pictor alpha* (2003) is a loop-based composition, a repeating theme-and-variations form with a repeating pulsar loop at 8–10 seconds as a central rhythmic figure, around which many other pulsations speed up and slow down. The loops are rarely perfect; rather, they are slightly "off" in timing or directly spliced into to break the regularity of the ostinato. Another rhythmic motif is a 13 Hz pulsation. A pivotal point around 2:14 sees 8 Hz pulses sustain and then explode. At 2:42, the rhythm splits into two contrapuntal streams. The finish is a fadeout of pulses at 4 Hz.

In contrast, in *Half-life* (1999), I wanted to shift the musical discourse away from continuous, stationary, and homogeneous signals (such as pitched tones) to intermittent, nonstationary, and heterogeneous emissions (pulses, grains, and noise bands). Thus the sound universe of "Sonal atoms" is a concentrate of punctiform transients, fluttering tones, and broadband noise textures. Only a few stable pitches appear as the epiphenomena of particle replications.

ECHOES AS RHYTHMIC ELEMENTS

To craft the rhythms of the sonic surface structure in detail requires many editing interventions. A common motive in some of my works is the echoed repetition of impulses at key transition points. While the underlying texture shifts abruptly, these echoes continue the past into the future. This is a signature of *Now* (2003)—a continuous granulation marked by undulations, spectral fluctuations, and accents. This work is the product of an asynchronous granulation with overlapping large grains, which created a 400 ms echo effect in many parts of the work. The piece is further characterized by sharp drum-like collisions of sound in the opening section (e.g., at 0:07, 0:12.6, 0:17.9, 0:33.1, etc.). I constructed these collisions by cutting off the swell of a granulation cloud (creating a sharp wave edge at the peak of the swell) and splicing it with a sound occurring several seconds before the swell. Over this junction, I layered particle streams to create hysteresis-like effects (figure 6.19), as if the previous sound was ricocheting or

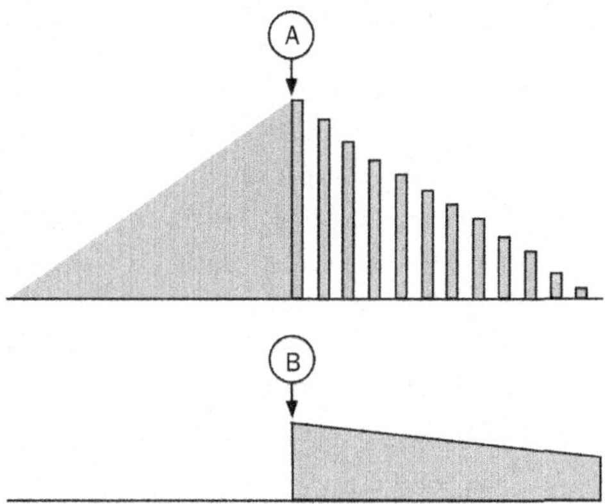

FIGURE 6.20 The initial sound crescendos to a peak at which point its last particle A echoes into the future as a kind of hysteresis effect over a new sound B.

rebounding from the collision. The final part of *Now* devolves into continuous granulation textures and a long quickly pulsating fadeout with a 24 Hz mean frequency, capped by a final echoed burst.

Nanomorphosis (2003) also unfolds as a continuous granulation marked by undulations, spectral fluctuations, and accents. The granulation sometimes breaks up into rapid-fire rhythmic figures with a typical density of 10–20 grains per second. In this piece, I sometimes mark transitions by inserting a *barrier particle* as a kind of punctuation mark into the flow. At the junction of a barrier particle, particles ricochet or rebound, while simultaneously the ongoing stream changes character. The behavior is similar to figure 6.20, but without an initial crescendo. This ricochet technique appears throughout *Nanomorphosis*.

Touche pas (2009) marked the beginning of a new rhythmic style, with "bouncing" particle figures, in which a particle echoes several times. This style reminded me of Subotnick's *Touch* (1969), hence the title. The phrases end on a strong accent that is sustained by a tag that is either (a) reverberation, (b) pitches alone or in chords, or (c) a sound that is pitch bending. This phrase-ending tag creates a breathing space in between phrases and serves as a cadence. The tags last anywhere from 2.6 to 9.2 seconds. Part 1 also introduces a bass line consisting of several deep sustained pedal points. Part 2 continues the rhythmic strategies of Part 1, with the addition of a more animated bass melody that serves as a rhythmic counterpoint to the granular figures. Brief particle pulsations overlay the central granulation theme. I also introduce the extensive deployment of brief (1 ms) and sharp impulse clicks scattered over the granulation like grains of salt and pepper. At 1:47, the central granulation texture is transposed down an octave, suddenly slowing the rhythmic pace for the rest of the piece. The unusual ending consists of seven iterations of a 3.4-second loop.

TAPE ECHO FEEDBACK

Another characteristic of my music is the deployment of analog tape echo feedback (see chapter 8, figure 8.7), with its unique palette of effects. These include pulsating discrete echos (as described in the previous section) whose period is determined by tape speed, to self-sustaining feedback with continuous pitch shifting and narrow filtered resonances. Feedback can be prolonged for several seconds or several minutes. The rhythmic component is a function of the fluctuations introduced by manual control of knobs and faders involved in regulating the process. A prime example appears in *Volt air*, Part 2, from 1:08 to 1:48, and in *Then* (2014).

Conclusion

Music is a dance of waves vibrating the air, the ear drum, the bones of the inner ear, and the auditory nerve, with the ultimate goal of stimulating electrical storms in the brain. In much electronic music, including my own, rhythm often emerges as the dominant element in a flux of ever-changing parameter interactions. Indeed, rhythm is the sum total of all parameter interactions.

Today, rhythm can no longer be viewed merely as a pattern of notes on a page of a score. We acknowledge the existence of a continuum from infrasonic fluctuations to events at all audio frequencies.

Microsonic processes introduce the possibility of evaporation, coalescence, and mutation of sound materials, analogous to the ever-changing pattern of clouds in the sky. As a result, the precise rhythmic pattern of certain sound phenomena is far from clear. As these microstructural processes unfold, they result in the phenomena of perceived pitch, duration, amplitude, space, and timbre, all of which function as articulators of rhythm. Thus rhythm occurs as an emergent quality of triggers, phasors, envelopes, and modulators on a micro timescale.

We have shown that the perception of duration can be modulated by musical processes and that human listeners construct rhythmic groups around events that are linked by Gestalt perception.

Tracing the history of rhythm, we saw that rhythmic notation evolved over time into hyper-complexity in the late 20th century, testing the limits of readability or playability. At the same time, the technology of electronic music made the design of complex rhythms ever more accessible.

Indeed, technology has changed the paradigm of rhythmic theory and organization. The liberation of time from meter was enabled by the technologies of recording (with variable speed and backward playback); editing, granulation, and programming have transformed the rhythmic playing field. Studio technology enables the exploration of polyrhythmic grids and fields. The new generation of sequencers and programmable clock sources leads into uncharted rhythmic territories. As Milton Babbitt (1962) observed, the precision of the electronic medium is especially compelling:

> Surely it is in the domain of temporal control that the electronic medium represents the most striking advance over performance instruments, for such control has implications not only for those events that are normally and primarily termed "rhythmic" but for all other notationally apparently independent areas: speed and flexibility of frequency succession, time rate of change of intensity, and important components of what is perceived in conjunction as tone-color, such as envelope–which is merely the time rate of change of intensity during the growth and decay stages—and deviations of spectrum, frequency, and intensity during the quasi or genuinely steady-state.

Ironically, the ability to stipulate rhythm precisely proved to be a barrier to naturally flowing rhythm in the early days of computer music, when the start time and duration of each event had to be typed in a long note list. The computer was an ideal vehicle for formally oriented composers who wanted to distance themselves from habitual phrasing, but this same built-in distance had to be overcome by composers and performers seeking more immediacy of expression (Ryan 1991). As music psychologists Bengtsson and Gabrielsson (1983) observed:

> A good performance, whether in speech, tennis, or music, is marked by acoustic and motor complexity. But a good performance is not perceived as complex; it is perceived as natural.

Thus an aesthetic tension remains between machine-generated timings and the subtle body rhythms we naturally associate with virtuosic performance. The challenge in generative rhythm is to tame the tendency to produce temporal minutiae that are fascinating only to the person who wrote the program that generated them.

Listeners organize rhythmic perceptions according to Gestalt expectations and tend to simplify or group events together into a limited range of rhythmic patterns. We are exquisitely sensitive to and compelled by pulsation. However, pulse is not only the ubiquitous beat of popular music, but any form of periodicity, however fleeting and temporary, like the repetition of slapback echo or the flutter of low-frequency amplitude modulation.

The traditional score presents a page, divides the page into lines and measures, and then divides lines and measures into fractional notes (whole, half, quarter, eighth, etc.). Thus the note-oriented composer tends to think of time as a quantity to be divided by fractional proportions.

However, as this chapter has shown, the possibilities of envelope control and the creation of liquid or cloud-like musical morphologies suggest a view of rhythm not as a fixed set of intervals on a time grid, but rather as a continuously flowing, undulating, and malleable temporal substrate upon which events can be scattered, sprinkled, sprayed, or stirred at will. In this view, composition is not a matter of filling or dividing time, but rather of generating it.

7

Pitch in electronic music

Pitch is an intrinsically fascinating phenomenon. Words fail to describe the emotional impact of a beautiful melody, harmonic progression, bass line, pitch cluster, or cloud of glissandi. Partly because of this concentrated aesthetic power, pitch is also a sensitive and culturally charged topic among musicians. It can be discussed in a variety of ways: abstractly as a branch of numerology and/or mathematics, experimentally in terms of psychoacoustic theories, or subjectively in terms of aesthetic preferences.

A composer's approach to pitch often defines his or her musical religion. Many creeds coexist, some dating back to antiquity. As the reader will see, I am "spiritual but not religious" about pitch. That is, I see many interesting approaches to pitch organization, yet I do not worship at the altar of one specific pitch scheme.

Pitch is the most zealously researched aspect of music. This obsessive focus has not resulted in a unified view. Pitch phenomena are studied from different angles by composers of various stripes, music theorists, psychoacousticians, and music psychologists. They import divergent biases and communicate in separate circles. The fundamental questions they ask are not the same, so ideas and beliefs veer off in disparate directions. Steering a straight line through the thicket of ideas on pitch is difficult, partly due to the gap between faith-based theories of abstract pitch organization and the reality check of scientific literature on the limits of acoustic perception and music cognition, such as Meyer (1967), Ruwet (1972), Dowling (1972), Lerdahl (1988, 2001), Lerdahl and Jackendoff (1983), and Bruner (1984). For references to more recent studies, see Huron (2006, chapter 7). Houtsma (1995) is a classic overview of pitch perception. Plack et al. (2005) focuses specifically on psychophysics and neurophysiology. This chapter is an attempt to wend a path through this conceptual forest.

The current musical situation prompts a reconsideration of the aesthetics of pitch. At least two developments motivate this. First, the inherent precision and programmability of digital synthesis removes limitations imposed by acoustic instrument design and human performance. This enables formerly speculative theorizing about pitch (such as precise microtonal performance) to be realized easily in practice. Second, musical aesthetics and technology have opened up to the entire universe of sound, placing the relatively narrow domain of scale-aligned pitched tones in a much broader sonic and compositional context.

In basic tonal music theory, notes and triadic chords are more-or-less unambiguous in identity and function. This is not the case in electronic music, in which a combination of pure frequencies could be considered a note, chord, or timbre depending on its composition and context (Sethares 2005). If the frequency of the tones varies in time, these static categories can break down completely.

The rest of this chapter mainly examines aspects of pitch that are not usually covered in standard music theory texts. It covers topics that tend to be enabled by electronic techniques. (I throw in the caveat that uncommon approaches to pitch have been tackled using acoustic instruments as well, but they are not the focus of this book.)

We assume that the reader has a basic knowledge of pitch relations in the European tradition: scales, tonal harmony, counterpoint, serial techniques, and so on.[40] First, we review the phenomenon of pitch from a scientific viewpoint, including the knotty concepts of consonance and dissonance. We then examine the design of early electronic instruments, including the Telharmonium, Thereminivox, Ondes Martenot, and Trautonium, all of which encouraged new pitch strategies. We explain how the aesthetic and functional role of pitch has evolved in view of distinctions such as the pitch-noise continuum, the harmony-noise continuum, and the pitch-rhythm continuum. In particular, as the role of pitch has expanded, its primacy as a compositional determinant has diminished due to the rise of other musical elements such as timbre and spatial interplay. We also introduce the concept of latent pitch, wherein pitch intervals can be articulated by non-pitched material. Twelve-note equal temperament has long dominated musical expression. What is its status in light of the possibilities opened up by other kinds of pitch games in electronic music? Microtonality is a vast topic. Our account merely pries open the door to further exploration. What if we give up the constraint of scales altogether, leaving us at liberty to explore the space of free intonation? We then explore the design of melody in electronic music, given that pitch can be considered a flowing, emergent quality. The concept of melody can be generalized beyond pitch. Finally, we look at the current musical context, in which pitch is one element out of many competing for the listener's attention.

What is pitch?

What is pitch? From a scientific viewpoint, pitch has no basis outside the mind. Pitch is a subjective mental impression, a reaction of the human auditory system to periodic waveforms in the range of about 40 Hz to about 5000 Hz (American National Standards Institute 1973; Houtsma 1995). The impression of pitch is especially strong for waveforms in which the fundamental frequency is strong. However, the impression of pitch can be induced when the fundamental is missing if harmonics of the fundamental imply its presence. This illusion, called *virtual pitch* (Sethares 2005), is common in music heard on tiny loudspeakers such as those on portable electronic devices.

Encapsulated within the notion of pitch are two concepts: linear frequency and pitch class. All pitches can be considered as occupying a position on an ascending line from low to high frequencies. In the scientific literature, this linear frequency attribute is called *pitch height*. For example, the pitch height of the 12-note equal-tempered (ET) C3 = 130.8 Hz is different from C4 = 261.6 Hz. In music theory, the term *pitch class* describes a 12-note ET note's position within an octave. For example, all Cs are of equivalent pitch class. In the scientific literature, pitch class is sometimes referred to as *pitch chroma*, and we use both terms in this chapter (Shepard 1999). Figure 7.1 depicts the space of pitches on the chromatic scale as a helix, showing both chroma and height.[41]

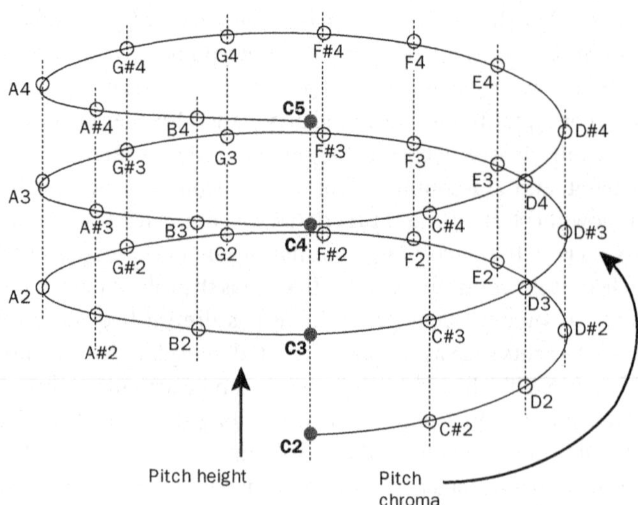

FIGURE 7.1. Pitch height relates to fundamental frequency, while the chroma refers to the pitch class. The horizontal nodes are half-steps of pitch in 12-note equal temperament. The vertically aligned nodes are octaves (after Snyder 2000).

Studies indicate that chroma and height are processed in different parts of the brain (Warren et al. 2003). As Shepard (1999) points out, one can suppress chroma while retaining height. We hear this in band-pass filtered noise, where the center frequency is sweeping up. There is no distinct pitch chroma, only a register or tessitura centered at a particular frequency. In many pieces of electronic music, the emphasis is more on height and less on chroma.

The *interval* between two stable pitches is the ratio between their fundamental frequencies: A pitch at 880 Hz is in a 2/1 or octave relationship with a pitch at 440 Hz. A *tuning* or *intonation* is a set of intervals that defines a sequence of pitches. Within a given tuning system, one can devise various scales or modes—arbitrary subsets of all possible pitches within the given tuning. (See, e.g., Slonimsky 1947 for a compendium of 1300 scales based on 12-note ET tuning.) The concepts of tuning and scale sometimes overlap when they refer to the same sequence of intervals.

Classical music theory treats pitch as a constant scalar quantity. Yet every musician knows that slight differences in pitch are common in ensemble performance, and pitches waver. Even in cases where the intonation is globally accurate, acoustic musical instruments can take dozens of milliseconds to achieve a stability of tone sufficient to induce a sense of pitch. Intentional variations in pitch are also common, including glissando and portamento effects, vibrato and trills (akin to frequency modulations in the range of 6–10 Hz), and flutter (frequency modulations in the range of 10–20 Hz).

As we will see, from a more general perspective, pitch can be viewed as a freely flowing periodic energy that emerges from instability, intermittency, and noise only in specific circumstances.

Tone and pitch are not identical terms. Any sound that is perceived to be continuous is a tone. This can include wide-band noises with no specific pitch quality, as well as sounds with ambiguous pitch. Acousticians speak of *complex tones* and *unpitched tones.* Thus pitch perception can be viewed as a subset of a larger phenomenon of tone perception.

The illusion of pitch

This section examines briefly the perception of pitch. As the acoustician Thomas Rossing (1990) observed, this topic is not fully understood by scientists:

> None of the current pitch [perception] theories is completely successful in explaining all the experiments.

This is a sentiment echoed by de Cheveigné (2005):

> Our current models may still be useful as tools to understand such a complex mechanism [as pitch detection]. Judging from yesterday's progress, however, it is wise to assume that yet better tools are to come.

We know that pitch is a cognitive illusion that occurs in the auditory systems of humans and other living beings (Pierce 1983). Why is pitch an illusion? Consider a laboratory impulse generator that can produce pulses in the range from 0.0001 Hz to 1 MHz. As the pulse sweeps upward in frequency, the physical circuit registers a linear increase in the rate of repetition. In contrast, when a human being hears these same impulses, the tone passes through major perceptual thresholds. Although the impulse generator accurately emits a pulse at 0.0001 Hz (one pulse every 2 hours 46 minutes and 40 seconds), a human being will not perceive it as periodic. Indeed, human beings are unable to synchronize accurately to periods greater than a few seconds. Somewhere around 0.1 Hz (one pulse every 10 seconds), a human being will be able to mark the beat with some accuracy. Between about 0.2 Hz (one pulse every five seconds or 12 beats per minute) and 20 Hz (1200 BPM), the body is exquisitely attuned to periodic rhythms. In this infrasonic frequency range, we easily sense a regular pulsation and meter and can track it to within a few milliseconds. Not coincidentally, it is in this same range that dance beats and many expressive effects transpire, such as vibrato, tremolo, fluttering, filter modulations, and spatial panning.

As the generator sweeps up beyond 20 Hz, another major change in perception takes place. The individual pulses become too fast to count; they appear to fuse into a continuous tone. A clear sense of identifiable pitch is not immediately evident between 20 and 40 Hz, however. Above 40 Hz, the illusion of identifiable pitch steps gingerly into the foreground. Hearing discrete sine tones between 40 and 80 Hz, we can begin to detect specific pitch intervals and recognize correspondences between chords and melodies. The pitch illusion takes center stage above 80 Hz. In the zone of acute pitch perception between

80 and 2000 Hz, melodies retain their identity even under drastic operations like transposition.

Still, it takes time to recognize a pitch, and the recognition time depends on its frequency. We need at least about 45 ms to recognize the pitch of the low-frequency tone at 100 Hz, but only 14 ms to recognize a pitch at 1000 Hz. Above 2000 Hz, pitch recognition times increase again.[42]

Certain pitched tones appear to be louder than others, even though they are physically the same in amplitude. Specifically, between 800 Hz and 1800 Hz, tones appear to become louder because of the ear's heightened sensitivity in this range. As the frequency increases beyond 4000 Hz, it becomes increasingly difficult to sense the precise interval of pitch changes.

At about 5000 Hz, the illusion of pitch evaporates into a looser sensation of high-frequency timbre. Specifically, it is impossible to distinguish an interval between tones above 5 kHz. (Some unusual individuals can reportedly detect pitches up to 16 kHz [Burns 1999].) As the generator reaches above 20 kHz (this threshold depends on age and the individual), the tone sweeps into the inaudible ultrasonic range.

It is clear that pitch perception takes place when individual periods speed up to the point when the auditory system can no longer discriminate individual periods. The periods fuse into a pitched tone due to the smearing effects of *forward masking* in the inner ear. Forward masking is the auditory equivalent of *persistence of vision*, which makes the illusion of cinema possible. Persistence of vision causes a rapid succession of discrete images to fuse into the illusion of a continuum. The perception of pitch is thus a beautiful cognitive illusion, bound by limits of attention, memory, and aptitude, but also conditioned by training. For all these reasons, it is not simple to train a computer to estimate pitch accurately. (For more on the topic of automatic pitch detection, see Roads 1996.)

Pitch perception is not unique to human beings. From the melodies of birds, to the cries of many animals, it is clear that pitch perception is shared by many other creatures (Weinberger 1999; Mithin 2006).

PERFECT PITCH

About one in 10,000 adults in North America have absolute or perfect pitch. This means they can identify a note without the benefit of a reference, or they can sing a named pitch. A few individuals can identify up to 75 different pitches over more than six octaves (Burns 1999).

Many scientists now believe that everyone is born with perfect pitch (Saffran and Griepentrog 2001; Saffran et al. 2006; Mithin 2006). Infants use it to learn speech; once a non-tonal language like English is learned, perfect pitch is lost unless it is deliberately cultivated through musical training. Experiments have shown that children can detect pitch differences that adults cannot, and that the skill of pitch labeling can be taught to anyone in the first six years of age. Afterward, however, this skill is quite difficult to reacquire (Carterette and

Kendall 1999). Only through rigorous training can adults attain a degree of perfect pitch proficiency (Ward 1999). This proficiency fades quickly without regular, sustained practice.[43] In contrast, a high percentage of people who speak tonal languages like Chinese, where the pitch of a word is important, have absolute pitch (Deutsch et al. 2009).

JUST NOTICEABLE DIFFERENCES AND CRITICAL BANDS

The precision of intervallic perception in humans is limited to a certain just noticeable difference or JND (defined in chapter 3). The JND is smallest in the middle range of pitch perception. When musicians are asked to compare tiny pitch intervals of simultaneous tones, they are accurate down to about 16 cents, or one sixth of a semitone. When the focus is tuning, the JND for experienced musicians can be as fine as 10 cents (Burns 1999). In any case, our ability to distinguish between the pitches of two sequential tones is greater than our ability to distinguish between those of two simultaneous tones (Wilkinson 1988; Houtsma 1995).

As explained in chapter 3, the JND limit is closely related to the critical band characteristic of the auditory system (Scharf 1961, 1970). Given two simultaneous sine waves that are very close to each other in frequency, the total loudness we perceive is less than the sum of the two loudnesses we would hear from the tones played separately. As we separate the tones in frequency, this loudness remains constant up to a point, but then a certain frequency difference is reached where the loudness begins to increase. Soon the loudness approximately equals the sum of the individual loudnesses of the two tones. This frequency difference corresponds to the critical band (Zwicker, Flottorp, and Stevens 1957).

The critical band is presumed to play a role in the sensation of *sensory dissonance* or *roughness* (Terhardt 1974). If two sine tones are very close together, they are heard as one tone with a frequency that lies between the two actual frequencies, together with a sensation of *beating* (an amplitude variation based on the difference frequency of the two tones) due to phase cancellation and reinforcement (Zwicker and Feldtkeller 1999; Sethares 2005). As the tones move farther apart, one senses roughness. Moving the tones still farther apart enables the ear to discriminate between the two frequencies, but the sensation of roughness continues until the frequency difference between the tones exceeds a critical bandwidth (Roederer 1975). Of course, the ear can discriminate between two non-simultaneous frequencies that are less than a critical bandwidth apart.

Despite a century-long debate, there is little consensus on how pitch is coded in the auditory system (Oxenham 2007). It is known that the human brain treats pitched tones in a special manner. In particular, neuroscientists suggest that pitch and harmony are processed primarily in the right hemisphere of the brain, while short events connected with rhythm and novel sounds are processed mainly in the left hemisphere (Weinberger 2004).

Pitch and timbre, consonance and dissonance

To analyze the combination of two or more pitches is to inevitably plunge into the ancient discourse on the nature of consonance versus dissonance. As the great acoustician Herman Helmholtz (1885) observed:

> The relation of whole numbers to consonance became, in ancient times, in the Middle Ages, and especially among Oriental nations, the foundation of extravagant and fanciful speculation. "Everything is Number and Harmony" was the characteristic principle of the Pythagorean doctrine. The same numerical ratios that exist between the seven tones of the diatonic scale were thought to be found again in the distances of the celestial bodies from the central fire. . . . In the book of Tso-kiu-mung, a friend of Confucious (BC 500), the five tones of the old Chinese scale were compared with the five elements of their natural philosophy—water, fire, wood, metal, and earth. The whole numbers 1, 2, 3, and 4 were described as the source of all perfection. . . . Even in recent times, theorizing friends of music may be found who will rather feast on arithmetical mysticism than endeavor to hear upper partial tones.

A century later, James Tenney (1988) mused:

> There is nothing in the language of discourse about music that is more burdened with semantic problems than are the terms consonance and dissonance.

Certain tone combinations appear to be "sweet," "smooth," or "restful," while others appear to be "sour," "rough," or "tense." It is not a question of an absolute binary opposition. As J. S. Bach knew (listen to the *Well Tempered Clavier*, 1722), the perception of the relative dissonance of two pitches depends on their context, which includes both subjective and objective factors. For example, what is the cultural and musical background of the listener? What is the musical idiom? On what instrument are the pitches being played? Is there a strong tonal center? How close is the interval in absolute frequency or pitch height (i.e., in what registers are the two tones)? How fast are the notes played? Are the tones equal in loudness? Are their spectra harmonic? Are they bathed in reverberation? These types of contextual questions qualify any narrow theory of consonance versus dissonance.

Certain historical arguments about consonance and dissonance appear as justifications for arbitrary cultural tastes. Thus it makes more sense to view questions of pitch preferences from a more general aesthetic point of view. I would liken the choice of tunings, scales, and intervallic combinations to a question of cuisine: a matter of taste and style, like oppositions between sweet and sour. As Tenney (1988) observed:

> Many 20th century composers evidently prefer dissonant textures.

Schoenberg (1926) spoke of the "emancipation of dissonance" and noted how consonance and dissonance differ not as opposites do, but only by degree. Balinese

Gamelan musicians are said to seek out-of-tuneness because the out-of-tune intervals are "more lively" (Taylor 1989). Gamelan instruments are often played in pairs, with one tuned slightly sharp such that a pronounced beating effect occurs.

Surveying the historical literature, Tenney found five different meanings for consonance and dissonance. Later, Huron (2009) identified 16 different theories to explain the phenomena. One of these definitions is based on beating, and it is this definition that was studied by Helmholtz and has been adopted by psychoacousticians as sensory dissonance.

For centuries, the idea of consonance has been associated with small integer ratios like 1/1, 2/1, 2/3, and 3/4 (Plomp and Levelt 1965; Hutchinson and Knopoff 1978). As Helmholtz's quote above notes, mystical powers have long been associated with simple ratios. From a physiological point of view, the reason why small integer ratios evoke an impression of consonance is not entirely clear. Burns (1999) and Sethares (2005) propose a number of hypotheses based on auditory physiology. In any case, the small integer ratio notion of consonance applies only to harmonic tones; inharmonic tone combinations can be shown to be more consonant at non-integer ratios (Sethares 2005).

In general, the greater the distance in pitch height between two tones, the greater their consonance. For example, on a Hammond tone wheel organ with only the fundamental drawbar engaged (a quasi-sine wave), a minor 17th formed by the pitches C4 + C-sharp 6 is audibly more consonant than a minor 2nd C4 + C-sharp 4. (C4 is middle C = 261.6 Hz.)

So far, we have discussed the notion of consonance in the context of dyads. The notion becomes thorny with the addition of more notes. Consonance in a triad correlates to its function with respect to a tonal center. Thus, with respect to a tonic (I) chord, most people would say that a dominant (V) chord is more consonant than a chord built on the tritone. However, this is already heading in the direction of cultural preferences. Chords based on quartal harmonies (e.g., C F B-flat, E-flat) would have been considered dissonant in the 1930s, but were accepted into common practice jazz in the 1950s. In an atonal piece, there is no tonal center, so the issue of consonance versus dissonance becomes less relevant. Attempts have been made to analyze the comparative roughness of arbitrary combinations of equal-tempered notes, but these models contain major simplifications (Parncutt 1989).

TIMBRE AND SENSORY DISSONANCE

Timbre has a strong effect on perceived roughness or sensory dissonance. Research in the last several decades has clearly demonstrated the role of spectrum in consonance judgments. Two chords may look the same on paper, but when they are played by different instruments, their sonic effect can be quite different (Carlos 1987; MacCallum et al. 2005). As Sethares (2005) observed:

> The more I experimented with alternative tunings, the more it appeared that certain kinds of scales sound good with some timbres and not with others.

Sethares has gone further to assert that almost any interval can be made consonant or dissonant by manipulating the spectra of the tones. For example, he created tones that sound more consonant (smoother) in a 2.1/1 ratio than in a simple octave 2/1 ratio, because the stretched harmonics of the tones beat with the octave but not with the 2.1/1 pseudo-octave. He also created a software "dissonance meter" to help one find the most consonant spectra for a given scale, or vice-versa (i.e., find a consonant scale to match a given spectrum). Using this meter, he created scales to complement bell, rock, and crystal spectra.

Pitch and the early history of electronic music

From its origins, the electronic medium prompted a fresh look at the phenomena of pitch intervals, tuning, and scales. This brief section describes how four early instruments, the Telharmonium, Thereminivox, Ondes Martenot, and Trautonium encouraged new approaches to pitch. We could continue to trace the entire history of microtonal electronic music instruments, but this would be something of a tangent. Our point here is simply to show that from the dawn of electronic music, the potential for expanded pitch resources was already recognized.

The world's first synthesizer, Thaddeus Cahill's gigantic Telharmonium (1906), could be played with a microtonal keyboard of 36 keys per octave: 12 standard equal tempered, 12 slightly sharp, and 12 slightly flat (Weidenaar 1995). In *Sketch of a New Esthetic of Music*, the composer Ferrucio Busoni speculated that the Telharmonium might lead to new solutions in microtonal scale construction (Busoni 1907).

Leon Theremin's Thereminovox (or Theremin), an instrument played by hand motions in the air, was played with continuous—rather than fixed—pitch control (figure 7.2).

Theremin (1927) was well aware of the implications of such an instrument for microtonal composition:

> My apparatus frees the composer from the despotism of the twelve-note equal-tempered scale. . . . The composer can now construct a scale of the intervals desired. He can have intervals of thirteenths, if he wants them.

The Theremin instrument, however, is fiendishly difficult to play in tune, so its microtonal pitch versatility has not been fully exploited.[44]

Maurice Martenot borrowed the synthesis circuit of the Thereminovox and connected it to a musical keyboard, calling his instrument the Ondes Martenot (first version 1928) (Laurendeau 1990). The keyboard made it easy to play, but the Ondes Martenot preserved pitch flexibility by providing an alternative to the discrete keys—a ring on a ribbon controller (figure 7.3). This controller lets a musician play pitch in a continuous manner to create ethereal glissandi, portamenti, vibrati, and intervals in between the keys. The most famous exponent of the Ondes Martenot was Olivier Messiaen, who used it in numerous pieces beginning in the 1930s. For example, his grand opera *Saint-François d'Assise* (1983) requires three of the instruments.

FIGURE 7.2 Leon Theremin and the Thereminvox instrument.

Oskar Sala's Trautonium (first version 1934), designed by Felix Trautwein, featured oscillators that generate a main pitch and several harmonics. These harmonics are not multiples of the fundamental tone, but fractions of it (figure 7.4). These are the *subharmonics*, corresponding to the *undertone series*. For example, for a tone at 440 Hz, subharmonics include 220 Hz (1/2), 146 Hz (1/3), 110 Hz (1/4), and 88 Hz (1/5), etc. Sala's album *Subharmonische Mixturen* (1997) showcases the evocative melodic and harmonic potential of subharmonic synthesis.

Sound example 7.1. Subharmonische Mixturen (1997) by Oskar Sala. 

The subharmonic realm has barely been tapped and remains a deep mine of possibilities.

The precision of electronic tone generators opened up another set of possibilities to the pioneers of the Cologne school of electronic music. As Herbert Eimert (1955) observed:

> Every musician is familiar with the note A at 440 cycles per second. The next whole tone above is B (492 cps). Within this major second from A to B, we are able to generate 52 different pitch levels of which, when ordered in a scale, at least each fourth level is heard as a different pitch interval.

FIGURE 7.3 Ondes Martenot showing the sliding ring on a ribbon controller played by the right hand. Image from blog.livedoor.jp/suo2005/archives/2005-03.html.

Not every oscillator was this accurate, however, and the state of analog technology in the 1950s made any such project arduous. As a result, only a handful of short studies of this type were made. With the advent of programmable digital oscillators, this limitation evaporated, and any desired frequency precision is possible. Unfortunately, even though such capability is trivial to implement, some synthesizer manufacturers (including developers of software synthesizers) still place arbitrary limitations on tuning.

The multiple roles of pitch

The phenomenon of pitch plays multiple roles in the music of today. This can be traced to aesthetic trends supported by the flexibility and precise control inherent in electronic means.

PITCH AS A CENTER OF GRAVITY

Following the ancient tradition of drone in Hindustani music, composers of electronic music have adopted the idea that a continuous pitch serves as a center of

FIGURE 7.4 Oskar Sala with his Mixtur-Trautonium (1991). Photograph by Curtis Roads.

gravity around which other events revolve. This seed idea has evolved into a form unto itself, consisting of long sustained tones with slight harmonic variations, sometimes played at high volume. Notable protagonists include Eliane Radigue and Pauline Oliveros, both of whom have focused on the drone form as a vehicle for meditation, as well as Jean-Claude Eloy, whose *SHÂNTI* (1973) lasts over two hours. In the words of Eliane Radigue (2009), these meditative works function as "mental mirrors," reflecting the mood of the listener.

PITCH AS A CONTINUOUS QUALITY

Whereas pitch was a frozen quantity in a traditional score, it is now a continuously time-varying quality. As Varèse (1954) observed:

> In our musical system we deal with quantities whose values are fixed. In the works that I dream of, the values will change continuously.

Not only can pitch glide freely, but the sensation of pitch itself can ebb and flow within a single event. With these changes, the discrete intervallic conception of pitch loses its former relevance. What is "the interval" between two freely varying pitches? In addition, we now recognize a continuum among pitch, chords, clusters, and timbre, between pitch and noise, and between pitch and rhythm.

Moreover, we see an organizational continuum around pitch at the higher timescale of mesostructural textures. That is, a texture can be tonal, atonal, free-toned, or unpitched altogether; these can be mixed in the same piece. We discuss this in more detail later.

Ironically, as the role of pitch has expanded, its primacy as a compositional determinant has diminished. Why is this? In traditional music, melody and harmony are the prime carriers of morphophoric burden; together with rhythm, they articulate musical structure. Yet in electronic music, other parameters such as timbre (in all its multidimensional variety), spatial choreography, density, register, etc., are just as likely to articulate the structure.

Sound example 7.2. *Musique douze* (1976) by Ragnar Grippe. In this work, pitch, although omnipresent, is essentially taken for a ride by other processes.

In certain works, acousmatic elements like vocalisms and references to specific places and situations can also play a major structural role. Rhythm remains of primary importance since it is bound up with the articulation of all the other parameters, as noted in chapter 6.

Additional roles of pitch

Though melody and harmony no longer necessarily dominate musical structure as they once did, pitch takes on additional roles that were not important in most traditional music. Specifically, pitch acts in the following capacities:

- As one pole of the pitch-noise continuum
- As one pole of the pitch-rhythm continuum
- As an articulator of register (pitch height) in a texture, where the precise pitch class is not important
- As a component of tone clusters and inharmonic sound masses
- As a component of timbre
- As a center of gravity in a drone
- As an articulator of interval in a sequence of pitch-shifted unpitched noises

We explore these roles in the next sections.

THE PITCH-NOISE CONTINUUM

Pitch stands at one end of a continuum of sonic effects and can be seen as an opposite pole to noise. Through the magic of sound transformation, we can move continuously through all intermediary states:

pure pitch → tuned noise → broadband noise

and back. This can be achieved in various ways: filtering, granulation, modulation, compression, additive synthesis, etc. To cite a historical example, Stockhausen passed white noise through band-pass filters to make a range of tuned (or band-limited) colored noises for *Gesang der Jünglinge* (1956). As Stockhausen (1989) observed:

> The discovery of the continuum between [pitch] and noise was extremely important because once such a continuum becomes available, you can control it, you can compose it, you can organize it.

Based on this principle, pitch can function as an emergent quality, as in Natasha Barrett's *Swaying to see* (1995), which features pitched concrète material morphing into noise and returning back.

THE PITCH-NOISE CONTINUUM AS A FUNCTION OF MODULATION

Zooming in to the center frequency of the pitch, stability and instability can be seen along the lines of a modulation:

> stable pitch → slightly unstable pitch → randomly varying pitch → noise

Depending on the rate and amount of modulation, the effect on pitch may be subtle or radically destructive. To achieve a mild periodic vibrato akin to the human voice or a cello, the rate of sinusoidal vibrato should be in the range of 6–8 Hz, with a modulation depth of about 50 cents. Using a random function as the modulator and increasing the depth of modulation creates an erratically varying pitch.[45]

When the rate of modulation increases to the audio frequency range, sideband frequencies appear on either side of the carrier (i.e., the frequency being modulated) (Chowning 1973). If the carrier and modulator frequencies are not related by a simple integer, the result will be inharmonic components in the spectrum, and the impression of pitch will be diminished.

Going beyond mild vibrato, one can push frequency modulation to induce nonlinear chaos. Specifically, as one increases the *modulation index* or degree of modulation, wild pitch fluctuations destroy the impression of stable pitch. Under certain conditions, the modulation of one sine wave by another at audio frequencies can generate tones so complex that they sound like white noise. Of course, if the modulation itself is a random audio signal, increasing the modulation induces a broad spectrum on any carrier waveform.

THE PITCH-NOISE CONTINUUM AS A FUNCTION OF ADDITIVE SPECTRUM

Another way to explore the pitch-noise continuum is by additively stacking tones on top of one another. For example, the addition of dozens of sine waves in a narrow band of frequencies (e.g., 90 sinusoids in one-third of an octave) results in an impression of noise. If the waveforms have a more complex spectrum, they converge to noise very rapidly. For example, additive synthesis of only 16 voices can become noisy if the waveform being added is a triangle wave.

THE PITCH-NOISE CONTINUUM AS A FUNCTION OF GRANULAR DENSITY

The physicist Dennis Gabor (1946, 1947) demonstrated that all sound can be considered as an agglomeration of microsonic grains. Taking this view as our starting point, we can view pitch as a region within a continuum of effects induced by increasing the density in time and varying the synchronicity of the granular flow. Figure 7.5 shows the gamut of these effects.

Viewed in this manner, the preconditions of pitch formation are fourfold:

1. Density of successive wavefronts remains in the range of 25 ms (corresponding to a frequency of 40 Hz) to 250 μsec (5 kHz)
2. Regular wavefront frequency
3. Regular grain emission
4. Consistent grain amplitude

When condition (1) is outside the stipulated limits, the resulting tone has no perceptible pitch. When parameters (2), (3), or (4) fluctuate, the result is an unstable pitch. For example, a symmetric positive-negative alteration in (2) induces vibrato or FM, which can turn into noise, as previously mentioned. When the alteration of (2) is asymmetric, the result is a pitch bend in the form of a portamento or glissando effect. When conditions (3) or (4) are not maintained, the result is an intermittent tone, with gaps or amplitude modulation (AM or tremolo). These modulations may be periodic or aperiodic. If the modulation frequency is in the audio range, the carrier or fundamental frequency is suppressed in favor of spectral sidebands (sum and difference frequencies); this destroys the impression of single pitch (Roads 1996). When the modulation is random, the result becomes noisier with increasing modulation.

Particle density	Synchronous emission	Asynchronous emission
Low	pulsation	irregular rhythms
	regular fluttering	irregular fluttering
	pitched tones	noise tones
	simple chords	bifurcated noise bands
	complex chords	multiple noise bands
High	tone clusters	noise clouds

FIGURE 7.5 The effects of temporal density on synchronous (periodic) grain emissions and asynchronous (aperiodic) grain emissions. Low density refers to less than 20 grains per second. The high-density limit is ultimately constrained by the sampling rate using Dirac delta functions (individual samples) as grains.[46]

The harmony-noise continuum

At the turn of the 20th century, tonal harmony was being extended by increasing exploration of non-triadic chord sequences. This included *altered chords* that replaced diatonic notes with neighboring chromatic pitches. As Roger Sessions (1951) observed, the increased use of altered progressions in the 20th century weakened the traditional notion of harmony:

> The principle of alteration runs actually counter to the notion of root progression. . . . Roman numerals [for chord labels] are really irrelevant. . . . The real point is that the "chord" as a valid concept, as an entity, has, in [an altered chord] progression, once more ceased to exist, much as it may be said to have not existed in the pretonal context. . . . The maintenance of two categories ("consonance" and "dissonance") has lost its meaning.

As the 20th century unfolded, it became clear that tonal harmony was one pole in a continuum of effects leading to atonality (lacking a tonal center or key), tone clusters, complex spectra (an attribute of timbre), and ultimately noise:

tonal chord → atonal chord → tone cluster → complex spectrum → noise

We have seen that pitch can be viewed as a pattern of wavefront periodicity on a micro timescale, and noise can be viewed as aperiodicity. We can also view pitch combinations along a continuum from relatively simple harmonizations to more complicated tone fusion effects that fall within the realm of spectrum or timbre.

Traditional Western harmony provides a set of rules for combining 12-note ET pitches in triadic sequences that form progressions related to primary key or tonality. Via the device known as modulation—a shift in tonal association—a harmonic progression in one key can move through pivotal harmonies that are common to two keys and then enter the second key. When the chords in a progression are affected by chromatic alterations, the concept of a root key can become ambiguous.

Common-practice harmony is an incompletely formalized system, based on triad chords separated by thirds. Chords that do not fit this model pose problems of classification. Consider a chord consisting of A, G, C-sharp, F-sharp, A-sharp (not to mention its various voicings). Such chords cannot be unambiguously classified outside the context of a specific chord progression.

A tone cluster is a chord (in any tuning system) with many close intervals. The sonority falls in between a chord and a timbre. An inharmonic tone cluster combines pitches that generally are not aligned to a fundamental frequency. Here the sound transcends intervallic perception and veers toward pure color or timbre. Henry Cowell (1930) described how a musical process could unfold as an accretion and decretion of notes in tone clusters, a process exploited fully in Ligeti's *Volumina* (1962) for organ. The pioneer of tone clusters in the electronic domain is Jean-Claude Risset, whose *Mutations* (1969) features melodies that morph into chords. Inharmonic tone clusters are a signature sonority in his music, appearing in works such as *Inharmonique* (1977) and *Sud* (1985) (Risset 1989). Going beyond synthesis, inharmonic tone clusters can also be produced by transformations such as including amplitude, ring, and frequency modulation, and nonlinear distortions such as dynamic range compression and waveshaping (Roads 1996). Any of these transformations can lead to distortions that we call *complex spectra*. A complex spectrum can also be synthesized as a sum of dozens of pure sinusoids (i.e., as a dense "chord").

Finally, broadband noise can be synthesized by combining hundreds of closely packed sinusoids with randomized phases.

THE PITCH-RHYTHM CONTINUUM

The human body is exquisitely attuned to periodic rhythms between about 0.2 Hz (one pulse every five seconds) and 20 Hz. If the periodic frequency is increased, the sensation of rhythm begins to give way to pitch chroma at about 40 Hz. Electronic generators make it easy to play across and between the pitch/rhythm boundaries as a compositional strategy. Figure 6.14 in the previous chapter showed the PulsarGenerator graphical interface based on envelope and waveform manipulations (Roads 2001). In figure 7.6, we see another example labeled with the zones associated with rhythm, tone formation, and chroma.

The frequency envelope shown in figure 7.6 crisscrosses freely among rhythm, tone, and pitch.

LATENT PITCH INDUCED BY PITCH SHIFTING

As discussed in the previous chapter, certain sounds are noisy and have no pitch, but can be induced to have latent pitch. As Natasha Barrett (1997) observed, latent pitch can be articulated by sequential contrast:

> Pitch content becomes perceptually evident when a composer applies methods of "sequencing."... When articulating a single [sound object], the sound may appear to contain little in the way of pitch. When articulating a series of [sound objects] in succession, one compares discrete articulations and detects differences of pitch or tessitura. . . . In *Earth Haze*, water droplets have been sequenced in this manner to expose a pitch contour.

In a similar manner, my piece *Touche pas* (2009) features sequences of unpitched impulsive sounds in which each successive sound is pitch-shifted by a perfect fifth. Shifting unpitched noise sounds like cymbals can bring out an impression of pitch through operations like pitch bending and pitch shifting.

Sound example 7.3. Glissando of an unpitched cymbal induces an impression of pitch change.

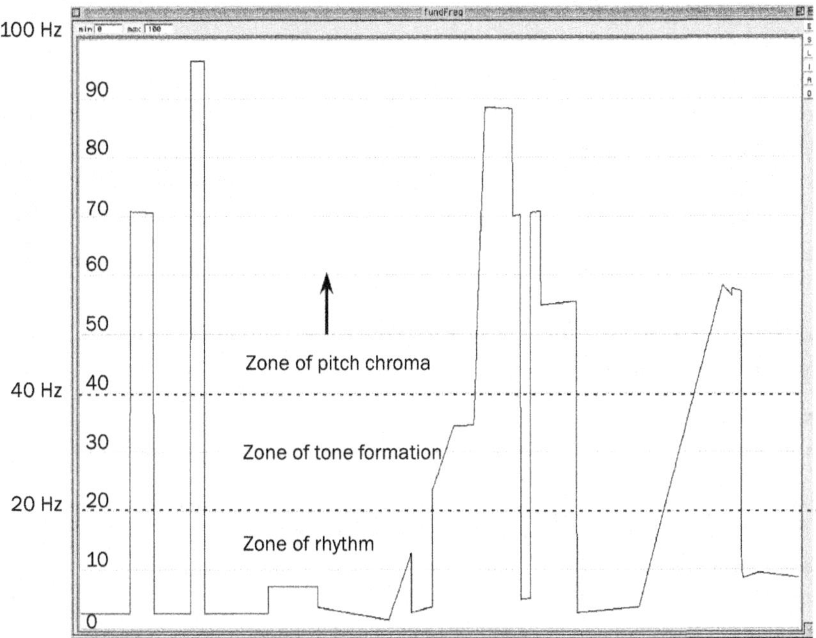

FIGURE 7.6 Detail of the fundamental frequency envelope window of PulsarGenerator. This window shows a span of frequencies from 0 to 100 Hz (vertically). The frequency range can be stipulated by the user by means of the min and max fields in the upper left corner. The timescale is 10 seconds. The dotted line at 20 Hz is the threshold between rhythm and tone formation. At about 40 Hz, the impression of pitch chroma begins.

Sound example 7.4. Pitch-shifting a cymbal crash by a perfect fifth several times in succession articulates this interval. 

Another means of articulating latent pitch is by additive superposition of pitch-shifted noises to articulate noise chords, including the reverberation chords described in the previous chapter. For example, in my composition *Epicurus* (2010), I superposed multiple pitch-shifted reverberation tails (which individually sound like colored noises) to create tuned reverberation chords (see figure 8.8).[47] My composition *Then* (2014) works with latent pitch in the continuous speeding up and slowing down of noise bands, inducing a sensation of pitch gliding.

The ambiguous zone of latent pitch is deeply fertile ground for experimentation. It shows again how a sound's perceived structural function depends on its musical context. For certain sounds, whether the sound is perceived as a noise or a pitch depends on its setting. Another technique that appears in *Epicurus* is the explicit introduction of pitched tones to imbue a harmonic shimmer to a reverberant cadence.

The range of pitch phenomena

Taking all that we have observed, we can situate pitch within a broad range of sonic phenomena on multiple timescales from the micro to the macro, as in table 7.1.

Although it is unlikely to find this entire range of phenomena explored in a single composition, it is possible to move through it as a continuous space.

TABLE 7.1
Range of pitch phenomena

Micro timescale	
Impulse	Unpitched point of sound (duration < 1 ms) with a broad spectrum
Grain	Pinpoint of sound, pitch emerges at durations > 14 ms, depending on the frequency
Sound object timescale	
Impulse sequence	Synchronous or asynchronous unpitched rhythms at infrasonic frequencies
Sustained tone	A sound object, either pitched or unpitched
Glissando	A sound object in which the pitch (pitched tone) or register (unpitched tone) is changing over time
Chord	Combination of simultaneous pitches (usually less than four or five); the musical function of the chord is defined by its relation to a tonic (tonal chord) or pitch-class set (atonal chord)
Cluster	Combination of multiple simultaneous pitches drawn from a scale (more than five notes, often closely spaced)
Inharmonic tone cluster	Combinations of simultaneous inharmonic sinusoids
Glissando cluster	Combination of multiple simultaneous glissandi
Meso timescale	
Harmonic melodies and progressions	Sequences of notes and chords related to a tonal center or root
Atonal melodies and chord sequences	Sequences based on enumeration and transformation of pitch class sets that avoid a tonal center or root
Free-intoned melodies and chord sequences	Sequences of pitches and chords unrelated to a scale
Glissando melodies and texture	Melody (sequence) or texture (combination) in which multiple pitches (for pitched tones) or registers (for unpitched tones) are changing over time
Noise cloud	Combination of dozens of pitched tones (e.g., chaotic frequency modulation noise) or thousands of granular events
Macro timescale	
Drone	In Hindustani music and some electronic music, it forms a canopy over the entire macrostructure.

The situation of 12-note equal temperament

> Today when science is equipped to help the composer realize what was never before possible . . . [here] are the advantages I anticipate from such a machine: liberation from the arbitrary paralyzing tempered system; the possibility of obtaining any number of cycles or, if still desired, subdivisions of the octave, and consequently the formation of any desired scale; unsuspected range in low and high registers; new harmonic splendors obtainable from the use of subharmonic combinations now impossible. . . .
>
> —EDGARD VARÈSE (1966)

> Our 12-tone equal-tempered tuning exists not because the number 12 is a nice number to divide things into or because it has interesting group-theoretical properties, which serial thinking might suggest, but because it developed as an approximation of 5-limit Just intervals.
>
> —JAMES TENNEY (2001)

Most European classical and popular music is based on the 12-note ET tuning, in which an octave is divided into 12 equal semitones according to the frequency ratio $\sqrt[12]{2}$, a ratio of approximately 89/84. This translates into a difference between semitones of about 6% (precisely 5.9463094%). This tuning was invented in the 1600s, but did not achieve dominance in Europe until the mid-1800s (Apel 1972). For historical, cultural, and economic reasons, 12-note ET is dominant in global musical culture.

A formidable advantage of 12-note ET over its predecessors was the equality of its intervals. For example, an ET "perfect" fifth interval will sound equivalent no matter which pitches are used to form it; this is not generally true of non-ET tuning systems. Such flexibility means that a composer can write functionally equivalent melodies and chord progressions in any key. It also enables harmonic modulation (i.e., a transition from one key to another by means of a chord common to both). The same flexibility fostered the rise of atonal and serial music and the promulgation of increasingly abstract operations on pitch class sets.

The mother lode of 12-note ET has been mined for 500 years by millions of musicians in innumerable compositions. The tuning is so ingrained that it is virtually impossible to musically express anything new about it. Consider a work for piano; it is constrained by its tuning and timbre from the start. If it is to find novelty, it must seek them not in tuning or timbre, but in other aspects of the composition. This is not to say that it is impossible to express anything new with 12-note ET. However, the new thing is not about the tuning. Rather, the novelty lies elsewhere, for example, in a new interpolation between existing genres, an unusual rhythmic organization, an atypical formal structure, a fresh combination of timbres, a philosophical message, etc.

The pop music industry sometimes manufactures songs that are attractive despite the use of 12-note ET in worn-out harmonic and rhythmic formulas. Yet some combination of elements in the voice, lyrics, audio production, fashion, face, camera angle, lens, setting, hairstyle, body language, stage show, animation, or attitude spawns mass fascination. The familiar melodic and harmonic formula—like the formulaic beat—serves as a comfortable backdrop.

CRITIQUE OF ABSTRACT 12-NOTE ET PITCH ORGANIZATION

This critique focuses on abstract 12-note ET pitch organization, but it could be generalized to any abstract system of musical organization.

The most important properties of 12-note ET were discovered long ago (modes, scales, major and minor chords and their alterations, harmonic progressions, cadential formulae, modulations of key, etc.). Today, only the dregs of novelty remain. In one style of contemporary music, novelty takes the form of mathematical transformations on pitch class sets, exploring abstract interval-based relationships (Lewin 1987; Morris 1987). The program notes for one such piece read as follows:

> [It] is based on eight simultaneously unfolding 55-note strings of pitches, quickly saturating the 88 notes of the piano. These strings completely exhaust all the basic 6-note harmonies of the twelve chromatic notes. The unfolding happens four times, the middle two involving direct (if camouflaged) octaves.

An obvious question with this approach is: How salient are such relationships to the ear and the mind? Surely they are extremely difficult if not impossible to hear in terms of the categories, structures, and processes designed by the composer (see the references below). This reflects a disconnection between the *composing grammar* and the *listening grammar*. As Cross (2003) wrote concerning Boulez's *Structures I* (1952) for piano:

> Though Boulez makes free choices regarding register, tempo, meter, and use of rests, his hands were tied by the system. The end result is so highly overdetermined that it ends up sounding almost completely random: the differences are not readily discernible between Boulez's *Structure 1a* and Cage's *Music of Changes*, where chance procedures of coin-tossing and use of the *I-Ching* were used to determine the musical parameters.

The same aesthetic disconnection was highlighted by Iannis Xenakis (1955) in his famous article "The crisis of serial music":

> Linear polyphony destroys itself by its very complexity; what one hears is in reality nothing but a mass of notes in various registers. The enormous complexity prevents the audience from following the intertwining of the lines and has as its macroscopic effect an irrational and fortuitous dispersion of

> sounds over the whole extent of the sonic spectrum. There is consequently a contradiction between the polyphonic linear system [of composition] and the heard result, which is surface or mass.

Transformations on pitch class sets can generate millions of permutations, combinations, and progressions (Nauert 2003). However, most such abstract transformations have questionable perceptual salience. That is, even an expert listener could not tell whether a derived sequence is "related to" a given original sequence.

Consider, for example, transformations based on even the simplest of concepts. The *interval vector* (or *Z-relation*) is a tally of the total intervallic content of a pitch class set (Forte 1977). Certain combinatorial transformations preserve the interval vector, so these are employed as compositional operations in a quest for "coherence." However, two sets can have exactly the same interval vector even though they have quite different musical qualities. As a simple example, a major triad and a minor triad have the same interval vector. Morris (1987) and Nauert (2003a), among others, have proposed elaborate mathematical derivations for calculating the relatedness of larger pitch class sets, but it is clear that a mathematical invariant is not the same as a perceptual similarity. Moreover, many of these derivatives fall into the category of detemporized or outside-time modulo-12 relationships, meaning that we cannot associate them directly with the time structure of a piece (Godoy 1997).

Perhaps if these relations were explored in straightforward progressional structures over time, they might be more comprehensible, but the serial aesthetic is often preoccupied with the goal of maximizing contrast (i.e., complexity) not only in pitch space, but in other dimensions as well. A common compositional process consists of the asynchronous superposition of disparate set forms in irregular and disjointed rhythmic patterns. In such works, the internal coherence is "deeply submerged" (Whittall 1999). The composing grammar is invisible.

Indeed, as Lerdahl (1988, 2001) has observed, serial organization tends to be *cognitively opaque*. Among his arguments are the following cognitive criteria:

- Permutational structures are difficult to learn and remember; the mind prefers tree-like structures with clear beginnings and endings.
- Even the most basic serial operations such as retrograde and retrograde inversion are difficult to perceive.
- Twelve items exceed the optimal number for comprehension.
- Serial music does not incorporate a psychologically coherent notion of skip or step, a primary means of generating a sense of directional motion
- Inventing a new row for each piece does not afford the listener consistent exposure to a limited number of pitch alphabets.
- Serial techniques do not take into account the psychoacoustic phenomena of sensory consonance and dissonance.

Lerdahl's observations were not meant as aesthetic judgments. Indeed, as he observed (1988):

> There is no obvious relationship between the comprehensibility of a piece and its value.

His theory means simply that listeners will not directly hear the structures that the composer designed. Many composers who use abstract pitch methods readily acknowledge as much. They take private satisfaction in creating intricate systems that they have no expectation of anyone perceiving.[48]

Myriad cultural factors transmit the value of a piece. For example, a famous virtuoso playing in a high-status venue can attach "value" to almost any score. Ultimately, appreciation of music is never totally dependent on its pitch organization. Other factors like rhythm, dynamics, orchestration, voice density, the actual performance, and other cultural norms (prestige, status, reputation, association with popular causes, etc.), as well as personal preferences, can inform a listener's appreciation. Music has many universal qualities that anyone can hear and appreciate (or not), regardless of training.

ABSTRACTION AND BEYOND

Going beyond basic operations on the serial 12-tone matrix, abstruse transformations derived from abstract algebra and category theory have been proposed for contriving an immense possible space of pitch sequences and combinations (Morris 2007; Mazzola 2002). The vast majority of these pitch collections, however, lack the unambiguous contrasts heard in the classical oppositions of tonal chord progressions. As research has shown (Huron 2006), two sets that are related in theory by means of a chain of algebraic transformations will just as likely be heard as unrelated. Perhaps, in purposefully designed clouds of notes generated by such means, our Gestalt perception of a statistical trend may result in the emergence of a distinguishable percept (Nauert 2003b). Otherwise, the only hope of applying such transformations in a manner that has any relevance to an audience is to apply the principle of *economy of selection* (see chapter 2), whereby a skilled expert composer selects a few perceptually salient choices from a vast desert of unremarkable possibilities.

Expert intuitive choices are important. As G. M. Koenig (1955) observed, the goal of art is not the enumeration of possibilities:

> Art . . . is qualitatively designed, aiming not at universal application, simplification, or efficiency, but at the most precise, most unique expression.

A composer who wants to make an original statement about pitch itself might search out other paths, including microtonal scales and strategies discussed later in this chapter, such as exploiting the pitch-noise continuum, the harmony-spectrum continuum, and polytonal or polyscalar combinations.

Microtonality

The design of scales is as integral to music as the design of instruments. As the microtonal music theorist Ervin Wilson (1960) stated:

> The act of scale formation is inseparable from the other creative aspects of music formation.

As Sethares (2005) observed:

> People have been organizing, codifying, and systematizing musical scales with numerological zeal since antiquity. Scales have proliferated like tribbles in quadra-triticale: just intonations, equal temperaments, scales based on overtones, scales generated from a single interval or pair of intervals, scales without octaves, scales arising from arcane mathematical formulas, scales that reflect cosmological or religious structures, scales that "come from the heart." Each musical culture has its own preferred scales, and many have used different scales at different times in their history.

Microtonality offers a vast realm of possibilities; this section presents but a brief overview. In contrast to 12-note ET, a *microtonal* tuning system is commonly defined as any tuning that is *not* 12-note ET; the intervals may be smaller or larger than a semitone (Wilkinson 1988). Microtonal music is sometimes referred to as *xenharmonic* music, the term deriving from the Greek *xenia* (hospitable) and *xenos* (foreign or strange) (Chalmers 1974; Darreg 1977; Wilson 2014). Although numerical arguments are often used to support microtonal intonations, Ivor Darreg (1975) emphasized their emotional impact:

> The striking and characteristic moods of many tuning-systems will become the most powerful and compelling reason for exploring beyond 12-tone equal temperament. . . . These moods were a complete surprise to me—almost a shock. Subtle differences one might expect—but these are astonishing differences. . . . I could explain here that the seventeen-tone system turns certain common rules of harmony upside-down: major thirds are dissonances which resolve into fourths instead of the other way round; certain other intervals resolve into major seconds; the pentatonic scale takes on a very exciting mood when mapped onto the 17 equally-spaced tones, and so on; but I can't expect you to believe me until you hear all this yourself.

For practical purposes, it is typical to define a microtonal tuning system in terms of a deviation from 12-note ET, commonly specified in *cents*, where 1 cent equals 1/100th of a semitone. A 1-cent deviation is a change of about 0.06% in frequency, an inaudible difference. On many digital synthesizers, each note can be retuned in cents to an arbitrary pitch, making it easy to program microtonal scales.

Microtonal pitch schemes have enormous untapped aesthetic and expressive potential. Inherent in digital sound synthesis is the capability of programming any tuning and scale precisely. Therefore, the easy exploration of microtonality is a strong incentive for working in the electronic medium. For example, a piece such as Charles Dodge's digitally synthesized *Fades, Dissolves, Fizzles* (1995) is a mathematically precise realization of just intonation.

All tunings can be categorized according to basic categories, for example: number of steps per gamut, logarithmic versus linear frequency, equal division versus unequal division, octaviating versus non-octaviating, cyclic or non-cyclic, and just-intoned or not.

NUMBER OF STEPS PER GAMUT

A basic difference between intonations is the number of steps they provide over a given range of pitches (gamut). For most scales, the gamut is an octave. For example, a simple pentatonic scale provides five steps per octave. The cent scale divides the octave into 1200 equal steps. We are, of course, not limited to octave (2/1) gamuts. For example, the Bohlen-Pierce scale, which we discuss later, has a gamut of 3/1. Ultimately, the gamut can be any arbitrary range.

LOGARITHMIC VERSUS LINEAR FREQUENCY

Most scales, such as 12-note ET, are based on a logarithmic (log) frequency grid so that perceived intervallic ratios are preserved no matter what the frequency is. Thus an octave 2/1 ratio is constant whether the frequencies are 440/220 or 4400/2200. However, it is also possible to experiment with frequency space divided in linear steps like differences of some number of Hz, which may be constant (e.g., 100 Hz, 200 Hz, 300 Hz, etc.) or vary according to a non-logarithmic scheme.

EQUAL DIVISION VERSUS UNEQUAL DIVISION

The 12-note ET is a classic equal division tuning that repeats the same 100-cent semitone interval. In contrast, many other tunings feature unequal intervals between adjacent intervals. An example of an unequal division is just intonation, which partitions the pitch continuum according to a series of different ratios. The same equal/unequal distinction can be applied to scales within a tuning. For example, a whole-tone scale in 12-note ET repeats the same interval while a diatonic scale does not.

One can devise an equal-tempered scale based on any interval. For example, Warren Burt composed *39 Dissonant Etudes* (1993), a series of highly expressive miniatures (90 seconds each), for electronic piano. Each etude is written using a different equal-tempered scale, from 5 to 43 tones per octave. The pieces range from the simple 6-note whole-tone scale, to the sharply contrasting sweet and sour pitch spaces of the 19-note ET, to the warmly dissonant chords of the 43-note ET (an homage to Charles Ives), in a jagged style reminiscent of Thelonious Monk.

Sound example 7.5. Excerpt of *Etude 22* (1993) by Warren Burt in 43-tone ET. 

OCTAVIATING VERSUS NON-OCTAVIATING

The traditional octaviating tunings cycle is at the 2/1 ratio or octave. In contrast, many non-octaviating tunings do not include the octave interval. Their gamut or repetition cycle (if there is one) is less than or greater than 2/1. As Xenakis (Harley 2002) observed:

> The first thing that you have to do is to understand how to create scales, which are not necessarily octaviating scales, that is, where every octave, or twelve notes, you have the same sounds. In fact, scales can be dispersed over the whole range of pitches.

Consider a tuning built on equal steps of an arbitrary interval such as 1.075, rather than the usual 1.059 of 12-note ET. Notice how after 11 steps, it approaches and then exceeds the octave without ever hitting it exactly.

9th step = 1.783/1
10th step = 1.917/1
11th step = 2.06/1

An interesting property of non-octaviating tunings is how they blur the standard concept of pitch class (which is usually tied to an invariant step within an octave).

Some notable examples of non-octaviating scales in electronic music include Stockhausen's *Studie II* (1954), which took the interval of 5/1 (a major third plus two octaves) and divided it into 25 intervals. Using a digital synthesizer, Wendy Carlos programmed several non-octaviating scales: alpha steps by 78 cents, beta jumps by 63.8 cents, and gamma steps by 31.5 cents (Carlos 1987). As Carlos said of her work *Beauty in the Beast* (composed in 1986 with the alpha and beta tunings):

> Both scales have nearly perfect triads (two remarkable coincidences!), neither can build a standard diatonic scale so the melodic motion is strange and exotic.

Finally, John Chowning's landmark opus *Stria* (1977) divides the ratio of the Golden Mean 1/1.618 into nine equal steps (Menenghini 2003).

CYCLIC VERSUS NON-CYCLIC TUNINGS

The notion of cyclic is related to octaviating. A cyclic tuning repeats a fixed set of intervals in different frequency ranges or registers. For example, the 12-note ET tuning is a typical cyclic tuning as it repeats the same intervals within the octave.

A non-cyclic tuning with respect to the octave would have unequal intervals in different octaves. For example, the Bohlen-Pierce scale (discussed later) repeats at the tritave 3/1, and so is cyclic with respect to the tritave but non-cyclic with respect to the octave. One can also easily imagine a scale of non-uniform degrees that never cycles at any simple integer ratio.

JUST-INTONED OR NOT

A just (also called perfect or rational) tuning is based on intervals constructed from ratios of small intervals (i.e., 1/1, 3/2, 4/3, 5/3, 5/4, 2/1, 6/5, etc.). The classic just scale introduced by Zarlino (1558) is as follows:

Note	C		D		E		F		G		A		B		C′
Frequency	1/1		9/8		5/4		4/3		3/2		5/3		15/8		2/1
Interval		9/8		10/9		16/15		9/8		10/9		9/8		16/15	

Notice that the intervals between tones are not equal. This stands in contrast to 12-note ET tuning, for example, which is based on the replication of a single interval $\sqrt[12]{2}$. The frequencies are all of the form $2^p \times 3^q \times 5^r$ where p, q, and r are integers and can be written:

C	D	E	F	G	A	B	C′
	32×2^{-3}	5×2^{-2}	22×3^{-1}	3×2^{-1}	5×3^{-1}	$(3 \times 5) \times 2^{-3}$	2

This is an example of a 5-*limit just intonation*, as all of the tones are powers of less than 5. The advantage of Zarlino's just intonation is that many of the intervals, most importantly the third and the fifth, are "pure" (i.e., without audible roughness for a variety of timbres). Of course, an unlimited number of just intonations besides Zarlino's can be devised. Indeed, it is possible to design just scales with arbitrary amounts of sensory consonance and dissonance.

The main limitations of just intonation have been known for centuries and gave rise to 12-note ET. First, in the case of tonal music, any just scale is correct only for one key. That is, in the key of C major, the interval between, say, C and D will be different from the interval between C and D in other keys. Thus, switching from one key to another requires retuning. (But see the following section on adaptive tuning.) Second, because of the inequality of the intervals between scale notes, successive transpositions generate new intervals. In an answer to this apparent shortcoming, theorist David Doty (1994) replied:

> [The] problem with twelve-tone equal temperament is that it supplies composers with an artificially simplified, one-dimensional model of musical relationships. By substituting twelve equally-spaced tones for a potentially unlimited number of tones, interconnected by a web of subtle and complex

> musical relationships, equal temperament not only impoverished the musical palette of Western music, but it also deprived composers and theorists of the means of thinking clearly about tonal relationships....

A large body of literature describes the theory of just intonation. For an introduction to the field, see Partch (1974), Doty (1994), and the Just Intonation Network (2009).

ADAPTIVE TUNINGS

Non-keyboard instrumental and vocal performers sometimes deviate significantly from a fixed scale for expressive effect, for example, in a vocal ensemble where a slightly altered pitch sounds more consonant than the corresponding pitch of a fixed scale. Such a variable scale is made possible by *adaptive tuning*, which allows the tuning to change dynamically in a context-dependent manner as the music is playing.

The computational flexibility of digital synthesis makes it possible to experiment freely with adaptive tuning strategies. To begin with, a computer can keep track of what notes have been played. This contextual knowledge enables retuning in real time in order to reset the root note to which all intervals are retuned, thereby enabling microtonal key modulation (Polansky 1987). The challenge is to maintain a desirable set of intervals (e.g., those based on small integer ratios) irrespective of starting tone, transpositions, and key modulations. Adaptive tuning can also be responsive to the spectrum of the instruments as they are played.

Given all these possible constraints, it is not surprising that a variety of strategies have been devised for implementing adaptive tuning. Waage (1984, 1985) designed a digital keyboard instrument that altered pitches according to the chords being played. On her album *Beauty in the Beast*, Wendy Carlos used one keyboard to set the root note, while another keyboard played the melody and chords. Clarence Barlow (1980, 1987) devised a software scheme for real-time pitch tuning that compared successive performed notes to achieve maximum harmonicity in subsequent notes (see the next section). Milne et al. (2007) invented a MIDI controller that facilitates adaptive tuning, and Sethares (2005) developed software that sought to minimize dissonance within a local context of notes.

BARLOW'S HARMONICITY MEASURE

Quantifying consonance is not simple (Graef 2002). Numerous measures have been proposed, such as Euler's *gradus suavitatis* (1739), Helmholtz's *harmoniousness measure* (1885), James Tenney's *harmonic distance* (1988), and Paul Erlich's *harmonic entropy* (1997). Clarence Barlow's *harmonicity* function is of special interest (1987, 2001, 2012). It produces a numerical rating for each note in an arbitrary scale, independent of timbre. (See Sethares 2005 for a similar but different measure.) Pitches with high harmonicity intensity values (such as unison, fifth, and octave) reinforce a sense of tonality. Barlow noted that ratios based on small integers and divisible (non-prime) integers were the most stable and contributed to a perception of tonality. Numbers such as primes were more *indigestible*, according to Barlow, meaning that they were less likely to reinforce tonality.

Going further, he created an algorithm for optimizing the harmonicity of any scale. He called this process *rationalizing* the scale, as it chooses the optimum ratio for each desired interval in the scale by retuning its intervals slightly to be just (i.e., ratios of small intervals).

> At first, all permissable tuning alternatives of the notes are investigated; the choice depends on two main factors: minimum [allowable] harmonicity and tuning tolerance. . . . The next step is to determine the quantity of tuning alternatives for each note; then the sum of the harmonic intensities (the absolute harmonicity value) of all intra-scalar intervals involving all tuning alternatives is evaluated—the tuning alternatives for any one note are excluded from mutual comparison: a tuning constellation is selected with the highest harmonicity sum. . . . The total number of intrascalar intervals . . . divided by the minimum sum of the indigestibilities is what I call the specific harmonicity of the optimal tuning of the pitch set.
>
> —BARLOW (2012)

Thus, given an arbitrary (not necessarily rational) scale, Barlow's software transforms the scale into a rational form in which each scale tone is close to the corresponding tone in the original scale while keeping to simple integer ratios. For instance, if the input is the usual 12-tone ET scale, then the result will be a just 12-tone scale.

For an example of a rationalized microtonal scale, see note 49.

Tonal, atonal, and unpitched systems

> The time lag between practice and theory, and the tendency for the theory to be created by theorists (rather than "great" composers), make music theory a somewhat idealized and simplified form of musical reality.
>
> —PARNCUTT (1989)

Nearly 300 years after Jean-Phillipe Rameau's *Traité de l'harmonie* (1722), the subject of Western harmony has recently received fresh scientific scrutiny. This is due mostly to expansion in the field of music science, in particular, psychoacoustics and music psychology (Huron 2006, 2009), but also fresh study by like-minded music theorists (Lerdahl 1988, 2001).

When I was a student of harmony, we were told that the theoretical foundation of Western 12-note ET harmony was the overtone series, that is, divisions of a string in ratios of 1/1, 1/2, 1/3, and so on (Sessions 1951). The teacher drew a fundamental C on a music blackboard and the 11 successive pitches corresponding to each of these ratios. Of course, with the exception of the octaves, no tones of equal temperament are harmonics. Moreover, as a basis for Western harmony, there is no way to derive a minor triad from the overtone series (Lerdahl and Jackendoff 1983).

Western harmony is a cultural-specific phenomenon. Studies indicate that the sense of tonality varies in different cultures (Huron 2006). What universal properties do all tonal systems share? Lerdahl and Jackendoff (1983) outlined the minimal conditions that any tonal system must fulfill, regardless of intonation and scale. Specifically, a tonal system requires only the following:

1. A scale or pitch collection
2. A tonic or basis tone and a dominant or secondary point of stability
3. A measure of relative stability in both melodic sequences and chordal harmony. In the simplest possible tonal music, only the tonic would be stable, and all other notes would be considered unstable, as in the chansons of the 13th-century troubadours. In Western classical music, the principles of relative stability are more elaborate. For example, a minor second is a stable melodic step but is unstable in the context of a chord, while an example of a stable harmonic progression is one that proceeds by a constant interval or circles back to the tonic regularly.

These conditions are easily fulfilled for any given scale, so a multiplicity of tonal systems can be designed.

In contrast, atonal music employs pitches but explicitly banishes a tonal center (Apel 1972). In much atonal music, the basic pitch material is transformed by means of mathematical permutations and combinations that are difficult for the ear to follow and segment into groups. Thus intuitions of musical tension and relaxation are based less on pitch and more on other factors such as rhythm, dynamics, note density, and timbre.

Scales versus regions, fixed or free intonation

> [In Western classical music] [w]e always hear pitches in terms of a closed external framework that precedes the piece—a system independent of the piece. We hear Beethoven, for example, not as an isolated experience at all but very much in relation to the entire tonal system, in fact to the whole history of tonal music. . . . I would say that Varèse's music is so formidably difficult to analyze because you cannot analyze it in terms of something outside of itself. . . .
>
> —ROBERT P. MORGAN (1979A)

A precondition of the serial approach to musical organization is that the material must be divided into a set of parameters, where each parameter is subdivided into a discrete ordered series or scale. One of the most zealous serialists, Karlheinz Stockhausen, established scales for many musical parameters besides pitch, including duration, amplitude, reverberation, position to strike a tam-tam, microphone position, filter bandwidth, etc. Going further, he designed scales for higher-order organizational parameters. For example, in *Zyklus* (1959), he set up a scale of nine degrees of indeterminacy. *Momente* (1964) was composed according to a "series of degrees of change." *Kontakte* (1960) featured 42 different scales, including a "scale of scales" (Maconie 1989).

Ordered sets and scales facilitate a kind of abstract uniformity. For example, one can apply the same intervallic operations to every musical parameter. Yet when abstract uniformity is not the ultimate compositional goal, there seems to be little reason to construct artificial scales. Indeed, it is often more interesting to consider parameters like pitch as continuous spaces, without steps. In this way, we can exploit the entire continuum—not just isolated points—and also use continuous transitions (such as glissandi), not just discrete intervallic jumps.

One such continuous space is a *pitch region*—a set of frequency boundaries within which pitches can be chosen (figure 7.7). Gottfried Michael Koenig called these bounded spaces *tendency masks* (Koenig 1971; Truax 1973, 1977). Thus a pitch region is a simple mechanism for constraining the range of pitches over a stipulated time interval. A pitch region articulates pitch height, presented earlier in the section on pitch perception. Pitch height refers to perception of register, independent of pitch. For example, one can easily judge the relative height of two band-pass filtered noise bands or tone clusters, without identifying a specific pitch.

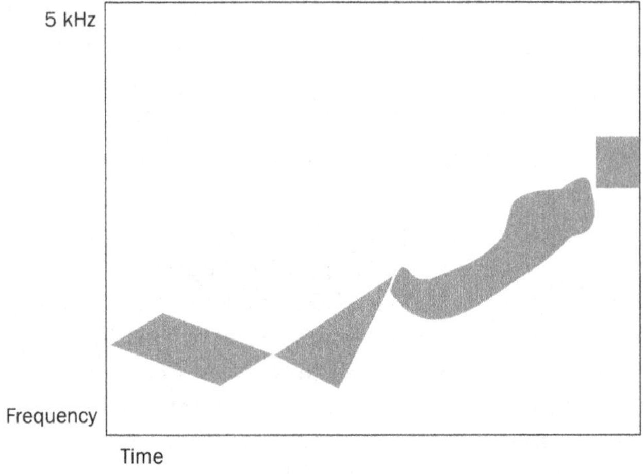

FIGURE 7.7 A sequence of pitch regions: parallelogram followed by triangle, surface bounded by a smooth function, rectangle.

Pitch height was as important as pitch class in the music of Varèse. As Solomos (1995) observed about *Ionisation* (1931) for percussion:

> Timbre in itself is not the principle concern in *Ionisation*. . . . The concern of Varèse was to relativize the role of pitches, a concern that the percussion instruments in *Ionisation* realize fully, because there the dimension of pitch is reduced to register.

As Varèse (quoted in Russcol 1994) himself stated:

> I think of D not as an artificial note of an imprisoning scale, but as . . . a specific frequency in relation to other frequencies.

The preface mentioned Ligeti's *Volumina* (1962) for organ—a sound mass composition in which pitch is reduced to a registral function rather than a harmonic/intervallic function. (See figure 9.7 for an excerpt of the graphic score.)

Within a given pitch region, there may or may not be a fixed intonation or scale. Consider the stochastic clouds in Xenakis's *Pithoprakta* (1956), *Analogique A* (1959), and *Syrmos* (1959) for stringed instruments. At different times, they combine unpitched col legno tapping, glissandi, and pitch regions in equal temperament.

In contrast, *free intonation*—not aligned with any scale—is featured in a large quantity of electronic music compositions, such as *Electronic Study No.2* (1962) by Mario Davidovsky, in which the pitch quality is sometimes wavering and unsteady.

Sound example 7.6. Excerpt of *Electronic Study No.2* (1962) by Mario Davidovsky.

Free intonation is also featured in many works by Morton Subotnick, such as *Silver Apples of the Moon* (1967), *The Wild Bull* (1967), *Touch* (1968), and *Sidewinder* (1971). These works were realized with Buchla 100 series analog synthesizers in which pitch was treated as a continuous, rather than discrete, quantity. The Buchla 100 had no traditional keyboard; rather it had a "touch controlled voltage source" (figure 7.8), where the voltage associated with each "key" could be tuned and the pressure of the finger on the surface continuously affected the voltage.

Sound example 7.7. Excerpt of *Sidewinder* (1971) by Morton Subotnick.

Free intonation was a focus of the earliest experiments in computer sound synthesis. Consider John Cage's description, quoted in Kostelanetz (1988), of Herbert Brün's *Infraudibles* (1968):

> I was very impressed . . . when I heard Herbert Brün's *Infraudibles*, which is sound output from computer, a sound that was different from the sound

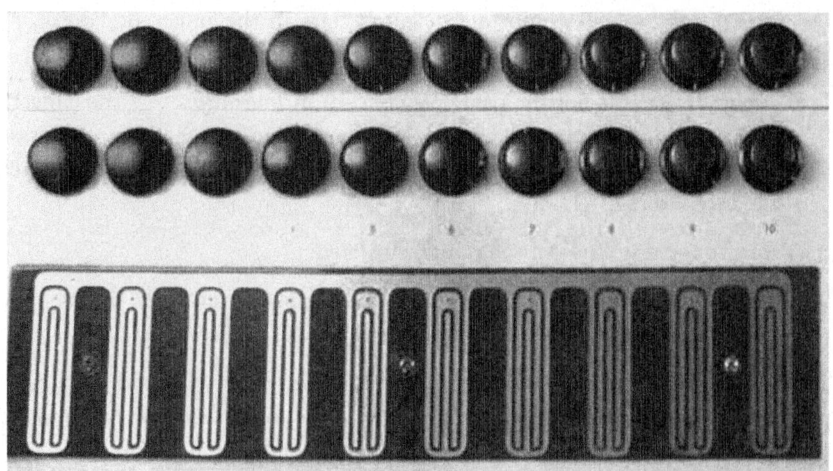

FIGURE 7.8 Buchla 100 touch-controlled voltage source module.

> of tape music and other forms of electronic music that are now familiar. It was an experience with which I was unfamiliar, not only with the sound qualities and juxtapositions of them and the delicate changes within a sound with respect to its timbre, but also the pitch relations which were microtonal and which were not arranged, as I understand it, according to any scale.

The synthesis of sound grains within pitch regions in free intonation is featured in the CloudGenerator program (Roads and Alexander 1995). Composers stipulate frequency band limits within which grains are scattered at random frequencies.

In the use of free intonation, the function of a specific pitch class is less important than register. Since no intonation, scale, or harmonic system is referenced, the significance of pitch is relative and reduced to a localized scope.

FREE VERSUS BARK SCALE

A mention of the Bark scale could be helpful in the context of free intonation. The Bark scale is a psychoacoustical frequency scale corresponding to the boundaries of the first 24 critical bands of hearing (see chapter 3), which range from 0 Hz to 15.5 kHz (Zwicker 1961; Houtsma 1995; Loy 2006).

To convert a given frequency f into the Bark scale, the following formula applies:

$$\text{Bark frequency} = 13 \times \arctan(0.00076 \times f) + 3.5 \times \arctan((f/7500)2)$$

Thus C261.6 = 2.63 Bark and A440 = 4.39 Bark. Clarence Barlow (2007) has demonstrated the Bark scale's utility in comparison to free intonation in musical situations where no traditional scale is desired. By subdividing the Bark scale into as many divisions as desired, one obtains a set of pitches that sound more "balanced" with respect to frequency, in comparison with randomized free intonation. What does "balanced" mean? A cloud of long grains with uniformly random pitches in Bark scale sounds more evenly spread throughout the entire frequency range, as opposed to a cloud of uniformly random pitches in free intonation. Specifically, the free intonation cloud sounds overly emphasized in the midrange of frequencies due to the ear's sensitivity to midrange frequencies. Similarly, a glissando that follows the Bark scale linearly sounds more perceptually linear and balanced than a corresponding simple linear frequency glissando.

Polytonal and polyscalar music

Polytonality refers to the practice of mixing keys in tonal music, a practice that has been explored by composers such as Bartok, Debussy, Ives, Koechlin, and Milhaud, among others. As Grout (1973) points out, we do not necessarily hear two simultaneous keys. In the music of Milhaud, for example, a second key tends to add a color of dissonance to another key. Most of Milhaud's chamber work *Machines agricoles* (1919) is in three keys simultaneously, lending an absurd air to this satirical composition (Haladyna 2008). Such a piece encourages a dual listening mode: One mode focuses on a single instrument, hearing its key clashing with the others; the other mode listens to the ensemble, hearing a mostly dissonant texture that weaves in and out of tonal associations.

The multitracking capabilities of electronic music studios make it trivial to layer tracks on top of one another, where each track corresponds to a particular tonal/harmonic scheme. These same capabilities allow us to mix scales within a single piece to make *polyscalar* music, in the manner of Stravinsky (Tymoczko 2002). The scales may or may not be aligned to the same intonation. An example of polyscalar music using two simultaneous intonations is the composition *Le loup en pierre* (2002) by Clarence Barlow. This piece features two organs: one in meantone temperament and one in 12-note ET. It unfolds as an interplay between common tones leading into extreme dissonance as the two scales diverge.

The challenge of polytonal and polyscalar organization is similar to the challenge of polyrhythm and plurirhythm: the eternal tension between attraction and repulsion. Specifically, do the multiple streams clash (dissonance), or do they come together in harmony (consonance)?

Exotic approaches to pitch organization pose many theoretical and aesthetic challenges, but they are attractive precisely because of their fresh and unfamiliar colors. Of course, any approach to composition based on exotic materials or operations faces the same aesthetic danger: novelty for novelty's sake.

Design of melody in electronic music

With the integration of unpitched noise elements and the rise of timbre and space as structural articulators in electronic music, melody is no longer the driving force that it was in the age of Mozart. This shift does not, however, imply that one should ignore melodic design. As Varèse (1923) aptly pointed out:

> The new composers have not abandoned melody.

Consider the lyrical quality of John Chowning's *Turenas* (1972), the first widely presented composition to make extensive use of frequency modulation (FM) synthesis.

Sound example 7.8. Excerpt of *Turenas* (1972) by John Chowning.

Melody remains a compelling musical component. However, it now finds itself in an aesthetic context alongside other elements. No longer always dominating, the role of pitch has changed from a stable solid substance to a flowing emergent quality. As we previously pointed out, the formation of a pitched tone can only occur when certain microsonic conditions prevail, and when these conditions are not present, pitch becomes unstable and can dissolve entirely.[50] Consider the sequence in sound example 7.9 from *Pictor alpha* (2003).

Sound example 7.9. Excerpt of *Pictor alpha* (2003) by Curtis Roads.

From a general point of view, a melody is a sequence of events in time. Any musical parameter can be sequenced: amplitude, duration, timbre, spatial position, etc. Here we focus on the pitch dimension. Later we look at the more general perspective of melody as parametric sequence.

The literature of melodic analysis is voluminous. Myriad theories and viewpoints abound, drawn from both music theory and musicology on the one hand, and psychoacoustics and music psychology on the other. The goal of this section is to examine melodic pitch design in the context of the electronic medium.

A melody can be defined loosely as a succession of pitches. This shape can be thought of geometrically, as a succession of positive and negative intervallic steps. However, as we explain in a moment, only under certain constraints can we perceive a melodic pattern or shape. It is this perceptually parsable quality that distinguishes what I will call *salient melody* from any possible succession of pitches. In the rest of this section, references to melody are synonymous with salient melody.

Salient melody emerges under certain conditions, constrained by perceptual limits. Obviously, the intervals cannot be imperceptibly tiny, and the tones cannot be inaudibly soft or dangerously loud; these lead to non-salient melodies. Moreover, the durations of the pitches and rests must not be too short or too long. As mentioned in chapter 3, a piece that flirts with the limits of parsable melodic velocity is *Synchronisms Number 6* (1970) for piano and electronic sound by Mario Davidovsky. The electronic part contains numerous bursts of rapid-fire tone sequences. Finally, a melody exists within a musical context, so the texture in which it appears must not be too thick with competing sounds.

Beyond these perceptual constraints, the construction of melody is governed by basic principles. A comprehensible—or as Lerdahl (1988, 2001) would say, *cognitively transparent*—melody can be recognized and memorized; thus it is limited in length. Melodic shapes tend to fall into a small number of general categories, often containing subdivisions or internal repetitions. As Schoenberg (1967) observed:

> Comprehensibility requires limitation of variety, especially if notes . . . follow each other in rapid succession. . . . Delimitation, subdivision, and repetition are most useful. Intelligibility in music seems to be impossible without repetition.

Melodies retain their recognizability when they are transposed. Yet psychoacoustic studies show that melodies in which the pitch classes are constant but the registers are scrambled lose identity (i.e., listeners no longer recognize them as being the same; Shepard 1999).

Melody is morphophoric, as articulated by Luciano Berio (2006):

> A melody . . . is . . . the meeting point for a number of functions of a primary nature (harmony, relative dynamics, timbre, rhythm, and meter) or a secondary nature (for example, a vocal or instrumental melody). A melody always carries with it the trace of these functions or a part of them: it evokes them in a more or less explicit way, or it contradicts them. Polyphony was built and held together on the melody of the cantus firmus or of the tenor. A symphony was constructed on its themes and on the harmonic relations which they signaled and embodied. Arias, lieder, canzoni, and cabalettas were made out of tunes. Fugues were guided by subjects and counter subjects.

Moreover, melody is rhetorical. That is, the precise manner of expression in which it is articulated or enunciated has a crucial impact on how it is received. For example, compare a bland MIDI sequenced score rendition of a Rodgers and Hammerstein melody such as *My Favorite Things* (1959) with the expressive 1961 recording by John Coltrane.

MELODIC TYPES

In traditional classical music, a well-formed melody features stepwise motion up and down the scale. This motion is functional, constrained by voice-leading considerations, and goal-directed, not a random walk. The position of the highest peak (in both pitch and amplitude) is important, usually occurring near the middle or end. Many traditional folk melodies are symmetrical, as they were originally aligned to dance steps or metered poetry. In contrast, in the 20th century, serial techniques and unconventional rhythms resulted in much more variegated melodic patterns, with wild intervallic leaps. In this music, it could be said that the notion of melody per se was replaced by the notion of the row or set.

Conventional classical and popular styles exhibit a great deal of redundancy in melodic patterns (i.e., parts of many melodies are identical). The tendency of composers to borrow or reinvent an existing tune has been long studied by musicologists (Karp 1970). As Thomas Alva Edison (1917) once observed:

> I had an examination made of the themes of 2700 waltzes. In the final analysis, they consisted of 43 themes, worked over in various ways.

One can classify conventional melodic forms into a number of types. For example, Szabolcsi (1965) classified Bach melodies into five types:

1. Sequence—variations on a theme
2. Declamation—rhetorical, using the dramatic impact of speech inflection
3. Passion—concentrated such that it cannot be expanded into a larger form
4. Runner or fantasia—a speech phrase set to music over an ostinato bass
5. Throbbing—a uniform insistent rhythm shapes the melody

If we try to generalize such a typology to all of music, however, we run into difficulties. For just as musical form is infinite in variety, so is melodic form. In a pioneering experiment, Baroni and Jacobini (1978) developed a grammar of melodic patterns in a generative computer program. They sharply delimited their study to the case of Bach chorale melodies, for which they derived 56 rules. The well-publicized experiments of Clarke and Voss (1978) attempted to show that fractal algorithms were more satisfying models of melodic generation than models based on uniform noise. Whether or not this is so (see Nettheim 1992 for a critique of Clarke and Voss), it is obvious that a simple fractal generator can only produce a crude approximation of expert melodic craft. The more sophisticated research of David Cope (1996) pointed out the possibility of extracting *signatures*, or frequently used patterns that signal a composer's style, to generate new melodies using recombinations of elements found in multiple works.

Mechanical pattern generation techniques only go so far, however. The charm of a chorale such as J. S. Bach's *Jesu, Joy of Man's Desiring* (1716) lies in the way that the melody and the harmony deftly exchange places as foreground and background. Melody is not simply sprinkled over the harmony; rather, it articulates a deeper structural function. These kinds of inspired processes are difficult to model algorithmically, because they are based on poorly understood mental processes of attention and expectation in music cognition. Indeed, one of the standard giveaways that a piece has been composed algorithmically is its "correct" but insipid or inane melodic choices. In defense of their scientific model of melody, Baroni and Jacobini (1978) wrote:

> At this point usually composers prick up their ears and start making objections about generated phrases. To such observations we usually answer that these pieces do not have to be beautiful but just correct.

In contrast, the principle of economy of selection means making the inspired choice. So far, inspired choice remains the domain of human talent. (See the preface, chapter 2, and chapter 10 on this topic.)

In traditional textbooks, the construction of melodic pitch patterns is sometimes treated as a sub-problem of harmony. In contrast, electronic music opens up to a vast range of expression when it treats melodic construction from the broader perspective of microtonality, tensions between stable and fluctuating pitches, the pitch-noise continuum, and the harmony-timbre continuum. That is, considering pitch as a variable and emergent quality rather than a stable constant construes the notion of melody within a broader context. A huge opportunity awaits. As Varèse (1925) observed:

> If history has taught us one thing, it is that the composer that one has reproached for absence of melody is perhaps the one that has developed it the most.

Melody is dead; long live melody.

THE SPECIAL CASE OF BASS MELODIES

The bass register is an especially interesting case of melody in electronic music. Whereas in traditional music, the bass line serves the function of reinforcing the meter and harmony, the role of the bass melody now serves a number of additional roles. Among these are the following:

- Articulating the bass register, irrespective of specific pitches and harmonic contexts; a balanced musical mix includes all registers—the entire spectrum
- Signaling the emergence of pitch in an otherwise noisy, unpitched context
- Adding an element of polyphonic interest
- Lending weight at critical climaxes and phrase boundaries through deep bass impact
- Articulating trajectories and shapes (regardless of the specific pitches or their relationship to an intonation or scale)
- Reinforcing or opposing the rhythmic pattern of the surrounding structure

All of these roles play out in my work *Epicurus* (2010).

Sound example 7.10. Excerpt of *Epicurus* (2010) by Curtis Roads.

MELODY GENERALIZED BEYOND PITCH: IMPLICATION-REALIZATION THEORY

The concept of melody as a parsable sequence of contrasting events can be extrapolated to the notion of timbre melody (Schoenberg's *Klangfarbenmelodie*). After World War II, the phenomenon of *integral serialism* extended the same method of organization to other musical parameters, such as dynamics, onset time, duration, and instrument. Theories of integral serialism introduced the notion of a row or series and applied the series to any conceivable parameter space, from concrete parameters like pitch, dynamics, onset time, duration, and instrument, to abstract qualitative parameters like "degree of change" or "degree of indeterminacy" (Roads 2013). The integral serial discourse was eventually supplanted by a set theoretical discourse, bringing with it a box of specific mathematical tools for organizing the sets. Lost in this discourse was the notion of a craft of melody; melody was treated as a byproduct of a generative process.

Eugene Narmour's theory of *implication-realization* serves as a counterweight to the set theoretical discourse. This theory provides analytical support for the generalization of the notion of melody to parameters other than pitch. Implication-realization is one of numerous theories of melody (e.g., Bharucha 1996; Lerdahl 2001) that share many features. As a model of music cognition, implication-realization could be tested through perceptual experiments, but this has not been Narmour's goal.

Implication-realization attempts to explain how a melody causes listeners to generate expectations about how it will proceed. The theory begins with the premise that perception of musical structure is driven by a continuous bottom-up "reality check" that informs our top-down conceptual hypotheses. An example of the latter would be our tendency to immediately hypothesize or extrapolate as to the style, historical period, form, etc., of a piece of music that we are hearing for the first time. As Narmour (1992) explains:

> That we hear the start of a major scale as a major scale evinces top-down processing, since from an ascending initial C-D-E, we envision . . . a continuation. However, were such a C-D-E suddenly to veer off into, say, a quarter-tone system . . . we would accurately perceive these changes since, simultaneously, our bottom-up processing always attends individually to the elements constituting individual parameters.

At the lowest level of implication-realization, any two consecutive notes form an *implicative interval* that implies a subsequent interval. That is, some notes are more probable than others to follow the implicative interval. Narmour codified these probabilities into a set of formal principles based on Gestalt laws of pattern perception: similarity, proximity, and common fate or direction. Human beings use these cues to group events but also to set up expectations. As we have stated before, Gestalt perceptual laws apply not only in tracking pitch sequences but to all perceived phenomena.

Certain patterns imply continuation, reversal, interruption, and closure. For example, the *principle of registral direction* states that a small interval implies an interval in the same registral direction, while a large interval implies a change in registral direction (a return to equilibrium, as it were). Another principle states that a small interval (less than five semitones) implies a similar interval while a large interval (greater than seven semitones) implies a smaller interval. Of course, in real music, parametric processes interact so that, for example, the rhythmic pattern may imply closure when the harmonic pattern does not, which is one way that musical tension is created. According to Narmour, this parametric theory can be applied to any musical element that serves a structural function. Recent psychological studies seem to support a number of Narmour's conjectures (Huron 2006). (For more on the theory of implication-realization, see Narmour 1977, 1984, 1990, 1992.)

This generalization extends beyond melodic sequences. The practice of Western counterpoint began by adding a note in parallel with every melodic note. It later evolved into a formal system of polyphony—combining multiple simultaneous voices. The rules of species counterpoint stipulate different ways of accompanying a pitch melody: the cantus firmus. Viewed more globally, however, most these rules describe patterns of rhythm (doubling, quadrupling, syncopation, etc.) and direction (inverting, imitating, etc.) that can be applied to any type of polyphony, whether pitched or not. Thus we can generalize the notion of counterpoint to include microtonal polyphony, as well as timbral and spatial counterpoint. In certain pieces of electronic music, counterpoint involves the interaction of parallel streams, overlapping granular clouds, or interplay between simultaneous pulse trains.

Pitch as a compositional determinant

Rhythm is primary in certain native musics, for example, that of Central Africa (Arom 1991). In contrast, in Europe, pitch achieved primacy in the early church music and still dominates teaching and practice in the conservatory tradition. It is still common to hear lectures by composers whose discussion of their compositional philosophy is limited to explaining why they chose certain pitches and pitch-related composition processes. Yet there is so much more to composition than this.

In electronic music, pitch tends to be less dominant; it more often plays either an equal role or a subordinate role to other morphophoric parameters such as rhythm, timbre, density, space, and acousmatic reference (Bodin

2004). The obsession with intervals is less pronounced. As Varèse (1952) observed:

> I work especially in the direction of "sound," which for me is the solid basis for music, my raw element. The intellectualism of the interval has nothing to do with our time and the new concepts.

As Henry Cowell (1928) observed:

> One key to a comprehension of Varèse's music is the fact that he is more interested in finding a note that will sound a certain way in a certain instrument and will "sound" in the orchestral fabric, than he is in just what position the note occupies in the harmony. . . . One must consider that besides the harmony of notes, which with Varèse is somewhat secondary, there is at any given time a harmony of tone-qualities, each of which is calculated to sound out through the orchestra . . . one finds that dynamic nuances on the same note, or repeated notes, often take the place of melody. He very frequently does away with melody entirely by having only repeated tones for certain passages. Removing from the listener's ear that which it is accustomed to follow most closely, sometimes to the exclusion of everything else, naturally induces a keener awareness of other musical elements such as rhythm and dynamics.

Or as Robert Morgan (1979b) stated succinctly about Varèse's 1925 composition *Intégrales*:

> With regard to pitch, there is virtually no development.

The early electronic music of Stockhausen is a classic example of the integration of pitched and non-pitched elements. *Gesang der Jünglinge* (1956) juxtaposed sung serial melodies and chords against such elements as "sine complex showers," "impulse complex showers," filtered and broadband noise, and "chords" of narrow noise bands. His *Kontakte* (1960) takes the contrasts even further. At any given instant, Stockhausen pits noise against pitch, fixed against moving, close against far, short against long, high against low register, soft against loud—always in sharp relief. This unrelenting counterpoint of contrasts marks *Kontakte* as an especially inventive composition, as Stockhausen discovered oppositions that were never before articulated.

Theodore Lotis's evocative *Arioso Dolente/Beethoven op.110* (2002) repurposes Beethoven's tonal opus (piano sonata number 31) by time-stretching it and juxtaposing it with wavering pitches and granular free-intonation pitch cascades.

Sound example 7.11. Excerpt of *Arioso Dolente/Beethoven op.110* (2002) by Theodore Lotis.

A piece in which pitch plays a subordinate role is the composition *Sud* (1985) by Jean-Claude Risset. *Sud* contains a pitch structure based mainly on the whole-tone scale, but the role of this scale is secondary in the overall scheme of the work, which is dominated by the interplay of timbral, spatial, and acousmatic oppositions, such as the contrast between closely miked ocean waves and reverberant clusters of inharmonic sinusoids.

Composition has seen an evolution from pitch-centric theories to more polycentric ones, such as the spectral school of composition. In today's electronic music, other elements, including timbre, density, noise, rhythm, space, and acousmatic reference, compete with pitch as the focus of musical interest. Listen to the treatment of granulated piano tones combined with concrète elements (e.g., train sound) in Laurent Delforge's *Dragonfly* (2011).

Sound example 7.12. Excerpt of *Dragonfly* (2011) by Laurent Delforge. 

Conclusion

To summarize this chapter, we have examined the illusion of pitch from both scientific and aesthetic perspectives and challenged the traditional view of it as a fixed, frozen quantity. Rather, pitch can be manipulated as a continuous and freely flowing substance. A fragile epiphenomenon of regular particle emission, pitch can be continuously deformed through mutations of its constituent grains. A comprehensive theory of pitch must take this fragility into account, as sounds can at any time coalesce, mutate, or disintegrate into noise or nothingness. Microtonal harmonies can become so complex that they mutate into timbre and texture. With so many pieces in free intonation, it is clear that pitch need not always be aligned to the grid of a fixed scale or intonation. As Xenakis (1995) mused:

> The scales are a basis, especially for instrumental music. But what is important is what you do with the sounds, the instruments, how you [combine them] and their evolution. The scales are not so important as they used to be. . . . This is why I made a theoretical study [of scales using sieve theory], because it was the end of them.

Varèse (1965b) went further:

> When I was eleven, I wrote an opera on Jules Verne's *Martin Paz*, in which I was already involved with sonority and unusual sounds. I detested the piano and all conventional instruments, and when I first learned the scales, my only reaction was: "Well, they all sound alike."

The scales that Varèse the boy reacted to were all 12-note ET. The electronic medium facilitates microtonal composition. With software synthesis in particular, any tuning is as easy to achieve as exactly as any other tuning.

Finally, from a functional perspective, pitch is no longer the dominant determinant in musical organization; it shares the stage with other musical parameters and can play subordinate roles. As Paul Lansky (quoted in Perry 1995) surmised:

> Telling complicated pitch stories is something that [traditional instrumental] performers do well, while machines have capabilities to create worlds and landscapes that have quite different agendas.

In general, the concept of pitch is much enlarged in electronic music by its application in the contexts of microtonal scales, the pitch-noise continuum, the harmony-timbre continuum, and polytonal and polyscalar combinations.

Sound example 7.13. Excerpt from the finale of *Strasser 60* (2009) performed live by Earl Howard.

8

Articulating space

To project in space is to choreograph sound: directing sources and animating movement. Recorded sounds articulate the space in which they were captured, but we can also compose virtual spatial characteristics for sounds. Immersing sound in deep reverberation, we bathe listeners in its lush ambience. With increasing use of *pluriphonic* or multichannel/multi-loudspeaker sound systems, we can articulate points, lines, chords (geometric forms), and spatial clouds in physical space (Roads et al. 2013).

Reasoning about spatial relationships is fundamental to human intelligence (Piaget and Inhelder 1967). Spatial perception is tightly integrated with both thought and action (Blauert 1997; Kendall 2010). Our body moves in space and must be aware at all times of its position in accordance with everything around it. We manipulate physical objects in space. Our mind needs to be able to recall (through spatial memory) the location of innumerable things, whether in physical space (e.g., our home) or virtual space (e.g., the location of a file). We plan and organize the spatial arrangement of objects in our home and in our garden.

We not only memorize and reason spatially, we feel it. Spatial experiences can be emotionally moving, including "breathtaking views," but also looking over a cliff or parachuting out of an airplane. To enter the Roman Pantheon or any sacred space can be an emotional experience. The sensations of intimate and vast spaces are especially powerful, as Denis Smalley (1991) observed:

> Our attitude to sounds which emerge into, intrude on, break into, close in on, or comfortably inhabit our space can create divergent emotional experiences: confrontation, threat, solace, and so on. If, on the other hand, the listener feels drawn outwards into an environment beyond the immediate listening space . . . then a further set of affective responses is activated: for example, distance and spaciousness can invoke feelings of insignificance faced with vastness, loneliness, peace-of-mind, calm, etc.

Visually, we respond to inspired dance choreography and all manner of sports involving the movement of the body in space. By cognitive analogy, the movement of sound reconnects us to the realm of kinesthetic experience.

Decades of experimentation have proven that spatial choreography is intrinsically interesting and meaningful to audiences. Listeners respond intuitively to creative spatial choreography, contributing to the meaningfulness of a composition. As a result, spatialization in the 21st century has assumed a newfound significance. Indeed, the spatial structure of a composition may be of equal or greater aesthetic importance than its organization in terms of pitch, rhythm, or timbre. As James Dashow (2013) observed:

> One could say that up to now, musical composition has been largely a question of What happens When. With spatialization, composition now becomes What happens When and Where. As more work is done to refine spatialization concepts and discover new modes of musical thinking in terms of space, it becomes clear that spatialization is our genuinely new contribution to musical art.

Yet while pitch and rhythm have been codified and schematized for centuries, there is little formal theory with respect to spatial relationships. Even without a formal theory, the practice of spatialization is becoming more sophisticated. This is due to increased awareness of the importance of spatial presentation in electronic music. Out of this awareness has come greater investment in pluriphonic sound systems and increasingly elaborate software for spatial sound manipulation.

As spatial theories (such as the one in this book) emerge, we must take into account that spatial perception is a limiting factor, even for experts with trained ears. As in our perception of other dimensions of music, the ear's ability to perceive spatial configurations and track changes in position is not unlimited. Blauert (1997) is largely an account of these limitations.

A substantial section of this chapter traces the history of sound spatialization, starting with instrumental/vocal music, and continuing into the digital age. The rest of the chapter outlines the scope and dimensions of spatialization as a compositional issue. Specially, we discuss spatialization on multiple timescales and the virtual/physical space distinction. The next sections focus on important topics of relevance to composition, including the use of spatial depth, audio cinematics, pluriphonic sound projection, the vertical dimension, sound rotation, superdirectional sound beams, and the growing field of immersive sound technology. The final section, "Articulating space," centers on a table of spatial oppositions: a basic set of possible spatial gestures.

History of spatialization in instrumental/vocal music

Historically, an awareness of the spatial and architectural possibilities of music came slowly to the fore of musical practice. The earliest published works using space as a compositional element date from the 1500s (e.g., Willaert's works for two spatially separated organs and choirs at the Basilica San Marco in Venice). Beyond this is a tradition of *polychoral* music, in which an ensemble or chorus is divided into two or more groups (Apel 1972). For example, W. A. Mozart wrote serenades for spatially separated orchestras (K. 239 and K. 286). Hector Berlioz (*Requiem*, 1837) and Gustav Mahler (*Symphony No. 2*, 1895) wrote for multiple orchestras and choruses, some of which were offstage. Similarly, Charles Ives's *Unanswered Question* (ca. 1906) used spatial separation of three groups of instruments as a structural focus of the composition (Zvonar 2005). After these experiments, however, there is little documentation of spatial techniques in composition until the post-WWII era.

The composer Henry Brant took up the gauntlet left by Ives. Starting in 1950, he began writing instrumental music in which the position of the performers in the hall, as well as onstage, was an essential factor in the composing scheme. Brant's *Antiphony I* (1953) called for five spatially separated orchestras. His catalog comprises over 100 such works, each for a different instrumentation, each requiring a different spatial deployment in a hall, and with maximum distances between groups prescribed in every case (Jaffe 2005). As Brant observed (Brant 1967; Harley 1998), and I paraphrase, spatialization serves fundamental compositional functions:

> Spatial separation clarifies the texture; this is particularly important if the music consists of several different layers located in the same pitch register.
>
> Spatial separation is equivalent to the separation by register or timbre. That is, just as one can hear separately layers of music that are located in different registers, one can also differentiate layers that originate from different points in space.
>
> Spatial separation facilitates greater complexity in the music; more unrelated elements can be heard simultaneously.

Other composers, such as Stockhausen, Xenakis, and Serocki, occasionally deployed spatially separated instrumentalists in the 1950s and 1960s (Harley 1998). For example, Stockhausen's *Gruppen* (1957) and *Carré* (1960) featured three and four spatially separated orchestras, respectively. Gérard Grisey's *Tempus ex machina* (1979) featured six spatially separated percussionists (Grisey 1987). These experiments were exceptional, however. Composed spatialization remains something of a novelty in instrumental/vocal literature and was never absorbed into pedagogy or common practice.

History of spatialization in electronic music

When we record a sound source, we inevitably capture the spatial environment in which it is recorded. This is because recorded sound is a double convolution; it represents the convolution of an acoustic event with the impulse response of the space in which the event takes place, further convolved by the impulse response of the microphone setup and recording device (Roads 1997b). Early recordings were monaural; today, stereo and surround recording are the norm.[51] It suffices to say that the choice of where and how to record a given sound allows for many technical and aesthetic options. Thus a recording can be *spatially composed* through the choice of recording space and the placement of microphones (Barrett 2008).

Dual to the microphone is the loudspeaker. The invention of the loudspeaker in the 1920s can be compared to the invention of the electric light bulb. Suddenly it was possible to project sonic energy in spaces small and large, at any angle or intensity. But the use of loudspeakers, in movie theaters, stadiums, railroad stations, phonographs, and home radios, remained plain and functional. Only by the 1950s, with the dawn of the first theories of electronic music, did composers begin to exploit the aesthetic possibilities of sound projection via loudspeakers.

Electroacoustic technology (amplifiers, loudspeakers, tape recorders, etc.) greatly expanded the potential of sound spatialization, permitting recorded spaces to be convolved with loudspeaker projection in physical halls. This section gives capsule descriptions of historically important examples of spatialization in electronic music, from the 1950s to the present.

ARTIFICIAL REVERBERATION (1930–1970)

The lush spatial effect of artificial reverberation is characteristic of the electronic medium. Early recordings used a real physical space—an echo chamber—to produce reverberation. Sounds were played into the echo chamber over a loudspeaker, and a microphone picked up the sound of the room. The echo chamber at Abbey Road Studios, London, was originally built in 1931 (figure 8.1).

Spring reverberators in electric organs date to the 1940s (Hammond 1941) and were later common in guitar amplifiers. In the 1950s, Elektro-Mess-Technik (EMT) introduced the massive (2.4 meters long, 200 kg) model 140 plate reverberator, a higher-quality reverberator renowned for its concert hall-like sound (figure 8.2). Plate reverberators consist of a large, thin piece of sheet metal suspended from a steel frame by springs. An electrical transducer mounted on the center of the suspended plate induces plate vibration, while pickups on the plate capture the effect. Equipped with vacuum tube electronics, these units were installed in early electronic music studios like the historic WDR studio in Cologne, where Stockhausen realized many of his electronic pieces, and the Columbia-Princeton Electronic Music Studio. Many of the early pieces from the Columbia-Princeton Studio are suffused with plate reverberation, which was

FIGURE 8.1 Echo chamber at Abbey Road Studios with tiled wall and pillars to enhance sound reflection.

FIGURE 8.2 EMT 140 plate reverberator.

then an exotic technique. A typical example is *Out of Into* (1972) by Bulent Arel and Daria Semegen.

Sound example 8.1. Excerpt of *Out of Into* (1972) by Bulent Arel and Daria Semegen.

The classic EMT 140 impulse response is accurately modeled by contemporary software reverberators and still marries well with electronic sonorities.

SPATIALIZATION OF MUSIQUE CONCRÈTE (1951–1952)

The first concert of musique concrète in 1950 involved a live element, using multiple turntables mixed in real time (Harrison 1998). By 1951, Pierre Schaeffer and his colleagues shifted to the medium of magnetic tape for concert playback. However, even in this fixed medium of tape playback, a device called a *space potentiometer* introduced live spatialization. The space potentiometer consisted of four metal hoops manipulated by a sound projectionist (Pierre Henry) onstage, which distributed a soundtrack to any of the four loudspeakers in the hall (Poullin 1957). This spatially moving track accompanied another four tracks that were distributed to individual loudspeakers (Manning 2004).

CAGE AND TUDOR'S SOUND INSTALLATIONS (1951–1973)

In the 1950s, John Cage created a number of installations involving multiple sources of sound. In these sound art installations, spatialization is achieved by having each member of the audience navigate freely through the gallery; in effect, each visitor creates their own performance. For example, Cage's *Imaginary Landscape No. 4* (1951) deploys 12 radio receivers. *Williams Mix* (1952), realized at the New York studios of Louis and Bebe Barron, featured eight monaural tapes, each playing through its own loudspeaker (Zvonar 2005). Together with David Tudor, Cage realized *Variations IV* (1965) in which multiple tape machines played back from locations inside and outside a Los Angeles gallery. Other multiple-source installations included Cage's *HPSCHD* (1969) and Tudor's *Rainforest* (1973), which featured multiple sound transducers in settings in which the audience circulated freely.

STOCKHAUSEN'S *GESANG DER JÜNGLINGE* (1956) AND *KONTAKTE* (1960)

Karlheinz Stockhausen's composition *Gesang der Jünglinge* was projected in a 1956 concert over five groups of loudspeakers in the auditorium of the West German Radio (Stockhausen 1961). His opus *Kontakte*, realized in 1960, was performed with the Telefunken T9 four-track tape recorder (Stockhausen 1968).

THE PHILIPS PAVILION, BRUSSELS (1958)

Long before the technology was available, Edgard Varèse (1936) dreamed of composing sounds moving in space. In 1958, he finally had a chance to realize this dream with his classic tape music composition *Poème Electronique*. This work, together with Iannis Xenakis's *Concret PH*, was projected over 400 loudspeakers[52] through an 11-channel sound system installed on the curved walls of the Philips Pavilion (figure 8.3). In a letter to Xenakis, Varèse (1958) observed:

> Since my music is based principally on the movement of unrelated sound masses, I have always sensed the need to move them simultaneously at different speeds and always hoped for this effect. And yet such a thing is possible. The very complex electronic [spatializer] device of the Philips Pavilion has demonstrated this in a striking way.

The Philips Pavilion was designed by Xenakis for Le Corbusier at the Brussels World's Fair (Xenakis 1971, 1992, 2008; Treib 1996). Amazingly, the shape of the building is a direct mapping of the glissandi in the score of Xenakis's *Metastasis* (1954) for string orchestra. For the spatialization of sounds, the Philips engineers

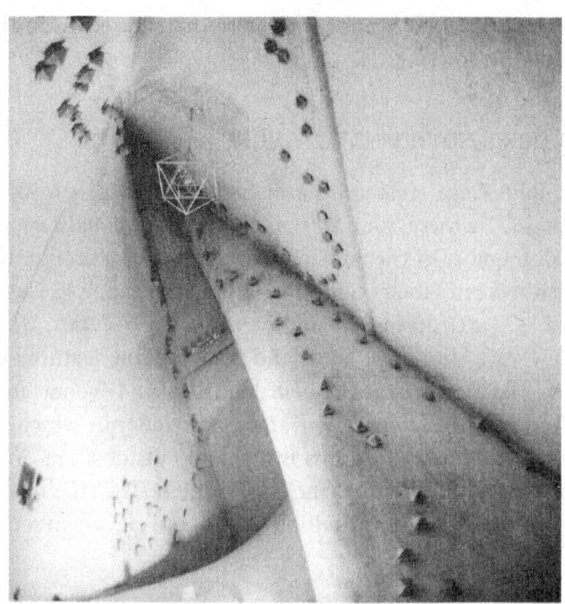

FIGURE 8.3 View, looking upward, of the inside of the Philips Pavilion. The objects on the surfaces are high-frequency loudspeakers in clusters, the patterns designed by Xenakis. Low-frequency loudspeakers were installed on the ground. From Treib (1996).

built a switching system so that the sounds would travel on programmed "sound routes" during the performance (figure 8.4).

The *Poème Electronique* was accompanied by a film of images chosen by Le Corbusier. Some two million visitors experienced this sound-and-light spectacle (Ouelette 1989).

VORTEX CONCERTS, SAN FRANCISCO AND BRUSSELS (1957–1959)

The Vortex Concerts (1957–1959) at the Morrison Planetarium in San Francisco featured visuals by Jordan Belson and music by Stockhausen, Ussachevsky, Takemitsu, Berio, and others projected via 38 loudspeakers (Horton 1996; Zvonar 2005).

> The elements of Vortex are sound, light, color, and movement in their most comprehensive theatrical expression. These audio-visual combinations are presented in a circular, domed theater equipped with special projectors and sound systems. In Vortex there is no separation of audience and stage or screen; the entire domed area becomes a living theater of sound and light. With the thirty-eight high-fidelity speakers, actual movement and gyration of sound was made possible by means of a special rotary console. Utilizing the elaborate Planetarium lighting system along with special projectors, coordinated full-scale visual effects gave promise of an exciting new form of theater. The premiere of Vortex on May 28, 1957 to a capacity audience established this audio-visual experiment as a true theater of the future with a

FIGURE 8.4 Playback and spatial switching system in the Philips Pavilion control room based on 35 mm sprocketed magnetic tape (*Philips Technical Review*).

> potential for directly reaching an audience with unique sensory experiences not based on the customary story, music, or entertainers. Vortex is direct. There is no age, linguistic nor aesthetic barrier to experiencing Vortex.
>
> —PROGRAM NOTES FOR VORTEX 4 (QUOTED IN HORTON 1996)

For the visuals, several projectors of various types were operating simultaneously so images from a variety of sources could be superimposed. Vortex ran for 100 performances including a stint at the 1958 Brussels World's Fair (Brougher 2005).

REVERBERATION BY DIGITAL MEANS (1961–PRESENT)

Dr. Manfred R. Schroeder of the Bell Telephone Laboratories was the first to implement an artificial reverberation algorithm on a digital computer (Schroeder 1961, 1962; Schroeder and Logan 1961). His designs used a combination of multiple time delays, filters, and mixing to achieve the illusion of sound scattering within a room. Schroeder (1970) later extended his original reverberation algorithms to incorporate a *multi-tap delay line* to simulate the early reflections that are heard in a hall before the outset of the fused reverberant sound. Thus to simulate a particular concert hall, a straightforward way to improve the basic model is to graft the measured early reflection response of the hall onto the generic global reverberator.

In Schroeder's time, computers were slow and reverberation algorithms absorbed hours of computation time. Modern reverberators based on Schroeder's model run in real time. (The Lexicon line of products such as the 300L and the

PCM96 are classic examples of Schroeder-inspired reverberators.) Control knobs and buttons on their front panels let musicians dial up a variety of effects. As we will see in the section on virtual spaces, digital reverberators have evolved considerably since Schroeder's era.

AUDIUM THEATER, SAN FRANCISCO (1960S–PRESENT)

In the 1960s, Stanley Shaff and Douglas McEachern mounted a series of concerts based on the notion of the *space audium*: "An electronic music concert . . . conceived and executed as movement through space." This eventually led to the construction of a special AUDIUM Theater in San Francisco that has been giving regular spatial music concerts since 1967 (AUDIUM 2008).

ENVIRONMENTAL SOUNDSCAPES IN FERRARI'S *PRESQUE RIEN* (1967–1970)

Portable field recorders enable composers to integrate natural spatial environments (both interior and exterior) into their work. Interior recordings bring us into living spaces, while recording the open space of the outdoors environment allows us to enter the realm of *free field acoustics*, characterized by a total lack of reflections. Of course, there can also be reflections outside, but the distance cue becomes especially important as we hear the natural foreground/background of the soundstage. As mentioned in chapter 4, Walter Ruttmann's *Weekend* (1930) pioneered this genre, depicting the urban soundscape of Berlin. Two decades later, musique concrète used natural sounds, but typically in short clips spliced together rapidly. In contrast, Luc Ferrari's breakthrough composition *Presque rien ou le lever du jour au bord de la mer* (1967–1970) began as a long, continuous recording of environmental sounds at a Yugoslavian beach. An inveterate recordist, Ferrari gathered sounds from around the world and integrated them into his compositions, creating amazing fictional soundscapes by layering one environment on top of another. By now, soundscape music is an established genre practiced by many artists (Schafer 1977).

SPATIAL MUSIC AT EXPO 70 OSAKA

EXPO 70 featured three major spatial sound systems. First, Karlheinz Stockhausen played his electronic music for 183 days over 55 Siemens loudspeakers distributed in seven rings on the interior surface of the geodesic dome of the German pavilion at EXPO 70 in Osaka (Stockhausen 1971a). Meanwhile, over in the Japanese Steel pavilion, Iannis Xenakis performed his 12-channel electroacoustic composition *Hibiki Hana Ma* on a system of 800 loudspeakers distributed in 250 groups around the audience, over their heads and under their seats (Matossian 1986; Xenakis 2008). At the same time, the Pepsi Cola pavilion at EXPO 70 featured a dome with 37 loudspeakers that could be driven by up to 32 sources: 16 line sources and 16 microphones. The project was curated by Experiments in Art and Technology (EAT), an organization promoting collaborations between artists and engineers.

MARTIRANO'S SAL-MAR CONSTRUCTION (1971–1972)

Beginning in 1969, the composer Salvatore Martirano and a team of engineers at the University of Illinois built a complex apparatus out of digital circuits (not a general-purpose computer in the conventional sense) called the Sal-Mar Construction. This interactive device controlled a custom analog synthesizer and distributed the sound in 24 channels to up to 250 Poly-Planar (styrofoam) loudspeakers suspended at various heights from the ceilings of venues.

XENAKIS'S *POLYTOPE DE CLUNY*, PARIS (1972–1973)

A 12-channel sound system animated Xenakis's computer-controlled sound-and-light spectacle *Polytope de Cluny*, projected on the interior of the ancient Cluny Museum in Paris (Xenakis 1975, 1992; 2008). The spectacle (figure 8.5) ran for 16 months and was experienced by over 200,000 people, including eight times by the author of this book, upon whom it made a deep impression.[53]

Sound example 8.2. Excerpt of *Polytope de Cluny* (1972) by Iannis Xenakis. 

FIGURE 8.5 Laser projections and flash-light scaffolding of the *Polytope de Cluny*.

THE ORCHESTRA OF LOUDSPEAKERS (1973–1974)

In early concerts of electronic music, the designs of the theatrical presentation and spatial projection were often neglected. As François Bayle (1989) observed:

> A theater, an empty stage, unflattering lighting, a few loudspeakers placed sadly in the corners, an accumulation of heterogeneous technical equipment, this is the caricature of an acousmatic concert on a small budget, thrown together hastily the day of the concert, thus revealing the difficulty of being true to experimental initiatives, as well as the mediocrity of the dialog between art and technique.

Recognizing the need for more organized design of public concerts, Christian Clozier and his colleagues at the Groupe de Musique Expérimentale de Bourges (GMEB) developed the idea of projecting sound over an orchestra of dozens of loudspeakers onstage and around the audience (Clozier 1997, 2001). This concept was first realized in the elaborate Gmebaphone, an orchestra of loudspeakers first heard in concert in 1973, with spatial projection performed manually by composers. The first concert of a similar configuration called the Acousmonium—an assemblage of dozens of sound projectors onstage by the Groupe de Recherches Musicales (GRM)—took place at the Espace Cardin, Paris, in 1974 (Bayle 1989, 1993). As we see in the next section, the idea of an orchestra of loudspeakers has since taken hold around the world.

COMPUTER-CONTROLLED SPATIALIZATION (1971–PRESENT)

Edward Kobrin's HYBRID synthesizer consisted of a digital computer controlling an analog synthesizer. As early as 1971, it was distributing sound to 16 independent loudspeakers in the composer's living room in Urbana, Illinois (Kobrin 1977). John Chowning (1971) was the first to develop software for spatialization with Doppler shift (simulation of angular velocity as a sound moves around a listener) in conjunction with a purely digital reverberator modeled after Schroeder's original design (Schroeder 1962). Chowning showcased 360-degree quadraphonic spatialization in his composition *Turenas* (1972), which also pioneered the use of frequency modulation (FM) synthesis.

The first hardware digital synthesizer to exploit pluriphony was the SSSP sound distribution system at the University of Toronto (Federkow et al. 1978). In 1987, researchers at Luciano Berio's Tempo Reale studio (Florence) developed a computer-based sound distribution system called Trails that could distribute sound to up to 32 audio channels, combining preprogrammed and real-time spatial patterns (Bernardini and Otto 1989). Since then, a variety of other computer-controlled multichannel sound spatialization systems have been developed, including the Halaphon (Freiburg) used by Luigi Nono, GRAME's Sinfonie (Lyon), the BEAST (Birmingham), Simon Fraser University's AudioBox, the Recombinant Media Lab's Cinechamber (San Francisco), the ZKM Klangdom

(Karlsruhe), and our own Creatophone and AlloSphere (Santa Barbara), among many others.

The market for spatial sound systems continues to grow and a multitude of software applications and plug-ins are available. At the same time, spatial sound has invaded the world of electronic art; it is now common to find gallery installations and sculptures that deploy distributed loudspeakers. The physicality of spatial sound is often a theme in these works. Multichannel sound systems have also become integral to many popular entertainment spectacles. For example, some cinemas are installing immersive sound systems to complement their 3D video projection systems (Jackson 2010). In outdoor venues, pluriphonic sound has been featured theatrically with accompanying light and water spectacles (McLean 1999).

MICHEL REDOLFI'S UNDERWATER CONCERTS (1981–PRESENT)

In the late 1970s, the Center for Music Experiment and the Scripps Institute of Oceanography at the University of California, San Diego, sponsored research by Michel Redolfi on broadcasting music underwater, a unique spatial environment. In 1981, he presented *Sonic Waters in the Pacific*, the first concert in history where music was played underwater for a large audience floating on the surface or submerged with scuba gear. Sound behaves differently in the medium of water, traveling 4.3 times faster, and waves within the water modulate the sound. Hearing is also changed, as the ear drums do not function underwater. Since that time, Redolfi and others have continued to conduct musical experiments in aquatic spatial environments like pools, coves, lakes, and the ocean (Redolfi 1991).

Spatialization on multiple timescales

In early electronic music, many compositions were characterized by a macroscale spatial perspective, such as a uniform blanket of reverberation applied to the entire composition. The lushly reverberated *Elektronische Impressionen* (1978) of Oskar Sala comes to mind. In other works, the spatial impression is more variegated, with reverberation added more selectively, following the contours of particular mesostructures. For example, Stockhausen's *Kontakte* (1960) contrasted sounds in foreground/background relationships on a timescale of phrases.

Going further, each and every sound can occupy a unique space. Compare the flat perspective of series of monaural electronic tones to a cascade of sounds, each emanating from a unique three-dimensional space, adding the dimension of depth to a phrase. As a phrase unfolds, the position of each sound object articulates a varying topography. Functional oppositions between stationary and moving objects articulate contrapuntal relations.

Spatial organization can be extended even further, down to the micro layers of sonic structure. Truax (1999b) used a spatializer to send each of eight granular streams to its own loudspeaker. Going further, our Cloud Generator program for granular synthesis (Roads and Alexander 1995) positioned each grain in a cloud of hundreds at an individual point in space. This is one example of *per-grain effects* in granular synthesis (Roads 2012). Per-grain effects enabled a new and interesting musical transformation called *granular spatial scattering.* This effect sprays a sound spatially in granular form, while leaving all other aspects of the sound (pitch, duration, timbre) intact. The sound can be panned or scattered randomly in space, creating spatial decorrelation. Directional swarming and flocking algorithms, borrowed from computer graphics, can also be applied to granular spatialization (Kim-Boyle 2005). The resulting sound cloud has a three-dimensional width, depth, and spaciousness.

Our Creatovox synthesizer (De Campo and Roads 2003) not only scattered each grain to a unique location, it also reverberated each grain individually (with different reverberation times) over an octophonic sound system in real time. Per-grain reverberation is effective when grain densities are low (no more than a few grains per second). However, as the grain density increases, the texture tends to fuse into a Gestalt impression of global reverberation (Roads 2001b).

NEW METHODS OF SPATIALIZATION BASED ON SOUND ANALYSIS

Recent experiments have led to new ways of spatializing sound on multiple timescales. These rely on spectrum analysis techniques that decompose a given sound into a *time-frequency* (TF) *representation.* This representation can be parsed by software that searches for specific features in the TF representation, such as transient events, specific frequency bands, harmonically related components, loud components, short components, etc. The events are then spatialized according to a script of rules.

For example, *dictionary-based pursuit* (DBP) decomposes a sound into a TF representation—essentially a collection of grains that are localized in time and frequency (Sturm et al. 2006, 2008, 2009).

We can parse the TF representation in many ways according to the different properties of the grains, and each parsing provides a basis for a novel spatialization. For example, all transient grains could be scattered in one way, while long grains could be scattered in another. Our Scatter application (figure 8.6) is a proof of the concept of spatialization based on TF analysis (Mcleran et al. 2008).

Another analysis technique that could enable such a strategy is the *tracking phase vocoder* and its extension, *spectral modeling synthesis* (SMS) (Serra and Smith 1990; Serra 1997; Roads 1996a). SMS reduces the analysis data into a *deterministic* component (modeled by sine waves) and a *stochastic* component (modeled by filtered noise). Like DBP, the TF representation generated by SMS can be parsed according to audio features that can be spatialized independently according to a script.

Even basic Fast Fourier Transform (FFT) spectrum analysis data can be used to control spatialization by assigning, for example, each of 64 frequency bands to a separate virtual location (Torchia and Lippe 2004).

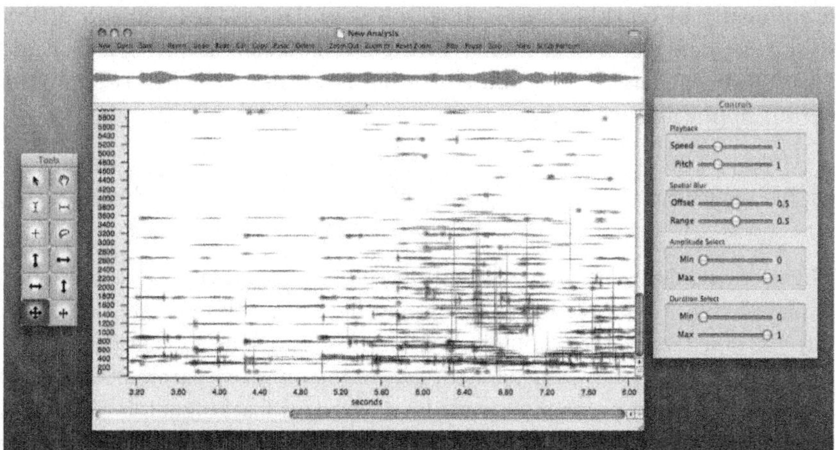

FIGURE 8.6 Screenshot from Scatter created to provide an interface for visualization and real-time transformation using dictionary-based TF decompositions. The time-domain resynthesis is shown at top, and the model wivigram is shown below this. A palette of tool icons on the left allows one to select groups of atoms for transformations including spatial "scattering."

These are all experimental methods. Analysis-based spatialization methods face both technical and aesthetic challenges in terms of choosing appropriate sounds for applying them, as well as issues of interactive control. Effective use of these techniques will likely require a great deal of testing and tuning.

Virtual spaces

Sound spatialization presents two facets: the virtual and the physical. In the studio, composers spatialize sounds by means of tape echo feedback, delays, spectral filtration, phase shift (for image displacement, widening, and narrowing), convolution, granulation, panning, Doppler shift (for simulation of moving sounds), and reverberation. These transformations give the illusion of sounds inhabiting and moving in imaginary virtual environments. This section looks at tape echo feedback, convolution, and pitch-shifted reverberation.

TAPE ECHO FEEDBACK

Tape echo feedback (TEF) is a classic tape-studio approach to sound transformation that creates a ping-pong panning echo effect, but it can also lead to a transmutation as the original input sound is submerged in distant feedback. There are many variations on TEF, but the classic version requires an analog tape recorder with a continuously variable speed control (known as varispeed). TEF was first developed by Werner Meyer-Eppler (1949, 1954) and his colleagues at the Cologne studio (Enkel and Schutz 1954) and was featured prominently in Stockhausen's *Kontakte* (1960). Despite the renown of this work, few composers explored it further. A notable exception is Bernard Parmegiani, who used TEF as the background canvas for the first two minutes of his *Capture éphémère* (1967).

Sound example 8.3. Excerpt of *Capture éphémère* (1967) by Bernard Parmegiani.

TEF is central technique in my recent composition *Then* (2014). In TEF, a sound is played into a tape recorder. This recording is then immediately fed back into the tape recorder, possibly filtered and mixed with new incoming sounds. A variety of effects can be generated, depending on many parameters. One of the most important parameters is the level of the feedback signal. If the level of the feedback is low, then a faint series of echoes are heard, corresponding to the distance between the record and playback heads and the tape speed. If the feedback is moderate, the echoes may be louder than the new incoming signal. As the feedback is increased, the entire circuit goes into self-sustaining oscillation, a rich shimmering sound. Analog tape hiss is an integral component of the classic sound. Varispeed control means that, as the feedback process is occurring, both the pitch and the echo rate can also be changed. This leads to dramatic accelerations and decelerations. Finally, by inserting variable filters into the circuit, the spectral bandwidth of the feedback can also be altered continuously, for example, from a broadband texture, to tuned noise, to a resonant sine wave (figure 8.7).

TEF is inherently unstable. The instability derives from the nature of feedback systems, which, in seconds, can explode into self-sustaining feedback loops with huge increases in amplitude. Thus TEF requires two people, as it requires careful control of feedback levels, as well as manual control of tape speed and variable filter settings, all in real time (Manning 2004). In musical applications, the goal of tape echo feedback is to surf on the edges of self-oscillation (a zone of morphosis) while also applying damping forces to the feedback process through spectrum shaping and control of the amount of feedback.

Sound example 8.4. Tape echo feedback experiment by Curtis Roads with an impulse generator as the source. From a work entitled *Then*.

A related technique is the method of multiple tape delay, where a sound is fed to a series of interconnected tape recorders, resulting in a multiple-stage delay line. *I of IV* (1966) by Pauline Oliveros is a classic example of this method.

Sound example 8.5. Excerpt of *I of IV* (1966) by Pauline Oliveros.

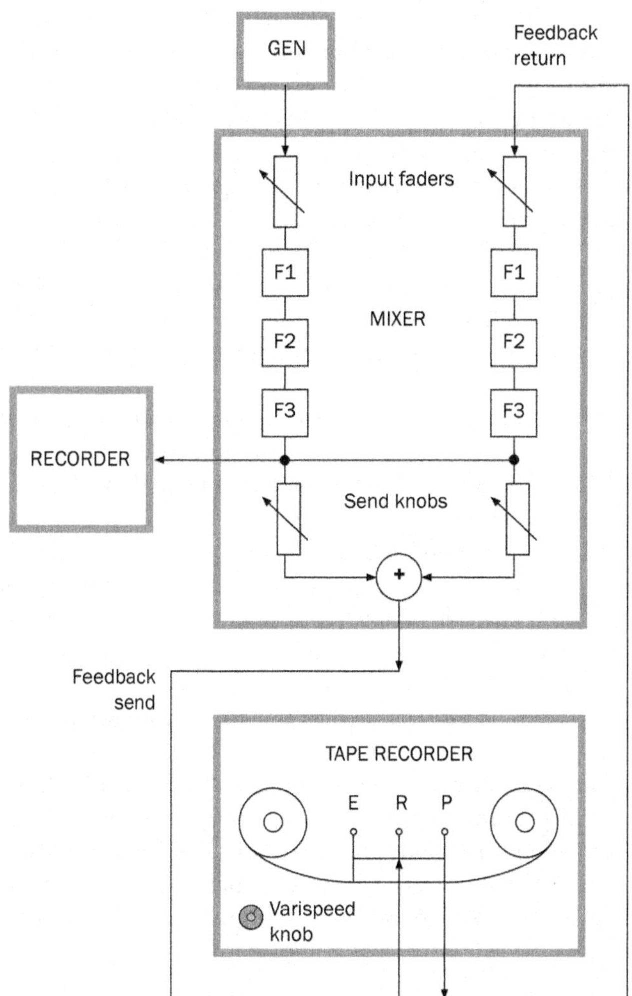

FIGURE 8.7 Tape echo feedback circuit as used by the author. GEN is an impulse generator or other sound source. F1, F2, and F3 are filters. E is erase head, R is record head, P is playback head. Note that in practice, all signals are two-channel. In order to create a ping-pong echo effect, the left send goes to the right input on the tape recorder.

NEWER REVERBERATORS

The virtual space of artificial reverberation is a staple of electronic music, putting otherwise spatially dead sounds into lively surroundings. Current research on reverberation has led to a multiplicity of new methods that go beyond Schroeder's model in terms of realism and flexibility. This includes methods based on physical models of simulated spaces, such as *geometric models* (beam and ray tracing), *waveguide networks*, and *feedback delay networks*. These provide the composer with a wide range of colors from which to choose. (For more on these techniques, see Roads forthcoming.)

Another class of reverberators based on convolution is especially interesting, as they open the door to a vast range of spatial transformations that imprint the acoustic signature of real and imaginary spaces onto any sound. Specifically, we can take the acoustic signature of an existing space such as a concert hall, and through convolution, impose its spatial characteristics on any sound, creating the illusion of sounds playing in the portrayed space (Roads 1993, 1997a). In the theory of convolution, the acoustic signature of a physical space is sampled by recording the response of a room to a sharp impulse. This is its *impulse response* (IR).[54] While Schroeder algorithms model generic spaces, convolution usually starts with a sampled IR of an actual hall. Convolving the sampled IR of the space with an input signal is a highly accurate means of simulating the reverberation of the space.

Since convolution itself is straightforward, the added value of convolving reverberator applications comes in the form of extensive libraries of proprietary IRs of exotic spaces, including concert halls, cathedrals, stadiums, theaters, churches, recording studios, rooms, scoring stages, clubs, tombs, car interiors, closets, and even acoustic instruments. For example, one might play a passage of electronic music that sounds as though it is emanating from the inside of a cello. Many libraries also contain the sampled IRs of vintage reverberators like the EMT 140 plate and the classic Schroeder-type digital reverberators. As we show later, it is also possible to create synthetic IRs that model strange imaginary rooms with otherworldly echo patterns.

Even "bad" (unrealistic, echoey, ringing, metallic, etc.) reverberators have their place in the toolkit of the electronic musician when used sparingly as a specific coloration for sounds. The result of all of these possibilities is that composers of today have a cornucopia of spatial treatments at their disposal. If desired, each and every sound in a composition can be placed in its own virtual space.

PITCH-SHIFTED REVERBERATION AND REVERBERATION CHORDS

Audio technology opens up the novel possibility of *pitch-shifted reverberation*. In this technique, which I used in pieces such as *Touche pas* (2009), *Never* (2010), *Epicurus* (2010), and *Modulude* (2015), I route a sound into a real-time reverberator and record the reverberation on a separate track. The reverberation track can then be pitch-shifted down for a deeper and longer effect. Going further, several copies can be made of the reverberated clip, each transposed by a different interval to form a *reverberation chord*. This echoes the point made in chapter 7 about latent pitch. While the reverberation tail itself may or may not be pitched, several pitch-shifted copies sequenced or layered articulate pitch intervals. Reverberation chords can be made out of non-pitched material (figure 8.8).

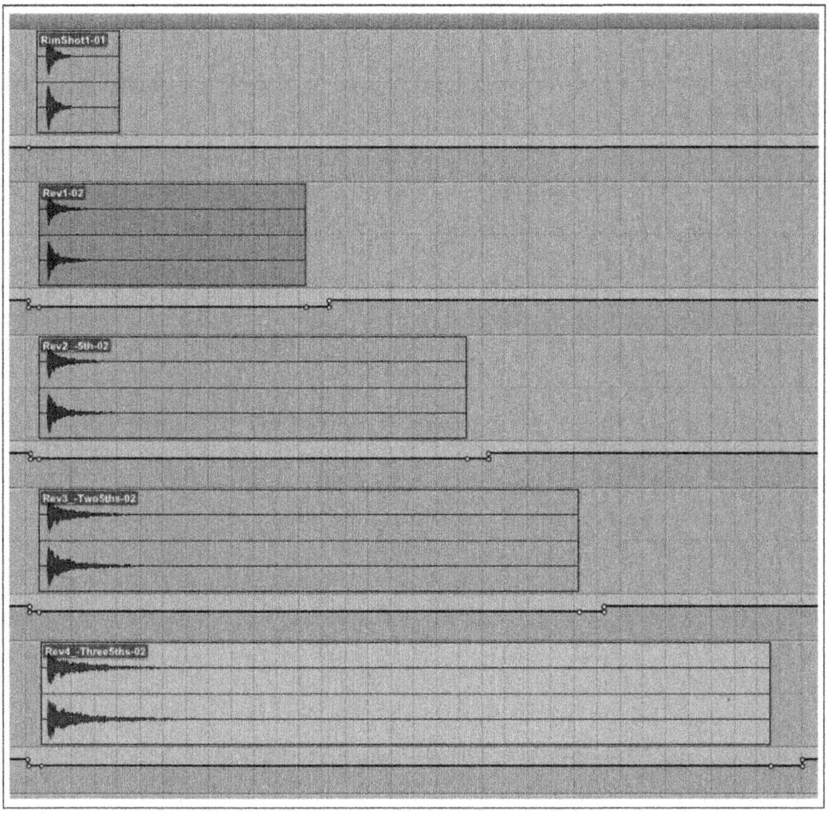

FIGURE 8.8 Superposition of amplitude-scaled pitch-shifted reverberation tails to form a reverberation chord. See the description of sound example 8.6.

Sound example 8.6. A reverberation chord constructed by applying reverberation to a drum sound. (a) Dry (non-reverberated) snare drum sound. (b) Reverberated drum sound. (c) Reverberated drum sound transposed down a perfect fifth (seven semitones). (d) Reverberated drum sound transposed down 14 semitones. (e) Reverberated drum sound transposed down 21 semitones. (f) Alignment of (a) through (e) to form a reverberation chord. (g) Sequence of transposed drum tones. (h) Equivalent chord played with pitched tones.

TRANSFORMATION OF VIRTUAL SPACE: SYNTHESIS OF ARTIFICIAL IMPULSE RESPONSES

In the virtual world, the morphology of space is utterly malleable. It can be transformed gradually or suddenly. For example, an intimate enclosed space can morph into a reverberant cathedral and back again. We can compose echo patterns that correspond to a fantastic voyage through a virtual world. Indeed, the central focus of a composition can be the evolution of its spatial morphology (Smalley 1991).

It is possible to generate artificial impulse responses by means of particle synthesis techniques (Roads 2001b). This opens a path to an infinite territory of virtual spaces. Many of the virtual spaces created in this manner would be difficult or impossible to realize in the physical world, such as spaces with time-varying echo densities or the simultaneous presence of different qualities of ambience.

Related to this line of research is the problem of building a visual model of the space corresponding to a given impulse response. This is a known engineering problem, prompted by the need to understand the geophysical structure of potential oil fields.

An inverse problem is the *auralization of virtual spaces*. What does a given virtual world sound like? How do we derive the impulse response of a virtual environment? Being able to recreate sound propagation in virtual worlds is useful in the design of concert halls, as well as the imaginary spaces found in interactive games. Methods drawn from physics can create realistic simulations using *beam* or *ray tracing*, which calculate the paths of waves in spaces as they encounter absorbing and reflecting surfaces (Vörlander 2008; Schissler 2012; Adams 2013).

Foreground and background in virtual soundscapes

Like a landscape, a soundscape integrates the notion of perspective or depth. We want to be able to place sounds anywhere within this spatial perspective—from extremely close to extremely far—and use this opposition (i.e., contrasts in proximity) in our composition methodology. Consider a piece like Martino Traversa's *Bianco, ma non troppo* (1996), which contrasts a live performance of a flautist playing extremely close to a microphone, accompanied by an electronic part that is deeply reverberated. Here intimacy confronts vastness. Similarly, in *Traversée des abysses* (1991), Michel Redolfi contrasts cavernous underwater spaces abruptly interrupted by close-up mechanical sounds. It sounds as if these noises were recorded in a closet-like space, so the listener is simultaneously within a tiny intimate enclosure surrounded by a vast submerged space.

Sound example 8.7. Excerpt of *Traversée des abysses* (1991) by Michel Redolfi.

In *Life in the Universe* (1998) by Ken Fields, we hear the apposition of distant sine wave "pad" tones contrasted with foreground granulation.

Sound example 8.8. Excerpt of *Life in the Universe* (1998) by Ken Fields.

With conventional loudspeakers in a typical room, the closest that a sound can appear to be to a listener is the edge of the sounding loudspeaker. Thus a listener using headphones can experience a more intimate soundscape than a listener hearing a loudspeaker that is several meters away, with its associated room reflections. (In special cases, such as wave field synthesis, sound can emerge from the loudspeaker and approach the listener; more on this later.)

Starting from the edge of the conventional loudspeaker, we can treat different sounds so that they appear to emanate from specific depths behind the loudspeaker. This leads to one of the more interesting possibilities in electronic music: the possibility of a counterpoint between foreground and background elements, where the perceived depth of each element is a function of its virtual acoustic properties. A low-pass filtered sound—bathed in reverberation and diminished in amplitude—recedes into the background, while a bright, present, loud sound jumps to the foreground.

Spatial depth is not the only determinant of a background texture, however. Any omnipresent, unobtrusive, or repeating figure tends to recede from our attention when strongly accented ephemeral elements intercede. Here the meaning of "background" is more abstract, referring to perceptually dominant and subordinate structural elements. Just as the background canvas of a painting need not be a neutral shade, the canvas of electronic music need not be silence. In Horacio Vaggione's compositions *Nodal* (1997) and *Agon* (1998), for example, a low-level granulose background texture "fills in the dots" to maintain tension between widely spaced foreground explosions.

Sound example 8.9. Opening of *Agon* (1998) by Horacio Vaggione. 

CINEMATIC USE OF SPACE

Some composers use microphone techniques and spatial processing in a manner similar to the cinematic use of camera angle, lens perspective (width), and depth of field. Accordingly, a trend toward cinematic use of space is seen in compositions that feature dramatic contrasts between sounds that are captured close in proximity and those that are distantly reverberated. Luc Ferrari's *Presque rien no. 1* (1970) pioneered this approach. (Notably, Ferrari was also visually sophisticated and directed several important films, including his series *Les Grandes Répétitions* [The Great Rehearsals].) Another classic example of audio cinematics is *Sud* (1985) by Jean-Claude Risset. In the first example, we hear wind in the background and insects in the foreground mixed with high-pitched synthetic flutterings and resonant filter effects.

Sound example 8.10. Excerpt of *Sud*, Part 1 (1985) by Jean-Claude Risset. 

In the second example, we hear the apposition of close-up recordings of water gently lapping onshore with inharmonic sine wave clusters.

Sound example 8.11. End of *Sud*, Part 3 (1985) by Jean-Claude Risset.

The sonic equivalent of zooming in on an image can be achieved by several means, most directly by a microphone in proximity to an acoustic source, but also in the studio by means of an increase in amplitude, a decrease in reverberation, or the application of "presence" filters that boost the low-frequency range. Another technique is to convolve a given sound with the impulse response of enclosed spaces such as closets and car interiors, or recording a sound playing through a loudspeaker with a microphone moving toward it in close proximity. Zooming out methods apply the same techniques in reverse, ending with a sound off in the distance. Changes of lighting correspond to changes in audio filter settings, and changes of camera angle correspond with directional microphone techniques and spatial signal processing. By means of all these methods, sound objects can be localized precisely in the soundscape of a work.

Virtual space meets physical space

An electronic music composer works in a specific studio, typically a modest-sized room with a fixed loudspeaker setup. When completed, the piece embodies its own virtual space, which can be heard in its purest form on professional studio monitors or headphones. The same composition, however, will likely be played in other physical spaces, from living rooms to concert halls. Conventional public address or sound reinforcement systems are designed to amplify conference speeches and popular music concerts. Their goal is to deliver uniform dispersion of sound throughout the audience. The ideal is that every listener hears more or less the same audio signal.

This is not necessarily the goal in a concert of electronic music, where *pluriphonic sound projection* (also called *spatialization* or *diffusion*) means that each listener can experience a unique spatial perspective (Clozier 2001). This is enabled by the installation of possibly dozens of loudspeakers around and even within the audience, and the fact that it is possible to move sounds through this network more-or-less continuously as a piece unfolds. In so doing, we create a sonic experience that can be appreciated from multiple angles, each of them evoking a different impression.

The projection of sound in a hall intersects virtual spaces in the music with a physical space and a specific playback system (figure 8.9). This intersection creates interplay between the static architecture of the hall and the dynamic virtual acoustics of the music.

Here the composer has an opportunity to add value to the performance, by tuning the playback and adapting it to the loudspeaker configuration and the hall. In its most basic form, this means optimizing the playback based on the

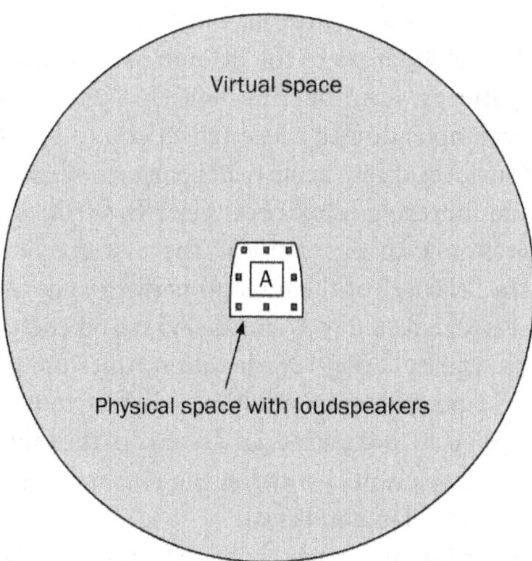

FIGURE 8.9 View of virtual and physical space from above. The box marked A indicates the audience in a concert hall. The perimeter of phantom images in virtual space is much larger than that of the physical space due to the possibility of reverberation and other distance cues.

venue. However, this can also go beyond optimization into the realm of reinterpretation, in particular, creative sound projection in real time that enhances and extends the virtual spaces recorded on the playback medium.

The rest of this section focuses on simple playback tuning, vertical projection, and headspace listening. Later we explore the possibilities opened up by creative sound projection.

The physical architecture of the performance venue colors the virtual sound. Even open-air performances can be affected by reflections and echoes.[55] Thus composers need to be aware of these factors:

- Room resonances
- Room reflections
- Room reverberation
- Ancillary vibration
- Loudspeaker type and configuration

Rooms resonate at frequencies that depend on their size and geometry. Thus the sound projection system should have variable equalizers that let the composer tune the mix. The most common resonances occur in the bass frequencies below 200 Hz. When loudspeakers are at a distance from listeners, it can be helpful to slightly boost the airy high frequencies in the range of 12 kHz to add presence.

When projected sound energy hits surfaces, some of it is reflected, some is absorbed, and some is transmitted through the surface. As mentioned in chapter 3, human clothing absorbs sound (Conti et al. 2003). Thus the acoustics of a concert hall can vary depending on the number of spectators and their attire.

Besides the *direct sound* emanating from the loudspeakers, every space imposes its own *room sound* through its pattern of sound reflections. Critical listening environments, such as mastering studios, are designed to absorb sound.

Good concert halls tend to have diffuse, random reflections, scattering reverberant energy equally to all areas of the listening space. Bad halls tend to have focused reflection patterns, resulting in echoes and uneven resonances in various locations. For example, domes cause reflections to be focused rather than dispersed. Parallel surfaces create acoustical problems such as *standing waves* or room resonances and fluttering echoes between two surfaces.

Room reverberation prolongs sounds. The amount of reverberation in a space determines the "clarity" of the musical performance. A space with a high ratio of direct and early reflected (< 80 ms delay) sound energy to later reverberant energy has more clarity. Long reverberation times are generally correlated with large rooms. In a performance situation, one way to mitigate the effects of excessive reverberation is to make a special dry mix of the music with no artificial reverberation. Another solution is moving the loudspeakers close to the audience, so the direct sound is loud and clear.

Another type of noise that is rarely discussed but is ubiquitous in real spaces is ancillary vibration: the buzzing and rattling sounds induced in various and sundry objects by low bass frequencies. Ancillary vibrations can be distracting, so it is necessary to neutralize these sources before the concert begins.[56]

The type of loudspeaker is critical to the performance of electronic music. High-quality speakers have a broad bandwidth and low distortion. However, the choice of specific loudspeakers depends on many factors, such as size, weight, power requirements, cost, and ultimately, the listener's subjective preference. In public performance, subwoofers are commonly used alongside conventional loudspeakers in order to reinforce the bass frequencies. The downside of subwoofers is a perception that the bass usually seems detached from the rest of the sound, especially when the sound is moving in space. A common myth says that "bass sounds are not directional," but this ignores the intensity cue. The source location of a loud bass tone can be readily detected in a non-reverberant hall. Indeed, directional cardioid-pattern subwoofers are available (d&b audiotechnik 2011).

The configuration of the loudspeakers (i.e., the number of loudspeakers and their position in space) is another critical factor in spatialization. Only a few configurations are common, such as stereo, quad, 5.1 surround, and octophonic surround. Loudspeaker configurations and spatialization technology remain areas of much scientific and artistic experimentation, resulting in a lack of common infrastructure. Thus sometimes a work will need to be remixed for a given configuration.

VERTICAL PROJECTION IN VIRTUAL AND PHYSICAL SPACES

Vertical sound sources offer a novel effect. Artistic experimentation with vertical projection of sound began in the early 1950s. Pierre Schaeffer's studio for musique concrète featured a loudspeaker mounted in the ceiling, and his group's performances featured live diffusion. Another pioneering configuration, for Stockhausen's *Gesang der Jünglinge* (1956), involved projection in five channels, with four loudspeakers in the corners of the performance hall and a fifth loudspeaker suspended above the audience. We have already shown an image of the Philips Pavilion with its loudspeakers mounted above the audience.

A simple but effective configuration for vertical sound projection is the *tetrahedral ambiphony* layout invented by Michael Gerzon (1973). This setup features four loudspeakers: two in front (one high and one low) and two in back (one high and one low). My experiences with this configuration confirm the dramatic impression it creates even with stereo source material. A simple pan from left to right also moves simultaneously from up to down, from down to up, and from right to left, due to the reversed configuration of the rear loudspeakers.

Overhead loudspeakers suspended above the audience make an even more striking effect. This contrasts with the virtual acoustic illusion that has been popularized in so-called three-dimensional (3D) sound systems in recent years. In the 1970s, it was demonstrated that certain vertical sound illusions could be achieved using headphones. In some cases, the illusion could be heard with a pair of loudspeakers positioned closely at ear level. This research inspired the development of commercial spatializers that were used in some popular recordings. In general, vertical 3D sound systems are based on research that shows that high-frequency sound (greater than about 6 kHz) reflecting off the outer ears (pinnae) and shoulders provides a critical cue to vertical localization. These reflections impose short time delays that manifest in the spectrum as a comb filter effect. (See Roads 1996.)

The virtual vertical illusion is, however, fragile and signal-dependent. Not all people perceive the illusion well, since it requires that the listener's pinnae bear an anatomical similarity to a model subject. Even in the best of cases, the front-back localization of the source is frequently ambiguous. Thus a robust and definitive solution to the vertical dimension can be provided only by a system that places physical loudspeakers in the vertical dimension, including one or more loudspeakers suspended above the audience. Another advantage of a physical acoustic approach is that it is not limited to sounds above 6 kHz; lower frequencies are perceived as a vertical source by means of the intensity cue, particularly sounds with a sharp attack transient. However, as Kendall (2010) points out, experiments show that we are not as sensitive to the precise location of the sound images coming from elevated loudspeakers as we are in the lateral plane:

> Elevation perception is confounded with the spectral characteristics of the source and this is particularly clear in the case of filtered signals. In general, the higher the spectral energy distribution of the source, the higher the perceived elevation.

FROM ROOM SPACE TO HEADSPACE

Beyond the public space of the concert hall is the private space of home listening and the ultimate personal space of *headspace*, based on headphone and earpod listening. As Denis Smalley (1991) observed:

> Headspace listening can encourage concentration when the listener is immobile in a room. However, when the listener is mobile, a more distracted

listening is encouraged since some attention must be paid to events in the surrounding environment.

Distracted listening is ubiquitous in contemporary culture, which is one reason why the focused concert hall listening experience retains its pertinence.

Pluriphonic sound projection

Pluriphonic sound projection or diffusion brings the virtual space embodied by the music to the physical space of the concert hall by means of an interface that maps the input channels to the loudspeakers in the hall. This mapping can extend to creative spatialization in real time that enhances and extends the virtual spaces recorded on the playback medium. The opportunity posed by diffusion was addressed by Horacio Vaggione (1991):

> There is a natural disjunction between the acoustic particularities of a room (such as random resonances) and the fine details in the inner space of a piece (the degree of play between near and far, between bright and dark, etc.). Given this disjunction, it is necessary to combine the two spaces by an additional stage of production in real space: this is the function of electroacoustic diffusion. . . . Being in command of [a spatialization system] gives us something more than the ability to enlarge a sound image: it also lets us newly create its virtual movement. Thus the sound comes to life, and the work's design—the multiple energies contained in composed morphologies—manifests to perception. The "readability" of these morphologies arises from their being set in motion by a kind of cinematic sound projection. The goal is not to maintain a stereotypical stereo image, but rather to break it to better reconstitute the plurality contained inside the work.

Thus a piece that was "finished" in the studio has the potential to be reinterpreted in a variety of ways through the process of diffusion. It is also true that reinterpretation can distort the composer's original conception, so it is not always recommended. However, in certain cases, diffusion revivifies and updates a work to new circumstances (figure 8.10).

The experience of projected sound evokes spatial impressions. These impressions include *dimensional* attributes like *direction, distance*, and *extent* (the size of the impression in terms of depth, width, and height), and *immersive* attributes like *presence* (e.g., the experience of realism) and *envelopment*, or being surrounded by sound (Rumsey 2002; Kendall 2010).

We have already cited the Gmebaphone—an innovative type of pluriphonic sound projection system designed expressly for the projection of electronic music. Its later incarnation, the Cybérnophone, proposed an "orchestra of loudspeakers" onstage along with a complement of supporting loudspeakers surrounding the audience (Clozier 1997, 2001). The goal of this type of diffusion is to *upmix*: project a small number of input channels to a large number of loudspeakers. In many concerts, this is a manual process, performed live. Live diffusion

FIGURE 8.10 The author at the 2010 open-air performance of the restored eight-channel version of *Persepolis* (1971) by Iannis Xenakis at the Los Angeles State Historical Park. The work was projected by means of a 48-loudspeaker sound system over a field of 650 square meters by the sound artist Daniel Teige. The performance was accompanied by searchlights and torches, as per Xenakis's original conception. Photograph by Stefanie Ku.

caught on quickly in France and has since been adopted all over the world (Roads et al. 1997a; Harrison 1999).

One can extend the pluriphonic concept to project sounds from a variety of positions above, below, and even within the audience. The sound sources need not be limited to fixed positions, but can emanate from rotating loudspeakers, mobile robots, or performers.

The art of pluriphony is based on three principles:

1. The experience of an electronic music composition in stereo format can be greatly enhanced by a spatial performance in concert, whether diffused by a musician in real time or semi-automated in real time. Alternatively, for a multichannel composition, the spatialization can be realized in the studio and mapped to a multichannel sound system in the concert venue.
2. The sound projection system can offer a variety of contrasting spatial images through the arrangement of multiple loudspeakers around the audience, across the front stage, above, within, and below the audience. Thus each listener has a unique perspective, and there is not necessarily a "correct" position from which to hear the music. Not all loudspeakers are used at all times. In performance, the composer selects particular spatial images to highlight certain aspects of his or her work and choreographs transitions from scene to scene. Deploying multiple

loudspeakers onstage makes it possible to project a sound image rivaling the complexity of an orchestra.

3. While a single type of loudspeaker guarantees a uniformity of sound quality, it is also possible to mix different types of loudspeakers in the same pluriphonic system, with the most common case being full-range versus subwoofers. Each type offers a particular voicing that may be useful in articulating a specific musical texture.

Let us elaborate point (1). The sound projection can be realized manually by a sound projectionist (typically the composer) working at a mixing console in the hall. This can add a spontaneous and virtuoso element to the concert.[57] When I project my music in this way, it is not so much a matter of physical skill but rather of intimate knowledge of the music being diffused (i.e., a sense of timing that enables me to anticipate and execute spatial gestures precisely on cue). The joy of manual spatialization was articulated by Annette Vande Gorne (1991):

> Nothing replaces the immense pleasure of feeling, together with the audience, multiple configurations of space—complex and changing—under the control of my fingers, a pleasure renewed each time I freely balance the levels of the channels, and become a listening for space.

To go beyond stereo and compose directly in a multichannel format can obviate the need for additional spatial performance (but see the next section). This poses a dilemma, as pointed out by Jonty Harrison (1999):

> Multitrack working also raises question over the nature of the signal itself—specifically over whether to use mono or stereo sources. Lateral movement in multimono works tends to gravitate to the speaker cabinets and the richness of a three-dimensional "stage" is rare. Many pieces composed in 4-channel format over the past four decades and many now being composed in 8- or 16-channel digital formats for replay in concert over the equivalent number of loudspeakers actually use mono source material. It seems glaringly obvious to me that the "space" of such pieces is unlikely to work, for there is little or no phase information. . . . Works which use stereophonic (i.e., three-dimensional) images within the multitrack environment tend to be the most spatially convincing. . . .

It will be interesting to see how emerging technologies, such as microphone arrays and sound field recording/synthesis, affect this issue. These make it possible to record and playback multichannel sound fields and not just stereo images. (See the section on "Immersive sound" later.)[58]

GENERATIVE UPMIXING

Two, 4, 8, . . . 1024 audio channels, mapped to 2, 4, 8, . . . 1024 loudspeakers—at what point does it become impractical to manually control the spatial projection of sound to such a system in real time? With the increasing prevalence of pluriphonic systems extending into dozens and hundreds of channels and loudspeakers, direct hands-on control of each source in real time is not feasible. Moreover, certain spatial gestures—multiple rotations at different speeds and angles, for example—are too complex to be controlled manually in real time.

A variety of solutions to the problem of pluriphonic spatialization have been developed in the form of interfaces and software. However, many of these tend to be customized for the unique requirements of a single piece or the unique capabilities of a specific sound system. Continuing experimentation in the design of pluriphonic sound has the unfortunate side-effect of system heterogeneity—leading to a lack of common infrastructure for spatial audio. Thus, apart from a few informal standard configurations like eight-channel surround, the approaches and solutions are heterogeneous. These range from a solution for a single piece, to a system that can be used by many composers through non-real-time scripting/sequencing or real-time interactive performance (Pottier 2012; Mooney 2008).

Non-real-time scripting/sequencing means that all channels are pre-spatialized in the studio, using whatever means are available. This self-contained solution enables portability, meaning that the piece can be played in multiple venues with minimal requirements. All the composer needs to do is bring a prepared *m*-channel audiofile (or *m* mono files) to the venue for playback through Pro Tools or a similar multichannel playback application with the same number of outputs.

Real-time control in concert requires an interactive diffusion system that lets one control the upmixing using semi-automatic high-level controls. The musician controls the timing of large gestures but delegates many low-level details to algorithmic control. Innumerable schemes can be designed, opening vast potential for generative upmixing as a compositional strategy.[59] Indeed, the spatialization algorithm itself can be made the central focus of the composition.

One upmixing strategy is related to the classic mono-to-stereo conversion problem. To create a stereo image from a mono file, one needs to decorrelate the two signals by operations like filtration, phase shift, delay, or granulation (Kendall 1995). So for an upmixing system that starts with *m* channels of audio and must produce *n* channels of output, where *n* is greater than *m*, one strategy is to generate decorrelated copies of the input tracks. The Scatter application mentioned previously could spatialize based on features found in a time-frequency analysis, a dissection of the sound into constituent grains. But even basic techniques such as filter banks, phase shifts, or delay lines can be used to separate different aspects of the sound. For example, the sound could be divided into one-third octave bands and each band could be spatialized separately.

A primary aesthetic challenge of pluriphonic diffusion is to articulate musical structure through its spatial projection. We have more to say about this in chapter 12.

PROJECTION OF SPATIAL CHORDS

Perhaps the most important strategy I followed when projecting sound from a stereo source to a pluriphonic sound system was that of *spatial chords*, or geometric forms (Roads 2011; Roads et al. 2013). A spatial chord deploys a combination of sources to present a unique spatial geometry. To give a simple example, instead of projecting a stereo sound to left-front and right-front speakers, I would project it to left-front and right-rear. In this case, a sound that normally pans from left to right now pans diagonally through the audience. A slightly more complicated situation might involve a third or fourth source loudspeaker to create a two-dimensional geometrical configuration in a ring of loudspeakers around an audience. This can be extended to three dimensions in the case of a space like the UCSB AlloSphere with dozens of loudspeakers (figure 8.11).

I cue the chords to change at critical structural junctures in the unfolding of a work. Here the spatial architecture coincides with the musical structure. Figure 8.12 indicates the types of geometrical forms that can be generated with such a system.

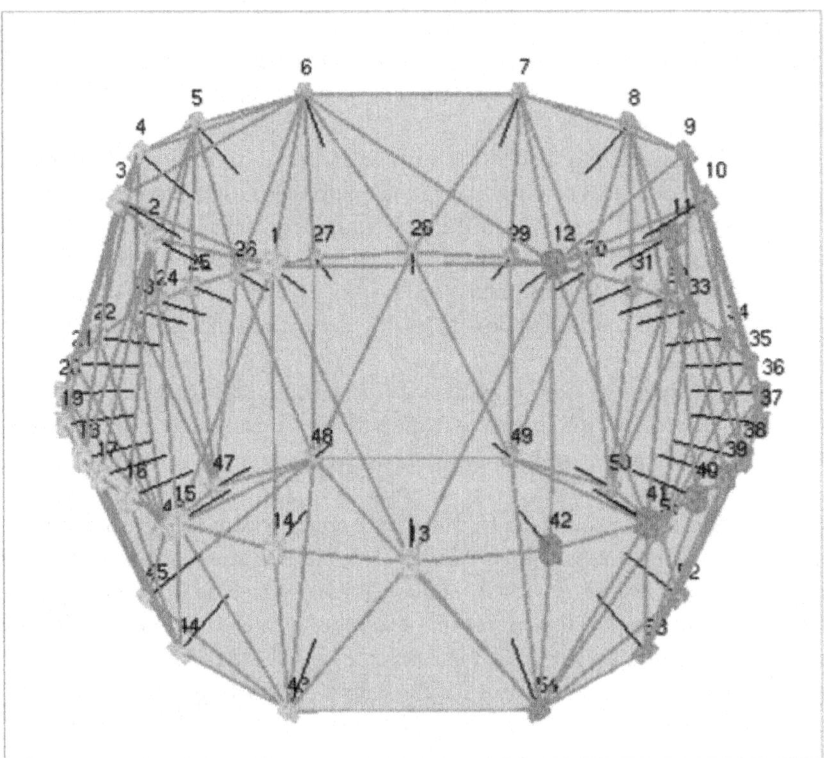

FIGURE 8.11 Loudspeaker configuration in the UCSB AlloSphere as of summer 2013, consisting of 54 Meyer Sound MM-4XP speakers in three rings, as depicted in the Zirkonium application. A 2250-watt Meyer 600-HP subwoofer is also supported.

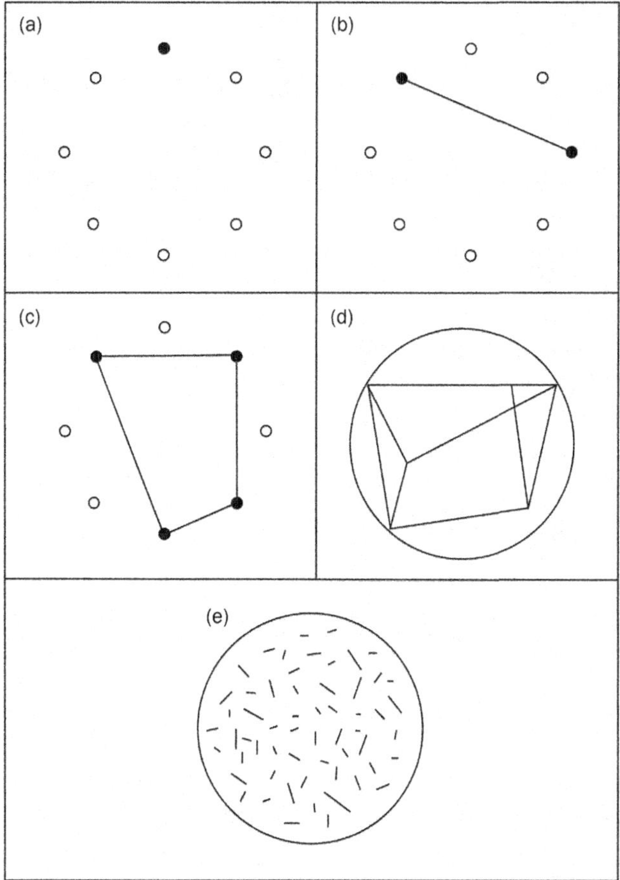

FIGURE 8.12 (a) Point in 2D octophony. (b) Line in 2D octophony. (c) Plane in 2D octophony. (d) Polyhedron in 3D sphere. (e) Cloud (multiple points with spatial jitter) in 3D sphere.

Changes in this geometry can be controlled in real time using a custom version of the Zirkonium spatial software (Ramakrishnan 2007) that allows the composer to stipulate:

1. The number of virtual sources in the chord
2. The spacing of the points, whether in a closely spaced cluster or scattered widely in three dimensions
3. Tilt or rotation selection (0 = no tilt or rotation)
4. Tilt angle
5. Rotation speed
6. Transition time from one chord to another, from sudden to smoothly interpolated

The composer can manipulate these parameters in performance at key structural junctures.

Rotating loudspeakers

Rotating loudspeakers open another dimension of spatial sound. To be in a room with a rotating speaker is to be surrounded by ever-changing reflections, like a spotlight on a rotating mirrorball. The physical rotation of a loudspeaker enlivens sounds, animating them with time-varying spatial and spectral qualities. The original rotating loudspeaker mechanism was the Leslie Tone Cabinet, which routed an incoming signal into two separate rotating mechanisms: a spinning horn for high frequencies and a rotating baffle (blocking and unblocking a stationary woofer) for low frequencies (Leslie 1949, 1952). A remote control for motor speed let musicians adjust the speed of rotation. The Leslie Tone Cabinet was designed to enrich the static sound emitted by electric organs, such as the Hammond, with its electromechanical additive synthesis engine (figure 8.13).

Sound example 8.12. Hammond organ tone: (1) static without Leslie rotation, (2) slow rotation, (3) fast rotation, (4) slow rotation, and (5) no rotation.

Later, musicians discovered that any sound could be enriched in this way.

In the late 1950s, engineers working at the Hermann Scherchen Experimental Studio Gravesano in Switzerland developed a spherical loudspeaker that rotated both horizontally and vertically (Loescher 1959; 1960; see photograph in Roads 1996).

Karlheinz Stockhausen manually rotated a loudspeaker affixed to a turntable to create the spinning sounds in his compositions *Kontakte* (1960) and *Hymnen* (1967; see photograph in Roads 1996). As he stated:

> I naïvely started to rotate any sound I produced, but it didn't work at all. I found that only certain rhythms can be moved in rotation or at certain speeds. . . . I say that in general the sharper the sound, the higher the frequency, the better it moves and the clearer its direction. But I would also say that the more a sound is chopped [amplitude modulated]—let's say in the region between three and twelve pulses per second, the better it moves in space. And the sharper the attack of each segment of a sound event, the better it moves.
>
> —COTT (1973)

"Sound chopping" by low-frequency square wave AM is a signature of Stockhausen's electronic technique. It markedly enhances the spatial salience of any broadband sound, whether rotated or merely panned.

Physically rotating speaker systems are available in the marketplace, and software plug-ins and effects units attempt to simulate this effect. The quest to model the complex effects of loudspeaker rotation involve Doppler shift vibrato, time-varying filtering, phase shifts, distortions caused by air turbulence, and echo reflections from adjacent surfaces—not to mention the transfer characteristics of the amplifiers and loudspeakers used. Much progress has been made

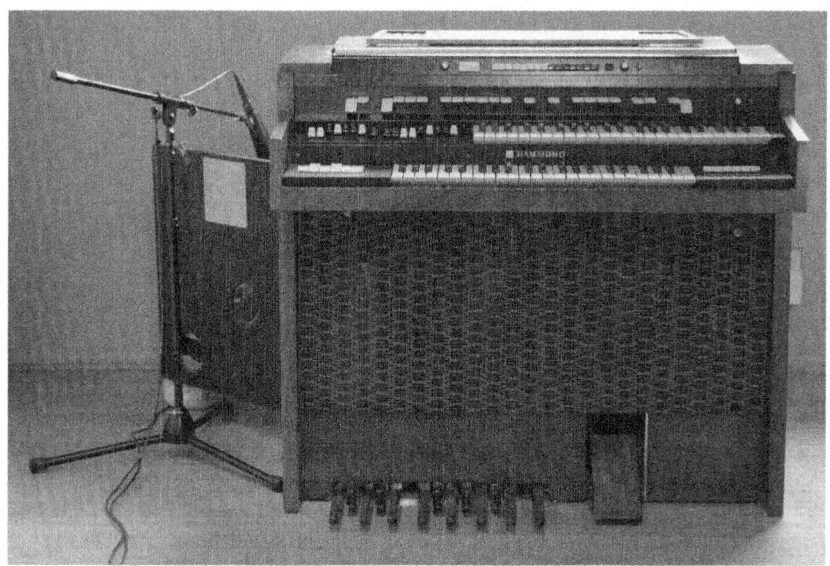

FIGURE 8.13 Recording a Leslie speaker built into a Hammond T422 organ with two Sennheiser 421 microphones. (a) Front view. (b) Rear view.

in recent years in simulating these complicated and interacting acoustical and electronic effects. The effect recorded in stereo, however, is not the same as being in the same room as a rotating loudspeaker, which is a three-dimensional immersive experience due to room reflections.

As an alternative to physically rotating loudspeakers, electronic rotation can also be realized on spherical loudspeaker systems with dozens of drivers around

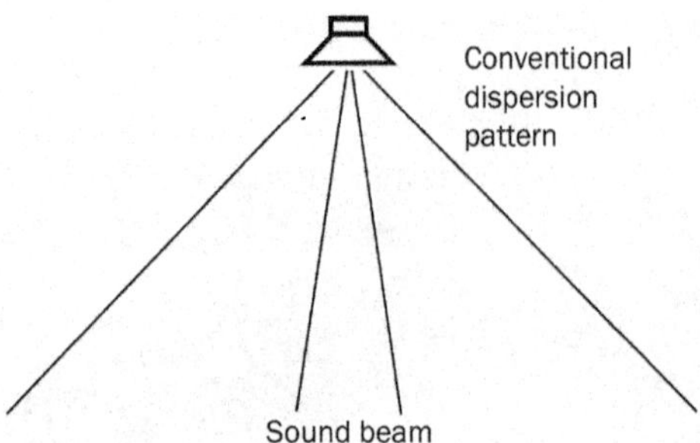

FIGURE 8.14. The conventional dispersion pattern of a loudspeaker is broad, while a superdirectional sound beam is narrow.

the surface (e.g., Avizienis et al. 2006). In this case, software generates a separate stream of audio for each driver. Such technology has also been used to emulate the radiation patterns of acoustic instruments, or to generate an omnidirectional radiation pattern. However, there is no reason why spherical speakers cannot be used more creatively to generate arbitrary radiation patterns—including rotations at various angles—adapted to specific pieces of electronic music (Hulen 2008).

Superdirectional sound beams

The directionality or dispersion pattern of a loudspeaker is a design feature and can vary from omnidirectional to superdirectional. Most conventional loudspeakers are broadly directional (i.e., they typically project sound forward through a horizontal angle spanning 80 to 90 degrees). So-called narrow coverage loudspeakers feature dispersion in the 50 degree range (Meyer Sound Laboratories 2010).

In contrast, loudspeakers that act as superdirectional sound beams behave like an audio spotlight, focusing sound energy on a narrow spot, typically about 15 degrees in width (figure 8.14). One person, for example may hear the sound, while someone outside the beam does not.

Superdirectional sound beams can be constructed using a variety of technologies. Here we look at loudspeaker arrays and ultrasonic devices. We discuss wave field synthesis later in the context of immersive sound systems.

It has long been known that loudspeaker arrays can form highly focused directional sound beams. Figure 8.15 shows a five-element array of loudspeakers. When the second and fourth elements are reversed in phase, the sound beam narrows to 26 degrees. A modern incarnation of this approach is found in the Yamaha YSP-1000 digital sound projector (figure 8.16). The device works by focusing sound into beams and then projecting them at angles into the room. The resulting sound waves—both direct and reflected—create a soundscape that seems to be coming from speakers placed throughout the room, but in reality, all the sound is emanating from the sound projector in the front.

An alternative technology for superdirectional sound beams employs ultrasound—the domain of high frequencies above the range of human

FIGURE 8.15 An early superdirectional loudspeaker array. After Kock (1971).

FIGURE 8.16 The Yamaha YSP-100 projects sounds from 42 loudspeakers to create surround-sound effects. Introduced in 2007, it was the first in a line of similar sound projectors.

audibility. Ultrasonic superdirectional loudspeakers are based on the scientific principle of *acoustic heterodyning* (Pompei 1999; American Technology Corporation 1998; Soundlazer 2013), first observed by Helmholtz. When two sound sources are positioned relatively closely together and are of sufficiently high amplitude, two new tones appear: one lower than either of the two original ones and a second one that is higher than the original two. The two new combination tones correspond to the sum and the difference of the two original ones. For example, if one were to emit two ultrasonic frequencies, 90 kHz and 91 kHz, into the air with sufficient energy, one would produce the sum (181 kHz) and the difference (1 kHz), the latter of which is in the range of human hearing. Helmholtz argued that the phenomenon had to result from a nonlinearity of air molecules, which begin to behave nonlinearly (to heterodyne or intermodulate) at high amplitudes.

Unlike regular loudspeakers, acoustical heterodyning loudspeakers project energy in a collimated sound beam, analogous to the beam of light from a flashlight. One can direct the ultrasonic emitter toward a wall, and a listener in the reflected beam perceives the sound as coming from that spot (figure 8.17).

At the time of this writing, there has been little experimentation with such loudspeakers in the context of electronic music. However, one could imagine coupling such a loudspeaker with a robot arm to create a spatial choreography of precisely controlled sound beams that are synchronized with a musical structure.

IMMERSIVE SOUND

One trend in music performance is moving away from the traditional stage-centered experience toward immersive audiovisual environments in virtual and augmented realities (Hollerweger 2006; Baalman 2010). Immersive sound systems extend the reach of spatialization to a three-dimensional enclosure. First, we briefly summarize three different approaches to immersive sound, and then we discuss their musical potential.

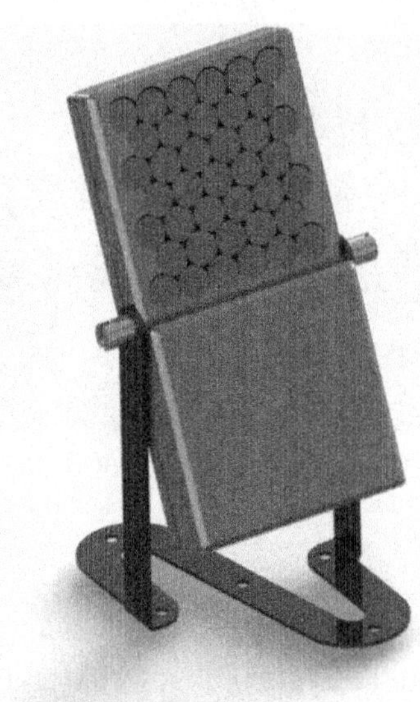

FIGURE 8.17 Soundlazer parametric array loudspeaker for highly directional sound projection. This experimental device is about the size of a mobile phone and is thus restricted in audio bandwidth. (Photo courtesy of SoundLazer.)

The realm of immersive sound or *sound field synthesis* is an active area of research and experimentation, with a number of experimental approaches in competition (Kolundzija et al. 2011). Among these are three techniques that have fascinating musical potential: *vector base amplitude panning, high-order ambisonics*, and *wave field synthesis*. All combine a physical infrastructure with spatial signal processing. The physical infrastructure consists of a regular array of many loudspeakers surrounding the listener in three dimensions including dome or sphere configurations. Spatial signal processing diffuses a potentially unique audio signal to each loudspeaker in the system to create an immersive spatial impression.

VECTOR BASE AMPLITUDE PANNING

Vector base amplitude panning or VBAP is a three-dimensional extension of stereophonic techniques (Pulkki 1997). Instead of projecting a signal from a stereo field with a phantom source between two loudspeakers, VBAP projects from triples of loudspeakers arranged in triangles, allowing for vertical as well as horizontal panning (figure 8.18). A typical VBAP configuration has regularly spaced loudspeakers around and above the audience. VBAP provides a simple but effective way to pan sound around the inner surface of a half-sphere, for example. VBAP produces virtual sources that are as sharp as is possible, since it uses the minimum number of loudspeakers needed, from one to three.

High-order ambisonics and wave field synthesis go beyond this to focus on the reproduction of *coherent wavefronts* rather than isolated phantom sound sources. A wavefront consists of all points in space that are reached at the same instant by a wave propagating through a medium. This approach is sometimes

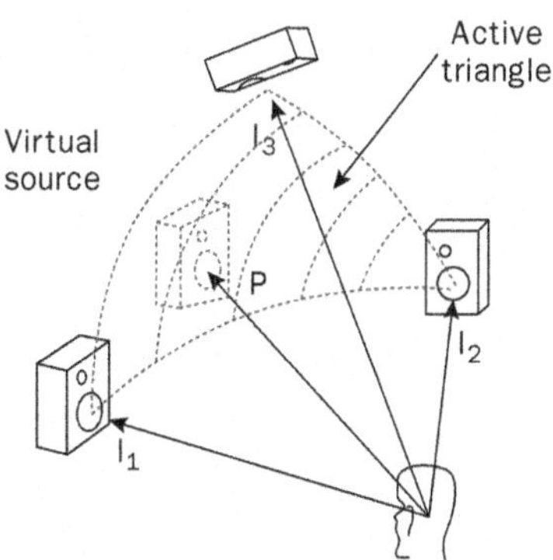

FIGURE 8.18 Vector base amplitude panning. The three-dimensional unit vectors l_1, l_2, and l_3 define the directions of loudspeakers 1, 2, and 3. The virtual sound source p is a linear combination of the gain factors of l_1, l_2, and l_3. Using these three loudspeakers, virtual sources can be created anywhere within the active triangle shown. This can be generalized to arbitrary spatial configurations. After Pulkki (1997).

called *holophony* by analogy to *acoustical holography* (Jessel 1973). The aim of these systems is the reconstruction of the acoustic sensations that listeners would perceive around them in a real immersive environment.

HIGH-ORDER AMBISONICS

High-order ambisonics (HOA) generates a *periphonic* (omnidirectional) *sound field* emanating from the edge of a sphere toward the listener in the center of the sphere. ("High-order" refers to greater than four channels.) A solution of the wave equation decomposes this sound field into a series of *spherical harmonic functions* (Malham and Myatt 1995; Malham 1998; Blauert 1997). The theory of spherical harmonic functions states that every point in any system of waves propagating in space can be considered as the source of an elementary spherical wave. By the superimposition of such waves, the wave field at any point can be calculated. Since the spherical harmonics form a set of orthogonal base vectors, they can be used to describe any function on the surface of a sphere. An HOA encoder takes a monaural sound and a virtual source position and generates a multichannel signal. In HOA reproduction, all speakers are generally used to localize a sound, as opposed to techniques that use only adjacent speakers such as VBAP. Scalability to multiple moving sources and multiple loudspeakers is one of the advantages of the HOA approach, which also enables unique operations on the encoded sound field, such as rotation and zoom (emphasizing sounds in the front). Rotation matrices have been defined for rotation about the *x* axis (*tilt* or *roll*), the *y* axis (*tumble* or *pitch*), the *z* axis (*rotate* or *yaw*), or any combination of these; these rotation capabilities are clearly of compositional interest.

WAVE FIELD SYNTHESIS

Wave field synthesis (WFS) is based on the Huygens principle, which states that any wavefront can be regarded as a superposition of elementary spherical waves (Berkhout 1988, Berkhout et al. 1993; Verheijen 1997; Baalman 2010).

The special feature of WFS is that it can create the impression of a 3D virtual point source located *inside the listening area* between the loudspeakers

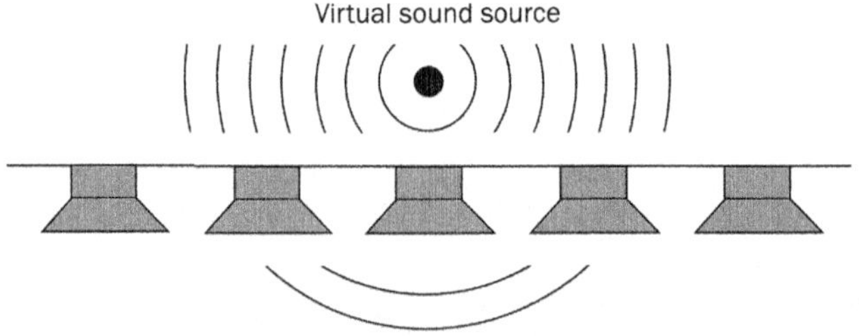

FIGURE 8.19 Multiple loudspeakers synthesizing a wavefront.

FIGURE 8.20 A wave field synthesis loudspeaker array in Eindhoven, the Netherlands, 2007, owned by Arthur Sauer. Photograph by Raviv Ganchrow, who designed the loudspeakers. Permission of Wouter Snoie.

and the listener. To achieve this effect, a computer controls a very large array of tightly spaced loudspeakers (typically hundreds) and actuates each one in exactly the same instant when the desired virtual wavefront would pass through it (figures 8.19, 8.20). The WFS algorithm calculates the delay times and attenuation factors for each sound source and speaker. All loudspeakers contribute to the reproduction of a virtual source.

However, translating the 3D illusion from theory to practice requires tightly controlled conditions. Imperfections in the system tend to diminish the 3D effect, which in any case is not as robust as a real source.

There is, of course, much more to the theory of immersive spatialization than we can delve into here. For technical details on VBAP, see Pulkki (1997). For more on HOA and WFS, see Gerzon (1973), Hollerweger (2006), Malham (1998, 2003), Malham and Myatt (1995), and Rumsey (2001).

MUSICAL POTENTIAL OF IMMERSIVE SOUND SYSTEMS

The musical potential of immersive sound systems has inspired a genre of music in which the spatial structure is the central narrative of the composition; all other elements serve the spatial organization. One concentration of recent musical works is inspired by the possibilities of ambisonic projection, coming from spatial sound research centers in Oslo, Belfast, Zürich, Karlsruhe, Santa Barbara, and others.

The most obvious game one can play with an immersive spatialization system is the illusion of presence: putting the listener inside a 3D soundscape, either from a real source or a virtual generated source. One can imagine how an artist such as Luc Ferrari, who often combined real soundscapes to create fictional ones, would have used immersive sound technology. The ability to rotate an entire sound field makes it possible to twist and turn the space around the listener, an incredible sensation.

Second, the ability to move multiple sources in three dimensions opens up the possibility of elaborate choreography, far beyond the ability of a musician to control directly in real time.

Third, in wave field synthesis, a sound can potentially emerge from the loudspeaker and occupy a defined physical space within a room. It can circulate within a room, being heard only when it meets a listener in a specific location. For example, in the acoustic chandelier shown in figure 8.21, only someone standing under the chandelier hears the sound, and the sound moves up and down one's body.

In 3D immersive sound spaces, sound morphology becomes a palpable presence. One can, in theory, walk through or around a sound, whose size, shape, and radiation pattern may vary in time. Silent areas can be sculpted within a sound

FIGURE 8.21 Acoustic chandelier, La Casa della Musica, Parma, Italy. The chandelier contains 224 loudspeakers for wave field synthesis.

field. Much research in immersive sound remains to be perfected, but the compositional potential of such capabilities is clearly attractive.

Articulating space

Music is a play of attracting and opposing forces. Attracting forces articulate similarities, while opposing forces articulate contrasts. (The similarities are implicit. For example, the opposition "put sound A in foreground/put sound B in background," implies the similarity "put sound A and sound B in foreground.") The art of spatialization plays out through specific tactics of attraction and opposition. Sonic space has multiple dimensions: lateral position, vertical position, image width, and image depth, all of which can vary on different timescales and in different frequency bands. As in all aspects of music, the density of voices is a prime structural element; the spatial trajectory of a single source contrasts with a texture consisting of 100 divisi elements, each emanating from its own unique point in space.

Table 8.1 is an attempt to list a basic repertoire of possible spatial oppositions. Such a list cannot be complete, as it will always be possible to invent new spatial operations and speaker configurations.

TABLE 8.1
Spatial oppositions

Foreground (present)	Background (obscured or reverberated)
Sole position in space	Multiple positions in space (spatial chords) forming geometrical shapes
Sole position in space	Spatial envelopment (sound from all sides)
Panning by related pairs of loudspeakers, e.g., from front left and right to rear left and right	Positioning and panning by arbitrary collections of loudspeakers, creating *spatial chords*, e.g., from upper front left and lower rear right to lower middle left and upper front right, generalized to *n* channels
Fixed position in space	Moving position in space
Fixed position in space	Scattered position in space (through granular decorrelation)
Fixed position in space	Oscillation between two positions in space, a kind of "spatial trilling"
Fixed dispersion pattern	Variable dispersion pattern (changes of apparent source width, possibly modeling the dispersion pattern of an acoustic instrument, horn, lens, or other source)
Sources positioned at two extreme poles	Sources filling in a stereo field, including the center
Fixed source geometry	Rotating source geometry
Slow motion	Fast motion
Periodic movement (sinusoidal, pulse, linear pan, exponential pan, logarithmic pan)	Random movement, juxtapositions in space

(continued)

TABLE 8.1 Continued

Spatialization is organized as an independent parameter, apart from pitch, rhythm, timbre, etc.	Spatialization linked to mesostructural musical function in coordination with other parameters; the spatial design helps to articulate structural transitions and "changes scene" on musical phrase boundaries. These changes can be linked with any of the oppositions in this table. For example, a transition from one phrase to another could be tied to a transition from one spatial chord to another.[60]
Global spatialization, such as global reverberation	Multiscale spatialization: phrases, objects, microsounds can be all given individual spatial characteristics
Spatialization is independent of frequency band and formant structure	Spatialization by spectrum, i.e., applying spatial filters that pan sounds depending on their frequency band (Wenger and Spiegel 2004; Sturm et al. 2008, 2009) or formant (as in pulsar synthesis, see Roads 2001, 2002)
Spatialization is independent of sound duration and amplitude	Spatialization by grain size and/or amplitude (Sturm et al. 2008, 2009)
Linear motions, from loudspeaker to loudspeaker	Coordinated geometric rotations at different speeds and directions (circular, elliptical, Lissajous, etc.)
Unidirectional rotation	Multidirectional rotation, including contrary motion (e.g., two sounds spinning in opposite directions)
Horizontal panning	Vertical panning (above and below the listener)
Circular rotation at a constant rate	Spiral rotation with acceleration
Panning without Doppler shift	Panning with Doppler shift
Spatial movement of multiple sounds with swarming or flocking behavior (sounds loosely follow one another; correlated movements)	Spatial movement of multiple sounds with independent trajectories (uncorrelated movements)
Fixed spatial perspective of virtual sounds	Variations in perspective ("cinematic" use of virtual space so that certain sounds appear to be recorded very closely while others appear to be distant)
Conventional loudspeaker dispersion pattern	Superdirectional sound beams
For fixed position sounds, fixed width of the sound image across multiple loudspeakers	Variations in the width of the image across multiple loudspeakers
Conventional spatial projection bounded on its inner surface by a perimeter of loudspeakers	Wave field synthesis in which the sound emerges from the loudspeaker perimeter and comes into the room
Multichannel spatial image	"Collapsed" spatial image to a single point or to an overall monaural image

Conclusion

The real world is pluriphonically spatial on every timescale. We can enrich our music by taking this into consideration. As a phrase unfolds, the position of each sound object creates a dynamic spatial dance. This choreography is intrinsically fascinating and meaningful to audiences. As a result, in electronic music, spatial strategy has become an integral facet of composition strategy. As Stockhausen (1958) observed concerning his composition *Gesang der Jünglinge (Song of the Youths)*:

> From which side, with how many loudspeakers, whether with rotation to left or right, whether motionless or moving, how the sounds and sound groups should be projected into space: all this is decisive for the understanding of the work.

Indeed, the art of spatialization has emerged as one of the most important topics in composition today. Even though a formal theory of spatial relations remains to be developed,[61] the compositional organization of sound spatialization is becoming increasingly elaborate, often assisted by sophisticated software. The combination of pluriphonic spatialization and 3D visual imagery creates strong perceptual impressions of presence, of total immersion in a world that seems physical and palpable (figure 8.22). The continued proliferation of pluriphonic sound systems fosters the development of ever-more-effective spatial

FIGURE 8.22 The UCSB AlloSphere viewed from outside. The AlloSphere is a three-story-high laboratory instrument for 3D immersive visual and audio projection with a multichannel Meyer Sound system (Amatriain et al. 2007, 2008, 2009). Photograph by Paul Wellman.

techniques and serves as a showcase for electronic music performance to the public.

Yet even with all this emphasis on amazing pluriphonic technology, we should not forget the profound impact of the humble stereo format—the universal standard for broadcast and distribution of music, where listeners drink at the source of the musical stream.

9

Multiscale organization

We live in an age of sonic wealth. One can record and store any sound, synthesize new ones, and transform them endlessly. This capability alone has dramatically changed the compositional landscape. The infusion of new sounds diversifies and deepens the emotional impact of music. It motivates a quest for fresh organizational strategies and leads to a new conception of musical organization involving any possible sound unfolding on multiple timescales. It takes into account the level of microsound, where granular processes often suggest fluid rather than fixed sound morphologies. This leads to new stream and cloud models, as well as processes of coalescence, evaporation, and mutation of sound that reach away from the conception of music as solely an interplay of fixed notes in metrically aligned rhythms.

This chapter is the core of the book, as it touches on the essence of composing: organizing sound. While other chapters examine different elements deployed in the game, this chapter addresses the game itself: the construction of mesostructure and macroform.

The concept of compositional organization is an abstraction—a mental plan for ordering sounds and spawning sound patterns. Any composition, not just an algorithmically generated one, can be seen as being produced by a set of operations that are constrained by a set of rules or grammar. This grammar, however, may not be explicit even to the composer, to whom it appears as elements of style. Moreover, the sonic result of composition seldom explicates the grammar or process that produced it.

Music analysts attempt to explain the internal relations within a work (i.e., a score) as a guide to explaining what we hear. Many analysts would freely admit that their deconstructions do not necessarily reflect how the composer organized the piece. In contrast, a composition strategy is the collection of ideas that a composer uses to organize his or her thoughts, to conceptualize and realize a piece. The latter topic is the subject of this chapter.

Considering music as a structure invites static architectural metaphors, while considering it as a process turns it into a recipe or algorithm. Either view taken alone is too constraining: Structure and process are entangled. That is, any musical structure is the result of a process, and every process results in a structure. The existence of one necessitates the existence of the other—like two sides of the same coin.[62]

Both of these views tend to objectify music as a logical design, removing it from the flow of real-time experience. Yet we experience music in real time as a flux of energetic forces. The instantaneous experience of music leaves behind a wake of memories in the face of a fog of anticipation.

Can we describe the organization that is heard by listeners? Neuroscientists use brain scans to try to find universal responses to musical sounds. Universals may exist, but ordinary experience teaches us that tastes vary widely. No two people listen with the same brain. Each listener imports prejudices of expectation, mood, and stylistic taste that impose a narrow filter on the sonic sensation. As they listen, their attention shifts and drifts. Musical form is apperceived in retrospect, through memory recall, which is subject to discontinuities and distortions. All of this means that a communication model of music—in which the composer transmits a message that is received and unambiguously decoded by listeners—is not realistic. Rather, "imperfect" communication, in which the message perceived by each listener is unique, is part of the fascination of music![63]

Multiscale perception

Nature is multiscale; different forces and laws come into play at different scales of space-time. Quantum laws reign at the nanoscale, while the laws of thermodynamics rule at the molecular level, resulting in the states of matter: solid, liquid, gas, or plasma (Goodstein 1985). Gravitation is a weak force at the level of atoms, yet it rules at the level of large-scale galactic evolution (Narkilkar 1977). Moreover, the rules governing the behavior of one thing are not the same as those governing a million things. Scientists are just beginning to develop models to describe the behavior of massive agglomerations of granular materials, how they collectively vibrate, flow, cluster, stabilize, and avalanche (Aranson and Tsimring 2009).

Multiple musical timescales are perceptual and physical reality (see chapter 3). We listen simultaneously on multiple timescales, from the microstructure of a single sound's timbral evolution to the parsing of global macrostructure. Musical meaning is embedded in layers and encoded in many simultaneous musical parameters or dimensions. We can listen to a sophisticated composition many times and each time recover another layer or dimension. Gestalt rules of perception govern how we parse or group events together. Thus we need a composition theory that is connected to the different scales and dimensions of human perception. As Gérard Grisey (1987) observed:

> [Musical] structure, whatever its complexity, must stop at the perceptibility of the message.

For the sake of formal coherence, it can be tempting to apply a single organizing principle to all timescales. Simple models, however, are not reflective of the multiscale world around us. As Horacio Vaggione (1996a) observed:

> The world is not self-similar. . . . Coincidences of scale are infrequent, and when one thinks that one has found one, it is generally a kind of reduction, a willful construction. The ferns imitated by fractal geometry do not constitute real models of ferns. In a real fern there are infinitely more accidents, irregularities and formal caprices—in a word—singularities—than the ossification furnished by the fractal model.

György Ligeti's important article "The metamorphoses of musical form" (1971) pointed out problems inherent in organizing all timescales according to a single abstract scheme, due to the lack of correlation with human perception. The musicologist Carl Dahlhaus (1970) adopted a similar tack in his critique of serial techniques applied to the organization of sound microstructure. Indeed, a main lesson of Stockhausen's 1957 iconic essay "How time passes" was to show how awkward it is to try to apply a proportional series developed for one timescale (e.g., pitch periods) to another timescale (e.g., note durations). Perception operates differently on these timescales, so it makes little sense to transpose the intervallic relations of the chromatic pitch scale into the domain of note durations. (See Roads 2001b.)

A truly multiscale approach to composition respects the peculiarities of each timescale. It recognizes that patterns are difficult to perceive or even imperceptible on extreme timescales—very small and very large time intervals. It also recognizes that a single pattern creates varying impressions on different timescales. Indeed, we may not even be able to identify the same pattern on different timescales.

We can transpose a pattern from one timescale to another, but the voyage is not linear. That is, pertinent cues may or may not be maintained. Specifically, the perceptual properties of a pattern are not necessarily invariant across dilations and contractions of time. To cite an example, a melody loses all sense of pitch when it is transposed very high or very low. This inconsistency does not prevent us from applying such transpositions; it merely means that we must recognize that each timescale abides by its own rules of perception.

Layers and dimensions of structure: hierarchy and heterarchy

Recall the tree structure of a simple musical composition from chapter 3 (figure 9.1).

This neat hierarchical form is highly idealized. Notice the symmetrical branching and perfect hierarchy, in which every sound object derives from exactly four layers of structure (phrase, subsection, section, and root). Children's nursery rhymes are an example of perfectly hierarchical and symmetrical structure (e.g., "Mary Had a Little Lamb," "Twinkle, Twinkle Little Star," etc.). These are trivial cases of musical structure.

Of course, symmetry is a beautiful concept. Starting from intuitive notions of symmetry, it has been codified by mathematicians as "invariance of a pattern under a group of automorphic transformations" (Weyl 1952). As pointed out in chapter 5, an automorphism maps a set into itself while preserving its internal structure. For example, a mirror image of an object is an automorphism because it preserves the geometric relations of the object in reflected form.

However, in music, one must distinguish between abstract properties like mathematical symmetry or logical consistency versus perceived properties that are experienced through the auditory system. The point is that abstract symmetry (codified visually on paper or in software) is not always perceived as such in the medium of sound.

Much music—including my own—is infused with asymmetric, imperfect, or broken hierarchies, characterized by the presence of juxtapositions, prunings,

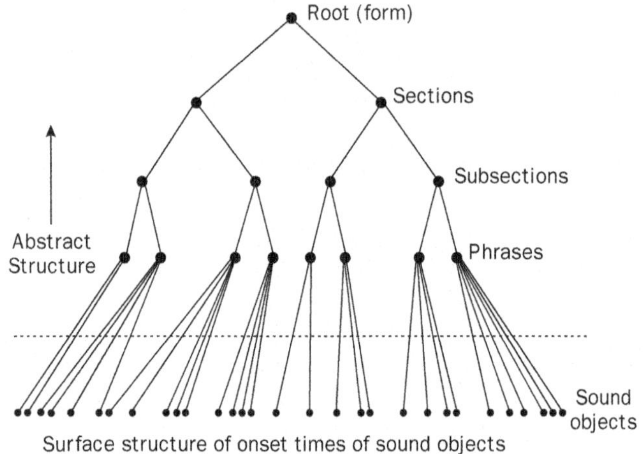

FIGURE 9.1 Idealized graph of musical structure.

and singularities (figure 9.2). Juxtapositions arise from unexpected additions or deletions—injecting surprise. They represent arborescences or prunings, respectively, of potentially hierarchical musical tree structure.

Nature is filled with *singularities*: unique events that never recur exactly the same way. When singularities appear on the sound object timescale, they juxtapose in between or superimpose upon phrases. In terms of the tree structure, they float unattached to intermediate layers of structure.

FUZZY TIMING, MUTATION, AND HETERARCHICAL ORGANIZATION

In electronic music, three additional factors work against perfect hierarchical models and are central to the enchantment of this art form: fuzzy timing, mutation, and heterarchical organization.

Fuzzy timing (for lack of a better term) means that certain sound materials have ambiguous beginning and ending times as they coalesce, evaporate, or mutate. This can be due to changes in particle density, crossfading and blending, or perceptual masking. For example, a sound can become sonically diaphanous and "evaporate" as another layer of sound rises in its place. By means of these processes, a sound can be continuously *mutating*—changing its identity through evolution in time.

Here we arrive at an important point. In music in which there is a combination of fuzzy timing and continuous mutation, we need to replace the outdated

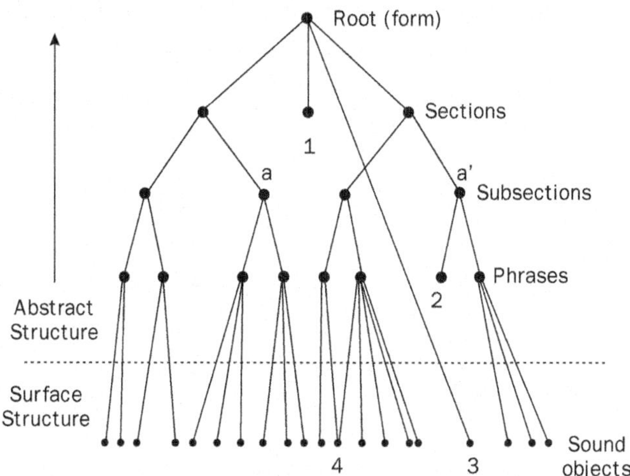

FIGURE 9.2 Imperfect tree structure: Objects 1 and 2 indicate prunings (i.e., structures that were composed and then deleted, or merely implied but not realized). For example, *a'* is a repetition of *a*, but without the initial phrase. Object 3 is a singularity that appears only once. It is not attached to any phrase and serves as a juxtaposition or element of surprise. Object 4 belongs to two phrases, serving as the ending of one and the beginning of the next. The microsonic hierarchy below the sound object level is not depicted.

notion of musical architecture as a structure that can be cleanly partitioned into discrete substructures. The situation was summarized by Denis Smalley (1997) as follows:

> Electroacoustic gestures and textures cannot be reduced either to note or pulse; the music is not necessarily composed of discrete elements. . . . Therefore it cannot be conveniently segmented.

This music often contains ambiguous and overlapping elements (on multiple levels) that cannot be easily segmented. Like layers of atmosphere, which are not neatly separated, electronic music often flows, billows, condenses, and vaporizes. Discrete elements can appear but they are not a necessity.

Another factor that works against simple hierarchical structure in music is the notion of *heterarchy*—a complex of simultaneous hierarchies (figure 9.3). These can take two forms: *parallel* and *multidimensional heterarchy.* A simple example of a parallel heterarchical structure is a set of superimposed rhythm tracks (*a, b,* and *n* in figure 9.3), each with an independent tempo. In this case, the terminal nodes are events in time. When combined, they form a polyrhythm. Digital mixing makes it easy to experiment with and manage parallel multitrack structures with shifting foreground-background relationships.

Multidimensional heterarchies arise because music speaks through multiple dimensions simultaneously: pitch, timbre, rhythm, space, and so on. A given dimension, such as pitch, for example, can be organized in a hierarchical manner independently (Morris 1987). This independence can be generalized to other dimensions. If each dimension is organized into a more-or-less independent hierarchy, the musical design presents a complex of simultaneous hierarchies. In this case, *a, b,* and *n* in figure 9.3 could be dimensions like rhythm, space, or

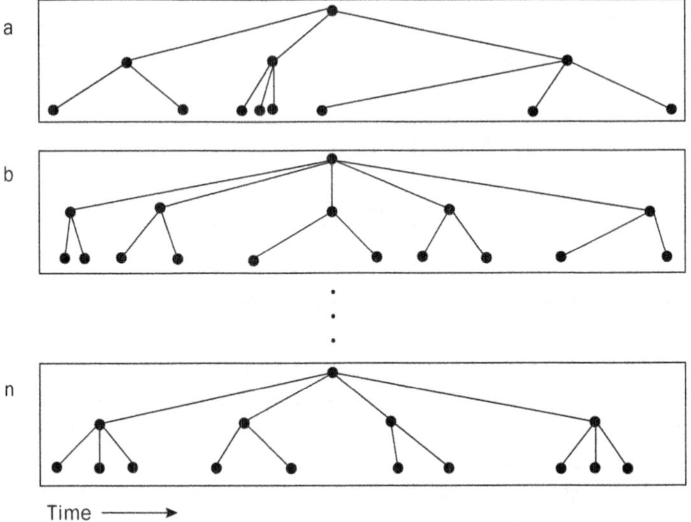

FIGURE 9.3 Heterarchical structure of multiple, simultaneous hierarchies.

pitch. In this case, the terminal nodes indicate the starting times of particular structures or behaviors.

The hierarchies can be coordinated or independent, so a slightly more complicated version of figure 9.3 could show cross-links or points of synchronization of the multiple hierarchies.

MUSIC DESIGN SPACE IS *N*-DIMENSIONAL

From a compositional point of view, music is an *n*-dimensional design space, in the sense that there are no intrinsic limits on the type and number of independent parameters that a composer can conceive of and manipulate. In the simplest case, we can organize a composition according to established dimensions or parameters such as pitch, timbre, rhythm, and spatial position. Going further, we can break any one of these dimensions down into any number of conceptual sub-dimensions. The pitch domain, for example, is a continuous space that can be subdivided into endless tunings, scales, chords, and their myriad combinations. The dimension of timbre can be articulated by variations in waveforms, spectra, filters, modulations, MPEG-7 timbral descriptors, etc., all operating simultaneously. The domain of space can be subdivided into lateral position, vertical position, image width, image depth, panning speed, rotation speed, and so on, all of which can vary on different timescales.

A given dimension can be further abstracted by means of higher-order organizing principles. For example, in Stockhausen's composition *Kontakte* (1960), the dimensions of organization concerned not a simple scalar parameter, such as amplitude, but degrees of change in a parameter, from static to dynamic. Another higher-order principle could be a degree of alignment to a meter, rhythmic pattern, harmonic mode, or scale. Any kind of opposition can be set up as a higher-order dimension of organization: static versus varying, fast versus slow, duple versus triple, statistical versus determinate, dense versus sparse, similar versus different, recognizable versus not recognizable, ad infinitum. The list is endless.

PARTIAL SYSTEMS

A composer can design a set of rules or system to govern one or many of these dimensions. But systems can also be set up and taken down like temporary scaffolding to be superseded by other forms of organization. Luciano Berio (2006) called them *partial systems*:

> Every musical work is a set of partial systems that interact among themselves, not merely because they are active at the same time, but because they establish a sort of organic and unstable reciprocity. Without that reciprocity we enter into a rather . . . uncomfortable musical space—we like to think about it but we don't have to listen to it—as is the case with works like Schoenberg's *Wind Quintet* or Boulez's first book of *Structures*.

As the parameters and the strategies used in different parts of a piece vary, the result may well be that the number of structural levels in a piece also varies. As Denis Smalley (1997) pointed out:

> There is no permanent type of hierarchical organization for all of electroacoustic music, or even within a single work. Undoubtedly there are structural levels, but they do not need to remain consistent in number throughout a work.

Given all these possibilities, it is no surprise that forms in electronic music are extremely heterogeneous.

Organizing macroform

The macro timescale covers the overall form of a composition. It is one thing to create an interesting sound or a clever phrase; it is quite another to design an original and convincing form. The test of composing is the delicate and dangerous business of piecing together a series of major sections that result in a form. Everything is at stake in this process. More than once, I have lost a composition on the emergency operating table of formal organization. These pieces did not make it into my repertoire. The importance of form was emphasized by Varèse (1949):

> Form is the dominant element in all works of art and my essential preoccupation, when I compose, is to focus on the form, on the structure of the work that I have conceived.

In the context of classical music, to discuss form is to reference a well-established taxonomy: a catalog of traditional organizational schemata such as march, rondo, minuet, and so on. In practice, however, a large number of compositions have been realized that do not correspond to the traditional catalog of forms. In particular, electronic music today exhibits a heterogeneous collection of macro morphologies. Traditional theory would classify these as "free forms" (Berry 1966).

The form of a work contextualizes the internal materials and structures, articulating their structural roles, rendering them what Krenek (1966) called "recognizable":

> The problem of modern music is one of recognition and understanding, because its inner technical problem is one of form. For in the aesthetic sense, form is a prerequisite of recognition. Formless content is . . . unrecognizable.

The *macroform* of a piece results from a compositional design or plan. As Varèse (1966) observed:

> Form is a result—the result of a process.

(a) **Top-down strategy**

1 Design macro form

2 Design Substructures

3 Create sound material that fills
in the higher-level structures

(b) **Bottom-up strategy**

3 Macroform emerges as the result of
lower-level processes

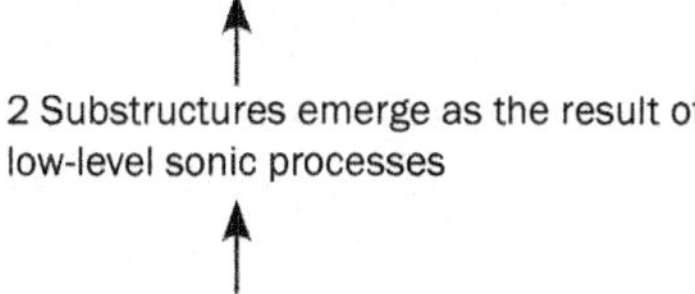

2 Substructures emerge as the result of
low-level sonic processes

1 Generate sound materials

(c) **Multiscale planning**

Macroform

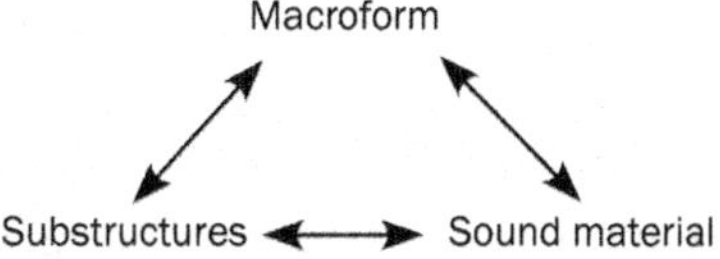

Substructures ⟷ Sound material

FIGURE 9.4 Three types of composition plans: (a) top-down strategy, (b) bottom-up strategy, and (c) multiscale strategy.

From a general perspective, plans can be divided into three basic types: *top-down*, *bottom-up*, and *multiscale* (figure 9.4). The next three sections discuss each of these basic approaches in turn.

This division into three cases is obviously a simplification; many compositions can be seen as combinations where one or another strategy dominates at any given time in the construction of the piece. An example would be a piece whose surface structure is mainly determined by a low-level formal process (bottom-up) but which has brief beginning and ending sections tagged onto it (top-down) (e.g., *Ensembles for Synthesizer* [1964] by Milton Babbitt). Notice how after a one-minute introduction, characterized by slow gestures, the core exposition of the work, characterized by a manic pace, takes over.

Sound example 9.1. Excerpt of *Ensembles for Synthesizer* (1964) by Milton Babbitt.

TOP-DOWN PLANNING

> The characteristic effort of the serious composer, as I see it, is not so much in the invention of musical ideas in themselves, as in the invention of interesting ideas that will also fill certain compositional requirements and allow for imaginative . . . phrases and their shape and content, the way he joins them, the type of articulation he uses, as well as the general drift or continuity of a large section, and the construction of the whole work. The small details . . . fall naturally into shape when one has interesting conceptions of the larger shapes.
>
> —ELLIOT CARTER (1960)

The top-down approach starts by predefining a macroform, a template whose details are filled in at later stages of composition. This approach corresponds to the traditional notion of form in classical music, wherein certain schemes have been used by composers as molds (Apel 1972). Music theory textbooks catalog the classical generic forms, such as song, march, waltz, rondo, and so on (Leichtentritt 1951; Berry 1966; Schoenberg 1967). The classical generic forms of occidental music originated in religious ceremonies (pagan rites, sung prayers, canticles, chants, hymns, masses, madrigals, motets) and social functions of the aristocracy and the military (dance fashions, fanfares, military exercises, gala symphony and opera concerts) (Grout 1973).[64]

Much great music has been written using the classical generic forms. Some of it follows the form schema closely, while in other cases, the schema is interpreted loosely. However, the strict use of classical generic forms was called into question at the turn of the 20th century. Claude Debussy, among others, discarded what he called sarcastically "administrative forms" and replaced them with fluctuating mesostructures through a chain of associated variations. In Debussy's *Jeux* (1913) for example, we hear undulating mesostructures—full of local detail—that resist classification within the standard catalog of textbook forms.

Since Debussy, a tremendous amount of music has been written that is not based on a previously defined classical form. The emergence of electronic music has rendered these historical forms even less relevant. This is due in part to fresh sonic materials, increased control over dimensions other than pitch, and new organizing principles that tend away from neatly hierarchical structures. Nonetheless, while musical form has continued to evolve in practice, the standard textbook repertoire of classical generic forms has not been updated over the past century.

Although the use of classical generic forms has diminished, the practice of top-down planning remains common in contemporary composition. Many composers design the macrostructure of their pieces according to a formal outline before a single sound is composed. (A-B-A form is alive and well.)

The most basic macroform is the continuous drone, as in the music of Eliane Radigue, for example, *Jetsun Mila* (1986) and *L'île Re-sonante* (2000). While drones typically revolve around a note or chord, Radigue also builds them around continuous noises.

Plans revolving around a systematic strategy often start from a top-down conception. In Charles Dodge's *Changes* (1970) for computer-generated sound, the entire work unfolds according to a detailed plan set out in advance:

> The texture of the composition comprises the same three elements throughout: lines, chords, and percussion; and each textural element delineates a different aspect of the composition's pitch structure. The chords play segments (3 to 6 notes) of the twelve-tone set that forms the basis of the work. In the course of the work the chords sound all 48 forms of the set. The lines play six-note segments of the set which are related to the original by rotation. The percussion duplicates the pitch-class content of the chords (i.e., the percussion linearizes the pitches of the chords). For the computer performance I designed an "orchestra" of "instruments" that emphasize the different types of pitch-delineation. For the lines, a family of registral instruments was created which consist of a pulse generator (of the type used in speech synthesis), which is fed into multiple banks of filters in series. As the amplitude of the banks of filters is varied, the timbre of the note changes. Further, the center-frequency settings of the filters are changed with each chord change, so that the timbre change itself changes as a function of the chord changes, which are themselves a function of the rate at which the lines sound all twelve tones. As the work progresses, each note in the lines incorporates more and more timbre changes, so that at the end each note changes timbre six times. All of the "percussion" sounds entail a timbre-change which is the result of different components decaying at different rates.

Discussion of top-down planning

An issue with strict top-down planning is its overemphasis on high-level concept and structure and its underemphasis on sound material. As pointed out in chapter 4, material and organization are intertwined. If the form is predefined, the sound material must be carefully chosen to conform to the package selected for it. The container tends to constrain free evolutions and mutations within the chosen sonic material. Moreover, if the form is identifiable (e.g., the well-known A-B-A form), then it is predictable.[65]

Accompanying top-down planning is a myth that composers proceed by conceiving an entire piece in their mind and then simply realizing it. Even Schoenberg (1967) promoted this myth:

> A composer does not, of course, add bit by bit, as a child does in building with wooden blocks. He conceives an entire composition as a spontaneous vision. Then he proceeds, like Michelangelo who chiseled his Moses out of marble without sketches, complete in every detail, thus directly forming his material.

The evidence left by many composers (notably Beethoven) indicates otherwise. Many important compositions are arduously pieced together out of little blocks during long periods of gestation, revision, major reorganization, and all manner of editing and refinement in which the final form is only discovered far into the process.

BOTTOM-UP PLANNING

Bottom-up planning is the opposite of a top-down approach. It constructs form as the final result of a process of internal development produced by interactions on low levels of structure—like a seed growing into a mature plant. In this approach, processes of attractive and repulsive pattern formation unfolding on lower levels of structure can lead to articulation of meso and macrostructure. Consonances, aggregations, synchronizations, and resolutions are types of attraction, while dissonances, scatterings, desynchronizations, and tensions are types of repulsion.

The rest of this section focuses on four approaches to bottom-up planning: development, sequence layering, indeterminancy, and generative algorithms.

Development

Traditional composition textbooks offer myriad ways to develop low-level structures into mesostructure. A classic example is variations on a theme. As Schoenberg (1967) observed:

> Smaller forms may be expanded by means of external repetitions, sequences, extensions, liquidations and broadening of connectives. The number of parts may be increased by supplying codettas, episodes, etc. In such situations, derivatives of the basic motive are formulated into new thematic units.

These same elaborations available in instrumental music are also available to the electronic music composer. In addition, the composer of electronic music can rely on other tactics for development. These could be, for example, processes of timbral mutation, spatial counterpoint, detailed control of complex sound masses, juxtapositions of virtual and real soundscapes, sonic coalescence and disintegration, and interplay between the micro timescale and other timescales that cannot be realized by acoustic instruments. For example, a common means of development in electronic music is dilation (time expansion) of a short sound fragment into an evolving sound mass, through granulation or another process. Here the continuous unfolding of the sonic patterns takes place over many seconds, on the same timescale as a harmonic progression.

Sequence layering

Sequence layering is another classic bottom-up strategy. In this approach, the composer constructs various patterns and then arranges them in sequences and layers. Very often, the patterns repeat or loop. In general, there is little emphasis on teleological development (goal-directed motion), although there can be variations in the repeating patterns. Common examples of sequence layering include the synchronic loops of techno music and the repetitive music of Steve Reich and others. The idea of loops or cycles repeating asynchronously is a signature technique in the oeuvre of Luc Ferrari, beginning in his *Visage I* (1956) and continuing through his installation *Cycle des Souvenirs* (2000) for four video projectors and six compact disc players.[66]

Indeterminacy

A different example of a bottom-up approach is found in the work of artists following in the wake of the composer John Cage. He conceived of form as arising from a series of accidents—random or improvised sounds (Cage 1973). For Cage, sound and form were epiphenomena: side effects of a conceptual strategy. Many of Cage's scores were detailed scripts that left the sonic result to happenstance. In *Imaginary Landscape 4* (1951) for 12 radio receivers, the sound is dependent on whatever radio shows are playing at the place and time of performance.

Such an approach often results in discontinuous changes in sound. Ironically, this was not mere chance; Cage (1959) planned for juxtaposition:

> Where people had felt the necessity to stick sounds together to make a continuity, we felt the necessity to get rid of the glue so that sounds would be themselves.

In many pieces, his instructions to the performer serve as designs for discontinuity. Paradoxically, ridding music of intentionality was Cage's intention. As Pritchett (1996) points out, his method of composition was willful:

> In composing these 44 pieces for *Apartment house 1776*, Cage had a goal that was clearly defined. His first attempts at making the piece in accordance with his goals were failures. Cage evaluated these intermediate results, making refinements and modifications to his way of working. Through this process, he eventually produced a finished product that he judged "beautiful," "brilliant," "marvelous."

Cage worked iteratively, trying experiments in which random choices were applied to different aspects of the piece, until he achieved a sonic result that was intuitively satisfactory to him. In this trial-and-error approach, he was not so different from many other composers.

Generative algorithms

The last approach to bottom-up planning that we discuss here involves generative algorithms. Although fascinating in many ways, this approach is not without its issues. To begin with, the quest for rigor through the use of formal processes is not a guarantee of artistic success. I will say more on this in a moment.

Another issue concerns strategies based on models in which a series or formula is expanded by permutation and combination into larger structures. A profound law of mathematics governs such combinatorial processes. Repeated permutations and combinations lead inevitably to higher states of entropy (i.e., increasing randomness; Ekelund 1988). As a simple example, take an ordinary deck of playing cards that begins completely ordered. Even a simple permutation such as "select every third card" leads to a randomization of the material. A popular term for permutation is *shuffling*—randomizing the order of a deck of playing cards. As Wolfram (2002) noted:

> Once significant randomness has been produced in a system, the overall properties of that system tend to become largely independent of the details of the initial conditions.

The effect of serial techniques on composition was described by Luciano Berio (2006) as follows:

> Serialists extracted from Webern's poetics those elements that would give concrete and conceptual drive to the break with the past. These elements were the autonomy and the equivalence of musical parameters often submitted to indifferent permutational procedures—so indifferent that the music could go on forever. It could not end; it could only stop. Grounded in permutational and equalizing criteria, and essentially lacking virtual or hidden dimensions, it was soon neutralized by the objective possibility of generating . . . evolving structures. . . . The excess of estranged formal order generated disorder.

Thus a quest for systematic procedures or rigor led to disorder in musical material. Many were caught up in a kind of apophenia—trying to find patterns in essentially meaningless data.

Another area of confusion is the focus on *emergent morphogenesis*, a variation on bottom-up planning. "Emergent" in a creative context means that the large-scale structure as a whole acquires complex properties through interactions among low-level automata, possibly augmented by feedback (Anderson 2005). Morphogenesis is a term from biology concerning the shapes of different tissues, organs, and organisms that grow out of cells that initially appear similar. Another term for this process is *cellular differentiation*, as cells acquire a type in the process of development.

> Emergence is associated with novelty, surprise, spontaneity, agency—even creativity. Emergent phenomena are associated with the appearance of order, structure, or behavior at a hierarchical level above that of the underlying system. . . .
>
> —JON MCCORMACK ET AL. (2009)

In algorithms designed to produce emergent morphogenesis, the automata themselves are usually simple procedures. The composer designs a low-level algorithmic process, whose control parameters may be only indirectly related to the acoustic result. Larger-scale sound structures are supposed to unfold as a byproduct of these low-level algorithmic processes.

An example of a generative approach with emergent behavior is Xenakis's GENDYN system for *dynamic stochastic synthesis* of sound. The GENDYN system generated sound waveforms using a system of interrelated probabilities (Serra 1992; Xenakis 1992; Harley 2004). The control parameters of this algorithm were only indirectly related to the acoustic properties of the generated waveform. That is, the algorithm was not designed or controlled in terms of acoustic properties like pitch, amplitude, phase, or spectrum. Thus the sonic result was unpredictable. A melody, for example, might emerge out of chaotic noise, only to dissolve into chaos, never to be heard again.

Sound example 9.2. Excerpt of *Gendy 3* (1991) by Iannis Xenakis. 

A composer who has focused on the generation of unpredictable emergent sonorities is Agostino Di Scipio (1997), who has used fractal algorithms and cellular automata in this quest, as well as purely acoustic feedback systems (Di Scipio 2012).

In related research, Wolfram (2002) documented numerous experiments with images generated by the interaction of simple automata. In particular, he showed how complicated visual patterns could be spawned by the interaction of multiple automata, each of which is governed by simple rules of behavior. He observed four basic classes of emergent behavior:

Class 1. Almost all initial conditions led to exactly the same uniform finite state.
Class 2. Many possible final states but all of them exhibit simple structures that repeat or loop.
Class 3. More complicated and random although triangles and other localized structures appear.
Class 4. Mixture of order and randomness, with the presence of persistent localized structures that move around and interact with other structures in complicated ways.

Is the multiscale nature of class 4 behavior a good model of generative music? This remains an open question. Wolfram's website (WolframTones) lets visitors generate, via similar rules, sound patterns in a variety of musical styles. These banal sound patterns, however, operate on only one level of organization; they lack narrative macrostructure, development, sectional organization, and macroform. They start without formal opening and continue mechanically ad infinitum, without taking into account higher forces operating above the sonic surface, for example, driving forces like birth, evolution, death, contrasts of attraction and repulsion, tension and relaxation.

Sound example 9.3. Four musical outputs from Wolfram Tones using the "classical" style selection. 

In general, a rigorous bottom-up algorithmic approach tends to romanticize logical process and pure conceptual schemes, sometimes to the neglect of the sonic result. There is, of course, nothing wrong about using formalist strategies (see chapter 11). However, mathematical elegance on paper is not equivalent to musical elegance in sound.[67] An "interesting" algorithm (however that is defined) cannot itself guarantee interesting musical results, if only because there are innumerable ways to map a given process onto sound. Some of these are inevitably more interesting then others. If the perceptual experience is boring, it is difficult to convince an audience that the concept behind a piece is fascinating.

Discussion of bottom-up strategies

Strict bottom-up strategies tend to be limited by a kind of conceptual purity that privileges low-level algorithms and underemphasizes narrative processes transpiring on higher timescales. As Smalley (1997) observed:

> It is fair to say that much electroacoustic music does not offer sufficient hierarchical variety. . . . With textured structures it is very easy for the composer, listening too hard to the textural material, to be deceived into thinking that there is lower-level interest in the material when there is not. . . . A rewarding balance of perceptual interest at a variety of structural levels is unfortunately more rare than it should be.

The surface structure produced by a low-level algorithm can be quite "complicated" (in the sense of being nonredundant) while lacking a rich hierarchical structure of clearly perceivable beginnings, middles, endings, pregnant pauses, directional transitions, juxtapositions, singularities, and sectional articulations. These do not simply "emerge" out of most bottom-up strategies.

MULTISCALE PLANNING

Both top-down and bottom-up planning privilege early decisions in the compositional process. In order to remain consistent, they mandate a commitment to the initial plan. In contrast, multiscale planning circumvents the preset and inflexible nature of strict top-down and bottom-up strategies. It takes into account the entire network of complicated relationships among timescales.

Multiscale planning encourages an interplay between inductive and deductive thinking, that is, from the specific to the general, and from the general to the specific. We use induction when we start working with a specific fragment and then see how many fragments can fit together within a larger framework. We use deduction when we conclude that a detail is inconsistent with the work as a whole. As Xenakis (1975) observed:

> Musicians are taught in schools to start with cells, that is, melodic patterns. . . . All polyphonic and serial music is based on a string of notes. Then they expand it by inversions and other polyphonic, harmonic, and orchestral manipulations. Now this is going from the detail to the large body, you see. In architecture, you must first take into consideration the large body and

> then go to details, or both simultaneously. However, in addition to that, you always have to think of the land, the entire scope. . . . That perhaps is one of the most important examples of what architecture gave to me, that is, how to think of music, not only from the detail to the generality, but conversely from architectural . . . to the details.

Details matter. The multiscale approach recognizes the detailed realm of microsound. As Horacio Vaggione (2000) observed:

> Once you are sensitive to a multiscale approach to composition, you do not see the note as an atomic entity—a primitive building block—anymore, but rather as a layered object containing many interacting timescales.

Sound example 9.4. Excerpt of *Points Critiques* (2012) by Horacio Vaggione. 

The core virtue of multiscale planning is flexibility; it mediates between abstract high-level concepts and unanticipated opportunities and imperatives emerging from the lower levels of sound structure. What are these imperatives? Certain objects and phrases cannot be neatly packaged within precut form boxes. (Consider sounds with a slow attack compressed into a rapid rhythmic sequence; there is not enough time for the attack to unfold before the sound ends.) Instead, they mandate a container (mesoform) that conforms to their unique morphology and moment. Thus, the multiscale approach tends toward variety and heterogeneity in mesostructures. This stands in contrast to bottom-up strategies, where there is little focus on building a rich hierarchical structure of clearly defined mesostructures: beginnings and endings, contrasting phrases, sections, transitions, and juxtapositions.

Multiscale planning is opportunistic

Multiscale planning is opportunistic. That is, at any point in the compositional process, the composer takes advantage of discoveries uncovered by exploration of material on any timescale. As Stravinsky (1942) noted:

> In the course of my labors I come across something unexpected. This unexpected element strikes me. I make a note of it. At the proper time I put it to profitable use. This gift of chance must not be confused with that capriciousness of imagination that is commonly called fancy. Fancy implies a predetermined will to abandon one's self to caprice. The aforementioned assistance of the unexpected is something quite different. It is a collaboration that is intimately bound up with the inertia of the creative process.

Berio (2006) expressed a similar view:

> The fascination of the studies of the itineraries of great musical minds (Beethoven, for example) does not lie simply in the account of the creative choices made, but above all in the description of the composer's ability to discover one thing when he was looking for something different.

Or as Maconie (1998) observed about Stockhausen:

> I soon came to discover that the serial principle in Stockhausen was nevertheless not as "pure" or transparent to analysis as for example in the music of Webern or Schoenberg. In practice, Stockhausen's formal structure is subject to reflective treatments, fantasies and elaborations that fly off at a tangent to the initiating program of synthesis and are treated literally as "diversions" [local decisions] to be followed up immediately, and not simply avoided or filed away. There is a point in *Kontakte* (17 min 38.5 sec in the published score, 33 seconds into cue 14 on the Stockhausen-Verlag CD) where the music settles on the note E below middle C, and having reached that point Stockhausen said he just wanted to go deeper into this one note, even though to do so was not part of his original scheme. As a novice codebreaker I found this disregard of laid-down procedure deliberately perplexing, even morally objectionable. It took me a long time to realize that Stockhausen was right. The series (or rigorous procedure) is not simply a yellow brick road or path of righteousness (Webern's "path to the new music") from which one is forbidden to stray. Nor is it there for your artistic protection; nor is it a guarantee of musical virtue. . . . Stockhausen's willingness to be diverted, however subversive it may seem to an academic observer, is in fact a key to his superior achievement as a composer.

Multiscale planning can begin from either a top-down or bottom-up starting point. For example, one might start from a high-level conception and then modify it as specific sounds are mapped onto it. Here the composer makes local decisions that take advantage of idiosyncratic or unexpected features that arise in building lower-level structures. Another top-down starting point would be a piece that is constructed by editing an existing sound file, for example, a long granulation. In this case, it is possible that major chunks of form are already built into the material. The construction of my piece *Tenth vortex* (2001), for example, began with subtractive carving and rearrangement of material from a long granulated sound file originally performed in real time. Beginning with this rough draft, I then began to rearrange the sound material on successively smaller timescales in the studio.

Sound example 9.5. Excerpt of *Tenth vortex* (2000) by Curtis Roads.

The construction of *Eleventh vortex* (2001) began in a similar manner. As I worked on the original material, however, I realized that the macroform would require structures that were not to be found in the original material, necessitating major surgery and new synthesis experiments. The realization of *Eleventh vortex* took much longer than the *Tenth*, and this shows in its idiosyncratic macroform.

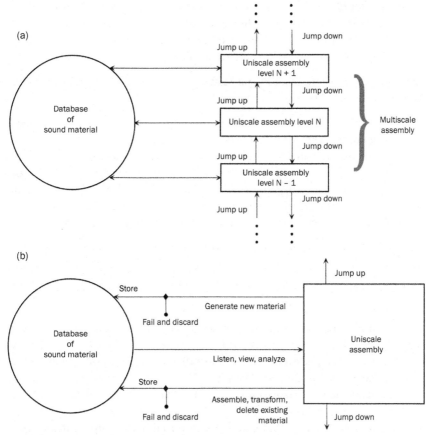

FIGURE 9.5 Multiscale strategies: (a) multiscale assembly, and (b) uniscale assembly on a single timescale.

Sound example 9.6. Excerpt of *Eleventh vortex* (2001) by Curtis Roads. 

Multiscale assembly

Figure 9.5a depicts three stages of multiscale assembly, each one corresponding to a different timescale of musical organization. At each stage of assembly, one can read from and write to a database of sound material (at left). The database can be as simple as a single sound file. The lines running out of the assembly boxes indicate actions. Figure 9.5b depicts possible actions on one timescale:

1. Trial-and-error generation of new material. If the composer judges the attempt to be a success, store the new structure in the database; otherwise discard it.
2. Listening, viewing, or analyzing existing sound material.

3. Trial-and-error assembly, transformation, or deletion of existing sound material. If the composer judges the attempt to be a success, store the new structure in the database; otherwise discard it.
4. Skip up or down one or more timescales.

The composer and conductor Bruno Maderna emphasized the flexibility inherent in this approach at Darmstadt in 1957:

> Whereas instrumental composition is preceded in most cases by a linear development of thought . . . the fact that in electronic music one can try out directly various possible sound structures and manipulate these ad infinitum to obtain new musical images, and lastly, that the composer can store away a vast amount of unfinished material, puts the composer in a completely novel position. Time appears as a field where he can experiment with an inordinate number of possible arrangements and permutations of material already produced.

His dense electronic composition *Continuo* (1958) no doubt reflects this process.

Sound example 9.7. Excerpt of *Continuo* (1958) by Bruno Maderna.

Just as sounds tend to suggest their own combinations, certain phrases suggest that they be organized together. In this way, increasingly larger mesostructures accumulate through editing. Such a bottom-up strategy is, however, driven by low-level detail and tends toward continuations. A typical example is the design of a melody, which in order to flow should be packed with transition notes in order to minimize discontinuities.

A common situation that occurs in an initial bottom-up strategy is that one builds up several mesostructures having little to do with one another. Now the composer needs to step back from the low-level material in order to analyze it and plan a larger-scale design. This can involve the construction of bridge sections to span the gap between disparate mesostructures, or the insertion of radical juxtapositions that would never have emerged from the bottom up.

As a last resort, it is sometimes necessary to discard part of the material or an entire piece. To know when it is not working and not worth additional effort is perhaps the greatest wisdom an artist can have.

Guessing, retreating, abandoning strategies

Multiscale composition is an experimental, trial-and-error process, full of risk. Behind every choice lies a hypothesis, or in simple terms, a guess. As the mathematician George Polya (1954) observed:

> Strictly speaking, all our knowledge outside of mathematics and demonstrative logic (a branch of mathematics) consists of conjectures. . . . We support our conjectures by *plausible reasoning.* A mathematical proof is demonstrative reasoning, but the inductive evidence of the physicist, the circumstantial

> evidence of the lawyer, the documentary evidence of the historian, and the statistical evidence of the economist belong to plausible reasoning. . . . Finished mathematics presented in finished form appears as purely demonstrative, consisting of proofs only. Yet mathematics in the making resembles any other form of human knowledge in the making. You have to guess a mathematical theorem before you prove it; you have to guess the idea of the proof before you work out all the details. You have to combine observations and follow analogies; you have to try and try again. The result of the mathematician's creative work is demonstrative reasoning, a proof; but the proof is discovered by plausible reasoning, by guessing.

Even at its most formalist, composition is a game of guessing. The formalist composer guesses an algorithmic tactic (one out of innumerable choices) that would be interesting to try.

Formalist or not, at each step of composition, one chooses an arbitrary path out of many possible forks. This is an experimental process. Experiments can fail, meaning that we need to retreat by discarding hours/days/weeks/months/even years of work. As Varèse (1949) observed:

> The most beautiful phrase must be abandoned if it is not part of the structure, otherwise it is nothing but a vagabond of the imagination.

Backtracking can be painful but also liberating. Discarding waste and clutter cleans house. Indeed, editing (modifying, rearranging, and cutting) is deeply creative work.

A great deal of my composition practice is subtractive: weeding out the unnecessary while conserving the essential. As in gardening, we remove dead material and detritus to reveal the simple living form hidden underneath.

A related strategy for compositional problem-solving is temporary abandonment: putting work aside for a while to come back to it with a fresh impression (Hamming 1997). In my case, this can be weeks, months, or years. In some instances, this has led to a reassessment resulting in permanent abandonment, a positive outcome for the world!

Multiscale planning as puzzle-solving

Multiscale planning can be likened to solving an n-dimensional jigsaw puzzle, where each piece in the puzzle is a sound object with a potentially unique morphology. How the pieces will ultimately fit together is not evident at the beginning. As the composer assembles the puzzle, certain objects appear to be natural matches: They fit in sequence or in parallel. Other objects seem out of place. Unlike a conventional jigsaw puzzle, however, one can construct new sound objects to fill in transitional gaps, or transform existing objects so that they fit better.

This process of solving a compositional puzzle can involve advance planning guided by predetermined design goals, but it can also be intuitive, exploratory, and open-ended. The process of aesthetic puzzle-solving can be quite difficult to describe precisely in words or in computer programs. How do human beings make aesthetic decisions? Our brains are designed to instantaneously tap largely unconscious preferences thousands of times a day in all of life's choices. As the master landscape architect Russell Page (1994) observed about this process:

> Whether I am making a landscape or a garden or arranging a window box, I must first address the problem as an artist composing a picture; my preoccupation is with the relationship between objects. . . . Take, for instance, a glass, a bunch of keys, and an apple and put them on a tray. As you move them around, their impact, the impression you receive from them, will change with every arrangement. Many of their interrelationships will be meaningless, some will be more or less harmonious, but every now and again you will hit on an arrangement that appears just.

The more objects in play, however, the more combinatorial possibilities accumulate. In such a case, the game of composition can slow down, as each object inserted carries additional implications, some of which can only be resolved by further editing or synthesis.

As the puzzle takes shape, the trial-and-error process of montage, of successive refinement and rearrangement, should lead to the illusion that the puzzle could be solved in only one way. In reality, there is no perfect solution. Along these lines, Stockhausen (1960) observed:

> I would probably still be working on *Kontakte* today if I had not finished it by deciding on a certain performance date. . . . The present ending appears to me to be a pseudo-conclusion at the most—it merely looks as though it cannot go on.

Yet this illusion of narrative functionality is basic to all music. Music is a loosely constrained system. That is, for any musical problem, there are usually multiple solutions. Composers choose a satisfactory solution, and if they have talent, this solution sustains a convincing illusion of being optimal and even inevitable.

The original database of sound is a constraint at the beginning of the process. But in a multiscale approach, we can generate new material at any point. We are not obliged to fit every sound in the database into the puzzle. The puzzle is solved when we are satisfied with the sonic result. Nor is this solution necessarily final. After the sonic feedback of a first audition, rehearsal, or performance, it is common practice for a composer to revise a work.

This reinforces my view that a composition is never "perfectly formed." Even great works have traces of arbitrary and capricious details, not to mention weak passages, stray threads, and loose ends. These imperfections can add to the charm of a work, even imbuing it with soul and spirit. I have already discussed compositions in which "trivial" or "insubstantial" sections are deliberately introduced in order to set up listeners for intense fireworks to come. Are these imperfections? Is every moment of a work supposed to carry the same weight as every other moment? Of course not. It makes no sense to talk of a perfect solution to a compositional puzzle: perfect according to what criteria, what context, what critic, what culture, what era?

The intellectually intensive and emotionally challenging puzzle-solving stage of composition can be far removed from the initial stages of inspiration and sound play. During this puzzle-solving stage, the composer must continuously make guesses and choices: whether to maintain the spirit of the original inspiration or to follow a more open-ended process of discovery, knowing that it may lead far away from the original conception. As Luc Ferrari (in Caux 2002) observed:

> When I put the sound objects into place with their times of action . . . inevitably I have urges to transform the [original] concept. Should I resist these urges in order to defend the concept or should I let myself go and please my imagination? Both possibilities seem equally acceptable. I am a creator who is, at any given moment, free with respect to the concept. I can follow the rules of the game that I have invented, but I also have the possibility to ignore them.

This freedom of choice, in which each work follows its own path, is inherent in the multiscale approach.

Analysis and the multiscale approach

Ongoing analysis of all levels of musical form and function is important in the multiscale process, especially in the later stages of construction. Problems in a composition must be confronted directly through analysis, a process akin to debugging software. One listens to each and every event in a work in progress, analyzing its function and implications. This allows one to identify extraneous elements that are neither implied by previous events nor imply any future events. One identifies the boundaries of basic narrative structures such as beginnings, motives, the outline of phrases, development sections, recapitulations, and endings. Sometimes, analysis poses bigger questions as to the nature of the material and the compositional process, which can even lead one to discard the piece altogether, not necessarily a bad thing. Composition is an experimental exploration, and not all experiments are grand successes.

Organizing mesostructure

Mesostructure encapsulates groups of sound objects on a timescale of notes (from about 100 ms to about eight seconds) into small and large phrases (from about eight seconds to several minutes). Within this category are all manner of patterns of sound objects and transitions from one mesostructure to another.

The range of potential sound morphologies is unlimited. In his *Traité*, Pierre Schaeffer attempted to create a taxonomy of sound objects, but he later recognized the need to account for the morphology of musical mesostructures as well (Schaeffer 1966, 1976, 1977; Chion 2009).

Taking up Schaeffer's challenge, *spectromorphology*, introduced in chapter 6, is a theory developed by the British composer Denis Smalley (1986, 1997) for categorizing various types of sound shapes and structural functions of mesostructure. Although it was not designed as a theory of composition, spectromorphology serves as an analytical catalog of possible compositional processes in electronic music. Smalley specifically characterized mesostructural processes according to their pattern of motion and growth. Such processes have directional tendencies that lead us to expect possible outcomes.

COMMON MESOSTRUCTURES

Certain mesostructures are common to both instrumental and electronic music. These include the following:

Repetitions—the most basic musical structure: iterations of a single sound or group of sounds. If the iteration is regular, it forms a pulse or loop.

Melodies—sequential strings of varying sound objects forming melodies, not just of pitch, but also of timbre, amplitude, duration, or spatial position.

Variations—iterations of figure groups under various transformations, so that subsequent iterations vary.

Polyphonies—parallel sequences, where the interplay between the sequences is either closely correlated (as in harmony), loosely correlated (as in counterpoint), or independent; the sequences can articulate pitch, timbre, amplitude, duration, or spatial position.

The next section focuses on polyphony, whose meaning has evolved in the age of electronic medium.

Polyphony and electronic music

Polyphony or counterpoint in traditional instrumental and vocal music refers to the use of two or more simultaneous but independent melodic lines: a pattern of note oppositions. Polyphony takes different forms in electronic music. We can categorize these according to the timescale. Polyphony on a micro timescale (as in granular synthesis) results in cloud, stream, or sound mass textures. While traditional polyphony depends on a counterpoint of stable notes, a texturally rich and mutating sound mass does not necessarily require a contrasting line to maintain interest. Of course, one or more independent lines (such as a bass line) playing against a sound mass can also be effective.

Polyphony on the level of sound objects is analogous to traditional note-against-note polyphony. Consider the tight counterpoint of Milton Babbitt's *Reflections* (1975) for piano and synthesized tape, where the two parts play a game of mirror/opposition that shifts back and forth on a second-by-second basis. The polyphony is not merely pitch contra pitch but also timbre contra timbre and pitch contra noise.

Sound example 9.8. Excerpt of *Reflections* (1975) for piano and synthesized tape by Milton Babbitt. 

Other kinds of polyphony frequently heard in electronic music include crossfading voices, repeating echoes, or reverberations that carry over other sounds.

On the mesostructural or phrase level, multitrack mixing systems enable free polyphony of independent lines that can be synchronized at pivotal moments. Such structural processes were foreshadowed by Charles Ives (1874–1954), for example, in his multilayered *Symphony Number 4* (1916).[68]

Intertwined with mesostructural interactions are higher-level processes governing the density of the polyphony. Polyphony in electronic music is also related to processes of *fission* (splitting of a sound) and *fusion* (merging of a sound). For example, in his piece *Kontakte* (1960), Stockhausen created compound sounds whose components split off from the main branch (Maconie 1989). In the inverse case, multiple independent branches can fuse to a single branch.

Xenakis called these processes *arborescences*. As figure 9.6 shows, he drew arborescences graphically and synthesized them directly with the UPIC system. He also transcribed them into instrumental notation (Varga 1996; Solomis 2004).

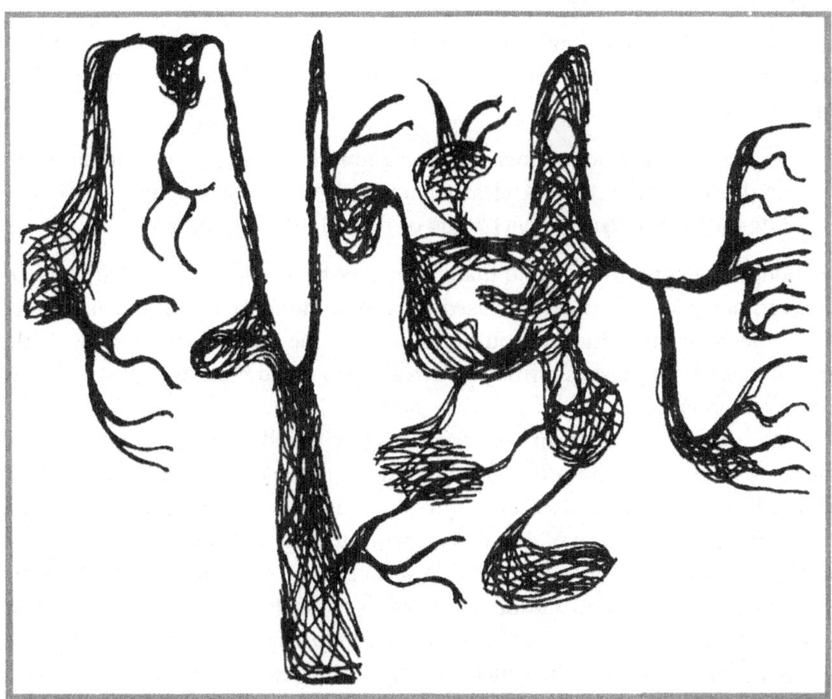

FIGURE 9.6 Arborescences in the graphic score of Xenakis's *Mycenae-Alpha* (1978) for UPIC synthesis. Reprinted with permission of Editions Salabert, 22 rue Chauchat, 75009 Paris, France.

Sound example 9.9. Excerpt of *Mycenae-Alpha* (1978) by Iannis Xenakis, corresponding to figure 9.6.

NEW MESOSTRUCTURES: MASSES, CLUSTERS, STREAMS, AND CLOUDS

New materials can take composition beyond note-based strategies of the past. As Annette Vande Gorne (1995) observed:

> Why still use the "note" as the foundation of a work, when access to sound itself, with all its qualities is possible? . . . Electroacoustic music is not only the result of a new instrumentarium, it is above all another way of thinking about sound and its organization.

Electronic synthesis lets us create structures that would be difficult or impossible to achieve with traditional instruments. These include sound masses, dense clusters, flowing streams, and billowing clouds, which we discuss next. These textures are characterized by qualities like their density, opacity, and transparency, and they call for fresh approaches to compositional organization.

Sound masses and clusters

Decades ago, Varèse (1936a) predicted that the sounds introduced by electronic instruments would necessitate new organizing principles based on the interplay of sound masses:

> . . . Taking the place of linear counterpoint, the movement of sound masses, or shifting planes, will be clearly perceived. When these sound masses collide the phenomena of penetration or repulsion will seem to occur.

Although the concept of sound mass has never been scientifically defined, here we consider it as a more-or-less fused texture or monolith of sound constructed from the superimposition of multiple sources. The density and opacity of the sound mass distinguishes it from the stream and cloud morphologies, which we discuss momentarily.

We hear sound masses in works such as Ligeti's brilliant and radical *Volumina* (1962) for organ, which unfolds as individual tones and stops add to or subtract from a broadband block of sound. Figure 9.7 is an excerpt of the graphical score of this work, an exploration of density and register with highly contrasting oppositions in these dimensions. In his middle period, Ligeti explored this approach in a variety of other pieces, including *Atmosphères* (1961) for strings and *Lux Aeterna* (1966) for chorus. A more recent example of a sound mass composition is *Clusters* (2010) by Hubert S. Howe Jr., which consists of sinusoidal pentachords spread out over three or four octaves. (See chapter 4 for sound examples of *Clusters*.)

As mentioned in chapter 7, the pioneer of inharmonic clusters and sound masses in computer music is Jean-Claude Risset, who has featured such textures

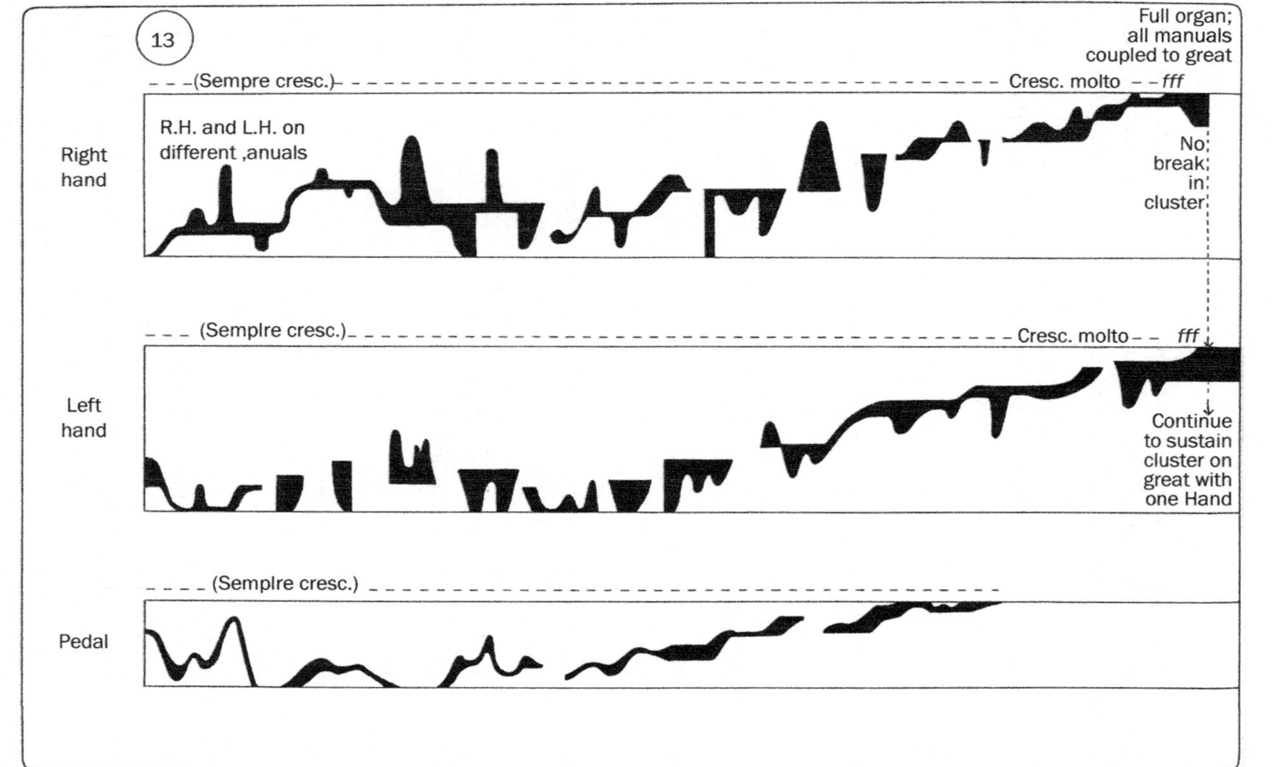

FIGURE 9.7 A page of the score of Ligeti's *Volumina* (1962) for organ, which is based on the unfolding of tone clusters and sound masses.

in many of his compositions. These include *Sud* (1985), which explores broadband noises processed through resonant filters.

Sound example 9.10. Excerpt of *Sud*, Part 3 (1985) by Jean-Claude Risset.

Risset (1989) offers recipes for making inharmonic clusters. These clusters are not static, but can evolve and mutate as they unfold. For example, in his classic piece *Mutations* (1969), the notes of a melody suddenly align to form a gong timbre:

> *Mutations* attempts to capitalize harmonically on the possibility offered by the computer of composing on the actual level of sounds. Thus the broken chord of the beginning is followed by a gonglike sound that is the chord's shadow: harmony mutates into sound.
>
> —RISSET (1987)

> The timbres of these [gong-like] textures are the result of the pitches of the chord.
>
> —RISSET (1982)

In Risset's *Inharmonique* (1977), the inharmonic clusters are often chord-like, since they consist of as few as five partials.

Sound example 9.11. Excerpt of *Inharmonique* (1977) for voice and tape by Jean-Claude Risset.

Another recipe for sound masses is to overlay a number of complex time-varying concrète sources obtained from natural and industrial sources. Classic examples include *Persepolis* (1971) and *Polytope de Cluny* (1972) by Xenakis, or the central part of his powerful *La légend d'Eer* (1978). In these long sound-mass compositions, we hear local chaos under the regime of a gradually unfolding macroscale mix.

Sound example 9.12. Excerpt of *Persepolis* (1971) by Iannis Xenakis.

Streams and clouds

A sound mass is a block of sound evolving relatively slowly. In contrast, streaming mesostructures seem to flow rapidly like liquids. Inside these fluidic processes is a model of sound as a continuous emission of microsonic particles. Here the rate of flow, or its equivalent—density of emission—is a key parameter (Wishart 1994). For example, using granulation processes, we can shape the flow of dozens of simultaneous audio streams (Truax 1988).

Closely related to streams are *sound clouds*—hundreds or thousands of sound particles controlled statistically—originally described by Xenakis (1960). Cloud textures suggest a different approach to musical organization, specifically, the unfolding of musical mesostructure through processes of statistical evolution. Cloud evolutions can take place in the domain of amplitude (crescendi/decrescendi), internal tempo (accelerando/rallentando), grain density (increasing/decreasing), harmonicity (pitch/chord/cluster/noise, etc.), and spectrum (high/mid/low, etc.).

Certain clouds resemble what statistics calls *stationary processes.* A stationary process has a constant mean value and fluctuates around the mean with a constant variance (i.e., within fixed boundaries). A stationary process is not necessarily static in time, but its variations remain within certain limits, so the global texture is predictable. Stationary processes are fertile material for composition. One can place them at low amplitude in the background, where they lend depth to the musical landscape. Positioned in the foreground, their constant presence introduces dramatic tension and sets up an expectation of change. The ear notices any change as a deviation from the stationary.

To impose a bias or trend transforms a stationary process into a *weighted stochastic process.* Any time-varying transformation can induce a trend, for example, by varying the bandwidth of a sound cloud, by altering its center frequency, by filtering, or by any other perceptible time-varying operation.

In contrast to slowly evolving trends, we can also induce sudden changes in sound clouds: accents, timbral or spatial contrasts, and juxtapositions.

One interesting class of sudden articulations is *intermittencies*: momentary silences. These fall into the general category of composing with silence, one of my standard techniques. Here one works like a sculptor, carving rhythmic and spatial patterns by subtraction. Algorithmic *cavitation* processes, which poke holes into continuous textures, also seem promising. A related type of intermittency is the juxtaposition of far (reverberant) elements spliced immediately after near elements, as in my piece *Touche Pas* (2009).

Xenakis's electronic compositions *Concret PH* (1958) and *Bohor I* (1962) feature dense, monolithic clouds, as do many of his works for traditional instruments. Stockhausen (1957) used "statistical forms" as a component of his early composition technique. Since the 1960s, cloud textures have appeared in numerous electroacoustic compositions, such as the remarkable *De natura sonorum* (1975) and *Capture éphémère* (1968) by Bernard Parmegiani.

Sound example 9.13. Excerpt of *Capture éphémère* (1968) by Bernard Parmegiani.

Varèse spoke of the "interpenetration" of sound masses. The acoustically diaphanous nature of cloud structures makes this possible. Density determines the transparency of the material. An increase in density lifts a cloud into the foreground, while a decrease in density causes evaporation, dissolving a continuous sound band into a pointillist rhythm or vaporous background texture. Crossfading between two clouds results in a smooth mutation.

Controls on multiple timescales regulate streaming and cloud formation processes. On the micro timescale of particles, we can control a particle's duration, waveform, frequency, and spatial position. On the sound object timescale, we can control amplitude and pitch envelopes, particle density, and spatialization. On the meso timescale, we regulate the flow of thousands of particles by means of parameters such as density, spatial trend, degree of synchronicity, etc. When the flow is sufficiently dense, the particles agglomerate into continuously scintillating textures.

In these fluid morphologies, we can create processes such as:

Coalescence—starting from silence, increasing particle density or increase of amplitude until a tone forms

Evaporation—regularly decreasing particle density or diminution of amplitude until silence

Intermittencies—irregular interruptions of particle density or amplitude

Points of attraction or repulsion—islands of high or low activity within a stream of particles. These can be articulated in multiple ways. For example, a point of attraction could be articulated through an increase in the density of sound events or layers, through a crescendo, or through an accelerando. In contrast, a point of repulsion could be articulated through increasing sparseness, a diminuendo, or a rallentando.

Transmutations and morphogenesis—continuous change of identity within a stream or cloud; for example, the material may at different times sound as if it is composed from dull matter, hard resonant matter, flowing liquid, bubbling liquid, or steam clouds.

Certain processes blur the border between microstructure and macrostructural organization, as Jean-Claude Risset (2005) observed:

> By bridging gaps between traditionally disconnected spheres like material and structure, or vocabulary and grammar, software creates a continuum between microstructure and macrostructure. It is no longer necessary to maintain traditional distinctions between an area exclusive to sound production and another devoted to structural manipulation on a larger temporal level. The choice of granulation, or of the fragmenting of sound elements, is a way of avoiding mishaps on a slippery continuum: it permits the sorting of elements within a scale while it allows individual elements to be grasped. The formal concern extends right into the microstructure, lodging itself within the sound grain.

In another realm, between and among the stars, outer space is swirling with clouds of cosmic raw material called *nebulae*. Cosmic nebulae form in great variety: dark or glowing, amorphous or ring-shaped, constantly evolving in morphology. Such forms too have musical analogies. Programs for sonographic synthesis such as MetaSynth (Wenger and Siegel 1999) provide airbrush tools that let one spray sound particles on a canvas of time (figure 9.8). On the screen, the vertical dimension represents frequency, and the horizontal dimension represents time. The images can be blurred, fragmented, or separated into sheets. Depending on their density, they may be translucent or opaque. Displacement maps can warp

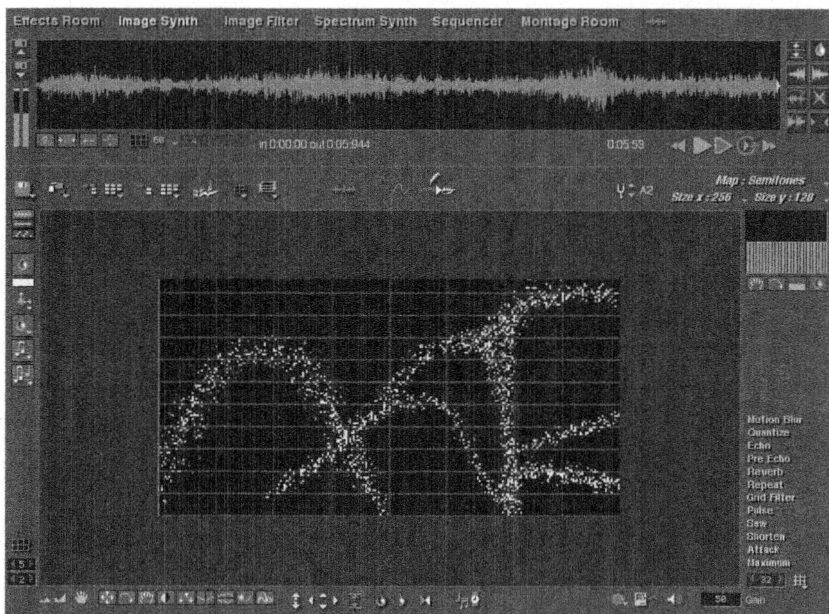

FIGURE 9.8 Sound cloud sprayed in MetaSynth.

the cloud into a circular or spiral shape on the time-frequency canvas. One can also import images of atmospheric clouds and cosmic nebulae.

Example of stream and cloud morphologies: *Half-life*

An example of a piece that uses cloud and stream morphologies is my composition *Half-life* (1999). This work explores the birth, replication, mutation, and decay of sound particles in stream and cloud forms. The fruit of a long period of study and experimentation, *Half-life* is deeply significant to me as a breakthrough and turning point in a long path of composition.

Although I first implemented granular synthesis in 1974, for many years, I did not have a clear idea of how to deploy it as the core of a composition. When I heard Horacio Vaggione's *Schall* in 1994 in Bourges, I knew that it was a landmark. *Schall* is composed completely out of sound particles derived from a piano that are projected on various timescales. In 1997, Ken Fields, a UCSB graduate student, played me his *Life in the Universe*, an intriguing mixture of granulated voice with distant sinusoidal textures. It became clear that I could combine techniques of phrase construction developed in my 1994 work *Clang-tint* (which used pulsar synthesis) with granulation processes. So 24 years after my initial experiments, I finally had a clear idea of how to proceed. *Half-life* and everything that I have composed since was the result.

Sound example 9.14. Excerpt of "Sonal atoms," Part 1, *Half-life* (1999) by Curtis Roads.

MOMENT FORM

In his electronic composition *Kontakte* (1960), as well as his instrumental pieces *Carré* (1960) and *Momente* (1965), Stockhausen introduced a paradigm called *moment form*, where a piece unfolds as a succession of unrelated episodes or moments:

> These forms do not aim toward a climax, and their structures do not contain the usual stages found in the development curve of the whole duration of a normal composition: the introductory, rising, transitional, and fading stages. On the contrary, these new forms are immediately intensive. . . . They are forms in a state of having already commenced. . . . Every present moment counts . . . a given moment is not regarded as the consequence of the previous one and the prelude to the coming one, but as something individual, independent, and centered in itself.
>
> —STOCKHAUSEN (1972)

Stockhausen likened moment form to the structure of Japanese Noh drama (Maconie 1989):

> In our Western tradition the composition of lyric forms is very rare, given the predominance of sequential and developmental conventions. Not so in the oriental traditions. . . . What counts is the here and now; they do not always feel compelled to base their composition on contrast with what has gone before or where a moment may be leading. . . . And for long periods of time you have no thought for the past or future, because there's nothing but the present moment. . . . The great difficulty in moment forming is the hair-raising problem of creating unity. It has to be the degree of immediacy, of presence that unites the individual movements: the fact that everything has presence to the same degree, because as soon as certain events are more present than others, then immediately we have a hierarchy: secondary events, transitions, accompaniments, preparatory event, echoes, and that means direction and development of a sequential kind.

This is not to say that *Kontakte* is devoid of directional processes—far from it. However, the directionality unfolds on the timescale of moments. (The duration of individual moments varies widely, with the average being about two minutes.) On a macro timescale, there is no overarching formal direction. From the beginning (which sounds like the middle of a piece and serves no introductory function) to the ending, each episode is a kind of non sequitur—a separate vignette that does not particularly follow from the previous vignette.

The macroform of *Kontakte* consists of a succession of 16 moment structures. Inside each moment is a struggle between sonic contrasts; Stockhausen pits pitch against noise, fixed against moving, close against far, short against long, high register against low register, soft against loud—always in sharp relief. It is this unrelenting salience and contrapuntal articulation that make *Kontakte* so remarkable.

Stockhausen (1989) cast the idea of moment form in a more general context, as one possible way of organizing form, but not the only way:

> Once we reach statistical ways of controlling it does not mean we forget about determinacy or directionality or variability, just as once we reach the lyric, we don't ignore the dramatic. Rather, what we are striving to reach is a universal conception, within which we may move in different directions from work to work and within individual works, but having all the possibilities of organization available to us in every composition.

Another composer who has explored moment form in the domain of electronic music is Natasha Barrett (2008).

Temporal junctions

At a musical junction, structure unfolds depending on the *rate of change* at that point, of which three cases are typical:

- Continuation (no change, stasis)
- Transition (moderate change)
- Juxtaposition (rapid change)

Continuations include sustaining, repeating, and time dilation processes. A continuation produces different results depending on the structural level on which the composer applies it. On the level of macroform, continuation results in a single movement without distinct sections. An example of a continuous mesostructure would be the prolongation of a tonal center containing many sub-phrases. Continuous phrases feature long and flowing gestures, rather than short and jagged patterns. On the timescale of sound objects, continuous tones contain an unbroken chain of wave periods and only gradual changes in waveform shape.

In contrast, a transition is a sequential change, moving either smoothly or stepwise from one state to another. Transitions are ubiquitous in music.[69] In traditional music, the possibilities for transition at the note level are limited. On a given monodic instrument, the pitch can stay the same, go up, or go down. Given the possibility of polyphony, a harmonic progression may unfold. The amplitude can increase or diminish; the tone quality may vary. The possibilities in electronic music include processes such as coalescence, disintegration, and mutation. In electronic music, a transition can involve a granular mutation from one sound to another over time, either continuously or in successive steps.

Sound example 9.15. Excerpt of granulation processes in *Dragonfly* (2011) by Laurent Delforge.

Abrupt juxtapositions articulate mesostructural boundaries. On the macroform level, a typical juxtaposed structure is a set of isolated movements, each distinct from the other. Within a movement, juxtaposed mesostructure appears as clearly demarcated sections. Within a section, juxtaposition interposes distinctly different phrases. Juxtaposition within a phrase occurs if it is constructed out of wildly different sound objects.

The possibilities of transition in electronic music devolve down to the level of acoustic structure, since any sound can mutate into any other sound at any time. Any given event may evolve in a multiplicity of possible directions including elaborate timbral and spatial developments. (See chapter 8 on spatialization.)

Repetition and intelligibility

Any musical statement can be made more obvious by repeating it. The repeating beat formula is the core of commercial pop music. Repetition encapsulates the appeal of certain works in the 20th-century minimalist style.

Gabriel Pareyon's text *On Musical Self-similarity* (2011) is an intriguing treatise in which repetition is generalized to several modes of self-similarity that are ubiquitous in musical discourse. These include functional similarity, statistical similarity, invariance relationships, analogies (e.g., the concept of pitch class), recursive processes, intersemiosis (translating one set of signs to another set of signs, such as playing a score), basis functions (elementary particles into which any sound can be decomposed), nested patterns, musical borrowings, proportional similarity, etc. As Pareyon observed:

> The human being is capable of multiplying its signs of reality by thanks to the operative principles of similarity and difference, and—especially—thanks to generalization and stereotyping achieved by these principles.

Based on functional substitution, one can also create an impression of repetition without literal repetition; this is of greater interest from a creative viewpoint. Moreover, in electronic music, repetition on multiple timescales leads from processes such as loops, meter, and beat formation, to echo and audio tone formation, as the timescale of repetition shrinks from seconds to microseconds.

An old cliché of composition says that repetition ensures closure. In other words, a repeated object or phrase marks off the boundaries of a mesostructure. However, repetition is only one strategy for closure. Another cliché states that there are only two ways to end a piece: by repeating the beginning or not. Xenakis's monumental 45-minute arch form *La légende d'Eer* (1978) has a three-minute closing whose sonic content mirrors its six-minute opening. However, a non-repeating ending is far more prevalent in the genre of electronic music.

Conclusion

The organization of a composition is intertwined with its materials and tools. (See chapter 4.) The unique materials and tools of electronic music lead to new forms of organization. Recording opened up the range of compositional material to include any sound possible. The tape machine liberated time: It could be cut up, rearranged, sped up or down, or played backward. The digital sound editor gave us immediate access to all timescales and the ability to transform them—from an entire piece to a single sample—in one operation. The studio-based practice of multiscale composition applies these tools directly to the organization of a work—in the presence of sound and aligned with human perception.

New materials such as grains and pulses led to novel mesostructures: sound masses, dense clusters, flowing streams, and billowing clouds. These textures are characterized by their density, opacity, and transparency; one sound can easily mutate into another. One can sprinkle grains like salt and pepper into any texture. These possibilities mandate fresh approaches to compositional organization.

The multiscale approach is above all flexible and opportunistic as a compositional strategy, intermingling top-down and bottom-up strategies for organization. Multiscale organization can be likened to a heterarchy of partial systems that come into and go out of being. It can employ generative processes but reserves the right for the composer to interact, intervene, edit, and transform at any time.[70]

On a fundamental physical level, music is a play of relationships among vibrations on multiple timescales. We call a specific pattern of energetic vibrations a composition. The universe itself is an infinitely rich interplay of relationships among vibrations on multiple timescales. As the physicist Fritjof Capra (1999) observed:

> Gradually, physicists began to realize that nature, at the atomic level, does not appear as a mechanical universe composed of fundamental building blocks, but rather as a network of relations, and that ultimately there are no parts at all in this interconnected web. Whatever we call a part is merely a pattern that has some stability and therefore captures our attention.

In composition, such patterns include syntactic relationships (e.g., before, after, overlaps, contains, is contained in), but also functional semantic relationships on multiple timescales (e.g., foreshadows, replicates, is a variation of, is a transposition of, perfect fifth, contrasts with, is the climax of, etc.).[71] The multiscale composer organizes all these elements in relation to each other and the overall form.[72]

10

Sonic narrative

A composition can be likened to a being that is born out of nothing. Like all of us, it is a function of time. It grows and ambles, probing and exploring a space of possibilities before it ultimately expires. This birth, development, and death make up a sonic narrative. Every level of structure, from sections to phrases, individual sounds, and even grain patterns, follows its own narrative. Individual sounds come into being and then form complementary or opposing relationships with other sounds. These relationships evolve in many ways. Sounds clash, fuse, harmonize, or split into multiple parts. The relationship can break off suddenly or fizzle out slowly. Eventually, all the sounds expire, like characters in a sonic play. As Bernard Parmegiani observed (Gayou 2002):

> If I have to define what you call the "Parmegiani sound," it is a certain mobility, a certain color, a manner of beginning and ebbing away, making it living. Because I consider sound like a living being.

Or as Luc Ferrari (quoted in Caux 2002) said:

> *Visage 1* (1956) should be discussed in terms of cycles, rather than repetitions. . . . I imagined the cycles as if they were individuals, living at different speeds. When they didn't meet, they were independent. When they met . . . they were transformed by influence or by confrontation. I have already said that this was a serial work. . . . However, I did not apply this technique in a systematic way, as I did not want the random encounters produced

> by the repetitions to systematically modify the individuals. . . . In this way a sort of sentimental or narrative mechanism could be articulated.

A compelling sonic narrative is the backbone of an effective piece of music. This chapter examines the important concepts of sonic narrative, including narrative function, sonic causality, nonlinear narrative, narrative context, humor/irony/provocation, narrative repose, and hearing narrative structure. Certain composers follow strategies that are intentionally anti-narrative, and we also consider these along the way.

Music is representational

The active human mind imbues perceptual experiences with meaning: What we see and hear signifies or represents something. Thus sound, like other sensory stimuli, is representational. Even abstract sounds (i.e., music) can establish a mood or atmosphere within seconds, setting the stage for narrative. Consider the pensive tone of Daphne Oram's *Pulse Persephone* (1965).

Sound example 10.1. Excerpt of *Pulse Persephone* (1965) by Daphne Oram. 

The fact that sound can signify and evoke moods means that it can be used to design a narrative structure. As the theorist Jean-Jacques Nattiez (1990) observed:

> For music to elicit narrative behavior, it need only fulfill two necessary and sufficient conditions: we must be given a minimum of two sounds of any kind, and these two sounds must be inscribed in a linear temporal dimension, so that a relationship will be established between the two objects. Why does this happen? Human beings are symbolic animals; confronted with a trace they will seek to interpret it to give it meaning.

I would go even further to say that a single sound can tell a narrative. A drone invites internal reflection and meditation. A doorbell alerts a household. An obnoxious noise provokes an immediate emotional reaction. Silence invites self reflection. An intense sustained sound commands attention (figure 10.1, sound example 10.2).

Sound example 10.2. Excerpt of *Process 5* (2010) by Xopher Davidson and Zbigniev Karkowski. 

The conundrum of musical meaning has been analyzed at length in the broad context of music cognition and music semantics. Library shelves are filled with books on musical meaning and the psychology of music. We have already cited Huron (2006) as an important source on music cognition. Imberty (1979) focused on broad issues of emotional and cultural semantics, including the role of spoken and sung language in music.

FIGURE 10.1 Setup for Xopher Davidson and Zbigniev Karkowski's album *Processor* (2010). The Wavetek waveform generators (left) are controlled by a Comdyna GP6 analog computer (right). Photograph by Curtis Roads in Studio Varèse at UCSB.

As Elizabeth Hoffman (2012) observed, composers of electronic music often use recognizable or *referential* sound samples. Such works project listeners into encounters with places, people, and things—the stuff of narrative. The composer places these referential elements in a deliberate order. In works that use sampled sound to present a sound portrait, the connection to narrative discourse is direct, as in Thom Blum's *Maroc* (1998), a collage of 500 sounds blended into a "sonic travelogue."

 **Sound example 10.3.** Excerpt of *Maroc* (1998) by Thom Blum.

In many acousmatic pieces, we eavesdrop on people talking to themselves, to others, or to us. Taken to a dramatic extreme, some works tend toward the literal story lines of audio plays. In these works, we experience sound effects rather than music per se.

While the connection to narrative is obvious in these cases, what about narrative articulated by *abstract sounds* (i.e., electronic sounds that are not sampled or not directly referential to events in the real world)? First, we must recognize that a distinction between abstract and referential sounds is clear only in extreme cases. An example of an abstract sound would be a burst of pink noise lasting one second. An example of a referential sound would be a recording of a conversation. As we will see, however, abstract sounds can serve structural functions in a composition. Thus they play a role in its narrative structure.

A similar fuzziness surrounds the distinction between *program music*, which projects extramusical ideas, and *absolute music*, which makes no explicit extramusical references. The distinction is imperfect because it is sometimes difficult to establish precise boundaries between "musical" and "extramusical" references, as we will see.

Throughout history, we see composers who attach themselves to extramusical references. They proselytize a social, cultural, or religious agenda. In contrast, many compositions propose no explicit social, cultural, or religious agenda. They transmit more diffuse impressions. Like an abstract painting, they convey a pattern of rhythm, tone, and texture (i.e., a spectromorphology). (See chapters 4 and 9 and Smalley 1986, 1997.) Spectromorphology categorizes patterns of motion and growth according to their sonic properties. Individual sound objects serve structural functions within these processes, such as beginning, transitional ascending element, climax, transitional descending element, pause (weak cadence), ending (strong cadence), juxtaposition, harmonizing element, contrasting element, and so on.

Inevitably, many sounds are charged with meaning beyond their purely spectromorphological function, for example, the spoken voice. We hear a spoken utterance not just as an abstract stream of phonemes but as human speech, full of expressive, linguistic, poetic, and conceptual ramifications. In music that relies on speech, the narrative often tends toward the literal, spilling outside the boundaries of "absolute" music per se. An example is a scripted *hörspeil* (audio drama) or soundtrack. Music based on spoken or sung text can recite a literal narrative, for example, Ilhan Mimaroglu's classic *Prelude 12 for Magnetic tape* (1967), featuring the evocative poetry of Orhan Veli Kanik.

Consider also soundscape compositions based on recordings of sonic environments (Truax 1984, 1999). These run the gamut from pure audio documentaries to combinations of pure and processed recordings, as in Maggi Payne's *Airwaves (realities)* (1987) or Paul Lansky's *Night Traffic* (1987). In Luc Ferrari's *Presque rien avec filles* (1989), we recognize the sound sources so the signification is direct: We are transported to a place where a brook babbles, a robin chirps, an airplane passes overhead, and Brunhild Meyer-Ferrari speaks in German overlaid by other women speaking Italian and French. In *Danses organiques* (1973) and *Far West News Episode Number 1* (1999), both examples of "cinema for the ear," Ferrari uses jump-cut splicing in the manner of filmmaker Jean-Luc Godard.

A primary strategy of self-described acousmatic music is precisely to play with reference (see chapter 4). Acousmatic works engage in games of recognition, mimesis, and semantic allusion, as in Elizabeth Hoffman's *Water Spirits* (2007).

Sound example 10.4. Excerpt of *Water Spirits* (2007) by Elizabeth Hoffman. 

The music of films often mirrors the scripted plot and its associated emotions (fear, happiness, anger, amusement, grief, triumph, etc.) in more-or-less direct musical form. Of course, in more sophisticated productions, the music can function independently or even as ironic commentary, such as a light song dubbed over a tragic scene.

Sound example 10.5. Excerpt of *Prelude 12 for Magnetic tape* (1967) by Ilhan Mimaroglu.[73]

In contrast to these directly referential materials and strategies, representation is more abstract in much music (both instrumental and electronic).[74] Consider a one-second sine tone at 261.62 Hz. It signifies middle C to someone with perfect pitch. It might also allude to the general context of electronic music, but other than this, it represents a structural function that varies depending on the musical context in which it is heard. It might harmonize or clash with another sound, for example, or start or stop a phrase.

In works like my *Now* (2003), for example, a sonic narrative unfolds as a pattern of energetic flux in an abstract sonic realm. We hear a story of energy swells and collisions, of sonic coalescence, disintegration, mutation, granular agglomerations, and sudden transformation, told by means of spectromorphological processes.

In such music, sounds articulate the *structural functions* of the composition. Structural functions in traditional music begin with basic roles like the articulation of scales, meters, tempi, keys, etc., and lead all the way up to the top layers of form: beginnings, endings, climaxes, developments, ritornelli, and so on. Analytical terms such as cadence, coda, and resolution directly imply scenarios. In a piece like J. S. Bach's *Art of Fugue* (1749), the narrative has been described as an exposition of "the whole art of fugue and counterpoint" as a process (Terry 1963). As Stockhausen (1972) observed:

> Whereas it is true that traditionally in music, and in art in general, the context, or ideas and themes, were more or less descriptive, either psychologically descriptive of inter-human relationships, or descriptions of certain phenomena in the world, we now have a situation where the composition or decomposition of a sound, or the passing of a sound through several time layers may be the theme itself, granted that by theme we mean the behavior or life of the sound.

That music can teach us about processes leads to the ambiguity between musical and extramusical references. Music can articulate many types of processes; some grew out of musical tradition while others did not. Some composers of algorithmically composed music consider the narrative of their works (i.e., their meanings or what they articulate) to be the unfolding of a mathematical process. Serial music, for example, derives from set theory and modulo arithmetic, originally imported from mathematics. After decades of compositional practice, are these still extramusical references? The distinction is not clear.

Another field in which sound articulates process is *scientific sonification* and *auditory display*. These have practical goals: mapping data onto sound, monitoring sensors, or providing auditory interfaces for computers and virtual reality systems (ICAD 2010). Stockhausen (1989) pointed out the difference between a scientific sonification and music composition.

> Of course, [the demonstration of a sound splitting into six parts in *Kontakte*] could be done more or less intelligently. . . . A physics professor would just have gone down six and a half octaves, and leave it at that. Someone else might just, well, vary it a little, make it a bit more inventive. If the same process is composed by different people and one is more imaginative that the other, then that's all there is to say about the process, and about the difference between a physics professor and a composer in this context.

Sonification is aligned with the current situation in the media arts. Today artists sonify data from diverse sources, blurring the lines of artistic and scientific projections (Kuchera-Morin 2011; Putnam 2012; Wakefield 2012).

Abstract sonic narrative

> Tonal music had the wonderful advantage of being stabilized for a long time so that people knew the predictable patterns. . . . A composer like Beethoven could play his music and say, "Okay, you're all for waiting for that type of modulation, but I—Beethoven—am going to design it differently. So I will trigger a surprise to the listener." So this game between predictability and unpredictability, expectation and surprises is what makes time living and musical. How can we now make such a game between predictability and unpredictability without an established musical language? My personal answer is that I am always trying to first establish the rules of the game rather clearly in order later on to be able to distort it or to change directions. I do not want to put the listener behind a wall of information through which he is incapable of finding his way. There must be some path, some thread, like Ariadne in the labyrinth.
>
> —GÉRARD GRISEY (QUOTED IN BUNDLER 1996)

> Many scholars of narrative have found the novel and the film quite enlightening, but they have generally ignored music, the quintessential art of time, perhaps because the musical world itself has rarely pondered the narrative.
>
> —JANN PASLER (1989)

What is narrative? In a general sense, it is a story that the human brain constructs out of our experience of the world, by anticipating the future and relating current perceptions to the past. We are constantly building stories out of sensory experiences:[75]

> I am sitting. The walls are wooden. I see a red and white checkered pattern. I see green colors. I hear broadband noises. I see a person sitting across from me. Out of these unconnected sensations I construct a narrative. The red and white checkered pattern is a window shade. The green colors are foliage outside the window. The noise is the burning wood in the fireplace. The wooden

> beams tell me I am in Cold Spring Tavern in the mountains above Santa Barbara. The person sitting across from me is a composer from Germany.

Our sensory experiences are continuously and immediately analyzed and categorized within a cognitive context. So it is with music. This musical narrative builder is our "listening grammar" in operation, as Lerdahl (1988) called it. Our listening grammar is how we make sense of the sonic world.

Part of how we make sense of the world is that we anticipate the future. Indeed, the psychological foundation of music cognition is anticipation. As Meyer (1956) observed:

> One musical event has meaning because it points to or makes us expect another event. Musical meaning is, in short, a product of expectation.

Thus a narrative chain can function because we inevitably anticipate the future. Huron (2006), in a detailed study of musical anticipation, described five stages of psychological reaction. They apply to music listening but also to any situation in which we are paying attention:

1. Imagination response—imagining an outcome
2. Tension response—anticipation: arousal and attention to see what will happen
3. Prediction response—when an event occurs, was it expected?
4. Reaction response—defensive and protection reflex
5. Appraisal response—reflection on what occurred

These reactions occur in time very quickly—moment to moment—as we listen; they inform a narrative understanding of our experiences.

As we have already pointed out, the narrative designed by the composer is not necessarily the same narrative heard by the listener (through the listening grammar).

In electronic music especially, musical narrative often revolves around processes of sonic transformation. Consider, for example, the famous transformation 17 minutes into Stockhausen's *Kontakte* (1960) in which a tone descends in frequency in a flowing down and up-down manner until it dissolves into individual impulses, which then elongate to re-form a continuous tone. Like a story from Ovid's fantastic *Metamorphosis* (8 CE), in which nymphs transform into islands, we are fascinated by the strange fortunes of this sound.

Metaphorically, we can think of sounds as abstract characters that enter a stage as we become aware of them, do something, and eventually leave the stage and our awareness, as follows:

- Enter—suddenly, through fade-in, or through coalescence
- Act—i.e., do at least one of these four things:
  - Stay the same (stasis)
  - Mutate—change in some way
  - Transmutate—become something else, change identity

    - Interact with other sounds, form harmonies, consonances, or contrasts/clashes
- Exit—suddenly, through slow fadeout, or through disintegration

This sonic play is a multiscale process; such a sequence can describe one sound, a phrase, a section, or a whole piece. For example, if a unique sequence of events occurs over one minute at the start of a 10-minute piece, we call it a beginning. At the close of a piece, we call it the ending. Within the act phase is a limitless realm of possible behaviors: repetitions, surprises, climaxes, relaxations, all manner of development and evolution, and interactions with other sounds.

How we interpret the sequence of musical events depends on our anticipation and our psychological reaction as to whether or not our expectations are met. As Huron (2006) noted:

> Minds are "wired" for expectation. . . . What happens in the future matters to us, so it should not be surprising that how the future unfolds has a direct effect on how we feel.

Sonic narrative is constructed by a succession of events in time and also by the interaction of simultaneous sounds. This is the realm of generalized counterpoint, as discussed in chapter 7. Do the sounds form a kind of "consonance" (resolution) or "dissonance" (opposition)? Is one sound a foil to the other? Does one serve as background while the other operates in the foreground? Does one sound block out another sound? Do the sounds move with one another (at the same time and in the same way), or are they independent? These contrapuntal interactions lead to moments of tension and resolution. As Varèse (quoted in Risset 2004) observed:

> One should compose in terms of energy and fluxes. There are interplays and struggle between the different states of matter, like confrontations between characters in a play. Form is the result of these confrontations.

Even static structures can elicit the experience of narrative. I vividly recall the wide range of emotions I experienced watching Andy Warhol's *Empire* (1964) for 45 minutes. (This silent film consists of eight hours and five minutes of continuous footage of a single shot of the Empire State Building in New York City.)

Morphology, function, narrative

> Design is a funny word. Some people think design means how it looks. But of course, if you dig deeper, it is really how it works.
>
> —STEVE JOBS

> Form ever follows function. This is the law.
>
> —LOUIS SULLIVAN (1896)

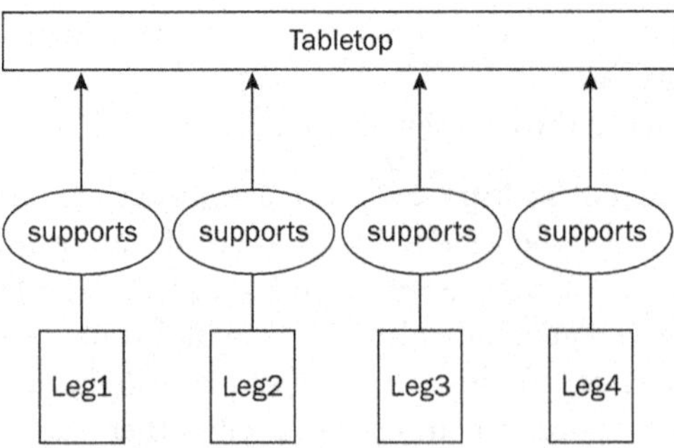

FIGURE 10.2 Functional representation of a table.

This section focuses on the relationship between morphology, structural function, and narrativity in music. Let us start with a simple nonmusical example in order to define terms. The *morphology* of a table is its shape—how it looks. Let us define its *structure* or *organization* as the way that the component parts are interconnected, how the legs attach to the top. As the biologist D'arcy Thompson (1942) observed:

> A bridge was once upon a time a loose heap of pillars and rods and rivets of steel. But the identity of these is lost, just as if they had fused into a solid mass once the bridge is built. . . . The biologist as well as the philosopher learns to recognize that the whole is not merely the sum of its part. . . . For it is not a *bundle* of parts but an *organization* of parts.

Figure 10.2 shows a simple diagram of the structure of a table. The oval elements connect and describe a *functional relationship* between the component parts. The basic function of the entire table is to support things placed on its top, but it can have other functions such as serving as a portable table, extendable table, or visual accent, etc. Thus there can be more than one functional relationship between two parts. For example, a table leg in steel might serve an aesthetic function of being a visual/material contrast to a marble tabletop.

Morphology in music is a pattern of time-frequency energy. Music articulates myriad structural functions: temporal, spatial, timbral, melodic, harmonic, rhythmic, etc. It can also serve and articulate social and cultural functions in all manner of rites and rituals, from the street to the palace.

Structural function refers to the role that an element (on any timescale) serves in relation to a composition's narrative structure. It was defined abstractly by music theorist Wallace Berry (1987) as follows:

> In music . . . actions (changes, events) involving various elements (lines of pitch change, tonal and harmonic succession, rhythm and meter, texture, and coloration) are so conceived and controlled that they function at hierarchically ordered levels in processes by which intensities develop and decline and by which analogous feeling is induced. . . . To see structural function in music as it concerns lines of intensity change is to see, in general, three

> possibilities: increasing intensity (progression), subsiding intensity (recession), and unchanging event succession (stasis).

Structural functions play out not just in pitch and rhythm but in all of music's features, as Berry (1987) observed:

> There are "dissonances" and resolutions in all of music's parameters.

Accordingly, to serve a structural function, an element either increases intensity, decreases intensity, or stays the same. Processes such as increasing intensity (heightening tension) and decreasing intensity (diminishing tension) are narrative functions. To give an example, an explosion at the close of the first part of my composition *Never* (2010) releases energy and fulfills a narrative function as "the end."

Changes in intensity imply trends and therefore imbue directionality. Quoting Berry (1987) again:

> The concept of musical motion is critically allied to the concept of progressive, regressive, and static events and event-complexes.

Of course, reducing all musical functionality to its effect on "intensity" begs the question of how this translates to specific musical parameters in actual works. Berry's book explores this question through analytic examples. The analysis can be quite complicated. As Berry, Narmour (1990, 1992), and many others have pointed out, real music plays out through the interplay of multiple parameters operating simultaneously and sometimes independently. Stasis in one dimension, such as a steady rhythmic pattern that serves a structural function of articulating a meter, can serve as a support for a process of increasing intensity in another dimension, such as the structural function of a crescendo, while another dimension undergoes a process of decreasing intensity.

Ultimately, structural functionality concerns the role and thereby the purpose of an element within a specific musical context. The context is extremely important. As Herbert Brün (1986) observed:

> Composition generates whole systems so that there can be a context which can endow trivial "items" and meaningless "materials" with a sense and a meaning never before associated with either items or materials.

To use an architectural analogy, a wooden beam that supports the roof of a traditional house would serve only a decorative function in the context of a steel skyscraper. Context is the key to meaning.

Sonic causality

A sonic narrative consists of chains of events. These chains can create an illusion of cause and effect, as if a subsequent event was the plausible or even inevitable consequence of an antecedent event. One way teleology can emerge in a musical narrative is by the design of chains of causal relationships.[76]

Before proceeding, we must separate two distinct uses of the term "causality" in the context of electronic music. In the acousmatic discourse (see chapter 4 on sound materials), causality is concerned with identifying the source that generated a given sound (i.e., what is its origin?). In contrast, my interest concerns a different issue, the idea that one sound appears to cause or give rise to another in a narrative sense, what Lars Gunnar Bodin (2004) called *causal logic*. That is, what if one sound was the necessary antecedent that appears to cause a consequent sound? We see this effect in the cinema, where a succession of sounds (often not recorded at the same time as the filming) spliced and layered together lends continuity to a visual montage (e.g., footsteps + yell + gunshot + scream + person falls to the ground). "Appears to cause" is the operative phrase; my use of the term "causality" is metaphorical.[77] As in the technique of cinema, we seek only an illusion of causality, suggested by a progression of events that indicates a direction leading to some inevitable result. As I wrote about *Half-life*, composed in 1999:

> As emerging sounds unfold, they remain stable or mutate before expiring. Interactions between different sounds suggest causalities, as if one sound spawned, triggered, crashed into, bonded with, or dissolved into another sound. Thus the introduction of every new sound contributes to the unfolding of a musical narrative.
>
> —ROADS (2004A)

As a sonic process emerges out of nothing, it may spawn additional musical events. These events, be they individual particles or agglomerations, interact with existing events, setting up a chain of implied causalities. Two sounds can converge or coincide at a *point of attraction* or scatter at a *point of repulsion*, leading to a number of consequences:

Fusion—multiple components fuse into a single sound
Fission—sounds split into multiple independent components
Arborescence—new branches split off from an ongoing sound structure
Chain reaction—sequences of events caused by a triggering event

An impression of causality implies predictability. If listeners are not able to correlate sonic events with any logic, the piece is an inscrutable cipher. Indeed, a hallmark of the beginner's style in composition is a smattering of seemingly unrelated events scattered haphazardly on the canvas of time. (This is not to deny the power of juxtaposition forms as a deliberate strategy, as in the notion of moment form, discussed in chapter 9.)

These fascinating scientific (and legal) questions must remain exterior to our discourse, which is only concerned with the illusion of causality. In the cinema, we see a closeup of someone pushing a switch, and the scene immediately cuts to a room scene in which a light goes on. The apposition of these scenes creates an illusion of causality. Similarly, in music, a swell of energy leading to a loud sound gives the illusion that the latter sound is a logical consequent of the swelling. It is through such quasi-dramatic illusions that structural functions in compositions articulate themselves.

Nonlinear or variable narrative

> A film should have a beginning, middle, and end, but not necessarily in that order.
>
> —JEAN-LUC GODARD (1966)

In the context of media, terms like "linear" and "nonlinear" are ambiguous metaphors with multiple meanings, like "light" and "dark." Something can be linear in one sense, yet nonlinear in another. Like many metaphorical adjectives, we need to be careful if we intend to speak precisely.

The term "linear narrative" has often been applied to a story with a beginning that introduces characters or themes, followed by tension/conflict resulting in a climax/resolution and final act. It was called a linear narrative partly because there was a sense of sequential time progression coupled with a sense of causality—a given event could be seen as being caused or implied by a previous event. A linear narrative presents a logical chain of events; events progress and develop; they do not just succeed one another haphazardly.

Contrast this with what is often called *nonlinear interactive media*, where each participant can choose their own path through a network. A classic example is a gallery exhibit, where each person can view artworks in any order. Another example is a videogame, where each player's experience is different depending on the choices they make. Yet another example is reading the news, where we tend to pick and choose what we will read and in what sequence. In the musical realm, an iconic example is the notion of *open form* in the scores of Earle Brown (1967), where the temporal order of the sections is determined by a conductor at the time of performance.

Notice, however, that there is linearity within nonlinearity. Each person in a gallery views a linear sequence of images. It is merely different from what another viewer sees. The videogame player experiences a linear sequence of events that seem like logical consequences of his or her actions. The newspaper reader scans an article from beginning to end, linearly. The musical listener hears a performance that has been designed with interchangeable parts so the order is of little consequence. Moreover, all of these experiences are taking place in time, which according to the metaphor, is a linear medium. What makes a medium "nonlinear" is its variability—everyone can do it a different way—whether by chance or choice. "Variable multipath narrative" is perhaps a more descriptive term than "nonlinear narrative."

Some would say that music and movies are linear, in that they unfold in time, and different audience members have no choice in what they hear. Similarly, a book is read from the beginning to the end. Here "linear" is again being used in place of "unvarying single path." A recording of a Beethoven symphony is essentially the same every time it is played.

Yet filmmakers, composers, and novelists often speak of nonlinearity in the organization of their works, even if they are ultimately presented in the form of an unvarying single-path narrative. It is obviously not necessary for a musical narrative to unfold in a linear chain. Artists use many techniques to break up or rearrange sequential narrative: ellipses, summaries, collage, flashback, flash-forward, jump cut, montage, cut-up, and juxtaposition. Narrative emerges out of nothing other than adjacencies, as Claude Vivier (1985) observed:

> My music is a paradox. Usually in music, you have some development, some direction, or some aim. . . . I just have statements, musical statements, which somehow lead nowhere. On the other hand, they lead somewhere but it's on a much more subtle basis.

Using digital media, sounds and images can play in any order, including backward, sped up, slowed down, or frozen. Granulation can pulverize a sound like a speaking voice into a cloud of phonemes, transforming a story into an abstract sonic narrative.

Moreover, music is polyphonic: Why not launch multiple narratives in parallel? Let them take turns, interrupt each other, unfold simultaneously, or twist in reverse. The possibilities are endless. As music psychologist Eric Clarke (2011) observed:

> Music's own multiplicity and temporal dynamism engage with the general character of consciousness itself.

Narrative design can be labyrinthine or kaleidoscopic, reflecting the true nature of consciousness and dreams.

Consider Luc Ferrari's comments on the construction of his *Saliceburry Cocktail* (2002):

> The Cocktail idea suggested that I hide things under one another. I took old elements, and since I didn't want to hear some of them, I hid them under some elements that I also didn't want to hear. And since I remembered some of the sounds, I also had no choice but to hide the images they evoked, and I had to hide some other realistic elements under synthetic sounds, and I had to dissimulate some of the synthetic sounds under some drastic transformations. Finally, I hid the structure under a non-structure or the other way around.

Sound example 10.6. Excerpt of *Saliceburry Cocktail* (2002) by Luc Ferrari.

Surprise is essential to a compelling narrative. Surprises are singularities that break the flow of continuous progression. The appearance of singularities implies that, like a volcano, the surface structure is balanced on top of a deeper layer that can erupt at any moment. What is this deeper layer? The traditional term is form, but if we look at what caused it, it is the will of the composer at the helm of a sonic vessel. The voyage of this vessel, as communicated by the sound pattern it emits, traces its narrative.

Anti-narrative strategies

Certain composers reject narrative as an organizing principle. The musicologist Pasler (1989) spoke of moment form (see chapter 9) as an example of what she calls *anti-narrative.* Stockhausen wrote of his orchestral work *Carré* (1959):

> This piece tells no story. Every moment can exist for itself. . . . I hope that this music may evoke a little quietude, depth, and concentration. . . .

Another example she cites is John Cage's *Freeman Etudes* (1980) for solo violin, which was composed with star maps and chance operations in such a way as to ensure absence of repetition and recognizable patterns. As Pasler said:

> As with viewing the stars, whatever shape the perceiver may hear in a *Freeman Etude* derives more from what he is seeking in it than from the work itself.

Yet a narrative impression is not so easily disposed. In this sense, narrative is like form, something rather hard to extinguish. As Earle Brown (1967) wrote:

> If something were really formless, we would not know if its existence in the first place. It is the same way with "no continuity" and "no relationship." All the negatives are pointing at what they are claiming does not exist.

The mind is apophenic—searching for patterns even in pure noise. As Pasler (1989) wrote about the *Freeman Etudes*:

> It is a strange coincidence then when in the fifth etude, the first nine notes—probably the most regular rhythmic succession of notes in the set—sound like a phrase when they end with a falling fourth and a diminuendo to *ppp*, and when they are followed by a another quasi-phrase of fifteen notes that ends with a falling fifth and a large crescendo.

Moreover, anyone who listens to Stockhausen's moment form works such as *Kontakte* (1960) or *Momente* (1964) hears teleological processes, patterns of increasing and decreasing intensity, convergence/divergence, coalescence/distintegration, and causal illusions, all elements of narrative. While the macroform is non-directional, on other timescales, we hear many familiar narrative elements: openings, development, cadences, counterpoint, transitions, etc. In any case, perceived randomness takes on well-known narrative identities: A series of unrelated juxtapositions is predictably chaotic, and white noise is predictably unchanging.

Synthesizing narrative context

Intimately related to the concept of narrative is the principle of context. A narrative context—on whatever timescale—determines the structural function and appropriateness of the sound material, since only a contextually appropriate sound serves the narrative structure. We see again the deep relationship between materials at lower levels of structure and the morphology of the higher-level context. Inappropriate sound objects and dangling phrases inserted into a structure from another context tend to work against their surroundings. If they are not pruned out of the composition, their presence may be detrimental to the structural integrity of the piece. Even a small anomaly of this kind can loom large in the mind of listeners. An inappropriate sound object or phrase can cancel out the effect of surrounding phrases, or call into question the effectiveness of an entire composition.

What determines the "inappropriateness" of a sound or phrase? This is impossible to generalize, as it depends entirely on the musical context. It is not necessarily a sharp juxtaposition—juxtapositions can be appropriate. It could be a sound that is unrelated to the material in the rest of the piece or an aimless dithering section that drains energy rather than building suspense.

For fear of inserting an inappropriate element into a piece, one can fall into the opposite trap: overly consistent organization. This condition is characterized by a limited palette of sounds and a restricted range of operations on these sounds. A hallmark of the "in-the-box" mindset, an overly consistent composition can be shown to be "coherent" in a logical sense even as it bores the audience.

In certain works, the synthesis of context is the narrative. For example, in Luc Ferrari's brilliant *Cycle des souvenirs* (2000), the composer is a master of fabricating context from unrelated sources: synthesizers, women speaking softly, bird and environmental sounds, a drum machine, and auditory scenes of human interaction around the world. In Ferrari's hands, these disparate elements magically cohere. Why is this? First, the sounds themselves are exceptional on a surface level, and their mixture is refined. On a higher structural level, we realize that the various elements each have a specific function in inducing a sensibility and mood. The combination serves to induce a kind of trance—made with everyday sounds that contextualize each other. When new sounds are introduced, they are often functional substitutions for sounds that have died out, thus maintaining the context. For example, the work is full of repeating pulses, but from a wide variety of sound sources. When one pulse dies out, another eventually enters, different in its spectromorphology but retaining the structural function of pulsation.

Humor, irony, provocation as narrative

Narrative context can be driven by humor, irony, and provocation. These need not be omnipresent—many serious works have humorous moments.

What is the psychology of humor in music? Huron (2006) describes it as a reaction to fear:

> When musicians create sounds that evoke laughter . . . they are, I believe, exploiting the biology of pessimism. The fast-track brain always interprets surprise as bad. The uncertainty attending surprise is sufficient cause to be fearful. . . . But this fear appears and disappears with great rapidity and does not involve conscious awareness. The appraisal response follows quickly on the heels of these reaction responses, and the neutral or positive appraisal quickly extinguishes the initial negative reaction. . . . In effect, when music evokes one of these strong emotions, the brain is simply realizing that the situation is very much better than first impressions might suggest.

Huron (2006) enumerates nine devices that have been used in music to evoke a humorous reaction, including material that is incongruous, oddly mixed, drifting, disruptive, implausible, excessive, incompetent, inappropriate, and misquoted. Humor can be derisive. As Luc Ferrari (quoted in Caux 2002) observed:

> To be serious in always working in derision is a permanent condition of my work. I am always preciously outside of anything resembling the idea of reason. Derision lets me disturb reason: who is right, who is wrong? It is also a question of power.

Dry humor is omnipresent in Ferrari's music, for example, in the incessantly repeating "Numéro quatro?" in *Les anecdotiques* (2002), or the changing of the guard sequence in *Musique promenade* (1969) with its absurdly contrasting sound layers.

Sound example 10.7. Excerpt of "Numéro quarto" from *Les anecdotiques* (2002) by Luc Ferrari.

Charles Dodge's humorous *Speech Songs* (1973) featured surreal poems by Mark Strand as sung by a computer. As the composer (2000) observed:

> I have always liked humor and had an attraction to the bizarre, the surreal. These poems were almost dream-like in their take on reality. So that made me feel very at home somehow. This unreal voice taking about unreal life situations was very congruent. The voices are . . . cartoon-like and that pleased me.

Dodge's *Any Resemblance is Purely Coincidental* (1980) warps the voice of Enrico Caruso to both humorous and tragic effect.

Sound example 10.8. Excerpt of Any Resemblance is Purely Coincidental (1980) by Charles Dodge.

A camp sense of humor prevails in the electronic pop music of Jean-Jacques Perrey, such as his rendition of *Flight of the Bumblebee* (1975) featuring the sampled and transposed sounds of real bees.

Irony is a related narrative strategy, letting music comment on itself and the world around it, often with humorous effect. Many techniques communicate irony: absurd juxtapositions, quotations of light music, and exaggerations, for example. Irony can also be conveyed in extrinsic ways, as in titles and program notes. An example is Stockhausen's program notes to the CBS vinyl edition of the *Klavierstücken* (CBS 32 21 0007). In the guise of documentation, the composer (1970) meticulously detailed all aspects of the recording, including the consumption habits of the pianist Aloys Kontarsky in the period of the recording sessions.

> . . . [The pianist] dined on a marrow consommé (which was incomparably better than the one previously mentioned) 6 Saltimbocca Romana, lettuce; he drank 1/2 liter of Johannisberg Riesling wine; a Crêpe Suzette with a cup of Mocca coffee followed; he chose a Monte-Cristo Havana cigar to accompany 3 glasses of Williams-Birnengeist, with an extended commentary on European import duties for cigars (praising Switzerland because of duty by weight) and on the preparation and packing of Havana cigars.

Another example of absurdist irony appears in John Cage's *Variations IV* (1964): "For any number of players, any sounds or combinations of sounds produced by any means, with or without other activities." The recording of the work unfolds as a Dada-esque collage that juxtaposes excerpts of banal radio broadcasts. These form a sarcastic commentary on American popular culture. Ironic re-sampling is a recurrent theme of artists influenced by the aesthetics of *cut-up* or *plunderphonics* (Cutler 2000).

Closely related to humorous and ironic strategies is provocation. Provocative pieces tend to divide the audience into fans versus foes. As Herbert Brün (1985) noted:

> We often sit in a concert and listen to a piece to which we do not yet have a "liking" relationship but of which we know already that it annoys the people in the row behind us—and then we are very much for that piece. I would suggest that my piece is just on a level where it invites you to a conspiracy with me and you like that. Yes, it annoys a few people in your imagination or your presence that you would like annoyed, and I am doing you this little favor.

Notice the two sides of the effect: Some people enjoy the piece at least in part because they think others are annoyed. Some artists are deliberately provocative; they seek to shock the audience. Shock is a well-worn strategy. Consider Erik Satie's *Vexations* (1893) for piano, in which a motive is repeated 840 times, taking over 18 hours. At the first full performance, which did not occur until

1963, only one audience member remained present through the entire event (Schonberg 1963).

Strategies for deliberate provocation follow known formulae. Certain artistic conceptions function as "audience trials" to see who can stand to remain. An exceptionally long, loud, noisy, quiet, or static piece tests the audience.[78]

The line between provocation and free artistic expression is blurry, since what is considered provocative is context-dependent, or more specifically, culturally dependent. To some extent, provocation is in the eye of the beholder. For example, Stravinsky's *Rite of Spring* (1913) was considered shocking at its Paris premiere but was celebrated as an artistic triumph in the same city a year later (Stravinsky 1936).

In some music, provocation occurs as a natural side-effect of a disparity between a composer's unconventional vision and the conventional mindset of an audience. For example, the music of Varèse was long considered provocative by many critics and labeled as "a challenge to music as we know it." The management of Philips Pavilion went so far as to attempt to have Varèse's *Poème Électronique* (1958) removed from the Philips Pavilion project (Trieb 1996). Similarly, Xenakis was a musical radical of an uncompromising nature; many of his pieces, both electronic and instrumental, challenged accepted limits:

> A tremendous furor was aroused in Paris in October 1968 at a performance of Bohor during the Xenakis Day at the city's International Contemporary Music Week. By the end of the piece, some were affected by the high sound level to the point of screaming; others were standing and cheering. "Seventy percent of the people loved it and thirty percent hated it" estimated the composer from his own private survey following the performance.
>
> —BRODY (1971)

I recall being present at the Paris premiere of Xenakis's composition *S.709* (1994), a raw and obsessive electronic sonority that dared the audience to like it.

Narrative repose

Compositional processes need a balance between sparsity, relaxation, and repose as well as density, tension, and action. As in the cinema, slowing down the action and allowing the direction to meander provides an opportunity to build up suspense–underlying tension. As Herbert Brün (1984) observed:

> Boredom is a compositional parameter.

Composers sometimes deliberately insert sections that stall or freeze the narrative, as preparation for intense fireworks to come. Stockhausen's *Gesang der Jünglinge* (1956) comes to mind, with its sparse and frozen middle section between 3:17 and 8:50 preceding a colorful finale (8:51–13:15). Consider also the quiet passage in the middle of Theodore Lotis's *Arioso Dolente/Beethoven op.110* (2002).

Sound example 10.9. Excerpt of *Arioso Dolente/Beethoven op.110* (2002) by Theodore Lotis.

Likewise, the long reposing phrases that characterize the style of Ludger Brümmer induce a sense of expectation for brief dramatic flourishes, as in works such as *The gates of H* (1993), *CRI* (1995), *La cloche sans valées* (1998), and *Glassharfe* (2006).

Sound example 10.10. Excerpt of *Glassharfe* (2006) by Ludger Brümmer.

Conclusion: hearing narrative structure

> In poetry and painting, and also in music, from the serial music of the 1930s to 1960s, rigorous abstraction was the proper way. . . . I was one of those musicians in the 1960s who felt that the time was ripe for escaping from this. . . . I thought that the best way to oppose abstraction in music was to introduce narrative and feeling, which had been banned for fear of a return to romanticism. . . . On the other hand . . . I like very much those things that are expressive without being swollen with sentiment.
>
> —LUC FERRARI (QUOTED IN GAYOU 2001)

A composer can design narrative structure, but will listeners hear it? Part of the pleasure of listening to music is decoding the syntactic structure as it unfolds. A clear and simple narrative design is decipherable to most listeners. A listener who cannot hear any patterns or organization in a piece of music will likely dismiss it as boring chaos.

At the same time, in a piece of new electronic music of sufficient complexity, it is unlikely that a listener will hear every detail that the composer designs. Like any craftsperson, composers of all stripes embroider patterns for their own amusement without expectation that audiences will decipher them. As mentioned in the preface and in chapter 9, a communication model of music—in which the composer transmits a message that is received and unambiguously decoded by listeners—is not realistic. "Imperfect" communication, in which the message perceived by each listener is unique, is part of the fascination of music.

Even if a listener was able to somehow perfectly track the narrative structure—to parse the syntax on all timescales—this does not account for the ineffable factor of taste in listening. Just because I understand how a work is organized does not mean that I will like it. Inversely, I do not need to understand how a work is constructed in order to marvel at it. As in all other aspects of life, there is no accounting for taste; the appreciation of beauty is subjective; nothing has universal appeal.

Recent research shows that our brains experience music not only as emotional stimulus but also as an analog of active physical motion (Echoes 2011). In effect, the composer sails the listener on a fantastic voyage. Let each person make up their own mind about what they experience.

11

Generative strategies

Models of process are natural to musical thinking.[79] As we listen, we absorb the sensual experience of sound while also setting up expectations—constructing hypotheses of musical process. The grail of composition—compelling and original form—is the result of a convincing process. For centuries, composers organized music compositions according to an evolving set of rules governing harmony and counterpoint.

It is a short leap from a set of rules to the coding of a computational process for composing music. As Wolfram (2002) observed:

> Just as the rules for any system can be viewed as corresponding to a program, so also its behavior can be viewed as corresponding to a computation.

Thus musical behavior can be modeled by a computational process (Hiller and Isaacson 1959). A composition algorithm serves as a generative engine for music creation.

The practice of algorithmic composition encompasses a broad spectrum of methods and philosophies, from hobbyists using commercial applications to produce songs in a popular style, to game soundtrack designers, to music scientists building models of existing musical styles. Most research goes to simulation of known styles, which is not surprising given the engineering and scientific tendency to build simulations. The justification given for some of these projects is to aid "musicians with writer's block" or to empower those "without the slightest bit of expertise" to compose music.

In this chapter, however, the focus is on creative composer-programmers who design their own generative composition systems according to a personal aesthetic vision in the pursuit of new and original styles.

Here we use the terms "formalized," "generative," and "algorithmic" interchangeably to describe any systematic rule-based approach to composition. This can include techniques that are not programmed, such as the systematic methods of Milton Babbitt, for example.

Sound example 11.1. Excerpt of *Vision and prayer* (1961) by Milton Babbitt. 

We begin with a look at the attraction of generative strategies: Why do they interest composers? We then review some of the pioneers in the field, who set the tone for the present era. Then we compare deterministic and stochastic algorithms, and show that both types are not always easy to define. The core of the chapter is devoted to a variety of issues raised by generative composition. As we point out, some of the philosophical justifications behind algorithmic methods are confusing or contradictory. One issue is that non-formal assumptions, preferences, and subjective choices permeate the design and application of formal processes. This can make it difficult to assess the meaning and significance of a generative approach.[80] We compare the premises and goals of sound-based composition with more conceptualist philosophies. Finally, we look at an especially intriguing application of generative algorithms: the control of sound synthesis and signal processing techniques like granular synthesis and automated mixing.

Attractions of generative strategies

Generative strategies are conceptually attractive. They offer the possibility of exploring novel musical processes and the creation of new musical structures according to freely invented strategies. As Ernst Krenek (1939) observed:

> The fundamental facts of a sound language have many formal points of similarity with an axiomatic system. . . . As the study of axioms eliminates the

> idea that axioms are something absolute, conceiving them instead as free propositions of the human mind . . . would . . . free us from . . . any systematized form of musical material as an irrevocable law of nature.

Another often-stated rationale for generative techniques is that they allow composers to reach beyond themselves (Berg 1987):

> To hear that which could not be heard without the computer, to think that which could not be thought without the computer, and to learn that which could not be learned without the computer. The computer can allow a composer to write music that goes beyond that which she is already capable of.

Unpredictability is part of the attraction (McCormack et al. 2009):

> It is not the indeterminacy that is of central importance here, but that the end product is something more than is specified in the instruction set . . . as the process gives rise to outcomes that "outperform the designer's specifications."

In Clarence Barlow's *Relationships for Melody Instruments* (1974–1986), his software improvised in real time using probability tables and played a digital synthesizer live onstage with two other musicians.

Sound example 11.2. Excerpt of *Relationships for Melody Instruments* (1986 version) by Clarence Barlow. Performers: Clarence Barlow on computer, Michael Riesslar on bass clarinet, and Jaki Liebezeit on percussion.

Romantic ideals can drive generative aesthetics, from purity of method to seductive metaphors of natural growth and evolution, life, and ecosystems. Josef Hauer, Schoenberg's contemporary, felt that following strict rules made his music more "spiritual," as Whittall (2008) observed:

> He detested all art that expressed ideas, programs, or feelings, demanding a purely spiritual supersensual music composed according to impersonal rules.

It is not self-evident, however, why and how logical rules accrue the quality of being sacrosanct.

In contrast to the view of composition as a form of spiritual expression, McCormack et al. (2009) likened generative composition to giving birth to a living organism:

> Another mode [of composition] exists within which compositions generate and self-organize, shifting and oscillating, adapting, developing, and becoming whole: like an organism.

When a composer frames her composition as the product of an elaborate technical process, this can make it seem more impressive. As Elliot Carter (1960) observed:

> With the help of [systems] a vast amount of music is being written, far more than can ever be played, than ever be judged or widely known. . . . The struggle

to be performed and to be recognized makes it very hard for one not to become some kind of system monger. . . .

Many institutions (academia, research centers, journals, conferences, etc.) reward systematic approaches to composition.

An indisputable attraction of generative techniques is that they let composers control sonic processes on a level that would be impossible without algorithmic assistance. We see this in the control of processes like granulation, additive synthesis, frequency modulation, spatial upmixing (see chapter 8), and live interactive performance (Collins 2003). Rather than giving up control, a composer actually gains control over a domain that is difficult or impossible to manage without machine assistance. As John Chowning spoke of his composition *Stria*, composed in 1978 (Roads 1985c):

> It was the first time that I tried to use a high-level programming language to realize a composition in toto. . . . There were rules for determining the details of the structure, from the microsound level up to the level of a phrase. In *Stria*, all frequency components are based on powers of the Golden Mean in the carrier:modulator ratios. So it is all very cohesive perceptually, even though it is inharmonic and sounds a little strange. But it does not take long, even for a naïve listener, to realize that even though it is strange, it is cohesive at a deep level. I believe this is because of the unified structure of spectral formation.

Sound example 11.3. Excerpt of *Stria* (1978) by John Chowning. 

Pioneers of algorithmic music

Composing according to rules dates back to ancient times (Da Silva 2002).[81] In the mid-century modern era, the turn toward formalized and systematic methods of composition in the 1950s is well documented. The serial or tone-row method of composition—promulgated 30 years earlier by Arnold Schoenberg—had been generalized from pitch to other musical parameters (note durations, dynamic markings, etc.) by Anton Webern, Olivier Messiaen, and others. Ever-more elaborate rationales dominated journals devoted to music. As the complexity of these procedures increased, so did the "precompositional" burden on composers. Herbert Brün (Hamlin and Roads 1985) observed this about his work from this period:

> I started writing a score for orchestra in which I used the method of having a table and precompositional material ready on the walls and on the table and on the floor—to an absurd state of completeness. I got, as could be predicted, totally stuck—confused. It was not really an unhappy affair, but it was a puzzling situation.

In an attempt to break out of the extreme determinism of serial composition, composers such as Karlheinz Stockhausen, Pierre Boulez, and John Cage, among

FIGURE 11.1 Lejaren Hiller, circa 1960, University of Illinois. Courtesy of the University of Illinois Archives, Photographic Subject File, RS 39/2/20.

others, experimented with *aleatoric* methods of composition: Certain details of the piece were left open to the interpreter (in the case of instrumental music), or else they were composed according to random or chance operations like throwing dice or coins and then mapping the outcome to a list of corresponding notes or note patterns.

Into this brew came Lejaren Hiller and the Illiac computer (figure 11.1). At the age of 23, Hiller received a Ph.D. in chemistry from Princeton, where he was also a student of Roger Sessions and Milton Babbitt in composition (Gena 1994). After five years as a researcher at DuPont, he joined the chemistry department at the University of Illinois to develop statistical models of chemical processes. While simultaneously gaining a master of music degree, he began to apply mathematical models to the generation of music. (See chapter 6 on rhythm for a description of his experiments in algorithmic rhythm generation.) The initial result was the algorithmically generated *Illiac Suite for String Quartet* (1956), a landmark in the history of music. The *Computer Cantata* (Hiller and Baker 1964) and *HPSCHD*, a collaboration with John Cage (Hiller and Cage 1968; Austin 1992) followed. As Hiller and Isaacson (1959) wrote:

> Music is . . . governed by laws of organization, which permit fairly exact codification. (. . . it has even been claimed that the content of music is nothing other than its organization.) From this proposition, it follows that

FIGURE 11.2 Iannis Xenakis. Photograph by Michel Daniel, courtesy of Les Amis de Xenakis (www.iannis-xenakis.org).

> computer-composed music which is "meaningful" is conceivable to the extent to which the laws of musical organization are codifiable.

Hiller's experiments proved that a computer could model any formal procedure: from the canons of traditional counterpoint to the tenets of serial technique; both deterministic and stochastic methods could be coded. Programs sped up the time-consuming labor associated with systematic composition. Software development emerged as a logical extension of the aesthetic of formalized composition (Hiller 1979, 1981; Hiller and Isaacson 1959). Outside the Illinois campus, the concepts behind Hiller's "experimental music" echoed throughout the music world (Hiller 1964).

A handful of brave composers followed in the immediate wake of Hiller. These include, among others, Herbert Brün and John Myhill at the University of Illinois, James Tenney at Bell Telephone Laboratories, G. M. Koenig at the University of Utrecht, and Pierre Barbaud, Michel Phillipot, and Iannis Xenakis (figure 11.2) in Paris. In some cases, they had already been composing according to formal procedures. Xenakis's *Metastasis* for orchestra, for example, composed according to stochastic formulas, was premiered in 1955—the same year Hiller began his computer experiments. His Stochastic Music Program was written in Fortran and was used to generate a number of works, including *ST/10* and *ST/48* (both 1962) among others (Roads 1973).

Sound example 11.4. *ST/48* (1962) by Xenakis composed with his Stochastic Music Program. 

By 1970, experimentation in algorithmic composition was sufficient to prompt the first historical survey of the field (Hiller 1970). After pioneering experiments in real-time interactive performance in the 1980s by composers like George Lewis, Clarence Barlow, and Ron Kuivila (Roads 1985b, 1986), the introduction of portable laptop computers in the 1990s brought real-time algorithmic music more widely to the concert stage and sound gallery.

Toolkits for algorithmic composition

While the algorithmic composition programs of the past were primarily standalone applications, the current trend is programming environments or toolkits: a collection of operators configured by the composer. The flexibility of the toolkit lets composers design custom strategies for composition. These environments are extensible, meaning that it is easy to add new functionality, in contrast to a closed application program.

The first toolkit for generative composition was the MUSICOMP library of assembly language subroutines developed by Robert Baker and Lejaren Hiller at the University of Illinois (Baker 1963; Hiller and Leal 1966; Hiller 1969). The MUSICOMP library included tools for selecting items from a list according to a probability distribution, randomly shuffling items in a list, tone row manipulation, enforcing melodic rules, and coordination of rhythmic lines. As Baker (1963) put it:

> MUSICOMP is a "facilitator" program. It presents no specific compositional logic itself, but is capable of being used with nearly any logic supplied by the user.

The output of MUSICOMP routines could be printed or formatted for input to sound synthesis programs. Hiller used the MUSICOMP routines to create a number of works including his *Algorithms I* (1968) for nine instruments and tape (Hiller 1981).

More recent toolkits include Max/MSP (Zicarelli 2002), SuperCollider (McCartney 2002), PD (Puckette 2007), and OpenMusic (Assayag and Agon 1996), among others (see also Roads 1996, chapters 17 and 18). These share the goal of providing kits that can be configured by individual composers. The most flexible environments are modular, meaning that composers need use only those functions that interest them.

Another approach is to use a standard programming language augmented by libraries that support music processing. Examples include Common Music, an extension of the Common Lisp language (Taube 1991, 2004), AC Toolbox (Lisp-based) (Berg 2003), Nyquist (Lisp-based) (Dannenberg 2013), and Clarence Barlow's MIDIDESK (1984–1999), a library of routines written in Pascal (Barlow 2009a). (Barlow used MIDIDESK to compose *Orchideae Ordinariae* [1989] for piano and orchestra.)

The choice of a model

A historical style of music can be analyzed scientifically as a kind of systematic process. It can be reverse-engineered into a set of rules: a generative model. Hiller and Isaacson's early experiments, for example, aimed at recreating 16th-century counterpoint (Hiller and Isaacson 1959). Their approach was like that of a typical engineer or scientist building a mathematical model of a known phenomenon and then running simulations to test it.

A key issue in simulating any process is the choice of representation and process model. Hiller and Isaacson favored Monte Carlo methods such as Markov chains. Three decades later, in modeling the style of composers like Bach, Mozart, and Mahler, David Cope (1993, 1996, 2004) used *augmented transition networks* (ATNs), an artificial intelligence model originally developed for understanding language. Engineering and science provide numerous other models for approximation and simulation of musical structure (Roads 1996, chapters 17 and 18).

Some models are *computationally equivalent*, meaning that they produce the same results but use different representations and processes, like separate paths that lead to the same endpoint (Chomsky and Schuetzenberger 1963; Wolfram 2002). Thus the choice of a specific model is somewhat arbitrary. This is an important point: The selection of any specific formalism is based on subjective preferences, intellectual fashions, or arbitrary technical criteria. For example, one model might be "compact," while another is "computationally efficient." Yet another model might be "accurate with respect to a test suite," while another is "complete over a broad corpus of cases" or "compatible with a standard model." Thus, for any given historical style, a dozen different people might each choose a different way to model it. None of these models purport to compose as a human being does.

This is where the goals of historical style recreation become murky. Given two models that reproduce the style of Mozart but in different ways, how should we compare them? See Pearce et al. (2002) for an analysis of the methodological problems raised by historical style recreation.

In any case, the aesthetic goal of creative composition differs from the model-based approach. It is not a matter of reverse engineering a historical style. Rather, the goal is to develop a new and original style. The main issue is this: How can generative strategies serve this goal?

Aesthetic issues in generative composition

As Jean-Claude Risset (2007) observed, the opposition between music-as-formalism versus music-as-perceived-sound is as ancient as Pythagoras and Aristoxenus. The ancient quadrivium defined music as "the discipline that treats of numbers in their relation to those things that are found in sounds" (Cassidorus quoted in Strunk 1950). (See Whitwell 2009 for a brief history of mathematics and music.) The tradition of linking music and mathematics continues today with organized conferences, journals, and books (Loy 2006; Barlow 2008; Benson 2007; Mazzola 2002). Let us distinguish between the mathematics of audio signal processing and the formalisms that have been employed in generative composition to represent higher levels of musical structure and process. The latter is the focus of this chapter.

The rest of this section is the core of the chapter. It dissects several intertwined issues. In particular, we examine certain contradictions that arise in strict formalism and contrast them with a more flexible, interactive approach. The contradictions can be summarized as disconnects between the ideals of generative formalism and the ground truth of human perception and music cognition.

DETERMINISTIC VERSUS STOCHASTIC ALGORITHMS

At the dawn of algorithmic music, an apparent conflict between deterministic versus stochastic algorithms was seen as a major aesthetic issue. Hiller and Isaacson (1959) experimented with both approaches. As Xenakis (1985) observed:

> One establishes an entire range between two poles—determinism, which corresponds to strict periodicity, and indeterminism, which corresponds to constant renewal. . . . This is the true keyboard of musical composition.

Deterministic procedures generate musical material by carrying out a fixed, rule-based compositional task that does not involve random selection. The variables supplied to a deterministic procedure are called the *seed data*. The seed data can be a set of pitches, a musical phrase, or some constraints that the procedures must satisfy. An example of a deterministic procedure would be a program to harmonize a chorale melody in the style of J. S. Bach. The seed data is the melody. The rules of harmonization, derived from a textbook, ensure that only certain chord sequences are legal. A deterministic algorithm might look for a solution that satisfies all the constraints of the harmonization rules. Another example of a deterministic algorithm is Clarence Barlow's formula for determining the dynamic marking at a given point in a stipulated meter (Barlow 1980). Like a calculator, a deterministic program fed the same seed data should produce the same result every time.

Stochastic procedures, on the other hand, integrate random choice into the decision-making process. A basic stochastic generator produces a random number and compares it to values stored in a probability table. If the random number falls within a certain range of values in the probability table, the algorithm generates the event associated with that range. By weighting the probability of certain events over others, one can guarantee an overall trend, while the filigree of local events remains unpredictable.

So far, the distinction between deterministic and stochastic seems clear. At a deeper algorithmic level, however, it is not so clear-cut. As we will see, both determinism and randomness are conceptual ideals based on simplistic assumptions.

In particular, the concept of randomness is impossible to define from a purely mathematical viewpoint (Chaitin 1975, 1994). To do so would take an infinitely long computer program according to the tenets of complexity theory (Kolmorogov 1968; Winter 2010). Wolfram (2002) took issue with this unattainable definition by asserting that his Rule 30 is "random for all practical purposes." Rule 30 serves as the *random* (integer) function in the Mathematica application. As the great numerical analyst R. W. Hamming (1973) noted:

> In the final analysis, randomness, like beauty, is in the eye of the beholder.

Any software function called "random," including Rule 30, is actually a deterministic algorithm, which will eventually repeat itself. In computer science, the proper term for such a function is a *pseudorandom number generator.* Meanwhile, the science of computation is moving away from determinism; the realm of quantum computation is based on probabilistic results.[82]

Scientists distinguish further between "random" processes and "chaotic" processes according to how much one knows about their inputs (Moon 1987):

> We must distinguish here between so-called random and chaotic motions. The former is reserved for problems in which we truly do not know the input forces or we know only a statistical measure of the parameters. The term *chaotic* is reserved for these deterministic problems for which there are no random or unpredictable inputs or parameters.

A deterministic chaotic process (such as a pseudorandom number generator) can be arbitrarily complex, repeating only after an astronomical number of iterations.[83] Yet determinism as an ideal has its own limits, as Sowa (2006) pointed out:

> Newton once claimed that the celestial bodies followed a more deterministic course than any clock that human beings could contrive. Yet today, atomic clocks, which are still not perfect, are routinely used to detect and accommodate minor fluctuations in the earth's orbit. A truly deterministic process is as elusive as a perpetual motion machine.

Certain deterministic algorithms exhibit such obvious mechanistic behavior that we can identify them by listening. Apart from such simple cases, however, it is not possible to ascertain by listening whether a given fragment of music has been generated by a stochastic or deterministic process. As Wolfram (2002) observed:

> There seem to be many kinds of systems in which it is overwhelmingly easier to generate highly complex behavior than to recognize the origins of this behavior.

Many generative algorithms in musical use are perceptually opaque. As Berio (2006) observed:

> Today we can find examples of complete estrangement between the practical and sensory dimension and the conceptual one, between the work listened to and the process that generated it.

The choice of algorithm is a matter of the composer's personal taste, influenced by the cultural and technical fashions of the day. Although some composers prefer to limit their options to one specific strategy for reasons of conceptual purity, there is no reason why different heuristically derived algorithms could not be intelligently mixed in one system and applied to various aspects of the composition process.

ALL-OR-NOTHING: BATCH MODE COMPOSITION

To compose in a logically consistent way is the ideal of the formalist composer. Yet as Herbert Brün (1986), a composer who experimented with generative methods, observed with some skepticism:

> If systems were consistent, then a consistent analysis of a system could also be consistent with the analyzed system. One fallacy to be mentioned is the assumption that in the case of an inconsistency between system and analysis, it is the analysis that has to be corrected. The other fallacy is the assumption that in such a case it is the system that has to be corrected. As if consistency were the goal.

Computer programs are nothing more than human decisions in coded form. Why should a decision that is coded in a program be more important than a decision that is not coded? This is the main question addressed in this section.

Some proponents of automated composition, notably Hiller and Barbaud, adhered to a strict "all-or-nothing" doctrine. In their view, the output score generated by a composition program should never be altered or edited by hand. If the user did not like the result, the program logic should be changed and run again. This doctrine stems from an aesthetic that values art that is, above all, formally consistent. According to this aesthetic, the concept and rules make the work. Some would say that the algorithms are the art. (We take up this idea in a moment.)

In the extreme, this type of artist resembles an experimental scientist who is neutral with respect to the results. Any outcome of a properly conducted experiment is a valid result. If formal consistency is all that matters, then one result should be as good as any other. However, almost all generative artists (in music and in the visual arts) exercise artistic prerogative to choose certain outcomes over others according to their personal taste. Even Barbaud said that if he did not like the output, he revised the algorithm. What is "liking" if not a subjective preference?[84]

There are two contradictions here. First, if one allows subjective preference in accepting certain results and rejecting others, why is it "inconsistent" to edit the results? Neither intervention is based on formal logic. Second, the design of the algorithm itself is based on intuitive subjective preferences. Why use a tessellation algorithm rather than a search process, hidden Markov model, genetic algorithm, grammar, cellular automaton or fractal, stochastic, or chaotic function? Underneath such decisions lies an arbitrary personal taste, subjective aesthetic goal, or cultural fashion.

Ultimately, there seems to be no deep reason why a decision that is coded in a program should be more privileged than a decision that is not coded. A fundamental limitation of the strict Hiller and Barbaud approach is the *batch mode* of interaction it imposes on the composer. The term "batch" refers to the earliest computer systems that ran one program at a time; there was no interaction with the machine besides submitting a deck of punched paper cards for execution and picking up the printed output. No online editing could occur; all decisions had to be predetermined and encoded in the program and its seed data.

In the batch mode of composition, the composer follows these steps:

1. Code the algorithm.
2. Enter the seed data.
3. Execute the program.
4. Accept or reject the output (an entire composition).

If we follow the batch doctrine and a single event is not to our taste, we must repeat these steps. We cannot simply correct the offending events without generating a new score. This is because in a batch approach to automated composition, the unit of composition and interaction are an entire piece.

A batch approach also characterizes the current generation of autonomous music systems that operate in real time, permitting neither intervention nor the selection of output (Collins 2002a).

Some have gone further, arguing that the composition is the program code itself, not the music it produces. This is similar to the position taken in the 1960s by composers such as Morton Feldman that the composition was the ink on paper, and that its rendition into sound was irrelevant. (See the section on "Generative rhythm and problems of notation" below.)

Advocates would argue that the rules of the program ensure logical consistency and originality in the generated output. However, simply because certain parameters of a piece conform to an arbitrary set of axioms is no guarantee that the listener will hear consistency or originality in the final product. Perceived musical consistency and originality are cognitive categories for which little theory yet exists.

A strong advocate of systematic methods, Ernst Krenek (1939) nonetheless took exception to the notion that formal consistency was the goal of composition:

> We cannot take the bare logical coherence of a musical "axiomatic" system as the sole criterion of its soundness! . . . The outstanding characteristic of music [is] its independence from the linguistic limitations of general logic.

As Vaggione (1997) noted, by convention, a rule must necessarily be followed many times; the artist, however, can invoke a rule only once. As a skeptical Debussy observed (Risset 2004):

> Works of art make rules, rules do not make works of art.

In certain masterworks, the composer escapes from the prison of self-imposed rule systems. Alban Berg, in composing *Lyric Suite* for string quartet (1926), alternated seamlessly between systematic and "free" strategies (Whittall 1999). As noted in chapter 9, "Multiscale organization," Stockhausen's practice combined systematic planning with intuitive interventions (Maconie 1989; Roads 2013). In the same vein, Xenakis treated the output of his composition programs flexibly. In particular, he edited, rearranged, and refined the raw data emitted by his Stochastic Music Program (Roads 1973).

> When I used programs to produce music like *ST/4*, *ST/10*, or *ST/48*, the output sometimes lacked interest. So I had to change [it]. I reserved that freedom for myself. Other composers, like Barbaud, have acted differently. He did some programs using serial principles and declared: "The machine gave me that so I have to respect it." This is totally wrong, because it was he who gave the machine the rule!
>
> —XENAKIS (VARGA 1996)

> "Formalized music" does not sound free, but it is. I wanted to achieve a general musical landscape with many elements, not all of which were formally derived from one another.
>
> —XENAKIS (1996)

In effect, Xenakis's interventions were part of a feedback loop between the algorithmic engine and the composer. In his later years, Xenakis no longer relied on computers for instrumental composition; he had absorbed algorithmic strategies into his intuition (Varga 1996; Harley 2004).

FORMAL/INFORMAL STRATEGIES IN HEURISTIC ALGORITHMS

Music interacts in deep ways with the memory and expectations of listeners (Huron 2006). Human beings respond intuitively to context-dependent cognitive impressions that are difficult to formalize, like wit, irony, tension, surprise, virtuosity, humor, and clever twists and transitions. One sound appears to cause another sound. Sounds converge on points of attraction or scatter at points of repulsion. In general, formal methods do not address these types of narrative dynamics. How do you codify narrative functions based on human expectation? This is not obvious, but it seems unlikely that it will emerge from a formula borrowed from an arbitrary branch of physics or mathematics.[85]

Yet I do not discount the power of mathematics to induce wonder. As the artist-engineer Lance Putnam (2011) said in a talk at the Southern California Institute for Architecture:

> Narrative is one of the key points. [Sound has] a very strong direction to it in time. We experience things. We encounter patterns and shapes in our lives. We can strip these down to their essence, but I do not expect to find a mathematical equation that gives us the same experience. But I think [mathematics] can capture some of the essence. We might remember things through these patterns or intuit them or feel them. Some of

> these curves have peculiar qualitative aspects to them that I am really curious about. In my research I am trying to understand the connection between these [qualitative] aspects and mathematics. Mathematics has been with us for a long time. To connect it to our human experience is an important step.[86]

As noted in chapter 2, the effect of music is magical–beyond logical explanation. Let us re-quote Francis Bacon's definition of magic:

> The science which applies the knowledge of hidden forms to the production of wonderful operations.

In the context of the 17th century, the "knowledge of hidden forms" involved mastery of esoteric skills—analogous to the knowledge of mathematics and programming languages today—but also how to apply them "to the production of wonderful operations." Criteria for the production of wonder have never been formalized. However, we observe that certain talented people make inspired choices from myriad possibilities to create fascinating designs. This remains the strong suit of human talent.

To produce wonderful forms, what is needed is a hybrid formal/informal approach, combining the computational power of algorithmic control with the magical influence of heuristics. What is heuristic influence? Heuristics is the art of experience-based strategies for problem-solving:

> Heuristic knowledge is judgmental knowledge, the knowledge that comes from experience—the rules that make up "the art of good guessing."
>
> —COHEN ET AL. (1984)

As the mathematician Gregory Chaitin (2002) once said of heuristic reasoning:

> When I was a kid I dipped into Euler's collected works, his *Opera Omnia*, in the Columbia University Math library. He does a lot of calculations, looks for different patterns, then he makes a conjecture, then there's a proof with a hole in it, and then a few more papers down the road he finds a way to fill in the hole, and later he polishes up the proof. So he shows his whole train of thought and he does a lot of experimentation. I think Gauss was the same, but he hid all the steps. Gauss said you have to remove the scaffolding when you finish a building. . . . So I do think there is an empirical component in math: it's computation. You do calculations and see patterns and make conjectures. . . . But when you publish, normally you hide all of that and present it like a direct divine revelation. . . . Mathematics in the process of discovery is a little bit like physics, The way you discover something new is "quasi-empirical." . . . You have to learn the art of discovery and that is heuristic reasoning [or] inspired guesswork.

The heuristic approach stands in contrast to brute-force computer models that enumerate and search millions of possibilities and then make choices based on short-term statistics. Such an approach may succeed in the realm of fixed-rule games like checkers and chess, but it has obvious limitations in the realm of art where the notion of "rules" is more fluid.

Heuristic methods include rules of thumb, educated guesses, intuitive judgments, and common sense—all based on experience. Heuristic methods are inevitably intertwined with an understanding of context, whether it is the state of a game, the state of a composition, or the state of a culture. While certain pieces, such as those of J. S. Bach, have a timeless quality, other pieces have an impact precisely because they articulate a critical juncture in culture: *The Rite of Spring* of Stravinsky comes to mind.

Heuristic methods are compatible with formalization. However, in practice, they implement tailor-made solutions that are domain-specific and context-dependent, rather than imported whole cloth from one area of study to another. For example, the visual artist Harold Cohen has long applied heuristic algorithms to aesthetic problems. Over a period of 40 years, Cohen has been developing a body of highly specific algorithms for drawing and coloring shapes. For the composition and spatialization of sound, we need music-specific algorithms.

Most important, heuristic algorithms are tested by experiments and refined by human perceptual judgments. Xenakis used stochastic processes in a heuristic manner, sometimes modifying and rearranging the results to better suit the piece. Poetic license is the ultimate heuristic.

For generative granular synthesis, one heuristic approach would be to borrow certain concepts from scientific models of granular processes but then rework them to serve more effectively in a musical context. In this sense, the physical model serves as a kind of metaphor for granular organization in music, rather than a strict model. The main point is that we can design heuristic algorithms to implement methods of mesostructural formation and multiscale behavior. These algorithms need to "work" according to testing and expert judgment.

INTERACTION WITH ALGORITHMS

By enriching an algorithmic system with interaction, we add a flexibility that is missing from a batch approach. In so doing, we gain direct access to the different layers and timescales of compositional structure and process. An interactive approach allows us to choose the processes that will be delegated to algorithms, versus those processes that will be handled by interaction. A motivation for this approach was expressed by McCormack et al. (2009) as follows:

> Our interest is in using the computer as an expressive, collaborative partner, one that answers back, interacts, and responds intelligently.

The scope, degree, and mode of interaction are compositional prerogatives. This approach concurs with the "formal and informal" philosophy articulated by Horacio Vaggione (2003). He proposed a plurality of diverse tactics (i.e., "a polyphony that integrates the idea of interaction"), rather than handing over control to an autonomous algorithm that rules over all aspects of a composition:

> To articulate a highly stratified musical flux is unthinkable using operations based on statistical means. On the contrary, this requires an approach based on singularities of discontinuity, contrast, and detail. This is why causal formulas are problematic in composition if their automation is not compensated by other modes of articulation, i.e., unique compositional choices—singularities—global as well as local, integrated explicitly within the composition strategy.

The scope of interaction can vary from the small (a single parameter, an envelope, a sound, individual grains), to the medium (a phrase, a voice, a procedure), to the large (all notes, the entire compositional strategy). The degree of interaction can range from the intense real-time performance onstage, where there is no going back, to the reflective interaction experienced in a studio, where there is time and opportunity to backtrack if necessary. In the studio, material produced by generative processes can be treated as a kind of "machine improvisation" that can be freely edited.

Moreover, we can choose the mode of interaction, from direct control of parameters via a musical input device, to interaction with performance software, to iterative transformation and live coding or programming in real time (Blackwell and Collins 2005; Roberts 2012). The iterative approach is exemplified by the practice of Clarence Barlow (2009b). His composition *Tischgeistwalzer* (2009) for two pianos involved an initial generative stage that produced the raw material of the work, followed by a series of transformations of the initial dataset in order to increase the composer's satisfaction with the material (Barlow 2001c).

ECONOMY OF SELECTION AND HUMAN INTERVENTION

> Poetry differs in this respect from logic, that it is not subject to the control of the active powers of the mind, and that its birth and recurrence have no necessary connection with consciousness or will.
>
> —PERCY BYSSHE SHELLEY (1821)

> We often speak of "making a choice" as though this were a deliberate act. However, that "action" may in fact be nothing more than the moment at which you stopped some process that was comparing alternatives. . . .
>
> —MARVIN MINSKY (2006)

The process of composition is essentially creative decision-making: up or down, long or short, sparse or dense, loud or soft, same or different, etc. Out of a universe of possibilities, we choose specific elements and order them in time to construct a musical morphology.

Computer-assisted composition means delegating certain decisions to the computer. Most compositional decisions are loosely constrained. That is, there is no unique solution to a given problem; several outcomes are possible. For example, I have often composed several possible alternative solutions to a compositional problem and then had to choose one for the final piece. In some cases, the functional differences between the alternatives are minimal; any one would work as well as another, with only slightly different implications.

In other circumstances, however, making the inspired choice is absolutely critical. Narrative structures like beginnings, endings, and points of transition and morphosis (on multiple timescales) are especially critical junctures. These points of inflection—the articulators of form—are precisely where algorithmic methods tend to be particularly weak.

Computers are excellent at enumerating possible solutions to a given set of constraints. This has led to optimal performance in well-defined tasks such as playing checkers, where the game has been entirely solved (Schaeffer et al. 2007). A computer can play chess at the grandmaster level by searching through all possible future moves and assigning a value to each move with respect to the goal of checkmate:

> Last year, [IBM's] Deep Blue . . . would examine and evaluate 100 million chess positions every second. This year we're hoping for a factor of two, or 200 million chess positions per second. Most human chess players, including Gary Kasparov, are very limited in the number of positions they can examine. Maybe two positions per second, but they have this talent, this intuition, which they aren't very good at describing how it works. That is, they can look at a position and almost always know the right move to play, without having to do any searching through possibilities. If we understood how a player like Kasparov can do this, then we could obviously make Deep Blue much stronger, but it's a mystery at this point how the human brain is able to play chess as well as it does.
>
> —M. CAMPBELL (1997)

As Noam Chomsky (2013) recently observed:

> When I was appointed at MIT in 1955, they were willing to appoint me in the Research Laboratory for Electronics to work on a program for machine translation. In my interview with the director of the laboratory, I told him that I would be happy to have the position . . . but I told him that I was not going to work on machine translation, because it was totally pointless. The way to do machine translation, I said, is by brute force. [Brute-force search means enumerating all possible translations for the solution and checking how well each one scores on a statistical basis.] There was still a belief at the time that enough was known about what a translator does that you could program it, and that would get you to machine translation. I felt then as I do now that this was pie in the sky. We just did not understand that much.

> Over the years that has turned out to be true. Google has a translator, which is kind of useful if you want to get a rough idea of what is in some scientific article, but it is done by brute force. It doesn't give any insight into the nature of translation [as done by human beings].

A pioneer in the field, Terry Winograd (1991), likened machine intelligence to mastery of rules and regulations:

> The most successful artificial intelligence programs have operated in the detached puzzle-like domains of board games and technical analysis, not those demanding understanding of human lives, motivations, and social interaction.

To compose is to solve a puzzle. However, in the artistic domain, this is as much a psychological and cultural puzzle as it a technical one. The decision-making powers of current computers in these kinds of complex aesthetic domains are minimal. Music composition is not a finite-state game; it has no simple well-defined solution like checkmate. The goal is complicated and hard to precisely define.[87] The overall aim is essentially to attract interest, awakening and delighting perception and consciousness, leading to a psychological or emotional response. As Xenakis (1992) put it:

> Art, and above all, music, has a fundamental function. . . . It must aim . . . toward a total exaltation in which the individual mingles, losing consciousness in a truth immediate, rare, enormous, and perfect. If a work of art succeeds in this undertaking, even for a single moment, it attains its goal.

As mentioned in chapter 2, economy of selection is the ability to choose one or a few perceptually and aesthetically optimal (evocative or salient) choices from a vast desert of unremarkable possibilities. A computer can only make decisions based on preset, formalized rules, whereas artists can make inspired choices based on intuitions fed by a lifetime of observations and experiences. Although a computer program can exhibit traits of intelligence—viz., it can solve well-defined problems—it would be naïve to call this "thinking" or "feeling," which are both part of the human decision-making process. As the computer scientist Edsger Dijkstra (2009) observed:

> The question of whether a computer can think is no more interesting than the question of whether a submarine can swim.

Without conscious awareness, a computer program has no stake in the game of art or life. It has no intuition, lacks lust and disgust, and cannot feel pain or joy, love or hate. Thus it cannot appreciate the meaning or significance of what it produces, much less any other works of art. Without cultural awareness, it has no capacity to appreciate or even to merely interpret a broader context. We see specialized computer programs that exhibit memorized awareness of pop-culture trivia in the manner of an idiot savant (e.g., IBM's Watson program, which beat human contestants at the game of *Jeopardy*). IBM is taking this technology in the general direction of an intelligent query system (Dweck 2011):

> Consider a human being that could read an essentially unlimited number of documents, understand those documents, and completely retain the information in those documents. Now imagine that you could ask that person a question. This is essentially what [Watson] gives you.

Composing is a different game. It involves design, synthesis, transformation, and organization informed by aesthetic criteria. One could program simple aesthetic heuristics so a computer could make less awkward and/or banal decisions. For example, one could apply evolutionary algorithms that search decision spaces using interactive suggestions from a human user (Dahlstadt 2004). Still, it will be a long time before a computer becomes a discriminating musical connoisseur. Humanlike general intelligence including something resembling intuition is a distant grail of research in the field of computer science (Horgan 2008). As Chomsky (2013) observed:

> What is a program? A program is a theory. It is a theory written in an arcane notation to be executed by a machine. You can ask the same questions of a program that you could ask about any other theory. Does it give insight and understanding? In fact these [brute-force artificial intelligence] theories do not. They were not designed with that in mind. What we are asking is: can we design a theory about being smart? We are eons away from that.

Nothing prevents a rule-based system from producing what an audience would consider to be a satisfactory composition. However, in a piece like the *Diabelli Variations* (1823) by Beethoven, which pianist Alfred Brendel called "the greatest of all piano works," a deeper emotional narrative operates beneath the technically contrived surface. The first 36 minutes of this 50-minute composition serve as a setup: After 28 more-or-less manic and sarcastic variations, there is a sudden change of mood to deep melancholy. This casts the previous variations under a shadow as a mindless mechanical process. The shift of mood sets the stage for the final serious and meditative section of the piece. We go from hearing a series of mechanical variations to hearing a reflection on the profundity of existence. This ability to embed a deep emotional narrative within a technical process reminds us that there is—at this time—no substitute for human genius.[88]

GENERATIVE RHYTHM AND PROBLEMS OF NOTATION

Since the 1950s, increasingly complicated approaches to rhythm generation have led inevitably to a conflict with common music notation, which was optimized for the relatively simple and regular patterns of classical music. For example, the notation of Stockhausen's *Klavierstück 8* (1955) reached an extreme rhythmic density, foreshadowing the "new complexity" school of the 1980s (figure 11.3). In these scores, notation evolved into a rococo style; notation for notation's sake became a kind of fetish. The density of these scores was, however, a sign of a weakening musical language. It took more and more symbolically to express less and less audibly.

Common music notation was not designed to describe music in which timbre, statistical texture, and spatial qualities are the primary focus. An aesthetic of notation for notation's sake appeared not only in hyper-complex pieces but also in extremely sparse scores. To some, the act of composition was not even related to the phenomenon of sound. To them, composition was essentially a sub-form of conceptual art:

> Morton Feldman gradually attached less and less importance to the actual realization of that which he notated, asserting "not only do I not care if they listen, I don't care if they play."
>
> —GAGNE AND CARAS (1982)

> The patterns of [Feldman's] late works exist purely as notational images, as isolated from the world of sound as the arcane rug patternings that so influenced Feldman are from our own (post) modern civilization. "My notational concerns have begun to move away from any preoccupation with how the music functions in performance."
>
> —FELDMAN (1988) (QUOTED IN PACCIONE AND PACCIONE 1992)

> I see Feldman's music as being more concerned with open field marking. He would lay out a 12-foot long piece of paper on the wall and then treat it like a field. He would make a mark in the center in relation to a mark to its left and one to its right and so forth, and then indicate the intervals between the marks as silences.
>
> —RICHARD SERRA (2011)

As Luciano Berio (2006) observed:

> An ultimate sign of the gap between thought and acoustic end-result came about when the musical score became an aesthetic object to be admired only visually—the eye becoming the substitute for the ear. . . . It may evoke the "beauty" of Bach's manuscripts or the "ugliness" of Beethoven's sketches; but that [visual] "beauty" and "ugliness" have nothing to do with musical processes and functions.

We return here to a familiar theme of this book: the opposition between a view of music as a concept/abstraction/symbolic representation versus a view of music as perceived sound. This opposition is nuanced, however; I appreciate the score of Stockhausen's *Klavierstücke 8* as a marvelous act of self irony.

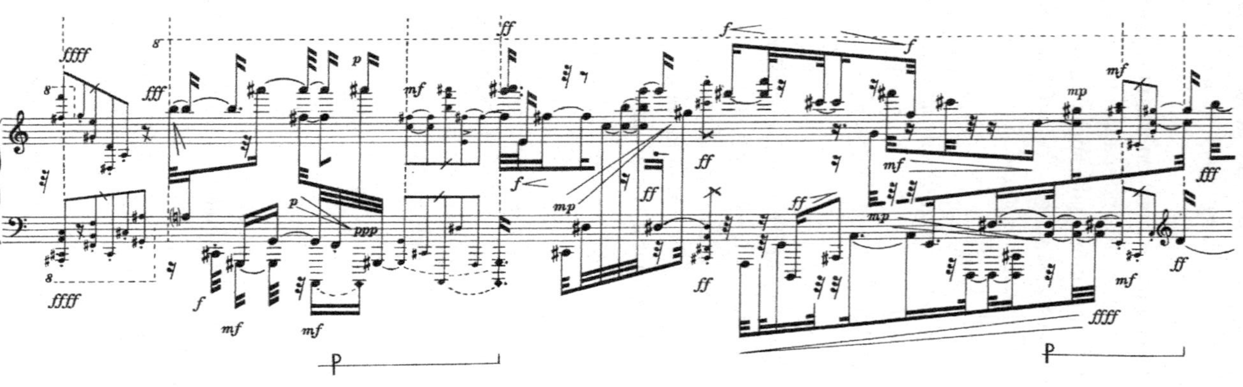

UE .°675 d LW

FIGURE 11.3 Excerpt from Karlheinz Stockhausen, *Klavierstück 8* | für Klavier | Nr. 4, Copyright © 1965 by Universal Edition Ltd. London/UE 13675D.

CONCEPTUALISM IN GENERATIVE SOUND ART

The world of generative sound art is broad and sometimes overlaps with music composition (LaBelle 2008; Licht 2009). One strain of sound art starts from a conceptual aesthetic and uses generative techniques in the realization. To such artists, the proof is primarily in the conceptual strategy used. In a famous essay on conceptual art, the artist Sol Lewitt (1967) wrote:

> In conceptual art the idea or concept is the most important aspect of the work. When an artist uses a conceptual form of art, it means that all of the planning and decisions are made beforehand and the execution is a perfunctory affair. The idea becomes a machine that makes the art.

Rather than evaluating the piece on a perceptual basis—the resulting sound—another set of aesthetic criteria often governs such art. For example, is the concept politically, culturally, and socially meaningful? How does it reflect, comment on, or critique society? What does it say about social connections between the artist and the community? What does it say about the technology and its influence on making art? If there is a live component, what about the performance?

An example of a piece that uses algorithms and takes in audio content from the public is the following (San Diego Museum of Contemporary Art 2008):

> The [sound art work] is an accumulation of mp3 files uploaded by visitors to a website that is made available as a streaming playlist. . . . Visitors are invited to listen ad contribute to the ever-changing archive of sounds on the site . . . [becoming] part of a shifting stream of music that both informs and reveals much about the growing informal community of users.

Here, the focus is on the process; the resulting sound can be anything. This is art as cultural probe. In some ways, it is akin to a poll, marketing experiment, or social media site that invites users to contribute content. The sonic result is the side-effect or byproduct of an invitation to the public to participate. These kinds of cultural probes, which try to challenge the limits of artistic creation, have a long tradition in the visual arts; some are more interesting than others.

Some sound artists design sounds but then delegate the activation of the sounds to the audience:

> In work that is interactive and site specific, audiences are essential to the fruition of the piece. In a way, the artist passes control even while inviting the audience to share in a dialogue, which, in a large piece, extends to include multiple participants acting simultaneously.
>
> —LIZ PHILLIPS AND PAULA RABINOWITZ (2006)

Here the concept of delegating control to a crowd is the central aesthetic theme, rather than any specific combination of sounds. This is but one of innumerable socially inspired conceptual strategies.

Contrast this with the aesthetic of Varèse (Risset 2004):

> [Varèse] believed social metaphors did not fully apply to art, which is not an ordinary production, but a creation of the visionary mind illuminated by "the star of imagination."[89]

Music has an ancient conceptual tradition. In the past, however, this tradition tended to gravitate toward formalist strategies rather than social gambits or cultural probes. However, art is opportunistic. When it becomes possible to experiment with technology-based social interaction, some artists will seize on this as a strategy for art-making just as others will make billions of dollars by inviting people to share their data.[90]

FROM ALGORITHM TO SOUND: THE MAPPING PROBLEM

It has long been possible to manipulate musical materials as symbols on paper or as objects in computer memory, separated from the act of producing sound in time. Therein lies a schism. Because formal symbols can be organized abstractly, symbolic manipulations have been closely identified with the organization of musical material. Many aspects of music theory can be codified without any need for sound. A deaf person can learn the rules of harmony, counterpoint, and serial/set techniques. As G. Mazzola (2002) asserted:

> Music is a system of signs composed of complex forms, which may be represented by physical sounds.

Notice the distinction: Music is signs, not sounds. This is a classic Platonist point of view. (See the section later on Platonism.)

A paper score (or its digital equivalent) is one possible representation of music. One can visually read a score and try to imagine its sound, but in electronic music, we focus on the sound itself as the final result. The experience of music comes through listening. Thus, music is more than a symbolic abstraction; music is finally rendered as perceived sound. As Varèse (1925) observed:

> [Music] has a well determined structure that one can apprehend much better by listening than by analyzing.

As we have emphasized repeatedly, the experience of music remains rooted in acoustics, auditory perception, the psychology of aesthetic preferences, and culture.

This means that the mapping from algorithm to sound is critical in generative music. In an unsuccessful generative work, it can be difficult to pinpoint precisely what failed. Was it a weak concept, a bad choice of sound material, a maladroit mapping from the algorithm to the chosen sound material, or a combination of all three?

GENERATIVE METHODS AND NARRATIVE STRUCTURE

We are all familiar with traditional musical rhetorical devices (e.g., cadential formulas in harmony) and traditional musical narrative (tension/release, conflict resolution, etc.). It is understandable that some composers seek a fresh alternative to traditional narrative formulas. Indeed, one justification that has been proposed for generative techniques is that they enable musical structure to "break away" from narrative form (Hansen 2009).

However, just by declaring that one is breaking away does not mean that one can escape narrative altogether. As stated in chapters 3 and 10, the mind relates what it has heard to the previous context and anticipates subsequent events; we inevitably react emotionally according to how expectations are met or denied. The construction of narrative is the human mind's innate response to perceived process and structure.[91]

GENERATIVE METHODS AND FORM

One of the great unsolved problems in algorithmic composition is the generation of coherent multilayered structures: mesoform and macroform. As G. M. Koenig (1971) observed:

> [The rules of] counterpoint and harmony, of course, tell us little about the construction of musical form, which has its own set of rules.

The design of form is the ultimate test of a composition. Many generative systems employ bottom-up strategies (see chapter 9) that do not take into account the meso and macro layers of form. As Wesley Smith (2011) observed:

> One of the major challenges in building a system that can increase in complexity as it runs is figuring out how to transfer complex structures in a lower level space into simple structures in a higher level space while still maintaining the essential qualities that the complex lower level structure represents.

The problem is not merely a question of scale. As we have already pointed out, music interacts on many levels with the psychology of the listener. We respond intuitively to context-dependent impressions that are difficult to formalize, like wit, irony, tension, surprise, release, etc.[92] It is not clear at this time how to formalize such narrative functions.[93]

GENERATIVE METHODS AND PLATONISM

The final aesthetic issue to mention is the association of generative methods with Platonist philosophy. Mathematics is a language invented and revised in the course of human history. Like everything else in human society, it is influenced by intellectual, educational, and cultural trends. An example of such a trend was the Bourbaki agenda of the 1950s to establish all of mathematics on a foundation of set theory (Struik 1967). Despite this, certain mathematicians and musicians adhere to a belief in the ontological existence of pure mathematical objects outside the realm of the human mind and human culture. According to this belief, human beings have not invented mathematics; rather, they have discovered it. This belief derives from Plato, who argued that what is real are eternal forms (perfect archetypes), such as ideal mathematical objects, whereas things experienced by human senses are merely copies (illusions). Such beliefs can be neither proven nor disproven by science.

Platonist philosophy in music posits that music is sign, symbol, and number, not sound (Johnson 2001), which is similar to the point of view of Morton Feldman (see above) who believed that real music existed as marks on paper and that its sound was secondary or even irrelevant. A Platonist music theorist could assert that the Werckmeister IV temperament (tuning system) was not invented but preexisted, waiting to be discovered. (One can only wonder whether other arcane nuggets of music theory, such as the Sequiquinquetone Progression invented by the scholar/prankster Slonimsky [1947], have always preexisted in an otherworldly realm.)

The Platonic view begs the question: What are the criteria for a mathematical object to gain entry into the preexisting otherworld? Do all mathematical expressions preexist? A computer program is a formal expression; thus do all computer programs preexist? Fortunately, it is not our duty here to disentangle these conundrums. For alternative views on mathematical ontology, stressing the role of mathematical structures as products of human cognition and culture, see Lakoff and Nunez (2000). For a more philosophical approach to the conundrum of mathematical ontology, see Castonguay (1972).

Generative algorithms in sound synthesis and processing

One domain where generative algorithms have vast untapped potential is in the control of sound synthesis and processing. This is an open territory for research.

Digital synthesis is effectively unlimited: Any possible sequence of bits can be created, and thus any possible sound can be created. However, by the 1970s, it became apparent that it was difficult to specify how to reproduce a sound heard in the mind's ear. The earliest experiments in digital sound synthesis showed that the computer could do only what it was told to do. Given simple rules, fixed envelopes, and basic waveforms, it invariably produced primitive sonic emissions. In digital synthesis, every aspect of the sound must be stipulated precisely. As I learned working at the MIT Experimental Music Studio, many composers had difficulty describing sound characteristics verbally, much less scientifically. It was not their fault. Without a reference example (e.g., "It should sound like an oboe"), it is hard to describe a sound heard in the mind's ear in any detail.

In order to create complex time-varying sounds, a synthesis system needs to be sophisticated, either in terms of the synthesis logic or in terms of the control data driving the process. Complex sounds often require large amounts of control data—too voluminous to be stipulated by hand. This data must be either obtained through analysis of an existing sound or generated by an algorithmic process, sometimes mediated by human interaction. A prime example of the latter is granular synthesis, which builds up sounds by combining hundreds or thousands of microsonic grains per second.

Max Mathews recognizing the need for scripted control of synthesis early in the history of digital synthesis. The PLF compositional subroutines of his widely used Music V sound synthesis program let one embed algorithmic control into the sound synthesis process (Mathews 1969). I used PLF routines in my first realization of automated granular synthesis. Another composer who has used PLF routines is Jean-Claude Risset. In his *Passages* (1982), they are used to control glissandi, modulation, spectral variations, choice of waveforms, and spatial variations (Pottier 2009).

Another synthesis technique that requires a large amount of control data is additive synthesis, which combines the output of dozens of sine wave oscillators (Roads 1996). Each sound object requires a dozen or more amplitude and frequency envelopes to control the oscillators. Here generative methods come to the rescue. For example, Eric Lindemann's Synful Orchestra application (2001) applies algorithmic control to produce acoustic instrument simulations with realistic note-to-note transition patterns.

Of course, composition goes beyond the creation of individual sounds. A given sound is only a starting point; any sound is only a pinpoint in a fabric of related sounds that form a composition. The compositional problem is to generate related families of sounds that articulate a specific musical context in support of a narrative structure. A possible way of creating families of sound is by means of algorithmic processes, such as interpolation and extrapolation of synthesis parameters, or the use of systematic transformations like modulations (Dashow 1980). (See the example of a family of related sounds in chapter 5.)

SOUND MIXING, REMIXING, AND UPMIXING AS GENERATIVE PROCESSES

The process of mixing many channels into a smaller number of channels is specific to the practice of electronic music. The composer plays the role—formerly delegated to a conductor—of artfully blending diverse sound sources. In the analog era, this was a manual task of moving knobs and faders in real time. Today the most common paradigm for sound mixing is a graphic mixing program (digital audio workstation or DAW) that displays waveforms, envelopes, and panning curves in tracks onscreen. These programs enable automated mixing by means of user-drawn envelopes.

Yet ever since the first music programming languages were developed, we have had the capability of mixing by script. A script tells the computer what sound files to mix, when to mix them, and with what envelopes. Preparing a mixing script for anything other than a simple piece is a tedious job of typing numerical lists—hence the popularity of graphical mixing programs. However, another possibility is to generate the script automatically. Using his Composer's Desktop Project software, Trevor Wishart observed:

> Despite being much less friendly than screen based mixing, this does allow for some powerful global procedures to be applied to mixes. . . . First of all, . . . any number of sounds can be superimposed. Secondly, global operations on the mix are available, from simple features like doubling (or multiplying by any number) the distance between event onsets, or randomizing them (very slightly or radically), to randomly swapping around the sound sources in the mix, automatically generating particular timing-sequences for event entry (from regular pulses, to logarithmic sequences, etc.), or redistributing the mix output in the stereo space in a new, user-defined way. More specialized procedures involve synchronizing the mix events (e.g., at their mid-point, or end, as well as at their start), or synchronizing the event-attacks (where the search-window for the attack peak can be delimited by the user). These latter procedures are particularly useful for building complex sonorities out of less rich materials, e.g., by superimposing transposed copies of the sound (over the original duration, or in a different duration) onto the original.

Given that such procedures are independent of the sounds they are manipulating (which can come from anywhere), it is easy to see the power of this approach in generating original montages. Today generative mixing is a largely unexplored territory of research.

A subfield of generative mixing is the domain of automatic remixing programs that take an existing sound file and reorganize it. An example of such a system is BBCut, a library of functions that assist those who want to work with automatic breakbeat cutting algorithms to create phrasing in the style of an artist like Squarepusher on his 2003 *Ultravisitor* album (Collins 2002b). Collins (2012) has also developed an "autocousmatic" algorithm that automatically creates electroacoustic music based on audio analysis of a directory of sound files.

Sound example 11.5. *Accordion Study* (2011) by Nick Collins.

A related topic is generative upmixing for sound spatialization. (See the discussion in chapter 8.)

Conclusion

Accelerated by ever-increasing computational power, the unlimited potential and experimental nature of generative music are inherently attractive as vehicles for compositional processes. As Gregory Chaitin (2009) observed:

> Bring someone from the 1200s here and show them a portable computer. You have this physical object, and when you put software into it, all of a

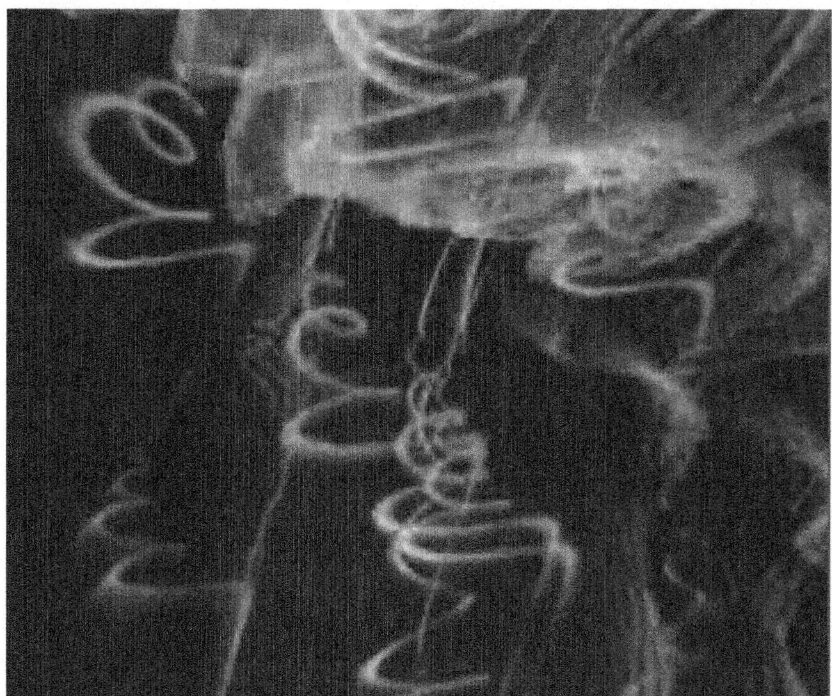

FIGURE 11.4 Still image from *S-Phase* by Lance Putnam.

> sudden it comes to life! So from the perspective of the Middle Ages . . . the perfect languages that we've found have given us magical . . . powers—we can breath life into inanimate matter. Observe that hardware is analogous to the body, and software is analogous to the soul, and when you put software into a computer, this inanimate object comes to life and creates virtual worlds. So from the perspective of somebody from the year 1200, the search for the perfect language has been successful and has given us magical, God-like abilities.

Any thought experiment involving musical process can be designed, coded, and tested. Algorithmic composition programs can handle more organizational details than would be possible by a human composer. They let composers shift their attention from arcane details (which can be delegated to the program according to instructions specified by the composer) in order to concentrate on a higher level of abstraction. At this level, the composer manages the meta-creation of the piece in terms of its process model.

Lance Putnam's *S-Phase* (2007) is an audiovisual work in which the same code generates the animated images and the sound (figure 11.4, sound example 11.6). As the artist explained:

> The score is a sequence of parameter state spaces with different interpolation curves and durations between them. The state spaces can be likened to the

notes and the interpolation the work going from one note to the next. The piece is effectively the journey taken between specific points of interest.

To compose the piece, I made an interactive editor to control all the compositional parameters with sliders and save presets of parameters. The parameter editor let me use sliders to change values or enter exact values with the keyboard. Several parameters, such as translate and rotation, were controlled with the mouse.

Sound example 11.6. Excerpt of *S-Phase* (2011) by Lance Putnam.

As we have argued, the incorporation of human interaction is a source of valuable feedback to a generative system, lending flexibility to an otherwise-brittle rule system.

Non-interactive algorithmic methods remain controversial. Part of the controversy revolves around the issue of responsibility. To what extent is the composer responsible for the resulting music? This issue is especially pertinent when someone uses a program conceived and written by a third party. The user's interaction may be limited to supplying a small amount of seed data, such as choosing from a menu prior to execution of the program. Since the compositional strategy is preset in the program, the user merely gathers the musical harvest. In its most extreme form, automated composition resembles a form of "found art." The user need only press a button and take the output. In this case, it makes little sense to speak of creativity or originality, as the engagement of the user is negligible. The process resembles online shopping.

Another source of controversy revolves around the issue of formalism. There is something to be admired about a composer who is able to completely formalize her composition process in order to maintain logical rigor. On the other hand, perhaps the process is formalizable precisely because it is simplistic and eliminates the steps of critical analysis that might lead to a messy revision. Many algorithms produce output that sounds either random or predictable, leaving listeners in anticipation of an already foregone conclusion.

One difference between algorithmic and non-algorithmic composition is that human composers commonly revise and edit their initial output. They modify, rearrange, and delete composed material. This is deeply creative work! How many generative systems incorporate this kind of self-critical feedback loop?[94]

Feedback and memory are integral parts of the composition process. A human composer is listening as she goes and remembers what has been composed. In contrast, it seems that few generative algorithms have any awareness of what they have done beyond a few stages in a Markov chain.[95] There is more situational awareness in a microbe than in most generative programs. Earlier we mentioned IBM's Deep Blue chess-solving engine, which searches through millions of possibilities at each step of the game. Yet Deep Blue had no knowledge of previous matches; it did not even remember its own previous moves. At the beginning of each new move, it started from scratch to assess the current situation and select the best possible next action (Hoane 1997).

We all know that machines can easily outdo us in certain tasks. If composition was merely a game of logic, then the technical virtuosity of the machine would already have relegated human efforts to a sideshow. The machine can execute formalized composition rules that are far more intricate than any human being could possibly manage. Like a sequencer racing through performances with superhuman speed and precision, the complex ratiocinations of machine composition inspire awe—up to a point. On a fundamental level, music is not a formal system of logical communication. It is a sensory experience involving acoustics, psychoacoustics, and subjective aesthetic response. As Varèse (1937) observed with characteristic bluntness:

> In art, an excess of reason is deadly. Beauty does not come from a formula.

The system can get in the way, as Jean-Claude Risset (2008) observed:

> I was very fascinated by the music of Pierre Boulez when I was a student, and I eagerly anticipated his book *Penser à la musique d'aujourd'hui* (1963). [After reading it] I was very disappointed by its enumeration of methods of permutational development, which seemed to me to be simple games, and it seemed to me that the richness, the volcanic power of pieces like [Boulez's] *Deuxième Sonate* or the *Marteau sans Maître* were a kind of miracle—traces of a titanic combat against the restrictions of algorithms.

A balanced perspective is in order, as Luciano Berio (2006) observed:

> The urge to split and divide, which has pervaded the musical world for the last few decades, has also postulated an opposition between the empirical musician (who has no need for [formal] "synthesis" and is subject to circumstances) and the systematic musician (who starts with a preconceived idea and follows an all-embracing strategy)—in other words, an opposition between the composer as *bricoleur* [tinkerer] and the composer as scientist. But creation is not [limited] to this unproductive dichotomy: the scientific or systematic musician and the empirical musician have always coexisted, they must coexist, complementing each other in the same person. A deductive vision has to be to be able to interact with an inductive vision. Likewise an additive philosophy of composition has to interrelate with a subtractive philosophy. Or again, the structural elements of a musical process have to enter into relation with the concrete acoustical dimensions of its articulation.

In another field, the master gardener Russell Page (1994) expressed a similar view:

> The discussion between adherents of "formal" and "informal" gardening still continues. This has always seemed to me to be a sterile argument. . . . For the "informalists" I would say that a garden, which is after all a humanization of nature and intended for convenience and delight, needs, like all man-made structures, a framework. Its different parts need connecting in

> some kind of order. The spaces for terraces, paths, lawns, vegetables, and different kinds of plantings must be related and there must be a sequence. Whether this order, this sequence of spaces be formal in its detail or not is really of secondary importance. . . . [With respect to the "formalists"] the limits of dullness in garden design seems to me to be achieved in the decadent formality of the later followers of Le Nôtre; one glance from the center of their dreary compositions is enough. There seems to be no point in setting out for a long and monotonous walk during which one will meet with no surprises and nothing of horticultural interest.

Indeed, the talent of composers who use generative methods is reflected in their skill in managing the logical excesses of their software prodigies.

12

The art of mixing

The act of mixing takes a collection of audio clips on a set of tracks and blends them into a finished composition. When this process takes a set of many tracks and blends them into a set of fewer tracks, we call it a *mixdown*. When this process take a small set of tracks and distributes them to a large set of tracks we call it *upmixing.*

This chapter looks at audio mixing from the perspective of electronic music composition, where mixing is implicated in many phases of the process. We briefly examine the history and technology of mixing before we present the core concept of the chapter: *multiscale mixing.* We then look at how the dimensions of time, amplitude, frequency, and space can be articulated through mixing and present a chart of "magic frequencies." The final sections examine the related topics of live spatial diffusion and mastering.

What is mixing?

To mix sound means to align a number of independent tracks in time and carefully blend them into a composite. In the audible range (from ~20 Hz–20 kHz, from 0–120 dB), air is a basically linear medium: Sound waves sum without distortion. In the domain of analog electronics, the same rules apply: Voltages add linearly. In the digital domain, audio signals take the form of sequences of numbers. Thus digital audio signals mix according to the rules of simple addition. As we move faders on a mixing console, we are scaling the amplitudes of the individual tracks. Scaling means simply multiplying the signals by a time-varying value from 0 (silence) to an arbitrary maximum.

The simplest case of mixing combines many tracks into a single monaural track. More typically, the result is intended for stereo or more tracks. In this case, the individual input tracks are not only scaled and summed, but also routed to specific output tracks. In an octophonic mix, for example, a given sound can spin around the listener. Clearly, the art of mixing is closely tied to the art of diffusion (performing a spatial mix of a piece in a concert situation), which I discuss later. In summary, from a technical point of view, mixing at its most basic is a process of time-varying multiplication (scaling), addition (combining), and routing.

Listen and learn

An orchestra combines a hundred instruments into a sonic totality. We hear sonic mixtures in the cacophony of a city street corner and the soundscape of a jungle. Like any animal, in order to survive in these complex sonic environments, we need to be able to instantly locate, identify, and classify individual sound sources. To pick out a single source within a complex soundscape is called the *source separation problem* in acoustics. For example, in loud restaurants, we try to isolate a friend's voice against a background cacophony. The ability to separate sources also serves us in music; following an individual line in an ensemble is an essential musical skill, as is following several simultaneous strands. The brain is naturally polyphonic and polyspatial. For a composer, developing a sophisticated ear (i.e., being able to recognize and analyze sonic qualities and patterns) is more valuable than any other musical skill.[96]

Human perception is highly malleable; otherwise, music education would be a waste of time. As the brain scientist Karl Pribram (2004) observed:

> In the 1960s, nomads in northern Somalia were unable to distinguish red from green, nor could they distinguish red from yellow or black in ordinary circumstances. In their semi-desert environment red was rarely if ever experienced. But they distinguished many shades of green and had names for these shades. Peace Corps volunteers were unable to differentiate between these many shades. Interestingly, some Somalis could distinguish colors such as red, orange and purple: they were tailors and merchants who dealt with colored fabrics. In short, they had been trained to perceive.

Thus we can learn by working with sound. Almost everything I have learned about mixing derives from listening.

The core problem of mixing

To combine sounds is one of the most common tasks of the electronic music composer. Yet surprisingly little analysis has focused on the art of mixing outside the context of pop music, where it is a central production technique.[97] Perhaps this is because pop music tends to separate music-making into discrete phases of production: song writing, performance, recording, editing, mixdown, and mastering. In contrast, in electronic music, all phases tend to be deeply intertwined, and mixing is central to every phase. Consider the sensitive mixing in the pioneering soundtrack to *Forbidden Planet*, which introduced the world to a new genre of musical expression.

Sound example 12.1. Excerpt of *A Shangri-La in the Desert Garden with Cuddly Tiger* from the soundtrack to *Forbidden Planet* (1956) by Louis and Bebe Barron.

From an aesthetic point of view, the core problem in mixing is to articulate opposing processes of fusion and fission. In this sense, mixing is deeply connected with the articulation of musical structure. Indeed, fusion and fission are structural functions. Fusion melds several sounds into a Gestalt—a composite whole. In contrast, fission comingles sounds while keeping them perceptually distinct. The art of mixing plays with and between these two poles.

Composers have always played with fusion and fission. Consider the fusion and fission in the harmonies of the string section in the fourth movement of Mahler's *Symphony No. 5* (1902) versus the divisi writing in *Also sprach Zarathustra* (1896) by Richard Strauss. In electronic music, fission and fusion take the form of transitional processes such as morphing or mutating sounds (one sound becoming another in a continuous fashion), splitting apart fused sounds, or the opposite of splitting: the convergence of disparate strands into a fused block. These kinds of coalescence/disintegration processes are featured prominently in iconic works like *Volumina* (1962) by Ligeti and *Kontakte* (1960) by Stockhausen.

An outstanding example of mixing in electronic music is Natasha Barrett's *Little Animals* (1997), which won first prize at the Bourges competition. This work stands out as a brilliant mixture of foreground and background, mixing multiple strands of abstract and referential sound material into richly textured sonic fabric (Barrett 1999).

Sound example 12.2. Excerpt of *Little Animals* (1997) by Natasha Barrett.

Sound mixing: historical background

The history of sound mixing dates back to the first synthesizer, Cahill's electromechanical Telharmonium, unveiled in 1906. The Telharmonium mixed sound signals electrically, summing many sine waves into a single complex waveform (Rhea 1972; Weidenaar 1995). The need to combine signals from several microphones became apparent in the early radio and talking-picture era. In order to provide this functionality, radio engineers designed the first mixing consoles using vacuum tube circuitry. By the late 1920s, the motion picture industry needed mixers to combine dialog, music, and sound effects in talking pictures. One of the most elaborate film mixes of the pre-WWII era was Disney's *Fantasia* (1940). The Philadelphia Orchestra conducted by Leopold Stokowski was recorded simultaneously on eight optical film recorders. Six channels were devoted to individual orchestral sections, one to a distant microphone, and another to a monaural mix (Klapholtz 1991). Later the sound from the eight synchronized recorders was balanced during mixdown to stereo. The concept of mixdown—combining multiple tracks into one or two composite tracks—was new at the time, but it is now standard procedure. (This process is also known in the industry as *downmixing* or *fold-down*.)

The mixing consoles of the early electronic music studios were custom-designed and built by hand (figure 12.1).

Commercially manufactured mono (one-track) magnetic tape recorders became available in 1948. Multitrack (two- and four-track) analog tape recorders appeared in the late 1950s (figure 12.2).

In the 1970s, companies such as Studer, Ampex, and MCI manufactured increasingly expensive 4, 8, 16, and 24-track analog tape machines. Professional

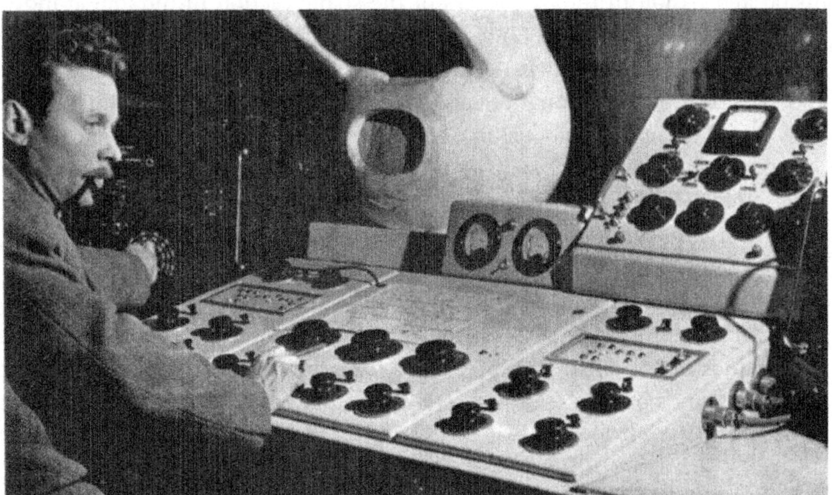

FIGURE 12.1 Jacques Poullin and his custom-built vacuum tube mixer for the Groupe de Recherche de Musique Concrète in Paris in the early 1950s. Notice the white loudspeaker with its "rabbit ear" projection horn (UNESCO, from Moles 1960).

quality multitrack tape recorders were large, heavy, and expensive (over $60,000 in 1980 dollars for a 24-track Studer machine weighing 400 kilograms). Multitrack machines enabled *overdubbing*, whereby individual tracks were recorded separately and later combined in a final mixdown to stereo. By the 1970s, a handful of boutique companies, such as Neve, built mixing consoles for professional studios. These were of high quality, but cost tens of thousands of dollars. In this period, small low-cost mixers were generally associated with poor audio quality: distortion, nasty equalizers, and high noise levels.

The 1990s brought a major change, as the home studio market propelled the spread of low-cost analog mixers of reasonable audio quality (e.g., Mackie and Soundcraft). At the same time, thousands of amateur musicians began to play with graphical software mixers like Pro Tools running on personal computers. Today such tools are ubiquitous. They are augmented by plethora of software plug-in effects, many of which emulate expensive hardware processors. As a result, the culture of sound mixing has evolved from an elite profession to a popular hobby. As with any hobby, the widespread availability of tools does not make everyone an expert.

The technology of sound mixing

Digital audio mixing can be performed either in software, hardware, or a combination of both. Software mixers generally operate in two steps: The composer

FIGURE 12.2 Studer J37 four-track tape recorder, introduced in 1964. This model was used to make the *Sgt. Pepper's Lonely Hearts Club Band* album by The Beatles, a tour-de-force of multitrack recording and mixing.

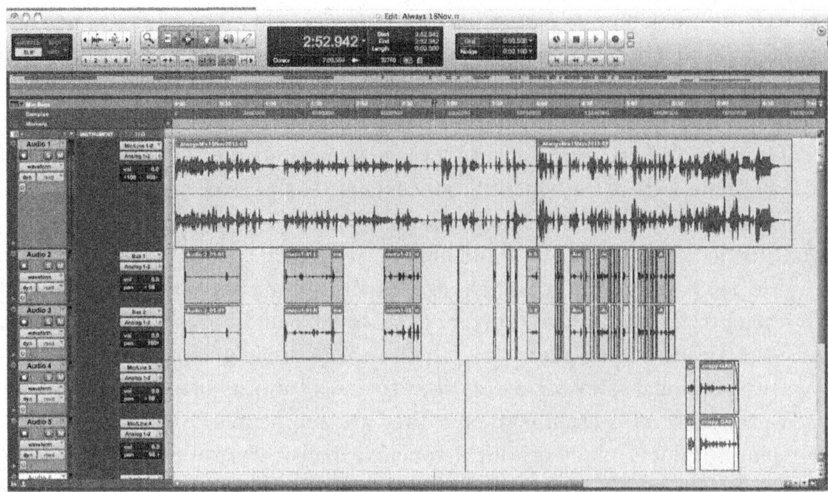

FIGURE 12.3 Pro Tools edit window showing six tracks of a mix of *Always* (2013) by the author.[98]

plans the mix (adjusting envelopes and effects), and then the software automatically performs it. By means of parameter automation, software mixers can carry out complex and precise operations that would be impossible to realize by any other means. For example, many software mixers can easily handle hundreds of sound files organized on dozens of tracks. The other advantage of software mixers is their ability to handle intricate tasks with precision on a micro timescale in a manner that would be impossible to perform manually.

Software mixers fit into two main categories: *graphical mixing* and *mixing by script*. Graphical mixing programs are widely available (figure 12.3). These applications mandate a preparation stage that gives the composer time to plan and rehearse a precise mix. By means of hand-drawn envelopes on the amplitude, spatial position, and effects parameters of an arbitrary number of tracks, an automated mix can be extremely detailed and complex, far exceeding the capabilities of an engineer manipulating faders by hand.

Mixing by script involves a music programming language of the Music-*N* type. Music-*N* refers to a series of music programming languages developed by Max Mathews (1969) and his colleagues, of which Csound (Boulanger 2000) is a classic example. Music-*N* languages let users design both *orchestras* (signal processing patches) and *scores* (note lists and envelopes). The text of the score serves as a mixing script.

Writing a mixing script necessitates detailed data entry (typing alphanumeric codes). Thus, for an ordinary piece of music, a graphical mixer is much easier to manage than a script. The power of mixing by script comes into play when the script is generated algorithmically, as the Paris-based composer Horacio Vaggione has done (Roads 2005). An algorithmically generated script can create complex structures that would be difficult to stipulate with a graphical mixer. Algorithmic mixing can be as complex as granular synthesis, combining hundreds of sonic events per second. Indeed, my first experiments with automated granular synthesis were realized using generative mixing scripts (Roads 2001b). Here is such a script; each line in this Csound score can name a sound file by number, stipulate when it will start, its duration, maximum amplitude (from 0 to 1), and spatial location (0 = left, 1 = right):

Start	Duration	Sound file	Amplitude	Location
0.000	0.136	8	0.742	0.985
0.281	0.164	10	0.733	0.899
0.346	0.132	12	0.729	0.721
0.628	0.121	1	0.711	0.178
0.748	0.174	3	0.693	0.555
0.847	0.062	6	0.687	0.159
0.974	0.154	8	0.686	0.031

The envelopes associated with each event are not shown. Note that a graphical mixer is simply an interface for generating such a script, which the user does not see.

Yet for all its flexibility and precision, software mixing has drawbacks. A major drawback is the lack of "feel" in software mixing. When there are no controllers to manipulate in real time, it is impossible to respond intuitively as one listens. Unless great care is taken in shaping envelopes on all timescales, the result may suffer from a stilted quality.

For these reasons, a hands-on mixing console (figure 12.4) or controller with precision faders is a reasonable alternative to software-only solutions. Consider the music of Luc Ferrari or François Bayle in the era of 1960s-to-1980s analog technology, where the ebb and flow of the mix is clearly shaped by expressive manual gestures. In musical situations that call for natural manual gestures, a mixing console with physical knobs and faders is the appropriate medium. It is also the preferred controller for many situations of live diffusion in concert, as discussed later.

Multiscale mixing

Here we arrive at the central concept of this chapter. A typical mixing strategy is to record and align tracks with a goal of ultimately mixing down all of them at once. This is the *multitrack mixdown* approach. In contrast, *multiscale mixing* is the practice of on-the-fly mixing on multiple timescales. A historical perspective helps to contrast these approaches.

Mixing technology was originally driven primarily by the needs of the pop music industry. In this production model, individual instruments are recorded on separate tracks. In order to keep each track untainted by other sounds, it is necessary to acoustically isolate the performers. Thus engineers use vocal and drum booths (isolated sub-rooms), and they position directional microphones

FIGURE 12.4 Neve 5088 analog mixing console. Photograph courtesy of Rupert Neve Designs, www.rupertneve.com.

in close proximity to each acoustic source. For electrical instruments such as electric bass, they bypass microphones altogether by plugging the output of the instrument into a direct box preamplifier connected to the recording device.

For decades, the number of tracks that could be mixed was limited by tape technology. The tape era peaked in 1991, when a digital 48-track tape recorder cost over $250,000 and a large mixing console to match it cost nearly the same. Simultaneously, a revolutionary change took place as inexpensive software-based recording and mixing programs reached musicians with personal computers. Mixing applications could support dozens of tracks. For example, the $400 Deck II application introduced by OSC in the early 1990s could mix up to 999 tracks, albeit not all in real time.

Expanding the number of tracks, however, made mixdown an ever-more complex process. How to control a mix of dozens or hundreds of tracks? The accumulation of track capacity fostered an aesthetic that favored postponing mixing decisions until the last minute, when dozens of tracks are mixed down at once. However, mixing is by definition a balancing act. That is, a change in the balance of one track affects the weight of every other track, making this approach difficult to manage in many circumstances. Thus many of us take an alternative approach to mixing, as explained in the next section.

SUBMIXING AND STEMS

Multiscale mixing proposes an alternative approach based on a divide-and-conquer strategy. Instead of postponing decisions to a grand finale mixdown, we mix as we go. This approach is not new. *Submixing* was a necessary discipline in the era of four-track recording. In order to add new tracks on a four-track tape, one had to mixdown the existing four tracks to two on another four-track tape machine, leaving two free tracks. This process could be done a couple of times (resulting in an eight-track mix) before the analog noise buildup became unacceptable. Stockhausen's *Kontakte* (1960) and classic pop albums like *Sgt. Pepper's Lonely Hearts Club Band* (1967) by The Beatles and *Are You Experienced* (1967) by Jimi Hendrix were mixed four tracks at a time as they went along (Johns 2000).

Today submixes are commonly called *stem mixes*, and they result in a mixed stem. For example, in a pop song, all tracks associated with drums can be reduced to a stereo pair of tracks to make up the drum stem. More generally, rather than accumulating dozens of tracks in a complicated mix, we can opportunistically mix a handful of tracks in order to render a given layer of mesostructure as a stem. Bouncing many tracks to a stem allows one to concentrate on a submix, thus greatly simplifying the problem of balancing the final mix at a later time. Operations such as "Render-in-place" in Cubase support this approach.

A submix enables a highly focused solution to a local compositional problem. In a multiscale approach, any stem is merely a consolidation, one step among many toward creation of the overall macroform.

The art of mixing

This section presents some basic aesthetic principles of the art of mixing. Mixing poses problems that were formerly separated in the traditional domains of composition, orchestration, conducting, and instrumental performance. In mixing, the composer must play the role of virtuoso interpreter, shaping a composition's raw energies into a refined and meaningful whole. Going beyond traditional roles, electronic music offers unique opportunities for musical expression. For example, any sound can mutate into any other sound at any time, and this is often achieved through mixing.

The key to mixing is efficient use of these aesthetic dimensions:

- Time
- Amplitude
- Spectrum
- Space
- Motion

One seeks to optimize aesthetic content by balancing diverse elements and processes, giving each a chance to articulate itself, whether in solo, simultaneous, or contrapuntal relationships.

Sometimes the goal of mixing a particular passage is fusion, such as merging voices into a unified chorus. At other times, the goal is fission: preserving the independence of each line in a contrapuntal lattice. The mixer articulates these processes through accentuation of the individual morphologies of each of the mix elements.

A goal of any mix is to avoid *clutter*—a jumble of simultaneous sounds that obscure each other in time, amplitude, spectrum, space, and motion. In a good mix, each element is salient (i.e., we can pick it out by ear).

ARTICULATING TIME WITH SILENCE

Aligning the mix elements in time is a critical factor. A typical problem in a poor mix is too many simultaneous elements, creating an indistinct mess. In contrast, in an efficient mix, one introduces each sound element only as it is needed. Any mix can be pruned down to essentials. In a sparse mix, the uniqueness of each sound stands out. Avoid long overlapping elements that do not complement one another. Keep non-complementary elements apart.

An unbroken continuum of sound is common in electronic compositions by beginners. Yet the most expressive sound is silence! To make music breath, intersperse silent rests. The silence does not have to be total; it can be a low-level "bed" or halo of reverberation, which I often use as a cadence. Electronic sound can be unrelentingly intense. Breathing points give listeners a momentary pause to digest what has just been heard. Consider this example from *Always* (2013), where I insert a 3.5 reverberation tail between two phrases. The cadence occurs 40 seconds into this sound example.

Sound example 12.3. Excerpt of *Always* (2013) by Curtis Roads.

Structural silence breaks articulate boundaries of meso and macrostructure: the elements of musical form.

Clearly, problems of mixing cannot be separated from those of composition. An experienced composer creates with an idea of how musical elements will fit together in a mix. A compositional problem may be solvable by creative mixing, particularly by judicious pruning: bringing in elements only as long as they are absolutely necessary.

ARTICULATING AMPLITUDE (DYNAMICS)

A fundamental task of mixing is balancing the relative amplitudes of many sound elements over the dimension of time. This is a trial-and-error process because it is based on a subjective quality: loudness. How loud a sound appears within a mix depends on many factors, including its context, attack profile, and spectrum. Auditory perception is especially attuned to pitch and vocalisms, so the presence of these elements leaps out in the midst of nebulous abstract timbres.

A composition that unfolds at a constant intensity is boring. Master composers use differences in amplitude to articulate macro and mesostructure. Sectional changes can be marked by contrasts in amplitude, as well as contrasts in pacing and materials. The power of gentle sounds and soft/loud appositions is too often overlooked in this age of constant loudness. Consider the dramatic level contrasts in Luciano Berio's classic piece *Thema (Omaggio a Joyce)* (1958).

Sound example 12.4. Dynamic range contrasts in an excerpt of *Thema (Omaggio a Joy2ce)* (1957) by Luciano Berio. 

In the real world of acoustic instruments, every note and drum stroke is unique. Thus we seek to avoid the bland impression of repeated sounds that never change. It is worthwhile to take the trouble to articulate a unique identity for each object by creative editing and processing. This includes stamping each sound with a unique dynamic profile. Such refinements can be extended down to the micro timescale, as exemplified in the details of granular rhythms in my *Touche pas* (2009) and *Epicurus* (2010).

It is remarkable how small changes in amplitude can affect the musical flow. A boost in one channel by 0.5 dB coupled with a cut in another channel by 0.5 dB can tilt the spatial image. A 3 dB boost or cut in a sound is easily noticeable.[99]

Related to the issue of balancing amplitudes in a composition is the question of the overall volume: How loud should the sound be as we mix? Since mixing can take hours, many audio engineers recommend working with sound at a relatively low level (well below 80 dB C-weighted as measured by a sound level meter, for example) in order to stave off ear fatigue. Ear fatigue affects our perception of high frequencies in particular. One can always check a mix at a higher level on an occasional basis.

ARTICULATING SPECTRA

To avoid clutter in the spectrum, it is important to separate sound elements by frequency band. Through compositional methods (pitch, timbral, and spatial counterpoint), synthesis techniques, recording techniques, and filtering, one can sculpt distinct registers in the spectrum.

Through long experience, I have identified a number of *magic frequency zones* that seem especially sensitive to the ears. Table 12.1 lists these frequencies; the rest of this section explains why each is important.

0 Hz refers to direct current (DC) offset. This is a constant or nearly constant signal that can creep into a signal from many sources, both hardware and software. For example, certain transformations produce it as a side-effect. It is recognizable in a time-domain display as a waveform that is not centered about the zero amplitude point (figure 12.5).

DC offset can rob a mix of apparent loudness and cause clicks at the beginning and end of tracks. It diminishes the available dynamic range, which is especially damaging to bass frequencies. The most pernicious problem occurs when a track with DC offset is mixed with other tracks. The result contains the sum total of all the DC offsets in any tracks, exacerbating the problem. The proper way to remove DC offset is to apply a high-pass filter with a cutoff frequency of 20 Hz.

TABLE 12.1

The magic frequences

Frequency (Hz)	Brief description
0	Pernicious DC offset. Must be eliminated.
6–9	Range of expressive natural tremolo and vibrato. Apply modulation in this range to make a sound more expressive.
16–18	Fluttering modulations.
< 20	Zone of infrasonic frequencies (rhythms)
> 20	Threshold of audio frequencies.
30–40	Lowest linear frequency range for a low-frequency woofer. There is no need to retain frequencies below this threshold.
50–60	AC line noise, also known as hum and buzz occur at 60 Hz (50 Hz in Europe and Asia) and multiples thereof.
80	Center of low frequency deep bass impact.
120–200	Zone of boomy and tubby mid-bass frequencies; to be deemphasized.
200–500	Important zone of midrange pitches. Middle C is usually posited as 261.63 Hz.
500–800	Expressive nasal pitches and formants.
800–1200	Zone of strident mid-frequency harsh pitches; to be attenuated.
1200–1800	Zone of mid-frequency harsh formants; to be attenuated.
2400–4400	Zone of transient articulation. The vocal fricatives and sibilants f, k, p, t, s, sh, and z have energy that falls within this zone.
5 k	Roll-off frequency for smooth vintage sound. With digital synthesis and processing techniques, it is easy to produce excessive energy above 5 kHz.
9–10 k	Zone of sharp mid-high frequencies; to be attenuated.
12.0–12.5 k	Zone of high-frequency "air." A slight boost adds sheen and sparkle to a mix.
> 20 k	Ultrasonic frequencies; watch for aliasing (see below).

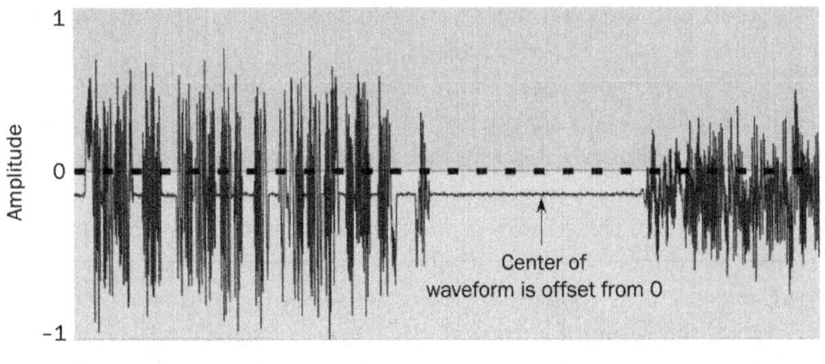

FIGURE 12.5 A classic case of DC offset, as seen in a sound editor. Notice that the waveform is not centered around 0 (dotted line), but is rather centered around a negative value.

6 to 9 Hz is the range of expressive natural tremolo and vibrato. One can start with a static electronic sound and apply modulation in this range to make it more expressive, in the same manner as a vibrato used by guitarists and violinists.

16 to 18 Hz is the range of fluttering modulations—a strong effect. The flute effect of flutter-tongue occurs in this range. In electronic music, I first noticed this range in *Kontakte* (1960) and *Hymnen* (1967) by Stockhausen. He modulated sounds using square waves at these frequencies to great effect. When spatializing sounds, fluttering tones stand out.

Below 20 Hz is the domain of infrasonic frequencies or rhythms. The range of tempos from 20 (*largissimo*) to 208 (*prestissimo*) beats per minute (BPM) corresponds to a repetition rate of between 0.3 Hz to 3.467 Hz.

30 to 40 Hz is the lowest linear loudspeaker frequency for a high-quality bass woofer in a full-range loudspeaker. By linear, I mean the lowest frequency that the loudspeaker can reproduce without attenuation or distortion. Most small loudspeakers cannot go below 60–80 Hz without compromise. This is not to say that near-field monitors cannot sound boomy! As the signal heads south of 200 Hz, one often hears an indistinct boominess, not tight and accurate deep bass reproduction.

50 or 60 Hz is the fundamental frequency of AC electrical line noise, also known as hum and buzz. In America, it is 60 Hz; in Europe and Asia, it is 50 Hz. Hum and buzz occur in myriad situations, whenever things electrical mingle. Typical sources are grounding problems, loose connections, and faulty cables. Moreover, certain performance venues have poor electrical systems in which the AC signal is already polluted. A power conditioner with filter can help, but once hum and buzz pollute a recorded signal, they are difficult to remove.

80 Hz (between D-sharp2 and E2) is the center of low-frequency deep bass impact. Even a slight boost of 1 dB makes a difference. My experience is that eliminating frequencies below 40 Hz removes DC offset and tightens up the reproduction of deep bass around 80 Hz; the loudspeaker no longer has to work at reproducing frequencies that it cannot handle efficiently and is free to resonate at 80 Hz.

120 to 200 Hz is the zone of boomy and tubby mid-bass frequencies. Being neither deep bass nor the preferred range of melodic exposition, it tends to muddy the sound when it is combined with deep bass. Thus it can be a good idea to deemphasize this zone.

200 to 500 Hz is the important melodic zone of mid-frequency pitches (middle C is usually posited as 261.63 Hz). Almost all pitches in traditional music fall in the zone between C2 (65.41 Hz) and C7 (2093 Hz).

500 to 800 Hz is another important zone of expressive nasal pitches and formants (akin to the American vowels ah, ee, ay, oh, you). Applying a band-pass filter in this range to any percussive sound will make it stand out. Taking advantage of this, the drummer of a well-known pop band tuned his snare drum to resonate at precisely 700 Hz in order to cut through wideband guitar spectra.

The zone between 800 and 1800 Hz deserves special consideration, as it is a most sensitive range of human hearing. Acoustical events in this zone naturally sound louder. A baby's cry falls within this zone; perhaps this is related to our extraordinary sensitivity to this region. More specifically, 800 to 1200 Hz is a

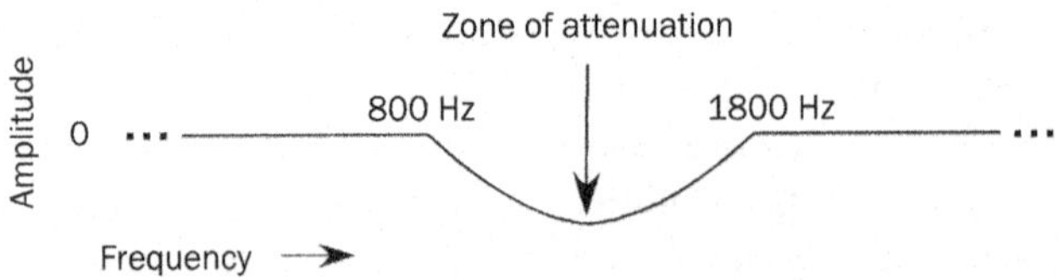

FIGURE 12.6 The "magic smile" equalization curve attenuates frequencies in the range between 800 and 1800 Hz.

zone of strident mid-frequency harsh pitches, and 1200 to 1800 Hz is a connected zone of mid-frequency harsh formants. Many sound engineers handle this zone by routinely applying a "magic smile" equalization curve (figure 12.6). The curve attenuates spectra in the harsh region between 800 and 1800 Hz. Such a curve is frequently applied in live sound systems, since it allows the sound engineer to play the music louder while retaining deep bass and crisp high frequencies.

2400 to 4400 Hz is the zone of transient articulation. Specifically, the vocal fricatives and sibilants f, k, p, t, s, sh, z, etc., fall within this zone. If a goal of a piece is to articulate the spoken word or any transient articulations, this zone should be salient.[100]

The threshold of 5000 Hz is a signpost. In acoustic music, the vast majority of sonic energy falls below 5 kHz (figure 12.7). This is not to say that instruments do not emit energy beyond 5 kHz. Indeed, many radiate into the ultrasonic range. For example, a key in the lowest octave of the piano, struck at a high intensity, radiates energy well beyond 20 kHz. The point is that the amount of energy emitted beyond 5 kHz is proportionally much lower. This observation is important because it contrasts with the situation in the digital domain. Many synthesis and processing techniques have no limits on frequency energy other than the obvious Nyquist frequency threshold (Roads 1996). Indeed, with digital synthesis and processing techniques, it is easy to produce sounds with strong energy above 5 kHz (figure 12.8).

It is common to be creating and processing sounds with equal energy above and below 5 kHz and to be so mesmerized as to not notice later how grating the result is. When we listen to early electronic music, we hear little energy beyond 5 kHz. For a natural and vintage sound quality, a smooth low-pass filter with a roll-off around 5 kHz can work wonders.

The zone around 9 to 10 kHz is an especially deadly region of ear-piercing high frequencies. The sharp energy here should be well controlled.

In contrast, what a relief to emerge into the zone of 12.0 to 12.5 kHz—a region of high-frequency air and sheen! Delicately boosting this zone brightens a dull mix. Boost this zone in concert situations when the audience is some distance from the loudspeakers to add crispness to the transients.

Beyond about 20 kHz lies the realm of the ultrasonic frequencies. Every recorder imposes a limit on frequency bandwidth. In digital systems, this is

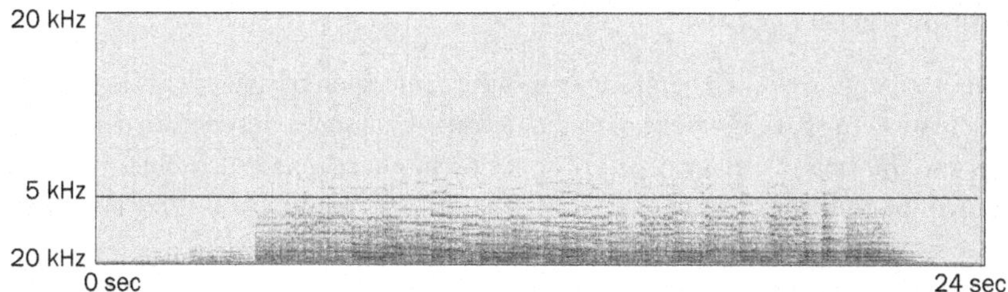

FIGURE 12.7 Spectrum analysis of the last 24 seconds of the finale to Mozart's *Symphony No. 40*. Sound energy that is more than 60 dB down from 0 dB is not shown. Notice that almost all of the sonic energy is below the line corresponding to 5 kHz.

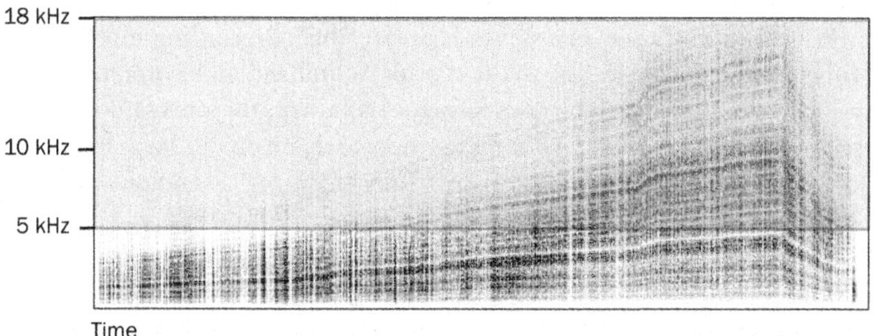

FIGURE 12.8 A sonogram of a three-minute granulation texture created by the author. Notice the shaded area indicating energy above 5 kHz. This material was ultimately shaped into the composition *Touche pas* (2009) after low-pass filtering to remove excessive high-frequency energy.

based on the sampling frequency. As the well-known Nyquist theorem states, the highest possible frequency that can be accurately recorded is half the sampling frequency. However, many technical factors (that need not be enumerated here) can compromise the recording process. One of the simplest ways to avoid them is to raise the sampling rate. Subjective sound quality tends to improve as the sampling rate increases (Howard 2005).

In sound synthesis applications, the lack of "frequency headroom" or spare bandwidth in a standard sampling rate such as 44.1 kHz poses serious problems. It requires that synthesis algorithms generate nothing other than sine waves above 11.025 kHz (44.1 kHz sampling rate) or aliasing distortion will occur. This is because any high-frequency component with partials beyond the fundamental has a frequency that exceeds the Nyquist rate. The third harmonic of a tone at 12 kHz, for example, is 36 kHz, which in a system running at a 44.1 kHz sampling rate will reflect down to an audible 8100 Hz tone. In sampling and pitch-shifting applications, the lack of frequency headroom suggests that samples be low-pass filtered before they are pitch-shifted upward. Yet such precautions are inconvenient in the midst of a fast-paced editing session.

ARTICULATING SPACE

A poor mix ignores and therefore wastes the dimension of space. This is a pity, for articulation in space is essential to a clear mix. One seeks to separate elements in space so they stand out and don't obscure each other. When each object occupies its own space, the mix takes on a three-dimensional quality, and there is room for more simultaneous mix elements.

Monaural ("mono") sources collapse to a point in the stereo plane. This point can be moved, but it remains without width. In contrast, stereo sources occupy a field in the stereo plane whose image width can be altered as part of the mix. Thus, when recording sound material, stereo is a better choice than mono. However, when many stereo files are superimposed with more or less the same image in the stereo plane, a mix can become spatially cluttered.

Presently, only a few microphones are capable of recording more than two channels simultaneously. The multi-capsule Soundfield ambisonic microphone developed by Michael Gerzon and colleagues is perhaps the most famous (Gerzon 1976). Microphone array recording, an approach involving large numbers of microphones, is not presently a mainstream recording technology (Weinstein et al. 2004).

Spatial depth (behind the loudspeakers) is another dimension. To separate foreground and background elements, reverberation, low-pass filtering, and diminutions in amplitude make sounds recede into the background. Spatial effects such as reverberation and panning can be applied to individual sound objects, resulting in a fantastic soundscape that is constantly shifting. Composers such as Berio exploited these possibilities in his work *Thema (Omaggio a Joyce)* (1958).

Sound example 12.5. Selective reverberation in an excerpt of *Thema (Omaggio a Joyce)* (1958) by Luciano Berio.

For sounds recorded by microphone, the old-fashioned approach of having a close microphone and a far microphone remains effective. The contrast between close and far sources adds depth to a mix. Some sources can be fixed in space, while others move. Listeners respond to spatially animated music, so it is important to pay close attention to spatial counterpoint.

It is easier to induce the illusion of a vertical source on headphones than on loudspeakers, so it could be interesting to exploit this dimension in a mix. A variety of effects processors are available to enhance the vertical dimension. When a vertically enhanced mix is played back on conventional loudspeakers in a lateral array, vertical effects often displace the spatial image in an interesting way, even if the vertical illusion itself is not robust.

Finally, I should mention the possibilities afforded by superdirectional loudspeaker systems, as discussed in chapter 8. Superdirectional technologies are still evolving, and much experimentation remains to be done. However, the potential of devices that could steer one or more beams of sound throughout an audience is intriguing from an aesthetic point of view. In theory, the sound could literally dance around the listener.

ARTICULATING MOTION: CHOREOGRAPHING THE MIX

Musical development is a play of sounds choreographed by the composer. The ear is extremely sensitive to motion in audio signals. This is not just spatial motion, but motion in amplitude, pitch, timbre, and rhythm. Such motion triggers expectations, for example, that the motion will continue. In contrast, static elements often set up expectations for change. The composer must know when and how to balance stasis and motion at measured intervals. Any dimension can serve as the dimension of change: pitch, rhythm, timbre, spatial position, or amplitude. One dimension can be active while others are static. An example of a masterfully choreographed mix is *Red Snow* (1998) by Natasha Barrett, which dances with the oppositions of soft versus loud, outside versus inside, real versus synthetic, near versus far, and static versus moving.

Sound example 12.6. Excerpt of *Red Snow* (1998) by Natasha Barrett. 

Upmixing: observations on live diffusion

Mixing and live diffusion (i.e., pluriphonic sound projection in performance) are closely related (see the discussion in chapter 8). If the goal of a traditional mixing session is to mixdown from a large number of tracks to a smaller number, the goal of live diffusion is the opposite: to mix up from a small number of input tracks to a large number of loudspeakers. In the audio industry, the term "upmixing" refers to the process of creating a multichannel surround version of a stereo original (Rumsey 2008). In many concerts, upmixing is a manual process, performed live, involving a certain degree of virtuosity (figure 12.9). As Francis Dhomont (2004) observed:

> If we speak of the live projection from stereo format using a mixing console, there is no doubt in my mind that there is a performance. The proof is that depending on how the work is diffused in space, it can either be expanded upon or reduced to nothing, just as a good or bad performance can affect an instrumental work.

Upmixed sound diffusion involves many variables. Each performance space is different, and the sound system can vary. If the loudspeakers are far away from the center of the audience, there can be a loss of sonic intimacy. Certain details noticed on headphones are lost in the translation to a larger venue.

The primary aesthetic challenge of upmixed diffusion is to highlight key features in the musical flow and route them to different loudspeakers in order to articulate musical structure. In practice, this is usually a controlled improvisation

FIGURE 12.9 Iannis Xenakis diffusing *La légende d'Eer* at a performance inside his Diatope structure in the center of Paris, 1978. Photograph by Mali.

with a certain number of preplanned gestures organized around specific cues. Diffusion can be arbitrarily complicated, but it is often limited in complexity by rehearsal time. In simple cases, the performer intervention may be minimal, planning around a few major gestures. In complicated cases, a score may guide the person doing the diffusion. This is usually a list of cues (timings and associated gestures) to be performed.

Bound with the task of diffusion is that of optimizing the overall dynamic range for a particular performance space. Freed from typical home-listening expectations, we can explore a wider range.[101] This means not just louder, but also softer. The impression of quietude can be enhanced by isolated projection from a solo loudspeaker, for example.

Playing with the contrast between solo loudspeakers and various combinations of loudspeakers is central to the task of sound diffusion. In a similar fashion, it can be useful to adjust the equalization on a time-varying basis according to the sound system and the resonances of the room.

When the number of input or output channels is large, manual upmixing is not practical or efficient. In these cases, it is necessary to develop alternative strategies. In a studio with a pluriphonic sound system that matches the system in another venue, a composer can design a complicated spatialization plan by hand that will be played back exactly as it was made in the studio. In some cases, however, the number of output channels in a specialized venue (such as the UCSB AlloSphere) exceeds that of any studio. Here the process of upmixing can be automated according to a preset compositional plan or an interactive real-time spatializer like Zirkonium (Ramakrishnan 2007). In some cases, such real-time performances can be captured in order to produce a definitive version.

Observations on mastering

To master is to prepare a mixed composition for distribution on a medium. Let us call the premastered mixture the *original.* Mastering is a practical craft based on skills and habits of detail that are not difficult to learn. It requires little mathematical or programming skills. However, as the last stage in production, it also stands as the final opportunity to save or ruin the original. Thus the stakes are very high. It is difficult to improve a bad original, but it is not difficult to ruin a good original. As the final stage of production before manufacturing, broadcasting, and streaming, mastering results in one of three outcomes:

- Optimizations and enhancements
- Subtle differences that are aesthetically neutral
- Distortions

One cannot underestimate the importance of this process, since the third outcome can be deeply disappointing, especially if the music is subsequently distributed in this form.[102]

In theory, mastering should be relatively straightforward: adjusting details, ensuring sonic balance, and adding polish. Why are the results so varied? Many factors contribute, and more important than any equipment deployed, they rest on mastery: the ears and skills of the mastering engineer. Mastery derives from a combination of experience, attention to detail, and aesthetic sensitivity, bolstered by solid knowledge of audio theory. The importance of experience is especially critical. In the studio, this means knowing one's tools and having a long period of learning through experimentation.

Next, we look briefly at how mastering has evolved from the days of the long-play (LP) record to now. We then look at the most important choices made in the mastering process. Finally, we examine production values that inform the mastering process.

ANALOG MASTERING FOR VINYL

Beginning with the introduction of analog Long Play (LP) vinyl records in 1948, mastering was an esoteric craft learned through apprenticeship. Only a few studios devoted to mastering existed. A mastering facility required a major investment in specialized hardware. The centerpiece was a diamond-tipped cutting lathe for discs (of lacquer, acetate, or copper), often mounted on a concrete slab for acoustical isolation (figure 12.10). Mastering engineers

FIGURE 12.10 Analog mastering studio with two disc-cutting lathes. Notice the black microscopes above each turntable.

not only listened on loudspeakers and headphones, but also inspected their labor through a microscope to examine the grooves of the disc's surface. After the master disc was sent to the pressing factory, the final product was a mass-produced vinyl LP.

For many people, LPs are still in vogue today, so analog mastering continues. Not only the sound, but the duration of a vinyl recording depends on choices made by the mastering engineer. The typical duration of a stereo LP is less than 25 minutes, but it can be made longer by keeping the audio level consistently low. This is because loud passages (especially those with strong bass frequencies) take up more space on the disc, thereby reducing the playing time (Huber and Runstein 1989). Thus the longer an LP side is, the quieter it must be. Unfortunately, a quiet disc calls attention to the noise floor. So when cutting a disc on a lathe, the mastering engineer has to constantly balance loudness and bass versus space and time in order to achieve a workable compromise. Moreover, as the playback stylus spins toward the center, it becomes harder to track high frequencies (Robair 2008). Thus inner grooves sound duller, which can influence the choice of track order.

MASTERING CHOICES

In the digital domain, the specialized expertise of the LP mastering engineer is not relevant; a loud bass signal takes no more memory space to store than a soft treble signal of the same duration. Anyone can download an application for audio mastering. More accessible technology is a blessing, but we should not think that technology can substitute for mastery. Mastery is not merely a skill set, but also a mindset or professional attitude. Like any skilled production task, it begins with attention to basics. These include a detailed inspection for noise and other technical flaws such as hum, clicks, pops, distortion, and DC offset, and taking appropriate corrective actions. On a higher plane, the mastering engineer makes choices in which technical considerations interweave with aesthetic issues. These choices include the monitoring system and issues involved in source-to-target mappings, spatial processing, and dynamic range processing.

Choice of monitoring system

The playback or monitoring system used in mastering is critical. Professional mastering houses invest in accurate listening environments. An accurate listening environment exhibits low distortion and linear frequency response over the entire audio bandwidth. This comprises all steps of playback, from the digital-to-analog converters, to the preamplifiers, amplifiers, loudspeakers, cables, and room treatment.

The reference monitors must be accurate, or the engineer has little idea what he or she is doing. At the same time, it is also essential to check a master on several different playback systems in addition to reference monitors. How does it sound on headphones, in a car, or on typical home loudspeakers? This is important because reference monitors, though supposedly faithful, do not account for all possible playback situations. It is especially important to examine bass response and loud passages. Car stereos, for example, tend to exaggerate bass, and home stereo systems can distort if they are fed more bass than they can handle.[103]

Checking a mix using high-quality headphones is like viewing sound under a magnifying glass. This is the best way to check a recording for subtle flaws like splice points, clicks, noise, distortion, and phase problems; these may not be as obvious on loudspeakers at moderate volume. However, the perception of deep bass, which is felt by the entire body, is impossible over headphones. Moreover, it is dangerous to listen exclusively on headphones, since subtle details like fades and pans that seem to work perfectly on headphones do not always translate well to loudspeakers, which tend to require more exaggerated gestures.

Mapping the original format to the master format

One task of mastering is to map a source format (specified by sample rate, quantization, number of channels, etc.) to a stipulated target format. For example, if the original is in stereo and the mastering medium is multichannel, the stereo version must be upmixed to the multichannel format. This means making a plan for spatialization to N channels. Suppose that the mastering medium is a surround format. Important questions come into play. How will the additional channels be used? Will there be panning motions that were not present in the original stereo format? These are not trivial issues, as they enter into the realm of compositional decisions. Considering the task more generally as a one-to-many automorphism to *N* channels, when *N* is a large number (as in wave-field synthesis), mapping can be a complex problem.

Spatial processing

Spatial processing can be applied even when the source and target format contain the same number of channels. For example, recordings that are excessively mono-centered can be spatially enhanced to have a wider soundstage. This may have the side-effect of adjusting the levels of sources panned to center (such as a vocal) up or down. Moreover, the depth of the soundstage can be enhanced by reverberation. Unless these effects are applied with great subtlety, we tread in the realm of compositional decisions.

Dynamic range processing

More than any other aspect of mastering, dynamic range processing remains the most controversial. Myriad aesthetic philosophies compete, and the goal is often a matter of taste. One goal is to make a piece sound louder, but this may conflict with other goals, such as keeping transients undistorted and ensuring dynamic contrast. Certain decisions cross into the realm of composition, such as when a crescendo is too strident and needs to be tamed.

In the audio industry, the standard tool for dynamic range processing is the ubiquitous dynamic range compressor (explained in chapter 5, "Sound transformation"). In an attempt to make recordings sound louder, pop music producers apply global compression with makeup gain to entire tracks. This has led to what Katz (2002) has called "the loudness war" as producers pursue ever-greater impacts (Bassal 2002). Such recordings not only have unvarying amplitude, they are also distorted. However, listeners tend to turn down the volume of loud tracks, which nullifies the benefit of compression. To an experienced listener, over-compression is an instantly recognizable and tiresome distortion that is characteristic of radio and television broadcasts, which are always compressed to make everything equally loud.

Compression is typically used as a global effect (i.e., it is applied to an entire piece without adjustment of its parameters). Yet no single setting of compression parameters is optimal for any more than one sound event. Thus the setting of compression parameters is usually a compromise between no processing on the one hand and audible distortion on the other. Sometimes it is precisely distortion that some pop music producers seek. Ultimately, compression is easy to overuse.

In mastering *POINT LINE CLOUD* (2004a), I developed an alternative to global compression that I call *manual compression*. This means manually re-enveloping the tracks in a sound editor on an event-by-event basis. Specifically, I went through each piece and applied makeup gain to passages that seemed too soft, while leaving transients intact. This approach to dynamic range optimization is much more time-consuming than running entire tracks through a compressor, but it represents the ultimate in detailed control of levels with a minimum of distortion.

PRODUCTION VALUES IN MASTERING

Mastering is driven by technical standards but also by aesthetic production values, such as the following:

- Accuracy with respect to the source—tracks are in their proper order, played at the proper speed, and all channels are aligned in time.
- Balanced spectrum—sonic energy in all regions of the spectrum.
- Airiness—transparent high end, not muffled.
- Nonabrasive midrange frequency band.
- Tightly articulated, not boomy, deep bass.
- Spatial breadth and depth.
- Intelligibility of vocal material.
- Imperceptible splices.
- Cleanliness—freedom from unintended noise, pops, hum.
- Lively dynamic range with freedom from audible compression distortion.
- Dynamic range consistent across tracks—the listener should not have to adjust the volume control when each new track starts playing.
- Natural sequential flow—the pacing from one piece to another flows smoothly, without awkward transitions. Pieces end fully and new pieces begin after an appropriate pause.

Of course, any production value can be stood on its head in a quest for artistic expression, and deliberately poor sound quality can serve as a foil to pristine quality. Low-quality reverberation, narrow-band filtering, distortion, and noise can all be applied as colorations. In general, these colorations are not applied globally, but rather to individual sound objects or brief passages. That is, they are usually associated with the step of composing rather than the step of mastering. In general, the mastering process seeks to preserve the aesthetic of the original tracks.

Conclusion

As a master chef once observed (Andries de Groot 1976):

> The amateur assembles the ingredients, measures them, mixes them, sets the oven temperature and timer, all by blindly following a set of fixed rules . . . often with no clear idea of the desired flavor, texture, and appearance of the completed dish; success is largely a matter of accident. The professional, on the other hand, understanding precisely the function of each ingredient, feels free to make substitutions and uses judgment in varying amounts. During the cooking, the professional will turn the temperature of the oven up or down, lengthen or shorten the time, reading the signals in the progress of the dish itself.

Mixing, diffusing, and mastering require more than equipment and technical craft; they demand musical insight and aesthetic judgment. Mixing in the studio, a composer plays a role analogous to a conductor, responsible for the overall balance of voices within a composition. As we have pointed out, the core problem in mixing is to articulate opposing processes of fusion and fission. Fusion (merging) and fission (splitting) are structural functions in composition.

In a concert situation, the art of sound diffusion tailors a piece for a specific venue, applying a spatio-dynamic projection and spectral finish that are unique to that time and place.

For the mastering engineer, attention to detail is the motto.

Electronic music introduced the notion that the design of sound morphology—on every timescale—is part of the composition process. Thus any operation that affects the sound crosses into the realm of composition.

APPENDIX A

Sound examples

Most examples are brief excerpts.

Introduction

0.1 *Strasser 60* by Earl Howard. Performed live at Roulette, New York City, 12 November 2009. From *Granular Modality.* New World Records 80728-2.
0.2 *Always* (2013) by Curtis Roads.
0.3 *Fluxon* (2003) by Curtis Roads. *POINT LINE CLOUD.* Asphodel ASP-3000.
0.4 *Brich dem Hungrigen dein Brot* (1726) by J. S. Bach. BWV 39. Collegium Vocale, Ghent, directed by P. Herreweghe. Virgin Classics 7243 5 62252 2 0.

1 The electronic medium

1.1 *Brandenburg Concerto No. 3, Allegro movement.* (1721) by J. S. Bach. From *Switched-On Bach* (1968) by Wendy Carlos. Columbia Records. Reissued 1999 on East Side Digital. ESD 81422.
1.2 *Sheep may safely graze, from Cantata 208* (1713) by J. S. Bach, from *Switched-On Bach II* (1973) by Wendy Carlos. East Side Digital. ESD 81422
1.3 *Underwater Waltz* (1952) by Vladimir Ussachevsky.
1.4 *Composition for synthesizer* (1961) by Milton Babbitt. *Columbia-Princeton Electronic Music Center.* Columbia Records MS 6566.
1.5 *Wall me do* (1987) by Carl Stone. Music and Arts Programs of America CD-276.

1.6 *String Quartet Opus 132* (1825) by Ludwig Beethoven, sequenced by Eric Lindemann. Internet: www.synful.com.
1.7 *Volumina* (1961) by Gyorgy Ligeti. Candide LP CE 31009.
1.8 *Purity* (1994) by Curtis Roads. from *Xenakis, UPIC, Continuum.* MODE Records 98/99.
1.9 *Epicurus* (2010) by Curtis Roads.
1.10 *Langsames Stück und Rondo für Trautonium* (1935) by Paul Hindemith. Performed on the Mixtur-Trautonium by Oskar Sala on the CD *Subharmonische Mixturern.* Erdenklang 70962.
1.11 *Presque rien no. 1, le lever du jour au bord de la mer* (1970) by Luc Ferrari. Musicdisc 245172.
1.12 *Industrial Revelations* (2001) by Natasha Barrett. *Isostasie.* empreintes DIGITALes IMED 0262.
1.13 *Now* (2003) by Curtis Roads. *POINT LINE CLOUD.* Asphodel ASP-3000.
1.14 *Love at the Swimming Hole* from the soundtrack to *Forbidden Planet* (1956) by Louis and Bebe Barron. Small Planet Records PR-D-001.

2 Aesthetic foundations

2.1 *Crystal Skull of Lubaantum* (1999) by Jeremy Haladyna. The sounds are produced entirely by sampled glass crystals, including a glass rod striking glass. Innova 818. American Composers Forum.
2.2 *Aquaforms* (2000) by JoAnn Kuchera-Morin.
2.3 *Utility of Space* (2000) by Natasha Barrett. *Isostasie.* empreintes DIGITALes IMED 0262.
2.4 *Harrison Variations* (2004) by Horacio Vaggione. *ETC.* EMF CD 053.
2.5 *Altars of Science* (2007) by Markus Schmickler. Editions MEGO 082.
2.6 *Tenth vortex* (2000) by Curtis Roads. *POINT LINE CLOUD.* Asphodel ASP-3000.
2.7 *Organic,* part 2 of *Clang-tint* (1994) by Curtis Roads.

3 The nature of sound

3.1 *Sonatina for CDC 3600* (1966) by Arthur Roberts.
3.2 *District Line II* (2004) by Squarepusher. *Ultravisitor.* Warp CD117.
3.3 *Synchronisms Number 6* (1970) for piano and electronic sound by Mario Davidovsky. *The Music of Mario Davidovsky, Volume 3*. Bridge Records 9171.
3.4 *Eleventh vortex* (2001) by Curtis Roads. *POINT LINE CLOUD.* Asphodel ASP-3000.

4 Creating sound materials

4.1 *Omaggio a Emilio Vedova* (1960) by Luigi Nono. Wergo 62292.
4.2 *Water Walk* (1959) by John Cage. Internet: www.youtube.com/watch?v=aLZ7yVszwgk.
4.3 *Dripsody* (1955) by Hugh LeCaine. Internet: www.hughlecaine.com/en/compositions.html
4.4 *Quatermass* (1964) by Tod Dockstadter. Starkland ST201.
4.5 *Prelude II* (1967) by Ilhan Mimaroglu. *Electronic Music III.* Turnabout/Vox TV 13477.
4.6 *Prelude XI* (1967) by Ilhan Mimaroglu. *Electronic Music III.* Turnabout/Vox TV 13477.
4.7 *corner* (2003) by Kaffe Matthews from *eb + flo.* Annette Works AWCD0005
4.8 (a) Coalescence of a sound by means of dictionary-based decomposition, transformation, and resynthesis.
4.8 (b) Coalescence of a sound by means of time-domain granulation.
4.9 The effects of cavitation on a sound.
4.10 *Thema (Omaggio a Joyce)* by Luciano Berio (1958). BMG Classics 09026-68302-2.
4.11 *L'oiseau chanteur* (1964) by François Bayle. Philips DSY 836 895.
4.12 *Synchronisms Number 5 for percussion ensemble and electronic sounds* (1969) by Mario Davidovsky. *Electronic Music.* CRI Modern Masters CD 611.
4.13 *Quartetto per viola solo* (2006) by Martino Traversa. *Manhattan Bridge.* NEOS 11023.
4.14 *Weekend* (1930) by Walter Ruttmann. Metamkine MKCD010.
4.15 *Hétérozygote* (1964) Luc Ferrari. BVHAAST CD 9009.
4.16 *Presque rien, numéro 1, le lever du jour au bord de la mer* (1970) by Luc Ferrari. Musicdisc 245172.
4.17 *Fizz* (2004) by Maggi Payne. Innova 783.
4.18 A long compound sound consisting of the superposition of a time-varying harmonic component, a broadband noise component, and an undulating bass component.
4.19 *In Winter Shine* (1983) by James Dashow. *Music for Instruments and Computer.* Experimental Music Studio. MIT Media Laboratory. YHDS 16.
4.20 *Analog #1: Noise Study* (1961) by James Tenney. Artifact FP001/ART 1007.
4.21 *Composition for Synthesizer* (1961) by Milton Babbitt. *Columbia-Princeton Electronic Music Center.* Columbia Records MS 6566.
4.22 *Live at Queen Elizabeth Hall* (1998) by Russell Haswell. *Live Salvage 1997-2000.* Editions MEGO 012.

4.23 *Scambi* (1957) by Henri Pousseur. BVHAAST CD 9010.

4.24 *Appearance* (1967) for three instruments, two oscillators, and two ring modulators by Toshi Ichiyanagi.

4.25 White, pink, and brown noise.

4.26 *19-tone Clusters* (2010) with sine waves by Hubert S. Howe. *Clusters.* Ravello Records RR-7817.

4.27 *19-tone Clusters* (2010) with instrumental samples by Hubert S. Howe. *Clusters.* Ravello Records RR-7817.

5 Sound transformation

5.1 *Santur Opera* (1977) for santur and electronics by Ivan Tcherepnin. *Flores Musicales; Five Songs; Santur Live!* CRI 684.

5.2 *E Cosi Via (And so on)* (1985) for piano and tape by Daniel Teruggi. Wergo 2028-2.

5.3 *Philomel* (1964) for soprano, recorded soprano, and synthesized tape by Milton Babbitt. New World Records 80466-2.

5.4 *Wind Chimes* (1987) by Denis Smalley. empreintes Digitales IMED 0409.

5.5 Deriving a family of sounds through a single transformation. We hear a vocal sample followed by eight variations, all produced with a multiband frequency-shifting effect (Virsyn PRISM).

5.6 *Terminus I* (1962) by Gottfried Michael Koenig.

5.7 *Mimetismo* (1992) for guitar and tape by Stéphane Roy. empreintes Digitales IMED 9630.

5.8 *de natura sonorum* (1975) by Bernard Parmegiani. INA C3001.

5.9 An impulse generated by the author in 1999.

5.10 An 800 ms sound object created by granulating the impulse of example 5.9.

5.11 *Volt air III* (2003) by Curtis Roads, much of which was derived from granulating the sound in example 5.10. *POINT LINE CLOUD.* Asphodel ASP-3000.

5.12 *Now* (2003) by Curtis Roads, much of which was derived by granulating *Volt air III* in sound example 5.11. *POINT LINE CLOUD.* Asphodel ASP-3000.

5.13 *Never* (2010) by Curtis Roads, much of which was derived by granulating *Now* in sound example 5.12.

5.14 *Always* (2013) by Curtis Roads, much of which was derived by granulating *Never* in sound example 5.13.

6 Processes of rhythm

6.1 *Sonal atoms* (Part 1 of *Half-life,* 1999) by Curtis Roads. *POINT LINE CLOUD.* Asphodel ASP-3000.
6.2 *Amériques* (1921, revised 1927) by Edgard Varèse. Cleveland Orchestra, Christoph von Dohnanyi, Conductor. Decca 443 172-2.
6.3 *Ionisation* (1931) by Edgard Varèse. *Varèse Orchestra Works 2.* Polish National Radio Symphony Orchestra, Christopher Lendon-Gee, Conductor. Naxos 8.557882.
6.4 (a) Speedup from pure pulsation to pitched tone and back.
6.4 (b) Speedup of burst pattern (3-on, 3-off) to pitched tone and back. Notice the subharmonic pitch.
6.5 *Electronic study number 3* (1965), Mario Davidovsky. Internet: avantgardeproject.conus.info/mirror/index.htm
6.6 *Laborintus 2,* part 2 (1965) by Luciano Berio. Musique Vivante. Harmonia Mundi HMA 190764.
6.7 *Cycle des souvenirs* (2000) by Luc Ferrari. Blue Chopsticks BC8.
6.8 *24 Variations* (2002) by Horacio Vaggione. ICMC 2002: Göteborg Sweden. International Computer Music Association.
6.9 *Points critiques* (2011) by Horacio Vaggione. INA/GRM 6032.
6.10 Pulsating grain echo in *Sonal atoms* (Part 1 of *Half-life*) (1999) Curtis Roads.
6.11 *Touch* (1969) Morton Subotnick. Wergo 2014-50.
6.12 Transition from tracks 8 to 9 on the album *Confield* (2001) by Autechre. Warpcd28 801061012823.
6.13 Pattern generated by Hammond Rhythm II percussion unit on a 1969 Hammond T422 organ by pressing pattern selection buttons and turning a tempo knob. The reverberation effect is provided by the built-in spring reverberator.
6.14 Sound created by the author using PulsarGenerator to crisscross between rhythm and tone corresponding to figure 6.14.
6.15 *Tiptop Z8000 Acid jam and experiments, Part 1* (2010) by Richard Devine and Josh Kay. The patch uses two Z3000 voltage-controlled oscillators, Doepfer A-145, and Tiptop's Z-DSP with Bat Filter card for processing.
6.16 Eardrill Pendulum/ratchet clock module demonstration. Internet: www.eardrill.com/modules/PendulumRatchet.
6.17 *Funktion Grau* (1969) by Gottfried Michael Koenig. *Acousmatrix 1/2.* BVHAAST CD9001/2.
6.18 *Silver Apples of the Moon* (1967) by Morton Subotnick. Wergo 2035-2 282 035-2.
6.19 *Volt air, part 1* (2003) by Curtis Roads. *POINT LINE CLOUD.* Asphodel ASP-3000.

6.20 *Volt air, part 2* (2003) by Curtis Roads. *POINT LINE CLOUD.* Asphodel ASP-3000.
6.21 *Touche pas, part 1* (2009) by Curtis Roads.
6.22 *Sculptor* (2001) by Curtis Roads. *POINT LINE CLOUD.* Asphodel ASP-3000.

7 Pitch in electronic music

7.1 *Subharmonische Mixturen* (1995) by Oskar Sala. Performed on the Mixtur-Trautonium on the CD *Subharmonische Mixturen.* Erdenklang 70962.
7.2 *Musique douze* (1976) by Ragnar Grippe. Caprice CAP 21471.
7.3 Cymbal glissando.
7.4 Cymbal crash followed by cymbal pitch-shifted by a perfect fifth three times.
7.5 *Etude 22* (1993) by Warren Burt. *39 Dissonant Etudes.* Tall Poppies TPO 93.
7.6 *Electronic Study Number 2* (1962) by Mario Davidovsky. *Columbia-Princeton Electronic Music Center.* Columbia MS 6566.
7.7 *Sidewinder* (1971) by Morton Subotnick. MODE 132.
7.8 *Turenas* (1972) by John Chowning. Wergo 2012-50.
7.9 *Pictor alpha* (2003) by Curtis Roads. *POINT LINE CLOUD.* Asphodel ASP-3000.
7.10 *Epicurus* (2010) by Curtis Roads
7.11 *Arioso Dolente/Beethoven op.110* (2002) by Theodore Lotis. Cache 2003. CA+UK.
7.12 *Dragonfly* (2011) by Laurent Delforge.
7.13 *Strasser 60* (2009) performed live by Earl Howard. From *Granular Modality.* New World Records 80728-2.
7.14 *Purity,* from *Clang-tint* (1994) by Curtis Roads. *Xenakis, UPIC, Continuum.* MODE Records 98/99.

8 Articulating space

8.1 *Out of Into* (1972) by Bulent Arel and Daria Semegen. New World Records 80521-2.
8.2 *Polytope de Cluny* (1972) by Iannis Xenakis. *Xenakis, UPIC, Continuum.* MODE 98/99.
8.3 *Capture éphémère* (1968) by Bernard Parmegiani. *La mémoire des sons.* INA-GRM 275 902.
8.4 Tape echo feedback experiment by Curtis Roads with an impulse generator as the source. From a study for *Then* (2014).
8.5 *I of IV* (1966) by Pauline Oliveros.

8.6 A reverberation chord constructed by applying reverberation to a drum sound. (a) Dry (non-reverberated) snare drum sound. (b) Reverberated drum sound. (c) Reverberated drum sound transposed down a perfect fifth (seven semitones). (d) Reverberated drum sound transposed down fourteen semitones. (e) Reverberated drum sound transposed down 21 semitones. (f) Alignment of (a) through (e) to form a reverberation chord. (g) Sequence of transposed drum tones. (h) Equivalent chord played with pitched tones.
8.7 *Traversée des abysses* (1991) by Michel Redolfi. Studio CIRM/ NAUSICAA Centre National de la Mer.
8.8 *Life in the Universe* (1998) by Ken Fields. MetaTools CD-ROM.
8.9 *Agon* (1998) by Horacio Vaggione. *IMEB Opus 30, Volume 2 1984-1999*. Chrysopée électronique 16.
8.10 *Sud* (part 1) (1985) by Jean-Claude Risset. INA/GRM C 1003.
8.11 *Sud* (part 3) (1985) Jean-Claude Risset. INA/GRM C 1003.
8.12 Hammond organ tone (1) static without Leslie rotation, (2) slow rotation, (3) fast rotation, (4) slow rotation, (5) no rotation.

9 Multiscale organization

9.1. *Ensembles for Synthesizer* (1964) by Milton Babbitt. *Columbia-Princeton Electronic Music Center.* Finnadar QD-9010.
9.2. *Gendy3* (1991) by Iannis Xenakis. Neuma 450-86.
9.3 Four musical outputs from Wolfram Tones using the "Classical" style selection. Internet: tones.wolfram.com.
9.4. *Points critiques* (2012) Horacio Vaggione. INA/GRM 6032.
9.5 *Tenth vortex* (2000) by Curtis Roads. *POINT LINE CLOUD.* Asphodel ASP-3000.
9.6 *Eleventh vortex* (2001) by Curtis Roads. *POINT LINE CLOUD.* Asphodel ASP-3000.
9.7 *Continuo* (1958) by Bruno Maderna. Stradivarius STR 33349.
9.8 *Reflections* (1975) for piano and synthesized tape by Milton Babbitt. New World Records 80466-2.
9.9 *Mycenae-Alpha* (1978) by Iannis Xenakis. *Electro-acoustic Music Classics.* Neuma 450-74.
9.10 *Sud* (part 3) (1985) by Jean-Claude Risset. INA/GRM C 1003.
9.11 *Inharmonique* for voice and tape (1977) by Jean-Claude Risset. INA/ GRM C 1003.
9.12 *Persepolis* (1971) by Iannis Xenakis. FractalOX.
9.13 *Capture éphémère* (1968) by Bernard Parmegiani. *La mémoire des sons.* INA-GRM 275 902.
9.14 *Sonal atoms,* which is part 1 of *Half-life* (1999) by Curtis Roads.
9.15 *Dragonfly* (2011) by Laurent Delforge.

10 Sonic narrative

10.1 *Pulse Persephone* (1965) by Daphne Oram. Paradigm Discs PD21.
10.2 *Process 5* (2010) by Xopher Davidson and Zbigniev Karkowski. *Processor.* SubRosa SR360.
10.3. *Maroc* (1998) by Thom Blum. Internet: www.thomblum.com/compositions.htm.
10.4 *Water Spirits* (2011) by Elizabeth Hoffmann. empreintes DIGITALes IMED 12115.
10.5 *Prelude 12 for Magnetic tape* (1967) by Ilhan Mimaroglu. *Electronic Music III.* Turnabout/Vox TV 13477.
10.6 *Saliceburry Cocktail* (2002) by Luc Ferrari from the compact disc *Son Mémorisé.* Sub Rosa SR252.
10.7 *Numéro quatro* from *Les anecdotiques* (2002) by Luc Ferrari. Sub Rosa SR207.
10.8 *Any Resemblance is Purely Coincidental* (1980) by Charles Dodge. New Albion NA 43.
10.9 *Arioso Dolente/Beethoven op.110* (2002) by Theodore Lotis. Cache 2003. CA+UK. CEC PeP. PEP 008 2004.
10.10 *Glassharfe* (2006) by Ludger Brümmer.

11 Generative strategies

11.1 *Vision and prayer* (1961) by Milton Babbitt. Bethany Beardslee, soprano. CRI CD 521.
11.2 *Relationships for Melody Instruments* (1986 version) by Clarence Barlow. Performers: Clarence Barlow on computer (controlling certain parameters of the algorithmic improvisation, such as tempo), Michael Riesslar on bass clarinet, and Jaki Liebezeit on percussion. *New Computer Music.* Wergo 2010-50.
11.3 *Stria* (1978) by John Chowning. Wergo 2012-50.
11.4 *ST/48* (1962) by Xenakis composed with his Stochastic Music Program. From *Xenakis Orchestral Works Volume 5*, Orchestre Philharmonique du Luxembourg, Arturo Tamayo, Conductor, Timpani 1C1113.
11.5 *Accordion Study* (2011) by Nick Collins. Internet: www.sussex.ac.uk/Users/nc81/music.html.
11.6 *S-Phase* (2011) by Lance Putnam.

12 The art of mixing

12.1 *A Shangri-La in the Desert Garden with Cuddly Tiger* from the soundtrack to *Forbidden Planet* (1956) by Louis and Bebe Barron. Small Planet Records PR-D-001.
12.2 *Little Animals* (1997) by Natasha Barrett. *Chillies & Shells*. Nota Bene Records, NB 980101M.
12.3 *Always* (2013) by Curtis Roads. A reverberation cadence occurs 40 seconds into this sound example.
12.4 *Thema (Omaggio a Joyce)* (1958) by Luciano Berio.
12.5 *Thema (Omaggio a Joyce)* (1958) by Luciano Berio.
12.6 *Red Snow* (1998) by Natasha Barrett. *Chillies & Shells*. Nota Bene Records, NB 980101M.

NOTES

Preface

i. As of January 2012, Wikipedia listed over 220 different genres of electronica (en.wikipedia.org/wiki/List_of_electronic_music_genres). Some of these divide into multiple subgenres.

ii. One reviewer questioned "the author's attention to microsound" as if this was an imbalance. Yet microsonic techniques are central to my aesthetic philosophy and practice. Indeed, I insist on pointing out the possibilities opened up by this realm.

iii. Translations of the texts of Varèse and other French authors are mine.

iv. The famous 1969 Moog synthesizer concert at the Museum of Modern Art in New York stands out (Glinsky 2000), but the tradition of live performance dates back to the dawn of electric music at the turn of the 20th century (Weidenaar 1995; Chadabe 1997; Pinch and Trocco 2002).

v. Permit me to thank my research partners Woon Seung Yeo, Garry Kling, Brian O'Reilly, James Ingram, David Thall, Bob Sturm, and Aaron McLeran.

vi. Indeed, how does one analyze a work so rich in scenery as *Les Anecdotiques* (2002) by Luc Ferrari? Perhaps with some kind of semiotic analysis borrowed from poetry?

vii. We can expect to see further advances in the methodology of electronic music analysis prompted by improved technology. The Acousmographe, developed at the Groupe de Recherches Musicales originally by Olivier Koechlin and Hughes Vinet (Bayle 1993; Roads 1996), is a step in the right direction (GRM 2008). This software starts from a sonogram analysis and provides graphical drawing tools to aid in decoding the sound signal into a repertoire of symbols. Using the Acousmographe, however, remains an interpretive manual process. Developing a tool that can automatically transcribe a sound file into a meaningful score has been attempted (e.g., Haus 1983) but requires more research.

viii. Guessing, trying, testing, and revising is the process. A recent edition of Ernest Hemingway's novel *A Farewell to Arms* includes 47 endings written by the author.

ix. It was not possible or practical to obtain legal permissions for certain sound examples. However, these are covered under the doctrine of fair use. All are short excerpts—analogous to quotations—that could not be used as a substitute for the complete original compositions. The excerpts appear in the context of a critical discussion in a scholarly book. Finally, their inclusion calls attention to these works and therefore enhances, rather than reduces, any commercial value of the original and complete sources from which they were drawn.

x. My book *Microsound* was chided by musicologist Joanna Demers (2010) for not citing enough musical examples from popular electronica. Ironically, her book also made this observation about the field of electronic music:

> Because of this breadth of activity, no one single participant or informant can speak about all of electronic music with equal facility.

Demers's book is an academic treatise on comparative aesthetics and sociology. It tried to find common threads among disparate genres. *Microsound* was never intended to be a study in comparative aesthetics or the sociology of aesthetics. Neither is this book. As I point out in the disclaimer above, since this is not my area of interest or expertise, it would be inauthentic for me to expound on it. In this book, I cite a number of independent artists like Autechre, Squarepusher, Tod Dockstader, Russell Haswell, and Richard Devine who are working creatively but not in the mainstream of pop.

xi. Many of the classic electronic music recordings of the period 1950–1990 are now online on sites such as avantgardeproject.org, wolffifth.blogspot.com. www.ubu.com, and others.

Chapter 1

1. It is amazing to read in this day and age a statement such as the following by a scientist studying music cognition:

> Why do timbral contrasts rarely serve as the basis for musical sound systems? . . . I believe that there are both physical and cognitive reasons why timbre is rarely used as the basis for organized sound contrasts in music. The physical reasons is that dramatic changes in timbre usually require some change in the way the instrument is excited. . . . [The cognitive reason is that] it may be that timbre-based music has not succeeded in the West because of the difficulty of organizing timbre in terms of intervals or scales.
>
> —ANIRUDDH PATEL (2008)

The author of this opinion has apparently never heard of electronic music! Remarkably, two pages before this, he notes that "timbral contrasts between instruments are quite organized and are used in systematic ways by composers from numerous cultures."

2. The rise of electronic music and musique concrète in the 1950s provoked strong reactions among conservative critics, who decried them as "unnatural." Natural music was viewed as music in 12-note equal temperament played on instruments such as the piano (Borio 1993). Ironically, both 12-note equal temperament and the piano are technological inventions; the theory of equal temperament can be likened to a software technology, while the piano is a mechanical hardware technology refined over many decades.

3. Varèse completed *Déserts* (1954) for orchestra and tape, and the famous *Poème électronique* (1958), which was originally accompanied by image projections selected by Le Corbusier. I finally experienced the audiovisual version in 2006 at a museum installation in Basel; it can also be viewed on the Internet.

4. Yet certain moments hint at possibilities to come. For example, the glissandi passages in Olivier Messiaen's otherwise traditional *Fête des belles eaux* (1936) for six Ondes Martenots foreshadow the cosmic sonorities of *Forbidden Planet* (1956) by Louis and Bebe Barron.

Sound example 1.14. Excerpt of *Love at the swimming hole* from the soundtrack to *Forbidden Planet* (1956) by Louis and Bebe Barron.

5. The MPEG-7 standard (Martinez 2004) introduced a catalog of mathematically defined descriptors for 18 attributes of timbre (Mintz 2007). Although these descriptors are limited to the acoustic properties of traditional instruments and voice, and not the vast realm of noises, they represent a starting point for building an objective scientific description of timbre.

6. For example, the obituary of the important and pioneering composer Luc Ferrari was not reported in any American newspaper.

7. Ambivalence and even distaste for loudspeakers and electronic sound remains a prejudice among certain composers groomed in the conservatory tradition. Yet for whatever reason, some of these composers dabble in the electronic medium. Afterward the same composers announce their break with the electronic medium in public statements. I have read many of these statements. A typical one is the following declaration made in a *Los Angeles Times* interview by a composer who rode a wave of publicity based on his electronic opera:

> I no longer find myself enamored with amplified sound or with things that sound electronic. I find that loudspeakers tend to flatten sound or simplify it.
>
> —TOD MACHOVER (1999)

This is a prevalent ideology. As Helmut Lachenmann stated in a 2003 interview:

> A loudspeaker is a totally sterile instrument. Even the most exciting sounds are no longer exciting when projected through a loudspeaker.

An example for success in the European contemporary music industry was set by early icons of electronic music, Stockhausen, Ligeti, and Berio. They abandoned the electronic medium in favor of opera productions within the mainstream of the European culture industry for which they were paid handsomely in commissions and royalties.

Pierre Boulez, one of the highest-paid musicians in the history of music, controlled much of the annual music budget in France for decades. Throughout his life, Boulez repeatedly attacked electronic music in polemic statements. The IRCAM Institute he founded, while making much hoopla about technology, never allowed electronic music to flourish as a compositional medium in and of itself.

Even pioneers in the field lost faith. Milton Babbit composed some of the classic early works of electronic music. Yet he repeatedly declared his antagonism to an aesthetic of new sounds. When the RCA synthesizer was decommissioned in 1979, Babbitt went back to writing instrumental music. A disillusioned Peter Zinovieff, the force behind the famous Electronic Music Studio (EMS) in London in the 1970s, summarized his gloomy perspective as follows:

> Electronic music is dead. It is doubtful that it was ever alive.
>
> —ZINOVIEFF (1983)

Pierre Schaeffer (1987) looked back on musique concrète as a failed experiment.

> Three circumstances compelled me to experiment in music: I was involved in music; I was working with turntables (then with tape-recorders); I was horrified by modern 12-tone music. I said to myself: Maybe I can find something different... maybe salvation, liberation, is possible. Seeing that no one knew what to do anymore with Do Re

> Mi, maybe we had to look outside that. . . . Unfortunately it took me forty years to conclude that nothing is possible outside Do Re Mi. . . . In other words, I wasted my life.

8. James A. Moorer (2000), a pioneer of the 1970s era of computer music, predicted:

> [In the year 2022] we should be able to process 9000 channels of audio in real time, doing million point FFTs [for convolution reverberation]. This is compute power far beyond what even the most starry-eyed fortune-teller could have imagined! It will change the nature of what audio is, and what audio engineers do, since it changes what is possible at a fundamental level.

9. It is not necessarily a golden age in other respects.

10. Consider the combination of the Sibelius common music notation program with Eric Lindemann's Synful Orchestra software, which emulates orchestral instruments. Here the means are all electronic, but the general approach to composition remains traditional.

11. As Horacio Vaggione (1998) has pointed out, operations like transposition preserve abstract intervallic relations, but they also shift the spectral centroid of the sound, which constitutes a tangible morphological change.

12. Stockhausen (1981) emphasized the role of performance in his studio practice:

> What I want is a studio set up rather like an airline cockpit, with at least four, if not six keyboards: two or three at the right and the same number at the left, with long joysticks to control the movement of sounds, and potentiometers. . . . I want it to respond instantly to the physical actions of my body, to the movements of my two hands on joysticks and keyboards and buttons, and if possible to my two feet on foot controls.

13. For Earle Brown, the "liberation of words, objects, time, etc." was enabled by assemblage strategies and was not specifically associated with electronic means. Inspired by the mobile sculptures of Alexander Calder, many of his compositions were designed in *open form*, in which a work consists of a set of modules scored on paper whose order is determined by a conductor at the time of performance on traditional instruments. Here "liberation" means freeing up the modules from being played in a fixed order. Of course, such strategies can easily be realized with electronic means as well.

Chapter 2

14. Vaggione's *Harrison Variations* is one of three works that are all derived from transformations of a single sound. The original work containing this sound is *. . . et ansi de suite . . .* (2002) by Jonty Harrison. Trevor Wishart's *Imago* (2002) is the third piece.

15. As the engineer Richard Hamming (1997) noted, it is easy to do something novel, or something that has never been done before. He suggested multiplying two randomly selected 10-digit numbers together, for example. Since there are 40 quintillion such products, it is very likely that this calculation will never have been done before. The point is that novelty in itself has no significance unless it has importance in our culture. What we call creativity, he argued, involves culturally important innovation. This often involves combining things that have a large initial psychological difference between them.

Chapter 3

16. Air, especially humid air, is a surprisingly weighty substance. A cubic meter of dry air weighs about 1.2 kg (2.64 pounds) (Solar balloons 2009). The total mean mass of the Earth's atmosphere is about five quintillion kilograms (NASA 2007). Thus when a current of air moves at high speeds, as in a hurricane, it can destroy things. Of course, music is transmitted not by air currents (wind) but by air waves (vibrations), which travel through the air without displacing it.

17. In audio signal processing work, the unit of the *millibel* (1/100th of a decibel) is convenient because it enables gain adjustments using computationally efficient integers rather than floating-point numbers (Thall 2012).

18. In 1967, a North American X-15 aircraft reached a speed of 7274 km/hour, or more than 4500 mph (Mach 5.9).

19. Most work in sound classification has been steered by commercial motivations like genre and song identification for marketing and licensing purposes.

Chapter 4

20. The great importance of Gabor's theory and experiments was not recognized until later, with such technical developments as *granular synthesis* (Xenakis 1960; Roads 1978, 2002), the *phase vocoder* (Flanagan and Golden 1966), and *dictionary-based methods* (Mallat and Zhang 1993; Sturm et al. 2008), among many other ramifications.

21. Ruttmann's pioneering sound montage *Weekend* (1930) was made by splicing fragments of film with an optical soundtrack. This "cinema for the ear," made with extremely bulky equipment, included sounds from everyday life. *Weekend* tells the story of an escape from Berlin to the countryside. Ruttmann died in 1941, and the film was long considered lost. A print was rediscovered in New York in 1978, and the soundtrack was produced on compact disc in the mid-1990s.

22. Original sound is apparently not valued by a certain segment of the composition community. For example, one of my composition students told me that her electronic music teacher in Los Angeles advised her to never create her own sounds, but to always use commercial sample libraries.

23. For a review of the principles of analog signal synthesis and voltage control from both musical and technical points of view, see Chadabe (1967), Wells (1981), Strange (1983), and Manning (1993).

24. According to Fourier, it is theoretically possible to add together sine waves at different frequencies and phases to produce any waveform, but this is especially difficult to manage in the analog domain.

25. A famous story from the 1980s was that in 99% of the Yamaha DX7 synthesizers returned for repair, the patch memory RAM had never been used. In other words, the vast majority of users had only used presets and had never edited a patch.

26. Csound is perhaps the only language for which one can say that a software instrument written 20 years ago will run today. However, perhaps Csound has not taken advantage of advances in language design in this period.

Chapter 5

27. In the electronic domain, it is not always easy to neatly separate synthesis (the creation of sound material) from transformation (a form of variation), since many synthesis techniques involve transformations of an existing sound. For example, subtractive synthesis carves a sound through filtering; granulation transfigures a sound by subdividing it into grains and scattering these on the canvas of time.

28. In 2008, I heard Helmut Lachenmann play his *Schattentanz* from *Ein Kinderspeil* (1980) in Los Angeles. I had not heard this piece before, so I was surprised by the new sounds coming from that most familiar of instruments, the unprepared piano. The sounds were created by striking the highest note on the piano with great force while also depressing other keys silently with various pedals engaged. The sounds were reminiscent of sending an electronic impulse into a comb filter with different delay times. While I was struck by the "freshness" of this sound, I also noticed that the piece was composed 28 years previously. I had to wonder, how many more new sounds can still be found in the piano? Certainly we can say that the pace at which new piano sounds are discovered is currently slow.

29. Schaeffer (1952) developed a similar but more complicated terminology to describe transformations.

Chapter 6

30. Pierre Schaffer called such fluctuations *allure* (Schaeffer 1966, 1976, 1977; Chion 2009).

31. I became aware of continuously flowing rhythm in my youth when I heard the drummer Tony Williams (1945–1997). Williams came to prominence at age 17 as the drummer for Miles Davis, and then went on to lead other groups. A key aspect of his style was extensive use of continuous rolls that would swell and ebb over several seconds, much like granular clouds.

32. As described later in the chapter, electronic drum machines, sequencers, and clock modules can easily generate events at extremely slow or fast rates beyond these perceptual ranges.

33. Music notation expert Donald Byrd wrote an entertaining article on the extremes of CMN (Byrd 2008). Another curious study was written by Perkins in 1976. He created a chart of notated durations (in the so-called Darmstadt notation) that span the range from ♩ to ♪ in 50 steps. At a tempo of MM60 = ♩, the entire span is 500 ms, and the difference between any two successive durations is 10 ms. This temporal resolution is beyond the limits of human performance. (At a tempo of 60 MM, the threshold of human performance accuracy is around a 32nd note or 125 ms, excluding double-stroke drum rolls.) Many of the rhythmic units in Perkins's chart are so precise as to be impossible to perform, such as playing a note at "9/13ths its usual duration," while another note is to be played at "13/9ths its normal duration."

34. Varèse's rhythmic strategies have not been formalized. Musicologist Robert P. Morgan (1979b) threw up his hands at the prospect of generalizing Varèse's rhythmic tactics:

From the point of view of rhythm, then, the essential question posed by Varèse is: How is the music to proceed—that is, to move forward—when the pitches have no inclination to move toward other pitches? The answer embodied in his work is complex and varies from composition to composition. In any event, a conclusive or systematic response is beyond my powers.

35. For a detailed analysis of *Ionisation*, see Chou (1979).

36. The Cologne studio even had a device for spooling loops of up to 150 meters, corresponding to over six minutes at a 38 cm/second tape speed (Enkel and Schutz 1954).

37. Examples of music programming languages that support algorithmic composition at the time of this writing include SuperCollider, Max/MSP, Pd, ChucK, Nyquist, OpenMusic, Common Music, and Autobusk.

38. Sieve theory was introduced into musical discourse by Xenakis in the 1960s. It remained an obscure topic until computer programs made it more accessible, beginning with the publication of Gérard Marino's program in the 1992 edition of *Formalized Music* (albeit with typographical errors introduced by the publisher). My encounter with sieve theory began in 1994, when I ported Marino's program to the Apple Macintosh at Xenakis's UPIC center (later CCMIX) in Paris.

39. It is interesting to compare Le Corbusier's visual and spatial grid system for architecture, the *modulor*, to Xenakis's more general concept of sieves. In 1948, Le Corbusier wrote *Le Modulor*, a book describing a scale of proportions for architecture, based on the human body. The modulor was inspired by the notion of musical scales. As Le Corbusier (1968) observed: "The modulor is a scale. Musicians have a scale; they make music that may be trite or beautiful."

Xenakis worked, first as an engineer, and later as an architect, under the management of Le Corbusier from 1950 to 1959. Xenakis used the modulor spatial scale for the design of the windows of their collaborative masterpiece, Le Couvent de la Tourette, begun in 1953 (Matossian 1986; Potié 2001). Figure 6.21 shows one façade of this design.

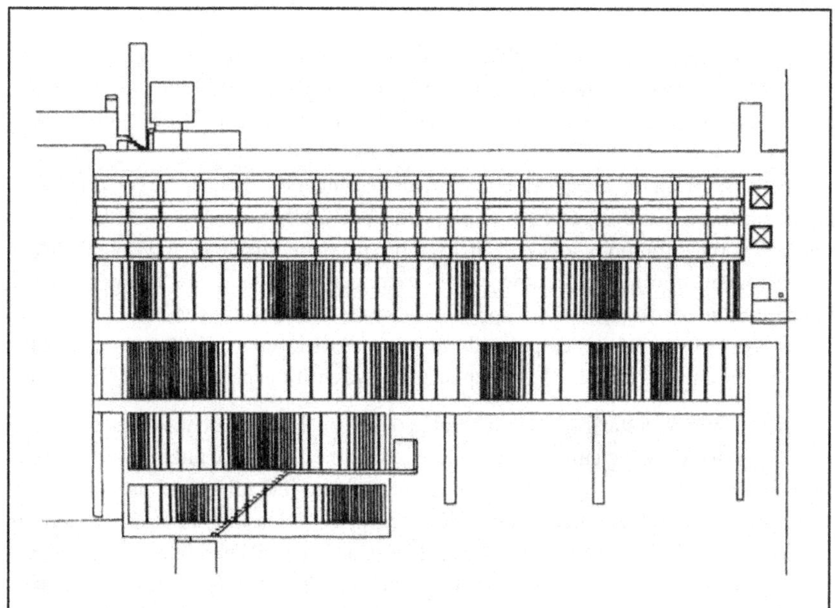

FIGURE 6.21 West facade of Le Couvent de la Tourette, showing the undulating composition of the windows according to the intervals of the modulor scale.

Xenakis's sieve theory, first published in 1967, generalizes scale-designing systems like the modulor and can be applied to any medium (Xenakis 1992):

> Sieve theory . . . is applicable to any other sound characteristics that may be provided with a totally ordered structure, such as intensity, instants, density, degrees of order, speed, etc. . . . This method can be applied equally to visual scales and to the optical arts of the future.

Chapter 7

40. See David Huron's (2001) interesting derivation of the rules of voice-leading according to perceptual principles:

> Traditionally, the so-called "rules of harmony" are divided into two broad groups: (1) the rules of harmonic progression and (2) the rules of voice-leading. The first group of rules pertains to the choice of chords, including the overall harmonic plan of a work, the placement and formation of cadences, and the moment-to-moment succession of individual chords. The second group of rules pertains to the manner in which individual parts or voices move from tone to tone in successive sonorities. The term "voice-leading" . . . refers to the direction of movement for tones within a single part or voice. A number of theorists have suggested that the principal purpose of voice-leading is to create perceptually independent musical lines. . . . The perceptual principles described will initially be limited to a core set of 6 principles that are most pertinent to understanding voice-leading. These principles can be treated in a manner akin to axioms in a formal system from which a set of propositions can be derived. . . . In the process of the derivation, several novel rules will arise that are not normally found in theoretical writings on voice-leading.

41. These definitions apply well to 12-note equal temperament. However, for a repeating scale that does not cycle at the octave, such a helix needs to be shrunk or expanded. For a set of frequencies in free intonation, the notion of pitch class or chroma is not necessarily defined.

42. Apart from the complexities of human hearing mechanisms, the laws of physics impose limits on the ability to distinguish pitch. Specifically, according to the law of convolution, as the duration of an event shrinks, its spectrum broadens, and the salience of pitch inevitably diminishes. In other words, extremely brief events are always noisy and thus cannot invoke the sensation of pitch. (See Roads 1996a, figure 5.17.)

43. As Morton Subotnick pointed out in a 2007 lecture at UCSB, perfect pitch is possessed by animals as well. This is supported by scientific experiment (Saffran 2005):

> When European starlings were presented with a pitch discrimination task that could be performed using either AP [absolute pitch] or RP [relative pitch] cues, the birds initially solved the task using AP cues, suggesting that birds first use AP cues to categorize novel auditory stimuli. However, when the task was changed to require transfer of the pitch sequences, the birds instead used RP cues. The authors suggest that the birds had access to both types of pitch cues, but that the demands of the task, particularly with respect to the structure of the input, determined which dimensions of the auditory stimuli were used during the test discriminations.

44. Theremin also constructed several electronic harmoniums. These were designed to facilitate microtonal performance, as each key could be tuned to an arbitrary pitch (Anfilov 1966).

45. It is quite interesting to induce vibrato in sounds that normally have fixed pitch. For example, adding vibrato and portamento to a sampled or physically modeled piano enlivens this familiar timbre.

46. Of course, the phenomena described in figure 7.5 need to be constrained in order for the figure to make sense. For example, a single long (≥100 ms) grain with a Gaussian envelope and a 1 kHz sinusoidal waveform already has pitch, regardless of density. The point is that this continuum is not a simple linear function of density alone. A precise combination of grain duration, envelope, waveform, frequency, and density would need to be adjusted to realize each of these states.

47. Reverberant chords are not a new phenomenon. Matthew Wright played an Afghan rubab, an ancient lute-like instrument with a highly resonant body and tuned sympathetic strings, for me. When the instrument is played, the sympathetic strings and the resonant body create a reverberation chord around anything played on the plucked strings.

48. In response to criticisms, defenders of abstract 12-note ET methods have penned ripostes in recent years. I summarize five of these arguments below.

Argument 1: This music is for experts

At one pole is the argument that the listener should definitely attempt to decipher the materials and operations used by the composer. Therefore, one needs to be an expert to appreciate this music (Babbitt 1958). Training and experience are needed because a given strain of modern music is like a foreign language; one cannot expect to understand a poem written in Greek if one does not invest the time to learn the language; one must be "well versed" (Barlow 2013). Moreover, these poems are not simple, as Morris (2010) states: "The complexity of Babbitt's music is staggering." Mead (1994) argues that appreciating complicated pitch structures is a matter of set theory training and "repeated listening to the same pieces" through what he calls "aggregate hearing" of "extremely demanding" music. Morris (2010) advises people to compare a given piece with another written with a similar pitch array:

> Once one has the row and has identified its hexachords and attendant row-regions, one can begin to sort out the notes into aggregates and blocks and recover the array.

Obviously this advice apparently presumes that the listener has the score and is strongly motivated to analyze the rows and practice repeated listening. Motivation is key, as Richard Toop (2004) observed:

> Naturally, how much of this detail one wants to follow . . . is a matter of personal choice.

Argument 2: Form-as-flow in the now

This view contradicts the studious approach advocated by Mead and Morris in argument 1, but it is put forth by Morris himself in another chapter of his book (2010, chapter 11). He argues against the expectation-based cognitive criteria put forth above by Lerdahl and Huron. To him, a sense of purpose, teleology, or causality in a composition smacks of "entertainment." Expectation-based music is even "addictive." Giving up expectations can only come through experiencing "form-as-flow" in the now. Morris asks:

> Is it possible to attend to music wholeheartedly but without the support of learning, knowledge, or habit? I'd rather not answer this question right away but simply insist that attention does not depend on cognition. If this is so, then the qualities of music are available to anyone who will listen. But this would mean there can be experience of quality without knowledge.

Drawing from long experience with meditation, he argues:

> We can now appreciate music that is unfinished, illusive, vague, ephemeral, mercurial, and so forth. . . . We no longer need to be programmed to understand the music.

Argument 3: Some of it is just murky

Certain pieces of serial music are difficult to listen to because they are not written clearly: Their structure is deeply submerged or muddled. For example, Morris (2010) criticized unnamed serial pieces as being "aurally opaque":

> They do not produce patterns of sound that are cognitively, psychologically, or phenomenologically intelligible to my ear and mind.

In another passage, Morris speaks of certain pieces of serial music as "dull and lifeless." At face value, this is apparently at odds with his argument 2, which suspends judgment and turns any given piece into a sonic meditation. (Perhaps he means that not all pieces are suitable for meditative listening.) Certain pieces present clear patterns, while others are so obscure that one could not follow their internal structure even if one tried. Richard Toop (2004) cites a number of complex works in which clarity of formal process can become apparent provided one knows what to listen for. He makes the excellent point that a bit of enlightened pedagogy on what to listen for can make a big difference in one's experience and understanding of a piece. I can testify that his preconcert lecture on Stockhausen's *Mantra* in Melbourne opened my ears to its structure by pointing out audible cues and landmarks that I otherwise might have heard "impressionistically," as the next argument describes.

Argument 4: Impressionistic listening

Even if it is impossible to follow the pitch organization in detail, one can hear it "impressionistically," as complicated patterns fade in and out of cognitive salience. Morris (2010) likens this to a game of "discovery" and "hide-and-seek" as patterns go in and out of recognition.

Argument 5: The composing grammar is irrelevant to the listener

The internal structures designed by the composer are of little or no concern to the listener of "modernist" music. Defenders of this view question a communication model in which music is supposed to transmit a message concerning its internal structure. As Amy Bauer (2004) wrote:

> I question [the] implication that an "order that can be heard" must serve as a paradigm for listening to music.

In her view, the experience of music listening is largely metaphoric:

The conceptual metaphors we use in language can be traced back, through a kind of recursive mapping process, to "image schemata," source domains based on bodily experience and action. We map elements of our concrete, physical experience of the world map onto our abstract, intellectual understanding, as when we label one musical pitch "higher" than another, or employ kinesthetic notions such as gesture, tension and release to structure musical experience.

However, the musical examples she uses to defend her assertions, Ligeti's *Lontano, Atmospheres*, and *Lux Aeterna*, are exceptionally transparent in audible structure, so they do not prove anything about structural opacity in the works of Boulez, which she cites numerous times as an example of "modernist" composition.

49. As an example of Barlow's scale rationalization method, we present the *Bohlen-Pierce* (BP) intonation (Bohlen 1978; Mathews and Pierce 1989; Loy 2006; Huygens-Fokker 2013). BP is not one scale but a family of related scales. A newcomer to the musical scene, BP has nonetheless attracted significant international interest (Hajdu 2010). BP is of particular interest to me, as I used it in *Purity*, the first movement of my composition *Clang-tint* (1994). I was attracted to this scale by its sound– a combination of sweet and sour intervals in which could hear melodic and harmonic potential–rather than its purely numerical properties.

Sound example 7.14. Excerpt from the middle of part one, *Purity*, from *Clang-tint* (1994) by Curtis Roads.

In contrast to 12-note ET, where each interval is derived from $^{12}\sqrt{2}$, or 1.05946, the BP tuning derives from the relation $^{13}\sqrt{3}$, or 1.08818. This means that the BP tuning has 13 chromatic tones and it cycles at 3/1–the *tritave*–in contrast to 12-note ET's 2/1 octave.

Several versions of the BP scale have been devised. Although Mathews and Pierce derived a 9-tone diatonic BP scale by selecting the steps 1, 2, 4, 7, 8, 10, 11, and 13, I used the total BP chromatic scale in *Purity*.

The just intonation Bohlen version derives from factors of 3, 5, and 7.

1	2	3	4	5	6	7	8	9	10	11	12	13	14
1:1	27:25	25:21	9:7	7:5	75:49	5:3	9:5	49:25	15:7	7:3	63:25	25:9	3:1

In contrast to the just BP, the equal-tempered BP applies the $^{13}\sqrt{3}$ value of 1.08818 per step, rather than integer ratios. In this version, the distance between each successive step is 146.304 cents. The conformity of ET BP to just BP is close, less than 1% or 16 cents.77

Table 7.2 presents a version of ET BP that has been retuned by Clarence Barlow's program for rationalizing scales. Barlow's program tries to find the optimum overall harmonicity for an entire scale within a given tuning tolerance (a maximum deviation in cents from the original scale step). The top row is the scale step. The second row **R** is result of the rationalization process. The third row expresses the rationalized intervals **R** in cents. The fourth row indicates the ideal frequency interval of the non-rationalized BP scale in cents. The bottom row shows the difference between the ideal and the rationalized interval in cents. Notice that the greatest deviation from the conventionally defined scale is at the ninth step, where the rationalization chooses the octave (2/1) as an approximation to 49/25.

TABLE 7.2

ET BP retuned by Clarence Barlow's program for rationalizing scales

ScaleStep	1	2	3	4	5	6	7	8	9	10	11	12	13	1
R	1:1	32:35	5:6	7:9	32:45	2:3	3:5	5:9	1:2	7:15	32:75	2:5	9:25	1:3
R in cents	0	155	316	435	590	702	884	1018	1200	1319	1475	1586	1769	1902
Ideal in cents	0	146	293	439	585	732	878	1024	1170	1317	1463	1609	1756	1902
Deviation	0	+9	+23	−4	+5	−30	+6	−6	+30	+2	+12	−23	+13	0

50. For example, in pieces like my *Half-life*, melody emerges as an epiphenomenon of microsonic processes, specifically, the replication of sound particles.

Chapter 8

51. Immersive recording using arrays of dozens or hundreds of microphones is in the experimental stage and may eventually become commonplace.

52. Various historical sources estimate from 300 to 450 loudspeakers. Some drivers were clustered, which could be a source of confusion.

53. In 2011, I had the privilege of projecting Xenakis's *Polytope de Cluny* at the REDCAT Theater, Disney Hall, Los Angeles (Swed 2011).

54. An alternative method of capturing the impulse response is to play a sine wave that sweeps the audible frequencies (Farina 2000).

55. I have performed at several open-air events where echo was an issue, including a 2007 courtyard concert at the New Venetian Fortress overlooking the Ionian Sea at Corfu. Sometimes the uniqueness of the venue trumps acoustics.

56. I recall a sound check before a concert at the Beijing Central Conservatory in October 2012 where the hall would rattle from both sides on every bass note produced by the powerful Genelec sound system. Walking around the hall, I noticed that the rattling was coming from the decorative metal light fixtures on the side walls. Standing on a chair, I was able to secure the two pieces of metal on every fixture that was rattling. The change was immediately noticed by composer Françoise Barrière, who walked into the sound check after the problem was solved, and asked: “How did you get rid of that rattling?”

57. The presence of a performer imbues a virtuosic aspect to the concert. Performance of spatial diffusion requires two types of expertise: expert knowledge of the piece being spatialized, so that changes in scene occur on cue, and expert knowledge of the sound system and the performance space. The composer has an advantage in the first case, while an experienced sound engineer may have an advantage in the latter case. For example, I recall an experience in Bourges with their unique Cybérnophone system (Clozier 2001) in which I was given a five-minute lesson and 15

minutes of rehearsal with their unique spatial control system that clearly required more time to fully exploit.

58. Using a two-dimensional microphone array, one can record and analyze the three-dimensional morphology of a wavefront of a sound source using the spatial Fourier transform. This technique, called *near-field acoustic holography* (NAH), produces a representation of the spatial propagation of a wavefront parallel to the microphone array. An established technique in acoustics engineering, NAH is often used for the localization of noise sources in machinery (LMS 2013).

59. In response to the heterogeneity of spatial audio schemes and systems for audio, the Spatial Sound Description Interchange Format or SpatDIF is a recent specification for storing and transmitting spatial audio scene descriptions to encourage portability and exchange of compositions between venues with different surround-sound infrastructures (Peters et al. 2013). Research is ongoing into how sound can be automatically upmixed, downmixed, or restructured for a variety of means of reproduction.

60. Another strategy that I have used in compositions such as *Epicurus* (2010) and *Always* (2013) is the introduction of reverberant space as a structural cadence. In these compositions, I take a particle explosion and submerge it in reverberation, thereby bringing a phrase or composition to an end.

61. Smalley (2007) presents a theory of spatial relations in acousmatic music. This includes a glossary of more than 40 terms invented by the author. As expected in an acousmatic approach, most of the terms describe situations in which sounds occur, taken from the viewpoint of the listener. One could liken them to Bregman's (1990) auditory scenes. Example: "Enacted space—Space produced by human activity, a space within which humans act. See also *agential space* and *utterance space*."

Chapter 9

62. When I say that "any musical structure is the result of a process," I am referring to perceived musical process internal to the work itself, not the process of composition. Thus the process here means the unfolding of the functional relations embedded in the work. William Verplank (2006) suggested that the duality of structure and process could be likened to the duality of a map (which points out where things are) versus a path (how to get there). One should be able to derive one from the other, more or less. The difference between the two representations is that a map provides additional context (what street is after the one you should turn on, in case you go too far), while a path sorts out a direct way through the maze of the map. The analogy would be that one could derive the structure from the process and vice-versa; however, Wolfram (2002) demonstrated the inherent difficulty in these tasks.

63. Reviewer Jennifer Logan asked: "Must the composer's method be perceivable for the result to have impact, especially considering each person hears uniquely? Is there a problem with the composer making these decisions for their own personal purposes while not particularly worrying about whether or not the audience perceives it, or maybe even preferring that the audience perceives something other than the architecture, such as the emotive/narrative material superimposed on the system?" I would draw an analogy with watching a film. When we watch a classic movie, everyone in the

audience understands the plot. Yet everyone has a different impression of the film. One person may think it brilliant, the other boring. One actor was convincing, another was not. The cinematography was inventive, but the soundtrack was hackneyed; innumerable other interpretations are possible. So even in a medium that tells a literal story, there is imperfect communication. At the same time, there are many details in a film that only the director can see because it is part of the craft, such as the particular focal length of a lens used in a scene, certain details of the set design, the pace of the cuts, and so on. So there is always organization of details that will not necessarily be spotted individually in the course of seeing the film once. Only someone who carefully studies the film in many repeated screenings or via frame-by-frame analysis will find these organizational details. Music, of course, tends to be more abstract than a literal story, leaving even more room for interpretation.

64. [Jean-Phillipe Rameau] had to compose or prepare music not only for concerts and church but also for balls, plays, festivals, dinners, ballets, and other special occasions (Grout 1973).

65. As reviewer Brian Hansen pointed out: "Just because a formal section is identifiable/predictable does not mean it is boring. Consider sonata forms or jazz forms. In sonata form, many anticipate the development section in order to see what directions the composer takes the music. In jazz, listeners anticipate the solo sections hoping to be amazed by the soloist's technique and musicianship. In each of these instances the form is identifiable and even predictable, but the music is not boring." The same could be said of Indian classical music, for example, where the forms are well known and much of the focus is on the virtuosity of the musicians.

66. *Cycle des souvenirs* is also available as a solo compact disc, Blue Chopsticks BC8.

67. As reviewer Nick Collins (2009) observed: "The failure of homomorphism between a mathematical space or dataset and music is because the structures in the originating domain are not actually equivalent in any way to the structures in music of importance to listening experience."

68. Due to the complexity and cost of mounting a production of this acoustic work, Ives never heard a complete performance in his lifetime. Today, the mixing of dozens or even hundreds of tracks is not especially difficult in the electronic medium.

69. The first transition in a piece has a special significance. In 1987, I served on the first Ars Electronica composition jury in Linz, Austria. We had to evaluate several hundred compositions in five days. Objectively, it was not possible to listen to every piece all the way through in the time allotted. A fellow member of this jury, the wise composer Gerard Grisey, pointed out that the handling of the first transition in a composition is a strong clue to the quality of what follows it. This was a great insight.

70. Reviewer Nick Collins likened my description of multiscale organization to the iterative design cycle in science and engineering. "Do something, see how it affects things. Keep on reacting. Trial and error eventually leads to deep consideration because of time spent in active contemplation, theory and practice in empirical feedback loop."

71. The distinction between syntax and semantics is not absolute, especially in the arts, where the syntax or arrangement of elements is an essential component of the meaning (e.g., in poetry).

72. Based on experiments, neuroscientist A. Patel (2003) proposed a hypothesis that syntax in language and music shares a common set of processes (instantiated in frontal

brain areas) that operate on different structural representations (in posterior brain areas). Language and music listening both involve structural integration as a key function of syntactic processing (i.e., mentally connecting each incoming element *X* to another element *Y* in the evolving structure). Both theories posit that integration is influenced by the distance between *X* and *Y* in an abstract cognitive space. For example, the processing of chords in a tonal context is influenced by their distance from one another in a structured cognitive space of pitch classes, chords, and keys.

Chapter 10

73. Mimaroglu's music was featured in Federico Fellini's extraordinary film *Satyricon* (1969).

74. Even in the most abstract music, a subtext is its cultural context: who is making it, why, and for whom? This kind of sociological analysis is important, but is not the topic of this book.

75. Of course, a goal of meditation is precisely to not anticipate or reflect. Its focus is on the now, not the past or the future. This is a special state of mind, however. The pioneering electronic music composer Pauline Oliveros has practiced and taught a form of sonic meditation for many years (Oliveros 2005).

76. Another way in which direction can emerge is by controlling trends in the spectromorphologies of sounds in time (e.g., a series of ever louder events that create a crescendo effect).

77. As a concept in the philosophy of science, causality is a deep and controversial topic (Williams and Colomb 2003; Owens 1992). A pioneer of algorithmic composition and artificial intelligence, John F. Sowa (2006), put it this way:

> *In modern physics, the fundamental laws of nature are expressed in continuous systems of partial differential equations. Yet the words and concepts that people use in talking and reasoning about cause and effect are expressed in discrete terms that have no direct relationship to the theories of physics. As a result, there is a sharp break between the way that physicists characterize the world and the way that people usually talk about it. Yet all concepts and theories of causality, even those of modern physics, are only approximations to the still incompletely known principles of causation that govern the universe.*

It can be argued that it is impossible to trace a given event to one specific cause. What caused the cause? Isn't the chain of causality infinite in extent? Wasn't the event also caused by the absence of innumerable disabling conditions that could have prevented the event? In other words, isn't everything dependent on everything else? (Williams and Colomb 2003). This is an interesting point of view, but for practical reasons, we often need to discern specific connections between things. In order to treat an epidemic, doctors need to know the illness; in order to fix a software crash, we need to find the bug that initiated it. D'Arcy Thompson (1942) responded eloquently to the philosopher's doubts:

> *The difficulties that surround the concept of the ultimate or "real" causation in Bacon's or Newton's sense of the word, and the insuperable difficulty of giving any just and tenable account of the relation of cause and effect from an empirical point of view, need scarcely hinder us in our physical inquiry. As students of mathematics and*

experimental physics, we are content to deal with those antecedents, or concomitants, without which the phenomena does not occur . . . conditions sine qua non.

These fascinating scientific (and legal) questions must remain exterior to our discourse, which is only concerned with the illusion of causality. In the cinema, we see a closeup of someone pushing a switch, and the scene immediately cuts to a room scene in which a light goes on. The apposition of these scenes creates an illusion of causality. Similarly, in music, a swell of energy leading to a loud sound gives the illusion that the latter sound is a logical consequent of the swelling. It is through such quasi-dramatic illusions that structural functions in compositions articulate themselves.

78. I once witnessed a concert of live electronic music by a solo performer in which hundreds of people walked out over the course of 45 minutes, virtually emptying a full concert hall. The mutual hostility in the air seemed to energize the performer.

Chapter 11

79. Some of the material in this chapter derives from chapter 18, "Algorithmic Composition Systems," in my book *The Computer Music Tutorial* (Roads 1996). It appears here with many revisions.

80. A personal note might illuminate my perspective on the subject. After encounters in my youth with pioneers of algorithmic composition Herbert Brün, Iannis Xenakis, and Gottfried Michael Koenig, I spent several years as a student writing a series of increasingly complicated algorithmic composition programs. Ultimately, my interest in writing composing programs per se waned (Roads 1992). It became clear to me that generative methods rested on arbitrary foundations. Formalism as an exclusive compositional strategy lost its special appeal. I found that I was ultimately more interested in sound and designing a sonic narrative than in designing an algorithmic process. I realized that designing a compelling sonic narrative would require methods that could not be easily formalized (e.g., performance in the studio, sampling, intuitive editing, and the use of analog technology and tape-based sound processing techniques). However, I do not deny the enormous potential of generative methods, especially in applications like granulation and generative spatial upmixing. I also remain interested in heuristic approaches to algorithmic composition.

81. For an overview of the history of formal processes in music, see chapter 18 of *The Computer Music Tutorial* (Roads 1996). For more detailed studies, good starting points for investigation are Hiller (1970), Barbaud (1966, 1968), Koenig (1978), Ames (1987), and Xenakis (1992).

82. An *N* qubit quantum computer is not in one state at a time but in 2^N superimposed states simultaneously. When this state is measured, the states collapse into an *N*-bit representation according to probability functions associated with the states.

83. Pseudorandom number generators are generally implemented in software. A "true random number generator" is a hardware device that generates a signal from an atomic-level noise in an analog circuit.

84. Consider the generative visual artist Harold Cohen (2008). Out of 100 images produced daily by his Aaron drawing program, he deletes 70, saves 30, and chooses two to print on paper. When asked how he chooses the ones to print, he said that he selects the outliers—the ones that look different from merely correct realizations.

85. Just about any process can be formalized, including narrative processes. In the commercial realm, a great deal of effort has been invested in building software models of narrative processes for interactive games based on IF-THEN rules and probabilistic decision trees. These include models of musical process in which the music must react to player decisions and important events that occur in the midst of game play. Up until recently, however, not much theoretical work has been done in this area. Only recently in the scientific world have there been initial attempts to develop a mathematical theory of narrative (Doxiadis 2005; Doxiadis and Mazur 2012).

86. See also Putnam (2012).

87. As Wittgenstein supposedly said, music is the solution to an undefined problem.

88. Much generative music is characterized by a weak narrative structure. It tends to operate on only one level of organization, beginning and ending in the middle of surface-level musical process. It lacks macrostructural forces, compelling sectional organization, and innovative form. In music composed by human beings, deeper and often conflicting forces shape the direction of the piece on a macro timescale.

89. The "star of imagination" metaphor derives from Varèse's preface to the score of his 1927 composition *Arcana*, which quotes the Renaissance physician, alchemist, and astrologer Paracelsus (1493–1541):

> One star exists higher than all the rest. This is the apocalyptic star. The second star is that of an ascendant. The third is that of the elements—of these there are four, so six stars are established. Besides there is still another star, imagination, which begets a new star and a new heaven.

90. Ultimately, the goals of most conceptual sound art seem not identical to those of most electronic music compositions. However, the aesthetic differences are not irreconcilable. For example, if one wanted to cover all the aesthetic bases, there is no reason why one could not create a piece that sounded fascinating, interacted with the audience, and was also motivated by a novel conceptual strategy and served as a vehicle for social change.

91. Human cognition seems to be designed to turn a temporal sequence of perceptions into a story and react to it accordingly. Thus, various attempts to escape narrative seem to have only succeeded in creating new narrative forms such as Stockhausen's moment form (a series of unrelated sections, where there can be linear progressions within a section) and John Cage's sound collages (viz., *Variations IV*, 1963), in which one quickly learns to anticipate the non sequitur. However, it is possible to hear music in a non-narrative manner by means of meditation. Meditation attempts to bypass the "thinking" mind to achieve a heightened state of awareness of the now. Meditation usually involves turning to a single point of reference, such as breathing, but can also focus on a sound, such as a drone, the flow of water, etc. Much of the practice of Pauline Oliveros (2005), for example, is directed to listening meditation:

> These exercises are intended to calm the mind and bring awareness to the body and its energy circulation, and to promote the appropriate attitude for extending receptivity to the entire space/time continuum of sound.

For more on music designed to be heard in meditation, see Kendall (2005).

92. Consider the transition in *Swaying to see* (1995) by Natasha Barrett, in which a modal cello melody emerges out of an inharmonic montage at around 7:25, building in

intensity as feelings of hope are evoked, leading to a climax at 8:49 in which the mood shifts instantly and unexpectedly to a dystopian soundscape.

93. Although it offers no specific solutions, Collins (2009) begins to address this problem conceptually. See also Doxiadis (2005) and Doxiadis and Mazur (2012).

94. In 1975, I wrote an algorithmic composition program called PROCESS/ING (Roads 1976a, 1976b). This Algol program modeled the interaction of 26 stochastic automata, where the interconnection between the automata was controlled by several levels of feedback and analysis. It was a first attempt to develop a composition program that could monitor its own output and change its mode of composition when the behavior became too predictable. Later, George Lewis developed machine listening algorithms for interactive improvisation (Roads 1985b). Going a step further, Robert Rowe (2012) described a "self-critical algorithmic composition" system that not only listens to other musicians interactively but also analyzes its own output before it is played, which could lead to changes in its musical output. Smith and Garnett (2012) describe a three-layer system based on neural networks in which each layer evaluates the output of the next lower layer in an effort to push the behavior of the system out of local minima (aimless wandering) and toward the formation of coherent larger-scale structures. See also Eigenfeldt and Pasquier (2012). Although it has been a long time coming, at least we can say that the goal of evaluation is now recognized as central to the task of generative music, or as Eigenfeldt (2012) put it:

> Autonomous aesthetic evaluation is the Holy Grail of generative music.

95. In order to study the behavior of simple generative algorithms, Stephen Wolfram (2002) produced millions of images. In order to find the exceptional ones, he wrote analysis procedures that would search through the images for unusual patterns. In this way, he was able to find the proverbial needle in a haystack.

Chapter 12

96. Commenting on ear training, the composer Markus Schmickler (2010) wrote:

> This skill should continuously be trained. One of the reasons for Stockhausen's popularity is that before his premieres he would stand in front of his audience and explain what they should pay attention to. He focused their listening to specific "streams." . . . In the domain of electronic music, special ear training is almost nonexistent and should be enforced in the future. . . . It should focus on the ability to separate distinct technical frequencies, synthesis techniques, levels, etc.

97. This chapter does not address the practice of remixing or creating an alternative version of a piece. With some notable exceptions (e.g., Karkowski and Humon 2002), remixing is mostly practiced in the domain of pop songs, where alternative versions for disk jockey (DJ) use are in demand.

98. The small number of tracks in this final mix of *Always* is typical of my stem-based mixing process, which breaks the assembly into multiple stages. (See the section on submixing and stems.) Notice that the top stereo track consists of a premixed "foundation" stem constituting the core of the piece. This stem derived from three previous mixing sessions. The initial mix session, which took place in February 2013, combined six highly

edited stereo sound files played back at 10 different transpositions simultaneously for a total of 120 tracks mixed in real time. The stem resulting from this mix was then extensively edited and incorporated into a second mix of eight tracks total in August 2013. The stem resulting from this mix was then edited and incorporated into a separate mix with six other tracks in October 2013. The result of this mix serves as the foundation stem for a final mix in November 2013. Thus the total number of tracks that went into this piece, not including the stems imported from the previous session, was 120 + 6 + 6 + 4 = 136.

99. Decibels can be confusing unless one is precise in their use and application. For example, a 3 dB boost in a sound doubles its *power* (measured in watts). However, it takes a 6 dB boost to double its *amplitude*. However, to double the *perceived volume* of a sound requires a boost of 10 dB sound pressure level (SPL). (See chapter 3 for more on decibels.)

100. The zone between 2100 to 3100 Hz has been targeted by weapons experts as the most likely to cause people to flee in the presence of a 150 dB sound beam (Associated Press 2004). Sound beams at 150 dB sound pressure level are physically intolerable. They are felt as a painful energy to the skin and result in permanent hearing damage in a matter of minutes. This frequency zone lies in the same range emitted by home smoke detectors, which beep at a merely annoying 90 dB SPL.

101. Too often, this means simply louder. Some venues provide massive amounts of sound power, and certain electronic musicians play with brute-force levels. In the audience, wearing ear plugs is the only reasonable solution.

102. Here is a personal anecdote for the reader's amusement. I was asked to submit compositions for three different compact disc anthology projects. On the first album, the mastering engineer somehow desynchronized one channel of the stereo sound file that I sent, resulting in a delay in one channel by 750 ms; the disc was manufactured and distributed anyway. For the second anthology, my composition was mastered (for reasons unknown) at half-speed, which pitch-shifted it down by an octave and doubled the length. For the third anthology, I specifically requested that the tracks I submitted not be altered in any way. When I heard the released disc, it was obvious that the piece had been dynamically compressed, and my composition, which was designed around accented transients and dynamic contrasts, was flattened and distorted. After these experiences, I no longer contribute to anthology productions. These episodes clearly demonstrate the dangers inherent in the critically important mastering process.

103. One reviewer asked if checking the master on several different loudspeakers (a standard practice in pop music production) was relevant in the creation of art music. My view is yes, that it is. One never knows what kind of system one's music will be heard on, so in order to avoid disappointing surprises, it is wise to check on a range of playback systems, from reference monitors to more modest systems. As a case in point, I found through experience that my B&W 802 Nautilus loudspeakers are effectively "too good." That is, they easily handle high-powered bass frequencies that overwhelm lesser monitors. Thus my current standard reference speakers are more modest (but still accurate) small-powered monitors: Dynaudio Acoustics BM5a. Mixes made on these tend to translate better to a wider range of loudspeakers.

REFERENCES

Adams, D. 2013. "Tracey: an acoustic ray tracer for music composition and sound design." M.S. project paper. University of California, Santa Barbara.

Adler, J. 2011. *Wheels within Wheels: A Study of Rhythm*. www.advancedrhythm.com.

Agon, C., G. Assayag, and J. Bresson, eds. 2006. *The OM Composer's Book*, Volume one. Paris: Editions Delatour France/Ircam-Centre Pompidou.

Ahlbäck, S. 2004. "Is the swing in the melody? Metrical analysis within a general model of melody cognition." In W. Brunson and J. Sundberg, eds. *Proceedings of the Conference on Music and Music Science*. Stockholm: Royal Conservatory. pp. 140–154.

Aldous, J., and R. Wilson. 2000. *Graphs and Applications: An Introductory Approach*. London: Springer-Verlag.

Aleksandrov, A., A. Kolmogorov, and M. Lavrentev, eds. 1963. *Mathematics: Contents, Methods, and Meaning*, Volume 3. Cambridge, MA: MIT Press.

Allen, J. B., and L. R. Rabiner. 1977. "A unified approach to short-time Fourier analysis and synthesis." *Proceedings of the IEEE* 65:1558–1564.

Amatriain, X., T. Höllerer, J. Kuchera-Morin, and S. Pope. 2007. "Immersive audio and music in the Allosphere." *Proceedings of the 2007 International Computer Music Conference*. San Francisco: International Computer Music Association.

Amatriain, X., J. Castellanos, T. Höllerer, J. Kuchera-Morin, S. T. Pope, G. Wakefield, and W. Wollcott. 2008. "Experiencing audio and music in a fully immersive environment." In R. Kronland-Martinet, S. Ystad, and K. Jensen, editors. *Sense of Sound*. Lecture Notes on Computer Science series. Berlin: Springer Verlag: 380–400.

Amatriain, X., T. Höllerer, J. Kuchera-Morin, and S. Pope. 2009. "The Allosphere: immersive multimedia for scientific description and artistic exploration." *IEEE Multimedia* 16(2): 64–75.

American National Standards Institute. 1973. *American National Psychoacoustic Terminology*. S3.20. New York: American National Standards Institute.

American National Standards Institute. 1999. *American National Standard Acoustic Terminology*. New York: American National Standards Institute.

American Technology Corporation. 1998. "HyperSonic sound." www.atcsd.com.

Ames, C. 1987. "Automated composition in retrospect: 1956–1986." *Leonardo* 20(2): 169–186.

Anderson, C. 2005. "Dynamic networks of sonic interactions: an interview with Agostino Di Scipio." *Computer Music Journal* 29 (3): 11–28

Anfilov, G. 1966. *Physics and Music*. Moscow: MIR Publishers.

Anthony, H. 1960. *Sir Isaac Newton*. New York: Collier Books.

Apel, W. 1972. *Harvard Dictionary of Music*. Cambridge, MA: Harvard University Press.

Aranson, I., and L. Tsimring. 2009. *Granular Patterns*. Oxford, UK: Oxford University Press.

Arbus, D. 2007. Quote. www.dianearbus.net/infocus.htm.

Ariza, C. 2005. "The Xenakis sieve as object: a new model and a complete implementation." *Computer Music Journal* 29(2): 40–60.

Arom, S. 1991. *African Polyphony and Polyrhythm: Musical Structure and Methodology.* New York: Cambridge University Press.

Ashby, A., ed. 2004. *The Pleasure of Modernist Music: Listening, Meaning, Intention, Ideology.* Rochester, NY: University of Rochester Press.

Assayag, G., and C. Agon (1996). OpenMusic architecture. In D. Rossiter, ed. *Proceedings of the 1996 International Computer Music Conference.* San Francisco: International Computer Music Association. pp. 339–340.

Associated Press. 2004. "Troops get high tech noisemaker." CNN.com, March 3, 2004.

AUDIUM. 2008. www.audium.org.

Austin, L. 1992. "An interview with John Cage and Lejaren Hiller." *Computer Music Journal* 16(4): 15–29. Revised version of Hiller and Cage 1968.

Avanzini, G., F. Faienza, D. Minciacchi, and M. Manjo, eds. 2003. *The Neurosciences and Music.* Annals of the New York Academy of Sciences, Volume 999. New York: New York Academy of Sciences.

Avizienis, R., A. Freed, P. Kassakian, and D. Wessel. 2006. "A Compact 120 Independent Element Spherical Loudspeaker Array with Programmable Radiation Patterns." Convention paper 6783. Audio Engineering Society, 120th Convention.

Baalman, M. 2010. "Spatial composition techniques and spatialisation technologies." *Organised Sound* 15(3): 209–218.

Babbitt, M. 1958. "The composer as specialist." Published as "Who cares if you listen?" in *High Fidelity* 8(2): 38–40, 126–127. Reprinted in S. Peles et al. 2003. *The Collected Essays of Milton Babbitt.* Princeton, NJ: Princeton University Press. pp. 48–54.

Babbitt, M. 1960. "The revolution in sound: electronic music." *Columbia University Magazine*, Spring 1960: 4–8. Reprinted in S. Peles et al. 2003. *The Collected Essays of Milton Babbitt.* Princeton, NJ: Princeton University Press. pp. 70–77.

Babbitt, M. 1962. "Twelve-tone rhythmic structure and the electronic medium." *Perspectives of New Music* 1(1): 49–79. Reprinted in In C. Boretz and E. Cone, eds. *Perspectives on Contemporary Music Theory.* New York: Norton. pp. 148–179.

Babbitt, M. 1964. "An introduction to the R.C.A. Synthesizer." *Journal of Music Theory* 8(2): 251–265. Reprinted in S. Peles et al. 2003. *The Collected Essays of Milton Babbitt.* Princeton, NJ: Princeton University Press. pp. 178–190.

Babbitt, M. 1988. "Composition in the electronic medium." In F. Roehmann and F Wilson, eds. *The Biology of Music-making.* Saint Louis, MO: MMB Music. pp. 208–212.

Babbitt, M. 1997. "Milton Babbitt on electronic music." http://www.youtube.com/watch?v=UHNG9rexCsg.

Babbitt, M. 2000. "Milton Babbitt talks about *Philomel*: by Jason Gross." www.furious.com/perfect/ohm/babbitt.html.

Backus, J. 1969. *The Acoustical Foundations of Music.* New York: Norton.

Baker, R. 1963. "MUSICOMP: MUSIc Simulator-Interpreter for COMPositional Procedures for the IBM 7090 electronic digital computer." Technical Report Number 9. Urbana, IL: University of Illinois Experimental Music Studio.

Barbaud, P. 1966. *Initiation à la musique algorithmique.* Paris: Dunod.

Barbaud, P. 1968. *La musique, discipline scientifique.* Paris: Dunod.

Barbosa, A, 2008. *Displaced Soundscapes: Computer Supported Cooperative Work for Music Applications*. Saarbrucken, DE: VDM Dr. Müller.

Barlow, C. 1980. "Bus journey to parametron." *Feedback Papers* 21–23.

Barlow, C. 1987. "Two essays on theory." *Computer Music Journal* 11(1): 44–60.

Barlow, C. 1999. Quoted in K. B. Roulès. "Satisfaction in artmaking as a function of æsthetic creativity and technical flexibility as well as of self-distance, remuneration and time pressure." Unpublished.

Barlow, C., ed. 2001a. "The Ratio Book." *Feedback Papers* 43.

Barlow, C. 2001b. "On the quantification of harmony and meter." In C. Barlow, ed. 2001a. "The Ratio Book." *Feedback Papers* 43.

Barlow, C. 2001c. "On the relationship between technology and artistic creativity–potentials and problems (with: satisfaction in artmaking as a function of aesthetic creativity and technical flexibility as well as of self-distance, remuneration and time pressure). In *Académie Bourges Actes VI*. Bourges, FR: Editions MNEMOSYNE. pp. 23–29.

Barlow, C. 2006. "On timbre in electroacoustic music." Unpublished.

Barlow, C. 2007. Personal communication.

Barlow, C. 2008. "Von der Musiquantenlehre." *Feedback Papers* 34.

Barlow, C. 2009a. Personal communication.

Barlow, C. 2009b. "The Making of *Tischgeistwalzer*." Unpublished.

Barlow, C. 2012. *On Musiquantics*. Report No. 51. Musikinformatik und Medientechnik. Mainz, DE: Universität Mainz.

Barlow, C. 2013. Personal communication.

Baroni, M., and C. Jacoboni. 1978. *Proposal for a Grammar of Melody: The Bach Chorales*. Montréal: Les Presses de l'Université de Montréal.

Barrett, N. 1997. "Structuring processes in electroacoustic music." Ph.D. diss. London: City University.

Barrett, N. 1999. "*Little Animals*: compositional structuring processes." *Computer Music Journal* 23(2): 11–18.

Barrett, N. 2002. "Spatio-musical composition strategies." *Organized Sound* 7(3): 313–323.

Barrett, N. 2007. "Trends in electroacoustic music." In N. Collins and J. Escrivan, eds. *The Cambridge Companion to Electronic Music*. Cambridge, UK: Cambridge University Press. pp. 232–255.

Barrett, N. 2008. Personal communication.

Bassal, D. 2002. "The practice of mastering in electroacoustics." cec.concordia.ca/pdf/The_Practice_of_Mastering.pdf.

Bauer, A. 2004. "Tone-color, movement, changing harmonic planes: cognition, constraints and conceptual blends in modernist music." In A. Arved, ed. *The Pleasure of Modernism*. Rochester, NY: University of Rochester Press. pp. 121–152.

Bayle, F. 1980. Program notes for *Tremblement du terre très doux*. LP. INA-GRM 9101 ba.

Bayle, F. 1989. "La musique acousmatique ou l'art des sons projetés." Paris: *Encyclopedia Universalis*. pp. 535–544.

Bayle, F. 1993. *Musique Acousmatique*. Paris: Institut National de l'Audiovisuel/Groupe de Recherches Musicales et Buchet/Chastel.

Bayle, F. 1997. Quoted in S. DeSantos. "Acousmatic morphology: an interview with François Bayle." *Computer Music Journal* 21(3): 11–19.

Bayle, F. 2006. Program notes for the CD "Les visiteurs de la musique concrete" in the collection *Archives GRM*. Paris: Institut Nationale de l'Audiovisuelle/Groupe de Recherches Musicale.

Bengtsson, I., and A. Gabrielsson. 1983. "Analysis and synthesis of simple rhythm." In J. Sundberg, ed. *Studies of Musical Performance*. No. 39. Stockholm: Royal Swedish Academy of Music.

Benson, D. 2007. *Music: A Mathematical Offering*. Cambridge, UK: Cambridge University Press.

Berg, P. 1987. "PILE—a language for sound synthesis." In C. Roads and J. Strawn, eds. *Foundations of Computer Music*. Cambridge, MA: MIT Press. pp. 161–187.

Berg, P. 2004. "Using the AC Toolbox." fc.mbs.net/~pfisher/fov2-0010016c/fov2-0010016e/FOV2-00100183.

Berio, L. 1958. *Thema (Omaggio a Joyce)*. CD program notes. New York: BMG 09026-68302-2.

Berio, L. 2006. *Remembering the Future* (based on lectures delivered in 1993 and 1994). Cambridge, MA: Harvard University Press.

Berkhout, A. J. 1988. "A holographic approach to acoustic control." *Journal of the Audio Engineering Society* 36: 977–995.

Berkhout, A. J., D. de Vries, and P. Vogel. 1993. "Acoustic control by wave field synthesis." *Journal of the Acoustical Society of America* 93(5): 2764–2779.

Berry, W. 1966. *Form in Music*. Englewood Cliffs, NJ: Prentice-Hall.

Berry, W. 1987. *Structural Functions in Music*. New York: Dover.

Bharucha, J. 1996. "Melodic anchoring." *Music Perception* 13: 383–400.

Bibby, N. 2003. "Tuning and temperament: closing the spiral." In J. Fauvel et al., eds. *Music and Mathematics: From Pythagoras to Fractals*. Oxford, UK: Oxford University Press. pp. 13–28.

Blackwell, A., and N. Collins. 2005. "The programming language as a musical instrument." In P. Romero et al. *Proceedings of the Psychology of Programming interest Group*. pp. 120–130. www.cogs.susx.ac.uk/users/nc81/research/proglangasmusicinstr.pdf.

Blades, J. 1992. *Percussion Instruments and their History*. Revised edition. Westport, CT: The Bold Strummer.

Blake, W. ca. 1798. Quoted in D. V. Erdman. 1982. *The Complete Poetry and Prose of William Blake* (second edition). New York: Anchor Books. p. 641.

Blauert, J. 1997. *Spatial Hearing: The Psychophysics of Human Sound Localization*. Cambridge, MA: MIT Press.

Bobrow, L. and M. Arfib. 1974. *Discrete Mathematics*. Philadelphia: W. B. Saunders.

Bodin, L.-G. 2004. "Music—an artform without borders?" Unpublished.

Bohlen, H. 1978. "13 tonestufen in der duodezime." *Acustica* 39: 76–86.

Borgo, D. 2005. *Sync or Swarm: Improvising Music in a Complex Age*. New York: Continuum.

Borio, G. "New technology, new techniques: the aesthetics of electronic music in 1950s." *Interface* 22(1): 77–87.

Bossis, B. 2006. "The analysis of electroacoustic music: from sources to invariants." *Organized Sound* 11(2): 101–112.

Boulanger, R. 2000. ed. *The Csound Book*. Cambridge, MA: MIT Press.

Boulez, P. 1958. "Concrète (Musique)." *Encylopédie de la musique*. Paris: Fasquelle. Reprinted in P. Boulez. 1995. *Points de repère I: Imaginer*. Paris: Christian Bourgois.

Boulez, P. 1986. *Orientations*. Cambridge, MA: Harvard University Press.

Bregman, A. 1978. "The formation of auditory streams." In J. Requin, ed. *Attention and Performance*. Hillsdale, NJ: Erlbaum. pp. 63–78.

Bregman, A. 1990. *Auditory Scene Analysis*. Cambridge, MA: MIT Press.

Brody, J. 1971. Program notes to *Iannis Xenakis: Electroacoustic Music*. Nonesuch Records H-71246.

Brougher, K. 2005. "Visual-music culture." In K. Brougher, J. Strick, A. Wiseman, J. Zilczer, and O. Mattis. 2005. *Visual Music: Synaesthesia in Art and Music Since 1900*. London: Thames and Hudson. pp. 88–179.

Brougher, K., J. Strick, A. Wiseman, and J. Zilczer. 2005. *Visual Music: Synaesthesia in Art and Music Since 1900*. London: Thames and Hudson.

Brown, E. 1967. "Form in new music." *Source: Music of the Avant-Garde* 1(1): 48–51. Reprinted in L. Austin and D. Kahn, eds. 2011. *Source: Music of the Avant-Garde*. Berkeley, CA: University of California Press. pp. 24–34.

Brown, S., M. Martinez, and L. Parsons. 2004. "Passive music listening spontaneously engages limbic and paralimbic systems." *NeuroReport* 15(13): 2033–2037.

Brün, H. 1984. Personal communication.

Brün, H. 1985. "Interview with Herbert Brün." Quoted in Hamlin and Roads (1985). p. 10.

Brün, H. 1986. *My Words and Where I Want Them*. London and Champaign, IL: Princelet Press.

Brün, H. 2004. *When Music Resists Meaning*. Middletown, CT: Wesleyan University Press.

Brunson, W., and J. Sundberg. 2006. *Music: Music Science*, Proceedings October 28–30, 2004. Stockholm: Royal Conservatory and Royal Institute of Technology.

Budon, O. 2000. "Composing with objects, networks, and time scales: an interview with Horacio Vaggione." *Computer Music Journal* 24(3):9–22.

Bundler, D. 1996. "Interview with Gérard Grisey." www.angelfire.com/music2/davidbundler/grisey.html.

Burns, E. 1999. "Intervals, scales, and tuning." In D. Deutsch, ed. *The Psychology of Music*. Second edition. San Diego, CA: Academic Press. pp. 215–264.

Busoni, F. 1907. *Sketch of a New Esthetic of Music*. Reprinted 1962. New York: Dover.

Byrd, D. 2008. "Extremes of conventional music notation." www.informatics.indiana.edu/donbyrd/CMNExtremes.htm.

Cage, J. 1980. Quoted in R. Kostelanetz, ed. 1988. *Conversing with Cage*. New York: Limelight Editions.

Campbell, M. 1997. "One-on-one with Murray Campbell." www.research.ibm.com/deepblue/meet/html/d.4.3.a.shtml.

Capra, F. 1999. *The Tao of Physics*. Boston: Shambala.

Carey, B. 2007. "Who's minding the mind." *New York Times*. July 31, 2007.

Carlos, W. 1987. "Tuning: at the crossroads." *Computer Music Journal* 11(1): 29–43.

Carter, E. 1960. "Shop talk by an American composer." P. H. Lang, ed. *Problems of Modern Music*. New York: W. W. Norton. pp. 51–63.

Carter, E. 1979. "On Edgard Varèse." In S. Van Solkema, ed. *The New Worlds of Edgard Varèse*. Brooklyn, NY: Institute for the Study of American Music. pp. 1–7.

Carterette, E., and R. Kendall. 1999. "Comparative music perception and cognition." In D. Deutsch, ed. *The Psychology of Music*. Second edition. San Diego, CA: Academic Press. pp. 725–791.

Carvin, A. 1993. "The man who would be king: an interview with Pierre Boulez." www.edwebproject.org/boulez.html.

Casey, M. 2001. "MPEG-7 sound recognition tools." *IEEE Transactions on Circuits and Systems for Video Technology* 11(6): 737–747.

Casey, M., A. De Cheveigne, P. Gardner, M. Jackson, and G. Peeters, eds. 2001. "Information Technology—Multimedia Content Description Interface—Part 4: Audio." *ISO15938-4 Final Draft International Standard*. Geneva: International Standards Association.

Casey, M. 2010. MPEG-7 Multimedia Software Resources. mpeg7.doc.gold.ac.uk.

Castine, P. 2002. Litter Power Package. Software documentation. www.bek.no/~pcastine/Music/programs.html.

Castonguay, C. 1972. *Meaning and Existence in Mathematics*. Vienna: Springer-Verlag.

Caux, J. 2002. *Presque rien avec Luc Ferrari*. Paris: Éditions Main'Oeuvre. Translated by J. Hansen, 2012, as *Almost Nothing with Luc Ferrari*. Los Angeles: Errant Bodies Press.

Chadabe, J. 1967. "New approaches to analog studio design." *Perspectives of New Music* 6(1): 107–113.

Chadabe, J. 1997. *Electric Sound*. Upper Saddle River, NJ: Prentice-Hall.

Chagall, M. 1963. *Les Lettres Françaises*. Quoted in E. Fischer. 1969. *Art Against Ideology*. New York: George Braziller.

Chaitin, G. 1975. "Randomness and mathematical proof." *Scientific American* 232(5): 47–54.

Chaitin, G. 1994. *The Limits of Mathematics*. Berlin: Springer-Verlag.

Chaitin, G. 2002. *Conversations with a Mathematician: Math, Art, Science, and the Limits of Reasoning*. London: Springer-Verlag. pp. 134–135.

Chalmers, J. 1974. "Computer-generated tuning tables." *Xenharmonikon* 1.

Chion, M. 1982. *La musique électroacoustique*. Paris: Presses Universitaires de France.

Chion, M. 2009. *Guide to Sound Objects, Pierre Schaeffer and Musical Research*. Translation of M. Chion. 1983. *Guide des objets sonores: Pierre Schaeffer et la recherche musicale*. Bibliothèque de recherche musicale. Paris: Buchet-Chastel. J. Dack and C. North, translators. 2009. Electroacoustic Research Site. www.ears.dmu.ac.uk/spip.php?page=articleEars&id_article=3597.

Chomsky, N. 1965. *Aspects of the Theory of Syntax*. Cambridge, MA: MIT Press.

Chomsky, N. 2013. "Noam Chomsky: The singularity is science fiction!" Interview by Nikola Danaylov. www.youtube.com/watch?v=okICLG4Zg8s.

Chomsky, N., and M. Schuetzenberger. 1963. "Algebraic theory of context-free languages." In Braffort and Hirschberg, eds. *Computer Programming and Formal Systems*. Amsterdam: North-Holland.

Chou, W.-C. 1979. "Ionisation: the function of timbre in its formal an temporal organization." In S. Van Solkema, ed. *The New Worlds of Edgard Varèse*. Brooklyn, NY: Institute for the Study of American Music. pp. 26–74.

Chowning, J. 1971. "The simulation of moving sound sources." *Journal of the Audio Engineering Society* 19: 2–6. Reprinted in *Computer Music Journal* 1(3): 48–52, 1977.

Chowning, J. 1973. "The synthesis of complex audio spectra by means of frequency modulation." *Journal of the Audio Engineering Society* 21(7): 526–534. Reprinted in C. Roads and J. Strawn, eds. 1985. *Foundations of Computer Music*. Cambridge, MA: MIT Press. pp. 6–29.

Clark, P. 1997. "Paul Lansky Interview." electronicmusic.com/features/interview/paullansky.html

Clarke, E. 1999. "Rhythm and timing in music." In D. Deutsch, ed. *The Psychology of Music*. Second edition. San Diego, CA: Academic Press. pp. 473–500.

Clarke, E. 2011. "Music perception and musical consciousness." In D. Clarke and E. Clarke, eds. *Music and Consciousness: Psychological and Cultural Perspectives*. Oxford, UK: Oxford University Press. pp. 193–213.

Clarke, J., and R. Voss. 1978. "1/*f* noise in music: music from 1/*f* noise." *Journal of the Acoustical Society of America* 63(1): 258–263.

Clayton, Martin. 2000. *Time in Indian Music*. Oxford, UK: Oxford University Press.

Clozier, C. 1997. "Composition-diffusion/Interpretation in electroacoustic music." *Composition/Diffusion in Electroacoustic Music, Proceedings of the International Academy of Electroacoustic Music*. Bourges, FR: Institut Internationale de Musique Éléctroacoustique. pp. 233–281.

Clozier, C. 2001. "The Gmebaphone concept and the Cybérnaphone instrument." *Computer Music Journal* 25(4): 81–90.

Cogan, R. 1984. *New Images of Musical Sound*. Cambridge, MA: Harvard University Press.

Cohen, H. 2008. "Art in Consumerland; Where, Exactly?" Lecture. University of California, Santa Barbara.

Cohen, H., B. Cohen, and P. Nii. 1984. *The First Artificial Intelligence Coloring Book*. Los Altos, CA: William Kaufmann.

Collins, N. 2002a. "Infinite length pieces: a user's guide." www.axp.mdx.ac.uk/~nicholas15.

Collins, N. 2002b. "The BBCut library." In M. Nordahl, ed. *Proceedings of the 2002 International Computer Music Conference*. San Francisco: International Computer Music Association. pp. 313–316.

Collins, N. 2003. "Generative music and laptop performance." *Contemporary Music Review* 22(4): 67–79.

Collins, N. 2007. "Live electronic music." In N. Collins and J. Escrivan, eds. 2007. *The Cambridge Companion to Electronic Music*. Cambridge, UK: Cambridge University Press. pp. 38–54.

Collins, N. 2009. "Musical form and algorithmic composition." *Contemporary Music Review* 28(1): 103–114.

Collins, N. 2012. "Automatic composition of electroacoustic art music utilizing machine listening." *Computer Music Journal* 36(3): 8–23.

Collins, N., and J. Escrivan, eds. 2007. *The Cambridge Companion to Electronic Music*. Cambridge, UK: Cambridge University Press.

Comscire. 2011. "R2000KU functional description." comscire.com/Products/R2000KU/.

Conti, S., P. Roux, D. Demer, and J. Rosny. 2003. "Let's hear how big you are." www.acoustics.org/press/146th/Conti.html.

Conti, S. P. Roux, D. Demer, and J. Rosny. 2004. "Measurement of the scattering and absorbtion cross sections of the human body." *Applied Physics Letters* 84(5): 819–821.

Cook, P. 1999. "Formant peaks and spectral valleys." In P. Cook, ed. *Music Cognition and Computerized Sound*. Cambridge, MA: MIT Press. pp. 129–138.

Cook, P. 2007. *Real Sound Synthesis for Interactive Applications*. Third edition. Wellesley, MA: A. K. Peters.

Cooper, G., and L. Meyer. 1960. *The Rhythmic Structure of Music*. Chicago: University of Chicago Press.

Cope, D. 1977. *New Music Composition*. New York: Schirmer.

Cope, D. 1993. A computer model of music composition." In S. Schwanauer and D. Levitt, eds. *Machine Models of Music*. Cambridge, MA: MIT Press. pp. 403–425.

Cope, D. 1996. *Experiments in Musical Intelligence*. Madison, WI: A-R Editions.

Cope, D. 1997. *Techniques of the Contemporary Composer*. New York: Schirmer.

Cope, D. 2004. *Virtual Music*. Cambridge, MA: MIT Press.

Couch, L. 2005 II. "Intelligence coding." In J. Whitacker, ed. *The Electronics Handbook*. Boca Raton, FL: CRC Press. pp. 1354–1367.

Cowell, H. 1928. "The music of Edgard Varèse." *Modern Music* 3(2): 9–19. Reprinted in H. Cowell, ed. 1933. *American Composers on American Music*. New York: Frederick Ungar. pp. 43–48.

Cowell, H. 1930. *New Musical Resources*. New York: A. A. Knopf. Reprinted in 1996 with notes by D. Nichols. Cambridge, UK: Cambridge University Press.

Cowell, H. 2001. *Essential Cowell: Selected Writings*. D. Higgins, ed. Kingston, NY: McPherson.

Cox, D. 1974. *Debussy Orchestral Music*. Seattle: University of Washington Press.

Cozarinsky, E., director. 1984. *Jean Cocteau: autoportrait d'un inconnu*. Film on DVD. Number 67. South Burlington, VT: Criterion Collection.

Cross, J. 2003. "Composing with numbers: sets, rows, and magic squares." In J. Fauvel et al., eds. *Music and Mathematics: From Pythagoras to Fractals*. Oxford, UK: Oxford University Press. pp. 131–146.

Crumb, G. 2011. Quoted in "Mario Davidovsky." en.wikipedia.org/wiki/Mario_Davidovsky.

Cutler, C. 1997. "SCALE." *The ReR Sourcebook* 4(2). Republished 2007. www.ccutler.com/ccutler/writing.

Cutler, C. 2000. "Plunderphonics." In S. Emmerson, ed. 2000. *Music, Electronic Media and Culture*. Burlington, VT: Ashgate. pp. 87–114.

d&b audiotechnik. 2011. "J-SUB Manual." www.dbaudio.com/fileadmin/docbase/J-SUB_Manual_1.3EN.PDF.

Dack, J. 1999. "Karlheinz Stockhausen's *Kontake* and narrativity." *eContact* 2(2): cec.concordia.ca/econtact/SAN/Dack.htm.

Dallapiccola, L. 1966. "Encounters with Varèse." *Perspectives of New Music* 4(2): 1–13.

Dahlstadt, P. 2004. "Sounds unheard of: evolutional algorithms as creative tools for the contemporary composer." Ph.D. diss. Chalmers University of Technology, Göteborg, SE.

Danielou, A. 1958. *Tableau Comparatif des Intervalles Musicaux*. Pondichéry, FR: Institut Français d'Indologie.

Dannenberg, R. 2013. *Nyquist Reference Manual*. www.cs.cmu.edu/~rbd/doc/nyquist/

Darreg, I. 1975. "New moods." www.furious.com/perfect/xenharmonics.html.

Darreg, I. 1977. "Two essays on xenharmonics." sonic-arts.org/darreg/dar13.htm.

Dashow, J. 1980. "Spectra as chords." *Computer Music Journal* 4(1): 43–52.
Dashow, J. 1985. Quoted in C. Roads. "Interview with James Dashow." C. Roads, ed. *Composers and the Computer.* Madison, WI: A-R Editions. pp. 26–45.
Dashow, J. 2013. "A letter on spatialization." Submitted to *Computer Music Journal.*
Da Silva, P. 2002. "Algorithms in music before the age of computers." Unpublished.
Davies, P. 1996. *About Time.* New York: Simon and Schuster.
Davis, J. "Subatomic pop: composing an electronic symphony, 0.001 second at a time." *WIRED* 16(5).
Dean, R. T. 2009a. "Envisaging improvisation in future computer music." In R. T. Dean, ed. 2009. *The Oxford Handbook of Computer Music.* New York: Oxford University Press. pp. 133–147.
Dean, R. T., ed. 2009b. *The Oxford Handbook of Computer Music.* New York: Oxford University Press. pp. 133–147.
DeCampo, A., and C. Roads. 2003. "The architecture of the Creatovox synthesizer." Unpublished report. University of California, Santa Barbara.
de Cheveigné, A. 2005. "Pitch perception models." In C. Plack, A. Oxenham, A. Popper, and R. Fay, eds. *Pitch: Neural Coding and Perception.* New York: Springer. pp. 169–233.
DeGroot, R. A. 1976. *Feasts for All Seasons.* New York: McGraw-Hill.
Demers, J. 2010. *Listening Through the Noise: The Aesthetics of Experimental Electronic Music.* New York: Oxford University Press.
DePoli, G., A. Piccialli, and C. Roads. eds. 1991. *Representations of Musical Signals.* Cambridge, MA: MIT Press.
DeSantos, A. 1997. "Acousmatic morphology: an interview with François Bayle." *Computer Music Journal* 21(3): 11–19.
Deutsch, D. 1982. "Grouping mechanisms in music." In D. Deutsch, ed. *The Psychology of Music.* New York: Academic Press. pp. 99–134.
Deutsch, D. 1999. "Grouping mechanisms in music." In D. Deutsch, ed. *The Psychology of Music.* Second edition. San Diego, CA: Academic Press. pp. 299–348.
Deutsch, D., K. Dooley, T. Henthorn, and B. Head. 2009. "Perfect pitch: language wins out over genetics." Presented at the 157th meeting of the Acoustical Society of America. www.acoustics.org/press/157th/deutsch.html.
Dickreiter, M. 1989. *Tonmeister Technology.* New York: Temmer Enterprises.
Dijkstra, E. 2009. Quoted in Wikipedia: en.wikipedia.org/wiki/Consciousness.
Di Scipio, A. 1997. "Interactive micro-time sound design." *Journal of Electroacoustic Music* 10: 4–8.
Di Scipio, A. 2007. "Formalization and intuition in *Analogique A et B.*" *Open Space* 8/9: 163–180.
Di Scipio, A. 2012. Personal communication.
Dodge, C. 1973. "Charles Dodge on *Speech Songs.*" www.furious.com/Perfect/ohm/dodge.html.
Dodge, C., and T. Jerse. 1997. *Computer Music: Synthesis, Composition, and Performance.* Second edition. New York: Schirmer.
Doornbusch, P. 2005. *The Music of CSIRAC.* Melbourne, AU: Common Ground Publishing.
Doty, D. 1994. *The Just Intonation Primer.* San Francisco: Other Music. www.justintonation.net.

Douglas, A. 1968. *The Electronic Musical Instrument Manual.* Fifth edition. New York: Pitman.

Douglas, A. 1973. *Electronic Music Production.* Bath, UK: Pitman.

Dowling, A., and J. Williams. 1983. *Sound and the Sources of Sound.* Chichester, UK: Ellis Horwood.

Doxiadis, A. 2005. "The mathematical logic of narrative." In M. Manaresi, ed. *Mathematica e cultura in Europa.* Berlin: Springer. pp. 171-181.

Doxiadis, A., and B. Mazur. 2012. *Circles Disturbed: The Interplay of Mathematics and Narrative.* Princeton University Press.

Dubnov, S., and G. Assayag. 2012. "Music design with audio oracle using information rate." *Musical Metacreation: Papers from the 2012 AIIDE Workshop.* AAAI Technical Report WS-12-16. www.aaai.org/ocs/index.php/AIIDE/AIIDE12/schedConf/presentations

Duckworth, W., and E. Brown. 1978. *Theoretical Foundations of Music.* Belmont, CA: Wadsworth.

Dudley, H. 1939. "Remaking Speech." *Journal of the Acoustical Society of America* 11: 167–177.

Dweck, J. 2011. Quoted in "IBM Watson: Watson after Jeopardy." IBM video. http://www.youtube.com/watch?v=dQmuETLeQcg&rel=0.

Eargle, J. 1995. *Music, Sound, and Technology.* Second edition. New York: Van Nostrand Reinhold.

Echoes. 2011. "Acoustics in the News." *Echoes: Acoustical Society of America Newsletter* 21(3): 8.

Edison, T. 1917. "New aspects on the art of music." *Edison Diamond Points.* May 1917. pp. 12–14. memory.loc.gov/ammem/edhtml/may171.html.

Eigenfeldt, A. 2012. "Embracing the bias of the machine: exploring non-human fitness functions." In *Musical Metacreation: Papers from the 2012 AIIDE Workshop.* AAAI Technical Report WS-12-16. www.aaai.org/ocs/index.php/AIIDE/AIIDE12/schedConf/presentations.

Eigenfeldt, A., and Pasquier, P. 2012. "Populations of populations—composing with multiple evolutionary algorithms." In P. Machado, J. Romero, and A. Carballal, eds. *EvoMU- SART 2012*, LNCS 7247. Heidelberg, DE: Springer. pp. 72–83.

Eimert, H. 1954. "Elektronische Musik." Translated as "Electronic Music." Translation by D. Sinclair of *Technische Hausmitteilungen des Nordwestdeutschen Rundfunks* 6, 4-5, 1954. Technical translation TT-601. Ottawa: National Research Council of Canada.

Eimert, H. 1955. "What is electronic music." *die Reihe* 1. English edition 1965. Bryn Mawr, PA: Theodore Presser. pp. 1–10.

Einstein, A. 1916. *Relativity: The Special and the General Theory.* Fifteenth edition, 1952. New York: Three Rivers Press.

Ekeland, I. 1988. *Mathematics and the Unexpected.* Chicago: University of Chicago Press.

Enkel, F., and H. Schutz. 1954. "Zur Technik des Magnettonbandes." Translated as "Magnetic tape technique." Translation by D. Sinclair of *Technische Hausmitteilungen des Nordwestdeutschen Rundfunks* 6, 16-18, 1954. Technical translation TT-604. Ottawa: National Research Council of Canada.

Erickson, R. 1975. *Sound Structure in Music.* Berkeley, CA: University of California Press.

Erlich, P. 1997. "On harmonic entropy." *Mills College Tuning Digest*. sonic-arts.org/td/entropy.htm.

Euler, L. 1739. Tentamen novae theoriae musicae ex certissimis harmoniae principiis dilucide expositae. St. Petersburg, RU: n.p.

Evans, B. 2005. "Foundations of a visual music." *Computer Music Journal* 29(4): 11–24.

Farina, A. 2000. "Simultaneous measurement of impulse response and distortion with a swept-sine technique." 108th AES Convention, Paris 2000, Preprint 5093.

Fauvel, J., R. Flood, and R. Wilson, eds. 2003. *Music and Mathematics: From Pythagoras to Fractals*. Oxford, UK: Oxford University Press.

Federkow, G., W. Buxton, and K. Smith. 1978. "A computer-controlled sound distribution system for performance of electroacoustic music." *Computer Music Journal* 2(3): 33–42.

Feldman, Morton. 1985. *Morton Feldman Essays* W. Zimmerman, ed. Hanover, NH: Frog Peak.

Ferrari, L. 2002. "Interview with Daniel Teruggi." Program notes for the CD *Luc Ferrari: Tautologos and other early electronic works*. EMF CD 037.

Fitz, K., and S. Fulop. 2009. "A unified theory of time-frequency reassignment." arxiv.org/abs/0903.3080.

Flanagan, J. L., and R. Golden. 1966. "Phase vocoder." *Bell System Technical Journal* 45: 1493–1509.

Forte, A. 1977. *Structure of Atonal Music*. New Haven, CT: Yale University Press.

Fraisse, P. 1982. "Rhythm and tempo." In D. Deutsch, ed. *The Psychology of Music*. New York: Academic Press. pp. 149–180.

Gabor, D. 1946. "Theory of communication." *Journal of the Institute of Electrical Engineers*, Part 3, 93: 429–457.

Gabor, D. 1947. "Acoustical quanta and the theory of hearing." *Nature* 159(1044): 591–594.

Galambos, R. 1962. *Nerves and Muscles*. New York: Anchor Books.

Gagne, C. and T. Caras. 1982. *Soundpieces: Interviews with American Composers*. Metuchen, NJ: Scarecrow.

Gayou, E. 2001. "Avec, de, sur . . . entre, entretien de Luc Ferrari avec Elisabeth Gayou." In E. Gayou, ed. *Luc Ferrari: Portraits Polychrome*. Paris: CDMC, INA-GRM. pp. 27–31

Gayou, E. 2002. "Mots de l'immédiat, entretien de Bernard Parmegiani avec Elisabeth Gayou." In E. Gayou, ed. *Bernard Parmegiani: Portraits Polychrome*. Paris: CDMC, INA-GRM. pp. 17–38.

Gayou, E., ed. 2011. *Denis Smalley: Portraits Polychromes*. Paris: CDMC, INA-GRM.

Gena, P. 1994. "Lejaren Hiller (1924-1994)." www.petergena.com/lhobit.html.

Gerzon, M. 1973. "Periphony: with-height sound reproduction." *Journal of the Audio Engineering Society* 21(3): 2–10.

Gerzon, M. 1975. "The design of precisely coincident microphone arrays for stereo and surround sound." *Preprint L-20, 50th Audio Engineering Society Convention, London*. New York: Audio Engineering Society.

Gerzon, M. 1976. "Unitary (energy preserving) multichannel networks with feedback." *Electronic Letters* 12(11): 278–279.

Gibson, B. 2001. "Théorie des cribles." In M. Solomos, ed. *Presences of/Présences de Iannis Xenakis*. Paris: Centre de Documentation de la Musique Contemporaine. pp. 85–92.

Glinsky, A. 2000. *Theremin: Ether Music and Espionage*. Urbana, IL: University of Illinois Press.

Godard, J.-L. 1966. Quoted in the commentary to *Masculin-Feminin*. DVD. New York: Criterion Collection.

Godoy, R. 1997. *Formalization and Epistemology*. Oslo, NO: Scandinavian University Press.

Goldman, L., and J. Paine. "Hip-hop cash kings." *Forbes Magazine*. August 16, 2007. Forbes.com.

Goodstein, D. 1985. *States of Matter*. New York: Dover.

Gouk, P. 1999. *Music, Science, and Magic in Seventeenth Century England*. New Haven, CT: Yale University Press.

Graef, A. 2002. "Musical scale rationalization—a graph-theoretic approach." Internet: www.musikwissenschaft.uni-mainz.de/~ag/q/scale.pdf.

Green, Tona. 1991. "Interview with Jean-Claude Eloy." *Computer Music Journal* 15(1): 14–19.

Grey, J. 1975. "An exploration of musical timbre." Report STAN-M-2. Stanford University.

Grey, J. 1978. "Timbre discrimination in musical patterns." *Journal of the Acoustical Society of America* 64: 467–472.

Griffiths, P. 1979. *A Guide to Electronic Music*. London: Thames and Hudson.

Griffiths, P. 1994. *Modern Music: A Concise History*. London: Thames and Hudson. pp. 131–133.

Griffiths, P. 2004. "Paul Griffiths Interview." www.compositiontoday.com/interviews/paul_griffiths.asp.

Griffiths, P. 2006. *A Concise History of Western Music*. Cambridge, UK: Cambridge University Press.

Grisey, G. 1987. "*Tempus ex machina*: a composer's reflections on musical time." *Contemporary Music Review* 2(1): 238–275.

Grout, D. 1973. *A History of Western Music*. Revised edition. New York: W. W. Norton.

Groupe de Recherches Musicales. 2008. Description of Acousmographe 3. www.ina.fr/sites/ina/medias/upload/grm/grm-tools/Acousmo_3.pdf.

Hajdu, G., ed. 2010. *Bohlen-Pierce Symposium and Concerts*. Boston: Boston Microtonal Society, Goethe Institute, Berklee College of Music, Northeastern University, and New England Conservatory.

Haladyna, J. 2008. "Machines and mystics." Program notes for Ensemble for Contemporary Music, March 13, 2008. University of California, Santa Barbara.

Hamblyn, R. 2002. *The Invention of Clouds*. London: Picador.

Hamlin, P., with C. Roads. 1985. "Interview with Herbert Brün." In C. Roads, ed. *Composers and the Computer*. Madison, WI: A-R Editions. pp. 1–15.

Hamming, R. 1973. *Numerical Methods for Scientists and Engineers*. New York: McGraw-Hill.

Hamming, R. 1997. *The Art of Doing Science and Engineering*. Amsterdam: Gordon and Breach.

Hammond, L. 1941. "Electrical musical instrument." U.S. Patent 2230836.

Handel, S. 1989. *Listening: An Introduction to the Perception of Auditory Events*. Cambridge, MA: MIT Press.

Hansen, B. 2009. "Current aesthetic views and practices." Unpublished.

Harley, J. 2002. "Iannis Xenakis in conversation: 30 May 1993." *Contemporary Music Review* 21(2/3): 11–20.

Harley, J. 2004. *Xenakis: His Life in Music*. New York: Routledge.

Harrison, J. 1999. "Diffusion: theories and practices, with particular reference to the BEAST system." *eContact!* 2.4. cec.sonus.ca/econtact/Diffusion/index.htm.

Harvey, L. 2010. Personal communication.

Harrison, J. 1998. "Sound, space, sculpture: some thoughts on the 'what,' 'how,' and 'why' of sound diffusion." *Organized Sound* 3(2): 117–127.

Haus, G. 1983. "EMPS: A system for graphic transcription of electronic music scores." *Computer Music Journal* 7(3): 31–36.

Hayes-Roth, B., and F. Hayes-Roth. 1979. "A cognitive model of planning." *Cognitive Science* 3: 275–310.

Hayward, J. 2004. "Musica futurista: the art of noises." Program notes to CD *Musica futurista: the art of noises*. Salon Limited CD 2401.

Heikinheimo, Seppo. 1972. "The electronic music of Karlheinz Stockhausen: studies on the esthetical and formal problems of its first phase." *Acta musicologica fennica* 6: 61–103.

Helmholtz, H. 1885. *On the Sensations of Tone as a Physiological Basis for the Theory of Music*. Reprinted 1954, A. Ellis, trans. New York: Dover.

Hetrick, M. 2010. Personal communication.

Hiller, L. 1964, "Informationstheorie und Computermusik." *Darmstädter Beiträge zur Neuen Musik* 8. Mainz, DE: Schott.

Hiller, L. 1969. "Some compositional techniques involving the use of computers." In H. Von Foerster and J. Beauchamp, eds. *Music by Computers*. New York: John Wiley and Sons. pp. 71–83.

Hiller, L. 1970. "Music composed with computers—a historical survey." In H. Lincoln, ed. *The Computer and Music*. Ithaca, NY: Cornell University Press. pp. 42–96.

Hiller, L. 1979. "Phrase structure in computer music." In C. Roads, ed. *Proceedings of the 1978 International Computer Music Conference*. Evanston, IL: Northwestern University Press. pp. 192–213.

Hiller, L. 1981. "Composing with computers: a progress report." *Computer Music Journal* 5(4): 7–21. Reprinted in C. Roads, ed. 1989. *The Music Machine*. Cambridge, MA: MIT Press. pp. 75–89.

Hiller, L., and R. Baker. 1964. "*Computer Cantata*: a study in compositional method." *Perspectives of New Music* 3: 62–90.

Hiller, L., and J. Cage. 1968. "HPSCHD: an interview by Larry Austin." *Source* 2(2): 10–19. See also Austin 1992.

Hiller, L., and L. Isaacson. 1959. *Experimental Music*. New York: McGraw-Hill.

Hiller, L., and A. Leal. 1966. "Revised MUSICOMP Manual." Technical Report 13. Urbana, IL: University of Illinois Experimental Music Studio.

Hindemith, P. 1941. *The Craft of Musical Composition*. New York: Associated Music Publishers.

Hinkle-Turner, E. 2006. *Women Composers and Music Technology in the United States: Crossing the Line*. Aldershot, UK: Ashgate.

Hirbour, L. 1983. See Varèse 1983.

Hoane, A. J. 1997. "One-on-one with A. Joseph Hoane, Jr." www.research.ibm.com/deepblue/meet/html/d.4.5.a.shtml.

Hodgkinson, T. 1987. "Pierre Schaeffer: an interview with the pioneer of musique concrète." www.ele-mental.org/ele_ment/said&did/schaeffer_interview.html. Originally published in *Recommended Records Quarterly* 2(1): 4–9.

Hoenig, U., S. Lindlar, and A. Schmidt. 2010. *Melodyne editor user manual.* Munich, DE: Celemony Software GmhB.

Hoffman, E. 2012. "I-tunes: multiple subjectivities and narrative method in computer music." *Computer Music Journal* 36(4): 40–58.

Hoffman, E. 2013. "On performing electroacoustic musics: a non-idiomatic case study for Adorno's theory of musical reproduction." *Organised Sound* 18(1): 60–70.

Hoffmann, P. 2000. "The new GENDYN program." *Computer Music Journal* 24(2): 31–38.

Hoffmann-Burchardi,R. 2008. "Digital simulation of the diode ring modulator for musical applications." *Proceedings of the 11th Conference on Digital Audio Effects (DAFx-08), Helsinki, Finland, Sept. 1–4, 2008*. pp. 165–168. www.dafx.de.

Hoffmann-Burchardi, R. 2009. "Asymmetries make the difference: an analysis of transistor-based analog ring modulators." *Proceedings of the 12th Conference on Digital Audio Effects (DAFx-09), Como, Italy*. pp. 98–101. www.dafx.de.

Hollerweger, F. 2006. *Periphonic sound spatialization in multi-user virtual environments.* Graz, AT: Institute for Electronic Music.

Höller, Y. 2001. Quoted in L. Brümmer et al. "Is tape music obsolete? Is spatialization superficial." *Computer Music Journal* 25(4): 5–11.

Holosonics. 2010. "Audio Spotlight Technical Specifications." www.holosonics.com/brochure/Audio_Spotlight_Specifications_Dimensions.pdf.

Honing, H., and O. Ladinig. 2008. "The potential of the Internet for music perception research: a comment on lab-based versus web-based studies." *Empirical Musicology Review* 3(1): 4–7.

Hopkins, J., and W. Sibbett. 2000. "Ultra-short pulse lasers." *Scientific American* 286(9): 72–79.

Horgan, J. 2008. "The consciousness conundrum." *IEEE Spectrum* 45(6): 36–50.

Horton, H. 1996. "The history of experimental music in Northern California." www.mcs.csueastbay.edu/~tebo/history.

Houtsma, A. 1995. "Pitch perception." In. B. Moore, ed. *Hearing.* London: Academic Press. pp. 267–295.

Houtsma, A. 1997. "Pitch and timbre: definition, meaning, and use." *Journal of New Music Research* 26: 104–115.

Houtsma, A., T. Rossing, and W. Wagenaars. 1987. *Auditory Demonstrations.* CD. Eindhoven, NL: Institute for Perception Research.

Howard, D., and J. Angus. 1996. *Acoustics and Psychoacoustics.* Oxford, UK: Focal Press.

Howard, E. 2009. Personal communication.

Howard, E. 2011. Personal communication.

Howard, K. 2005. "Ringing false." *Stereophile* 29(1): 57–65.

Huber, D., and R. Runstein. 1989. *Modern Recording Techniques.* Third edition. Indianapolis, IN: Howard Sams and Co.

Hulen, P. 2008. "A low-cost spherical loudspeaker array for electroacoustic music." *Proceedings of the 2008 International Computer Music Conference.* San Francisco: International Computer Music Conference.

Hultberg, T. 2001. *SoundArt: The Swedish Scene*. Stockholm: STIM/Svensk Musik.

Huron, D. 2006. *Sweet Anticipation: Music and the Psychology of Expectation*. Cambridge, MA: MIT Press.

Huron, D. 2009. "Consonance and dissonance: the main theories." dactyl.som.ohio-state.edu/Music829B/main.theories.html.

Hutchins, B. 2012. *The Musical Engineer's Handbook*. electronotes.netfirms.com.

Hutchinson, W., and L. Knopoff. 1978. "The acoustic component of Western consonance." *Interface* 7(1): 1–29.

ICAD 2010. International Community for Auditory Display. www.icad.org.

IMA. 1983. "MIDI musical instrument digital interface specification 1.0." Los Angeles: International MIDI Association.

Imberty, M. 1979. *Entendre la musique: sémantique psychologique de la musique*. Paris: Dunod.

International Standards Organization. 2002. "Multimedia Content Description Interface Part 4: Audio." International Standard 15938-4. Geneva: ISO/IEC.

Jackson, B. 2010. "Beyond 5.1: the race for greater playback dimensionality heats up." *MIX* 34(9): 20–22.

James, R. S. 1970. "The relationship of electro-acoustic music to pre-1950s music and ideas." In 1988. C. Comberlati and M. Steel, eds. *Music from the Middle Ages Through the 20th Century: Essays in Honor of Gwynn S. McPeek*. New York: Gordon and Breach: pp. 235–263.

Jan, S. 2004. "Meme hunting with the Humdrum Toolkit: principles, problems, and prospects." *Computer Music Journal* 28(4): 68–84.

Jenkinson, J. 2003. *Squarepusher: Ultravistor*. Warp CD 177. London: Warp Records.

Jenny, G. 1955–1956. "L'Ondioline, conception et realization, initiation à la lutherie électronique." *Toute la Radio* (September 1955): 289–294, (November 1955): 397–404, (December 1955): 455–459, (January 1956): 23–26, (February 1956): 67–72.

Jessel, M. 1973. *Acoustique Théorique: Propagation et Holophonie*. Paris: Masson.

Johns, A. 2000. "Andy Johns." In C. Owinski. *The Mixing Engineer's Handbook*. Boston: Thomson Course Technology. pp. 175–179.

Johnson, T. 2001. "Found mathematical objects." www.editions75.com/Articles/Found%20Mathematical%20Objects.pdf.

Jones, E. 2001. "Residue-class sets in the music of Iannis Xenakis: an analytical algorithm and a general intervallic expression." *Perspectives of New Music* 39(2): 229–261.

Jordà, S. 2007. "Interactivity and live computer music." In N. Collins and J. Escrivan, eds. 2007. *The Cambridge Companion to Electronic Music*. Cambridge, UK: Cambridge University Press. pp. 89–106.

Jot, J.-M., and T. Caulkins. 2008. *Spat Reference Manual*. support.ircam.fr/forum-ol-doc/spat/3.0/spat-3-ref/c0/spat-3.html.

Just Intonation Network. 2009. www.justintonation.net.

Kadis, J. 2012. *The Science of Sound Recording*. Oxford, UK: Focal Press.

Kaegi, W. 1967. *Was ist elektronische Musik?* Zürich, CH: Orell Füssli Verga.

Kandinsky, W. 1926. *Point et ligne sur plan*. 1991 edition. Paris: Gallimard.

Karkowski, Z., and N. Humon, curators. 2002. *Iannis Xenakis, Persepolis Remixes, Edition 1*. CD 2005. San Francisco: Asphodel Ltd.

Karp, T. 1970. "A test for melodic borrowings among Notre Dame *Organa Dupla.*" In H. Lincoln, ed. *The Computer and Music*. Ithaca, NY: Cornell University Press. pp. 293–298.

Katz, R. 2002. *Mastering Audio*. Oxford, UK: Focal Press.

Kendall, G. 1995. "The decorrelation of audio signals and its impact on spatial imagery." *Computer Music Journal* 19(4): 71–87.

Kendall, G. S. 2005. "Qosqo: Spirituality, Process and Structure." www.garykendall.net/publications.html.

Kendall, G. 2010. "Spatial perception and cognition in multichannel audio for electroacoustic music." *Organized Sound* 15(3): 228–238.

Kendall, M. 1973. *Time Series*. London: Charles Griffin.

Kennedy, J., and L. Polansky. 1996. "Total Eclipse: the music of Johanna Magdalena Beyer: an introduction and preliminary annotated checklist." *Musical Quarterly* 80(4): 719–778.

Kim-Boyle. D. 2005. "Sound spatialization with particle systems." In A. Sedes and H. Vaggione, eds. *12e Journées d'Informatique Musicale 2-3-4 juin 2005*. Paris: Université de Paris VIII.

Klapholz, Jesse. 1991. "Fantasia: innovations in sound." *Journal of the Audio Engineering Society* 39(1/2): 66–70.

Klee, P. 1925. *Pedagogical Sketchbook*. 1984 edition. London: Faber and Faber.

Klein, H. 1974. *The Science of Measurement*. New York: Dover Books.

Klemm, F. 1964. *A History of Western Technology*. Cambridge, MA: MIT Press.

Kling, G., and C. Roads. 2004. "Audio analysis, visualization, and transformation with the matching pursuit algorithm." In G. Evangelista, ed. *Proceedings of DAFX 2004*. Naples, IT: Federico Due University of Naples. pp. 33–37.

Klug, A. 2008. nobelprize.org/nobel_prizes/chemistry/laureates/1982/klug-speech.html.

Kobrin, E. 1977. *Computer in performance*. Berlin: DAAD.

Kock, W. 1971. *Seeing Sound*. New York: Wiley-Interscience.

Koenig, G. M. 1978. "Composition processes." Published as "Kompositionsprozesse" in Gottfried Michael Koenig. 1993. *Aesthetische Praxis / Texte zur Musik, Band 3, 1968–1991*. Saarbrücken: PFAU Verlag. pp. 191-210. English version available at Internet: www.msu.edu/~sullivan/KoenigCompProcFull.html.

Koenig, G. M. 1955. "Studio technique." *die Reihe* 1. English edition 1965. Bryn Mawr, PA: Theodore Presser. pp. 52–54.

Kollmeier, B., T. Brand, and B. Meyer. 2008. "Perception of speech and sound." In *Springer Handbook of Speech Processing*. New York: Springer-Verlag. pp. 61–76.

Kolmogorov, A. 1968. "Three approaches to the quantitative definition of information." *International Journal of Computer Mathematics* 2(1): 157–168.

Kolundzija, M., C. Faller, and M. Vetterli. 2011. "Reproducing sound fields using MIMO acoustic channel inversion." *Journal of the Audio Engineering Society* 59(10): 721–734.

Kostelanetz, R. 1988. *Conversations with Cage*. New York: Limelight Editions.

Krenek, E. 1939. *Music Here and Now*. New York: Norton.

Krenek, E. 1966. *Exploring Music: Essays by Ernst Krenek*. London: Calder and Boyars.

Krohn-Hite. 1978. *Variable filter model 3550. Operating and Maintenance Manual*. Avon, MA: Krohn-Hite Corporation.

Kuchera-Morin, J. 2011. "Performing in quantum space: a creative approach to n-dimensional computing." in Special Section "Transactions." *Leonardo* 44 (5): 462–463.

Ladd, A. 1953. Quoted by Ivan Moffat in the audio commentary of the film *Shane: Special Edition*. DVD. 2000. Hollywood: Paramount Pictures.

Laitinen, M., S. Disch, and V. Pulkki. 2013. "Sensitivity of human hearing to changes of phase spectrum." *Journal of the Audio Engineering Society* 61(11): 860–877.

Lakoff, G., and R. Nunez. 2000. *Where Mathematics Comes From*. New York: Basic Books.

Landy, L. 2007. *Understanding the Art of Sound Organization*. Cambridge, MA: The MIT Press.

Laurendeau, J. 1990. *Maurice Martenot: Luthier de l'Électronique*. Croissy-Beaubourg, FR: Divery-Livres.

Le Corbusier. 1968. *The Modulor*. Cambridge, MA: MIT Press.

Leichtentritt, H. 1951. *Musical Form*. Cambridge, MA: Harvard University Press.

Leighton, T. G., and A. Petculescu. 2009a. "The sound of music and voices in space: Part 1: theory." *Acoustics Today* 5(3): 17–26.

Leighton, T. G., and A. Petculescu. 2009b. "The sound of music and voices in space: Part 2: modeling and simulation." *Acoustics Today* 5(3): 27–29.

Lerdahl, F. 1987. "Timbral hierarchies." *Contemporary Music Review* 1: 135–160.

Lerdahl, F. 1988. "Cognitive constraints on compositional systems." In J. Sloboda, ed. *Generative Processes in Music: The Psychology of Performance, Improvisation, and Composition*. Oxford, UK: Oxford University Press. pp. 231–259.

Lerdahl, F. 2001. *Tonal Pitch Space*. Oxford, UK: Oxford University Press.

Lerdahl, F., and R. Jackendoff. 1983. *A Generative Theory of Tonal Music*. Cambridge, MA: MIT Press.

Leslie, D. 1949. "Rotatable tremulant sound producer." U.S. Patent 2,489,653.

Leslie, D. 1952. "Apparatus for imposing vibrato on sound." U.S. Patent 2,622,693.

Lewin, D. 1987. *Generalized Musical Intervals and Transformations*. New Haven, CT: Yale University Press.

Lewis, G. 2009. "Interactivity and improvisation." In R. T. Dean, ed. 2009. *The Oxford Handbook of Computer Music*. New York: Oxford University Press. pp. 457–466.

Lewitt, S. 1967. "Paragraphs on conceptual art." *Artforum* 5(10): 79–83.

Licata, T. ed. 2002. *Electroacoustic Music: Analytical Perspectives*. Westport, CT: Greenwood Press.

Licht, A. 2009. "Sound art: origins, development, and ambiguities." *Organized Sound* 14(1): 3–10.

Lidov, D. 1975. *On Musical Phrase*. Monographies de sémiologie et d'analyses musicales, volume 1. Université de Montréal.

Ligeti, G. Undated. Program notes to *György Ligeti*. LP. New York: Vox Candide CE 31009.

Lindemann, E. 2001. "Musical synthesizer capable of expressive phrasing." U.S. Patent 6,316,710.

LMS. 2013. "Acoustical holography." www.lmsintl.com/acoustic-holography.

Lombardi, D. 1978. "Realization of F. P. Marinetti's 1933 Cinque Sintesi Radiofoniche." On the CD *Musica Futuristica: The Art of Noises*. Undated. London: Salon LTMCD 2401.

London, J. 2002. "Cognitive constraints on metric systems: some observations and hypotheses." *Music Perception* 19(4): 529–550.

London, J. 2006. "How to talk about musical metre." people.carleton.edu/~jlondon/UK%20PPT/HTTAM%20Web%20Version.htm.

Lorrain, D. 2009. "Interpolations." In L. Pottier, ed. 2009. *Le calcul de la musique: composition, modèles, et outils*. Saint Etienne, FR: Publications de l'Université de Sainte Etienne. pp. 366–399.

Loy, D. G. 2006. *Musimathics*. Two volumes. Cambridge, MA: MIT Press.

Lyon, M., and B. Teruggi, eds. 2002. *Bernard Parmegiani: Portraits Polychromes*. Paris: Centre de documentation de la musique contemporaine/GRM Institut national de l'audiovisuel.

Maass, W., and C. Bishop. 1998. *Pulsed Neural Networks*. Cambridge, MA: MIT Press.

MacCallum, J., J. Hunt, and A. Eindbond. 2005. "Timbre as a psychoacoustic parameter for harmonic analysis and composition." In H. Richter and X. Serra, eds. 2005. *Proceedings of the 2005 International Computer Music Conference*. San Francisco: International Computer Music Association. pp. 825–828.

Machover, T. 1999. Quoted in M. Swed. "This does compute." *Los Angeles Times*. December 26, 1999.

Maconie, R., ed. 1989. *Stockhausen on Music*. London: Marion Boyers.

Maconie, R. 1998. "Stockhausen at 70: through the looking glass." *The Musical Times* 139 (1863).

Malham, D. 1998. "Approaches to spatialisation." *Organized Sound* 3(2): 167–178.

Malham, D. 2003. "Space in Music—Music in Space." Ph.D. diss. University of York, UK.

Malham, D., and A. Myatt. 1995. "3-D sound spatialisation using Ambisonic techniques." *Computer Music Journal* 19(4): 58-–70.

Mallat, S. 1998. *A Wavelet Tour of Signal Processing*. San Diego, CA: Academic Press.

Mallat, S. and Z. Zhang. 1993. "Matching pursuit with time-frequency dictionaries." *IEEE Trans. Signal Proc.* 41(12):3397–3414.

Manning, P. 1993. *Electronic and Computer Music*. Second edition. Oxford, UK: Oxford University Press.

Manning, P. 2004. *Electronic and Computer Music*. Revised and expanded edition. Oxford, UK: Oxford University Press.

Margulis, E. 2007. "Silences in music are not silent: an exploratory study of context effects on the experience of musical pauses." *Music Perception* 24: 485–506.

Marin, O. S. M. 1982. "Neurological aspects of music perception and performance." In D. Deutsch, ed. *The Psychology of Music*. New York: Academic Press. pp. 453–477.

Marple, S. 1987. *Digital Spectral Analysis*. Englewood Cliffs, NJ: Prentice-Hall.

Martinez, José, ed. 2004. "MPEG-7 Overview." www.chiariglione.org/mpeg/standards/mpeg-7/mpeg-7.htm#E11E8.

Mathews, M. 1969. *The Technology of Computer Music*. Cambridge, MA: MIT Press.

Mathews, M. 1999. "Introduction to timbre." In P. Cook, ed. *Music Cognition and Computerized Sound*. Cambridge, MA: MIT Press. pp. 79–87.

Mathews, M., and F. R. Moore. 1970. "GROOVE—a program to compose, store, and edit functions of time." *Communications of the Association for Computing Machinery* 13(12): 715–721.

Mathews, M., and J. R. Pierce. "Musical sounds from digital computers." *Gravesaner Blätter* 6: 109–118.

Mathews, M., and J. R. Pierce. 1989. "The Bohlen-Pierce Scale." In M. Mathews and J. R. Pierce, eds. 1989. *Current Directions in Computer Music Research*. Cambridge, MA: MIT Press. pp. 165–173.

Mattosian, N. 1986. *Xenakis*. New York: Taplinger.

Mazzola, G. 2002. *The Topos of Music: Geometric Logic of Concepts, Theory, and Performance*. Basel, CH: Birkäuser Verlag.

McAdams, S., and A. Bregman. 1979. "Hearing musical streams." *Computer Music Journal* 3(4): 26–43, 60.

McCartney, J. 2002. "Rethinking the computer music language: SuperCollider." *Computer Music Journal* 26(4): 61–68.

McCormack, J., A. Eldridge, A. Dorin, and P. McIlwain. 2009. "Generative algorithms for making music: emergence, evolution, and ecosystems." In R. T. Dean, ed. 2009. *The Oxford Handbook of Computer Music*. New York: Oxford University Press. pp. 354–379.

McLeran, A., C. Roads, B. Sturm, and J. Shynk. 2008. "Granular methods of sound spatialization using dictionary-based methods." In *Proceedings of the Sound and Music Computing Conference, Berlin, Germany*. smcnetwork.org/files/proceedings/2008/session2_number4_paper20.pdf.

McLuhan, M. 1971. *From Cliché to Archetype*. New York: Pocket Books.

Mead, A. 1994. *An Introduction to the Music of Milton Babbitt*. Princeton, NJ: Princeton University Press.

Menenghini, M. 2003. "*Stria* by John Chowning: analysis of the compositional process." *Proceedings of the XIV Colloquium on Musical Informatics (XIV CIM 2003), Firenze, Italy, May 8-9-10, 2003*.

Merwin, N. David. 2009. "What's bad about this habit." *Physics Today* 62(5): 8–9.

Messiaen, O. 1944. *Technique de mon langage musical*. Paris: Alphonse Leduc.

Messiaen, O. 1976. Quoted in C. Samuel. *Conversations with Olivier Messiaen*. Translated by F. Aprahamian. London: Stainer and Bell.

Messiaen, O. 1994. *Traité de rhythm, de couleur, et d'ornithologie*. Tomes I, II, and III. Paris: Alphonse Leduc.

Meyer, F., and H. Zimmermann, eds. 2006. *Edgard Varèse: Composer, Sound Sculptor, Visionary*. Woodbridge, Suffolk, UK: Boydell Press.

Meyer, L. 1956. *Emotion and Meaning in Music*. Chicago: University of Chicago Press.

Meyer Sound Laboratories. 2010. "UPQ-2P: Narrow Coverage Loudspeaker." www.meyersound.com/pdf/products/ultraseries/upq-2p_ds_b.pdf.

Meyer-Eppler, W. 1954. "Mathematisch-akustische Grundlagen der elektrischen Klang-Komposition." *Technische Hausmitteilungen des Nordwestdeutschen Rundfunk* 6: 29–39. Translated by H. Nathan as "The mathematical-acoustical fundamentals of electrical sound composition." *National Research Council of Canada Technical Translation* TT-608.

Meyer-Eppler. W. 1960. "Zur Systematik der elektrischen Klangtransformation." *Darmstader Beitrage zur Neuen Musik III*. Mainz, DE: Schott. pp. 73–86.

Miller, D. C. 1935. *Anecdotal History of the Science of Sound*. New York: Macmillan.

Miller, J. D. 1978a. "Effects of noise on people." In E. Carterette and M. Friedman, eds. *Handbook of Perception*, Volume 4. New York: Academic Press. pp. 609–640.

Miller, J. D. 1978b. "General psychological and sociological effects of noise on people." In E. Carterette and M. Friedman, eds. *Handbook of Perception*, Volume 4. New York: Academic Press. pp. 641–676.

Miller, J. D. 1978c. "General physiological effects of noise." In E. Carterette and M. Friedman, eds. *Handbook of Perception*, Volume 4. New York: Academic Press. pp. 687–686.

Milne, A., W. Sethares, and J. Plamondon. 2007. "Isomorphic controllers and dynamic tuning: invariant fingering over a tuning continuum." *Computer Music Journal* 31(4): 15–32.

Mimaroglu, I. 1967. *Six Preludes for Magnetic Tape*. Program notes. TV 34177. New York: Turnabout Records.

Mimaroglu, I. ca. 1968. Program notes for the vinyl disc *Musique concrete*. Candide CE 31025 LP.

Minsky, M. 2006. *The Emotion Machine*. New York: Simon and Schuster.

Mintz, D. 2007. "Toward Timbral Synthesis: a new method for synthesizing sound based on timbre description schemes." M.S. thesis. University of California, Santa Barbara.

Molavi, D. 2005. "The Washington University School of Medicine Neuroscience Tutorial." thalamus.wustl.edu/course.

Moon, F. 1987. *Chaotic Vibrations*. New York: Wiley-Interscience.

Mooney, J., and D. Moore. 2008." Resound: open-source live sound spatialisation." In *Proceedings of the 2008 International Computer Music Association*. quod.lib.umich.edu/i/icmc.

Moore, F. R. 1990. *Elements of Computer Music*. Englewood Cliffs, NJ: Prentice-Hall.

Moorer, J. 2000. "Audio in the new millennium." *Journal of the Audio Engineering Society* 48(5): 490–498.

Morgan, R. P. 1979a. Quote from "Discussion." In S. Van Solkema, ed. *The New Worlds of Edgard Varèse*. Brooklyn, NY: Institute for the Study of American Music. pp. 75–90.

Morgan, R. P. 1979b. "Notes on Varèse's rhythm." In S. Van Solkema, ed. *The New Worlds of Edgard Varèse*. Brooklyn, NY: Institute for the Study of American Music. pp. 9–25.

Morris, R. 1987. *Composition with Pitch-Classes*. New Haven, CT: Yale University Press.

Morris, R. 2007. "Mathematics and the twelve-tone system: past, present, and future." *Perspectives of New Music* 45(2): 76–107.

Morris, R. 2010. *The Whistling Blackbird: Essays and Talks on New Music*. Rochester, NY: University of Rochester Press.

Morse, P. 1981. *Vibration and Sound*. New York: American Institute of Physics.

Murail, T. 1991. "Spectres et lutins." In D. Cohen-Lévinas. *L'Itinéraire*. Paris: La Revue Musicale.

Nancarrow, C. 1987. "Composer Conlon Nancarrow: A conversation with Bruce Duffie." http://www.bruceduffie.com/nancarrow2.html.

Narklikar, J. 1977. *The Structure of the Universe*. Oxford, UK: Oxford University Press.

Narmour, E. 1977. *Beyond Schenkerism: The Need for Alternatives in Music Analysis*. Chicago: University of Chicago Press.

Narmour, E. 1984. "Toward an analytical symbology: the melodic, durational, and harmonic functions of implication and realization." In M. Baroni and L. Callegari, eds. *Musical Grammars and Computer Analysis*. Florence, IT: Leo S. Olschki Editore. pp. 83–114.

Narmour, E. 1990. *The Analysis and Cognition of Basic Melodic Structures.* Chicago: University of Chicago Press.

Narmour, E. 1992. *The Analysis and Cognition of Melodic Complexity.* Chicago: University of Chicago Press.

NASA. 2007. Quoted in "Earth's atmosphere." http://en.wikipedia.org/wiki/Air.

Nattiez, J.-J. 1990. *Music and Discourse: Toward a Semiology of Music.* Carolyn Abbate, translator. Princeton, NJ: Princeton University Press.

Nauert, P. 2003a. "The progression vector: modeling aspects of post-tonal harmony." *Journal of Music Theory* 47(1): 103–124.

Nauert, P. 2003b. "Field notes: a study of fixed-pitch formations." *Perspectives of New Music* 41(1): 180–239.

Nettheim, N. 1992. "On the spectral analysis of melody." *Interface* 21(2):135–148.

Newton, I. 1687. *The Principia: Mathematical Principles of Natural Philosophy.* Translation 1999 by I. Bernard Cohen and Anne Whitman. Berkeley, CA: University of California Press.

Norman, K. 2004. *Sounding Art: Eight Literary Excursions Through Electronic Music.* Aldershot, UK: Ashgate.

Norris, E. G. 1999. "Acoustic heterodyne device and method." U.S. Patent 5,889,870.

Oliveros, P. 2005. *Deep Listening: A Composer's Sound Practice.* Lincoln, NE: iUniverse.

Oliveros, P. 2009. "From outside the window: electronic sound performance." In R. T. Dean, ed. 2009. *The Oxford Handbook of Computer Music.* New York: Oxford University Press. pp. 467–472.

Olson, H. 1952. *Musical Engineering.* New York: McGraw-Hill.

Olson, H., and H. Belar. 1955."Electronic music synthesizer." *Journal of the Acoustical Society of America* 27(5): 595.

Oram, D. 1972. *An Individual Note: Of Music, Sound, Electronics.* London: Galliard.

Ord-Hume, A. W. J. G. 1973. *Clockwork Music.* New York: Crown Publishers.

Owens, D. 1992. *Cause and Coincidence.* Cambridge, UK: Cambridge University Press.

Oxenham, A. 2007. "Pitch perception in normal and impaired hearing." *Journal of the Acoustical Society of America* 121(5), Part 2: 3067.

Paccione, M. and P. Paccione. 1992. "Did modernism fail Morton Feldman?" *Ex tempore: A Journal of Compositional and Theoretical Research in Music* 6(1): 13–21.

Page, R. 1994. *The Education of a Gardener.* New York: New York Review of Books Classics.

Pape, G. 2008. Personal communication.

Pareyon, G. 2011. *On Musical Self-similarity: Intersemiosis as Synecdoche and Analogy.* Helsinki, FI: *Acta Semiotica Fennica* XXXIX.

Parncutt, R. 1989. *Harmony: A Psychoacoustical Approach.* Berlin: Springer Verlag.

Parncutt, R., and H. Strasburger. 1994. "Applying psychoacoustics in composition: "harmonic" progressions of "nonharmonic" sonorities." *Perspectives of New Music* 32(2): 88–129.

Partch, H. 1974. *Genesis of a Music.* New York: Da Capo Press.

Pasler, J. 1989. "Narrative and narrativity in music." In J. Fraser, ed. *Time and Mind: Interdisciplinary Issues. The Study of Time VI.* Madison, CT: International Universities Press. pp. 233–257.

Patel, A. 2003. Language, music, syntax and the brain. *Nature Neuroscience* 8(7): 674–681.

Patel, A. 2008. *Music, Language, and the Brain.* Oxford, UK Oxford University Press.

Pearce, M., D. Meredith, and G. Wiggins. 2002. "Motivations and methodologies for automation of the compositional process." *Musicae Scientae* 6(2): 119–147.

Pellegrino, R. 2010. *Emergent Music and Visual Music: Inside Studies,Part One: The Book.* www.ronpellegrinoselectronicartsproductions.org.

Peretz, I., L. Gagnon, and B. Bouchard. 1998. "Music and emotion: perceptual determinants, immediacy, and isolation after brain damage." *Cognition* 68: 111–141.

Perkins, J. M. 1976. "Note values." In B. Boretz and E. Cone, eds. *Perspectives on Notation and Performance.* New York: W. W. Norton. pp. 63–73.

Perkis, T. 2009. "Some notes on my electronic music improvisation practice." In R. T. Dean, ed. 2009. *The Oxford Handbook of Computer Music.* New York: Oxford University Press. pp. 161–165.

Perry, J. 1995. "The inner voices of simple things: a conversation with Paul Lansky." silvertone.princeton.edu/~paul/perry.interview.html.

Peters, N., T. Lossius, and J. Schacher. 2013. "The spatial audio description interchange format: principles, specifications, and examples." *Computer Music Journal* 37(1): 11–22.

Phillips, L., and P. Rabinowitz. 2006. "On collaborating with an audience." www.lizphillips.net.

Piaget, J., and B. Inhelder. 1967. *The Child's Conception of Space.* New York. W. W. Norton.

Pierce, J. R. 1983. *The Science of Musical Sound.* New York: W. H. Freeman.

Pierce, A. D. 1994. *Acoustics: An Introduction to Its Physical Principles and Applications.* Woodbury, NY: Acoustical Society of America.

Pinch, T., and F. Trocco. 2002. *Analog Days: The Invention and Impact of the Moog Synthesizer.* Cambridge, MA: Harvard University Press.

Plack, C., A. Oxenham, R. Fay, and A. Popper, eds. 2005. *Pitch: Neural coding and Perception.* New York: Springer Science.

Plomp, R. 1970. "Timbre as a multidimensional attribute of complex tones." In R. Plomp and G. Smoorenburg, eds. *Frequency Analysis and Periodicity Detection in Hearing.* Leiden, NL: A. W. Sjthoff. pp. 397–414.

Plomp, R., and W. Levelt 1965. "Tonal consonance and critical bandwidth." *Journal of the Acoustical Society of America* 38: 548–560.

Polansky, L. 1983. "The early works of James Tenney." eamusic.dartmouth.edu/~larry/published_articles/tenney_monograph_soundings/index.html.

Polansky, L. 1987. "Paratactical tuning: an agenda for the use of computers in experimental intonation." *Computer Music Journal* 11(1): 61–68.

Polansky, L. 1996. "Morphological Metrics." *Journal of New Music Research* 25: 289–368.

Polansky, L., and T. Erbe. 1996. "Spectral mutation in SoundHack." *Computer Music Journal* 20(1): 92–101.

Polya, G. 1954. *Induction and Analogy in Mathematics: A Guide to the Art of Plausible Reasoning.* Princeton, NJ: Princeton University Press.

Pompei, F. J. 1999. "The use of airborne ultrasonics for generating audible sound beams." *Journal of the Audio Engineering Society* 47(9): 726–731.

Posner, M. 2005. "Timing the brain: mental chronometry as a tool in neuroscience." *PLoS Biology* 3(2). dx.doi.org/10.1371/journal.pbio.0030051.

Potié, P. *Le Corbusier: Le Couvent Sainte Marie de la Tourette.* Basel, CH: Fondation Le Corbusier/Birkhauser.

Pottier, L. 2009a. ed. *Le Calcul de la Musique: Composition, Modèles, et Outils.* Saint-Étienne, FR: Publications de l'Université de Saint-Étienne.

Pottier, L. 2009b. "Le contrôle de la synthèse sonore par ordinateur." In L. Pottier, ed. 2009. *Le calcul de la musique: composition, modèles, et outils.* Saint-Étienne, FR: Publications de l'Université de Saint-Étienne. pp. 225–330.

Pottier, L. ed. 2012. *La Spatialisation des Musiques Electroacoustiques.* Saint-Étienne, FR: Université de Saint-Étienne.

Pribram, K. H. 2004. "Consciousness reassessed." *Mind and Matter* 2(1): 7–35.

Pritchett, J. 1996. *The Music of John Cage.* Cambridge, UK: Cambridge University Press.

Puckette, M. 2007. *The Theory and the Technique of Electronic Music.* Singapore: World Scientific Publishing.

Pulkki, V. 1997. "Virtual sound source positioning using vector base amplitude panning." *Journal of the Audio Engineering Society* 45(6): 456–466.

Putnam, L. 2011. "Sonic space-time structures." Lecture in the symposium "Polytopes: The Architecture Of Soundscapes." Southern California Institute for Architecture, Los Angeles. February 11, 2011. sma.sciarc.edu/subclip/polytopes-part-two-the-architecture-of-the-soudnscapes-clip_3783.

Putnam, L. 2012. "The harmonic pattern function: a mathematical model integrating synthesis of sound and graphical patterns." Ph.D. diss. University of California, Santa Barbara.

Quartz, S. 2009. Quoted in D. Brooks. "The end of philosophy." *New York Times*, April 7, 2009. www.nytimes.com/2009/04/07/opinion/07Brooks.html.

Raaijmakers, D. 2000. *Cahiers «M» A Brief Morphology of Electric Sound.* Leuven, BE: Leuven University Press.

Rabiner, L., and B. Gold. 1975. *Theory and Applications of Digital Signal Processing.* Englewood Cliffs, NJ: Prentice-Hall.

Radigue. E. 2009. *Portrait of Eliane Radigue.* vimeo.com/8983993.

Ramakrishnan, C. 2003. "Musical effects in the wavelet domain." M.S. thesis. University of California, Santa Barbara.

Ramakrishnan, C. 2007. *ZIRKONIUM.* Software manual. Karlruhe, DE: Zentrum für Kunst und Medientechnologie.

Rameau, J.-P. 1722. *Traité de l'harmonie.* Reprinted 2009. Bourg-la-Reine, FR: Zurfluh Éditeur.

Read, G. 1978. *Modern Rhythmic Notation.* Bloomington, IN: Indiana University Press.

Read, G. 1979. *Music Notation.* New York: Taplinger.

Redolfi, M. 2008. "Ecouter sous l'eau." In F. Dhomont, dir. *Espace du son II.* Ohain, BE: Musiques et Recherches. pp. 41–44.

Rees, M. 2004. Quoted in J. Wakefield. "Doom and gloom by 2100." *Scientific American* 291(1): 48–49.

Reich, S. 1974. *Writings About Music.* New York: New York University Press.

Rhea, T. 1972. "The evolution of electronic musical instruments in the United States." Ph.D. diss. Nashville, TN: Peabody College.

Rimsky-Korsakov, N. 1891. *Principles of Orchestration.* New York: Dover.

Risset, J.-C. 1965. "Computer study of trumpet tones." *Journal of the Acoustical Society of America* 38: 912 (abstract only).

Risset, J.-C. 1969. "Catalog of computer-synthesized sound." Bell Telephone Laboratories. Reprinted in *The Historical CD of Digital Sound Synthesis*. 1995. WER 2033-2. Mainz, DE: Wergo Music Media GmbH.

Risset, J.-C. 1982. "Interview with Jean-Claude Risset." In B. Schrader. *Introduction to Electro-acoustic Music*. Englewood Cliffs, NJ: Prentice-Hall. pp. 194–201.

Risset, J.-C. 1985. "Computer music experiments 1964– . . ." *Computer Music Journal* 9(1): 11–18.

Risset, J.-C. 1987. Program notes to *Mutations*, CD edition. Paris: INA C-1003.

Risset, J.-C. 1989. "Additive synthesis of inharmonic tones." In M. V. Mathews and J. R. Pierce. *Current Directions in Computer Music Research*. Cambridge, MA: MIT Press. pp. 159–163.

Risset, J.-C. 1991. "Timbre analysis by synthesis: representations, imitations, and variants for musical composition." In G. De Poli, A. Piccialli, and C. Roads, eds. 1991. *Representations of Musical Signals*. Cambridge, MA: MIT Press. pp. 7–43.

Risset, J.-C. 2004. "The liberation of sound, art-science and the digital domain: contacts with Edgard Varèse." *Contemporary Music Review* 23(2): 27–54.

Risset, J-C. 2005. "Horacio Vaggione: towards a syntax of sound." *Contemporary Music Review* 24(4/5): 287–293.

Risset, J.C. 2007. Comments accompanying the lecture "Fifty years of digital sound for music." In C. Spyridis et al. *Proceedings of the SMC'07 4th Sound and Music Computing Conference*. Athens: National Kapodistrian University of Athens. pp. 3–8.

Roads, C. 1973. "Analysis of the composition *ST/10* and the computer program Free Stochastic Music by Iannis Xenakis." Unpublished student paper.

Roads, C. 1978. "Automated granular synthesis of sound." *Computer Music Journal* 2(2): 61–62. Revised and updated version printed as "Granular synthesis of sound" in C. Roads and J. Strawn, eds. 1985. *Foundations of Computer Music*. Cambridge, MA: MIT Press. pp. 145–159.

Roads, C. 1984. "An Overview of Music Representations." In M. Baroni and L. Callegari, eds. 1984. *Musical Grammars and Computer Analysis*. Florence, IT: Leo S. Olschki Editore. pp. 7–37.

Roads, C. 1985a. "The realization of nscor." In C. Roads, ed. 1985. *Composers and the Computer*. Madison, WI: A-R Editions. pp. 140–168.

Roads, C. 1985b. "Improvisation with George Lewis." In C. Roads, ed. 1985. *Composers and the Computer*. Madison, WI: A-R Editions. pp. 74–87.

Roads, C. 1985c. "John Chowning on composition." In C. Roads, ed. 1985. *Composers and the Computer*. Madison, WI: A-R Editions. pp. 17–26.

Roads, C. 1986. "The second STEIM symposium on interactive composing in live electronic music." *Computer Music Journal* 10(2): 44–50.

Roads, C. 1991. "Asynchronous granular synthesis." In G. De Poli, A. Piccialli, and C. Roads, eds. *Representations of Musical Signals*. Cambridge, MA: MIT Press. 143–186.

Roads, C. 1992. "Composition with machines." In J. Paynter, R. Orton, P. Seymour, and T. Howell, eds. *A Compendium of Contemporary Musical Thought*. London: Routledge. pp. 399–425.

Roads, C. 1996a. *The Computer Music Tutorial*. Cambridge, MA: MIT Press.

Roads, C. 1996b. "Early electronic music instruments: timeline 1899–1950." *Computer Music Journal* 20(3): 20–23.

Roads, C. 1997a. "Design of a granular synthesizer: 1992–1997." Unpublished.

Roads, C. 1997b. "Sound transformation by convolution." In C. Roads et al., eds. 1997. *Musical Signal Processing*. London: Routledge. pp. 411–438.

Roads, C., S. Pope, A. Piccialli, and G. DePoli. eds. 1997. *Musical Signal Processing*. London: Routledge. pp. 411–438.

Roads, C. 2001a. "Sound composition with pulsars." *Journal of the Audio Engineering Society* 49(3): 134–147.

Roads, C. 2001b. *Microsound*. Cambridge, MA: MIT Press.

Roads, C. 2003. "The perception of microsound." In G. Avanzini et al., eds. *The Neurosciences and Music*. Volume 999 of the *Annals of the New York Academy of Sciences*. New York: New York Academy of Sciences. pp. 1–10.

Roads, C. 2004a. "The path to *Half-life*." *POINT LINE CLOUD*. DVD. ASP 3000. San Francisco: Asphodel.

Roads, C. 2004b. "*Half life* score." *POINT LINE CLOUD*. DVD. ASP 3000. San Francisco: Asphodel.

Roads, C. 2005. "The art of articulation: the electroacoustic music of Horacio Vaggione." *Contemporary Music Review* 24(4): 295–309.

Roads, C. 2011. "Software and interface for the projection of spatial chords." Unpublished manuscript.

Roads, C. 2012. "Grains, forms, and formalization." In S. Kanach, ed. 2012. *Xenakis Matters*. Hillsdale NY: Pendragon Press. pp. 385–409.

Roads, C. 2013. "Deciphering Stockhausen's *Kontakte*." Unpublished manuscript.

Roads, C. Forthcoming. *The Computer Music Tutorial, Revised Edition*. Cambridge, MA: MIT Press.

Roads, C., and J. Alexander. 1995. Cloud Generator. Software. www.create.ucsb.edu.

Roads, C., J. Kuchera-Morin, and S. Pope. 1997a. "The Creatophone Sound Spatialisation Project." Out of print.

Roads, C., S. Pope, A. Piccialli, and G. De Poli, eds. 1997b. *Musical Signal Processing*. London: Routledge.

Roads, C., and D. Thall. 2008. *EmissionControl Quick Start Manual*. www.create.ucsb.edu/downloads.

Roads, C., C. Ramakrishnan, and M. Wright. 2013. "An interface for projection of multichannel spatial geometries live in concert." Unpublished manuscript.

Robair, G. 2008. "Vinyl mastering." *Electronic Musician* 24(3): 54–59.

Roberts, C. 2012. Personal communication.

Roederer, J. 1975. *Introduction to the Physics and Psychophysics of Music*. Second edition. New York: Springer-Verlag.

Rodgers, Tara, ed. 2010. "Introduction." *Pink Noises: Women on Electronic Music and Sound*. Durham, NC: Duke University Press. pp. 1–23.

Rosner, B., and L. Meyer. 1982. "Melodic processes and the perception of music." In D. Deutsch, ed. *The Psychology of Music*. New York: Academic Press. pp. 317–341.

Rossing, T. 1990. *The Science of Sound*. Second edition. Reading, MA: Addison-Wesley.

Rostand, C. 1965. "Music?" Program notes to *Xenakis: Metastasis, Pithoprakta, Eonta*. CD LCD 278368. Paris: Le Chant du Monde.

Rowe, R. 1993. *Interactive Music Systems*. Cambridge, MA: MIT Press.

Rowe, R. 2001. *Machine Musicianship*. Cambridge, MA: MIT Press.

Rowe, R. 2012. "Iannis Xenakis and algorithmic composition: pre-cursors, co-cursors, post-cursors." In S. Kanach, ed. *Xenakis Matters*. Hillsdale, NY: Pendragon Press. pp. 39–52.

Roy, S. 2003. *L'Analyse de la musique électroacoustique: modèleset propositions*. Paris: l'Harmattan.

Rumsey, F. 2001. *Spatial Audio*. Oxford, UK: Focal Press.

Rumsey, F. 2002. "Spatial quality evaluation for reproduced sound: terminology, meaning, and a scene-based paradigm." *Journal of the Audio Engineering Society* 50(9): 651–666.

Rumsey, F. 2008. "Signal processing for 3-D audio." *Journal of the Audio Engineering Society* 56(7/8): 640–645.

Russcol, H. 1994. *The Liberation of Sound*. New York: Da Capo Press.

Russolo, L. 1916. *The Art of Noises*. Translated 1986 by Barclay Brown. New York: Pendragon Press.

Ryan, J. 1991. "Some remarks on musical instrument design at STEIM." *Contemporary Music Review* 6(1): 3–17.

Saffran, J., and G. Griepentrog. 2001. "Absolute pitch in infant auditory learning: evidence for developmental re-organization." *Developmental Psychology* 37: 74–85.

Saffran, J. R., K. Reeck, A. Niehbur, and D. Wilson. 2005. "Changing the tune: the structure of the input affects infants' use of absolute and relative pitch." *Developmental Science* 8: 1–7.

San Diego Museum of Contemporary Art. 2008. Notes on the exhibition "Soundwaves: The Art of Sampling." www.mcasd.org/soundwaves.

Schaeffer, J., N. Burch, Y. Björnsson, A. Kishimoto, M. Müller, R. Lake, P. Lu, S. Sutphen. 2007. "Checkers is solved." *Science* 317(5844): 1518–1522.

Schaeffer, P. 1952. *A la recherché d'une musique conrète*. Paris: Editions de Seuil. Translated by C. North and J. Dack. 2012. *In Search of a Concrete Music*. Berkeley, CA: University of California Press.

Schaeffer, P. 1957. "Vers une musique expérimentale." *La Revue Musicale* 236.

Schaeffer, P. 1966. *Traité des objets musicaux*. Paris: Éditions du Seuil.

Schaeffer, P. 1976. "La musique par exemple (positions et propositions sur le *Traité des objets musicaux*." *Cahiers Recherche/Musique* 2: 55–72.

Schaeffer, P. 1977. *Traité des objets musicaux*. Second edition. Paris: Éditions du Seuil.

Schaeffer, P., G. Reibel, and B. Ferreyra. 1967. *Solfège de l'objet sonore*. Paris: Editions ORTF. Second edition 1998. Paris: Institut Nationale de l'Audiovisuel et Groupe de Recherches Musicales.

Schafer, R. 1977, new edition 1994. *The Soundscape: Our Sonic Environment and the Tuning of the World*. Rochester, VT: Destiny books.

Scharf, B. 1961. "Complex sounds and critical bands." *Psychological Bulletin* 58: 205–217.

Scharf, B. 1970. "Critical bands." In J. Tobias, ed. 1970. *Foundations of Modern Auditory Theory*. Orlando, FL: Academic Press.

Schillinger, J. 1946. *The Schillinger System of Musical Composition*. New York: Carl Fischer. Reprinted 1978. New York: Da Capo Press.

Schissler, C. 2012. "Gsound: Fast sound propagation and rendering for games." http://www.carlschissler.com.

Schonberg, H. 1963. "A Long, Long Night (and Day) at the Piano; Satie's 'Vexations' Played 840 Times by Relay Team." *New York Times*, September 11. p. 45.

Schoenberg, A. 1926. "Opinion or insight?" Cited in Schoenberg 1975.

Schoenberg, A. 1967. *Fundamentals of Musical Composition*. London: Faber and Faber.

Schoenberg, A. 1975. *Style and Idea*. Edited by L. Stein. New York: St. Martin's Press.

Schroeder, M. 1961. "Improved quasi-stereophony and colorless artificial reverberation." *Journal of the Acoustical Society of America* 33: 1061.

Schroeder, M. 1962. "Natural sounding artificial reverberation." *Journal of the Audio Engineering Society* 10(3): 219–223

Schroeder, M. 1970. *Journal of the Acoustical Society of America* 47(2): 424–431.

Schroeder, M. R., and B. F. Logan. 1961. "Colorless artificial reverberation." *Journal of the Audio Engineering Society* 9(3): 192–197.

Schuller, G. 1971. "Conversation with Varèse." In C. Boretz and E. Cone, eds. *Perspectives on American Composers*. New York: Norton. pp. 34–39.

Schwanauer, S. and D. Levitt. 1993. *Machine Models of Music*. Cambridge, MA: MIT Press.

Seife, C. 2000. *Zero: The Biography of a Dangerous Idea*. New York: Penguin.

Serra, M.-H. 1992. "Stochastic Composition and Stochastic Timbre: Gendy3 by lannis Xenakis." *Perspectives of New Music* 31.

Serra, R. 2011. "Richard Serra with Phong Bui." *Brooklyn Rail* July/August: 22–26.

Serra, X. 1997. "Musical Sound Modeling with Sinusoids plus Noise." In C. Roads et al. 1997b. *Musical Signal Processing*. London: Routledge.

Serra, X., and J. Smith. 1990. "Spectral modeling synthesis: a sound analysis/synthesis system based on a deterministic plus stochastic decomposition." *Computer Music Journal* 14(4): 12–24.

Sessions, R. 1951. *Harmonic Practice*. New York: Harcourt, Brace, & World.

Sessions, R. 1971. "To the editor." In C. Boretz and E. Cone, eds. *Perspectives on American Composers*. New York: Norton. pp. 108–124.

Sethares, W. 2005. *Tuning, Timbre, Spectrum, Scale*. Second edition. London: Springer-Verlag.

Sethares, W. 2008. *Rhythm and Transforms*. Electronic edition. London: Springer-Verlag.

Shepard, R. 1999. "Pitch perception and measurement." In P. Cook, ed. *Music Cognition and Computerized Sound*. Cambridge, MA: MIT Press. pp. 149–165.

Simon, H. 1969. The Sciences of the Artificial. Cambridge, MA: MIT Press.

Simoni, M., ed. 2006. *Analytical Methods of Electroacoustic Music*. New York: Routledge.

Slonimsky, N. 1947, republished 1997. *Thesaurus of Scales and Melodic Patterns*. London: Music Sales Corporation.

Smalley, D. 1986. "Spectro-morphology and structuring processes." In S. Emmerson. *The Language of Electroacoustic Music*. New York: Harwood Academic.

Smalley, D. 1991. "Spatial experience in electro-acoustic music." In F. Dhomont, ed. *L'espace du son*. Ohain, BE: Musiques et Recherches. pp. 123–126.

Smalley, D. 1993. "Defining transformations." *Interface* 22(4): 279–300.

Smalley, D. 1994. "Defining timbre—refining timbre." *Contemporary Music Review* 10(2): 35–48.

Smalley, D. 1997. "Spectromorphology: explaining sound shapes." *Organised Sound* 2(2): 107–126.

Smalley, D. 2007. "Spaceform and the acousmatic image." *Organised Sound* 12(1): 35–58.

Smith, O. 2010. *Physical Audio Signal Processing.* W3K Publishing. https://ccrma.stanford.edu/~jos/pasp/pasp.html.

Smith, L., and H. Honing. 2008. "Time-frequency representation of musical rhythm by continuous wavelets." *Journal of Mathematics and Music* 2(2): 81–97.

Smith, W. 2011. "Hierarchies of spaces: building from the bottom up." moniker.name/worldmaking.

Snyder, B. 2000. *Music and Memory: An Introduction.* Cambridge, MA: MIT Press.

Solar balloons. 2009. "Phenomena which affect a solar balloon." pagesperso-orange.fr/ballonsolaire/en-theorie1.htm.

Solomos, M. 1995. "Lectures d'*Ionisation*." *Percussions* 40. phillal.club.fr/PAGES/IONISA/ionisation.html.

Solomos, M. 2004. "Xenakis et la nature: entre les mathématiques et les sciences de la nature." *Musicalia* 1: 133–145.

Soundlazer. 2013. "Soundlazer: the open-source, hackable, parametric speaker." www.soundlazer.com.

Sowa, J. F. 2006. "Processes and causality." www.jfsowa.com/ontology/causal.htm.

Sowa, J. F. 2008. "Semantic networks." www.jfsowa.com/pubs/semnet.htm.

Steiglitz, K. 1996. *A Digital Signal Processing Primer: With Applications to Digital Audio and Computer Music.* Upper Saddle River, NJ: Prentice-Hall.

Stockhausen, K. 1955. "Structure and experiential time." *die Reihe* 2. English edition 1959. Bryn Mawr, PA: Theodore Presser. pp. 64–74.

Stockhausen, K. 1957. " . . . How time passes . . . " *die Reihe* 3. English edition 1959. Bryn Mawr, PA: Theodore Presser. pp. 10–43. Reprinted with revisions as ". . . wie die Zeit vergeht . . . " in K. Stockhausen. 1963. *Texte zur elektronischen und instrumentalen Musik.* Band 1. Cologne, DE: DuMont Schauberg: pp. 99–139.

Stockhausen, K. 1959. Program notes for *Carré* on Deutsche Grammaphon LP 104 989.

Stockhausen, K. 1960. "Momentform: Neue Zusammenhänge zwischen Aufführungsdauer, Werkdauer und Moment." Text for a program of the West German Radio (WDR) "Die unendliche Form." Reprinted in K. Stockhausen. 1963. *Texte zur elektronischen und instrumentalen Musik.* Band 1. Cologne, DE: DuMont Schauberg. pp. 189–210. English translation by S. Heikinheimo (1972).

Stockhausen, K. 1963. *Texte zur elektronischen und instrumentalen Musik.* Band 1. Cologne, DE: DuMont Schauberg.

Stockhausen, K. 1964. *Texte zu eigenen Werken zur Kunst Anderer Aktuelles.* Band 2. Cologne, DE: DuMont Schauberg.

Stockhausen, K. 1971. *Texte zur Musik 1963-1970.* Band 3. Cologne, DE: DuMont Schauberg.

Stockhausen, K. 1972. *Four Criteria of Electronic Music with Examples from* Kontakte. Film of lecture at Oxford University. Kürten, DE: Stockhausen Verlag. (See also Maconie 1989, which contains the edited text of this lecture.)

Stockhausen, K. 1978. *Texte zur Musik 1970-1977.* Band 4. Cologne, DE: DuMont Schauberg.

Stockhausen, K. 1981. "Some questions and answers." In Stockhausen (1989), pp. 129–171.

Stockhausen, K. 1989. "Four criteria of electronic music." In *Stockhausen on Music.* R. Maconie, compiler. London: Marion Boyers. pp. 88–111.

Stockhausen, K. 1992. "Studie II." Program notes. *Elektronisches Musik 1952–1960*. CD 3. Kürten, DE: Stockhausen-Verlag.

Stockhausen, K. 2007. "Karlheinz Stockhausen, Colonia 08-08-07." Video interview by G. Sanchristoforo. www.gleetchplug.com/gleetchplug/works. See also vimeo.com/25862906.

Strange, A. 1983. *Electronic Music: Systems, Techniques, Controls*. Second edition. Dubuque, IA: W. C. Brown.

Stravinsky, I. 1936. *Stravinsky: An Autobiography*. New York: Simon and Schuster.

Stravinsky, I. 1942. *The Poetics of Music*. Cambridge, MA: Harvard University Press.

Strawn, J. 1985. "Modelling musical transitions." Ph.D. diss. Stanford University.

Streicher, R., and F. A. Everest. 1998. *The New Stereo Soundbook*. Second edition. Pasadena, CA: Audio Engineering Associates.

Struik, D. 1967. *A Concise History of Mathematics*. Third revised edition. New York: Dover.

Strunk, O. 1950. *Source Readings in Music History*. New York: W. W. Norton.

Stuckenschmidt, H. 1970. *Twentieth Century Music*. New York: McGraw-Hill.

Sturm, B. 2006. "Adaptive concatenative synthesis and its application to micromontage composition." *Computer Music Journal* 30(4): 46–66.

Sturm, B., L. Daudet, and C. Roads. 2006. "Time-frequency alteration of audio signals using sparse atomic approximations." *Proceedings of the ACM Multimedia Conference*. New York: Association for Computing Machinery. pp. 45–52.

Sturm, B., C. Roads, A. McLeran, and J. J. Shynk. 2008. "Analysis, visualization, and transformation of audio signals using dictionary-based methods." *Proceedings of the International Computer Music Conference*. San Francisco: International Computer Music Association. Online document. Internet: quod.lib.umich.edu/cgi/t/text/text-idx?c=icmc;view=toc;idno=bbp2372.2008.054

Sturm, B., C. Roads, A. McLeran, and J. J. Shynk. 2009. "Analysis, visualization, and transformation of audio signals using dictionary-based methods." *Journal of New Music Research* 38(4): 325–341.

Subotnick, M. 1992. *All My Hummingbirds Have Alibis*. CD-ROM. Santa Monica, CA: Voyager Co.

Sullivan, L. 1896. "The tall office building artistically considered." In I. Athey, ed. 1947. *Kindergarten Chats and Other Writings*. New York: Courthope Press. pp. 202–213.

Swed, M. 1999. "This does compute: music is in the air, and the furniture, for the leader of MIT's opera of the future lab." *Los Angeles Times*. December 26.

Swed, M. 2011. "A blast of electric brilliance." *Los Angeles Times*. February 1.

Szabolcsi, B. 1965. *A History of Melody*. London: Barrie and Rockcliff.

Tanaka, A. 2009. "Sensor-based musical instruments and interactive music." In R. T. Dean, ed. 2009. *The Oxford Handbook of Computer Music*. New York: Oxford University Press. pp. 233–257.

Taube, H. 1991. "Common Music: a music composition language in Common Lisp and CLOS." *Computer Music Journal* 15(2): 21–32.

Taube, H. 2004. *Notes from the Metalevel: An Introduction to Computer Composition*. London: Taylor and Francis.

Taylor, E. 1989. *Musical Instruments of South-east Asia*. Oxford, UK: Oxford University Press.

Tcherepnin, A. 1971. "The world of sound." In R. Cummings, ed. *They Talk About Sound.* Rockville Center, NY: Belwin/Mills.

Tenney, J. 1963. "Sound generation by means of a digital computer." *Journal of Music Theory* 7(1): 24–70.

Tenney, J. 1988. *A History of 'Consonance' and 'Dissonance.'* New York: Excelsior.

Tenney, J. 1991. Program notes for the compact disc: *Conlon Nancarrow: Studies for Player Piano Vols. I and II.* WER 6168-2, 6169-2. Mainz, DE: Wergo.

Tenney, J. 2001. "The several dimensions of pitch." In C. Barlow, ed. "The ratio book." *Feedback Papers* 43: 102-115.

Terhardt, E. 1974. "On the perception of periodic sound fluctuations (roughness)." *Acustica* 30(4): 201–213.

Terry, C. S. 1963. *The Music of Bach: An Introduction.* New York: Dover.

Teruggi, D. 2008. "Après un écoute de Sud." In Teruggi, D., and E. Gayrou, eds. 2008. *Jean-Claude Risset: Portraits Polychromes.* Paris: INA/GRM. pp. 83–89.

Teruggi, D., and E. Gayrou, eds. 2008. *Jean-Claude Risset: Portraits Polychromes.* Paris: INA/GRM.

Thall, D. 2004a. "A scheme for generalized control of particle synthesis." M.S. thesis. University of California, Santa Barbara.

Thall, D. 2004b. "Experiments in sound granulation and spatialization for immersive environments." Presented at the Interactive Digital Multimedia IGERT Annual Research Review, sponsored by the National Science Foundation. University of California, Santa Barbara.

Thall, D. 2012. Personal communication.

Thompson, D. 1942. *On Growth and Form.* Cambridge, UK: Cambridge University Press.

Tingley, G. 1981. "Metric Modulation and Elliott Carter's First String Quartet." *Indiana Theory Review* 4(3): 3–11.

Toop, R. 1999. *György Ligeti.* London: Phaidon Press.

Toop, R. 2004. "Are you sure you can't hear it?: some informal reflections on simple information and hearing." In A. Ashby, ed. 2004. *The Pleasure of Modernist Music: Listening, Meaning, Intention, Ideology.* Rochester, NY: University of Rochester Press. pp. 23–45.

Torchia, R., and C. Lippe. 2004. "Techniques for multi-channel real-time spatial distribution using frequency-domain processing." In *Proceedings of the 2004 Conference on New Instruments for Musical Expression (NIME04).* pp. 116–119.

Trieb, M. 1996. *Space Calculated in Seconds: The Philips Pavilion, Le Corbusier, Edgard Varèse.* Princeton, NJ: Princeton University Press.

Truax, B. 1975. "The computer composition—sound synthesis programs POD4, POD5, and POD6." *Sonological Reports Number* 2. Utrecht, NL: Institute of Sonology.

Truax, B. 1977. "The POD system of interactive composition programs." *Computer Music Journal* 1(3): 30–39.

Truax, B. 1984. *Acoustic Communication.* Norwood, NJ: Ablex Publishing.

Truax, B. 1988. "Real-time granular synthesis with a digital signal processing computer." *Computer Music Journal* 12(2): 14–26.

Truax, B. 1999a. *Acoustic Communication.* Second edition. Westport, CT: Greenwood Press.

Truax, B. 1999b. "Composition and diffusion: space in sound in space." *Organised Sound* 3(2): 141–146.

Tymozko, D. 2002. "Stravinsky and the octophonic: a reconsideration." *Music Theory Spectrum* 24(1): 68–102.

Tyndall, J. 1875. *Sound.* Akron, OH: Werner.

Ulmann, B. 2013. *Analog Computing.* Munich, DE: Oldenbourg Verlag.

Ungeheuer, E. 1994. "From the elements to the continuum: timbre composition in early electronic music." *Contemporary Music Review* 10(2): 25–33.

Ussachevsky, V. 1958. "Musical timbre by means of the 'Klangumwandler.'" Preprint No. 65. Presented at the 10th Annual Meeting of the Audio Engineering Society. New York: Audio Engineering Society.

Ussachevsky, V. 1965. Program notes for the LP *Electronic Music.* Turnabout Stereo TV 34004S.

Vaggione, H. 1982. "Le courant and le maintenu." *Révue d'esthétique* 4: 132–137.

Vaggione, H. 1991. "Jeux d'espaces: conjonctions et disjonctions." In F. Dhomont, ed. *L'espace du son.* Ohain, BE: Musiques et Recherches. pp. 119–124.

Vaggione, H. 1996a. "Autour de l'approche électroacoustique: situations, perspectives." In G. Bennett, C. Clozier, S. Hanson, C. Roads, and H. Vaggione, eds. *Esthétique et Musique Électroacoustique.* Bourges, FR: Éditions Mnémosyne. pp. 101–108.

Vaggione, H. 1996b. "Articulating micro-time." *Computer Music Journal* 20(2): 33–38.

Vaggione, H. 1996c. "Analysis and the singularity of music: the locus of an intersection." In *Analyse en Musique Électroacoustique, Acts de l'"Académie Internationalde Musique Électroacoustique.* Bourges, FR: Éditions Mnénosyne. pp. 268–274.

Vaggione, H. 1998. "Son, temps, objet, syntaxe: vers une approche multi-echelle dans la composition assistée par ordinateur." In A. Soulez, F. Schmitz, and J. Sebestik, eds. *Musique, rationalité, langage.* Volume 3 of *Cahiers de philosophie du langage.* Paris: L'Harmattan. pp. 169–202.

Vaggione, H. 2003. "Composition musicale et moyens informatique: questions d'approche." In M. Solomos, A. Soulez, and H. Vaggione, eds. *Formel-Informel : Musique-Philosophie.* Paris: L'Harmattan. pp. 91–116.

Vaggione, H. 2006. "Timbre et absence de causalité dans la musique électroacoustique." Bourges, FR: Éditions Mnémosyne.

Vande Gorne, A. 1991. "Espace et structure." In F. Dhomont, ed. *L'espace du son.* Ohain, BE: Musiques et Recherches. pp. 127–128.

Vande Gorne, A. 1995. "Une histoire de la musique électroacoustique." In *Esthétique des arts médiatiques,* Tome 1. L. Poissant, ed. Montréal: Presses de l'Université du Québec. pp. 291–317.

Vande Gorne, A. 2011. "L'analyse perceptive des musiques électroacoustiques." *Lien: Revue d'esthétique musicale.* www.musiques-recherches.be/edition.php?lng=fr&id=110.

Vande Gorne, A. 2012. "L'espace comme cinquième parameter musicale." In L. Pottier, ed. *La spatialisation des musiques électroacoustiques.* Saint-Étienne, FR: Publications de l'Université de Saint-Étienne. pp. 53–80.

Varèse, E. 1916. "Credo." Quoted in Varèse (1983) p. 23.

Varèse, E. 1923. "Musique expérimentale." Quoted in Varèse (1983) pp. 31–38.

Varèse, E. 1924. "La musique de demain." Quoted in Varèse (1983) pp. 38–40.

Varèse, E. 1925. "En quête d'un melodist." Quoted in Varèse (1983) pp. 41–42.

Varèse, E. 1926. "Comments on *Amériques*." Quoted in Vivier (1973): p. 35.

Varèse, E. 1930. "La mécanisation de la musique." Quoted in Varèse (1983) pp. 58–63.

Varèse, E. 1936a. "Nouveaux instruments et nouvelle musique." Quoted in Varèse (1983) p. 91.

Varèse, E. 1936b. "Musique de notre temps." Quoted in Varèse (1983) pp. 88–90.

Varèse, E. 1939. "Liberté pour musique." Quoted in Varèse (1983) pp. 100–107.

Varèse, E. 1936. "La forme." Quoted in Varèse (1983) p. 124.

Varèse, E. 1952. "Lettre à Dallapiccola." Quoted in Varèse (1983) pp. 125.

Varèse, E. 1954a. "Comments on *Déserts*." Quoted in Vivier (1973) p. 153.

Varèse, E. 1954b. "Intégrales." Quoted in Varèse (1983) pp. 128.

Varèse, E. 1955. "Les instruments de musique et la machine électronique." Quoted in Varèse (1983) pp. 144–147.

Varèse, E. 1958. "Le destin de la musique." Quoted in Varèse (1983) pp. 152–160.

Varèse, E. 1959. "Rhythm, form, and content." Quoted in Varèse (1971) pp. 28–31.

Varèse, E. 1965a. "L'artiste «d'avant-garde»." Quoted in Varèse (1983) pp. 169–171.

Varèse, E. 1965b. "Conversation with Varèse." Gunther Schuller, interviewer. Perspectives of New Music 3(2): 32–37.

Varèse, E. 1966. See Varèse and Wen-Chung 1966. (Wen-Chung assembled this paper out of existing texts by Varèse. It was awkward to cite both authors in places where Varèse is speaking.)

Varèse, E. 1983. *Écrits*. L. Hirbour, ed. Paris: Christian Bourgois.

Varèse, E., and C. Wen-Chung. 1966. *Perspectives of New Music* 5(1): 11–19. Reprinted in C. Boretz and E. Cone, eds. 1971. *Perspectives on American Composers*. New York: W. W. Norton. pp. 26–34.

Varga, B. A. 1996. *Conversations with Iannis Xenakis*. London: Faber and Faber.

Verheijen, E. 1997. *Sound Reproduction Via Wave Field Synthesis*. Ph.D. diss. Delft, NL: Delft University of Technology.

Verplank, W. 2006. Personal communication.

Vivier, C. 1985. Quoted in "Hommage a Claude Vivier 1948–1983." *Almeida International Festival of Contemporary Music and Performance*. June 8–July 8, 1985, Islington, London. oques.at.ua/news/claude_vivier_klod_vive_works/2010-06-21-28.

Vivier, O. 1973. *Varèse*. Paris: Éditions de Seuil.

von Amelunxen, H., S. Appelt, P. Weibel, and A. Lammert, eds. 2009. *Notation: Kalkül und Form in den Künsten*. Berlin: Akademie der Künst.

Vörlander, M. 2009. *Auralization: Fundamentals of Acoustics, Modelling, Simulation, Algorithms and Acoustic Virtual Reality*. Berlin: Springer Verlag.

Waage, H. 1984. "The varitonal scale of primetones, pentones, and septones." *EAR* 9(1) 2–9.

Waage, H. 1985. "The intelligent keyboard." *1/1* 1(4): 1, 12–13.

Wakefield, G. 2012. "Real-time metaprogramming for the computational arts." Ph.D. diss. University of California, Santa Barbara.

Ward, W. 1999. "Absolute pitch." In D. Deutsch, ed. *The Psychology of Music*. San Diego, CA: Academic Press. pp. 265–298.

Warren J., S. Uppenkamp, R. Patterson, and T. Griffiths. 2003. "Separating pitch chroma and pitch height in the human brain." *Proceedings of the National Academy of Sciences* 100(17): 10038–10042.

Watson, C. 2009. Quoted description of *Weather Report* album. www.chriswatson.net.
Weidenaar, R. 1995. Magic Music from the Telharmonium. Metuchen, NJ: Scarecrow Press.
Weinberger, N. 1999. "Music and the auditory system." In D. Deutsch, ed. *The Psychology of Music*. Second edition. San Diego, CA: Academic Press. pp. 47–87.
Weinberger, N. 2004. "Music and the brain." *Scientific American* 291(5): 89–95.
Weinstein, E., K. Steele, A. Agarwal, and J. Glass. 2004. "LOUD: A 1020-Node Modular Microphone Array and Beamformer for Intelligent Computing Spaces." MIT/LCS Technical Memo MIT-LCS-TM-642. Cambridge, MA: MIT Laboratory for Computer Science.
Wenger, E., and E. Spiegel. 2009. *MetaSynth 5.0 User Guide and Reference*. Redwood City, CA: U&I Software.
Wessel, D. 1979. "Timbre space as a musical control structure." *Computer Music Journal* 3(2): 45–52. Reprinted in C. Roads and J. Strawn, eds. 1985. *Foundations of Computer Music*. Cambridge, MA: MIT Press. pp. 640–657.
Westercamp, H. 2006. "Soundwalking as ecological practice." www.sfu.ca/~westerka/writings%20page/articles%20pages/soundasecology2.html
Weyl, H. 1952. *Symmetry*. Princeton, NJ: Princeton University Press.
Whelan, R. 2000. *Stieglitz on Photography*. New York: Aperture Foundation.
Whistler, J. M. 1916. *The Gentle Art of Making Enemies*. New York: G. P. Putnam's Sons.
Whitfield, J. 1978. "The neural code." In E. Carterette and E. Friedman. *Handbook of Perception, Volume IV, Hearing*. New York: Academic Press. pp. 163–183.
Whittall, A. 1999. *Musical Composition in the Twentieth Century*. Oxford, UK: Oxford University Press.
Whittall, A. 2008. *The Cambridge Introduction to Serialism*. Cambridge, UK: Cambridge University Press.
Whitwell, D. 2009. "Essay Nr. 19: Music defined as mathematics." www.whitwellessays.com.
Wiener, N. 1961. *Cybernetics or Control and Communication in the Animal and the Machine*. Cambridge, MA: MIT Press.
Wikipedia 2006. "Timbre." en.wikipedia.org/wiki/Timbre.
Wilkinson, S. 1988. *Tuning In: Microtonality in Electronic Music*. Milwaukee, WI: Hal Leonard Books.
Wilson, E. 1960. "The act of scale formation." www.anaphoria.com/wilson.html.
Wilson, E. 2014. "The Wilson Archives." www.anaphoria.com/wilson.html.
Williams, J., and C. Colomb. 2003. "Arguments about causes." In *The Craft of Argument*. New York: Addison Wesley Longman.
Wilson, S. 2008. "Spatial swarm granulation." In *Proceedings of 2008 International Computer Music Conference*. San Francisco: International Computer Music Association.
Winograd, T. 1991. "Thinking machines: Can there be? Are we?" hci.stanford.edu/~winograd/papers/thinking-machines.html.
Winter, M. 2010. "Structural metrics: an epistemology." Ph.D. diss. University of California, Santa Barbara.
Wishart, T. 1993. "From architecture to chemistry." *Interface* 22: 301–315.
Wishart, T. 1994. *Audible Design*. York, UK: Orpheus the Pantomime.
Wishart, T. 1996. *On Sonic Art*. Amsterdam: Harwood Academic Publishers.

Wishart, T. 2000. "Computer sound transformation: a personal perspective from the U. K." www.trevorwishart.co.uk/transformation.html.

Wold, E., T. Blum, D. Keislar, and J. Wheaton. 1996. "Content-based classification, search, and retrieval of audio." *IEEE Multimedia* 3(2): 27–36.

Wolf, D. "Alternative tunings, alternative tonalities." *Contemporary Music Review* 22 (1–2): 3–14.

Wolfram, S. 2002. *A New Kind of Science*. Champaign, IL: Wolfram Media.

Woolman, M., ed. 2000. *Sonic Graphics: Seeing Sound*. London: Thames and Hudson.

Wright, M. 2002. "Open Sound Control Specification." www.cnmat.berkeley.edu/OSC/OSC-spec.html.

Wright, M. 2005. "Open Sound Control: an enabling technology for musical networking." *Organized Sound* 10(3): 193–200.

Wright, M. 2008. "The shape of an instant: measuring and modeling perceptual attack time with probability density functions (if a tree falls in the forest, when did 57 people hear it make a sound?)." Ph.d. diss. Stanford University.

Wright, M. 2009. Personal communication.

Wright, M. 2011. "A scientific view of musical rhythm." In J. Berger and M. Turow, eds. *Music, Science, and the Rhythmic Brain: Cultural and Clinical Implications*. New York: Routledge. pp. 73–85.

Wright, M., and A. Freed. 1997. "Open Sound Control: a new protocol for communicating with sound synthesizers." *Proceedings of the 1997 International Computer Music Conference*. San Francisco: ICMC. pp. 101–104.

Wright, M., J. Beauchamp, K. Fitz, X. Rodet, A. Röbel, X. Serra, and G. Wakefield. "Analysis/synthesis comparison." 2000. *Organised Sound* 5(3): 173–189.

Xenakis, I. 1955. "La crise de la musique sérielle." *Gravensaner Blätter* 1: 2–4.

Xenakis, I. 1960. "Elements of stochastic music." *Gravensaner Blätter* 18: 84–105.

Xenakis, I. 1967. "Vers une métamusique." *La Nef* 29: 117–140.

Xenakis, I. 1971. *Formalized Music*. Bloomington, IN: Indiana University Press.

Xenakis, I. 1975. Quoted in M. Zaplitny. "Conversations with Iannis Xenakis." *Perspectives of New Music* 14(1): 87–101.

Xenakis, I. 1978. Program notes for *La Légende d'Eer*, quoted in *Xenakis: Electronic Music 1*. DVD. Mode 148. New York: Mode Records.

Xenakis, I. 1980. "Preface by Iannis Xenakis, 1980." In I. Xenakis. 2008. *Music and Architecture*. Translated, compiled, and presented by Sharon Kanach. Hillsdale, NY: Pendragon Press. pp. xvi–xx.

Xenakis, I. 1989. "Concerning time." *Perspectives of New Music* 27(1): 84–92. Reprinted in French as "Sur le temps" in I. Xenakis, 1994, *Kéleütha*. Paris: L'Arche.

Xenakis, I. 1990. "Sieves." *Perspectives of New Music* 28(1): 58–78.

Xenakis, I. 1992. *Formalized Music*. Revised edition. Stuyvesant, NY: Pendragon Press.

Xenakis, I. 1995. "Iannis Xenakis and Harry Halbreich in conversation." *La Légende d'Eer: Xenakis Electronic Works 1*. DVD 148. New York: Mode Records.

Xenakis, I. 1996. "Eskhaté Ereuna: extending the limits of musical thought—comments on and by Iannis Xenakis." *Computer Music Journal* 20(4): 11–16.

Xenakis, I. 2008. *Music and Architecture*. Translated, compiled, and presented by Sharon Kanach. Hillsdale, NY: Pendragon Press.

Yeston, M. 1976. *The Stratification of Musical Rhythm*. New Haven, CT: Yale University Press.

Young, J. 2004. "Sound morphology and the articulation of structure in electroacoustic music." *Organized Sound* 9(1): 7–14.

Zatorre, P. Benin, and V. Penhune. 2002. "Structure and function of auditory cortex: music and speech." *TRENDS in Cognitive Sciences* 6(1): 37–46.

Ziccarelli, D. 2002. "How I learned to love a program that does nothing." *Computer Music Journal* 26(4): 44–51.

Zinovieff, P. 1983. "Compositional attitudes to electronic music." *Composer* 144: 6–11.

Zölzer, U., ed. 2002. *DAFX: Digital Audio Effects*. New York: Wiley.

Zölzer, U., ed. 2011. *DAFX: Digital Audio Effects*. Second edition. New York: Wiley.

Zuccarelli, H. 1983. "Ears Hear by Making Sounds." *New Scientist* 100(1383): 438–440. www.acousticintegrity.com/acousticintegrity/Holophonics.html.

Zvonar, R. 2005. "A history of spatial music." www.zvonar.com/writing/spatial_music/History.html. See also cec.sonus.ca/econtact/Multichannel/spatial_music.html.

Zwicker, E. 1961. "Subdivision of the audible frequency range into critical bands." *Journal of the Acoustical Society of America* 33(2): 248–249.

Zwicker, E., and R. Feldtkeller. 1999. *The Ear as a Communication Receiver*. Woodbury, NY: Acoustical Society of America.

Zwicker, E., G. Flottorp, and S. Stevens. 1957. "Critical band width in loudness summation." *Journal of the Acoustical Society of America* 29: 548–557.

Zwislocki, J. 1978. "Masking: experiments and theoretical aspects of simultaneous, forward, backward, and central masking." In E. Carterette and E. Friedman, eds. *Handbook of Perception*, Volume IV, *Hearing*. New York: Academic Press. pp. 282–336.

COMPOSITION INDEX

NAME INDEX

SUBJECT INDEX

CPSIA information can be obtained
at www.ICGtesting.com
Printed in the USA
BVOW06s0046250118
506110BV00002B/69/P

9 780195 373240